RACE & DEMOCRACY

Adam Fairclough

THE UNIVERSITY OF GEORGIA PRESS

ATHENS & LONDON

Race  Democracy

THE CIVIL RIGHTS STRUGGLE IN LOUISIANA,

1915–1972

Paperback edition, 1999

© 1995 by The University of Georgia Press

Athens, Georgia 30602

All rights reserved

Set in Galliard by Tseng Information Systems, Inc.

Printed and bound by IBT, Inc.

Printed in the United States of America

10   09   08   07   P   5   4   3   2

The Library of Congress has cataloged the hardcover edition of this book as follows:

Library of Congress

Cataloging-in-Publication Data

Fairclough, Adam.

Race & democracy : the civil rights struggle in Louisiana, 1915–1972 / Adam Fairclough.

xxix, 610 p., [16] p. of plates : ill., map ; 25 cm.

Includes bibliographical references (p. 557–583) and index.

ISBN 0-8203-1700-4 (alk. paper)

1. Civil rights movements—Louisiana—History—20th century. 2. African Americans—Civil rights—Louisiana. 3. Louisiana—Race relations. I. Title. II. Title: Race and democracy.

E185.93.L6 F35 1995

323.1′196073′009041—dc20   94-22563

Paperback ISBN-13: 978-0-8203-2118-9

ISBN-10: 0-8203-2118-4

British Library Cataloging-in-Publication Data available

To my mother, Marion Wills,

and my aunt, Margaret Skea

Pure hell broke loose. . . .
Apparently, the first thing that
touched them off was the historical
section as it related to "Creoles"
and "free men of color" as opposed
to slaves. I learned from the rather
heated discussion that we presumably have "white Creoles" as well as
"Colored Creoles," among other
types of Creoles, and I think that it
is pretty hard to say Creoles in any
way without offending someone.
— J. Westbrook McPherson,
    executive secretary of the
    New Orleans Urban League,
    on the reaction of the white
    board members to a study of
    "The Negro in New Orleans"
    (1950)

In Louisiana, the term "Creole"
has no reference to the offspring of
interbreeding whites and Negroes.
— political scientist Allan P. Sindler
    (1956)

It just meant a mixture of two racial
groups or more.
— black civil rights lawyer
    Alexander Pierre Tureaud (1968)

You could feed all the "pure
whites" in Louisiana with a nickel's
worth of red beans and a dime's
worth of rice.
— attributed by blacks to
    Huey P. Long

Honey, we's all Creoles as far as I
can see. We don't ask what it is, we
just be's it. . . . Everything down
here is Creole.
— anonymous black woman, quoted
    in Velesta Jenkins, "River Road"
    (1973)

CONTENTS

PREFACE

W hen I began this study, in 1987, my perceptions of the civil rights movement had been formed during ten years of research into the history of the Southern Christian Leadership Conference and the career of Martin Luther King Jr. That work both derived from and reinforced the commonly held perception that the black activism of 1955 to 1965 displayed a unity and momentum that set it apart from what came before and what came after. Here, finally, were a powerful mass movement and a leader worthy of the cause; here, at last, was the decisive breakthrough. Embarking upon a study of Louisiana, I imagined not only that an examination of the civil rights movement at the state and local levels would broaden our understanding of black insurgency, but also that it would confirm rather than challenge the Montgomery-to-Selma framework that seemed self-evidently correct. Like most historians of the movement, I realized that black militancy had quickened in the late 1930s and during the Second World War, but I intended passing lightly over this period, confining it to a chapter, perhaps two, on the "origins" of the civil rights movement. The focus of the book, as with my history of SCLC, was to be on the late 1950s and 1960s.

As I plunged into research, however, it soon became apparent that the contours of the struggle in Louisiana bore little resemblance to the Montgomery-to-Selma story. For one thing, black activism between the late 1930s and the *Brown* decision was so multifaceted, broadly based, and militant that it seemed to merit the same kind of scholarly attention as the period 1955–65.

The black activism of the Roosevelt-Truman era has not been neglected by historians. There are books and articles weighing the impact of the Depression, assessing the influence of the New Deal, studying blacks and the labor movement, and examining how the Second World War changed race relations. In addition, several community studies, notably Robert J. Norrell's book on Tuskegee, Alabama, have argued that the civil rights movement, at the local level, actually got under way in the late 1930s and had already gathered considerable momentum by the 1950s. But although such works have cast doubt on the prevailing interpretation of the civil rights movement, they have often done so implicitly rather than explicitly, and no larger synthesis has appeared to challenge the Montgomery-to-Selma perspective. It is a central thesis of this work that black protest between the late 1930s and the mid-1950s constituted more than a mere prelude to the drama proper: it was the first act of a two-act play. It therefore made no sense to begin my analysis in the mid-1950s: the Montgomery bus boycott had an important impact, as did the Greensboro sit-ins, but black activism did not so much escalate to a higher level as change in shape. What Bayard Rustin called the "classical period" of the civil rights movement needs to be placed within the context of a struggle that stretched over three full decades.[1]

Measured in the lifetimes of dedicated individuals, some elements of continuity appear even longer. Alexander Pierre Tureaud, for example, joined the NAACP in 1922 and fought against racial discrimination for fifty years. The dean of civil rights lawyers in Louisiana — and for a time the *only* black lawyer in the state — his name appeared on virtually every suit filed by the NAACP: working with Thurgood Marshall, he integrated schools, universities, buses, parks, and public buildings; he won voting rights suits; he equalized the salaries of black teachers. In 1960 he represented students arrested in the sit-in movement, arguing the first such case to reach the Supreme Court.

Tureaud's life spanned, almost precisely, the rise and fall of white supremacy in post-Reconstruction Louisiana. He was born in 1899, three years after the Supreme Court upheld Louisiana's railroad segregation law in the *Plessy* case, one year after a new state constitution disfranchised black voters en masse. He died in 1972, the same year that the state legislature expunged all its Jim Crow laws, the year that black voters helped elect Edwin Edwards governor, and one year before a new state constitution, borrowing the language of the once-despised Fourteenth Amendment, outlawed racial discrimination. But his life was more than a mere chronological link between the two periods: Creoles like Tureaud had a consciousness of history and of their place within it. Tureaud's uncle served in the Reconstruction legislature; his protégé and law partner, Ernest N. Morial, became the first black mayor of New Orleans.

Historians can become obsessed with the question of continuity and change. The search for the origins of a social transformation invariably goes further and further back in time, until often one does not know when to stop. Hence the perspective of time, while a useful antidote to present-mindedness, can also distort. Too much stress upon continuity smooths out history's peaks and valleys, producing a bland, featureless landscape. Awareness of continuities, therefore, should not blind us to the shifts, the twists and turns, the periods of retrogression and stagnation.

History may be a seamless web, but we must not mistake fragile threads for sturdy cords. Some historians of the Old Left, for example, contend that the radicalism of the Roosevelt-Truman era paved the way for the later civil rights movement. Of course, it is always possible, by a kind of "honor by association," to discover links between 1930s radicals and 1960s activists. But such links were tenuous: McCarthyism smashed the Old Left and marginalized its ideas. One of the most striking aspects of Robin Kelley's fascinating study of Alabama Communists is how quickly and completely the Communist Party's influence faded during the 1950s.[2]

Indeed, the impact of McCarthyism was so profound that one could argue that a fundamental discontinuity separated the period 1940–54 from the following decade. The Cold War and the deradicalization of organized labor exhausted the possibilities of New Deal liberalism, and the movement that arose after 1955 drew its strength from new sources: the southern black church, the ideas of Gandhi, the leadership of Martin Luther King, and the élan of a younger generation of black college students. Many therefore resist the idea that the black protest of that period should be lumped together with pre-Montgomery activism. As Richard King reminds us, "The freshness of the movement should not be underplayed for the sake of an historical pedigree." Or as Hugh Murray put it more tartly, "The people who were involved in the movement in the 1950s and 1960s called it the civil rights movement. Historians in pipe-smoke filled rooms ought not to try to rename it." The very term "movement" implies something new and special: it connotes not only organization but also mass participation, not only activism but also direct action. It evokes marches, sit-ins, demonstrations — new methods of organization, mobilization, and protest.[3]

The relationship between the pre-1955 and post-1955 phases of the black struggle is a complex one, but an awareness of discontinuities and an appreciation of the distinctive characteristics of the Montgomery-to-Selma years do not negate the argument for treating the two periods as equally important and inextricably linked. The laserlike focus with which historians have concentrated on the period 1955–65 has served as an historical blinder. By exaggerating the extent of the mass mobilization that took place during the 1960s, it slights the scope of popular involvement during the 1940s and early 1950s. By highlighting the role of nonviolent direct action after 1955, it has neglected the importance of litigation and drawn too sharp a distinction between litigation and direct action. By placing Martin Luther King Jr. at the center of the narrative, it has exaggerated the importance of the black church, placed too much emphasis upon "leadership," and obscured the crucial importance of local activists. And by highlighting the three organizations most oriented towards direct action — SNCC, CORE, and SCLC — it has neglected the role of the NAACP.

The NAACP is, paradoxically, the most important but also the least studied of the civil rights organizations. Most histories of the movement give it short shrift, barely mentioning it after the *Brown* decision save for an occasional comment disparaging its effectiveness. The reasons for this scant treatment are not hard to fathom. The NAACP lacked a charismatic leader; Roy Wilkins, its executive secretary, was an uninspiring figure. The association also lacked a cadre of action-oriented young field-workers of the kind that gave SNCC its hard-hitting edge and appeal to youth. The NAACP was slow-moving and bureaucratic; local initiatives were too often stifled by committees, hierarchies, and procedural complexities.

The habit of ignoring the NAACP and highlighting the 1960s has been reinforced by the generation gap. Most SNCC workers, for example, were in their teens or early twenties; James Forman, executive secretary of SNCC at the age of thirty-three, was considered an old man. The generation of 1960 tended to be curtly dismissive of older NAACP activists. The words "Uncle Tom" came easily, and too often unthinkingly, to their lips. The CORE workers who fanned out across Louisiana between 1962 and 1965 knew little, and cared less, about the history of the civil rights struggle in the communities to which they were assigned. What had happened in 1956, let alone 1946, was ancient history.

To a great extent our own image of the civil rights movement continues to be shaped by the generation of 1960. The veterans of SNCC and CORE are still relatively young; they are often educated and articulate; many are now quite influential. It is noteworthy that while SNCC alumni, in particular, regularly speak at historical conventions, one rarely if ever encounters a veteran of the NAACP.

The result has been a kind of historical amnesia. In Louisiana (and I suspect that the same was true in South Carolina and several other states) the

NAACP provided the backbone of the civil rights struggle. It furnished crucial continuity from the 1940s through the 1970s. By the time of *Brown*, the NAACP's victories had already started to transform the South. In Louisiana, for example, black policemen had been hired, the salaries of black teachers equalized, state colleges integrated, and some 150,000 black people registered as voters. Lynching, at least in its most barbarous form, had been eliminated.

These were monumental achievements. And, as Mark Tushnet and Genna Rae McNeil have shown, they testified to the effectiveness of the NAACP Legal Defense Fund, which, first under Charles Houston and then under Thurgood Marshall, used the federal courts as a lever for social change at a time when blacks had virtually no political influence. But the advances that black southerners made before *Brown* did not flow ineluctably from court decisions engineered by NAACP lawyers: they also took agitation, organization, and sheer guts on the part of ordinary people. Indeed, the bedrock strength of the NAACP lay in its local branches; as Ray Gavins has written of North Carolina, studies of the organization at the local level "present a less bureaucratic and more people-oriented NAACP." This observation is equally applicable to Louisiana. In fact, as both Houston and Marshall recognized, legal strategy and grassroots activism were mutually dependent. An accurate history of the civil rights struggle must therefore recognize the differences between the NAACP Legal Defense Fund and the NAACP (after 1939 they were distinct entities, and by 1957 the Legal Defense Fund had complete organizational independence) as well as analyze the complex relationship between the two.[4]

To focus on the glamorous, direct-action phase of the black struggle, then, is to risk overlooking a rich and often continuous history of NAACP activity, not only in local communities but also, from about 1940 on, at the state level. Historians have long recognized the existence of local NAACP activists but have often accorded them significance only insofar as they linked up with CORE, SNCC, or SCLC, enabling those organizations to enter and organize communities. Thus we know about Rosa Parks and E. D. Nixon because of Martin Luther King; we know of Amzie Moore because of Bob Moses. As Julian Bond once put it, these older activists constituted the "prehistory" of the civil rights movement. But they were actually much more than that. Such people could be found throughout the South: men and women of great courage and integrity, whose struggles lasted a lifetime and provided the strong base, the bedrock, of the civil rights movement. They deserve more than footnotes; their stories rightly belong in the mainstream history of the movement.[5]

A reassessment of the NAACP also illuminates the complexity of the social networks that sustained black activism. The NAACP derived its strength not only from the dedication of individuals but also from the fact that such people were part of the fabric of the community; black organizations and institutions provided the social context within which they could accumulate influence. Labor unions, Masonic organizations, insurance companies, newspapers, Catholic societies, and teachers' associations provided the NAACP with important building blocks. The church was only one such unit. The history of the NAACP, in fact, brings into question the belief that the black church furnished the driving force behind the civil rights movement. The church emerged as a distinct force only when the NAACP came under state persecution in the late 1950s, and only in Alabama, where the organization was suppressed altogether, did ministerial leadership entirely supplant that of the NAACP. There were, to be sure, black ministers who became strong leaders, but such men were few and far between. In Louisiana, and perhaps in other states, the civil rights struggle seems to have been a largely secular affair. Ministers were often conspicuously absent from local movements; not only did they fail to provide leadership, often they refused to participate at all.

The fact that men usually monopolized the positions of formal leadership in the NAACP (and later in CORE) has obscured the importance of women. Andrew Young once noted that black women — respected matriarchs, businesswomen, teachers — often wielded more authority than allegedly influential male leaders. As Vicki Crawford has argued, through their churches, sororities, and other community organizations, women provided networks of support and information that nurtured and sustained civil rights efforts. Courageous individual women, moreover, often became "powerful catalysts" in the formation of local movements. When CORE workers first entered West Feliciana Parish, for example, two elderly women housed them when everyone else in the community feared associating with them. And although women rarely headed local NAACP branches, they often occupied the less prominent but equally important office of secretary. In Shreveport women, not ministers, formed the backbone of the branch's voter registration drives. And generally women were often far more willing to attempt to register to vote than men were. Women also provided support for the NAACP through their activities in the teaching unions and the education associations. Indeed, women dominated the teaching profession, accounting for two-thirds of all black teachers. Black women figured prominently in the biracial work of organizations like the Commission on Interracial Cooperation and the Southern Regional Council.[6]

Any interpretation that focuses on activists can be accused of exaggerating the extent and durability of black protest. The NAACP never had more than twelve thousand members in the entire state. Even at the height of 1960s militancy, the number of people who took part in demonstrations was tiny, the number who went to jail smaller still. Civil rights lawyer Lolis Elie thought the common image of the civil rights struggle as a "mass movement" a myth. Only a few hundred activists, he believed, underpinned black protest in Louisiana.[7]

It would be facile to suggest that blacks in the South were continually resisting racial discrimination in overt ways. Before the 1940s, when lynching was a fact of everyday life and the edifice of white supremacy impregnable, to protest meant risking life and limb. Outside New Orleans, where city life afforded some degree of protection, only the very brave and the very foolhardy raised their voices or put their heads above the parapet. Accommodation — getting along with the white man — was an essential survival skill that parents drummed into their children at an early age. And as long as blacks accepted their place in the racial order, whites could be remarkably friendly.

One might justify an emphasis on black protest as a necessary corrective to the reluctance of whites in Louisiana to acknowledge its existence. Between the disfranchisement of blacks in 1898 and the New Orleans schools crisis of 1960, whites who wrote about the state and its history virtually ignored the black community. To read the files of the *New Orleans Times-Picayune*, for example, one would never realize that blacks constituted a third of the state's population; they were hardly mentioned at all. A recent memoir by a prominent white politician failed to name a single black person, contained no reference to the black population, and neglected even to discuss race as an issue.[8]

There is a more cogent reason for stressing protest rather than accommodation, however. Given leadership that inspired confidence and a perception that things could change, blacks repeatedly showed themselves ready to take assertive action against inequality and white supremacy. In the late 1930s they advanced their economic interests through collective action in the labor movement. During the Second World War they expressed their dissatisfaction with the racial order in a thousand different ways. During the 1950s and 1960s they supported boycotts that often proved 99 percent effective. After the Voting Rights Act of 1965 they flocked to the registration offices and lined up outside the polling stations. To admit that black protest was sometimes fitful and that overt defiance was not always well supported is not to concede that the activists, either in the 1930s or the 1960s, were atypical.

Moreover, as Robin Kelley has argued, historians have often defined resistance and protest far too narrowly. Instead of confining their purview to membership in organizations and to formal political activity, they should recognize that blacks resisted white supremacy in a variety of informal, indirect, and individual ways. A black passenger might dispute a streetcar conductor but never dream of joining the NAACP. A black worker might subtly resist his or her white employer without ever belonging to a union. In the context of the rural South, even the most innocuous act — reading the *Pittsburgh Courier,* driving a flashy car, failing to yield the sidewalk — represented a subversion of white authority and an assertion of equality.[9]

Organization, nevertheless, proved critical to black progress; if resistance is defined too broadly the concept loses its explanatory power. Organization, formal and informal, provided the vital transmission shaft transmuting individual feelings into the *only* kind of resistance — purposive and collective — that could force change. This study, then, focuses on the organizations, especially the NAACP and CORE, that advanced the struggle for equality most effectively.

I also analyze organizations that fell by the wayside without bequeathing a tradition of protest or a legacy of tangible change. To state that an organization failed is not to commit the pragmatic fallacy of dismissing its historical significance. It is vital, for example, to grasp the importance of the constellation of forces loosely known as the Old Left. The Communist Party and its satellite organizations — the Louisiana Farmers Union, the Southern Negro Youth Congress, the Civil Rights Congress, the Young Progressives — helped to fertilize the growth of black militancy during the 1930s and 1940s and thus had a great indirect effect upon the struggle for equality. Moreover, even if they failed in their goals, and failed even to survive, those failures had profound repercussions. It is impossible to understand the evolution of the civil rights struggle without examining how anticommunism, in all its various manifestations, affected black protest. An evaluation of anticommunism, moreover, might soften the sometimes harsh judgments that have been rendered on the anticommunism of the NAACP. During the McCarthy years survival became the name of the game; the NAACP survived.

Black resistance, therefore, cannot be properly understood divorced from its political context. Emulating the best of the existing community studies, I have attempted to overcome a major weakness of much civil rights historiography: the tendency to segregate history by race. Most histories have examined *either* white actions *or* black actions; only rarely have the twain met. We need to marry the two perspectives. Racial change entailed a dialectic between black and white, and in studying this dialectic within particular communities we can discard the crude stereotypes that often reduce the history of the period to a simpleminded morality play. It is absurd to generalize about "whites" without differentiating — to name the most obvious categories — between political factions, business lobbies, trade unions, the Ku Klux Klan, and the Catholic Church. Hence while organized black protest provides the focal point, the analysis explores, in considerable depth, the structures of race relations and political power.

I am well aware of the pitfalls and difficulties of local history. Although no longer the refuge of antiquarians that it once was, it still often suffers from narrowness of vision. It conveniently limits large subjects, but often dodges large questions. Historians face a constant tension between the need to generalize in order to make a welter of facts comprehensible and the need to convey a sense of history's complexity. Local history tends to stress complexity at the expense of comprehension. In his humorous handbook *One-Upmanship*, Stephen Potter recommended a conversational ploy that he called "Yes, but not in the South." It works in the following way: a listener interrupts a learned discourse on a particular country by interjecting, in a knowledgeable but slightly irritated tone, "Yes, but not in the South" (of Italy, France, India, England, the United States, and so on). Framed narrowly, a study of the civil rights movement in Louisiana might yield little more than a more refined version of this ploy: "Yes, but not in Louisiana," or even, "Yes, but not in *south* Louisiana."[10]

Local history must be much more than a vehicle for "local color" or a handy geographical limitation: it should be a constructive analytical tool. Studying the civil rights movement within a particular state offers a fresh approach to the subject, one that avoids the tendency of community studies to fragment our knowledge but retains a sense of the movement's diversity and local roots. One can explore how a state's distinctive political culture affected the responses of local communities to black protest. The state also provides a canvas that is broad enough to contain materials for comparison. By contrasting black activism in rural areas, small towns, and large cities the historian can move from individual case studies to a broader synthesis, achieving breadth as well as depth.

I chose Louisiana because it is the most diverse and unique southern state, with historic differences that provide an illuminating counterpoint to the rest of the South. Louisiana's singular characteristics include its French-Spanish origins, its Creole and Cajun cultures, the influence of the Roman Catholic Church, the special character of New Orleans, the peculiar ethnic mix of places like Plaquemines Parish, and the political influence of Huey and Earl Long. This diversity invites fascinating comparisons between the Protestant north and the Catholic south, between the rural and urban areas, and between New Orleans and the more typically "southern" cities of Baton Rouge and Shreveport.

A state study is also, of course, an exercise in comparative history. The history of the civil rights movement in each state departed from the Montgomery-to-Selma narrative. The picture that emerges from Louisiana is of a moderate, legalistic, incrementalist movement. There seems to have been less class tension than in Mississippi and less Black Power militancy than in, for example, North Carolina. The federal judiciary was, taking the state as a whole, more liberal than that of other Deep South states. Moreover, the tradition of bifactional politics bequeathed by Huey Long discouraged the rabid racism of those other states. The Catholic Church and a Latin tradition of race relations also gave the racial struggle in Louisiana its own flavor. As NAACP field secretary Harvey Britton put it, "There was always an underlying feeling in Louisiana of some kind of comradeship between blacks and whites. . . . We had worked out our own pace, and things were going to generally get better, but it was not on a national time schedule, it was on Louisiana's time schedule."[11]

Yet the history of Louisiana, for all its peculiarities, also illustrates the force and centrality of race. On balance, Louisiana was more like other southern states than unlike them; the white population resisted the civil rights movement with as much determination there as it did elsewhere. While throwing light on the nuances and peculiarities of one state, the Louisiana story is also, in important respects, typical of how the civil rights struggle unfolded in the South.

Local history is not, therefore, a world unto itself. It can give a richness of texture that broader histories cannot match, but it must also retain a sense of perspective. Emphasis on the purely local can lead to insularity and incoherence. It is an error, for example, to assume a simple dichotomy between local history and national history: local struggles had a state, a regional, and a national context, and these intersected in complex ways. While local movements formed the backbone of the civil rights struggle, they could rarely pursue their goals without reference to the federal government or assistance from national organizations. For example, the Bogalusa Voters League, perhaps the most dynamic local movement in the entire South, worked with CORE and the Lawyers Constitutional Defense Committee; it negotiated with the Crown-Zellerbach Corporation and the paperworkers' unions; it prompted a crackdown on the Ku Klux Klan by the FBI; and it achieved signal court victories with the aid of the Justice Department and the federal judiciary. Local history is not merely a building block of national history; nor is national history simply local history writ large. The two approaches are two sides of the same coin.[12]

This study makes no claim to be a comprehensive survey. Because of its emphasis upon organized struggle, certain cities have been passed over lightly. Thus New Orleans, Baton Rouge, and Shreveport receive extended treatment, while Alexandria, Lake Charles, and Lafayette are mentioned only briefly. Southwest Louisiana generally, which experienced relatively little racial conflict over voting and desegregation, is accorded comparatively little attention. Other communities have been neglected in order to avoid repetitiveness; the Bogalusa movement, for example, is analyzed in detail, while the movement in Jonesboro, which developed along similar lines, is quickly summarized. The availability of sources, too, has influenced the selection of examples. Obviously, it is much easier to chronicle the history of black protest in a community with an active NAACP branch that kept good records. Yet the history of black activism can also be reconstructed through oral history, by scanning the pages of black newspapers, and by extensive but judicious use of FBI reports. In constructing a narrative, I have tried to retain a sense of chronology. However, in tracing the path of school integration after 1964, I have paralleled the main narrative in order to achieve thematic coherence.

Reflecting current usage, I have used the words *black* and *African-American* interchangeably. I have also retained the word *Negro,* the term preferred by most African-Americans from the 1920s to the 1960s, when appropriate to the historical context.

Inevitably, upon the completion of a book one belatedly realizes that certain themes have been neglected or overlooked. I wish, for example, that I had investigated the structuring of black protest by age and gender more systematically. I also wish that I had considered the effects of black out-migration from Louisiana. The movement of blacks to northern and western cities surely had profound consequences for the black struggle within the South. The existence of family ties between North and South diminished the feeling of isolation felt by blacks in the rural South and without doubt encouraged a greater sense of militancy. Migration also established escape routes: there are scattered instances, for example, of blacks fleeing to the safety of northern family members when threatened by white violence. In Washington, Chicago, and Los Angeles, moreover, Creoles of color retained a sense of Creole identity and remained in close touch with their communities of origin. Migration created support networks and information networks. But that, perhaps, will be the subject of another book. This one is already long enough.

ACKNOWLEDGMENTS

I laid the groundwork for this book during six months in New Orleans in 1987, a solid stint of research made possible by an American Studies fellowship from the American Council of Learned Societies. Without the generosity of the ACLS, which backed what was then only a vague proposal, this book would probably never have been written. As well as facilitating my research within Louisiana, the ACLS fellowship enabled me to consult the invaluable civil rights archive of the State Historical Society of Wisconsin.

In 1990–91 I had the good fortune to be a postdoctoral fellow at the Center for the Study of Civil Rights, part of the Carter G. Woodson Institute at the University of Virginia. For a full year, I had the luxury of being able to write and research, free of any other responsibilities save voluntary participation in the institute's intellectual and social activities. My fellowship year in Charlottesville was enriched by friendships both professional and personal. Patricia Sullivan and Nelson Lichtenstein encouraged my work simply by expressing interest in it. And the members of my Tuesday evening reading group–poker game, Penny Russell, Connie Curry, and Mary Ellen Curtin, provided laughs and company as well as discussions about African-American history. It was one of the most enjoyable and productive years of my life, and I shall always remember it with gratitude and affection. Most of this book was written during that year.

It is a pleasing obligation to thank two other sources of funding. The Lyndon Baines Johnson Foundation provided a grant that enabled me to visit the Johnson Presidential Library in Austin, Texas. And my previous employer, Saint David's University College (now called the University of Wales, Lampeter), helped to defray the cost of travel to the United States during my year at the Woodson Institute. Lampeter also paid for all of my Freedom of Information Act requests, enabling me to acquire tens of thousands of pages of FBI documents.

During eleven years at Lampeter, I benefited from two periods of study leave, a total of six months relief from teaching. I also received sympathetic encouragement from my department chairs, Colin Eldridge and Malcolm Smith. I am particularly grateful to Dr. Smith, who gave me every possible encouragement to complete this book at a time when I definitely needed such support. I saw the book through the final stages of publication during a fellowship year at the National Humanities Center. I am grateful to the University of Leeds for partially funding this leave of absence from my job.

I wish to thank those fellow historians who supported my numerous applications for grants and fellowships, even though, in some cases, they knew me only through my work. Steven F. Lawson, August Meier, J. Mills Thornton III, David J. Garrow, Mary Ellison, and Anthony J. Badger all expressed confidence in my work. Tony Badger, in particular, expressed enthusiasm for this project and helped me in ways too numerous to mention. Tony continues to encourage British historians of the civil rights movement in a spirit of academic generosity that is rare and admirable. Mary Ellison, a friend and mentor of more than twenty years, is similarly unselfish in helping younger scholars; I owe her more than I could possibly say in this brief paragraph.

A number of Louisiana scholars, or rather scholars of Louisiana, helped and encouraged me during the early stages of my research. I wish to thank Michael L. Kurtz, Edward F. Haas, and Arnold R. Hirsch for providing me with positive thoughts and suggestions. Some scholars also generously shared research materials with me. Keith Weldon Medley sent me articles on New Orleans history, including his valuable studies of Ernest J. Wright. Patricia Rickels of the University of Southwestern Louisiana arranged for me to consult her oral history interviews. Hugh T. Murray Jr. allowed me to read two important unpublished manuscripts that deal with civil rights activism in New Orleans. Joseph L. Logsdon of the University of New Orleans permitted me to read his important oral history interviews with John Henry Scott and A. P. Tureaud. (I should add that Joe Logsdon's unsurpassed knowledge of the civil rights movement in New Orleans proved of inestimable help to me. In lengthy conversations, as well as in a detailed critique of the manuscript, he gave me many helpful suggestions and much food for thought.)

The extent to which I depended upon the help and efficiency of librarians and archivists is reflected in the footnotes to this book. I depended upon some libraries more than others, and the staffs of the following institutions went out of their way to assist my research. Working for months on end at the Amistad Research Center at Tulane University — a veritable treasure trove for anyone interested in African-American history — was sheer delight. Its staff were helpful, attentive, and welcoming. I am grateful, in particular, to Clifton Johnson, Florence Borders, Lester Sullivan, Kenneth Coleman, and Andrew Simon. Patricia L. Meadors, head of Archives and Special Collections, Noel Memorial Library, at Louisiana State University in Shreveport, helped me plan my visit to northern Louisiana and made a special effort to track down possible "leads." The archivists at the Earl K. Long Library of the University of New Orleans were unfailingly helpful, as were those at Tulane's Howard-Tilton Library. During long spells of research at the New Orleans Public Library, the overworked and dedicated staff of the Louisiana Collection always cheerfully attended to my requests. Finally, I wish to thank the staff of the microforms department at the University of Virginia's Alderman Library.

To a historian accustomed to Britain's stifling climate of official secrecy, the Freedom of Information Act is a marvel. Although the results were usually disappointing — the most interesting documents were also the most censored — the Federal Bureau of Investigation processed my requests efficiently and with reasonable dispatch. (The same cannot be said of the Department of Justice: seven years after my initial requests, I have yet to receive the relevant documents.) One can only hope that Congress strengthens the Freedom of Information Act so that scholars can fully utilize the rich potential of FBI and other federal documents.

There are two other specific sources of help I wish to mention. The following people granted me interviews, which varied in length from forty-five minutes to three hours: William Bailey, James H. Henderson, Harvey R. H. Britton, John J. McKeithen, Jesse N. Stone, John R. Martzell, Tom Dent, Joseph L. Logsdon, Thomas H. Clancy, Harold N. Rouzan, Lolis E. Elie, Raphael E. Cassimere, and John E. Rouseau, who also showed me his complete file of the *New Orleans Sentinel*. I also wish to thank the authors of the many theses and dissertations that I consulted. All professional historians rely, especially in the initial stages of their research, upon the work of graduate students — many of whom, through the vagaries of the job market rather than through any fault of their own, never become university professors. My footnotes and bibliography document the extent to which I have depended upon these scholars, and it is right that I acknowledge that debt.

To call my ten-year association with the University of Georgia Press "trouble-free" would be to understate just how smooth and rewarding that relationship has been. Hearing the horror stories of other authors, I can only congratulate myself on having found such a fair, efficient, and friendly publisher. As well as thanking Charles East for finding the illustrations and Mark Pentecost for editing the manuscript so skillfully, I owe a special debt to Karen Orchard, the associate director. Karen has always been my principal point of contact with the Press, and I could not have hoped for a more sympathetic and helpful editor.

Finally, I have incurred debts of a more general nature. My friends in Wales, fellow members of the Carmarthen Labour Party, followed the progress of this book with amused interest. Whenever things seemed bleak, our Wednesday night political discussions always buoyed me. Thank you Tom, Judy, Richard, and Keith. Nigel, Carol, and Matthew Rigby have also been wonderful friends, not least by looking after Tostig during my frequent and extended absences in the United States. My mother, Marion Wills, provided help and support during a period when the completion of this book seemed all but impossible. My aunt, Margaret Skea, has encouraged my interest in American history for more than thirty years, ever since an eight-year-old boy became fascinated (for all the wrong reasons) by the American Civil War. Jennifer, my daughter, contributed to this book simply by being a presence in my life. During the time it took me to write it she has grown from a baby into an eight-year-old girl. It seems fitting that she is now a native of Louisiana, a New Orleanian, and that she is enjoying, in large ways and small, the legacy of the civil rights movement. Finally, Mary Ellen opened my eyes to new ways of looking at history, as well as new ways of approaching life. Thank you, M.E.

ABBREVIATIONS

AAA	Agricultural Adjustment Act
ADA	Americans for Democratic Action
AFSC	American Friends Service Committee
AMA	American Missionary Association
ANP	Associated Negro Press
ASWPL	Association of Southern Women for the Prevention of Lynching
BRC	Biracial committee
BVL	Bogalusa Voters and Civic League
CABL	Committee for a Better Louisiana
CCGNO	Citizens Council of Greater New Orleans
CCHR	Catholic Commission on Human Rights

CCHR	Catholic Council on Human Relations
CCS	Catholic Committee of the South
CIC	Commission on Interracial Cooperation
CIO	Committee for Industrial Organization (later Congress of Industrial Organizations)
COPE	Committee for Public Education
CORE	Congress of Racial Equality
CRC	Civil Rights Congress
CRS	Community Relations Service
FEPC	Fair Employment Practice Committee
FSA	Farm Security Administration
HANO	Housing Authority of New Orleans
HUAC	House Un-American Activities Committee
ILA	International Longshoremen's Association
ILD	International Labor Defense
ILWU	International Longshoremen's and Warehousemen's Union
JLC	Joint Legislative Committee to Maintain Segregation
LCDC	Lawyers Constitutional Defense Committee
LCHR	Louisiana Committee on Human Rights
LCRC	Louisiana Civil Rights Congress
LCTA	Louisiana Colored Teachers Association (see LEA)
LDF	NAACP Legal Defense and Educational Fund (Inc. Fund)
LEA	Louisiana Education Association (formerly LCTA)
LFU	Louisiana Farmers Union
LSC	Louisiana State Conference of NAACP Branches
LSUNO	Louisiana State University in New Orleans
MIA	Montgomery Improvement Association
NAACP	National Association for the Advancement of Colored People

NAPE	National Alliance of Postal Employees
NMU	National Maritime Union
NOPSI	New Orleans Public Service, Inc.
OPPVL	Orleans Parish Progressive Voters League
PDL	People's Defense League
OKKK	Original Knights of the Ku Klux Klan
SAC	Special Agent in Charge
SCEF	Southern Conference Educational Fund
SCHW	Southern Conference for Human Welfare
SCLC	Southern Christian Leadership Conference
SEDFRE	Scholarship, Education, and Defense Fund for Racial Equality
SNYC	Southern Negro Youth Congress
SOS	Save Our Schools
SRC	Southern Regional Council
SUNO	Southern University in New Orleans
TWU	Transport Workers Union
UCM	United Christian Movement
UDL	United Defense League
VEP	Voter Education Project
WPA	Works Progress Administration

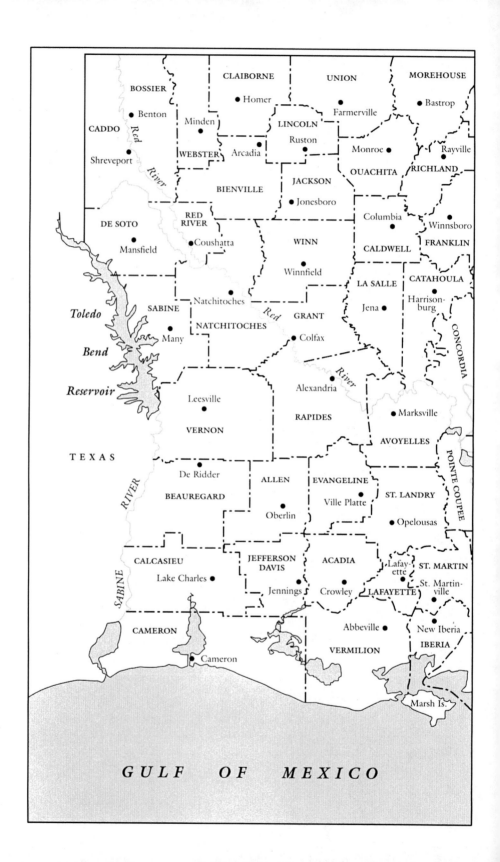

CLAIBORNE
UNION
MOREHOUSE
BOSSIER
• Homer
• Bastrop
• Benton
• Farmerville
CADDO
Minden •
LINCOLN
Shreveport •
WEBSTER
Ruston
Monroe •
• Rayville
Arcadia •
RICHLAND
OUACHITA
BIENVILLE
JACKSON
• Jonesboro
Columbia •
• Winnsboro
DE SOTO
RED
RIVER
WINN
CALDWELL
FRANKLIN
Mansfield •
• Coushatta
Winnfield •
LA SALLE
CATAHOULA
Toledo
SABINE
Natchitoches •
GRANT
Jena •
Harrison-
burg
NATCHITOCHES
Bend
Many •
• Colfax
CONCORDIA
Reservoir
River
Alexandria •
Leesville •
• Marksville
VERNON
RAPIDES
AVOYELLES
POINTE COUPEE
TEXAS
• De Ridder
ALLEN
EVANGELINE
ST. LANDRY
BEAUREGARD
Ville Platte •
Oberlin •
• Opelousas
CALCASIEU
JEFFERSON
DAVIS
ACADIA
Lafay-
ette
ST. MARTIN
Lake Charles •
St. Martin-
ville
Jennings
Crowley •
LAFAYETTE
CAMERON
Abbeville •
• New Iberia
IBERIA
• Cameron
VERMILION
Marsh Is.

GULF OF MEXICO

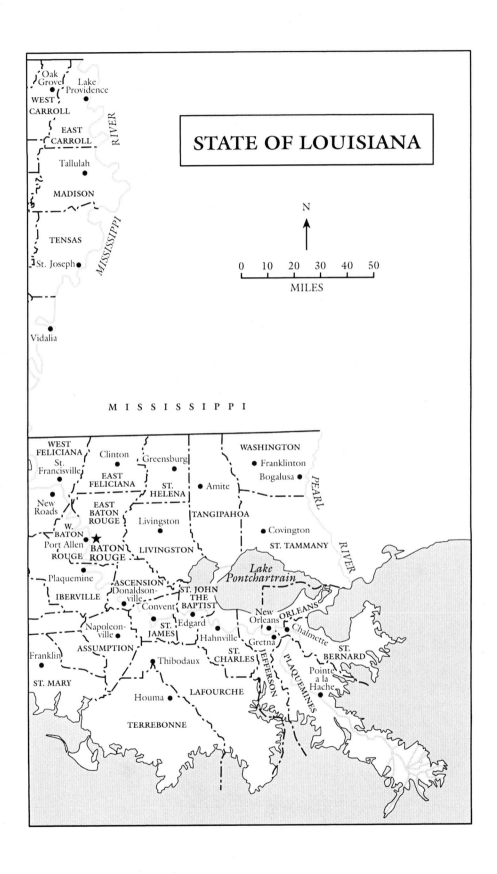

STATE OF LOUISIANA

N

0 10 20 30 40 50
MILES

Oak Grove
Lake Providence
WEST CARROLL
EAST CARROLL
RIVER
Tallulah
MADISON
MISSISSIPPI
TENSAS
St. Joseph
Vidalia

M I S S I S S I P P I

WEST FELICIANA
Clinton
Greensburg
WASHINGTON
St. Francisville
Franklinton
EAST FELICIANA
ST. HELENA
Amite
Bogalusa
PEARL
New Roads
EAST BATON ROUGE
Livingston
TANGIPAHOA
W. BATON ROUGE
Port Allen
BATON ROUGE
LIVINGSTON
Covington
ST. TAMMANY
RIVER
Plaquemine
ASCENSION
Donaldson-ville
ST. JOHN THE BAPTIST
Lake Pontchartrain
IBERVILLE
Convent
Napoleon-ville
ST. JAMES
Edgard
New Orleans
ORLEANS
Chalmette
Franklin
ASSUMPTION
Hahnville
Gretna
ST. BERNARD
ST. MARY
Thibodaux
ST. CHARLES
Pointe a la Hache
JEFFERSON
PLAQUEMINES
Houma
LAFOURCHE
TERREBONNE

RACE & DEMOCRACY

Chapter 1

CREOLE LOUISIANA

A traveler to Louisiana in the 1930s would have been hard pressed to distinguish much of that state from the rest of the South. The Black Belt that once contained the bulk of the Old South's slaves still stretched in a giant arc, embracing hundreds of counties, from Virginia to Texas. Here, where African-Americans still commonly outnumbered whites, black farm families eked out an existence producing the same crops as their slave forbears, their daily lives marked by extreme poverty and harsh subjection to white authority.

Louisiana contained many Black Belt counties; they clustered along the Mississippi River, the Red River, Bayou Teche, and Bayou Lafourche. Apart from the fact that in south Louisiana they were devoted to sugar, a crop peculiar to the state, they differed from plantation areas in other states chiefly in being called "parishes" rather than counties. North of Alexandria, the geographical center of Louisiana, and in the "Florida Parishes" that lay north and east of Baton Rouge (so called because they had once been part of the "Free and Independent State of West Florida") a traveler might easily suppose he or she were in Alabama or Mississippi.

Yet its origins as a French colony and its cultural diversity make Louisiana different from other southern states. In the rest of the South, the population is overwhelmingly Protestant; the population of Louisiana is half Catholic. Elsewhere, most whites are descended from British and Irish stock; those in Louisiana make up a mélange of Cajuns, Creoles, old stock Americans, and the descendants of more recent European immigrants such as Irish, Germans, and Italians. And while Louisiana's foreign-born population is now relatively small, during the nineteenth century it exceeded that of any other southern state; indeed, in 1850 it had the highest proportion of immigrants in the nation with the exception of Wisconsin.[1]

Louisiana's black population is also distinctive and in some respects unique. Whereas the English colonies imported most of their slaves from the British West Indies, Louisiana's first slaves came directly from Africa. In Louisiana, moreover, most of the slaves imported under French and Spanish rule were Bambara people from Senegambia. These two circumstances produced "an unusually cohesive and heavily Africanized slave culture — arguably the most Africanized slave culture in the United States." From the interplay between African and French came that mysterious and politically contested culture known as "Creole."[2]

After the Civil War the descendants of Louisiana's French and Spanish settlers came to insist that all "Creoles" be pure-blooded whites; blacks or people of racially mixed ancestry could not legitimately lay claim to the term. Descendants of African slaves, however, regarded themselves as Creole if they had racially mixed ancestry and/or French cultural attributes as reflected in name, religion, or language.

Historical evidence gives little support to exclusive white claims to the name *Creole*. The term originally meant, quite simply, native to Louisiana; it described blacks and whites alike. The Creole culture of the eighteenth and early nineteenth centuries was, in fact, heavily influenced by the black population, which for most of that period actually composed a majority of Louisiana's people. For example, the type of French that came to be spoken in Louisiana was not simply a modified version of the metropolitan tongue that the French colonists imparted to their slaves, but rather a simplified form of the language fashioned by the slaves themselves and subsequently adopted as a lingua franca. Louisiana Creole, notable for the pleasing musicality of its speech patterns, came to be spoken by many whites as well as by newly imported African slaves.[3]

Immigration from the French Caribbean both diversified and strengthened Afro-Creole culture. Of the ten thousand people from St. Domingue (Haiti) who sought refuge in Louisiana after fleeing the successful slave insurrection of 1794–1803, about a third were slaves and another third *gens de couleur libre* (free people of color). This influx doubled the population of New Orleans virtually overnight.

The free people of color, most of whom boasted white as well as African ancestry, testified to another aspect of Creole culture that whites subsequently denied and disclaimed: the large degree of racial intermixture that characterized antebellum Louisiana. True, in 1860 upper South states like Maryland and Virginia had many more free and mulatto (mixed race) Negroes than Louisiana, but the racially mixed population of these older states was for the most part descended from interracial unions that dated from colonial days. In Louisiana, by contrast, miscegenation persisted much later. The white Creoles had a more permissive attitude towards interracial sex than the British and Irish who settled the rest of the South; miscegenation was more flagrant, and even, in some circles, socially acceptable. Indeed, Louisiana's antebellum racial order resembled the Latin American tripartite system of white, mulatto, and black rather than the dichotomous black/white system that prevailed throughout the rest of the southern United States. The largely mulatto population of free blacks came to acquire an exceptional degree of wealth, education, and freedom. These Creoles of color composed a skilled, assertive, and self-confident group; from the Civil War to the present day, they and their descendants have furnished many of the most militant leaders in the black struggle for racial equality.[4]

In the twentieth century the people of Louisiana became more homogeneous, as the proportion of foreign-born immigrants declined. New Orleans acted as a veritable melting pot; by 1930 the Germans and Irish had long since been assimilated, and the Italians were rapidly becoming so. Creoles of both races ceased speaking French; indeed, the Crescent City acquired an accent that evoked Brooklyn rather than Paris. Louisiana also became predominantly white: out-migration caused the proportion of blacks to decline from 50 percent to 36 percent.

Yet Louisiana, especially southern Louisiana, continued to exude an exotic flavor that sometimes prompted visitors to imaginatively locate it in Central America or the Middle East. The semitropical look of the place contributed to these flights of fancy. The natural flood plain of the Mississippi, much of south Louisiana lies below sea level; in this shifting and imprecise border between land and water, levees, spillways, and pumping stations mean the difference between life and death. A lush, swampy region of alligators and armadillos, live oaks and spanish moss, cane fields and rice paddies, shrimping fleets and crayfish farms — there is none other quite like it.

But Louisiana's distinctiveness had as much to do with culture as with topography. Compared with other southern states Louisiana exhibited an amazing ethnic variety. Dotted around New Orleans, small, tightly knit white ethnic communities flourished. Canary Islanders (*Islenos*), Croats, and Serbs fished and trapped among the swamps and bayous south of the city. Italians and Hungarians worked truck farms in the parishes north of Lake Pontchartrain. Numbers of Syrians and Lebanese could be found in New Orleans and Lafayette.[5]

French culture remained strong. Immigrants from France continued to arrive in Louisiana during the nineteenth century; settling mainly in New Orleans, they rivaled the Irish and the Germans in total numbers. South and west of New Orleans, "Cajuns" still inhabited the bayous and prairies that their ancestors had first settled in 1765 after fleeing British rule in Nova Scotia. In Acadiana, a vast triangle whose apex lay in Avoyelles Parish, Cajun French thrived, and its status as a lingua franca had encouraged the assimilation of German, Spanish, Dutch, and English-speaking immigrants. According to one estimate, almost half the 1940 population of Louisiana could be accounted "French" in terms of language, religion, cuisine, and other cultural traits.

That definition of "French" applied to a substantial portion of African-Americans. Although blacks in Acadiana were not regarded as Cajuns, either by themselves or by whites, the black and Cajun cultures overlapped. Many blacks spoke French, and some spoke nothing else. Blacks ate a similar cuisine and evolved a type of music, "Zydeco," which resembled Cajun dance music in both its rhythms and its reliance on the accordion. And while the black population of southern Louisiana was not as solidly Catholic as the white, the diocese of Lafayette, in the Acadian heartland, contained more black Catholics than any other diocese in the United States.[6]

In New Orleans, the number of black Francophones diminished and in time all but disappeared. Yet many people of color — in the 1930s they did not dream of using the word "black" — remained fiercely proud of being in some sense "Creole." Moreover, while the migration of black Protestants to the city "Americanized" the black population, these incomers were to some extent "Creolized" by the receiving culture. New Orleans blacks had evolved a distinctive social milieu that embraced jazz, a passion for parades, a unique cuisine, and peculiar religious practices, including voodoo. Black Protestants soon adopted the Creole traditions of "good food, dance, music, gambling halls, ritualized festivals, and marching bands."[7] In addition, both Creole and American blacks took pride in claiming Indian ancestry, and during the Carnival season black "Mardi Gras Indians," attired in gorgeous handmade costumes, strutted around their tribal territories, uttering strange "war cries" and fighting with rival "tribes."

How many Mardi Gras Indians actually had Indian forbears is a matter of conjecture. Growing up in New Orleans during the 1930s and 1940s, Andrew Young remembered that "most black folk were still trying to say they were one-fourth Indian, or something — anything but *all* black." Yet black claims to Indian ancestry had historical validity. Black and Indian slaves had worked together and run away together. "Matings between Africans and Indians took place both on and off the plantations throughout the eighteenth century," writes Gwendolyn Midlo Hall. Most black-Indian offspring were called Negroes or mulattoes; some became free people of color, others a "distinctive, self-conscious group among slaves." In the 1930s a few descendants of black-Indian unions could still be found living in separate communities scattered along the Gulf Coast and western Louisiana; they called themselves "Sabines" and "Redbones" and kept aloof from the rest of the black population.[8]

In one crucial respect, however, Louisiana closely resembled the rest of the South: slavery, segregation, and white supremacy described the evolution of race relations. A third of a million slaves, half the state's population, had underpinned Louisiana's antebellum economy, and white Louisianians — Creoles, Acadians, and Anglo-Americans alike — had put aside their cultural differences to defend the "peculiar institution."

Distinctions within the black population itself also seemed to pale into insignificance beside the overwhelming fact of slavery and race. Louisiana's *gens de couleur libre* may have enjoyed a more exalted status than free Negroes in other southern states, but they numbered only eighteen thousand, and no matter how great their admixture of white blood (three-quarters of them were light-skinned "mulattoes") whites still considered and treated them as an inferior caste. During the 1850s, moreover, Louisiana, like other slave states, further restricted their rights and displayed mounting intolerance of black-white sexual liaisons.[9]

Reconstruction and its aftermath made old distinctions within the white and Negro populations of diminishing importance. White Creoles and Acadians made common cause with Anglo-Americans in their struggle to reestablish white hegemony; the free people of color joined the liberated slaves in a crusade for racial equality under the banner of the Republican party. With the overthrow of Reconstruction, the tripartite social structure of antebellum days — slaves, *gens de couleur libre*, and whites — gave way to a caste system that admitted two categories only: the superior white and the subordinate black.[10]

It took several decades to perfect this system of white supremacy. Meanwhile the "color line" remained imprecise and the status of the old *gens de couleur libre* and their descendants unclear. In 1890, however, the Louisiana legislature enacted a bill requiring railroads to segregate Negro passengers; sustained by the United States Supreme Court in *Plessy* v. *Ferguson* (1896), this measure provided a legal bulwark for discriminatory legislation. Ten years later Louisiana adopted a new constitution that effectively disfranchised the Negro population. And in 1910 the legislature banished the last vestige of the old distinction between slave and *gens de couleur libre* by abolishing the lingering difference in law between dark-skinned Negroes and light-skinned people of color. Henceforth no favored status would be accorded to people of mixed racial ancestry. Quite the reverse: the legal definition of the inferior caste embraced people with *any* traceable black forbears. Interracial sexual relationships were still fairly common after the Civil War, and not only in south Louisiana: in the sparsely populated northern parishes white farmers often replaced a wife who had died with a young black woman. However, antimiscegenation laws, abolished during Reconstruction, were reenacted in 1894, and in 1908 the legislature made concubinage between whites and blacks a felony.[11]

With a tradition of assertive protest and independent politics that survived the demise of Reconstruction, black leaders in New Orleans vigorously resisted white supremacy. Forming a *Comité des Citoyens* in 1890, prominent Creoles of color lobbied against the bill outlawing intermarriage and challenged railroad segregation in federal court. Between 1890 and 1898 the *Crusader,* the city's last black daily newspaper, continued to articulate militant opposition to racial discrimination. The three black colleges in New Orleans, each tied to northern-based Christian denominations, continued to foster dissent from white supremacy well into the twentieth century.[12]

The Louisiana Constitution of 1898, however, stripped blacks of all political influence. The number of black voters fell from 130,344 to 5,320; by 1904, after the poll tax came into force, it had dwindled to 1,342. Thereafter the number of black voters varied, but the total rarely exceeded 2,000 and in 1940 stood at 886. In the early twentieth century, blacks were in no position to mount an effective challenge to white supremacy.[13]

Their political exclusion seemed all the more galling to blacks when Italian immigrants, Americans of only a few years standing, were rapidly gaining influence within the reigning Democratic party. "Unlike the myriads of hyphenates, who infest our country's shores, the Negro is the solid American," protested black journalist James B. LaFourche. Such cries fell on deaf ears. During the 1890s the Italians had been subjected to vicious discrimination: the public lynching of eleven Italians in New Orleans provoked an international incident in 1891; eight years later five Italians were lynched outside the courthouse in Tallulah, in Madison Parish. Nevertheless, Italians were exempted from the literacy test enacted by the Constitution of 1898 and quickly incorporated into the New Orleans Democratic machine. They gained social and political acceptance, at least in part, by subscribing to the anti-Negro attitudes of their adopted country.[14]

Louisiana's Creole and Catholic culture did little to stem the tide of racism that engulfed the South at the turn of the century. White Creoles ardently championed white supremacy; historians and romanticizers of white Creole culture insisted on the "racial purity" of their people and, in a semantic ruse of Orwellian proportions, denied the very existence of Creoles who were also blacks.[15]

In 1895 Archbishop Francis Janssens of New Orleans established the first "national" or Negro parish in Catholic Louisiana. Blacks successfully resisted further segregation for another twenty years, but in 1916 Archbishop James Blenk established Corpus Christi, the first segregated parish in downtown New Orleans, the heart of the black Catholic community. During the next ten years segregated churches were organized throughout the state. Until the twentieth century, most priests had been born in France and were often resistant to segregation, but the growing number of clerics from Ireland, Poland, and the northern states more readily conformed to the South's racist mores. A few blacks stayed in mixed congregations, but an increasingly strict segregation code assigned them separate pews in the rear of the church. Segregation became the rule in all public parades and ceremonies. As one church official put it, Catholic principles had to be carefully qualified "to meet temporal necessities."[16]

The temporal necessity of supporting white supremacy also ensured that no black priests served in Louisiana. The St. Joseph's Society of the Sacred Heart, which ministered to black Catholics, tried to remedy this lack, but its efforts proved unavailing. The three blacks whom the Josephites raised to the priesthood were rejected by Louisiana's white clergy. John Plantevigne, a colored Creole ordained in 1907, found himself banned from conducting services in New Orleans by Archbishop Blenk; repeatedly humiliated, he suffered a nervous breakdown. Disgusted by the racism of the hierarchy, the first head of the Josephites, John R. Slattery, left the church. Except for an order of black nuns, the Sisters of the Holy Family, the Catholic hierarchy remained all white. In 1934, under considerable pressure from Rome, the Society of the Divine Word assigned four black priests to the diocese of Lafayette, but they served under the strict supervision of a white pastor who insisted that they adhere to southern racial etiquette, "including never offering a hand to shake on meeting white priests." The Archdiocese of New Orleans had no black priests until the 1950s. Small wonder that by the 1930s the Catholic Church retained the allegiance of, at most, only a quarter of the black population of New Orleans.[17]

Regardless of the state's cultural peculiarities, race relations in Louisiana followed the ugly pattern of the region. Indeed, historian William Ivy Hair has suggested that Louisiana's unique meld of English-speaking and Creole-

Cajun cultures, far from softening the edges of caste, actually produced an "unusual insensitivity to human rights" on the part of the whites. What Eric Foner has described as the "bloodiest single instance of racial carnage in the Reconstruction era," the Colfax massacre of 1872, occurred in Louisiana. The worst act of racial violence in the post-Reconstruction era, the butchering of dozens of striking sugar plantation workers in 1887, took place in Thibodaux, in the heart of Catholic south Louisiana. According to the most plausible tallies, lynching claimed at least 355 black lives between 1882 and 1952, a total second only to Mississippi as a proportion of population. Such outrages occurred throughout the state. In 1900 a race riot in New Orleans claimed six black lives.[18]

Despite its reputation as a sophisticated, cosmopolitan, and "Latin" metropolis, New Orleans, with a quarter of the state's population, played an important role in maintaining white supremacy in Louisiana. The Tammany Hall-style machine that dominated New Orleans politics, the Regular Democratic Organization or "Old Regulars," welcomed black disfranchisement. Despite the city's past record of miscegenation and informal racial contact, by the 1920s the color line had hardened. Streetcars were segregated in 1902. In 1924 the city passed an ordinance mandating residential segregation.

Shreveport, the largest city in north Louisiana and in those years the second most populous in the state, presented an even harsher face to blacks. Founded in the nineteenth century as a regional hub of the Red River valley cotton lands and developed in the twentieth as a major oil center, Shreveport was in its own way as insular as New Orleans. Situated at the northwestern edge of the state, looking as much toward Texas as toward the Louisiana hinterland, the city felt little identity with the distant, culturally alien populations of Acadiana and New Orleans. Conservative even by the standards of the South, Shreveport's planter-business elite enforced white supremacy with an iron fist. Between 1900 and 1931 at least nineteen blacks were lynched in Caddo Parish, more than any other Louisiana parish. There was no ambiguity about the color line here. "This place is one of the most intolerant in the whole southland," wrote a local NAACP member in 1923. Over the next half-century, Shreveport furnished some of the most determined defenders of white supremacy. In the 1920s it was the Klan's most fertile recruiting ground; during the 1950s and 1960s it became the bastion of the segregationist Citizens Council movement.[19]

Whites in Louisiana, then, appeared to treat blacks with the same contempt, exploitation, and violence as did whites in other southern states. Yet there remained subtle differences between Louisiana and the rest of the South: race relations in the "Pelican State" were harsh, but not as harsh as in Alabama or Mississippi.

Those differences were most evident in the southern, predominantly Catholic half of the state. Catholicism itself, for all its conformity to the practices of white supremacy, softened, albeit slightly, the harder edges of racism. The ameliorative influence of the Catholic Church was discernible, for example, in the lynching statistics. Between 1889 and 1922, the peak years, the north Louisiana parishes of Caddo, Ouachita, and Morehouse, all overwhelmingly Protestant, witnessed more lynchings than any other counties in the nation. Over half the lynchings that occurred in Louisiana between 1900 and 1931 took place in seven parishes, all of them mainly Protestant, and all but one in the northern part of the state.[20]

The significance of religion was also apparent in the bitter opposition of Louisiana Catholics to the resuscitated Ku Klux Klan, which began organizing in Louisiana in 1920. Because of this opposition, the Klan never attained the degree of political influence in Louisiana that it gained in other states. The abduction and murder of two white opponents of the Klan in Bastrop in Morehouse Parish in 1922 prompted Governor John M. Parker to press hard for the indictment and prosecution of the killers. Although the state failed to win convictions, the Klan issue dominated the gubernatorial election of 1924, with two of the three candidates condemning the organization. After the election of Henry L. Fuqua, the state legislature approved three anti-Klan laws. One required organizations to file their membership lists with the Secretary of State — lists that would be open to public inspection — and another made it a misdemeanor to appear in public wearing a masked disguise (except during the New Orleans Carnival season).[21]

New Orleans itself retained a reputation for relaxed and easygoing relations between black and white. That reputation was to a large extent undeserved, but not entirely so. Geographically isolated by river, lake, and swamp, the "Crescent City" was in many ways a world unto itself, and its lazy, hedonistic culture seemed to discourage extreme racism. During the annual ritual of Carnival, for example, both races abandoned themselves to good-natured exhibitionism; white and black spectators crowded the sidewalks together, yelling "Throw me something, mister!" with equal demented fervor to the masked figures on the passing floats. The city also had a relatively low level of housing segregation: most blacks and whites lived in mixed neighborhoods, sometimes in adjacent sides of "double shotgun" houses. Many white families, moreover, employed black cooks and nurses, who inhabited small wooden "shotguns" located on side streets close by the prestigious avenues and boulevards.[22]

New Orleans also had a history of labor solidarity that bridged the racial divide. The most striking example of interracial cooperation could be seen on the docks, where black and white longshoremen "more often than not

. . . joined forces in order to wrest concessions from their employers." In 1901, after three decades marked by intermittent racial conflict, dockworkers formed the Dock and Cotton Council. This body united all thirty-six dock unions and provided for equal representation between black and white. Each union furnished two delegates, one of each race, and the council's offices were divided equally, with blacks and whites rotating in each position. In 1902 the council agreed to share work between blacks and whites on a fifty-fifty basis. For nearly two decades, the Dock and Cotton Council functioned as a model of black-white labor unity.[23]

At the other end of the class structure, the city's Creole legacy encouraged a modicum of communication between the social elite of each race. Although white Creoles jealously guarded their "racial purity" and insisted that "Creoles" were by definition white, they allowed that "creole Negroes" might use the term as an adjective, and even admitted with a certain pride that, to quote Judge John Minor Wisdom, "New Orleans has had an unusually superior class of blacks." Even civil rights activists acknowledged that race relations in New Orleans were peculiar. There had been more racial mixing there, Donald Jones, a prominent NAACP member, explained in 1940; the presence of so many mulattoes resulted in more social contact and friendly understanding. Nearly forty years later Oretha Castle, a leader of the Congress of Racial Equality in the 1960s, conceded that there were always lines of communication "between some white folks and some black folks."[24]

During the 1920s and 1930s, Louisiana's Republican party served as one such line of communication. Numerically insignificant and bereft of any influence in state politics, the party gave blacks indirect access to white officials and politicians by bringing a few members of the black social elite into contact with prominent whites. Black Republican leader Walter L. Cohen served as the principal go-between, often interceding with judges and politicians, especially in police brutality cases. Sometimes criticized as an "Uncle Tom" for conveying the excuses and evasions of white officialdom to disbelieving blacks, Cohen, in the words of civil rights lawyer A. P. Tureaud, was "just as aggressive as the times permitted." Whatever influence he exercised depended upon white goodwill, and within that circumscribed sphere of action he did whatever he could. Other black Republicans, such as B. V. Barranco Jr. in Baton Rouge and John G. Lewis Jr. in Natchitoches, played a similar role, approaching whites as supplicants rather than militants.

Louisiana's black Republicans were the proud inheritors of the legacy of Reconstruction, and however ineffectual as a political force, they kept alive their party's original ideals of citizenship and democracy. To black Republicans Reconstruction was not a distant era lost in the mists of history; it was a vivid historical memory of a time — a relatively recent time — when blacks voted, sat in the state legislature, and wielded political power. Some boasted fathers or uncles who had held office in the late nineteenth century; many retained memories of proudly uniformed black Union veterans. Even after the black vote was extinguished, moreover, black Republicans retained a share of the federal patronage well into the twentieth century.

By the 1920s, however, the vestigial influence of the black Republicans was waning fast as successive Republican administrations favored the "lily-white" faction over Cohen's "black-and-tans." The "lily-whites" never succeeded in banishing blacks from the Republican party altogether, as in Alabama and elsewhere, and blacks continued to serve as delegates to the national convention. But after Cohen's death in 1929 the "lily-whites" were in the ascendant, and by 1936, when the state attorney general ruled that they were the only legally constituted Republican party, they firmly controlled the Louisiana organization.[25]

The Commission on Interracial Cooperation offered another channel of communication between the races. Formed in Atlanta in 1919 after the appalling "red summer" of lynchings and race riots, the CIC launched a regional program to dispel the vicious racism that dominated white attitudes. During the twenty-four years of its existence, the commission encouraged interracial discussion, campaigned against lynching, published well-researched studies of southern problems, and undertook innumerable projects under the broad heading of "Negro welfare." It functioned as the principal vehicle of southern liberalism during the interwar period.

The CIC's most important achievements were in the field of black education. Acting as a conduit for northern philanthropy, the commission helped to establish Dillard University in New Orleans, a merger of two older black colleges. The CIC also facilitated the building of thousands of black schools with money from the Julius Rosenwald Fund, a Chicago-based charity founded with profits from the Sears, Roebuck business. Across the South, the Rosenwald Fund financed 5,000 schools between 1914 and 1922. In rural Louisiana, the 372 Rosenwald schools accounted for a quarter of all black schools, a third of the total enrollment, and a half of all the teachers.[26]

The resulting educational improvements were dramatic. In 1915 fewer than half of Louisiana's black children were enrolled in schools, and on a typical day fewer than a quarter attended. The comparable figures for white children were 79 percent enrollment and 57 percent attendance. By 1940, two-thirds of black children were enrolled, and the daily attendance averaged 60 percent. The equivalent rates for whites were 78 percent and 73 percent. In the elementary grades, the disparity was narrower still: of children 5 to 9 years old, 67 percent of blacks attended school compared with 68 percent of whites. In the 10-to-14 age range, school attendance stood at 87 percent for blacks and 95 percent for whites.[27]

The universalization of elementary education had a profound effect on black Louisianians. Between 1920 and 1930 their rate of illiteracy declined from 38 percent to 23 percent. Equally important, the school-building program mobilized local black communities in a collective effort that enhanced their solidarity and gave them a tangible stake in education. The Rosenwald Fund and state taxes combined paid only 70 percent of the cost of new schools: blacks themselves raised about a quarter of the total by contributing money, materials, land, and labor. In many cases, the black contribution was far higher. In St. Helena Parish, for example, the local school board provided only the lumber: blacks furnished the land, paid for a carpenter, and provided the labor. In Palmetto, St. Landry Parish, "We raised the money, cut the trees, cleared the land and built a school 24 feet by 20 feet. . . . We pulled out nails from scrap lumber. The boys made their own benches." Yet it was a condition of the Rosenwald Fund that all schools receiving any Rosenwald money be deeded to local school boards. Small wonder that blacks became increasingly resentful of the persisting inequalities between black and white schools.[28]

For all its good works, however, the interracial movement was small, weak, fitful, and beset by internal contradictions. When blacks and whites sat down together and engaged in calm, rational discussion, it could only be judged a step forward. However, blacks and whites interpreted interracialism quite differently. Blacks saw it as a stepping-stone toward complete equality, including, ultimately, the abolition of segregation. Most whites, on the other hand, contemplated improvements within the structure of racial segregation. By the 1930s, as the Depression eliminated the scope for amelioration and made southern blacks more militant, this basic contradiction rendered the CIC increasingly ineffective.[29]

In Louisiana the flame of interracialism flickered dimly, could rarely be seen outside New Orleans, and in the early 1930s expired. The movement's basic ethos was apparent from the program adopted in June 1920 by a conference of whites top-heavy with planters, bankers, and businessmen. Scattered throughout the proposals for improving black health, recreation, and education were condescending comments that implied that blacks were to blame for their own low status. "Negroes are not fully awakened to their opportunities in Louisiana," the document lamented, and it went on to chide blacks for, among other things, "lack of civic pride" and a tendency to "spend their idle time in shooting craps, [and] to stay awake half of the night . . . in emotional orgies." To remind blacks that they did not have racial equality in mind, the white conferees noted that "Louisiana has wisely passed miscegenation laws," and they praised segregation as "wise and proper" and "in the interest of both races."[30]

Outside New Orleans, interracial committees either failed to materialize or lapsed into inactivity after one or two meetings. Many blacks treated the movement with suspicion, regarding it as a ploy to preserve the status quo. Blacks "doubt the sincerity of the white men who have been suggested as members," explained one white, referring to the absence of a local committee in Shreveport; blacks also suspected that "the Colored men on the committee would be entirely dominated by the White members." That was in 1922. Nine years later, when Jesse Daniel Ames was organizing the Association of Southern Women for the Prevention of Lynching, an offshoot of the CIC, she also drew a blank in north Louisiana. "I failed utterly in securing someone to represent this part of the state," lamented her Shreveport contact.[31]

A third line of interracial communication ran through the Roman Catholic Church. At first sight, the continuing allegiance of many blacks to that institution appears perverse: the all-white hierarchy seemed to do everything possible to offend and alienate the church's black adherents. Indeed, the church's racism contributed to a dramatic falling away of the black faithful after the Civil War, and the institution of segregated Negro parishes led to further defections. Some blacks left for Protestant denominations; others remained nominal Catholics but ceased attending services. Arthur J. Chapital, who became a mainstay of the New Orleans NAACP, joined a Congregational church. A. P. Tureaud's father simply stopped going to church when he was reassigned to the all-Negro Corpus Christi Parish.

Yet, ironically, the creation of segregated Negro churches helped to preserve the church's core support among black Catholics. While some objected in principle to separate churches, many came to recognize their practical advantages and learned, at the very least, to acquiesce in the new system. When blacks had attended mixed churches the discrimination was gross and visible: they usually stood or sat at the back, A. P. Tureaud recalled, and "the priests simply didn't take any interest in us." In the Negro parishes, by contrast, at least blacks did not have to endure segregation within the church, and their white priests, many of them members of the Josephite order, were much more likely to have a sincere concern for their spiritual and material welfare.[32]

Black Catholics saw education as the most tangible benefit of all-Negro parishes. After the Civil War the church made practically no provision for Negro education; nearly all of the black secondary schools in New Orleans were Protestant institutions located uptown, distant from the center of the Creole-Catholic population. For primary education, blacks had to rely on the public schools, which taught all classes in English and became, in the words of one authority, "a powerful instrument of Americanization" for French-speaking black Creoles. By the end of the nineteenth century the Catholic hierarchy recognized that the decline of the French language was eroding the number of black Catholics. Parochial schools would help stem these losses: in an era when white support for black education was at a low ebb, schooling offered blacks a strong incentive for remaining within the faith. Black Catholics finally acceded to a segregated church, argues John B. Alberts, "in order to get new schools."[33]

As they ceased to speak French and their social status declined, allegiance to the Catholic Church became an increasingly important part of Creole self-identity in New Orleans. Although not all Creoles were Catholics and not all Catholics Creoles, the church loomed large in the lives of many Creoles of color. Corpus Christi Parish, founded in 1916 and located in the Seventh Ward, boasted twelve thousand members; it claimed to be the largest Negro church in the world. In 1941 the Catholic Church operated sixty-three colored grade schools and eight Negro high schools in Louisiana, about half of them in New Orleans. Xavier University in New Orleans, founded in 1915, was the nation's only Catholic institution of higher learning for blacks. New Orleans was also home to the national headquarters of the Knights of Peter Claver, a Catholic fraternal society for black laymen founded in 1909. The society had more members in Louisiana than any other state.[34]

Acceptance of a segregated church, however, reinforced a tendency in the Creole community to look inward, regarding itself as separate and distinct from the black population as a whole. Indeed, visitors to New Orleans frequently commented that the cultural divide between the Creoles of color and the "American" Negroes aggravated black disunity and weakened black capacity for collective action.

According to the common stereotype, Creoles of color were the light-skinned descendants of the antebellum *gens de couleur libre*. They lived "downtown," below Canal Street, mainly in the Seventh Ward. They belonged to the Catholic Church and had their own clubs and societies: the two social hubs of Creole life in the Seventh Ward were Corpus Christi church and the Autocrat Club, a men's club on St. Bernard Avenue founded in 1914. The more numerous "Americans," on the other hand, descended from the darker-skinned slaves; they lived "uptown," attended public schools, and worshipped in Protestant churches. The American blacks were on the whole poorer, although they also tended to dominate business and the professions.

In the early part of the century it was quite possible for Creoles and blacks to live their lives rarely encountering members of the other group. "The Creoles of the 7th Ward had a society almost exclusively of their own," A. P. Tureaud recalled of his childhood days before World War I. "Back in those days there wasn't too much mingling between Creole Negroes and what we called the American blacks above Canal Street." The two groups were such strangers to each other that men faced the risk of assault if they strayed into unfamiliar territory.[35]

To outsiders, the Creoles of the Seventh Ward still resembled a clannish elite. Indeed, there were always some blacks who suspected that Creoles hankered after the kind of privileged position that the *gens de couleur libre* had enjoyed before the Civil War. After all, the antebellum free blacks had often prospered at the expense of the slave population. During the colonial period they had served, in the words of historian Ted Tunnell, as "white society's strongest ally against servile revolt." By 1830, almost one thousand free blacks were slaveholders themselves, and when the Civil War came, the free people of color formed volunteer militia units to help defend the Confederacy. Even after Emancipation, many of them had proposed restricting black suffrage to the former *gens de couleur libre*. When they finally endorsed universal suffrage, embracing the cause of the ex-slaves, they were responding, in Tunnell's view, less to a "genuine awakening of liberal conscience" than to a "realistic perception of class interest." Long after the Civil War, some blacks nursed the suspicion that Creole egalitarianism masked a desire to regain a privileged status or even "pass" for white.[36]

But the charge that Creoles thought and acted as if they were a superior caste was a gross exaggeration of one tendency within Creole society. An awareness of their peculiar cultural identity did not prevent most Creoles of color from identifying with the plight of the larger black population; indeed, Creoles provided many of the most militant leaders in the struggle against racial discrimination. Former free people of color dominated the black leadership during Reconstruction, and their descendants included some of the most vigorous opponents of segregation. A Creole group, the *Comité des Citoyens*, fought the establishment of Jim Crow streetcars in New Orleans and organized the challenge to the 1890 Separate Car Act, requiring segregated railway carriages, that resulted in the *Plessy* v. *Ferguson* decision. The same group resisted the introduction of segregation in the Catholic Church. "These persons," complained Archbishop Janssens in 1895, "aim at a greater equality with the whites, politically and socially." In 1925 the Creole Dejoie family founded the *Louisiana Weekly*, whose eloquent editorials flayed the hypocrisies of racism. There was no more dedicated servant of the NAACP and foe of racial discrimination than A. P. Tureaud. In truth, black notions of Creole exclusiveness were to a large extent distorted by ignorance and myth. The widespread belief, for example, that Creole social clubs employed a "brown bag test" to exclude people of dark complexion had no basis in fact. Nevertheless, the belief persists to this day.[37]

There was, to be sure, another side to the Creole coin. Creole pride embodied a feeling of cultural superiority that stuck in the craw of many blacks. Although not all Creoles were light-skinned, some Creole families placed a high social value upon light skin and European-looking features. Even if, as A. P. Tureaud insisted, color was less important than hair texture in defining one's social acceptability in Creole circles, a light complexion was still advantageous: straight hair could "compensate" for dark skin, but a light skin needed no such compensation. And if the "brown bag test" was a myth, the formation of social networks on the basis of light skin color was very much a reality. When some Creole families spoke of a "mixed marriage" they were making unfavorable reference to a match between a light-skinned Creole and a dark-skinned non-Creole.[38]

Such attitudes were even more pronounced among some of the Creoles of rural Louisiana. Along the Cane River south of Natchitoches, in the Frilot Cove area near Opelousas, and in small towns like White Castle in Iberville Parish, light-skinned people of color, many descended from *gens de couleur libre* who had been wealthy slaveholders, continued to live in self-contained communities. They attended separate schools, sat as a distinct group in church, married only among themselves, and maintained a strict social distance from the dark-skinned blacks around them. In Plaquemines Parish the Catholic Church provided a separate school for mulattoes. The people of Frilot Cove made life so difficult for the dark-skinned teachers appointed to their local elementary school in 1937 that the school board replaced them with light-skinned staff. Writing in 1940, T. Lynn Smith and Homer L. Hitt described such groups as "suspended between two worlds, reflecting in their lives the tragedy of people doomed to racial isolation."[39]

Outside observers frequently exaggerated the extent to which skin color differentiated black Creoles and black Americans. In the rural parishes of southwestern Louisiana, for example, color had far less social significance than it did in enclaves like Frilot Cove. Yet although tiny, often too small to appear on the map, communities like Frilot Cove represented an important ideological pole, an extreme manifestation of a pervasive attitude. For many blacks, Creole and non-Creole alike, color remained an important point of reference. Mixed ancestry and light skin implied higher social status. It could even involve the possibility of "passing" for white, a fairly common phenomenon that evoked mixed feelings of resentment, envy, and satisfaction in the community that the "passablanc" left behind. Conversely, it was praise indeed to observe that a light-skinned black refused to pass, even when — the example of A. P. Tureaud was often mentioned — he "looked like a white man."[40]

If color represented a source of division among blacks in Louisiana, it also constantly reminded them of the hypocrisy, inconsistency, and illogicality of segregation. The very ubiquity of light-skinned blacks, many of whom could or did "pass," testified to the imprecision of the South's racial categories and made a mockery of the white claim to "pure blood."

Blacks delighted in stories that revealed the inability of whites to distinguish between the races. A. P. Tureaud recalled an occasion in court when the opposing lawyer suggested that they "have some fun with these niggers," apparently confusing his race. Opelousas lawyer Marion O. White related how, traveling by bus, he was once ordered to find another seat because the driver mistook his light-skinned companion for a white child. The only Negro to serve as a juror in Orleans Parish was selected in the erroneous belief that he was white. According to Ernest J. Wright, New Orleans hired its first black social workers believing them to be whites. During the Second World War, when the shipyards refused to employ black welders, numerous blacks gained employment by "passing." Dr. Leonard Burns remembered that the New Orleans police once raided a social event at Municipal Auditorium after receiving a complaint that blacks and whites were dancing together. Hearing an explanation that none of the couples were in fact "mixed," a puzzled cop scratched his head and complained, "I can't tell who's who around here!"[41]

Such anecdotes, apocryphal or real, subverted the racial ideology of segregation and mocked white efforts to enforce the color line. Tales attributing Negro ancestry to prominent whites performed the same function. When St. Bernard Parish dropped the prosecution of eight couples it had indicted for miscegenation, blacks speculated that district attorney Leander Perez feared the exposure of many other interracial liaisons; Perez himself, a fanatical white supremacist, was rumored to have a "colored auntie." The people of New Orleans "don't know whether they're white or black," averred one civil rights activist. "I say the ones as black as me don't know whether they're white, and the ones as white as snow don't know whether they're black." To this day, blacks still chuckle over Huey Long's observation that all the "pure whites" in Louisiana could be fed "with a nickel's worth of red beans and a dime's worth of rice."[42]

For the most part, the differences between black Americans and black Creoles reflected culture rather than color: dark-skinned Creoles abounded, as did light-complexioned Americans. At the same time, the distinction between Creole and American became increasingly blurred through intermarriage, social mobility, the decline of the French language, and the sheer weight of white supremacy. Writing at the close of the 1930s, Allison Davis noted that "the Creole group itself is merging socially and biologically into the American Negro group."

Yet the contrast between Creole and American remained a cultural landmark of black life in New Orleans, subtly influencing perceptions and interactions. Members of the NAACP's executive committee tried to explain to a visiting researcher the superior virtues of the "downtown" Negroes. "The 'downtown' group has a traditional culture which the 'uptown' group cannot understand," asserted one. "When leadership comes from 'uptown' it is bizarre as only it can be from an uncultured group." Chimed in another: "The 'downtown' people came in close contact with the European old-world culture; the quadroon mistresses mingled with the best European whites. Poor whites are just as crude as the poorest, darkest and most-kinky-headed Negroes 'uptown.'"[43]

The New Orleans branch of the NAACP, founded in 1915, provided Creoles and Americans with a common vehicle for opposing racial discrimination. Cultural differences, however, remained an irritant, especially before 1930. Lighter-skinned African-Americans were insufficiently militant, complained Ernest Cherrie, a young physician. "Our population of Negro descent is so thoroughly mixed that approximately seventy-five percent have what is termed 'white complex.' Although they associate with those of darker hue, they are not willing to assist in righting wrongs." The branch's long fight in the 1920s against the city's segregated housing ordinance marked one of the first occasions on which the two groups made common cause, forming "a joint committee of Creoles and colored people."[44]

The NAACP also had to contend with a neighborhood parochialism that complicated the uptown/downtown division. In the 1930s, despite the defeat of the segregation ordinance, housing in New Orleans became increasingly segregated, and the construction of separate public housing projects accelerated the trend. Even so, blacks were still scattered across a handful of relatively small neighborhoods, and many still lived in largely white parts of the city. Hundreds of "social aid and pleasure" clubs reinforced the identity with neighborhood, block, and street. The dispersed population presented another obstacle to black unity.[45]

Neighborhood localism was not wholly divisive, however; neighborhoods provided the building blocks of organization and mutual aid. Social clubs like the Autocrat Club and the San Jacinto Club bridged the Protestant/Catholic division and served, in the words of historian Arnold Hirsch, "as neutral meeting places for those leery of attending gatherings in churches not their own." Such clubs also provided bedrock support for the New Orleans NAACP.[46]

Even more vital to the NAACP's development was the network of doctors, pharmacists, and businessmen associated with the black insurance industry. Growing out of neighborhood-based benevolent societies that furnished health care, sickness pensions, and funeral benefits, the insurance companies became the most important black-owned businesses in Louisiana. At a time when there were only 1,600 Negro-owned businesses in the entire state, when Louisiana had only two or three black lawyers, and when the census identified only 656 blacks in New Orleans as professionals or semiprofessionals, the significance of the insurance industry as a source of race leadership can scarcely be overstated. Moreover, the larger ones maintained offices throughout the state, providing an important network of communication. Dr. Joseph A. Hardin, cofounder of the Seventh Ward Civic League, Walter L. Cohen, Republican politician, and the Dejoie family, owners of the *Louisiana Weekly,* all founded insurance companies. NAACP stalwarts like George W. Lucas, A. M. Trudeau, and Daniel Byrd all at one time worked for insurance companies.[47]

The New Orleans NAACP scored some notable successes during its early years. In 1927 it achieved a legal triumph when the United States Supreme Court struck down the city ordinance establishing segregated residential areas. Three years later it hired a lawyer to assist in the prosecution of Charles Guerand, a white man who shot and killed a fourteen-year-old girl, Hattie McCray, who had resisted his sexual advances. In a courtroom hushed into stunned silence, an all-white jury found Guerand guilty — probably the first time that a white had been sentenced to death for the murder of a Negro.

Such successes were ephemeral, however, and had little impact on the lives of black people. Housing segregation continued to advance. Guerand escaped hanging when he was declared insane, and in 1936 he won a new trial. Not surprisingly, the branch found it difficult to translate such paper victories into popular support for the NAACP. "We attribute this indifference to the general characteristic of our group," explained Dr. George W. Lucas, the branch's president. "Fighting for the race is very unpopular with our people."[48]

Some of its own characteristics, however, contributed to the branch's weakness. The formal democracy of the NAACP, with its emphasis upon correct parliamentary procedure, discouraged mass involvement while encouraging internal "politicking." In New Orleans, moreover, the faction fights of the Republican party sometimes spilled over into the branch. In 1929, for example, the death of Walter L. Cohen triggered a fight for control within the "black-and-tan" faction that exacerbated rows within the branch over the selection of lawyers. The ostensible cause of the quarrel was the branch's insistence on choosing a white lawyer to handle a court challenge to the voter registration laws. In 1931 A. P. Tureaud angrily quit the NAACP executive committee when branch president George Labat berated colored lawyers for venality during a Republican meeting. Tureaud, five years out of Howard Law School, was incensed not only with the selection of Henry Warmoth Robinson, a prominent member of the "lily-white" faction, but also with the branch's professed lack of confidence in black lawyers. "Colored attorneys are sought only on occasions when free services are required," he complained. "Or to make speeches for the cause." The NAACP national office, however, rejected Tureaud's request to charter a rival branch.[49]

Outside New Orleans, the NAACP had a tenuous existence. A branch had been organized in Shreveport as early as 1914, the first in the Deep South, but after ten years of intermittent activity it lapsed into silence. "The NAACP is thoroughly hated in this section," the branch president, Dr. Claude Hudson, wrote in 1923. The previous year, angry newspaper editorials and threats from city officials caused the branch to cancel a visit from field secretary William Pickens. "The great trouble here," Hudson explained, "is that they do not want the southern Negro to have much dealings with his northern brother." By 1930 seven other branches had been chartered, but few managed to survive, let alone translate the initial burst of enthusiasm into sustained effort. The prospects for a statewide black movement were bleak. An attempt in 1920 to band the branches into a state conference came to nothing. The barriers to statewide organization were many: long distances and bad roads, endemic poverty and widespread illiteracy, suspicion and jealousy of New Orleans, and a paucity of black professionals, especially lawyers. In south Louisiana there was the additional problem of language; many blacks in the rural parishes spoke only French.[50]

During the first two decades of the twentieth century the legal, political, and economic status of blacks had stabilized into one of across-the-board inferiority. Protests had been unavailing. At the end of the 1920s, however, the world of all Louisianians, black and white, began to change. The election of Huey Long as governor in 1928 inaugurated a political upheaval, and the following year the Wall Street Crash ushered in an economic disaster. For black Louisianians the 1930s were to begin in desperation and end in hope.

Chapter 2

RACE AND POWER IN THE LONG ERA

L ongism" built upon Louisiana's well-established traditions of political thuggery, electoral chicanery, flagrant disregard for civil liberties, and racial oppression. Huey Long and his supporters, who between them controlled the state government between 1928 and 1940, did little for black Louisianians. Long himself did not question white supremacy. Equally important, he did not challenge the structure of local political power that kept African-Americans in subjugation. True, Long retaliated against opponents by withholding patronage, gerrymandering electoral districts, and sundry other punitive acts, but local politicos who supported him ruled with a relatively free hand. Long struck deals with whomever he could, and how his allies dealt with blacks did not concern him. In fact, as far as race was concerned, supporters and opponents alike were free to treat blacks as they would.[1]

Long's henchmen included some of the South's most vehement racists, such as Leander H. Perez, boss of Plaquemines Parish and a staunch Longite until he broke with Huey's brother Earl in 1950. A ferocious anti-Semite as well as a vitriolic negrophobe, he spearheaded the Dixiecrat revolt of 1948. During the 1950s he devised many of the laws and legal tactics that hampered black voting and blocked school desegregation, and in 1960 he championed the racist mobs of New Orleans and ensured that school integration there was a shambles. Ruling over his bailiwick with the power of a medieval baron, he remained one of the most formidable and unyielding foes of the civil rights movement until death removed his malignant presence in 1969.[2]

In the Deep South of the 1920s and 1930s, Long's own racism was relatively restrained. Virtually every southern politician exploited the prejudices of the white electorate, reasoning that if they did not, their opponents would. But there was a distinction, some have argued, between the politician who framed his public appeal around racism, who deliberately stirred up white racial hatred in a vicious and calculating manner, and the one who merely resorted to "nigger-baiting" as an occasional political device. Huey Long was a politician of the second type. His principal rhetorical targets were the "thieving" oil companies, the "lying" newspapers, and the "crooked" politicians, not blacks.

But if Long's racism was subdued compared with that of Bilbo of Mississippi or Talmadge of Georgia, he was by no means unschooled in race-baiting as a political tactic. During a 1924 campaign he professed dismay that an opponent "would ever openly accept a negro's political help against a white Democrat." In 1930, he angrily denounced as an "outrage" the opening of a movie theater for Negroes in the New Orleans downtown business district. Two years later, Long smeared gubernatorial candidate Dudley LeBlanc as a "nigger-lover" because he ran a burial society that had a mainly black clientele. He also ridiculed LeBlanc's proposal for state-funded old-age pensions on the grounds that "you white people will be working the year round to pay pensions to niggers." In private and in public, Long lampooned blacks as slow-witted "niggers" and "coons."[3]

Long sometimes presented himself as a friend of blacks. He boasted to Roy Wilkins, a young NAACP official sent to interview him, that his personal power enabled him to do things "quietly for the niggers" when others "would have been murdered politically" had they shown similar concern. He had provided blacks with schools and free textbooks "so they could learn to read and write and figger." He had given them free hospitals and clinics. He had even found jobs for black nurses in New Orleans's Charity Hospital by decrying the fact that white nurses risked catching awful diseases by attending black patients. "I'm for the poor man," he told Wilkins, "all poor men. Black and white, they all gotta have a chance. They gotta have a home, a job and a decent education for their children. 'Every Man a King' — that's my slogan. That means every man, niggers along with the rest." When he launched his "Share

Our Wealth" movement, designed as a national springboard for a presidential campaign in 1936, blacks were encouraged to join. Even in the South, Negro "Share Our Wealth" clubs sprang up.[4]

But the extent to which blacks in Louisiana benefited from Long's program is unclear. Long "certainly had no intention of positively aiding blacks," writes one authority. For all his boasts about reducing black illiteracy, spending on Negro schools was drastically curtailed during the Long regime, and although white schools also suffered during the Depression, the burden of retrenchment fell unevenly. In 1930, for example, the average salary of black teachers stood at about 40 percent of the white average; by 1935, the year of Long's assassination, that figure had dropped to 32 percent. During the same period, per capita spending on black children fell from 22 percent of the white level to only 17 percent. The most that can be said is that if Long's reforms benefited blacks, it was largely inadvertently. "The case for Huey Long as an active friend of black Louisianans," writes Alan Brinkley, "is little stronger than the case for him as an active enemy."[5]

Ultimately, Long's attitude to race was strictly and shrewdly political. "He wouldn't hesitate to throw Negroes to the wolves if it became necessary," Roy Wilkins guessed; "neither would he hesitate to carry them along if the good they did him was greater than the harm." Writer Carleton Beals offered a similar judgment shortly after Long's death. "Huey's sectional racial prejudice was about average. He could, if necessary, submerge it — in a political sense he had no prejudices at all." Appealing to whites primarily on the basis of class, Long had little to gain by exacerbating racial antagonism. Moreover, he nurtured national as well as state ambitions, and as his presidential aspirations swelled he became aware of the growing black vote in the North and the necessity of surmounting the common stereotype of the race-baiting southern politician.[6]

In Louisiana, however, blacks were a political cipher, and Long intended to keep it that way. When he became governor of Louisiana in 1928, about two thousand blacks were registered voters out of an adult black population of about three-quarters of a million. They represented 0.5 percent of the total electorate.

Black interest in voting waned but never died. In 1927 the San Jacinto Club invited the Orleans Parish registrar of voters to explain the registration procedures; his statement to the effect that Negroes lacked the education to qualify caused such resentment that it prompted the formation of the Seventh Ward Civic League, the Eighth Ward Civic League, and two years later the citywide Federation of Civic Leagues. The civic league movement stimulated interest in voting by encouraging blacks to pay the poll tax and by coaching black applicants. It was not the procedures themselves, however, that kept blacks off the rolls, but the unfair administration of the registration process. The registrar of voters, appointed by the governor, rejected black applicants as a matter of course, usually because of alleged errors in filling out the application form.

Few applicants proceeded to the literacy test or to the alternative test for illiterates, each of which required applicants to "understand and give a reasonable interpretation of any section" of the U.S. or Louisiana constitutions. If they did, the excuses for rejection were limitless. "A third grade student holding the position of deputy registrar," wrote Tureaud, "will insist that a college graduate can not give him a reasonable interpretation of the Constitution."[7]

In 1931 the New Orleans branch of the NAACP filed a test case to challenge Louisiana's "understanding clause." Huey Long's law partner, Hugh Wilkinson, represented the Orleans Parish registrar of voters and conferred closely with Long during the litigation. When the suit came to trial, Judge Wayne G. Borah ruled against the plaintiff, and in 1933 the Fifth Circuit Court of Appeals affirmed his judgment. The "understanding clause" applied to all voters alike, the appeals courts reasoned, and did not discriminate on its face. Moreover, the Louisiana Constitution of 1921 allowed rejected applicants to complain to the state courts; this the plaintiff, A. M. Trudeau, had failed to do. "We cannot say, and refuse to assume," the appeals court piously stated, "that, if the plaintiff had pursued the administrative remedy that was open to him, he would not have received any relief." Blacks in Louisiana knew otherwise: the right of appeal to a state court was worthless.[8]

In 1934 Long induced the state legislature to abolish the poll tax; henceforth voters merely had to sign a poll book in order to obtain, without charge, a poll tax "receipt." This reform augmented the white electorate by about two hundred thousand and boosted voter turnout by 10 percent. Blacks were rapidly disabused of the expectation that repeal of the poll tax would open the door to black voting. "It doesn't change the status of the nigger one bit," insisted R. J. Gregory, the registrar of Orleans Parish. "Some of these niggers don't even know when they were born. It's comical as hell, we get a regular picnic out of it. Oh, sure, they're coming down here alright but we're turning 'em down by the hundreds because they don't qualify."[9]

Harold Rouzan, a black insurance agent and a light-skinned Creole, recalled his first attempts to register:

> You'd fill out the application, and the white fellow behind the desk looked at you, and as soon as you put "Negro" down there he'd look at you and tear it up with a face as ugly as he possibly could and say, "It's wrong!", and tear it up and throw it in the waste basket, and say it loud to embarrass you all over the place. And then you'd have to eat humble pie and say, "Well, I'm sorry, sir," and walk away. Then I'd go back the next week, fill out another one, and I'd keep going back til they got tired of seeing this,

and they must have said, "This nigger is persistent," and they'd allow me to vote.

Robert Perry, a minister, remembered making sixteen attempts before his application was accepted. A. P. Tureaud suffered repeated rejections. "I know you can qualify if anybody can," a sympathetic registration clerk once told him, "but we have to do this on orders from above." Most blacks never applied or simply gave up after the first few rejections.[10]

Outside New Orleans, black efforts to register could be dangerous. When A. C. Terrance, a physician, applied to vote in Opelousas, the registrar sent him to the sheriff, who directed him to a local judge, who sent him back to the sheriff. Although Terrance, whose white patients included the local police chief, eventually registered, the next black applicant, an electrician by trade, was beaten unmercifully outside the court house. The sheriff witnessed the assault impassively. No other blacks besides Terrance were allowed to register, and few even attempted to do so. In Claiborne, a majority-black parish in northern Louisiana, the sheriff warned Frederick Douglass Lewis, a black farmer, that if he ever tried to vote he would "get the hell knocked out of him." Long himself was quite explicit that eliminating the poll tax would make no difference to blacks. "Do you think I could get away with niggers voting?" he asked Roy Wilkins. "No sirree!"[11]

It actually became more difficult for blacks to vote during the Long years. Charles H. Myers, president of the Monroe branch of the NAACP, had registered as a Republican since 1926. But since repeal of the poll tax, he complained to NAACP special counsel Charles H. Houston, "the parish officers have refused to let any colored people register. . . . I says to the sheriff, 'I need and wishes to sign the poll book, so I will be eligible to hold office in the Republican party.' He replies, 'nobody cares no body wants the office.' So on December 2, 1935 I goes back to the court house and asked to be permitted to sign the poll book. I was told to 'Get out no niggers were allowed to sign the poll book.'" When the Long regime fell from office in 1940 after twelve straight years in control of the state government, black registration had fallen below one thousand and represented a miniscule 0.16 percent of the electorate.[12]

The persistence of lynching strengthens the impression that the years of Longite control failed to improve the status of blacks in Louisiana. After declining during the 1920s, the early 1930s saw an upsurge of lynchings. It would be unfair to blame this trend on Long; the onset of the Depression was undoubtedly the main cause. Nevertheless, Long did little to curb lynching. This failure not only attested to his indifference to black welfare but also underlined the fact that outside the cities the sheriff still remained the kingpin of local politics. While Long was apt to clip the wings of local bosses, frequently interfering in their political backyards, the sheriff was still an official of immense power, especially when allied with the district attorney. And in dealing with blacks, the power of the "high sheriff" remained absolute. During the Huey Long era, and for many years afterward, union organizers, NAACP activists, Negro plaintiffs, and blacks seeking to vote risked being threatened, beaten, jailed, "run out of the parish," or slain.[13]

The involvement of sheriffs in lynchings was the most chilling evidence of their power over blacks. Blacks were usually lynched because sheriffs allowed them to be, in some cases permitting mobs to enter jails, at other times meekly surrendering prisoners to the mob before they ever reached the jail. Three of the four lynchings that occurred in 1933 involved the complicity of law officers. On February 19, Sheriff Jordan of Bienville Parish let a mob storm the parish jail and seize Nelson Cash, a suspected murderer and bank robber, and hang him on the spot. On August 26, near Opelousas, prisoner John White was "taken from a deputy sheriff . . . by a group of white men and hanged." On October 11, Freddy Moore, a sixteen-year-old boy, was taken from the Assumption Parish jail and hanged from a railroad bridge at Labadieville.[14]

The wonder is that blacks ever resisted white authority, yet fight back they sometimes did. In 1934 a farm boy shot a deputy sheriff who tried to arrest him without a warrant. The following year an agent of the Arkansas-Louisiana Gas Company was killed trying to evict a family from company property. In 1936 a farmer in St. John the Baptist Parish shot a constable who came to arrest him for allegedly stealing a plough four years earlier. In Lafayette Parish, a man riding a freight train killed three policemen when they challenged him.

Some believed that such acts deterred whites from pushing blacks too far. Perhaps. But the killing of whites, whatever the circumstances, brought swift retribution at the hands of a lynch mob or official executioner. Born of desperation, such deeds underlined the futility of opposing whites with force.[15]

Two lynchings merit particular attention. The first involved just such an example of resistance to white authority; the second exemplified in a particularly stark manner the utter powerlessness of the NAACP to investigate mob killings. Both illustrate the untrammelled power of the sheriff, even to the extent of flouting the state supreme court.

The first lynching stemmed from a dramatic shootout that took place on July 21, 1934, on the farm of John and Tempie Wilson near Franklinton in Washington Parish. John Wilson was a landowner, and a prosperous one at that; his recent purchase of eighty more acres made his farm several times the size of the typical black holding and on a par with the white farms around him. With five sons and three daughters, who all lived at home, Wilson grew corn, cotton, and sugarcane, and had a keen eye for a bargain when it came to buying and selling livestock. Locals respected him as an upright and honest man.[16]

On the day in question, a white stock inspector named Joe Magee visited the Wilson farm. Magee told Jerome, John's twenty-eight-year-old son, that one of his mules needed to be dipped under the tick eradication law. Jerome replied that he would have to wait for his father to return from Franklinton, whereupon an argument developed. Magee threatened to seize the mule there and then; Jerome ordered Magee off the farm and promised to shoot him if he laid hands on the animal.

When the enraged Magee returned an hour or two later with Deputy Sheriff Delos C. Wood and two other deputies, Jerome Wilson realized that his wisest course was to surrender the mule. But Wood had come for more than the mule. "Go with me, boy," he told Wilson, and walked toward the house to place him under arrest. Wilson refused to budge and, with his brother Moise, insisted on seeing a warrant. When the deputy sheriff made to grab Jerome, a tussle broke out, with Moise Wilson and Wood wrestling over Wood's pistol. Wood managed to pull his arm free and shot Moise in the stomach; either Wood or another deputy shot Jerome in the thigh. Jerome staggered into the house, fetched his shotgun, and fired at Wood. The blast hit Wood in the head, killing him instantly. The other deputies quickly overpowered the Wilsons, and shot two other brothers, including a twelve-year old boy, as they tried to flee. The entire family was jailed, including the mother, the sisters, an uncle, and — even though he had missed the entire incident — John Wilson. Moise Wilson died of his wounds later that day. A mob gathered outside the jail each night with a view to lynching the prisoners. The promise of a speedy trial and swift punishment kept it at bay.

On July 24, Jerome Wilson, his brother Luther, and their mother Tempie were charged with Wood's murder. John Wilson and four of his other children were held as material witnesses. The counsel appointed by the trial judge to defend them had three days to prepare his case; a second attorney had only two days. The fact that Jerome Wilson was seriously ill, and that the entire Wilson family was in jail, each in a separate cell, made their task impossible. Furthermore, they did not know until the morning of the trial whether the three defendants were to be tried together or separately.

The trial of Jerome Wilson, who had to be carried into the courtroom on a chair, opened on July 30 in Franklinton. In the second floor courtroom it was standing room only, and some whites perched themselves on the window sills outside. Apart from the defendant, no blacks were present: a relative of the Wilsons managed to squeeze his way into the room only to retreat before a rain of blows from elbows and fists. The selection of a jury consumed most of the day, and the trial proper did not get under way until late afternoon. The defense claimed that Jerome had only fetched his gun after Wood had shot Moise. Magee and deputy McCain countered that Jerome went for the gun before any shots had been fired. When the jury finally retired at 9:30 P.M. on July 31, the whites surrounding the courthouse were impatient. Seeing Jerome Wilson being carried back to the jail, someone shouted, "Get him!" and the crowd surged toward the prisoner. In the courthouse, the jury could hear Sheriff J. L. Brock pleading with the mob "to give the jury a chance." On August 1 Jerome Wilson was found guilty. The following day Judge C. Ellis Ott rejected the defense lawyers' motion for a new trial. On August 6 Ott sentenced Wilson to death by hanging.[17]

In Chicago, Percival L. Prattis of the American Negro Press news agency followed the trial with interest. On August 3 he alerted Roy Wilkins, a member of the NAACP's national staff and a seasoned journalist, to the story's potential. "It's as clear as crystal that convictions in these cases cannot stand," Prattis wrote. The speed of the trial, the lynch-mob atmosphere, and the circumstances of the shootout made it "a case in which you cannot lose and which will enable you to sensationally contrast the Association's methods with those of the [Communist] I.L.D." The stout defense of the Scottsboro boys by the International Labor Defense had made the NAACP appear slow and timid. In 1934, moreover, the ILD had made an appearance in Louisiana, publicizing the lynching of Freddy Moore.[18]

At the urging of Walter White, the NAACP's executive secretary, the New Orleans branch retained a white criminal lawyer, G. Wray Gill, to appeal Jerome Wilson's sentence and prepare the defense of Tempie and Luther Wilson. When the state asked for a continuance in the case of Tempie Wilson on November 5, it became evident that the prosecution was losing confidence. Two days later the Louisiana Supreme Court ordered a new trial for Jerome Wilson on the grounds that the defense had been given inadequate time to prepare their case. "It is only natural that there should be public indignation when it might appear that a foul and brutal killing took place," the court reasoned, "but it should not be permitted to interfere with the orderly process of justice in such a way as to deprive the accused of his constitutional rights and guaranties." On January 11, Walter White received a letter from James E. Gayle, president of the New Orleans branch, informing him of the successful appeal.[19]

Jerome Wilson never got his second trial. Earlier that day, in the small hours of the morning, a group of whites had entered the Washington Parish jail in Franklinton. They killed Wilson with a hammer, and then dumped his body in a ditch. The reaction of Sheriff J. L. Brock, who gave the reporters a detailed account of how Wilson met his death, spoke volumes: "There wasn't any lynching. There wasn't any mob either. . . . They were just about six or eight men who were going about their business." Thus did a local sheriff flout the highest judicial tribunal in the State of Louisiana.[20]

With the Costigan-Wagner antilynching bill before Congress, Wilson's fate gave the NAACP more ammunition in its propaganda war against the South's Capitol Hill solons. In a sarcastic telegram to Huey Long, now a senator, White noted that "it is widely reported . . . that you are virtual dictator of State of Louisiana and that you are able to accomplish anything you choose to attempt in State." If so, White taunted, would Long make good his recent statement, delivered in opposition to the Costigan-Wagner Bill, that the southern states would themselves wipe out lynching? In an angry letter to President Roosevelt containing a lengthy account of the case, White restated his perennial demand for forceful presidential action against lynching. The Writers League Against Lynching, whose letterhead read like a who's who of the literary world, added its own protests. And on January 30 in New Orleans, sixty-two community organizations sponsored an antilynching rally at the Pythian Temple. The protests availed little. The Costigan-Wagner Bill fell before the brick wall of a southern filibuster; Jerome Wilson's killers went unpunished.[21]

The day after the lynching, speaking to Roy Wilkins of the NAACP, Huey Long made light of the affair. It was "too bad," he lamented, "but those slips will happen." Still, he noted, "that nigger was guilty of cold-blooded murder." Wilkins protested that the Louisiana Supreme Court had just granted him a new trial. Long brushed away the point. "This nigger got hold of a smart lawyer somewhere and proved a technicality. He was guilty as hell." It would be pointless to pursue the lynchers because "it might cause a hundred more niggers to be killed. You wouldn't want that, would you?"[22]

Three years later, on October 13, 1938, a group of whites lynched W. C. Williams, nineteen years old, near Ruston in north Louisiana. They committed the deed in broad daylight with a crowd of hundreds urging them on.

Williams was suspected of murdering a white paper-mill worker and beating his girlfriend, a waitress, as the couple kept a lover's tryst in the rear seat of a car; he had surrendered to a posse after being tracked for two days. His captors marched him to the scene of the crime and tortured a confession from him. When Sheriff Bryan Thigpen arrived, one of the mob held a gun to Williams's head and threatened to kill him on the spot. The sheriff and the mob talked back and forth for a few minutes. "I promised to ask for a special session of the grand jury at once, and emphasized that a speedy trial and hanging would follow," Thigpen later explained. "I told them I would hang the negro myself." A college professor, L. F. Fox, and, according to one account, relatives of the beaten waitress pleaded for Williams's life. Thigpen then assented to what he surely knew was a ruse: the mob proposed to walk Williams through the woods to a side road, where they promised to meet the sheriff and surrender their prisoner. With members of the state police in tow, Thigpen got in his car and drove round the hill.

Members of the mob then stabbed and beat Williams, hanged him from an oak tree, and shot at his body for about ten minutes. When Sheriff Thigpen heard the shots he immediately returned to Ruston, believing there was "nothing further I could do." By the time Williams's corpse was cut down, thousands of whites had visited the scene. At one time cars were parked along the highway for over a mile.[23]

The New Orleans NAACP dared not investigate the affair. Even the *Shreveport Sun,* the nearest black newspaper, feared sending a reporter. In Baton Rouge, Dr. H. Horne Huggins, an officer in the local NAACP branch, discussed the lynching with Gordon McIntire, the white organizer of the Louisiana Farmers Union. With Huggins's encouragement, McIntire made an overnight drive to Ruston, completing the two-hundred-mile journey shortly after daybreak. He found whites still poring over the scene of the lynching "hunting for shells, drops of dried blood on leaves, pieces of bark from the oak tree and other souvenirs." From the whites he spoke to, McIntire judged that "public sentiment in Lincoln Parish is 95% with the lynchers." Fox, the sociology professor who interceded for Williams, had been roundly criticized. A white minister refused to comment on the lynching, admitting to feeling "very nervous." A student at a local college described his feelings when he saw Williams's bullet-riddled body: "I let out a big whoop. I felt just like the home team had won." Local blacks clammed up when McIntire approached them; only one talked to him.[24]

Almost a month later, the president of the Monroe NAACP branch, Charles Myers, supplied Walter White with a rumor that was going the rounds, that the murdered mill worker, R. R. Blair, had not been killed by Williams at all, but by his paramour's irate husband. White had no way of checking this story, however, knowing that if any local Negro became connected with it "his life would not be worth a plugged nickel." Howard Kester, a white North Carolinian who had probed the lynching of Claude Neal in Marianna, Florida, in 1934, agreed to visit Ruston in an effort to track down the rumor, but afterward he advised White to drop the case. "What I could discover did not cause me to feel that it was the sort of case to which the NAACP could absolutely tie to without any misgivings or doubts." He thought that Williams had probably been guilty.[25]

State judge E. L. Walker convened a grand jury, but after hearing twenty-five witnesses it failed to return any indictments. Walker thanked the jurors for having "fully and honorably discharged their duty." All the NAACP could do was get maximum mileage from the case in terms of publicity and propaganda, but the prospects of Congress passing an antilynching bill were fading. In February, southern senators had talked out the latest proposal, with Louisiana's Allen J. Ellender contributing a marathon speech of twenty-seven hours, holding the floor for a record six days. During the course of his "speech" Ellender openly disparaged blacks, advocated repeal of the Fifteenth Amendment, and urged federal legislation to ban interracial marriages. Rubbing salt in his wounds, Walter White received an unsolicited and abusive letter from Sheriff Thigpen, which opined that even if the bill were passed, it would have "about as much affect [sic] on lynchings as the pouring of a mere drop of water in the Atlantic ocean."[26]

Yet the killing of Williams turned out to be the last time a Louisiana mob lynched a black person in broad daylight. Lynching had been on the wane since the early 1920s, thanks in part to the NAACP's campaign for an antilynching law, which induced the southern states to discourage lynchings in order to avert congressional action. In addition, the tireless efforts of the Association of Southern Women for the Prevention of Lynching had slowly but inexorably changed white attitudes. The ASWPL repeatedly refuted the traditional justifications for lynching: that lynching "protected" southern white womanhood; that southern courts could not adequately punish Negro criminals; and that southern sheriffs were powerless to stop lynch mobs.[27]

A further sharp decline in lynching at the end of the 1930s reflected the heightened fear of federal intervention felt by southern politicians. Although the New Deal focused on the South's economic problems, Roosevelt sympathized with the cause of black citizenship; his dependence on southern Democrats in Congress limited his scope for action, but he nevertheless encouraged southern liberals to challenge the status quo. In 1938 he cautiously backed the formation of the Southern Conference for Human Welfare (SCHW), an interracial coalition of liberals and radicals that held its first meeting in Birmingham, Alabama. In 1939 he created the Civil Rights Section of the Justice Department, which instigated FBI investigations of lynchings and initiated the first federal prosecution of a police brutality case. Without doubt, the existence of the section had a tonic effect on southern officials. When Clinton Clark, an organizer for the Louisiana Farmers Union, was detained in Natchitoches jail in July 1940, state attorney general Eugene Stanley phoned the local district attorney and warned him to keep the prisoner alive. "We've got to be careful," Stanley insisted. "The State is on the spot. Can't afford that kind of thing with the federal government like it is. Remember now, no lynching!"[28]

Within days of Stanley's admonition, the *Louisiana Weekly* reported a legal decision that must have given southern sheriffs, who were fond of saying, "I *am* the law around here," pause for thought. This unusual case arose out of the lynching of Freddy Moore in October 1933. The lynchers accused him of murdering Annie Mae LaRose, a seventeen-year-old white girl. Later, however, the girl's stepfather confessed to the crime. Moore's parents sued Sheriff Lezin H. Himel for $10,000 in criminal damages, claiming that two of his deputies assisted the lynchers. Attorney Johnson Armstrong succeeded in having the case removed to a federal court on the basis that the action involved an interstate dispute, Moore's father being a native of Arkansas. An all-white jury awarded the Moores $2,500 in a judgment against the sheriff, an award that took four years to collect.[29]

As the "classic" lynching died out, however, lynching became increasingly difficult to define. For example, on October 31, 1935, Sheriff Frank Clancy of Jefferson Parish announced that two prisoners, Henry Freeman and Dave Hart, had been killed in Gretna jail trying to escape; they had somehow obtained a gun, he alleged, and wounded one of his deputies. Freeman and Hart were being held as suspects in a rape and robbery case, the latest of a series. Whites in New Orleans were appalled by the crimes, convinced of the pair's guilt, and indifferent to their fate. Rumors of a mob lynching were all over the city.[30]

Did the deaths of Freeman and Hart constitute a lynching? Blacks considered it one in all but name. "No one here believes the story of the smuggled gun," reported James E. Gayle of the New Orleans NAACP. Gayle requested the services of a white investigator, and Walter White sent Howard Kester. But Kester gloomily reported that it would be difficult if not impossible to establish the truth: he had been unable to locate any of the dead men's relatives, and a rumor that Freeman and Hart had been hanged from a bridge could not be substantiated. Walter White's principal white contact in the city, businessman and philanthropist Edgar B. Stern, discouraged the investigation. It would only cause trouble, he advised. This had been a "particularly atrocious" rape, and few whites doubted the dead men's guilt. The newspapers had even played down the rape "for fear of a race riot." In any case, Stern pointed out, the jailers' story would be impossible to disprove. Kester considered recruiting a black volunteer who would have himself arrested in order to get inside Gretna jail. Nothing, apparently, came of the idea.

Tom Tippett, a lecturer with the New York-based Affiliated Schools for Workers, happened to be in New Orleans at the time the prisoners died. "The thing that floored me most," he wrote White, "was the attitude of these people — liberals, radicals, advanced thinkers — on the lynching before it took place and their refusal afterwards to do a single thing about it." Blacks seemed afraid, and the local chapter of the NAACP was weak. "I understand why they are impotent and afraid . . . much better than I ever did before." The truth about how Hart and Freeman met their deaths remained elusive. "That the men were lynched," wrote Kester, "I haven't any doubt whatever. Exactly when, where and by whom we don't know positively."[31]

The Gretna killings provide an essential context for judging the decline of "classic" lynchings. Blacks well knew that racial murders were still commonplace. As the *Louisiana Weekly* commented in 1940, the Tuskegee Institute had erred to the point of fatuity in claiming that the first six months of that year had been free of lynchings. "The illegal police murders . . . and various mysterious homicides are lynchings and have not ceased." Shortly after this editorial appeared, as if to underscore the point, a white resident of Jefferson Parish wrote to Walter White regarding the Gretna jail where Hart and Freeman had met their deaths five years earlier. Police chief Beauregard H. Miller, he alleged, "not only . . . beats his negro prisoners but recently has killed two of them under the pretext that they were either resisting arrest or fleeing."[32]

If the Long regime's racial liberalism turns out to be a myth, its championship of the poor was equally phoney. Huey Long's battles against the corporations were mock-heroics, his "Share Our Wealth" program a political gimmick. While he was vociferously attacking the oil and utility companies, he was also enriching himself by taking their bribes and favors.

Oil, in particular, greased the wheels of the Long machine and fed the ravenous corruption that became a hallmark of state politics during the Long era. First discovered in Jennings in 1901, oil had subsequently been found in virtually every nook and cranny of the state. By the 1930s squat, ugly symbols of the twentieth century, oil derricks, pockmarked the countryside, making Louisiana the nation's third biggest producer of crude petroleum and second biggest supplier of natural gas. With the exception of Texas, no other southern state enjoyed the blessing of such mineral wealth, and almost every town and city shared in its attendant benefits. Indeed, oil helped to make Louisiana the most urbanized of the southern states: it boosted the growth of Shreveport, Monroe and Lafayette, fostered Baton Rouge and Lake Charles as ports and industrial centers, and gave the stretch of the Mississippi between Baton Rouge and New Orleans one of the world's biggest concentrations of refineries and petrochemical plants. Oil became Louisiana's second largest industrial employer, and oil revenues helped the Long dynasty to finance a welfare system that provided services and benefits unmatched in the rest of the South.

Oil also enriched Long and his cronies, wealthy men who grew even fatter by fixing state contracts, cutting deals with the Mafia, stealing public money, and exploiting Louisiana's mineral wealth for their private gain. Leander Perez, perhaps the worst corruptionist, manipulated the lease of oil- and sulphur-bearing public lands in Plaquemines Parish to amass a colossal personal fortune. "The plunder of state mineral lands is one of the most shameful episodes in Louisiana history," writes Glen Jeansonne. "Millions of dollars that should have gone to the state or local governments were diverted to a handful of Long's unscrupulous allies."

After Long's assassination, the notion of "Longism" as an assault on the rich became increasingly implausible. Long's cronies quickly dropped the "Share Our Wealth" movement and its chief organizer, Gerald L. K. Smith. "Share Our Wealth was a lot of bullshit," recalled Robert S. Maestri, a prosperous businessman whose interests ranged from furniture to prostitution. "Hell, Huey only used it to get attention, but Smith wanted to take *my money* and give it to the poor." Installed by the "Longites" as mayor of New Orleans in 1936 without having to stand for election, Maestri soon presided over a ferocious attack on organized labor.[33]

When the Committee for Industrial Organization (CIO) commenced an organizing drive in the Crescent City, Chief of Police John J. Grosch unleashed a campaign of violence and intimidation that rivalled in ferocity anything perpetrated by "Bull" Connor in Birmingham or "Boss" Hague in Jersey City. Grosch's men broke up meetings, raided homes and offices, seized documents, arrested strikers, threatened union lawyers, turned a blind eye to the AFL's thugs, and beat up CIO organizers in the back room of the Tenth Precinct. Meanwhile, a "Red Scare" whipped up by the right-wing Coalition of Patriotic Societies (founded by Dr. Emmett Lee Irwin, a future leader of the segregationist Citizens Council) filed charges of "subversion" against Mack Swearingen and Herman C. Nixon, professors of history at Tulane University. Both eventually resigned. In 1939 the ACLU condemned New Orleans as one of the three worst cities in America from the standpoint of civil liberties.

It would be unfair, perhaps, to hold Maestri and the Longites wholly responsible for this state of affairs. The police often employed union-busting violence at the behest of anti-Long businessmen; Emmett Irwin was himself anti-Long. Moreover, beating up labor organizers was nothing new for the New Orleans police, who had long been, and would long remain, virtually a law unto themselves. Still, the Longites made little effort to restrain the anti-CIO violence. They did even less to discourage police brutality against blacks.

"When police beat up white people as well as Negroes," the president of the New Orleans NAACP wrote despairingly, "when they get them in prison and not only beat them up but kill them just as they kill Negroes, there is little that anyone can do to curb such brutality." Police violence against blacks was so routine that it caused little comment outside the pages of the Negro press. Every year, two or three blacks were shot dead in dubious circumstances. The police thought nothing of beating confessions out of prisoners — in one case torturing a suspect for thirty-three days — a practice openly defended by Chief Grosch. Prisoners sometimes died in their cells, the victims of overzealous interrogators or trumped-up "escape attempts."[34]

By 1940 the Long machine was being rocked by scandal, with members of its inner circle accused of embezzling state funds to the tune of $100 million. Deluged by evidence of malfeasance unearthed by O. John Rogge of the Justice Department, federal grand juries handed down over two hundred indictments. Governor Richard W. Leche received a ten-year sentence for fraud, and dozens of other state officials and private individuals went to jail. Four of the accused committed suicide before they could be tried. Huey's brother Earl, elected lieutenant governor in 1936, had stepped into Leche's shoes and was doing his best to obstruct the investigations. In the judgment of his latest biographers, Earl Long had plenty to hide, being "in the forefront of the corrupt politicians of the era." Even if he avoided prosecution, Long faced the fight of his life to keep Sam Jones, an anti-Long reformer, from booting him out of the governor's mansion.[35]

In a tight election dirty even by Louisiana standards, both Jones and Long appealed to white racial prejudice. Long, however, made the running in the bigotry stakes. His paper, the *Louisiana Progress,* carried a photograph of two black children holding Jones placards. Longite Senator Allen Ellender scored the election-watching activities of John Rogge, warning, "If you people don't watch out, in 10 or 15 years the federal government will be in charge of all your elections and the darkies will be voting."

As he approached the second, runoff primary, staring defeat in the face, Earl Long plumbed the depths of race-baiting. A fictitious "Committee on Political Enfranchisement" endorsed Jones in the black newspapers. "The election of Mr. Jones will probably pave the way for the wholesale registration of Negroes in Louisiana," the advertisements enthused. The Long machine then reprinted the fake endorsements and distributed them far and wide. "Sam sure is making gains with the coons," the *Progress* sneered. "He charms them with some kind of sex appeal. Look what this nigger newspaper says about Sam." Jones disclaimed any intention of letting blacks vote, threw the accusation back at Long, accused his opponent of "consorting with Negroes," and warned that Earl planned to hire Negroes for state jobs now held by whites. Long responded by firing all the black janitors, maids, and firemen at the state capitol. As the *New Orleans Item* commented, Earl Long's tactics in 1940 were all the more reprehensible because "even in the days of his wildest depradations," Huey Long "was above this sort of cruel abuse of his state's unfortunate Negroes."[36]

With the election of Sam H. Jones, twelve years of Longite rule came to an end. Set against Huey Long's boasts of helping "teach niggers to read and write and figger," the appalling condition of black schools was an ironic monument to Longism. During the 1930s the black school-building program came to a virtual standstill, and black schools were starved of funds in order to maintain the white schools. Money apportioned by the state for black education was diverted by parish school boards to white children. In 1936–37 fifty-eight of Louisiana's sixty-four parishes spent less than the $14.17 it received from Baton Rouge for each black child. Twenty-six parishes spent less than half that amount; St. Martin, the most stingy, spent only $2.16. Statewide, the underspending amounted to $991,000. "The money allocated to the colored children is spent on the education of white children," admitted the school superintendent of a delta cotton parish. "That's unfair, and I know it, but that's the only way we can have decent white schools here." Blacks thus labored under what James D. Anderson has called a system of "double taxation." Receiving little in return for their tax dollars, they had to look to their own resources to maintain, repair, and supply their schools.[37]

As the national leadership of the NAACP formulated a strategy to attack racial discrimination in the South, education loomed into their sights as an obvious target. Here the discrimination was gross, easily documented, and readily admitted by the state. The official figures spoke for themselves: in 1940 the amount allocated for each black child amounted to 24 percent of the amount allocated to whites; black teachers were paid, on average, 64 percent less than white teachers; the average school year in black schools was thirty-seven days shorter than in white schools. Three-quarters of all black schools were housed in churches, Masonic halls, or ramshackle structures erected by blacks themselves. "The crowded conditions in these schools is appalling," noted a 1939–40 survey of the Baton Rouge Negro community. "In many rooms there were more than sixty pupils, all under the direction of one teacher." Only the Rosenwald schools provided adequate accommodation, and these were fast deteriorating. Thus the combined value of Louisiana's black schools was estimated at less than $6 million, $60 million less than the estimated value of the white schools.[38]

When Charles Houston, the NAACP's chief legal strategist, complained about the disparities to T. H. Harris, Louisiana's respected Superintendent of Education, he elicited some frank and damaging admissions. Yes, Harris replied, discrimination was "frequently very pronounced," and it was undeniable "that a great deal more will be spent upon the white schools than upon the Negro schools." Harris, according to his own lights, was doing his best to improve black schools. In 1938, in a letter to all parish school boards and local superintendents, he complained that "there is no serious intention in most of the parishes to provide school facilities for Negro children." Louisiana needed at least a thousand new schools, Harris believed, to bring black education up to a bare minimum standard.

Yet even the vision of an enlightened educator like Harris embodied white supremacist assumptions. When he spoke to Houston of providing blacks with "educational opportunities that would best serve them in making good and useful citizens," he meant, in effect, providing a lower standard of education, one that encouraged blacks to stick to their traditional roles. "Negro children should be instructed in the communities where they live," he believed, "and . . . they should be schooled in the idea that when they grow into manhood and womanhood they should remain in these communities and make their living on the farms." Whereas white rural schools were being consolidated and children bussed to large facilities, blacks were to remain in one- or two-room schoolhouses, relying on their legs for transportation. For most black children, moreover, schooling would be confined to the elementary level; Harris advocated secondary education only in "the large centers of Negro population."

Even in the cities, however, black high schools were few, and local school boards showed considerable reluctance to expand secondary provision lest blacks become trained beyond their station and begin competing for "white" jobs. In 1931, for example, the Orleans Parish school board declined to back a Rosenwald Fund proposal for a Negro "industrial high school," in spite of assurances that it would educate blacks for "negro trades" only. One school board member warned that an institution of such excellence would lead to "all the negroes in the entire state coming to New Orleans." In 1934 the city had one four-year public high school to serve a black population of 130,000, "an old brick structure considered unsafe for white children, gloomy rooms, the wooden walls creaky." In Hoffman Junior High twenty-six teachers had to serve 1,250 children. By 1940 the situation had begun to improve, the number of black high schools in the state increasing from four to thirty-nine. There were also eight Catholic high schools. Louisiana's white children had access to 383 high schools, however, and their rate of enrollment was four times higher. For most black children, schooling ended at the age of fourteen or earlier.[39]

A fortunate few attended Gilbert Academy, a private school situated on stately St. Charles Avenue in New Orleans. With an enrollment of about four hundred, this Methodist institution was, in the view of educator Horace Mann Bond, "one of the best, if not the best, secondary schools for Negro youth in the country." By the time it closed in 1949, a list of Gilbert Academy's alumni read like a who's who of black New Orleans. Xavier Preparatory School, located on Magazine Street and run by the same order of nuns who controlled Xavier University, also set excellent standards.[40]

As for higher education, the state maintained Southern University in Baton Rouge, which eventually became the largest state university for blacks in the nation. Yet while the Long regime lavished money on white Louisiana State University, its funding of Southern remained parsimonious. In 1936–37 Southern, the sole state-supported institution of higher learning for blacks, had only five hundred students and a faculty of sixty-seven. The two other universities worthy of the name, Xavier and Dillard, were both private institutions dependent upon northern philanthropy.[41]

If Huey Long and his followers exhibited, at best, indifference to blacks, that was hardly surprising: few whites in the 1920s and 1930s expressed any concern for their welfare. The state had evinced little interest in black schooling until the Rosenwald Fund started its building program, and the most important advance in black higher education during the Long era, the founding of Dillard University, also resulted from private philanthropic initiatives. The pattern of race relations was so rigid, moreover, that white Louisianians who supported black uplift programs usually articulated a strong commitment to racial segregation.

The role of Edgar B. Stern in the birth of Dillard University provides an instructive commentary on the racial climate of the Long years and the strengths and limitations of Louisiana's best-known white philanthropist. A wealthy cotton broker, Edgar Stern was married to Edith Rosenwald, whose father founded the Julius Rosenwald Fund from his Sears, Roebuck fortune. The match gave Stern the wherewithal to spend most of his time, in the words of one friend, "administering his wife's large fortune." Over the years, his good works earned him a reputation as the "best white friend" that Negroes had, a man who selflessly represented their interests. Stern worked hard to create Dillard from a merger of two old but moribund institutions, New Orleans University and Straight University, one a Methodist college, the other a Congregationalist one.[42]

Throughout the lengthy, delicate, and sometimes acrimonious negotiations that led to Dillard's birth, Stern insisted on the need to preserve the goodwill of local whites. Blacks could achieve nothing, he believed, without the assistance of "friendly southern white men," especially "white men of leadership and influence." Any challenge to "local tradition," that is, racial segregation, would antagonize such men and jeopardize the entire project. "The people in this section are very sensitive about the social implication of the Negro question," he told a northern member of Dillard's board of trustees. If the trustees selected a Negro president, "we cannot have a mixed faculty" as this would place a black in authority over whites. A white president, on the other hand, would need to "avoid giving offense to Southern tradition" by engaging in "social contact" with black students and faculty members; indeed, he would be well advised to live off campus. Stern was horrified by the maladroit attempts of some white presidents of Negro colleges to "meet what they thought were the social requirements of their situation," even allowing their wives to dance with Negro men. "I can tell you straight from the shoulder," he told Edwin Embree, director of the Rosenwald Fund, "that the day the wife of the white president of Dillard does this, you will find me among the missing of the trustees of that institution."[43]

Stern's social conservatism brought him into sharp conflict with some of the other trustees, particularly Fred Brownlee of the American Missionary Association. An arm of the northern-based Congregational Church, the AMA had long championed black education in the South, and had resisted the narrow vocationalism associated with Booker T. Washington and championed by the General Education Board, a philanthropic instrument of northern industrialists. The AMA stressed liberal values and viewed its black colleges, to quote James D. Anderson, "as social settlements that imported the culture of New England . . . along with the culture of the Greeks and Romans." The AMA sought to produce black leaders who would transform southern society, not meekly accept second-class citizenship.[44]

Interracialism was central to the AMA's vision. Reluctantly accepting that Dillard's first president should be a white man, Brownlee insisted that the person appointed should "identify himself self-forgettingly with the Negroes, their interests and their welfare" and that he could only do this by establishing intimate, friendly relations with his black faculty members. "Assisting underprivileged people . . . is as much, if not more, a psychological and spiritual problem as it is a physical and economic one," Brownlee explained. "You cannot do much for people until first of all they are satisfied that you are one with them." Edwin Embree endorsed Brownlee's reasoning, telling Stern that if students and faculty were to develop self-respect "as scholars and as men," the president must associate with them "on the basis of scholarly equality." This would entail "seeing the faculty in their homes, at student receptions, and in all normal relationships, including probably the ceremony of breaking bread." Stern considered this emphasis on "personal relationships" dangerously misguided, but hoped that Will Alexander, who reluctantly agreed to take the job, would adhere to the racial etiquette expected of a southern white man.[45]

The question of the racial composition of the faculty prolonged the dispute over what kind of university Dillard ought to be. To Brownlee there was "something basic and fundamental about maintaining a high-grade interracial faculty." But to Alexander an interracial faculty was an expensive luxury: few whites would apply to teach at a black college, fewer still at the salaries being offered. "In every case," he told Brownlee, "I have discovered a Negro with better training and ability than any white person who was applying for the job." For Brownlee and his allies the basic principle outweighed such practical arguments. "I would deplore having only one member of the faculty white, especially if the only one were at the head," wrote Mrs. L. R. Eastman, another AMA trustee. The next generation of black leaders would be "warped and biased," she warned, if it had no "first-hand contacts with members of another group."[46]

Another Dillard trustee, Dr. John J. Coss of Columbia University, weighed in on Alexander's side with the argument that black leadership would be better nurtured within an all-black faculty. "Negroes understand their own folk," he argued. Even if whites were "devoid of all sense or attitude of superiority," their presence was still a "complicating factor in the welding together of a pre-dominantly Negro group." Adopting a position that foreshadowed elements of the "Black Power" position of the late 1960s, Coss stressed that "Negroes must feel security and leadership within their own race." But such arguments cut no ice with the high-principled Brownlee. After much acrimony, the two sides adopted a compromise that, in effect, committed Alexander to hiring three or four "token" whites, even if it meant paying them more. After Dillard moved to its new campus in 1935, Alexander turned over the job of president to William Stuart Nelson, a black theologian. He was succeeded in 1941 by Albert W. Dent, a graduate of Morehouse College and the business manager of Flint-Goodridge Hospital, an adjunct of the University.[47]

To Stern, Brownlee and his ilk were impractical sentimentalists whose in-sistence on interracialism would actually isolate blacks and even endanger "the very survival of the race itself, physical and economic." Stern was interested in results, and it took southern white goodwill to achieve them. If powerful whites — lawyers, bankers, and publishers — had not been willing to fight for Dillard, the city council would never have sold it a site in Gentilly, a white neighborhood, and a local fundraising drive would have fallen far short of the $250,000 it raised. Moreover, Stern was quite prepared to appease white prejudices to attain his goal. For example, when local white residents objected that buses to and from Gentilly would be crowded with blacks, he arranged for New Orleans Public Service to lay on special, all-black buses during the peak hours. "In the South at the present moment," he insisted, "we can only make progress in Negro matters by being willing to make concessions as we go along." The creation of a viable university and of a hospital that would serve the impoverished and disease-ridden black population were life-and-death matters. Beside them the question of interracialism paled into insignifi-cance. Stern was, in any case, a convinced believer in racial segregation, and he noted approvingly that President and Mrs. Dent had "given not the slightest evidence of wanting to seek what is called 'social equality' with the whites."[48]

Stern's abhorrence of anything that hinted at "social equality" was not unusual. Many whites frowned upon even the most innocuous interracial contacts. Typical were the fulminations of W. J. Avery, the school superintendent of Rapides Parish, upon learning that the Hi-Y Club of a local black school had performed "Heaven Bound" at a white high school. "These negro high school students will not be permitted to appear in the white schools," he informed H. B. Burkee, state secretary of the YWCA. "The churches may do just as they please about things of this kind. Should they be invited to Emmanuel Baptist Church, of which I am a member, I shall doubtless be absent on that occasion." Proposals to afford blacks courtesy titles were equally unacceptable. "Only new-comers in Alexandria say Miss, Mr., or Mrs. when addressing or speaking of Negroes," stated Avery. Most newspapers felt the same way. "It is our policy not to refer to negro men, or negro women as Mr. or Mrs.," explained the publisher of the *Baton Rouge Morning Advocate* in 1941. "This policy, I have no idea of changing." The convention covered written correspondence as well: whites avoided the "Dear Mr./Mrs." form and usually opened letters with "Dear Sir" or just "Sir."[49]

Such conventions illustrated a central weakness of the interracial movement of the 1920s and 1930s. For many whites, the concept of interracialism could only imply equality. They were not persuaded by the protestations of the Commission on Interracial Cooperation that civility and cooperation need not undermine racial segregation. Segregation did not merely denote separateness; it also embodied the white belief in black inferiority. Being civil to blacks as one might be civil to whites subverted segregation, because the caste system demanded an etiquette that made explicit, in *all* social interaction, the superiority of the white and the inferiority of the black.

By the early 1930s the Commission on Interracial Cooperation had run out of steam, and blacks were increasingly inclined to dismiss it as irrelevant. As Fred Brownlee told Will Alexander, the CIC's director, "You know as well as I do that there isn't one educated Negro in a hundred who is willing to be honest with us who believes that our inter-racial movements . . . are anything but superficial fussing around the fringes of the problem." The decline of the movement in Louisiana confirmed this assessment: only the New Orleans committee survived, and barely. In 1934 Burkee of the YWCA complained that the chairman of the committee had stopped calling meetings because the blacks had been getting "ever more sharp" and the whites "ever more restive."[50]

By then the Great Depression had swamped the efforts of racial uplift organizations, as both blacks and whites struggled to keep their heads above water. Blacks were especially hard hit. Black institutions were financially shaky at the best of times, and the Depression wrought enormous damage to the infrastructure of black society. Banks folded; businesses went under; insurance companies saw their receipts dry up; churches and Masonic halls were mortgaged up to the hilt; universities had to go cap in hand to white philanthropists. Some black institutions — even the *Louisiana Weekly* — passed into white ownership.

For black wage earners, the rule of "last hired and first fired" was applied with a vengeance. Even in the boom years of the 1920s blacks were being ousted from some of their traditional occupations, as economic change exacerbated competition between black and white workers. The onset of the Depression saw the wholesale firing of black workers and attempts by the New Orleans city government to restrict municipal and public works jobs to "qualified voters." Only a federal injunction and opposition from the Board of Trade and the Steamship Association halted a city plan, endorsed by the white longshoremen's union, to exclude blacks from the municipal wharves.

In Monroe, a candidate for the city commission in 1936 pledged to employ "only white labor" for skilled work. Two years later Charles Myers of the NAACP reckoned that "there is hardly ten Negroes on the city pay roll now, they have been replaced by whites." In the Monroe railroad shops, black workers were downgraded and laid off when the Missouri Pacific stopped dealing with the company union, in which blacks had enjoyed equal representation, and signed contracts with the all-white unions affiliated with the American Federation of Labor.

In the early 1930s, at least half the South's urban black population depended on state and federal relief. In New Orleans, blacks made up about a third of the population but half of the unemployed and two-thirds of the families on relief. "Black employment opportunities were nil," one historian has written. The city set lower relief payments for blacks, and during the recession of 1937–38 the city's Department of Public Welfare began turning black families away, insisting that blacks compose no more than half of relief rolls. In the opinion of Katherine Radke, director of Xavier's school of social work, these restrictions threatened "the slow starvation of a large section of the population."[51]

Such desperate urban conditions discouraged migration from the country to the city. Although Louisiana had a more diversified economy than other Deep South states, the bulk of the black population remained on the land. In 1930 at least half of the male workforce and more than a third of the female workforce toiled in agriculture, and the state's 74,000 black farmers, only 8,000 of whom owned their own land, still accounted for a good 45 percent of the total. Despite grinding poverty throughout the countryside during the 1930s, Louisiana's farm population remained steady, even growing slightly.

The New Deal agricultural programs brought a measure of relief to farmers, but whites reaped most of the benefits. The Agricultural Adjustment Act, writes Harvard Sitkoff, "did nothing to lift the Afro-American from the lowest rungs on the agricultural ladder or to insist that black farmers be treated equally with whites." Whites monopolized the AAA county committees that determined crop reductions, and black farmers suffered disproportionately. Black tenants expecting AAA subsidies found their white landlords reluctant to pass on the money they received from Washington. "Even now the Negroes who operates their own farms havent got any of their Penney Money yet," an NAACP member reported from East Carroll Parish in 1938. "And them who are farming with the Big land owners never see a Govement Check. The Land Owner gets them and . . . just splits the difference with the Tennants. Gives him just what they wants them to have." When the AAA revised its rules to provide direct payments to tenants, many landlords shifted to wage labor. In Louisiana, the number of black farm operators decreased by about 10,000 during the 1930s.[52]

The Farm Security Administration had been specifically designed to assist small farmers; its resettlement program created new communities of family-sized farms on land purchased by the government. Administered by Will Alexander, the FSA made a determined effort to avoid discrimination, and blacks made up about a third of its resettlement units in Louisiana, 791 farms. Never a major program, however, the FSA's impact on rural poverty was negligible. Moreover, Alexander's attempt to eliminate discrimination within the FSA bureaucracy ran up against the New Deal's tacit acceptance of segregation. According to Sitkoff, "the FSA employed a higher percentage of Negro supervisors than any other New Deal agency." But in Region Six, which embraced Arkansas, Mississippi, and Louisiana, the FSA employed only thirty-five blacks in 1939, seven of them in Louisiana. T. Roy Reid, the regional director, resisted Alexander's pressure to employ more. "A negro supervisor," he explained, "could work only with negro clients, while it is possible for the white supervisor to work with all groups of clients."[53]

As the history of the Transylvania project in East Carroll Parish illustrated, FSA projects usually brought mixed blessings as far as blacks were concerned. In 1939, for example, some 250 black families were compelled to leave the Transylvania area to make way for a resettlement project dedicated to white farmers. Their protests elicited some concessions from the FSA, including new schools and a school bus, but their campaign to prevent the removals proved unavailing. Some of the displaced families moved onto all-Negro projects near the town of Lake Providence; others moved into neighboring Madison Parish. Their new farms, however, could not match "the rich loam soil, real delta land," that they left behind in the Transylvania area.[54]

But if the New Deal advanced blacks little and the Long regime helped them even less, both Roosevelt and Long had a profound impact upon the expectations of black Louisianians. New Deal programs *included* blacks, and the fact that they also discriminated against them should not be allowed to obscure this crucial point. "State and local welfare agencies had essentially ignored black needs before 1933," writes Anthony Badger. "Any assistance from New Deal agencies was therefore a bonus." Hence, while the Public Works Administration spent more per capita on whites than blacks, "it spent four times as much on building black schools and hospitals between 1933 and 1936 as had been spent by governments in the previous thirty years."

Equally important, especially in the long term, was the way that the New Deal, to quote Badger again, "showed to black leaders in the South the potential of federal solutions to black problems." The New Deal involved an enormous extension of federal power, which, as Patricia Sullivan has argued, "implicitly challenged the southern structure of states' rights supported by legalized white supremacy." This was especially true in Louisiana, where the Roosevelt administration first compromised with the Long regime but later attacked it, wresting control of federal programs away from Long's successors. The New Deal imparted a sense of hope to blacks and an awareness of the possibility of change. Traditionally committed Republicans, by the end of the 1930s most black southerners aspired to cast ballots for Roosevelt.[55]

As for the Louisiana Kingfish, historians are nowadays inclined to view Huey Long as an unprincipled demagogue and a racist, not the populist hero of T. Harry Williams's 1969 biography. Historical revisionism, however, cannot alter the fact that Long, for all his faults, also helped to rouse blacks from the political torpor that had overtaken them after losing the vote at the turn of the century. Blacks recognized the constraints under which Huey Long operated and appreciated the way he usually eschewed gratuitous abuse of the Negro. Like his white supporters, they were awed by Huey Long's oratory and lapped up his vituperative attacks on the rich. Even Long's below-the-belt attempts to insinuate that political opponents had "nigger blood" evoked wry amusement — blacks relished his observation that you could feed all the "pure whites" in Louisiana "with a nickel's worth of red beans and a dime's worth of rice."

Above all, blacks watched in awe as Long mobilized the white lower class and gave them unprecedented political power. He inspired hope in the Negro community, explained the Reverend J. H. Scott; blacks "saw the poor whites who had not been voting begin to vote and to get recognition." As A. P. Tureaud put it, Long "awakened [blacks] to the possibility of what an aggressive leader could do" and to what they themselves could do "if only they could become a part of this aggressiveness and leadership." The exciting political ferment of the Depression years led, eventually, to a reawakening and broadening of black militancy. By 1940 the NAACP was poised to take advantage of this new spirit: the struggle for racial equality would soon take a great leap forward.[56]

Chapter 3

THE LABOR MOVEMENT, THE LEFT, AND

THE TRANSFORMATION OF THE NAACP

T he onset of the Great Depression exacted a heavy toll on the NAACP. Branches that had barely kept alive during the 1920s fell silent. The Alexandria branch regrouped in 1930 but soon became inactive. The chronically unstable Shreveport branch reorganized in the same year but collapsed again in 1932, when pressure from whites forced it to cancel a talk by Oscar DePriest, the black congressman from Chicago and at the time the only African-American in Congress. "They felt that DePriest is not a representative type of Negro," the branch president reported, "that his talks are injurious to the Negro in the South, that encouraging the Negro along political lines was not what they felt should be done at this time." In many cases the national office simply lost contact with branches; by 1933 even the New Orleans branch had become so quiet that New York assumed that it had gone under.[1]

The fortunes of the association slowly picked up as economic conditions improved. The New Orleans branch showed signs of activity in 1934 and, under the leadership of James E. Gayle, expanded its membership to 750. New branches appeared in Jennings (1935), Plaquemine (1935), and Lake Charles (1936). Reorganizations revived dormant branches in Shreveport (1936) and Lake Providence (1938). By 1940 the Baton Rouge branch had 800 members. Many branches owed their survival and vitality to the dedication of individuals. In Baton Rouge, for example, insurance man Benjamin J. Stanley, who served as a branch officer from 1930 to 1955, supplied the essential stability, and the Reverend John Henry Scott served as president of the Lake Providence branch for thirty years.[2]

The role of Charles H. Myers in leading the Monroe branch was especially noteworthy. By the 1960s this branch had declined into virtual oblivion, and civil rights workers regarded Monroe as one of the most repressive towns in Louisiana. Yet between 1928 and 1948 Monroe boasted the strongest, the most stable, and arguably the most militant NAACP branch in the state, thanks in large part to Myers's leadership. A native of Texas, Myers moved to Monroe during the 1922 railroad strike and, like many other blacks, became a beneficiary of the companies' efforts to defeat the unions. Recruited as a mechanic by the Missouri Pacific, he quickly gained promotion and gladly joined the company union, since the AFL unions and the independent railroad brotherhoods systematically excluded blacks. Myers also became a successful businessman (at one time he operated two movie theaters in Shreveport) as well as an accomplished magician. As president of the NAACP, he protested the disfranchisement of blacks, took up cases of police brutality, and peppered local editors with complaints about discrimination. When the growing power of the railroad unions caused black workers to be demoted and displaced, Myers wrote to Charles H. Houston, the NAACP's chief legal strategist, who pressed the issue until the Supreme Court declared the unions' discriminatory practices illegal. In 1940 Myers threatened to boycott and picket a Monroe movie theater that had replaced its Negro manager with a white man. He won his point.[3]

Building popular support, however, often proved difficult, especially in the rural areas. As J. H. Scott reported from East Carroll Parish, "one of the biggest problems our branch has had is to have people believe that the association can be helpful in the South. . . . Also in the farming community where old boss has had the say about everything it is hard to get the tenant to stand for the right." Complaints about opposition from teachers and ministers cropped up regularly in branch letters to the National Office; Scott was a rare example of a black preacher providing strong leadership. According to E. L. Fair, secretary of the Lake Providence branch, some preachers urged blacks not to join the NAACP on the grounds that "if the white folks knew that they were organizing anything to go against them they would run them out of the Country." An agent for the *Pittsburgh Courier,* Fair could find only two ministers willing to distribute this militant black newspaper. "Where we gets most of our trubble from is the 2×4 pastors." Charlie Myers informed Walter White that he had almost thrown one minister down some stairs "as he attempted one of his Uncle Tomish talks."[4]

In the mid-1930s the NAACP was surviving, in the sense that it could claim a handful of active branches in Louisiana, but it still had no statewide structure to foster its growth and coordinate its activities. With the exception of Monroe, and possibly Baton Rouge, it had failed to attract mass support. This state of affairs reflected the weakness of the organization nationally; as late as 1940 the NAACP had only fifty thousand members.

Black political scientist Ralph J. Bunche deplored the NAACP's failure to recruit a mass base. In a lengthy monograph he wrote for the Carnegie-Myrdal study, "The Negro in the United States," he complained that "the control of the branches rests largely in the hands of an exclusive, often class and color snobbish, self-appointed Negro upper class group, and they are run, more frequently than not, as closed corporations." Bunche further contended that the association's unimaginative pursuit of court cases rendered its program irrelevant to the vast majority of blacks, whose primary concerns — poverty and unemployment — it largely neglected. The NAACP's national leadership, he went on, "has shown a pitiful lack of knowledge of mass technique and of how to pitch an appeal so as to reach the ears of the masses." Bunche's criticisms were tendentious and overstated: as the example of Charles Myers showed, individual branch leaders could sometimes be militant and populist. However, as applied to many of the big-city branches, Bunche's description did not stray far from the truth.[5]

In 1939, for example, the executive committee of the New Orleans branch read like a who's who of the black bourgeoisie. It included nine top executives of the leading black insurance companies, two members of the most prestigious undertaking business, and the city's most eminent black surgeon, Dr. Rivers Fredericks. Actually, this group was not so much middle class as upper class: they were men of considerable means. When he died in 1954 Fredericks left assets worth $1.5 million.[6]

Fredericks, the chief surgeon of Flint-Goodridge Hospital and president and principal stockholder of the Louisiana Industrial Life Insurance Company, could hardly be described as typical. Indeed, his early life would challenge the imagination of a Hollywood screenwriter. Born into a Creole family in Pointe Coupee Parish, he studied medicine in New Orleans and Chicago and returned to Louisiana in 1900 to take over the practice of a white doctor. That same year, at age twenty-six, he acquired a 210-acre plantation. Upon marrying a white woman, however, he left the country for eight years. He first moved to Honduras, where he served in turn as chief surgeon of the government hospital and chief surgeon to the rebel army. When the rebels were vanquished he fled to Belize, returning to New Orleans in 1908. By the 1930s he had become the preeminent black doctor in Louisiana and one of the best surgeons in the South. An outstanding man by any standard, Fredericks was nevertheless representative of his class. He stood at the center of an interlocking directorate of doctors, insurance men, and funeral directors that all but monopolized the branch's leadership.

These men had served the NAACP well, nurturing the branch through its difficult infancy. As businessmen and professionals serving a black clientele, they enjoyed the economic independence that enabled them to provide protest leadership as well as vital financial support and organizational competence. Fredericks himself preferred to stay in the background, yet his wealth and social status gave him considerable influence. Some of his protégés, moreover, became community leaders elsewhere: through Fredericks, for example, Dr. A. C. Terrance established a practice in Opelousas. Like other black doctors in rural Louisiana, Terrance kept in touch with the NAACP despite the absence of a local branch.[7]

A social gulf, however, separated the leaders of the New Orleans branch from the black lower classes, inhibiting the NAACP's ability to attract popular support. In their struggle to achieve wealth and status, moreover, black professionals tended towards elitism and clannishness; they prized their credentials, wore their learning proudly, and sometimes regarded others with patronizing condescension. Aspects of lower-class black culture that white folklorists celebrated, educated blacks looked upon with embarrassed disapproval. The arguments that swirled around the annual Mardi Gras parade of the Zulu Social Aid and Pleasure Club typified this conflict between lower-class hedonism and middle-class respectability. As the Zulus and their "second-liners" reveled in a display of drunken buffoonery, the people whom they regarded as "stuck-up niggers" condemned the spectacle as grotesque and distasteful. As A. P. Tureaud recalled from the perspective of old age, "Once we climbed the so-called ladder of middle-class America we . . . felt that that was not a good image of middle-class life — to be parading and having the men and women in the streets carrying on these body gyrations; 'shaking,' as they'd say on the street." The persistence of "hoodoo" evoked similar disdain, especially among the physicians and pharmacists who felt they had had to contend against the "credulity and faith of the ignorant."[8]

Thus the New Orleans branch was almost a caricature of the "closed corporation" described by Bunche in 1940. Yet by the time Bunche's views found their way into *An American Dilemma*, published in 1944, his analysis was already out of date. The NAACP's national membership had increased almost tenfold and was approaching the half-million mark. New branches were sprouting like mushrooms, and in most big cities, working-class blacks gained representation on branch committees, sometimes winning outright control. In New Orleans, a two-year struggle resulted in a group of Young Turks, nearly all of them middle class or working class, taking over the leadership.

The spectacular growth of the NAACP during the 1940s is usually attributed to the Second World War, which had a dramatic effect on the outlook and behavior of African-Americans. Yet the cycle of growth started *before* the war. In New Orleans, the Young Turks made their first bid for leadership in 1939, and they took control of the branch before Pearl Harbor. By 1941 the NAACP was showing signs of fresh vigor throughout Louisiana. By then, moreover, the NAACP's national legal staff, led by Thurgood Marshall, had secured important court victories that enabled branches in the South to go onto the offensive. The NAACP was already being transformed.

The leadership shift that took place in New Orleans was closely linked to the explosion of labor militancy associated with the rise of the CIO. The growth of industrial unionism in the late 1930s transformed the political climate and to some extent radicalized the black working class, hitherto discouraged by apathy and fear. The NAACP was a direct beneficiary of this political awakening.

With the arrival of organizers from the Committee for Industrial Organizations in 1936, New Orleans, once a union stronghold but by 1939 a bastion of the "open shop," echoed to the din of industrial strife. On the waterfront the International Longshoremen's and Warehousemen's Union, fresh from its triumphs on the West Coast, slugged it out with the International Longshoremen's Association. The conflict came to a head in the summer of 1938 with a simultaneous strike of dockworkers and truck drivers. After a federally supervised election attended by fraud, bribery, and intimidation, the notoriously corrupt ILA emerged victorious.

The CIO drive thoroughly alarmed city and state authorities. The legislature urged the city to "suppress, stamp out, and eradicate communism," condemning the CIO's "organization of negroes" as a "threat to white supremacy." One organizer was beaten up in a police station and told he "had no business coming down to New Orleans . . . telling the niggers about their rights." But while it lost out to the ILA on the waterfront, the ILWU won bargaining rights with several warehouses; with a foothold in the city, the CIO began to organize other industries. It recruited with equal zeal, moreover, both blacks and whites.[9]

The CIO unions soon boasted half a million black members nationwide, and they placed themselves "in the vanguard of efforts to transform race relations." The National Maritime Union promoted blacks to leadership positions and insisted that its contracts with the shipping companies include antidiscrimination clauses. The majority-black National Union of Marine Cooks and Stewards was an exemplar of racial equality. As Jane Record noted, the union's Negro members, mostly from the South, "found in the NUMCS hiring hall the most satisfying hiring experience of their lives." On the New Orleans waterfront the small ILWU local was, to quote Dave Lee Wells, "an example of union democracy, racial solidarity and militance unmatched . . . in the Jim Crow era." Local 206 of the Transport Workers Union "played a significant role in anti-racist activities of all sorts," according to the most thorough history of the TWU. Comprising about six hundred New Orleans truck drivers, most of them blacks, it conducted a successful strike against a contractor who, at the insistence of the Louisiana and Arkansas Railway Company, refused to employ black drivers. The Communist Party exerted a strong influence within each of these unions and played a major role in shaping their egalitarian policies.[10]

The Communist Party also entered rural parishes, trying to organize blacks and whites into a farmers' union. The drive began in 1936 when Clyde Johnson, Communist organizer of the Alabama-based Sharecroppers Union, moved his headquarters to New Orleans. This was the union's first attempt to operate openly — the Party itself still led a twilight existence in Louisiana, police harassment forcing it to operate under cover of a bookstore. Johnson began building what became the Louisiana Farmers Union, soon handing over its leadership to fellow party member Gordon McIntire, a young, tall, gaunt, white Texan. McIntire was assisted by Peggy Dallet, whose brother, Joe, died in Spain as a member of the International Brigade.[11]

The union first established itself as a going concern in St. Landry Parish, where it fought the eviction of twenty farming families, most of them blacks, by the Resettlement Administration. However, although the LFU recruited both blacks and whites, its leaders decided to draw back from directly challenging segregation after an incident in Opelousas. At a mass meeting in the courthouse square a white man yelled, "Nigger union!" The gathering stayed calm, but McIntire recognized the potential for violence if black union members appeared to "crowd out" whites in public. Thereafter the union stuck to a policy of separate locals and separate meetings.[12]

White planters and merchants did not take kindly to the LFU's activities. In Simmesport, Avoyelles Parish, Sheriff J. J. Jeansonne arrested organizer John Moore for "criminal libel" after he proposed boycotting a storekeeper who had threatened union members. When Moore's wife protested, the sheriff explained that "a lot of things can happen at night, like a mob beating him up, and I might not come in time." After his release Moore left town. "If we let whites and niggers organize," commented the mayor of Simmesport, "things might happen like they are happening in Arkansas. We don't like the word strike and we don't like the word boycott." Landowners in DeSoto Parish formed a "White Farmers' Legion" to combat the union. "It is a troublemaking organization," the FBI agreed, "in that it puts ideas in the minds of the negro tenant farmers . . . which could not possibly have originated there."[13]

In West Feliciana Parish the violent backlash from local planters stopped the union in its tracks. Other things being equal, the LFU would not have chosen that parish as a primary target. Two-thirds black (the highest ratio in Louisiana), West Feliciana was the most conservative and planter-dominated parish in the state. In the spring of 1936, however, Willie and Irene Scott began to organize farmers on their own initiative, having learned of the LFU from visits to neighboring Pointe Coupee Parish.

The Scotts were encouraged by their white landlords, Sarah and Alberta Reed, who had inherited a plantation in the heart of the Black Belt. The Reed sisters taught in the public school system of New Orleans and were women of radical views. Sarah, in particular, was an indefatigable and outspoken political activist. At a time when women teachers had to be single, Sarah Reed kept her marriage a secret. In the mid-1930s she organized the Classroom Teachers Federation of New Orleans, becoming president after it affiliated with the AFL, and helped black teachers organize their own AFL local. In 1938 she attended the organizational meeting of the Southern Conference for Human Welfare. Formed with the encouragement of Franklin and Eleanor Roosevelt (and with strong covert support from the Communist Party), the SCHW brought together the most liberal and progressive elements in the South. It was therefore entirely in character that the Reed sisters encouraged their tenants to join the LFU. With help from Gordon McIntire and another white, Reuben Cole, the Scotts established four locals, with a combined membership of about two hundred people.[14]

On June 23, 1937, a group of white farmers broke down the door of the Scott cabin. One of them, a prominent landowner and storekeeper, beat Irene Scott with a pistol and demanded to know the whereabouts of Willie Scott and Reuben Cole. After feigning unconsciousness, she slipped out of the house to warn her husband. The Scotts fled to New Orleans.

Gordon McIntire visited St. Francisville, the parish seat, to reason with local whites. "We don't want people interfering with our niggers," an irate planter lectured him. "We won't have it. You keep out of here. We take care of them when they're sick and bury them when they're dead. . . . We don't mind burying societies but we won't have a union. You all let the niggers alone." McIntire tried to respond, but the planter cut him off. "Get out of this parish and get out before nightfall." McIntire drove back to New Orleans as fast as his dignity permitted.[15]

When the incident came to the attention of the recently formed Louisiana League for the Preservation of Constitutional Rights, the league sent George Dreyfous, a white lawyer, and Mack Swearingen, a Tulane history professor, to investigate. After a day in West Feliciana they returned to New Orleans without "the slightest hope" that local whites could be converted to "a more enlightened policy and attitude." When it came to acts of violence against blacks, they concluded, juries would neither indict nor convict, and no help could be expected from the state authorities. Although scarcely a hundred miles, the drive upriver had taken Dreyfous and Swearingen five hours and brought them into a different world.[16]

Three years later, the authorities in Natchitoches suppressed an LFU meeting and ran the union organizer, Clinton Clark, out of the parish. On the day of the meeting, July 27, 1940, about six hundred blacks had arrived in the town "on mules, horses, in wagons, trucks or jalopies." Whites believed they were there to demand forty cents an hour for picking cotton and planned to strike if they failed to get it. The mayor warned Clark to leave town lest he wind up floating down the Cane River inside a sack. The police then arrested him, together with six union men from New Orleans. The latter were held for three days, Clark for three weeks. Upon his release, Clark stated, "They filled my automobile with gas, gave me an escort to the Texas border, and told me to 'keep moving.'" State attorney general Eugene Stanley had sternly instructed local officials to prevent Clark being lynched.[17]

In the early 1940s the union collapsed. Tuberculosis forced Gordon McIntire into a sanatorium in upstate New York; his successors proved unable to hold the organization together at a time when the approach and onset of war diverted the attention of white supporters and produced confusing and divisive contortions in Communist Party policy. In January 1942 Clinton Clark and state secretary Kenneth Adams tried to organize a local in Concordia Parish; they were arrested and held for three months. The LFU expired soon afterwards.[18]

On the face of it, the LFU vanished without a trace, its efforts leaving little or no mark on the black struggle for equality. The parishes that it had cultivated most assiduously saw little subsequent activity in terms of black organization; they remained areas of NAACP weakness. While participation in the union may well have politicized many blacks, attempts by some historians to link the work of the farmers' unions to the civil rights movement of the 1960s are unconvincing. Still, as Dreyfous and Swearingen emphasized, the very appearance of the union signified "growing race or class consciousness among the negroes." Blacks were overcoming their illiteracy, they noted, and were "coming to believe themselves as able individually as the white people." Indeed, they judged blacks to be more politically aware than whites, and some impressed them as "quite capable of determined, courageous and effective leadership." Whites had restored the status quo, but they would not be able to maintain it indefinitely. "It would be well for the whites to realize *soon* that they will no longer have to deal with the old time subservient negro, but with a species of negro of whom they have no knowledge or understanding."[19]

If rural Louisiana proved to be a graveyard for black political organization, New Orleans in the late 1930s and early 1940s was a veritable training ground. The CIO unions instructed blacks in unity and mass action, nurturing a new black leadership, and in the wake of the CIO came the Communist-inspired Southern Negro Youth Congress (an offshoot of the National Negro Congress), organized in Richmond in 1937. Raymond R. Tillman, later to lead Local 206 of the Transport Workers Union, coordinated the SNYC's activities in New Orleans. The SNYC held labor schools, organized a "People's Community Theater," and, with help from left-wing lawyer Herman Midlo, instructed people on voter registration. In 1940 the SNYC chose New Orleans to hold its fourth annual conference, launching a right-to-vote campaign that featured leafleting, lobbying, mock elections, and outdoor rallies.[20]

The rise of the People's Defense League (PDL) provided another illustration of how the labor militancy and leftist activism of the 1930s spilled over into the civil rights drive of the 1940s. The PDL was synonymous with Ernest J. Wright. Born in Kenner, just outside New Orleans, Wright attended Xavier University in the 1930s, where he came under the tutelage of Katherine Radke, a German-born nun and head of Xavier's school of social work. With Radke's encouragement, Wright studied social work at the University of Michigan, working on placement in Detroit. Returning to New Orleans, he joined the staff of the *Louisiana Weekly* to promote a "community responsibility program." Using his weekly column as a platform, Wright soon became a well-known lecturer and activist. "Every week in churches, community centers, and labor halls throughout the city," wrote one student of Wright's career, "hundreds turned out as he spoke on the need to obtain the ballot, [and] reviewed the latest local and national developments." He also became a leading light in the SNYC.[21]

A strike of black insurance agents marked the beginning of Wright's career as a labor organizer and served as the launching pad for the People's Defense League. The dispute started in September 1940 when the four biggest black-owned insurance companies (the Unity, the Louisiana, the Douglas, and the Good Citizens) attempted to quash efforts by their collection agents to form a CIO union. In 1934 the companies had signed a secret anti-union compact, which they now put into effect. At the Unity, the two instigators of the union were fired in the presence of the assembled agents.

The ensuing strike became a contest for black public opinion, with the outcome partly turning on the willingness of policy holders to pay their weekly premiums to "scab" agents, some of whom carried pistols or were accompanied by white "goons." The black owners, headed by Dr. Rivers Fredericks, orchestrated a barrage of publicity — sound trucks, radio spots, newspaper advertisements — attacking the union. The strikers held mass meetings in Shakespeare Park, at which Ernest Wright and striking agent Daniel Byrd excelled as speakers. The union also recruited "goons" of its own — two seafarers known as "Battling Siki" and "Poydras Street Black" — to discourage the scabs. On October 8, Wright was arrested with five others and charged with assault with a deadly weapon, and by November owners had broken the strike at three of the companies. At the Good Citizens, however, the owners decided to recognize the union, the United Office and Professional Workers, in the hope of winning away business from the others. The strike made a martyr and a hero of Ernest Wright. After serving a sixty-day sentence, he stepped through the gates of Orleans Parish prison to the acclaim of thousands of cheering blacks. Shortly afterward he joined the regional staff of the CIO. He helped to organize three thousand laundry employees; the CIO Industrial Union Council elected him secretary.

In August 1941 Wright founded the People's Defense League, which soon became, in the FBI's estimation, "the most powerful negro organization in New Orleans," thanks to Wright's "personal magnetism and unlimited energy." Wright held regular meetings in Shakespeare Park and wrote a weekly column in the *Louisiana Weekly*. He crisscrossed New Orleans and Louisiana addressing churches, unions, NAACP branches, PTAs, graduation classes — every conceivable audience. He hammered away at the same themes: police brutality, discrimination, organized labor, the vote. In March 1943 he teamed up with the Reverend Abraham Lincoln Davis, pastor of New Zion Baptist Church, to form the Louisiana Association for the Progress of Negro Citizens, which focused exclusively on obtaining the ballot.[22]

The prominence of ministers like Davis in the right-to-vote movement furnished another yardstick of blacks' heightened aspirations and rising self-confidence. During the 1930s black intellectuals had lambasted ministers for their timidity and conservatism. Davis, however, who had moved to New Orleans in 1936 as a young man of twenty-two, embraced social and political causes; through his leadership of the Interdenominational Ministerial Alliance he did more than any other minister to identify the black church with the fight for the ballot. Other ministers joined the fray, among them L. L.

Haynes, pastor of Mount Zion Baptist Church, and Gardner C. Taylor, who left New Orleans in 1942 to become pastor of Mount Zion First African Baptist Church in Baton Rouge, one of the largest in the state. Other like-minded ministers included Jetson Davis, A. L. Davis's brother, a pastor in Plaquemine; and Maynard T. Jackson, president of the Baptist Ministerial Union in Lake Charles. As Davis told a meeting in Shakespeare Park in October 1941, "The church cannot, must not and will not distance itself from the everyday problems which face the Negro people."[23]

The revival of white liberalism in New Orleans reflected the rise of the labor movement, the growth of race consciousness among blacks, and the climate of political openness encouraged by Roosevelt and the New Deal. In 1938 the National Urban League organized a branch in New Orleans; numerically, conservative, segregation-minded whites dominated its board, but a handful of Jewish liberals and a prolabor Josephite Catholic priest wielded disproportionate influence. The year 1939 saw the formation of the Catholic Committee of the South; staunchly prolabor and strongly antidiscrimination, the CCS established a stronger presence in New Orleans than in any other city. In 1940 the Southern Conference for Human Welfare organized a Louisiana committee with an office in New Orleans.[24]

Against the political ferment that provided a backdrop to the late 1930s, the New Orleans branch of the NAACP looked increasingly timid and isolated. Under the presidency of James Gayle, a publisher of church music, the branch staged occasional protest meetings but did little else. His successor, Dr. Aaron W. Brazier, a physician, spurned an opportunity to identify the branch with the defense of Hugh Pierre, a headline-making case that resulted in the first instance in which the U.S. Supreme Court reversed a Louisiana verdict because of the exclusion of blacks from the jury. Brazier attributed the branch's poor showing to the apathy of the masses and the inertia of the membership, but A. P. Tureaud thought that Gayle and Brazier showed "little or no aggressiveness at all. They were just keeping the organization alive." In 1938 James B. Lafourche, a writer at the *Louisiana Weekly,* challenged Brazier and, when defeated, asked the national office to revoke the branch's charter. New York refused — Lafourche was a slippery character who inspired distrust — but it expressed concern over the branch's weak leadership and lack of popular support, especially when the Communist Party was assiduously courting the Negro.[25]

For Brazier's critics, the humiliating outcome of a suit against the Municipal Auditorium proved to be the final straw. The auditorium is an imposing structure that lies on the site of Congo Square, the open space on the edge of the French Quarter that was famous in antebellum days for the dancing of African slaves. Built in the 1930s in the plain, modernist architectural style typical of WPA-financed public buildings, it was run by a commission appointed by the City of New Orleans. In 1937, when a black minister, denied permission to hire the building, decided to take the commission to court, the NAACP agreed to back his action. But the case went awry from the start. Instead of hiring a competent attorney, the branch retained a white man who worked as a postal clerk and lawyered in his spare time. This amateur lawyer then submitted a brief that alleged that the minister had been discriminated against as a taxpayer rather than as a Negro. The failure to allege racial discrimination allowed the federal court to dismiss the case for want of jurisdiction. "You know, he only had to say he was a nigger," the judge told A. P. Tureaud. "I would have had to hear the case." [26]

The loss of the suit discredited the Brazier administration and spurred a group of younger blacks into fielding their own slate of candidates. The insurgent faction called itself "The Group." It included truck drivers, insurance agents, letter carriers, postal clerks, and a doorman at Godchaux's department store. None of these men were remotely upper class, and none of them, with the exception of lawyer A. P. Tureaud and a couple of schoolteachers, could be classified as professionals. The core of The Group consisted of a trio of post office workers: John E. Rousseau Jr., Donald Jones, and Arthur J. Chapital. Jones and Rousseau were clerks, Chapital a letter carrier. With insurance agent Daniel E. Byrd, Jones became The Group's principal ringleader.

The prominence of postal employees in The Group was not fortuitous. Although the job of letter carrier, or even postal clerk, might seem relatively humble, it ranked highly in the black social structure. Postal workers were federal employees, and they enjoyed a degree of job security that most blacks envied. Moreover, compared with the average black wage, post office jobs paid well. The postal service offered other attractions: segregation was less oppressive — black and white clerks worked alongside each other — and the hours were flexible, allowing blacks to devote time to college, journalism, or the NAACP. With so few middle-class careers open to blacks, "black postal workers tended to have more education than their white coworkers, and that made them a force to contend with." In 1913 black mailmen formed the National Alliance of Postal Employees, which fought discrimination in the service. In New Orleans NAPE was led during the 1930s by W. W. Kerr, an articulate and militant letter carrier. Described by his foreman as "bold and defiant," the light-skinned Kerr was repeatedly reprimanded for sitting in the white section of buses. Kerr responded by quoting the Fourteenth Amendment. In 1941 NAPE won a major victory when, after the postmaster general's intercession, the local postmaster hired the first black clerks since 1929. [27]

Numbering at the outset about two dozen people, The Group sought to recruit enough new members to vote the existing executive committee out of office. Donald Jones told Thurgood Marshall of the planned "coup" and solicited his advice. Marshall encouraged him, but warned The Group to play by the rules. By November 1939 The Group had signed up 319 new members, and it put forward a "balanced ticket" that included Creoles and non-Creoles, people who lived downtown and uptown. As the election approached, a rival ticket led by J. Edwin Wilkins came forward, referring to itself as the "Progressive" ticket. A pharmacist at Flint-Goodridge hospital, Wilkins was also president of the Autocrat Club, a well-known Creole institution. Rivers Fredericks had induced him to stand, promising office space in the Louisiana Life building and money for a full-time secretary. Both factions wrote to New York predicting electoral skullduggery; Walter White admonished them to behave properly.[28]

The election took place in an atmosphere of high excitement. The ticket fielded by The Group held a preelection pep parade through the Seventh Ward, culminating in a rally at Jeunes Amis Hall with music and refreshments. When the votes were counted the following evening, the "Progressive ticket" defeated The Group by 324 to 294. Brazier himself, who received but seven votes, praised the "hectic and enthusiastic" campaign. "The sight was unbelievable," he wrote Walter White. "More than one thousand people came out, including spectators to watch the contest and spur their friends on."[29]

This healthy exercise in democracy swelled the branch's membership and brought about a near clean sweep of the offices: only three members of the old guard won places on the seventeen-member executive committee. But the clash of "tickets" produced a badly divided branch. The Group complained that Fredericks had hastily cobbled together a slate of wealthy "big shots" for the sole purpose of excluding them. Wilkins had won, moreover, with the help of a bloc vote from the corrupt longshoremen's union, the ILA, which had purchased memberships for all its men. "Practically the entire interested NAACP membership remains under the leadership of the losers, The Group," Donald Jones complained. "In other words, you have there a Democratic cabinet and a Republican congress."[30]

Actually, Jones overstated the matter: although the new board was dominated by businessmen and professionals, it also included Clarence Laws, the young executive secretary of the Urban League and himself a member of The Group. Wilkins also reached out to The Group by inviting A. P. Tureaud to serve as the branch's legal adviser; the old leadership had strenuously opposed using Negro lawyers. Responding to charges that he had presented his slate of candidates as the "downtown," or Creole, ticket, Wilkins insisted that he wanted to bridge the old division between downtown and uptown. "The objective of the NAACP is to get the 180,000 Negroes of New Orleans together," he explained. "The southern white man tries to divide them — to make the educated Negro feel he is superior to the uneducated Negro, the urban to the rural, the light to the dark. . . . But Negroes must come together under all conditions."[31]

A renewal of the Municipal Auditorium controversy gave Wilkins a chance to practice what he preached. In the spring of 1940 Marian Anderson was booked to give a concert in New Orleans. Then at the height of her fame as a singer, Anderson had just won "a smashing victory over segregation" in the nation's capital that thrilled blacks everywhere. When the Daughters of the American Revolution denied her permission to sing in Constitution Hall, Secretary of the Interior Harold Ickes, a longtime supporter of the NAACP, invited her to give her recital on the steps of the Lincoln Memorial. Widely condemned for its bigotry, the DAR later lifted its color bar on Constitution Hall.[32]

Marian Anderson, however, was neither a racial crusader nor a political activist: her art and her career came first. Thus she accepted the invitation to sing in New Orleans despite the fact that the organizers of the concert planned a whites-only event. After vociferous black protests, the auditorium allocated seats for blacks in the balconies. The NAACP protested that "horizontal" segregation of this kind insulted blacks: only "vertical" segregation, whereby blacks and whites sat on opposite sides of the hall but on the same level, would be acceptable. When the auditorium commission rejected this demand, refusing to allow blacks to sit on the ground floor, the NAACP voted to boycott the concert. The branch's action split the black community. The fraternities and sororities wanted the concert to go ahead, seeing it as an opportunity for an internationally renowned black singer to perform in New Orleans. The *Louisiana Weekly* lashed Wilkins in print, accusing him of "fighting to keep Negroes from hearing a great Negro artist." The NAACP failed to persuade Anderson to cancel her appearance and failed to dissuade blacks from attending. The branch found itself out on a limb.

Frederic Morrow, the NAACP's coordinator of branches, saw the split in the black community as evidence of the old "class-caste fight between the native Negroes and the Creoles," who had never managed to cooperate. "The biggies are fighting," he believed, "because cancellation will deny them an opportunity to put on the dog and entertain." Actually, Morrow cited the Creole/American division to explain something considerably more complex. After all, the branch's leaders, largely Creole and upper class, were themselves "biggies," yet they instigated the boycott. The Group, largely Creole too, but mainly working class and middle class, supported the boycott. In fact, the protest generated support that cut across both class and cultural lines. The dispute over the Anderson concert seems to have been a division between the race-conscious NAACP and the black upper class, not between Creoles and non-Creoles.[33]

Outsiders frequently made the same error when viewing New Orleans black society, explaining everything in terms of the alleged conflict between Creoles and Americans and equating that division with a light-skinned/dark-skinned dichotomy and a split between the upper class and the lower class. Thus simplification was piled upon simplification until caricature obscured reality. By the 1930s there was little correspondence, in fact, between the black class structure and the division between Creole and non-Creole. And while many Creoles still placed a high social value on light complexion, culture rather than color had become the main reference point of Creole identity. A Creole such as A. P. Tureaud remained proud of what his ancestors, the free people of color, had achieved in antebellum days, but he did not believe that Creoles could remain apart from other blacks. Nor did he draw attention to his light complexion.

The celebration of the free people of color by black writers such as Marcus Christian, Clarence A. Laws, and Octave Lilly Jr. expressed a similar outlook. Employed by the Federal Writers Project to produce a study of "The Negro in Louisiana," these scholars described with pride the literary, military, and economic achievements of the *gens de couleur libre,* but they stressed that after Emancipation the free colored class had united with the freed slaves, realizing that they shared a common interest in obtaining equal rights. As Joan Redding has pointed out, to these writers "the convergence of the freed and free black cultures . . . provided a model for solutions to the political and social issues of their own day." Thus they viewed cultural differences as a source of strength rather than a source of division: "Rather than finding professionalism and elite culture at odds with the interests of the black masses, they found both folk and elite culture integral to the improvement of the race." In this way they could prize their Creole heritage and their own educational attainments while pressing the cause of all blacks through the NAACP. Clarence Laws and Octave Lilley both joined The Group.[34]

The controversy surrounding the Marian Anderson concert marked a watershed in the evolution of the NAACP in New Orleans: the boycott movement represented the branch's first serious protest against inequalities within segregated public accommodations. Although the NAACP lost that fight, the affair illustrated a marked tendency for blacks to unite across class and cultural lines, exemplified by large public meetings and cooperation between organizations. The NAACP won the backing of the Interdenominational Ministerial Alliance and the Southern Negro Youth Congress; one mass meeting drew three thousand people. Shortly afterward an array of organizations, and black leaders of virtually every political persuasion, jointly lobbied the city's public housing authority, HANO, to employ black managers in its new Negro projects. Under the auspices of this coalition, the Committee of 100, blacks attended protest meetings and boycotted the Magnolia project's "open house" day. Faced with such opposition, HANO agreed to take on black personnel.[35]

The Group, however, remained dissatisfied with the NAACP's leadership and frustrated by their own exclusion from power. They also complained that the existing black newspapers in New Orleans, the *Louisiana Weekly* and the *Sepia Socialite*, were insufficiently militant. Worse, in the recent gubernatorial election, they had allowed themselves to be manipulated by the Long organization. The Group therefore decided to launch its own weekly newspaper, each man chipping in $100 of his own money. The first issue of the *New Orleans Sentinel* appeared in June 1940. It was edited by the two postal clerks, Donald Jones and John E. Rousseau (three years earlier Rousseau had founded NAPE's local newsletter, *The Postscript*). A. P. Tureaud contributed copy, including occasional editorials, and Ernest Wright wrote a regular column. The paper supplemented its local material with articles from the *New York Times* and press releases from the NAACP and the Southern Negro Youth Congress. The *Sentinel* was left-of-center and prolabor. "We dared to publicize the coming of Negro candidates on the Socialist ticket with Norman Thomas," Tureaud recalled. In contrast to the *Louisiana Weekly*, the *Sentinel* supported the agents in the insurance strike of late 1940.[36]

That strike exemplified the way in which the old division between Creole and non-Creole had to a large extent been superseded by the economic conflict between class and class. It also showed how such conflicts could spill over into the NAACP: the leaders of the strike were all members of The Group; the branch's executive committee included five representatives of the struck companies. Daniel Byrd specifically charged J. E. Wilkins of favoring the owners because he owed his election to Rivers Fredericks, president of Louisiana Industrial Life. The "insurance vote" had indeed assisted the Wilkins ticket; the Louisiana, for example, counted forty-seven NAACP members among its employees. The strike damaged the standing of the branch leadership, and at the 1940 annual general meeting, held during the tail end of the dispute, Rev. C. C. Taylor defeated Wilkins. But The Group still failed to elect its own ticket, and two of the insurance owners, Rivers Fredericks and Henry E. Braden, remained on the board.[37]

Nevertheless, The Group stayed together, with the *Sentinel* their campaigning organ. Impatient with the branch leadership and keen to find an issue that would boost the paper's circulation, The Group laid plans for a suit in federal court to challenge the differential in the pay of black and white schoolteachers. Black teachers in New Orleans were keen to file an equalization suit, and in March 1939 three high school principals advanced the money to bring Thurgood Marshall to New Orleans to discuss strategy. Despite their defeat in the 1939 and 1940 branch elections, The Group kept in touch with Marshall, proceeding with their plans independently of the local NAACP.[38]

Those plans meshed closely with the legal strategy that had been developed by Charles Houston, the NAACP's special legal counsel, to attack inequalities in public education. Houston envisaged a campaign of litigation in the federal courts based on the contention that gross disparities between the provision for blacks and whites arose from racial discrimination that violated the Fourteenth Amendment. His immediate goal was to improve black schools and colleges according to the "separate but equal" principle of *Plessy* v. *Ferguson,* but his ultimate goal was to overturn *Plessy* and abolish segregation root and branch. The absence of any provision for graduate education for blacks (particularly in law) and the gap in the pay of black and white teachers provided the immediate lines of attack. In 1936, under the direction of Thurgood Marshall, the NAACP took on its first suit to compel school districts in the South to equalize their salary scales. Three years later, the NAACP Legal Defense and Education Fund became a separate wing of the NAACP under Marshall's direction. Marshall believed that salary equalization suits promised not only to win important legal precedents but also to strengthen the NAACP's grassroots support.[39]

The teaching profession certainly appeared to offer the NAACP a fertile recruiting ground. By 1940 there were over 4,000 black schoolteachers in Louisiana, one for every 57 black children of school age. Women greatly outnumbered men: a survey of 196 schools counted 464 teachers of whom 390 were women. Even in the high schools, women outnumbered men three to one. According to the same survey, conducted by Fisk University sociologist Charles S. Johnson, the median salary of black teachers constituted but 36 percent of the average for whites. Yet they were well off in comparison with the black population as a whole; over half, for example, owned their own homes, a figure that rose to 63 percent in the cities. Johnson also found teachers to be relatively well informed: nearly all of them read at least one black newspaper, and over two-thirds regularly read the *Pittsburgh Courier,* generally regarded as the most militant and influential black paper in America. Nearly 14 percent of the survey already claimed membership in the NAACP.[40]

Recruiting teachers, however, depended upon effective cooperation with the Louisiana Colored Teachers Association. Founded in 1901 by J. B. Lafargue, the principal of Peabody Training School in Alexandria, the LCTA had not been a militant protest organization. Moreover, it had long been troubled by divisions between New Orleans and the rest of the state: teachers in the rural parishes, especially in north Louisiana, resented the dominance of Crescent City teachers and sometimes felt threatened by their more outspoken positions. Furthermore, teachers had little job security. During the Long era, education, like everything else, was highly politicized; white teachers were frequently sacked for failing to back the right faction. The legislature passed a tenure law in 1938, but teachers still felt insecure, black teachers even more so: they remained at the mercy of white school superintendents and the black principals whom they favored. Whites expected, and usually received, abject deference from blacks, and teachers were no exception. Lafargue himself offered a ripe example of the deferential style in a letter he submitted to an Alexandria newspaper, thanking the paper for an editorial that urged whites not to fire their black servants. "How noble and consoling was the news to the poor and almost destitute colored people of our city," wrote the president of the LCTA, "when the news was flashed across the city by our evening friend."[41]

In the late 1930s, however, the LCTA beefed up its organizational structure and edged, albeit cautiously, toward a more militant posture. It obtained an official charter, opened a permanent office, and started the *LCTA Journal*. In 1938 George S. Longe, a New Orleans high school principal, became president; Longe supported The Group's efforts to initiate a salary suit and tried to prize money from the LCTA. By 1940 the organization claimed 2,000 members, with branches in all but thirteen parishes.[42]

Securing the LCTA's backing for the equalization suit proved no easy task. Donald Jones reported that Longe had to "fight like hell out of a tight little Uncle Tom clique composed of four or five out-of-town school principals who are 'in good' with the school board bigwigs."[43] Fruitless negotiations to win over the white public school teachers caused further delays. Finding a plaintiff also proved difficult, for it was widely predicted that anyone putting his name to a suit would be immediately sacked. Jones's brother, Clyde, was willing, but his mother insisted that he pull out. By 1941, however, Jones had found a plaintiff and obtained promises of money from the LCTA. On June 14, A. P. Tureaud filed suit against the Orleans Parish School Board on behalf of Joseph McKelpin — the first action of its kind in Louisiana.[44]

The outcome rested with the federal judiciary, but the prospects of success were fair. The NAACP's legal strategy was increasingly in tune with judicial trends: by the late 1930s the U.S. Supreme Court, liberalized by Roosevelt's appointments, was expressing impatience with the flagrant character of southern racism. Indeed, the Court's readiness to grasp the nettle of racial discrimination sometimes surprised the NAACP.

In *Pierre* v. *Louisiana* (1939), for example, the Court addressed the exclusion of blacks from Louisiana juries. A crippled black farmer living in St. John the Baptist Parish, Hugh Pierre was sentenced to death for the 1936 shooting of Ignace Roussell, a constable who attempted to arrest him for the theft of a plough. The alleged theft had taken place in 1932, and the white man who claimed ownership, Leonard Ory, had tried without success to recover the implement. When Ory returned with his two sons and constable Roussell, Pierre fled into his house. He then shot Roussell, claiming that he fired his shotgun in self-defense when the constable broke down his door and entered with a drawn pistol. Pierre's sister, an articulate and literate widow living in New Orleans, persuaded a white lawyer, Maurice R. Woulfe, to defend him. Woulfe convinced the trial judge, Robert L. Rivarde, that blacks were systematically excluded from juries in St. John the Baptist Parish. Rivarde ordered a new jury to be selected from a panel that included blacks but refused to quash the indictment handed down by the grand jury. Woulfe appealed.

The state supreme court rejected Pierre's appeal. In a decision that defied logic and common sense, it conceded that no blacks had served on local juries since 1896 but pointed out that four had been included on the list of three hundred people from which both the grand jury and the trial jury had been selected. Asserting that St. John the Baptist Parish contained only about one hundred black men who could read and write — a figure that assumed an illiteracy rate of well over 90 percent — the court declared that four out of three hundred seemed a reasonable proportion. The court also thought it reasonable that jury commissioners should prefer members of their own race. "It is not their duty to search the parish for members of the colored race who possess the proper qualifications merely in order that there be the names of such persons on the rolls."

When Woulfe appealed to the U.S. Supreme Court, the NAACP's legal top brass declined to participate: they considered Woulfe incompetent, and reckoned the chance of the Supreme Court taking the case, let alone rendering a verdict, slight. It turned out to be an embarrassing misjudgment.[45]

In an opinion delivered by Justice Hugo L. Black, the Supreme Court reversed Pierre's conviction, arguing that the Louisiana court's estimate of black literacy was unworthy of belief. According to the 1930 census, 70 percent of the parish's black population of ten years and older were literate. The local superintendent of schools put the figure at 83 percent. Applying the precedent of *Norris* v. *Alabama* (1935), one of the famous Scottsboro cases, the Supreme Court decided that Pierre had been deprived of a fair trial because "negroes had been systematically excluded — because of race — from the Grand Jury." In several respects, however, *Pierre* v. *Louisiana* was a paper victory. The decision proved little use to Hugh Pierre: after two further trials he was executed. Blacks continued to be excluded from Louisiana juries, in some parishes until the 1960s. But as a weather vane decision, it indicated how the judicial wind was blowing, and that gave blacks hope and encouragement.[46]

A more far-reaching Supreme Court decision, which had important implications for black political rights, involved the federal prosecution of election irregularities in Louisiana's 1940 Democratic primaries. It was no coincidence that this precedent-setting case, *U.S. v. Classic* (1941), concerned the Pelican State: the Justice Department had mounted a major crackdown on political corruption in Louisiana and was on the alert for electoral shenanigans by the Long machine. Ironically, the boot turned out to be on the other foot: Long supporters tumbled to ballot rigging by members of the anti-Long "reform" faction. Assistant Attorney General O. John Rogge took the case to a federal court. Five Sam Jones workers were found guilty of conspiring to deprive people of their civil rights. The Supreme Court upheld the convictions, arguing that Democratic primaries, being an integral part of Louisiana's electoral machinery, were subject to the federal safeguards contained in the First Amendment, which guarantees the right of qualified voters to cast their ballots in congressional elections and have them counted fairly.

The *Classic* decision did not concern the question of racial discrimination, and the Court explicitly refrained from invoking the Fourteenth Amendment. Nevertheless, the case had a clear bearing on the black struggle for the vote. In 1935 the Supreme Court had decided that it lacked jurisdiction over primary elections because political parties were private organizations; their discrimination did not constitute "state action," and they could exclude blacks without violating the Fourteenth Amendment. The Court now abandoned the fiction that primaries lay outside federal law. *Classic* opened the door to suits against the "white primary," one of the principal disfranchising devices in the southern states.[47]

A few months later, The Group finally captured control of the New Orleans branch of the NAACP. Daniel Byrd, Donald Jones, Raymond Tillman, Ernest Wright, Arthur J. Chapital, John E. Rousseau, and A. P. Tureaud all joined the executive committee. So did Rev. A. L. Davis. The social and class character of the branch's leadership had altered decisively. If not exactly a revolution, it did signal the most important change in the branch's history: members of The Group dominated the New Orleans NAACP for the next twenty years, some of them remaining active into the 1960s and even the 1970s. Three of them, A. P. Tureaud, Daniel E. Byrd, and Arthur J. Chapital, merit particular attention, for they provided stable and strong leadership for both New Orleans and Louisiana.[48]

Of the three, A. P. Tureaud deserves to be considered first, for his name became virtually synonymous with that of the NAACP in Louisiana. Like other black lawyers in the South at that time, Alexander Pierre Tureaud used his initials rather than his given names so that whites would not address him on a first-name basis. Known to all as "Tureaud," he first joined the NAACP in 1922 after hearing James Weldon Johnson, the organization's first executive secretary, give a speech at Howard University, and he remained active in the association until his death in 1972. For most of that half-century, Tureaud's name appeared on every school and university integration suit filed by the NAACP in Louisiana, as well as on suits integrating buses, parks, and public buildings. Tureaud represented the first Louisiana students to be arrested in the sit-in movement of 1960, and his case resulted in the first Supreme Court decision quashing the convictions of sit-in demonstrators. The fact that Tureaud was the most experienced and competent black lawyer in Louisiana — indeed, in 1947 he was the *only* black lawyer in the state — made him uniquely important. He always worked closely with the experts of the NAACP Legal Defense Fund, particularly Thurgood Marshall, the fund's top lawyer and chief strategist between 1940 and 1961; in key integration cases the briefs filed by Tureaud were drafted, partially or in their entirety, by the fund's New York staff. Yet Tureaud himself participated in the formulation of legal strategy and tactics, and his local knowledge enhanced the value of his contribution.[49]

Tureaud's professional ambitions as a lawyer cannot be disentangled from his role as a litigator for the NAACP, for his involvement in the salary equalization cases finally enabled him to give up his job in the New Orleans Customs House and practice law full-time. He had fought long and hard to persuade the New Orleans branch to accept the services of black lawyers, and he bitterly resented its adamant refusal to do so throughout the 1920s and 1930s. Having to contend with the racism of whites was bad enough — Tureaud was convinced that the Louisiana bar routinely failed black entrants at least twice before allowing them to qualify. Far more galling, however, was the refusal of most blacks to retain Negro lawyers, stereotyping them as incompetent and ineffective. Even black-owned businesses, with a handful of exceptions, disdained black lawyers. Thus, after a "long, tedious, harassing experience . . . in getting admitted to practice law," he could not attract enough business to support himself. Taking a job in the Customs House in 1926 (a post secured through the patronage of black Republican leader Walter Cohen) Tureaud hoped to return to full-time practice within a couple of years. But he had so few clients that he was forced to stay in that job until 1941.[50]

Mark Tushnet has speculated that Tureaud may have regarded NAACP work simply as an opportunity to earn fees. Such a view, however, is only a partial truth. Understandably, Tureaud seethed with indignation when the NAACP paid white lawyers generously and then expected blacks like himself to give their services for free or for next to nothing. As he complained to Thurgood Marshall when the New Orleans teachers balked at his bill: "When I first came here white lawyers were in the habit of getting the fees while I helped to raise the money to pay this fee in every case we had. . . . I made fights for recognition as attorney in these cases and lost. I concealed my feelings and went on working believing that a future day would change this situation." Yet Tureaud had no interest in enriching himself: he and his family lived a modest life in the heart of New Orleans's Seventh Ward. Tureaud identified his own personal struggle to establish himself as a lawyer with the advancement of the black legal profession as a whole. And this was not a self-serving belief: he had a deep interest in the history of black lawyers in Louisiana. When he finally established himself in full-time practice, he nurtured the careers of many younger attorneys.[51]

Tureaud's role in the NAACP, moreover, extended far beyond the courtroom. Like Thurgood Marshall, he regarded litigation as a crucial means of building popular support for the association, and he became fully involved in every phase of its activities. He raised funds, spoke at branch meetings, headed the New Orleans branch for a time, and served four years as president of the statewide organization, the Louisiana State Conference of NAACP Branches (LSC). He helped to drum up support for the NAACP among black Catholics. He took part in voter registration drives and helped to organize the black vote, both in New Orleans and across the state. In 1958 he ran for Congress; his protégé, law partner, and campaign manager, Ernest N. Morial, became the first black mayor of New Orleans. In short, A. P. Tureaud's career as a lawyer and activist formed the most important strand of the complex fabric that made up the civil rights movement in Louisiana.

Tureaud had little time for the Left, and in the 1950s wanted nothing to do with alleged Communists. By the 1960s he appeared to many younger militants as a staid, old-fashioned, conservative figure, his faith in litigation at odds with the turn towards boycotts, demonstrations, and other forms of direct action. The NAACP's legal strategy, which in the 1940s and early 1950s won spectacular victories, became a slow, plodding process in which cases took years, even decades, to wind their way through the courts.

Yet Tureaud's commitment to legalism did not simply reflect professional self-interest or political conservatism: it must also be understood in terms of his background, generation, personality, and religious faith. Tureaud had a sense of history, an appreciation not only of his particular Creole heritage but also of what black Louisianians had achieved as a whole. His knowledge of the past gave him a faith in the future; temporary setbacks did not faze or discourage him. Moreover, Tureaud grew up during the so-called nadir of the Negro's post-Emancipation odyssey. Born three years after *Plessy* v. *Ferguson* and one year after Louisiana disfranchised virtually all black voters, he passed his youth and early adulthood during a time when lynching was commonplace. As with many of his generation who made the decision to stay in the South, Tureaud had no choice but to practice patience and forbearance, enduring setbacks and humiliations in the faith that God and the Constitution would enable blacks to ultimately triumph. Tureaud did not wear his religion on his sleeve, and he was privately critical of the racism that sullied the Catholic Church. Yet like other Creoles of color who stayed within the church, his faith reinforced his commitment to a certain methodical, patient, and moderate approach to social and political change.

Patience and moderation, however, were also part of Tureaud's personal makeup. As long as he could do so without compromising his principles, he preferred to do things amicably; he would bend over backward to appear reasonable and moderate. White politicians sometimes shamelessly exploited this characteristic. DeLesseps S. "Chep" Morrison, mayor of New Orleans, often prevailed upon him not to press NAACP suits during his all-too-frequent election campaigns. But Tureaud's palpable fairness, and his unfailing courtesy, won him universal respect. He was a man of complete integrity, relentless dedication, and uncommon decency.

Daniel E. Byrd played almost as big a part in the NAACP's litigation as Tureaud and Marshall. Between 1950 and 1977 he served as the Louisiana field secretary of the NAACP Legal Defense and Education Fund, popularly known as the "Inc. Fund." Before that, during the 1940s, he did more than anyone else to revitalize the New Orleans branch and boost its membership, first as branch president and then as its full-time executive secretary. In 1943 he also took on the job of president of the LSC, preceding Tureaud in that post. Byrd's career in the NAACP thus spanned almost forty years. He functioned as a vital link between Marshall, Tureaud, black plaintiffs, and local branches. He also investigated lynchings, worked on voter registration, and helped to research the *Brown* case.

Byrd was not a native of Louisiana. Born in Arkansas, he spent his teens in Gary, Indiana, graduated from Northwestern University, and played professional basketball with the Harlem Globetrotters before settling in New Orleans in 1937 and marrying a local schoolteacher. His wife, Mildred, was herself a dedicated member of the NAACP who served for many years as branch secretary. Byrd found a job with the Unity Life Insurance Company and in 1940 helped to organize the black insurance agents in their strike against the "Big Four" companies. This strike cost him his job. The following year he became president of the NAACP.

The tall, mustachioed Byrd was a born rebel. As a high school student he led a successful protest to stop the segregation of blacks during the annual ROTC Victory Day parade and also led a student strike that earned him a semester-long suspension. As a college student in Cleveland and Chicago during the early 1930s, he joined the "Don't Buy Where You Can't Work" campaigns that boycotted and picketed A & P and other chain stores. Byrd was a rare example of a northerner who became part of, and was completely accepted by, the tightly knit black leadership circles in New Orleans. Like Tureaud, he earned widespread respect as a model of dedication and integrity.[52]

Arthur J. Chapital was New Orleans born and bred, and his importance as an NAACP activist stemmed largely from his long service to the New Orleans branch. Born in 1901, Chapital attended the public schools and Straight University. Raised a Catholic, he rebelled against the church's segregation policy and joined Beecher Memorial Congregational Church, which had both black and white members. A postal worker for thirty-eight years, he helped to organize NAPE and served as the union's branch president. He joined the NAACP in 1939 and, elected to the executive board in 1941, was a mainstay of the New Orleans branch until his death in 1969. He served as branch president between 1951 and 1962 and briefly held the post of full-time executive secretary in the late 1960s.

Chapital was stubborn, argumentative, and cantankerous, but also utterly dedicated and completely honest. That earned him the kind of respect accorded to Byrd and Tureaud. Moreover, Chapital had deep and wide roots in the New Orleans black community. His breadth of contacts and network of personal relationships made him a key individual — *the* key individual — when it came to rallying and uniting blacks around a particular issue. "The association's strength was in individuals as opposed to being in an organization," recalled Harvey Britton, who became the NAACP's Louisiana field secretary in 1966. "You had individuals who could issue a call, like Arthur J. Chapital. When Chapital wanted to pull people together, he was part of the fabric of the community, he could pull those people together."[53]

Britton was right to stress the importance of key individuals in the NAACP, yet the association also derived its strength from black organizations and institutions. These provided the social context within which individuals could accumulate influence. Arthur Chapital, for example, was not only a respected and well-known individual, he was also a leader of the postal workers union and the Supreme Commander of the Scottish Rite Masons in Louisiana. Similarly, A. P. Tureaud could drum up support for the NAACP among black Catholics by virtue of his high rank within the Knights of Peter Claver.[54]

The ability of the NAACP to build popular support depended on these institutional building blocks. The two black Masonic orders were an obvious example; by the 1940s they boasted a combined membership of twenty thousand in three hundred lodges. Their histories went back a long way, and they both functioned as quasi-political organizations.

The history of the Prince Hall Masons in Louisiana dated from 1842, when free Negroes formed the first of several lodges in New Orleans. Repressed and forced underground in the late 1850s, the lodges reemerged during the federal occupation and, under the leadership of Oscar J. Dunn, combined to form the Eureka Grand Lodge. Dunn himself went on to become lieutenant governor of the state, and the Eureka lodge of the Prince Hall order, to quote Joseph Logsdon and Caryn Bell, "provided an important nucleus for political activism" during the Reconstruction years. The link between the Prince Hall Masons and the Republican party survived the demise of Reconstruction. James Lewis Sr., who headed the lodge after Dunn's death, held public office long after 1877 and remained active in the party until his death in 1914. The son of a white planter and a mulatto slave, Lewis had raised the first black regiment for the U.S. Army during the Civil War. In the 1890s he supported the challenge to segregation mounted by the *Comité des Citoyens*. His son James Lewis Jr. continued the family tradition of Republican politics, attending every national convention between 1928 and 1940.

Another Lewis dynasty revived the fortunes of the Prince Hall Masons in the early twentieth century and dominated the order for a remarkable span of seventy years. John G. Lewis Sr. took over the state organization in 1903; his son Scott became grand master in 1931, and another son, John G. Lewis Jr., headed the order between 1941 and 1979. The elder Lewis was born either in England or Canada — accounts differ — in 1851 and came to New Orleans in 1865. After serving as an inspector of Customs for the Port of New Orleans at the tender age of eighteen, he moved to Natchitoches and opened a school (according to Masonic lore, "the first public school north of Rapides Parish"). By the turn of the century he had become a substantial businessman and landowner; in 1910 he started *The Plumb Line,* a Masonic paper produced by his own printing company, the Dawn of Light.

Under the leadership of John G. Lewis Jr., the Prince Hall Masons became closely associated with the NAACP. The Masons provided members and meeting places; they organized voter registration schools; they furnished generous financial support. Lewis himself played an important part in the formation and growth of the Louisiana State Conference of NAACP Branches. Daniel Byrd was a keen Mason, and another Mason, Dr. E. A. Johnson, succeeded Tureaud as president of the LSC.

The Masonic network was national in scope. Like Byrd, his staff worker in Louisiana, Thurgood Marshall was a devoted Mason. He counted John Lewis Jr. among his closest friends, and he provided free legal representation when the Prince Hall order took its rivals to court. Substantial donations to the Inc. Fund — sometimes exceeding twenty thousand dollars a year — cemented the Prince Hall-NAACP alliance at the national level.[55]

The second black Masonic order, the Scottish Rite, had a fascinating lineage in Louisiana. White refugees from St. Domingue founded New Orleans's

Étoile Polaire lodge in 1794. After the Civil War, on the instructions of the Grand Master of France, Felix Vogeli of Lyons, the Louisiana lodges of the Scottish Rite decided to admit black members. This bold commitment to racial equality produced a deep schism within the ranks of the Prince Hall order, as many of its members defected to the Scottish Rite lodges. The Prince Hall lodges viewed the latter as renegades and to this day have refused to accept their legitimacy. But as Joseph Logsdon has argued, for many French-speaking Creoles of color the integrated Scottish Rite order embodied the political ideal of egalitarian republicanism. By the end of the nineteenth century, as the older white members died and no younger whites joined, the Scottish Rite lodges had become all black. Nevertheless, to men like Arthur J. Chapital, who would never willingly join a segregated organization, the Scottish Rite order still represented the principle of racial integration. The Scottish Rite Masons were never as closely identified with the NAACP as the Prince Hall order, but they too constituted an important source of support.[56]

The Louisiana Colored Teachers Association also gave the NAACP vital backing. Under the presidency of George Longe (Arthur Chapital's predecessor as Grand Commander of the Scottish Rite Masons) the LCTA made its first solid commitment to the NAACP by agreeing to help defray the cost of the Orleans Parish salary equalization suit. The alliance became firmer under Longe's successor, J. K. Haynes. A native of Lincoln Parish, Haynes assumed the presidency in 1942, and his election softened the old rivalry between New Orleans and the northern part of the state, smoothing the way for a formal agreement in 1943 between the LCTA and the NAACP Legal Defense and Education Fund. Under its terms, the LCTA undertook to finance all the Inc. Fund's education suits, with A. P. Tureaud handling the litigation under the supervision of Thurgood Marshall. The arrangement represented a kind of "package deal" whereby the LCTA secured the Inc. Fund's assistance by placing Tureaud on a permanent retainer. The pact also enabled black teachers to support the NAACP without putting their jobs on the line — an especially important consideration in north Louisiana, where the repressive atmosphere made teachers doubly reluctant to take out memberships. In Bossier Parish, for example, where the NAACP had no branch, teachers financed a successful voter registration suit litigated by the NAACP.[57]

Although historians of the civil rights movement have often exaggerated the importance of the black church, some Baptist and Methodist ministers did support the NAACP. Ministers headed perhaps a third of the association's branches, including, at one time or another, those in Shreveport, Alexandria, Monroe, and New Orleans. But the significance of ministerial support did not lie merely in their individual participation, or even in their general prestige within the black community; in many instances, ministers brought about the bloc enrollment of their congregations. In New Orleans, for example, Rev. L. L. Haynes persuaded 820 members of his 900-strong congregation to join the NAACP. Unfortunately, black ministers often proved to be poor organizers. They were accustomed to acting unilaterally, especially the Baptists, and their authoritarian style was ill-suited to the NAACP's democratic and bureaucratic structure. Branches headed by ministers tended to be weak ones. However, there was one outstanding exception: Rev. J. H. Scott led the Lake Providence branch, one of the strongest in rural Louisiana, for thirty years.[58]

The paucity of NAACP branches in southwestern Louisiana can be explained, in part, by its large population of black Catholics. The Catholic churches, in every case pastored by white ministers, provided the association with no direct assistance. The Knights of Peter Claver, which had more members in Louisiana than in any other state, supported the NAACP financially, but it did not have the same close association with the NAACP that, for example, the Prince Hall Masons did.[59]

Throughout Louisiana, but especially in the Catholic half of the state, black professionals still provided the strongest leadership. Doctors, dentists, and pharmacists composed an influential elite; although few in number (black doctors and dentists actually *declined* in number during the 1930s and 1940s) they were educated, organized, and economically independent. A black physician, Dr. E. A. Johnson, founded the NAACP branch in Natchitoches; a group of medics organized the New Iberia branch. These professionals, moreover, often had interlocking business interests with insurance companies and funeral homes, the largest black-owned enterprises in the state. The insurance companies, with 2,500 employees and branches throughout Louisiana, provided a network of communication and another source of NAACP leadership. Even in communities without NAACP branches, doctors and insurance agents provided a point of contact with the state and national organization. In Opelousas, for example, A. P. Tureaud worked with Dr. D. D. Donatto, president of the Negro Chamber of Commerce. Another local doctor, A. C. Terrance, served on the NAACP's National Medical Committee.[60]

Black newspapers prepared the soil for the NAACP's growth. Virtually all literate blacks read at least one paper a week, and many read more than one. Apart from the *Shreveport Sun* and the New Orleans-based *Louisiana Weekly*, which had both achieved commercial stability, other local papers were launched from time to time and had a short-lived impact: the *Alexandria Observer*, the *Monroe Broadcast*, the *New Orleans Sentinel*, and the *Sepia Socialite*, also published in New Orleans. Blacks in southwestern Louisiana sometimes read the *Houston Informer*; copies of the *Kansas City Call* and the *Oklahoma City Black Dispatch* found their way to northern Louisiana. Far more influential than any of these local papers, however, were the nationally distributed *Chicago Defender* and *Pittsburgh Courier*. The latter included a Louisiana supplement, a single sheet that covered the paper front and back, four pages of state news. A New Orleans schoolteacher, O. C. W. Taylor, provided the local copy and arranged for the *Courier*'s sale in Louisiana. John E. Rousseau Jr. later became its Louisiana correspondent. By the 1930s, both papers reached every corner of the state; their distribution networks formed important lines of communication. They also provided the NAACP with priceless free publicity, and their news coverage and militant editorials helped to mold the political and racial consciousness of two generations. "It was the *Defender* that kindled in me a fire for civil rights," recalled Rev. J. H. Scott.[61]

After 1940 the NAACP experienced exponential growth. By 1944 its membership had increased from 50,000 to 429,000, and the number of branches had tripled. Most of that expansion took place in the South, and Louisiana shared in it. By 1944 the branches in Baton Rouge, Shreveport, Monroe, and Lake Charles each claimed at least a thousand members. The New Orleans branch, which in 1938 had barely three hundred members, now boasted six thousand.[62]

Criticized by the left and loathed by the right, slow-moving and bureaucratic, often riddled with factionalism and petty rivalries, the NAACP emerged during the early 1940s as the spearhead of the civil rights struggle in Louisiana. By 1943 A. P. Tureaud had filed salary equalization suits in the parishes of Orleans, Jefferson, and Iberville. In 1944 the NAACP intensified its campaign for the ballot, and in the months leading up to the autumn elections blacks registered in larger numbers than any time since 1896. The following year Edward Hall sued the registrar of voters of St. John the Baptist Parish in what Tureaud expected to be a decisive test case. By 1945 the NAACP had been transformed. Previously ineffectual and largely inactive outside New Orleans, it was now a statewide organization with a fast-growing membership and increasing legal clout.

Of all the factors contributing to that transformation, one deserves a chapter to itself: World War II. The war revived the economy and boosted union membership. It placed some blacks in skilled jobs from which they had formerly been excluded. It put black men in uniform and sent them overseas. It eroded the isolation and parochialism of rural communities, facilitating travel and involving blacks in home-front activities. Above all, the war interrupted the status quo and gave blacks an all-pervading sense that white supremacy, increasingly discredited as an ideology, could be successfully challenged.

Chapter 4

TREMORS OF WAR

Today, America is at war," the *Louisiana Weekly* reminded its readers. In January 1942 no sensible person could have been unaware of the fact, but the *Weekly* was simply adding dramatic emphasis to what followed: "Tonight, Negro youths in khaki uniforms are down on Lee Street shedding blood in a battle for equal rights." Louisiana's first racial conflagration of the war had ignited in Alexandria, Rapides Parish.

Barely a month had elapsed since Pearl Harbor, but the nation had been gearing up for war since the Fall of France; Alexandria, surrounded by three military camps and three airfields, was "bursting its britches." On an average weekend this city of 65,000 played host to 30,000 off-duty servicemen.

On January 10, 1942, black soldiers were enjoying a respite from the humiliating discipline of a segregated Army in the bars and taverns of Lee Street. But the arrest of a drunken soldier caused a fracas that, with the arrival of sixty white MPs, a score of policemen and a contingent of state troopers, promptly turned into a riot. For two hours, Lee Street echoed to a cacophany of brawling, cursing, shattering glass, exploding tear gas, and the report of firearms. When the donnybrook subsided the authorities herded thousands of civilians off the streets and trucked 3,000 black GIs back to camp. According to the newspapers, thirteen blacks — twelve soldiers and a woman civilian — had been shot. One white, a state trooper, sustained a minor injury. The military authorities denied reports of fatalities, but the War Department later conceded that "civilian policemen and one military policeman indulged in indiscriminate and unnecessary shooting." Ten months later a reporter from the *Weekly* found Alexandria still gripped by tension and fear.[1]

The Second World War placed every facet of the South's racial system under pressure. Mobilization uprooted millions from homes and farms, herding them to factories, shipyards, and military bases. In the cities whites and blacks crowded together cheek by jowl, in a physical proximity unknown since slavery. The transience and turmoil of war placed people in new situations and assigned them new roles. Traditional relationships were ruptured, and the apparent certainties of the color line gave way to challenge, doubt, resentment, and fear. Beneath the blare of patriotism and propaganda, racial tensions simmered and sometimes exploded, in outbursts of violence ranging from barroom fisticuffs to full-fledged riots. And in this tinder box atmosphere, rumor and speculation magnified anxieties: whites feared a black insurrection; blacks anticipated a wave of postwar lynchings.

The war years saw a generation of African-Americans slough off the humility and resignation with which most black southerners had formerly accepted their lot. Blacks now clamored for fair employment, agitated for the ballot, insisted on better public facilities, and held meeting after meeting to protest police brutality. The new militancy was infectious: the mere fact of being at war seemed to encourage a devil-may-care attitude that easily translated into racial assertiveness. "People were in a belligerent mood," remembered Ernest Wright, one of the most outspoken black leaders of the period. When once blacks would have swallowed their pride, many now stood their ground. Soldiers clashed with the military authorities; civilians argued with bus drivers and policemen; shipyard workers walked off the job. Blacks were speaking and acting in a way not seen since Reconstruction.[2]

Black Americans contemplated war in 1941–42 in a very different mood from that of 1917–18. Notwithstanding the blaze of patriotism that followed Pearl Harbor, many blacks evinced a palpable lack of enthusiasm for the war, exhibiting varying degrees of cynicism, resentment, and indifference. In 1918, as editor of the NAACP's *Crisis* magazine, W. E. B. Du Bois had urged blacks selflessly to put aside their "special grievances" and "close ranks" with their white compatriots. "We shall not bargain with our loyalty," he wrote. "We shall not profiteer with our country's blood." Black veterans returned from the western front, however, to be greeted not by the waving flags of a grateful nation but by race riots, lynchings, and Jim Crow. With that experience seared into the collective memory of the race, pleas for unconditional loyalty fell on deaf ears. As the *Crisis* argued after Pearl Harbor, "Now is the time *not* to be silent about the breaches of democracy here in our own land." The onset of World War II brought no letup in racial discrimination, and by 1942 black attitudes toward the war were informed by mounting anger and a determination to shake up the status quo.[3]

Hence, the assertiveness that characterized black speech and behavior not only reflected the heightened emotions of wartime, it also stemmed from a clearsighted recognition that the war represented a rare political opportunity. Their contribution to the war effort gave blacks a powerful argument for equal treatment. If blacks bought war bonds, served in the armed forces, and helped to build ships, tanks, and planes, they were surely entitled to the rights of American citizens. Complete participation in every aspect of America's war effort thus represented an essential step in the wider struggle for equality. Even before Pearl Harbor, black trade union leader A. Philip Randolph, president of the Brotherhood of Sleeping-Car Porters, used the threat of a mass "March on Washington" to wrest from President Roosevelt a federal ban on job discrimination and a Committee on Fair Employment Practices (FEPC). Blacks also demanded the right to fight, to be recruited into each of the armed services in numbers that reflected the overall ratio of blacks to whites. When the White House endorsed the principle of Negro quotas in 1940, blacks insisted that they should be given combat assignments on the same basis as white troops, and that they ought to stand shoulder to shoulder with their white compatriots, in integrated units.[4]

On the home front, blacks bitterly resented any exclusion from patriotic activities. When it learned of plans for an "I Am an American Day" rally at the Municipal Auditorium, the New Orleans Press Club, composed of black journalists, asked to be represented on the organizing committee. Their request granted, they laid plans for a parallel Negro ceremony at Xavier University. At a stormy public meeting, however, blacks opposed the holding of a separate event, insisting that blacks should either participate alongside whites in the Municipal Auditorium rally or not take part at all. Blacks ended up boycotting the event. Blacks were quick to perceive and protest any hint of discrimination in fundraising work. "This insult and slight was the result of racial prejudices, pure and simple," wrote O. C. W. Taylor, ranking black official in Louisiana's War Finance Committee, upon learning of a whites-only meeting of war bond personnel. "Our pride has been hurt," he added. "Our feelings have been wounded."[5]

Blacks likened their battle against discrimination to the struggle against

Nazism, describing the Axis ideology as the quintessence of racism and the antithesis of democracy. Echoing the "Double V" slogan popularized by the *Pittsburgh Courier*, the *Louisiana Weekly* urged blacks to fight for a victory at home as well as victory abroad, describing white supremacy as a domestic version of Nazism. "Democracy will never survive the present crisis as a frozen or half-caste concept," thundered one editorial, barely six weeks after Pearl Harbor. "The struggle to preserve it must on all fronts be linked with the struggle to extend it. The victory must be complete if it is to be at all. We must overthrow Hitlerism within as well as Hitlerism without."

Black newspapers everywhere rang the changes on the "Double V" theme, a stance that proved popular with readers, who bought more copies than ever. Perhaps, as historian Lee Finkle argues, the black press was not as radical as it appeared to be. True, the "Double V" campaign of World War II struck a consistently militant note, explicitly rejecting the "close ranks" position expounded by Du Bois in 1918. However, while blacks pressed their grievances in no uncertain terms, few contemplated noncooperation with the war effort as a bargaining position. In practical terms, the "Double V" focused on "getting blacks to serve faithfully and fully so they would be able to seek concessions later." According to Finkle, the "Double V" campaign emerged as a rallying point for the black press only after blacks seemed to reject pleas for unconditional unity. By the end of 1942, moreover, black newspapers, fearing the wrath of the government, had moderated their tone. Still, that did not stop them from hammering away at discrimination, nor did it prevent the Army from trying to stop the sale of black newspapers on military bases. The press could articulate black militancy in more restrained words but could not ignore it.[6]

Tensions within the military both reflected and contributed to black militancy. The mistreatment of black soldiers aroused especially strong passions. Writing to the NAACP national office shortly before Pearl Harbor, A. P. Tureaud attributed disorders at New Orleans's Jackson Barracks to "cracker over-lords who are . . . resentful of 'northern' Negroes." But the problem became much wider than that, with black servicemen from all regions clashing with white authority in every shape and form — officers, MPs, policemen, and civilians.[7]

Doubtless some of these incidents had much to do with the timeless character of "licentious soldiery." As the *Louisiana Weekly* complained in June 1943, "It doesn't make a pleasing picture to see Negro soldiers drunk and cursing all up and down the street with some tramp . . . or to see the same soldiers speaking to every Negro woman they see." However, in the context of segregation both within the military bases and without, every confrontation between white and black carried a racial meaning and the potential for violence. The Alexandria riot of January 1942 was the first and the worst, but by no means the last. November witnessed a near-riot in New Orleans when city policemen entered a Rampart Street saloon and tried to arrest a soldier for disorderly conduct. The following summer rioting erupted on five southern Army camps, including one near Lake Charles.[8]

The NAACP also took up countless individual acts of violence and injustice. In Alexandria, Private Edward Green, finding the black section of a bus full, took a seat on the last row of the white section. The driver ordered him off the bus and then shot him. Also in Alexandria, a state trooper killed a black MP, Private Raymond Carr, for no good reason. A state grand jury refused to indict the trooper, and the Department of Justice declined to put the case before a federal grand jury. NAACP executive secretary Walter White cited the case in hearings before the Senate Military Affairs Committee, but Congress failed to enact legislation to protect servicemen.

The concentration of military bases around the city made Alexandria a constant focus of racial tension, and the local branch of the NAACP became a hive of activity. Led by Georgia M. Johnson, businesswoman and newspaper editor, and Louis Berry, a student at Howard University law school and the son of a wealthy local businessman, the branch saved a number of blacks from the electric chair. Plagued by internal schisms, however, the branch soon lost its effectiveness; a disputed election in 1944 paralyzed the branch for three years. Nevertheless, in 1942 the branch succeeded in making the "three soldiers' case" a black cause célèbre that attracted national attention. Lawrence Mitchell, Richard Adams, and John Bordenave were sentenced to death for allegedly raping a white waitress in Camp Livingston. After the NAACP took up their cause, Thurgood Marshall convinced the Supreme Court to set aside the verdict of the U.S. District Court on a technicality. The defendants were retried before a military tribunal, however, and again found guilty. In 1944 President Roosevelt commuted their sentences to life imprisonment; they were paroled in 1947. This case provided the stimulus for the formation of the Louisiana State Conference of NAACP Branches in January 1943.[9]

Goaded by discrimination, blacks occasionally took matters into their own hands. In August 1944, for example, some black soldiers in Camp Claiborne went on a rampage, wildly firing their guns and assaulting white officers and MPs. Fourteen culprits were court-martialed for riot and mutiny, and the ringleader, Private Leroy McGary, received a death sentence. He sent a stream of pathetic letters to Tureaud describing his "immense sorrow, and worries; from the effect of shattered nerves and mind, dued to the horrid situation I'm in." Tureaud and Marshall persuaded a review board to commute his sentence to forty years. When black servicemen inflicted violence upon whites, even in self-defense, blacks were cynical about the chances of a fair trial. In Shreveport, a black soldier killed an off-duty policeman in a dance hall; Tureaud considered it an open-and-shut case, but many blacks faulted the conviction because an all-white jury had sat in judgment.[10]

The files of the NAACP and the black press also bulged with allegations of police brutality against civilians, ranging from wrongful arrest and the use of arbitrary dragnets to the most sadistic forms of torture and death. How accurate were such charges? A. P. Tureaud, a cautious man who rarely overstated the facts, had no doubt about the prevalence of police brutality. "We have so many of these cases happening every day," he wrote in 1942. "In recent times we have had cases of the police actually killing Negroes while handcuffed right here in New Orleans." Harold Newton Lee, the Tulane professor active in the League for the Preservation of Constitutional Rights, found that "in the large majority of cases" he investigated personally, "the abuse is substantially as reported." But while the level of black protest grew louder during the war, complaints against police behavior remained exercises in futility. Lee argued that the difficulty lay in the reluctance of blacks to come forward as witnesses: unless they did so, he told Ernest Wright of the People's Defense League, "protest meetings and grumbling" would achieve nothing. However, Tureaud went to the heart of the matter when he spelled out the deeper problems: lawyers generally refused such cases; juries rarely convicted; the culprits were adept at covering their tracks; district attorneys, even if sympathetic, considered police brutality cases "hopeless."[11]

Blacks who retaliated against policemen faced a dismal future. In August 1943 the president of the Alexandria NAACP, Georgia Johnson, asked Tureaud to represent Herbert Anderson, who had shot and killed W. H. Bishop, the police chief of Oakdale, in Allen Parish. Despite the mitigating circumstances — the police chief had beaten the man's fiancée and tried to kill Anderson himself — no local attorney would handle the case. "There are so much brutality in this section," Johnson reminded Tureaud. "Persons of color are being beaten by officers every day." Tureaud was not optimistic. "The Alexandria branch have taken on a hard case," he replied. "There is an unwritten law in Louisiana that any man who kills a policeman . . . either goes to the electric chair or the police will kill him." When the NAACP appealed against the inevitable guilty verdict and death sentence, the state supreme court quashed the conviction on the grounds that blacks had been systematically excluded from local juries throughout the thirty-one-year history of Allen Parish. Successful appeals, however, invariably led to new trials and reconviction.[12] Anderson was executed in 1945.

That policemen could arrest, beat and kill blacks without cause or provocation underlined black powerlessness in the cruellest possible manner. In *An American Dilemma,* that probing analysis of race relations published in 1944 but based on research carried out on the eve of the war, Gunnar Myrdal argued that police brutality functioned as an integral part of white supremacy. The caste system demanded that "even minor transgressions of caste etiquette should be punished," and with the decline of lynching and other forms of private violence, that task increasingly fell to the police. White supremacy required the courts, the agencies of government, and white public opinion generally to endorse police actions unquestioningly. As the *Louisiana Weekly* put it, the "killers behind the badge" functioned as "the tools by which suppressive measures have been enforced upon an entire people."[13]

In October 1942 the secretary of the New Orleans Press Club, Leon Lewis, wrote President Roosevelt that "general unrest among Negroes" was "growing by leaps and bounds." As black militancy grew, however, so did the danger of violent white reaction, especially when some candidates for political office deliberately sought to arouse white fears.

Racial tensions increased dramatically during the 1942 U.S. Senate race when challenger E. A. Stephens warned of "social equality" being "forced down the throats of white people" and alleged that "colored organizations are sitting around midnight candles" plotting the overthrow of white supremacy. He also accused local draft boards of "depleting the South of its white manhood" by rejecting disproportionate numbers of blacks. "I wish you would caution Mr. Stephens about the negro draft matter," a nervous white woman wrote Senator Ellender, "and advise him not to incite race trouble at a time like this, when people's nerves are keyed up to the breaking point. . . . Some of the draftees are taking it seriously and threatening the negroes." Ellender tried to calm white racial fears by stressing his segregationist credentials. He let Senator John Overton speak on his behalf. "We do all that we can to avoid any racial antagonism. In order to do this we let the negroes understand — and they do understand — that here in Louisiana we have a white man's government, run by white men. Here in Louisiana we permit neither social nor political equality." Ellender won handily, but the tensions remained.[14]

In February 1943 white members of the New Orleans Urban League, including Archbishop Joseph F. Rummel, chastised the black press for exacerbating racial tensions and promoting views with which the "average Negro" did not agree. The atmosphere became more highly charged still when Ernest Wright organized weekly mass meetings in Shakespeare Park to protest against police brutality. By the end of April New Orleans was awash with rumors of an impending racial explosion. Whites were "scared to death," reported NAACP field secretary Donald Jones; they whispered that blacks had acquired hidden caches of arms and planned a "race uprising" for May 1. On April 29 Wright called at the offices of the FBI to state that the rumors were groundless and needed to be quashed lest whites initiate preemptive violence. The next day a committee of blacks met Mayor Robert Maestri to deny the rumors and ask for police protection. May 1, 1943, passed without incident.[15]

During the following months a flurry of interracial discussion took place with the aim of steadying nerves, yet whites showed marked reluctance to engage in anything resembling negotiation. When the Chamber of Commerce appointed a "race relations committee" it selected whites only — the Chamber had no black members — and they refused at first to meet black spokesmen. Such meetings would entail negotiation, and negotiation implied a relationship between equals. In November 1943 the merchants' committee finally agreed to hear suggestions from Tureaud, Wright, and the Reverend A. L. Davis on how to improve race relations, but the businessmen had little disposition to even discuss, much less act upon, their demands for the vote and complaints about police brutality. Committee chairman Edgar B. Stern attempted to steer the discussion toward jobs, but black leaders declined to pursue the talks as long as the committee remained exclusively white. "My people are getting tired of the report that 'the committee is working out something for you,'" complained Albert Dent, president of Dillard University. "My students, my friends, and Negroes throughout the nation . . . want some action from these race relations groups."[16]

At Dent's instance the Council of Social Agencies, which had been instrumental in setting up a branch of the National Urban League, took the initiative in organizing a race relations committee worthy of the name. With the help of Rabbi Emil Leipziger, Dent recruited over eighty members to a "Citizens Committee on Race Relations," under the chairmanship of Tulane professor John M. Fletcher. The committee tried to improve black access to the lakefront, it pressed for the employment of black police, and it attempted to defuse white opposition to the establishment of a hostel for black seamen in the French Quarter in the old Senator Hotel (a plan that Congressman F. Edward Hebert had denounced as a "diabolical scheme" to "equalize the negroes and the whites" and promote "a permanent mixture of the races").[17]

Little of substance, however, emerged from any of these efforts, an experience common to interracial groups in the South. Race relations committees helped to relieve tension and may even have prevented violence, but blacks were unsuccessful in turning them into vehicles of social change. Blacks had no political pressure to exert, and little pressure of any other kind. The whites who engaged in interracial discussions were, in their own way, equally powerless. As Gunnar Myrdal noted, the South's white liberals were few in number and bereft of popular support, and their political isolation bred a caution that verged on timidity, especially over the issue of segregation. In New Orleans they suffered the additional handicap of being, oftentimes, recent migrants, many of them Jews, rather than natives of Louisiana. Interracial groups tended to have short lives. By 1945 the Citizens Committee on Race Relations had ceased to function. As for the businessmen's committee, it was little more than an ad hoc effort to head off rioting and soon lapsed into inactivity.

In the absence of compelling pressure to do otherwise, most whites acted under the assumption that increased racial tension stemmed from temporary wartime conditions that would soon subside. This short-term view, if complacent, was not wholly inaccurate. As historian Neil Wynn has argued, the dislocations of war prevented institutions from functioning normally, delaying the resolution of grievances and creating intolerable pressures. When those conditions abated, on the other hand, so did some of the overt friction between blacks and whites. It is possible, therefore, to exaggerate the significance of wartime conflicts and the extent to which they signified a deliberate attempt by blacks to challenge established racial patterns.[18]

Throughout the South, for example, whites complained that blacks on buses and streetcars jostled white passengers, were boisterous and rude, and refused to occupy the rear seats as required under the segregation laws. Such incidents were indeed commonplace, and they sometimes led to violence. However, whereas whites tended to see a concerted effort to subvert segregation, a perception that encouraged overreaction, blacks viewed these clashes in terms of abusive and aggressive drivers, the mistreatment of black soldiers by white civilians, and overcrowded vehicles that frayed tempers and made segregation onerous and physically difficult.[19]

Much of the friction stemmed from the sheer inadequacy of public transportation. Systems that had been shrinking for two decades were suddenly overloaded, as urban populations swelled with defense workers and servicemen. To make matters worse, rationing and the switch to war production curtailed the use of private cars, including taxicabs. As Tureaud informed a national official of the NAACP, it was this lack of transportation, coupled with discrimination on the part of the crews, that created the "constant threat of racial outbreaks." In allocating scarce seats on crowded vehicles, white drivers were far more likely to favor their own race; "It is common," Tureaud noted, "to see busses and streetcars pass up Negroes waiting for transportation."

As Robin Kelley has argued, buses and streetcars afforded a public theater in which blacks could express, in a direct and dramatic manner, their opposition to Jim Crow. Looking at Birmingham during a twelve-month period in 1941–42, Kelley found fifty-five instances in which "African-American passengers either refused to give up their seats or sat in the white section." In addition, there were innumerable cases of black passengers, especially women, challenging drivers and conductors by arguing, cursing, or merely complaining.

In September 1943, a New Orleans bus driver ordered a black soldier to vacate a front seat, despite the absence of white riders. In the ensuing row, the driver left his route and headed for the nearest police station, whereupon all twenty-four black passengers were arrested and jailed. At the end of the year Tureaud told a sympathetic white of two representative incidents:

> I was told of an incident on the Galvez bus in which the motorman pulled out a pistol on a Negro passenger. Last week a Negro school teacher was arrested by an ex-policeman in retaliation for an alleged "insulting" remark of some other Negro passengers. . . . The teacher was just about to board the bus when this ex-policeman . . . pulled her outside and had her arrested because he wanted to teach "you niggers" how to respect a white man. A charge of disturbing the peace and reviling the police was made against her.

As Tureaud made clear, however, blacks did not always suffer in silence; one woman "threw a conductorette out of the street car when the conductorette attempted to strike her with the controls."[20]

The countless instances of individual defiance did not add up to collective resistance, however, even though a consensus was emerging among Southern blacks rejecting the principle of segregation. The Congress of Racial Equality was founded in Chicago in 1942 for the specific purpose of fostering nonviolent direct action against Jim Crow; in 1943 A. Philip Randolph proposed that blacks in the South register their opposition to Jim Crow by conducting one-day boycotts of segregated schools, railroads, streetcars, and buses. Yet blacks were not yet ready for a direct assault upon segregation. As the signatories to the 1942 "Statement by Southern Negroes" averred, it was more "sensible and timely" to concentrate on obtaining the vote and tackling pressing problems of discrimination and neglect. CORE's protests were confined to the North and involved a mere handful of people; Randolph's proposals for mass boycotts elicited no practical response in the South. Blacks in Louisiana, and elsewhere in the South, did not perceive segregation to be vulnerable to such tactics; indeed, direct action would seem to invite a violent white response.[21]

The New Orleans lakefront controversy underlined the limitations of wartime militancy. Blacks had long complained about the chronic shortage of parks and playgrounds, a deeply felt grievance in this densely populated city that endured subtropical temperatures for much of the year. Barred from the two main open spaces, Audubon Park and City Park, blacks had to make do with Shakespeare Park, an uptown area scarcely the size of two city blocks, and a handful of cramped playgrounds. A single swimming pool served a black population that approached two hundred thousand. For most blacks, saloons, "juke joints," and the streets offered the only means of escaping their stifling homes.[22]

Blacks sought access to the city's five-mile shoreline along Lake Pontchartrain in order to swim, go crabbing, and cool off in the southerly breezes; whites virtually monopolized this pleasant strip of land. In earlier years, with the lakefront largely undeveloped, blacks had used certain stretches on an informal basis; Seabrook, a section approximately the length of a city block, about one-sixtieth of the entire lakefront, eventually became the unofficial Negro beach. By the 1920s, however, white suburbs were creeping northward toward the lake, and residents of Gentilly, a new district south of Seabrook, protested against the presence of black bathers. Pressure to remove blacks from Seabrook intensified when the shoreline itself was expensively landscaped and redeveloped, becoming front yard to the most affluent white residential area in New Orleans.[23]

In 1939, as an inducement for blacks to quit Seabrook, the Orleans Parish Levee Board set aside 2.3 acres for a segregated black beach. Lincoln Beach, however, lay fifteen miles from the central business district, was ill-served by public transportation, and had virtually no facilities (the concession, in fact, was in the hands of a white racketeer). Worse, it was so polluted that the Board of Health, upon discovering quantities of raw sewage in the water, declared the beach contaminated. Blacks preferred Seabrook and continued to bathe there despite being periodically chased away by police and, after the siting of an Army Air Force base nearby, by MPs. In 1943 the base commander slapped a complete ban on bathing at Seabrook. Blacks protested, warning of mounting racial tension and the possibility of large-scale violence. But the ban stayed in place.[24]

Dire predictions of violence, in fact, seemed to have little influence on the white authorities, notwithstanding the constant rumors of impending riots and insurrections. In reality, the danger posed by black militancy was less one of black violence than of violent white retaliation.

The events that occurred in New Iberia in the spring of 1944 forcibly reminded blacks of their powerlessness and vulnerability. During the week of May 15, a group of blacks, including the leadership of the NAACP, was expelled from the town; despite affidavits from the victims, protests from the national office of the NAACP, and an extensive FBI investigation, the Department of Justice failed to secure the indictment and prosecution of the perpetrators. Nevertheless, if the incident illustrated the fury with which whites sometimes responded to wartime black militancy, it also provides a fascinating case study of the first, fumbling attempts by the federal government to protect the civil rights of black southerners.

The issue that moved whites to rid New Iberia of the NAACP's leadership, the demand for a school to train black welders, laid bare one of the principal causes of wartime racial tension: competition for jobs.

Mobilization for war had a tonic effect on Louisiana's economy. The New Orleans shipyards strained to keep up with the demands of the Navy and merchant marine; the Beaird company in Shreveport turned out shell casings and armored tank parts; a vast shell-loading plant, covering 6,000 acres and including 430 buildings, was established near Minden; Baton Rouge became a major depot for Army supplies. By 1943 Louisiana's 7,300 oil wells, to be found in fifty-six parishes, produced 8 percent of the nation's output; the giant Standard Oil complex in Baton Rouge provided the fuel for one plane out of every fifteen.[25]

Blacks wanted to share in this economic boom. They wanted, especially, to work in the shipyards as welders, but white workers bitterly opposed the recruitment of black skilled labor. In New Orleans, for example, the whites-only Brotherhood of Boilermakers, Iron Shipbuilders and Helpers of America monopolized the welding jobs. Although the docks and shipyards were crying out for welders, management colluded with the unions to exclude blacks, fearing "an explosion if Negroes should be employed while whites were still seeking jobs in large numbers."[26]

Faced with a national manpower shortage, the federal government funded an industrial training program, but state and local officials did not wish to draw blacks away from the agricultural areas and place them in competition with white workers. The Orleans Parish school board offered courses to blacks in printing, shoe repairing, and motor mechanics but refused to run welding courses. When a state commission recommended improving black schools, it spoke of "the value of the Negro as a plantation worker, as a tenant farmer, as a farm owner, as a domestic servant, as a laborer, as a mechanic, [and] as a professional man or woman rendering service to his own race." Whites held fast to the notion of separate occupational niches for blacks, and skilled industrial worker was not one of them.[27]

As the expanding industrial economy absorbed the white unemployed, blacks found themselves squeezed between job discrimination on the one hand and the termination of New Deal relief programs on the other. By March 1942 blacks in New Orleans were being thrown off the relief rolls faster than the labor market could absorb them. According to social workers, blacks made up a third of the overall population but half of the eleven thousand families on relief and most of six thousand needy families who could not be accepted because of cutbacks. "Their desperate status is obvious."

Agent John Beecher of the Fair Employment Practices Committee reported that Delta shipyard's six-thousand-man workforce included only sixty blacks, half of them office porters and half common laborers. The Boilermakers union, in a cosmetic attempt to parry charges of discrimination, set up a Negro auxiliary, but the union's international representative delayed giving it a charter because a group of white workers threatened to kill him if he did. The Negro organizer, Beecher noted, "hardly dares enter the white offices, where he says he is subjected to abuse, cursing, and even blows from the white members who happen to be lounging about." The school board had received six hundred applications from blacks who wanted training in welding, the Urban League another two thousand, but no black welders were being trained. Nothing would change, Beecher predicted, without "strong and *immediate* measures originating in the highest quarters of the government."[28]

The FEPC stepped up pressure on Southern shipyards to hire skilled black workers, sometimes with explosive consequences. In May 1943, obeying an FEPC directive, the Alabama Dry Dock Company in Mobile placed twelve newly upgraded black welders alongside white workers. The white workforce erupted in violence, and federal troops had to quell the outbreak. The following month white shipyard workers rioted in Beaumont, Texas.

In Louisiana, Xavier and Southern Universities began welding classes for blacks, but the problem of employment remained. A state official placed ten black trainees in a Morgan City shipyard to help build minesweepers; the white workers were so hostile that he whisked them away "unhurt but still unemployed." In New Orleans, the Delta shipyard continued to flout FEPC directives to hire black welders. Welding involved close teamwork, management argued; to place blacks alongside whites would provoke, at the very least, a strike of white workers. In February 1944 two thousand black workers walked off the job after state troopers hired as shipyard guards failed to prevent blacks being beaten on three different occasions.[29]

Blacks made some gains. A survey of 175 firms in New Orleans revealed that by June 1943 twenty-seven had recruited blacks to their previously all-white workforce, but only nineteen employed blacks and whites in the same jobs, and only ten practiced no workplace segregation of any kind. Blacks and whites worked together, moreover, at the menial level only; indeed, blacks employed above the menial level were virtually impossible to find. "We cannot put Negroes in our office," explained one employer. "Everybody would quit, beginning with the manager." Many admitted that only the labor shortage had induced them to take on blacks, and that they looked forward to demoting and shedding black workers when the war ended.

Most employers assumed that blacks were naturally suited to hot and heavy manual labor (the only category in which they rated them superior to whites) and believed that FEPC pressures were causing blacks to become arrogant and overpaid. "To many Southern whites," writes historian Merl Reed, "the committee was no less feared and hated than the enemy overseas." Shreveport chose to forgo $67,000 in federal funds for a health center rather than accept a hiring quota of twelve blacks for every hundred workers. "We are not going to be bribed by federal funds," the mayor explained, "to accept the negro as our political or social equal." The FEPC, he complained, wanted to "cram the negro down our throats."[30]

In the cotton and sugar parishes, planters feared that FEPC pressures would aggravate labor shortages by speeding up the migration of blacks to the cities. Their traditional supply of cheap, docile workers had already been threatened by the Louisiana Farmers Union, whose efforts to organize sharecroppers and farm laborers evoked threats, beatings, arrests, and near lynchings. The Farm Security Administration, which helped set up black tenants as independent farmers, also incurred planter enmity. Threats and political pressure caused the FSA to withdraw its black supervisors from Natchitoches Parish during the tense 1942 Senate campaign; southern congressmen weakened and eventually killed the FSA.

In some parishes, planters reportedly employed coercion to stop their tenants leaving. In Alexandria, the *Louisiana Weekly* claimed, blacks were "picked up off the streets" and forcibly dispatched to the cane and cotton fields. In 1943 the Department of Agriculture forbade farmworkers to leave their home counties unless a "labor surplus" had been officially declared. By 1944 sugar planters resorted to employing 4,600 German prisoners of war, labor that had the added benefit of causing black workers to worry about being displaced. "As a result," one planter reported, "the negroes are working better and are staying on the job throughout the week."[31]

New Iberia, a town of about fifteen thousand people 125 miles west of New Orleans, lay in the heart of a sugar-growing area. When the state Department of Education set up a whites-only welding school there, Lawrence Vilitz, an African-American, wrote to the War Manpower Commission complaining of racial discrimination. According to one report, the sheriff virtually ran a black WMC representative out of the city in the fall of 1942. A few months later the WMC sent two white field examiners to investigate.

Lloyd G. Porter, superintendent of the Iberia Parish schools, invited a group of "prominent colored citizens" to meet the WMC agents in the company of the sheriff, a district judge, the state senator, and an assistant district attorney. In the presence of the WMC officials, the handpicked blacks nervously assured Porter that they knew nothing about Vilitz's letter and denied any desire for a welding school. The WMC turned the case over to the FEPC.[32]

Blacks in Iberia Parish had no civic or political organization. They did, however, have a recently organized federal credit union, and in the summer of 1943 the officers of the union founded a branch of the NAACP. By June the branch had recruited over one hundred members, and it gained thirty more on July 24 when A. P. Tureaud and Daniel Byrd attended the formal installation of the branch officers.

The NAACP leadership in New Iberia was unusually strong for such a small town. A dentist, Ima A. Pierson, and a schoolteacher, Herman Joseph Faulk, became president and vice president of the branch. The executive committee included two physicians, Howard Scoggins and Luins H. Williams, another schoolteacher, Franzella Volter, and an insurance agent, Octave Lilly Jr. Another prime mover was J. Leo Hardy, a former insurance agent currently employed as a bartender. Hardy had been active in the NAACP since 1927, having once served as secretary of the Monroe branch under the militant leadership of Charles Myers. As an insurance agent, Hardy had traveled about the state. Octave Lilly Jr., whose father founded the People's Life Insurance Company, had been born and raised in New Orleans. In the late 1930s he had worked for the Federal Writers Project; some of his poems had been published in *Opportunity,* the magazine of the National Urban League.

The doctors, in particular, gave the branch strength and respectability. These were well-educated and prosperous men; one owned a pharmacy, another operated a ten-bed private hospital. In addition, they had connections with the white community. Iberia Parish boasted one of the best public health clinics in the state; located in the courthouse, it was staffed by both black and white doctors. "The [black] doctor and nurse have desks in the office," observed Charles Johnson. "There are many Negro patients and they are served freely by members of both the Negro and white staff." For the South, the black doctors worked in unusually close proximity with whites. They had little inkling, however, that such proximity was setting white tongues wagging.[33]

Leading whites looked with alarm upon the formation of the NAACP branch. Spurning an invitation to attend the installation of the branch officers, the mayor asked a Catholic priest, the pastor of a Negro parish, to warn the blacks against disturbing the town's "harmonious" race relations. Shortly after the NAACP's inaugural meeting, Sheriff Gilbert Ozenne summoned the branch officers and sternly warned that they would be "personally held responsible for anything that may happen in New Iberia." In December, Ozenne confided to a disbelieving FBI agent that the NAACP was stockpiling ammunition. The newly elected sheriff, a former Highway Patrolman, began girding himself for an armed confrontation. These repeated warnings produced a division within the branch's executive committee about how to proceed, with branch president Pierson advocating caution and others adopting a more militant approach.[34]

In 1944 J. Leo Hardy, one of the militant group, became branch president. "Most of the Old Timers use the argument 'The time is not ripe' for us to attempt to Vote and Register," he informed the National Office. Hardy thought otherwise. In March, oblivious to the mounting tension, the branch invited Ernest Wright to speak. As expected, Wright emphasized the absolute necessity for blacks to gain the vote. On April 28 the branch celebrated the NAACP's victory in *Smith* v. *Allwright*, which declared Texas's whites-only Democratic primary to be unconstitutional. As the church echoed to the "Amens" of the audience, Hardy decried the fact that white children rode to school while Negro children had to walk, and that white neighborhoods boasted paved roads and sidewalks while the streets fronting Negro houses were made of dirt and mud. Now was the time, he concluded, for Negroes to secure the ballot.[35]

The branch took up Lawrence Vilitz's complaint about the lack of industrial training for blacks, and on March 6, 1944, a black official of the FEPC, Virgil Williams, visited New Iberia to resolve the dispute. He left with the understanding that the school board would establish a welding school for blacks, the state Department of Education providing the equipment and Gulf Public Service Company furnishing the power. School superintendent Porter undertook to operate the school on two six-hour shifts, five days a week. Hardy gave him a list of over one hundred prospective trainees. "This case . . . promises to turn out an interesting affair," mused Carlos Castaneda, Williams's FEPC superior.

When the welding school opened on May 7 it operated one shift only, and at 8:00 P.M., two hours after the first class began, Porter told the instructor to finish at 10:00 rather than midnight. White residents, he explained, were complaining about the noise. The following day the school began operating a daytime shift that ended at 7:00 P.M., causing several trainees to drop out. The NAACP sent a deputation to ask that the welding class be moved to a black neighborhood, but Porter, allowing only one of them into his office, pointed out that the black school had no electric power and that he had no money to run in cables. Hardy asked the FEPC to intercede again, alleging that the school's location on the edge of a white neighborhood was a deliberate attempt to deter blacks. When Hardy attended the welding class on May 15, he was the only person there apart from the instructor.[36]

Precise responsibility for the ensuing expulsions is difficult to establish, but the sequence of events is clear. On the afternoon of Monday, May 15, two sheriff's deputies picked up Hardy at the welding school. Within minutes, he found himself standing in the sheriff's office, facing Sheriff Ozenne and Superintendent Porter. According to the account written by Hardy a few days later — the only evidence directly linking Ozenne and Porter to the expulsions — the Sheriff began to browbeat him. Did Hardy know who was talking to him? Did he realize that his letters to Porter (one of which asked for "an immediate answer") were insulting? Terrified, Hardy became obsequious. He apologized and punctuated every sentence with "yassuhs."[37]

Then Porter spoke. Hardy would not be writing any more letters to the FEPC or to anyone else. He, Porter, would run the welding school as he saw fit; not even the President of the United States could make him do otherwise. Hardy's repeated "yassuhs" infuriated Porter. "You yellow son of a bitch," he shouted. "You are saying 'yes sir,' but deep down in your heart you would cut my throat." With Porter's assent, Ozenne gave Hardy until ten o'clock the next morning to get out of town. Hardy, however, lingered in New Iberia throughout the next day, despite warnings from friends not to spend the night in his home or stay with any of his relatives.

At about eight o'clock in the evening Hardy was nonchalantly chatting with friends outside Uncle Tom's Saloon when a black car carrying four deputy sheriffs drew up. They ordered Hardy into the car and took him to the sheriff's office. After threatening to kill him, one of the deputies asked Hardy where he wanted to go. When Hardy suggested that they take him by his house, the deputy retorted, "Hell, no. Do you want to go east or west?" Ozenne then kicked and pummeled Hardy while two deputies held his arms. After half an hour in a cell, he was bundled into a car and driven out of town. A deputy in the backseat grabbed hold of his necktie and punched him in the face. Dumped in the road, he was ordered to walk fast, not look back, and never return. The deputies drove behind him for a time; one fired a parting shot with his pistol. Reaching the hamlet of Burke, Hardy phoned Dr. Howard Scoggins for help. Scoggins found him standing by the roadside about five miles out of town, bleeding from the nose and mouth. After applying first aid, he took his injured friend to Lafayette. The following day, the doctor drove back to Lafayette with clean clothes, and Hardy took an overnight train to Monroe, two hundred miles distant.[38]

The expulsions had only just started. On the evening of Wednesday, May 17, Walker and two other deputies picked up Dr. Ima A. Pierson, Dr. Luins H. Williams, and Herman Joseph Faulk. One was taken as he sat in a barber's chair, another dragged half-clothed from his bed. The deputies drove them out of town and dumped them by the roadside. All suffered beatings of varying severity: Pierson and Williams were pistol-whipped, Faulk "clubbed over the right eye, knocked to the ground, and stomped in the face by [deputy] Gus Walker." Faulk left a particularly vivid account of his ordeal. Before letting him loose, one deputy held him against the bonnet of the Plymouth sedan while Walker slapped his face and berated him. "You are a damn smart nigger, eh? . . . Nigger, you mean to tell me that you and your wife work for Mr. Porter, knowing he doesn't like that damn organization you niggers got, and you wouldn't quit it? . . . You are one of those niggers going around telling other niggers they will be voting soon. We are going to beat the hell out of you for the first ballot you cast."[39]

News of the expulsions coursed through New Iberia's black community. Some fled. Octave Lilly Jr. visited Pierson in Lafayette and, seeing his bandaged head and hearing his tale, decided to leave New Iberia forthwith. Schoolteacher Franzella Volter, the NAACP branch secretary, also left town. So did Dr. E. L. Dorsey, who owned a clinic, an insurance company, and a funeral home. When a black barber saw Williams being taken away, he went to warn Dr. Scoggins, who barricaded himself in his house that night and drove to Lafayette on the morning of May 18. Roy Palmer, the black welding instructor, also took flight.[40]

In New Orleans, A. P. Tureaud tried to piece together the facts for the NAACP's national office. "All attempts to talk with the people of New Iberia have failed," he told Thurgood Marshall. "I called a Catholic priest there and he said he could not discuss the matter over the phone." According to the *Louisiana Weekly,* the black schools closed early and an unofficial curfew kept blacks off the streets. NAACP field secretary Donald Jones wrote to Walter White to underline the seriousness of the affair. If the whites of New Iberia get away with the expulsions, "our small town southern branches, already timid, will practically freeze up on us."[41]

The NAACP pressed the Civil Rights Section of the Justice Department to prosecute the culprits. Victor Rotnem, head of the section, passed on Tureaud's information to the Criminal Division. Malcolm Ross, chairman of the FEPC, also demanded action. On May 25, Assistant Attorney General Tom Clark authorized the FBI to enter the case, and five days later FBI Director J. Edgar Hoover ordered the New Orleans office to conduct a "preliminary investigation." SAC (Special Agent in Charge) A. P. Kitchin assigned two "G-men" to the case.[42]

Even before the FBI formally entered the case, one of its agents in New Orleans had heard about the affair during a social event. A white woman from New Iberia told him that a vigilante committee had been organized and several black leaders had been given thirty days to leave town. Local blacks, she added, had been instructed by the NAACP not to work for the white people. Shortly afterward, visiting the town, Agent Dill learned from a member of the sheriff's department that some deputies had employed "strong methods against some of the local negroes" because "the negroes were becoming very sassy and [they] had to keep them in order." Sheriff Ozenne had planned a raid on black bars and nightclubs to confiscate "razors, knives, guns and other weapons," but he cancelled the crackdown when he decided that local blacks were sufficiently intimidated already. Ozenne and other white officials had talked to the blacks "and apparently scared them plenty"; further repression might cause the blacks to " 'fold up or leave town' and would not leave any colored help for the merchants and planters."[43]

When Agent Dill finally interviewed Ozenne on June 10, he found him in a belligerent mood, armed to the teeth and apprehensive about possible retaliation. The sheriff complained that blacks were insubordinate and alleged that deputy sheriff Gus Walker recently had his telephone go dead when a Negro cut through the line. Boasting that his men were prepared "for anything that might happen," Ozenne showed Dill his gun vault. The agent noted two Thompson machine guns, six shotguns, five rifles, and quantities of tear gas — a veritable arsenal. "It seems about time that several negroes resist arrest," said Ozenne ominously. "Then they will quieten down for a while." When asked about the expulsions, however, he claimed that no such incidents had taken place. Sitting beside the sheriff was Lloyd Porter, the superintendent of schools, a revolver strapped to his waist. Ozenne asked Porter if he needed more ammunition.[44]

On June 20, SAC Kitchin forwarded a thirty-one-page report, the result of a six-day inquiry by two agents. The FBI had failed to identify the men responsible for the expulsions, but one informant, a Catholic priest, admitted that local gossip singled out two particular sheriff's deputies. One of them was Gus Walker, also known as "Rough House Walker" and "Killer Walker." However, the only black witness interviewed in New Iberia, the barber who witnessed the abduction of Dr. Williams, had been unable or unwilling to name any of the whites involved.[45]

The NAACP accused the Justice Department of dawdling. In late July Thurgood Marshall and Leslie Perry, chief of the NAACP's Washington bureau, met Victor Rotnem of the Civil Rights Section. Why had the government failed to make a case against Gus Walker, they asked, when all the victims had positively identified him? And why had the FBI visited New Iberia without interviewing possible black witnesses?[46]

Genuinely sympathetic — and concerned that publicity surrounding the case might lose black votes in the presidential election — Assistant Attorney General Tom C. Clark asked for a full investigation. Anxious to secure a prosecution, Clark prodded the Bureau to follow up all leads that might clearly identify who carried out the expulsions. He also asked that "discreet efforts" be made to ascertain whether the deputies were acting under Ozenne's orders. In September, Hoover impressed upon his agents that "the Criminal Division has expressed great interest in this case" and that they should report within two weeks, but the New Orleans office moved slowly, not reporting until December 8. In the meantime, Leo Hardy visited Washington to relate his experience to Victor Rotnem, a meeting that apparently helped convince the Justice Department to present the case to a federal grand jury. The department's renewed interest prompted Hoover to press New Orleans to follow up some leads that had still not been covered; a further report followed on December 28. On January 16, 1945, U.S. Attorney Herbert W. Christenberry presented the evidence to a federal grand jury in New Orleans. The government's case collapsed, however, when the jurors refused to return any indictments.[47]

The New Iberia outrage contained a multitude of meanings. Most obviously, it exposed the difficulties facing the federal government when it came to prosecuting civil rights violations. Since the creation of the Civil Rights Section in 1939 the Justice Department had certainly become more sensitive to the maltreatment of southern blacks. By 1944, however, it had yet to secure the conviction of a single lyncher, and only three police brutality cases had resulted in guilty verdicts. White jurors were still loath to indict and even more reluctant to convict whites accused of violence against blacks, especially when the accused included law enforcement officers. Moreover, the Reconstruction-era statutes under which such prosecutions were brought had been so weakened by the federal courts that they had atrophied through lack of use. Reviving them proved to be an uphill struggle. As Victor Rotnem admitted in 1945, "Unusually exceptional elements must be present if we are to have a successful case in this field."[48]

The Justice Department's dependence on the FBI posed another difficulty: the Bureau's performance in the New Iberia investigation typified its palpable lack of enthusiasm for civil rights cases. Hoover disliked such cases because, in part, they proved difficult to prosecute, and too many failures marred the Bureau's public image. In addition, police brutality probes endangered the FBI's close relations with local law enforcement agencies, jeopardizing its investigations in other areas. The FBI's reluctance to take on civil rights cases also reflected the political conservatism that suffused the agency, as well as the thinly veiled racism that permeated the Bureau from top to bottom. In the field of race relations, the New Orleans office spent most of its time monitoring the black population for signs of "foreign-inspired agitation," investigating labor unions and civil rights organizations for "Communist infiltration," and compiling reports on alleged "Communists" like Ernest Wright. It pursued the New Iberia investigation only because of continual prodding from Justice.[49]

To be sure, FBI agents faced problems in gathering evidence. Although many whites in New Iberia admitted that the black leaders had been run out of town, none would sign a statement confessing direct knowledge of the affair. Blacks were loath to testify for an entirely different reason: fear. A man who witnessed Hardy's abduction refused to name the deputies "because if he did he would be found dead in a gutter somewhere." Two other witnesses were similarly reticent. Eventually, in the relative safety of the Federal Building in New Orleans, one of the frightened blacks named the three deputy sheriffs who had accosted Hardy. The FBI found three other witnesses who identified Gus Walker. In the context of the southern courts, however, the federal case was flimsy. All the government witnesses were blacks, and only one of them, Hardy, could link Ozenne and Porter to the expulsions. One deputy admitted to being present during Hardy's questioning on May 15, but when pressed further he became "vague and evasive." Against the government was arrayed virtually the entire white community of Iberia Parish, including its men of wealth, status, and political influence.[50]

The credibility of the black witnesses, however, was not enhanced by the FBI's dismissive attitude towards the case. The FBI reports exhibited a veneer of impartiality. They scrupulously included contradictory opinions and made extensive use of the word "alleged." But the investigating agents shared the view of their white informants that Hardy and the others had violated the rules of the racial caste system and were thus the authors of their own misfortune. Leo Hardy, they wrote, had been employed as a card dealer and bartender at Uncle Tom's saloon before being fired "because of his constant trouble making and impudence." As president of the NAACP, he had been "endeavoring to incite trouble." Octave Lilly had a "chip on his shoulder" and was considered a "trouble maker." Herman Faulk had been "a constant source of trouble" as a schoolteacher. Scoggins was "hot-headed" and "bitter about the racial situation." Williams had become "very arrogant." Dorsey was "flashy and showy" and wore a "perpetual grin on his face" that might be interpreted as a "grin of arrogance." Pierson had been "increasingly more arrogant just prior to his leaving New Iberia." Hardy was a born troublemaker, who would "never do anything that he was told to do without an argument," and "tried to agitate the colored people who came into the bar and tell them how they should have equal social rights with the white persons."

Summarizing the case on October 4, the Bureau argued that while Hardy and others "may have suffered mishandling at the hands of law enforcement officials," the evidence "failed to substantiate" that they had been beaten and run out of town. The local agents placed little credence on Hardy's testimony. Agent Dill described him to Tureaud as "a bad character . . . a gambler and a trouble maker."[51]

The FBI reports provide valuable insights into white attitudes. For whites, the welding school controversy symbolized a growing challenge to the traditional pattern of race relations. They detected racial threats all about them: in black demands for the vote, for skilled training, and for industrial jobs; in the shift in black leadership from docile teachers and preachers to independent businessmen and professionals; above all, in the assertive demeanor of ordinary blacks. Again and again, whites used the words "arrogant" and "sassy" in complaining of black behavior; they were unnerved and felt physically threatened by blacks who failed to display the traditional signs of deference and humility. "The negro [welding] students would crowd up on the sidewalk," complained one resident, "and then when some of the women in the neighborhood tried to pass, they would not move." The Catholic pastor cited a similar incident: black children had ganged up on a white child, shoving him off the sidewalk and beating him. Alert to every gesture and nuance, whites sometimes attributed insult and insubordination to the most innocent action. Dr. Luins Williams, for example, caused a minor scandal when he began entering the public health clinic by the front door, hanging his coat and hat on the "white" rack and even on one occasion allowing the tail of his coat to brush the shoulder of a female clerk.[52]

Some prominent whites cast the issue in economic terms. Iberia Parish was primarily agricultural, the mayor pointed out, and its sugar plantations and salt mines depended on black labor. He could not understand, therefore, why New Iberia needed a welding school for blacks, especially when sugar was such a critical war material. The state Director of War Production Training made the same point, adding that the white welders in Morgan City had vigorously objected to the opening of the New Iberia welding school. In light of the recent race riots in Mobile and Beaumont, the sensitivity of the state authorities to a violent "white backlash" should not be underestimated. Leo Hardy suggested another economic reason for the expulsions: whites wished to destroy the credit union because it loosened the strings of dependency between blacks and whites.[53]

Who ordered the expulsions? Walker and the other deputies clearly acted under orders from Sheriff Ozenne. Ultimate responsibility for the episode, however, is more difficult to determine. The Catholic priest interviewed by the FBI doubted that Ozenne would have instigated the expulsions by himself "inasmuch as the Sheriff was an ignorant man who had apparently been put into office by one Paulin Duag [sic], a wealthy oil man." The priest also testified to the longstanding concern of the city fathers, including the mayor and the city attorney, about the activities of the NAACP. There may even have been collusion with state officials. In early May Lloyd Porter had traveled to Baton Rouge to attend the inauguration of Governor James H. Davis and Lieutenant Governor J. Emile Verret and may well have discussed the welding school problem. Verrett himself was surely aware of it: as president of the parish school board for thirty years — he stepped down in 1944 — he was Porter's close colleague. Certainly, officials in the Departments of Education and Public Health were well aware of the mounting white concern in New Iberia that the NAACP leaders needed restraining.[54]

The evidence points to a carefully planned operation, approved by local bigwigs and acquiesced in by state officials, to rid New Iberia of selected black activists. This was not the indiscriminate violence of a mob. On the contrary, the people who ordered the expulsions wished to avoid the kind of mob action that might cause blacks to flee the area, exacerbating the labor shortage. Ozenne's deputies knew who they were looking for and expelled the victims with clinical efficiency, and the mayor boasted that not a single black family had left New Iberia apart from those involved in the incident. Whites also congratulated themselves that the departure of the town's black doctors had not led to any increase in black ill-health. The expulsions achieved their desired end: the "troublemakers" left town but there was no general black exodus.[55]

The *Louisiana Weekly* speculated that many whites privately disapproved of the expulsions, but the FBI reports did not support this view. Of course, caution is needed when generalizing about white racial attitudes on the basis of FBI reports. For one thing, the agents spoke mainly to officials; the attitudes of these middle- and upper-class informants were not necessarily representative of the white community as a whole. When the agents interviewed white residents in the vicinity of the welding school, for example, most stated that the black trainees had not bothered them in any way. Secondly, the FBI tended to be dismissive of dissenting white opinions. One nurse at the public health clinic flatly disbelieved the claim that Dr. Williams had exhibited rudeness to the female clerks. She acquitted the doctor of arrogance and praised his "gentlemanly manner" — but the FBI men did not place much credence in this woman when told that she was a patrician type well known for her heterodox opinions. Finally, fear may have silenced some whites who disapproved of the expulsions. One person claimed that Ozenne had threatened him over the telephone. The frightened informant begged to be left alone "because he could be liquidated by the Sheriff's office without too much difficulty."[56]

New Iberia's "most substantial citizens," however, seemed to agree that "the job done by the sheriff was a job expertly done." Another informant, "one of the most outstanding citizens in town," deplored the "Gestapo methods" of the sheriff's department but described the expulsions as the "best thing that could have happened." The blacks "were beginning to get the upper hand," he explained. "The fact that these negroes were run out of town quieted the negro situation down for a while at least." Even the Catholic priest, pastor of a black parish, shared this sentiment. The blacks had been increasingly arrogant, he told the FBI. His own parishioners had petitioned him to exclude the few whites who attended the church. Of course, the priest decried Ozenne's

"Gestapo tactics," but he thought it just as well that the "trouble makers" had left town. Ozenne certainly paid no political penalty for his actions: a few weeks later the Louisiana Sheriff's Association elected him to the post of vice president.

At the same time, paradoxically, whites boasted about their community's friendly race relations. They pointed out that in New Iberia, as in other parts of southern Louisiana, whites and blacks had traditionally mingled in a degree of physical proximity unknown elsewhere. Local whites had never been especially "race conscious"; the races had lived and worked together quite amicably. Blacks in the town and the surrounding sugar belt were treated exceptionally well, claimed the mayor; the planters looked after their workers when they were sick, pensioned them off in old age, and attended their funerals when they died. Only intervention by outsiders, whites agreed, had disturbed the friendly and easygoing atmosphere. Several blamed "all of this trouble" on black newspapers imported from New Orleans. The mayor claimed that blacks had been "sent into New Iberia for the purpose of organizing and agitating the negro situation." If they were not northerners, he stated, they had been "sent in by northerners." Another white suggested that the NAACP had deliberately picked on New Iberia, thinking the town's "excellent racial relations" would enable it to gain a foothold. In another parish, claimed one informant, the blacks would have been run out of town long ago.[57]

Clearly, the emergence of a black cadre prepared to organize the black population in direct opposition to New Iberia's political elite presented whites with a new and frightening development that revived folk memories of Reconstruction.

How did blacks feel about the expulsions? Surprisingly, some of the FBI's black informants agreed that the NAACP leaders were irresponsible "hotheads" who only had themselves to blame. Several blacks took pains to disassociate themselves from the NAACP. One explained that he had only joined "because he was afraid if he did not join the negroes of that community would attack him." Two others claimed to have resigned from the NAACP after Hardy became president because, as one of them put it, "he saw trouble brewing." Some praised Lloyd Porter's efforts to improve black schools and accused Faulk of spreading discontent among teachers at the colored high school in an attempt to undermine and possibly oust principal A. B. Simon.[58]

There was another side to the picture. Some blacks spoke up for the victims and refused to supply the FBI agents with derogatory information. The expulsions were outrageous, said one. "He had never heard of any trouble in which any of these people had been involved." All the doctors "had very good reputations," another insisted; Faulk had been "brutalized." The testimony of the one black druggist who remained in New Iberia is particularly illuminating. This man, who had been active in the NAACP, admitted that many blacks had criticized him for journeying to Lafayette after the expulsions and persuading one of the doctors there to set up practice in New Iberia. The absence of black doctors, they argued, would keep the memory of the expulsions alive and highlight the need for federal intervention. Indeed, some told him he ought to leave town too in order to show solidarity with his race. The FBI agents also encountered obstruction and distrust. An official of the People's Life Insurance Company refused to divulge Octave Lilly's personnel records; one of Lilly's former supervisors greeted the agents with a hatchet and "kept the hatchet in his hand during the entire interview" because "he just wanted to be on the safe side."

Which set of reactions most accurately expressed the feelings of New Iberia blacks can only be guessed at. However, an anti-NAACP bias in the FBI reports is easy to detect. The agents seized upon any criticisms of Hardy and the other activists, however minor, in order to bolster their thesis that the victims had caused the expulsions through their own provocative behavior. Some blacks needed little prompting to denounce the NAACP leaders. However, the frequency of words like "arrogant" and "hot-headed" leads to a suspicion that the FBI men put words into the mouths of their black informants or, at the very least, sometimes distorted or exaggerated what they were told. A. P. Tureaud, for example, may well have described Scoggins as "hot-headed" and stated that "the white people and the negroes had gotten along well in New Iberia," but it is unlikely that he would have agreed with the way his words were interpreted. It seems safe to conclude that while many blacks were wary of the NAACP, many more were shocked and angered by the expulsions.[59]

Blacks could take little comfort in any aspect of the affair. The welding school ceased operation; the doctors never returned; Leo Hardy died a year after his beating. Amazingly, however, the expulsions failed to kill off the New Iberia NAACP. Gus Baronne, a funeral director, and F. M. Boley, a minister, stepped into the leadership. "Our branch . . . is yet alive," they assured Walter White. When Thurgood Marshall visited the town with Tureaud in late June, "Nothing happened," he noted, "didn't even get threatened." Both men believed that the FBI investigation, however inconclusive, had produced a salutary effect on local officials. As Tureaud put it, "These pecks down in Louisiana fear no government agency as they do the Department of Justice."[60]

Still, some historians have argued that white violence, especially the Beaumont, Mobile, and Detroit race riots, dampened black militancy. Black newspapers, for example, seemed to edge toward a more cautious, less strident tone. They cooled towards A. Philip Randolph's proposal for an all-black movement employing mass direct action, speaking more favorably of conventional tactics like litigation, political action, and interracial cooperation.

Perhaps, as Finkle has suggested, black editors softened their voices because they feared government censorship; perhaps they were intimidated by criticism from prominent white liberals who castigated black newspapers such as the *Pittsburgh Courier* for irresponsible militancy.[61]

Yet it would be an error to suppose that black leaders timidly retreated from their earlier militancy, feeling content, in the words of historian Harvard Sitkoff, to "entrust white liberals with the job of winning the Negro his rights." The thrust of black protest, to be sure, was directed toward politics and the courts, but it would be a misreading of reality to dismiss such action as tame gradualism. In the South of the 1940s *all* forms of activism entailed high risks: to organize a branch of the NAACP, file a lawsuit, or appear before the registrar of voters implied no lack of militancy. When any challenge to the status quo violated the laws and customs of white supremacy, the difference between direct action and conventional action was often academic. Another generation of activists learned this very lesson in Mississippi two decades later.[62]

Set beside the grand panorama of war, the NAACP's campaign to equalize teachers' salaries might seem a trivial affair. The issue "aroused little excitement, even in the Deep South," writes historian George B. Tindall. "The tedious pace, the limited results, the manifest equity of the claim prevented any shock or alarm" on the part of whites.[63]

Tindall's sanguine assessment, however, underestimated both the depth of white opposition and the importance of the campaign. Salary equalization represented a clear-cut legal victory for blacks, one of their first, and signaled an increasing willingness by the federal courts to strike down obvious forms of "official" discrimination. It strengthened the NAACP by creating a close partnership with the Louisiana Colored Teachers Association, which in 1943 agreed to finance all the NAACP's education cases and retained A. P. Tureaud as its legal advisor. It also set the pattern for the NAACP's modus operandi in all its school and college cases, which relied upon a smooth working relationship between the LCTA, Tureaud, and the NAACP Legal Defense and Education Fund under Thurgood Marshall. However, the campaign also demonstrated some drawbacks of the NAACP's litigation strategy, foreshadowing some of the problems that ensued in the wake of *Brown* v. *Board of Education*. Salary equalization was no easy victory.[64]

The New Orleans suit went deceptively smoothly. After the usual legal shadowboxing, Judge Wayne G. Borah came down firmly on the side of the plaintiff when the case came up for trial in June 1942. Thurgood Marshall watched the litigation with an attentive eye, instructing the inexperienced Tureaud in tactics. "The thing we have to bear in mind is that the pressure is on the school board, and not on us," he advised. "They are trying the strategy of playing upon a 'war of nerves.' . . . It is just like a checker game, and it is now their move; and I don't see why we should make a move and leave ourselves open." Tureaud wanted the support of the city's white teachers and, influenced by Sarah Towles Reed, local president of the American Federation of Teachers, he told Marshall that equalization over three years was the best that the school board could offer without imposing an across-the-board pay cut. But a skeptical Marshall warned him not to fall for the school board's ploy. "Maybe I do not know the New Orleans school board," he wrote, "but I do know about fifty other school boards . . . and they all pull the same stuff. . . . They always have loose money lying around." Accepting Marshall's advice, Tureaud rejected the three-year plan, winning an agreement to equalize salaries by September 1943. This result delighted Tureaud, and he looked forward to the speedy capitulation of school boards throughout Louisiana.[65]

Tureaud's rejoicing proved premature. School boards in other parishes evinced no willingness to follow the New Orleans precedent, and their resistance necessitated a hard legal slog by the NAACP. Finding teachers willing to sue their employer, however, was no easy task, for suits exposed complainants to retaliation. In October 1943, the Jefferson Parish school board dismissed Eula Mae Lee, the plaintiff, an example followed by Iberville, Rapides, and Lincoln parishes. "It has been a difficult problem to get the teachers organized for these fights," Tureaud admitted, "because no one wants to sacrifice his job." In Baton Rouge, teachers expressed interest in filing a suit but then backed off when the superintendent of schools assured them that legal action would not be needed. It took three years to find a plaintiff.

Nor had Tureaud reckoned with the opposition of white teachers who, fearful that black salaries would be topped up at their expense, backed a plan for payment according to qualification, experience, and ability, a system that might preserve the racial differential. Teachers in New Orleans opposed this plan but, according to the *Louisiana Weekly,* they were booed down at a meeting of the Louisiana Teachers Association in Baton Rouge "packed with anti-Negro sentiment." In July 1943 the State Board of Education added "merit" and "responsibility" to the criteria that parishes could use in determining salaries. The president of Tulane University "fought the passage of this resolution to the last ditch," but his was the sole dissenting voice. First off the mark, the Iberville Parish school board commenced to rank its teachers according to the new criteria, devising a new pay scale based on "merit."[66]

The salary cases also yielded fewer organizational dividends than the NAACP had anticipated. Teachers did not flock to join the association, and the strategy of creating "citizens committees" to finance the suits caused resentment among the local branches. The citizens committee reaped the credit if the case went well, Daniel Byrd complained, while the local NAACP bore the blame if something went wrong. The creation of separate committees also caused money quarrels; in Iberville Parish, for example, a dispute over funds raised in the name of a "Teachers Club" all but paralyzed the NAACP branch.[67]

In 1943 Tureaud gloomily predicted that equalization would take fifty years "unless some quicker means is found." He cast about for a way of attacking the problem on a statewide basis, but the National War Labor Board disclaimed any jurisdiction over the matter, and his proposal for a suit against the state Superintendent of Education proved unworkable. There seemed no alternative to filing suits in parish after parish until black teachers accumulated enough victories to convince whites that further resistance would be futile.[68]

The resolution of the Iberville Parish case became the key to the equalization struggle statewide. At a meeting with parish and state officials in Baton Rouge, Tureaud and the Reverend Gardner C. Taylor, who headed an NAACP-backed Citizens Committee for Equal Education, resolutely resisted accepting the "merit" system as a basis for settling. Another conference took place on January 19, 1945, but blacks again emphatically rejected "merit" pay. "It is now clear to the officials of Louisiana that the Negroes in Louisiana are together," noted Thurgood Marshall, who attended the session, "and that the so-called conservative Negroes are likewise in favor of equalization." The conference had the additional significance, in Tureaud's opinion, of being the first time that blacks and whites had met "on a basis of equality as far as the right of free discussion is concerned." Four days later both sides endorsed an LCTA plan to equalize salaries, standardize the nine-month school year, and provide every child with "a school of suitable grade . . . with adequate buildings and physical facilities and a competent teacher in every classroom." Governor Jimmie Davis appointed a biracial commission to consider the plan. In order to win white support for this ambitious statewide program, Tureaud agreed to a consent decree in the Iberville Parish case that would equalize salaries over a five-year period. He also undertook to forgo further litigation for the time being.[69]

The anticipated breakthrough, however, did not materialize, and Tureaud found himself the recipient of some sharp criticism. The *Pittsburgh Courier,* the most influential black newspaper in the country, blasted the LCTA proposals as vague, weak, and a flimsy basis for settling the Iberville Parish suit. Tureaud, incensed, threatened a libel suit. Thurgood Marshall, however, also found fault with the proposed consent decree: it failed to find the school board in violation of the Fourteenth Amendment; it stretched equalization over five years; and it failed to renounce payment by "merit," which the U.S. Court of Appeals for the Eighth Circuit had recently found unconstitutional in a case involving Little Rock. But when Marshall arrived in Louisiana for another legal strategy session, bad news awaited him: the U.S. Court of Appeals for the Fifth Circuit had upheld a merit system used in Miami. "This decision will really hurt," he complained. "The Iberville case is much harder now." [70]

When Iberville superintendent of schools Linus P. Terrebonne implemented a "merit system," he placed eighty-four of eighty-five white teachers in the top two ranks and forty of forty-four blacks in the bottom two. No black teacher was ranked above a white one, no white teacher below a black. The prospect of a negotiated settlement disappeared altogether when the school board fired fourteen of the teachers behind the suit. Terrebonne also, it seems, attempted to blacklist them. By 1945 Iberville Parish had become the symbol of white resistance to equalization. Unless Terrebonne were stopped, warned W. W. Harleaux, "then all superintendents will follow in his footsteps, when such suits are filed." [71]

There was no comfort to be had, either, from the governor's biracial commission: in June 1945 it had still not met. "I am tired," complained Gardner C. Taylor. "We who have been a part of the negotiation stand in danger of having our influence and leadership repudiated by a people who are understandably impatient." Many believed that only political pressure would induce the state legislature to enact across-the-board equalization. Having seen whites wield it so effectively and guard it so jealously, blacks appreciated the power of the ballot. [72]

In April 1944 word finally came from Washington that the Supreme Court had struck down the whites-only primary. Hailing the decision as "the Negro's Second Emancipation," blacks in Louisiana steeled themselves to demand the franchise in the most forthright and concerted voice they could muster.

The months preceding the August 1944 registration period saw a flurry of voter registration activity by the NAACP, the People's Defense League, the CIO's Political Action Committee, the Prince Hall Masons, and the Knights of Peter Claver. With strong backing from activist ministers like Gardner C. Taylor of Baton Rouge and L. L. Haynes of New Orleans, black leaders formed a new organization, the Louisiana Progressive Voters League, to stimulate and coordinate these registration drives. [73]

When blacks visited the registration offices in August, Tureaud monitored the results with a sense of elation. "Reports have been coming in of Negroes registering in many places where they have never been registered before," he enthused. In Alexandria, the NAACP selected a committee of nine to be the pioneer applicants; although five fell by the wayside, the remaining four, who included branch president Spencer Bradley and lawyer Louis Berry, succeeded in registering. During the following days Alexandria "broke all precedent," Tureaud reported, by registering thirty Negroes. About four hundred blacks registered in Shreveport, an "exceptionally good" total for that city. According to the *Louisiana Weekly,* significant numbers of blacks also registered in East Baton Rouge, Orleans, Ouachita, Iberville, and Ascension parishes. "In many of these parishes Negroes are being given friendly assistance by whites."[74]

Assessing the overall picture, however, Tureaud struck a note of caution. In Calcasieu and St. John the Baptist parishes, registrars turned away all black applicants. In most parishes "Negroes are afraid to even try to register because of repeated examples of brutality." Even when registrars accepted some blacks, they employed arbitrary standards and sometimes rank intimidation to keep black enrollments to a trickle. In Baton Rouge, for example, the registrars flagrantly ignored *Smith* v. *Allwright* by refusing to let blacks register as Democrats. In Alexandria the registrar refused to register more than two applicants a day. Blacks in New Orleans found themselves turned down "on any pretext suitable to the deputy registrar," a favorite excuse being slight errors in filling out the application form. Many registrars required applicants to confirm their identity by producing two witnesses from their precinct, both of them registered voters — often an impossible requirement, for in most parishes there had been no black voters since 1896. In Shreveport, blacks were subjected to abuse and threats; one applicant was literally booted out of the office.[75]

Whites, in fact, were not ready to dilute their political power and frankly avowed their determination to keep the great mass of blacks disfranchised. As the assistant registrar of Tangipahoa Parish wrote her husband, no Negroes had yet applied and "we don't intend to let any register." The registrars, of course, obeyed the dictates of the politicians who, virtually without exception, frowned upon black voting. After weighing the implications of the *Smith* v. *Allwright* decision, the Committee on Elections of the state legislature reported that the existing registration laws were quite adequate to keep blacks off the rolls. "Louisiana is bursting over with anxiety to knock out this iniquitous law," Tureaud informed Marshall. "The money is here awaiting the first sign to go forward."[76]

Although inundated by affidavits from aggrieved black applicants, the Department of Justice was not inclined to assist black registration. Jonathan Daniels, Roosevelt's advisor on race relations, warned that a federal suit against voter discrimination "would translate impotent rumblings against the New Deal into an actual revolt at the polls." When he discussed the Louisiana situation with Attorney General Francis Biddle, therefore, Marshall received tea and sympathy but no promise of federal action. Indeed, Justice Department lawyers were skeptical that a private civil suit in federal court would get very far. According to *Trudeau* v. *Barnes,* they argued, the federal courts had no jurisdiction over registration complaints when the plaintiff had failed to use all the remedies theoretically available in the state courts.

But Marshall thought otherwise. In *Lane* v. *Wilson* (1939) the Supreme Court had ruled that a plaintiff alleging deprivation of voting rights on the grounds of race could resort to the federal courts "without first exhausting the judicial remedies of state courts." This decision now governed, Marshall believed, and he set out to test his theory.[77]

On August 4, 1944, Edward T. Hall, president of the St. John the Baptist Parish branch of the NAACP, led a group of blacks to the courthouse in Edgard, on the left bank of the Mississippi. Instead of asking them to fill out an application form, the registrar of voters, T. J. Nagel, asked each applicant a series of questions. What judicial district did they live in? Which parishes made up their judicial district? What congressional district did they live in? What was their senatorial district? Nagel rejected Hall, along with the others, as unqualified. The group immediately complained to Joseph Thornton, Tureaud's ailing law partner, who telephoned Nagel and threatened him with a civil suit. When the applicants returned, however, Nagel still refused to give them application forms.

This was the case Tureaud and Marshall had been looking for, and in July 1945 Hall sued Nagel in federal court. "We've been begging too long for what lawfully belongs to us," Marshall told a rally in New Orleans. "Take them to court and you'll hear from them." When federal district judge Adrian Caillouet dismissed the suit for want of jurisdiction, Tureaud promptly filed an appeal. Visiting St. John Parish, however, he found his client badly frightened and reluctant to talk. Hall was weakening, Tureaud wrote Marshall, and had been warned "not to be caught out at night away from home."[78]

In April 1946, Marshall argued *Hall* v. *Nagel* and *Mitchell* v. *Wright,* an Alabama case, before the U.S. Court of Appeals for the Fifth Circuit. Tureaud and Birmingham lawyer Arthur Shores assisted him. It was standing room only when the trial opened, and Marshall noted with satisfaction that "the audience was practically all Negroes with the exception of a few lawyers." The *Louisiana Weekly*'s correspondent penned an admiring portrait of the handsome, debonair Marshall, with his "dark suit and polka dot tie, his unusual height towering above others and his . . . speeches touched off with a sparkling bit of dry, sarcastic humor." Ridiculing the defense attorneys, the reporter noted how one white lawyer's southern drawl mangled the word "Negroes" into "Nig-gras." From time to time "a murmur of controlled laughter" filled the courtroom "when the defense was caught napping." Marshall thought it ironic that the Alabama registrars were represented by an attorney from the law firm headed by Lister Hill, "that great liberal." The future would reveal another irony: that lawyer was none other than Richard Rives, destined to become one of the staunchest advocates of civil rights on the federal bench.[79]

In a unanimous opinion written by Judge Edwin Holmes of Mississippi, the federal appeals court reversed Caillouet's decision and, setting a crucial precedent, affirmed the plaintiffs' right to sue in federal court without first going through the state courts. *Trudeau* v. *Barnes* had been knocked on its head. Daniel Byrd hailed the decision as "the turning-point of registration in Louisiana."[80]

After the Second World War drew to a close, returning veterans stiffened the determination of blacks in Louisiana, and throughout the South, to claim their rights as equal citizens in a democracy. Some, like Zelma C. Wyche of Madison Parish, had seen their white comrades cast absentee ballots in the 1944 presidential election, only to be denied that right themselves. Others witnessed elections in the newly liberated countries, noting the absence of complicated registration procedures and the speed with which recent enemies were granted democratic rights.

William Bailey of Bogalusa summed up the view of many a black veteran when he recalled, some forty years later, how the war had shaped his attitudes. "I have always had a feeling that I was just as much entitled to register to vote as anybody. This thinking seemed to take on momentum after getting out of the service, knowing the price that I had paid, the problems that I had faced — my life, you know, had been at stake, and why shouldn't I exercise the rights and privileges of any citizen? . . . If I could go over there and make a sacrifice with my life I was willing to do it here, if it meant death. There had to be a beginning. Everything here was stalemated. The resistance was overwhelming. Somebody had to make up their mind, and do something about it, if there was to be changes."[81]

Chapter 5

BRUTALITY AND BALLOTS, 1946–1956

Between 1946 and 1956 the structure of white supremacy in Louisiana appeared to crumble, as one racial barrier after another fell. Blacks registered to vote in sixty of Louisiana's sixty-four parishes, and the black electorate increased from 7,000 to 161,000. In 1954 two blacks were elected to the city council of Crowley, in Acadia Parish, the first blacks to hold elective office for more than fifty years. In 1950 Louisiana State University became the first state university in the Deep South to admit a black student, and did so without violence. In the same year New Orleans recruited two black policemen, its first since 1915. Black policemen also began serving in Shreveport, Lafayette, Lake Charles, Monroe, and a dozen smaller towns. In 1952 blacks gained admittance to City Park in New Orleans. Two years later, the city's public libraries were quietly integrated.

Some of the most dramatic changes could be found in public education. In 1947, white resistance to the equalization of teachers' salaries suffered a decisive blow when, after four years of legal sparring, Judge Wayne Borah ruled for the plaintiffs in the Iberville Parish case. The existing salary schedule, he decided, clearly discriminated against blacks, notwithstanding the "merit system" devised by Superintendent of Schools Linus P. Terrebonne. The following year Judge Herbert W. Christenberry signed a consent decree in the Jefferson Parish case, where the school board had fired the plaintiff, Eula Mae Lee. The agreement represented a complete victory for the black teachers: the board agreed to full equalization and offered Lee her job back.[1]

By then the NAACP had widened its equalization strategy to cover the entire spectrum of education — schools, colleges, and universities. The beauty of equalization suits was that they were simple to file, easy to argue, and had an excellent chance of success.

The wide disparities between black and white schools were easy to document. In St. Charles Parish all the white schools were two-story brick edifices; every black school was a two-room wooden building. In East Carroll Parish, forty-three teachers served 1,460 white pupils while forty-six teachers coped with 2,064 black pupils. Not one school for blacks contained a library; not one taught home economics. The parish provided bus transportation for white children but not for black ones. Twelve parishes failed to provide high schools for blacks of secondary age.[2]

In East Carroll and other parishes of the upper Mississippi Delta, the rhythms of the cotton season still dictated the black school year: terms were "split" to enable children to hoe cotton in late spring and harvest the crop in early fall. Split terms did Negroes a favor, the local district attorney informed Tureaud; keeping black children in school at these times would deprive their families of income and compel farmers to further mechanize, thus forcing more blacks off the land. Tureaud conceded that many blacks were glad to see their children toiling in the fields, but such parents, he wrote, were "the victims of the economy under which they must survive and are not aware of their rights or of the broader outlook on life for the future of their children who have no intention of remaining cotton pickers in competition with the mechanical devices now in use." He tartly reminded the D.A. that state law required a minimum school year of 180 days and compulsory attendance, regardless of whether local school board members owned plantations.[3]

In the cities, where black migration compounded the problem of neglect, conditions were little better. The 1950 "Shreveport Negro Survey" described the Northside school as "typical." It had no electricity and "old type outhouses." An antique galvanized iron cistern contained the water for both washing and drinking. Students were crammed into two classrooms and attended only seven months of the year. Another school was so overcrowded that a church housed the overflow; children sat on pews or benches and used their laps as desks.[4]

Overcrowding was especially acute in New Orleans, where black enroll-ment increased by 28.9 percent in 1947 and a further 10.8 percent in 1948. "At no time in the history of public education in New Orleans has there been even a semblance of adequate housing for Negro children," admitted Super-intendent of Schools Lionel J. Bourgeois. "The situation at the present time is critical." While fifteen white elementary schools were half-empty, twenty-three of the Negro schools operated the "platoon" system of double shifts. Even so, the *Louisiana Weekly* estimated that perhaps a quarter of the city's black children were not in school.[5]

By 1948 Tureaud had filed additional salary suits in Lincoln, Rapides, Ouachita, and Union parishes, suits against Louisiana State University, and a school equalization suit in St. Charles Parish, the first of its kind in the state. The strategy, Tureaud explained to Marshall, was "to get as many cases filed in Louisiana as possible to force the legislature into action when it meets in May 1948." By that criterion, the strategy paid off handsomely: with Earl Long triumphantly installed as governor, an obedient legislature boosted education expenditure and appropriated $8 million to raise and equalize teachers' sal-aries. Tureaud kept up the pressure, with equalization suits soon to follow in Iberville, St. Landry, and Orleans parishes.[6]

In New Orleans, Superintendent Bourgeois all but invited the NAACP to sue the school board. In 1947 he had urged Tureaud to forgo litigation, as-suring him that "I stand squarely upon a platform of equal opportunity for all children." Accordingly, in January 1948 he submitted an ambitious plan for the improvement and equalization of the city's public schools. It called for a building program of $40 million, 63 percent of which would be earmarked for Negro schools, an additional $2 million a year to be spent on teaching, and the conversion of eight underutilized white schools to black use. If it were im-plemented in full, blacks stood to gain eleven new schools, four rebuilt ones, and about two hundred additional teachers. However, when voters approved only a fraction of the building program, and when the school board caved in to pressure from white residents who protested the conversion plan, Bour-geois realized that he had failed. Choosing his words carefully, he told Daniel Byrd that he was no longer counseling patience. "Please understand me. I am not advocating court action, nor am I opposing such action." Six weeks later, Tureaud filed *Bush* v. *Orleans Parish School Board*. He had little reason to expect this litigation to last for twenty years.[7]

By any standard, the equalization strategy worked. By 1950, despite being one of the poorest states in the union, Louisiana spent a greater proportion of its per capita income on education than any other state in the South and all but two states outside the South. In absolute terms, too, Louisiana out-spent every other southern state. Overall, between 1940 and 1955, the average per capita sum allocated to black children each year increased from $16 to $116, from 24 percent of the amount spent on white children to 72 percent. Although black and white schools were still far from equal by the time of *Brown* v. *Board of Education,* the gap had narrowed significantly. Black enrollment had caught up with white enrollment, the level of daily attendance was the same, the length of the school year was equal, hundreds of new buildings had been erected, and the salaries of black teachers had all but reached that of their white counterparts. At the college level, funding for both Southern University and Grambling College rose sharply, and in 1947 a law school had been established at Southern to fend off the integration of LSU's law school.[8]

Such gains were all the more remarkable in light of the seeming impregnability of white supremacy in the immediate aftermath of World War II. In 1946 whites in Louisiana were no more disposed to make concessions to black demands than they had been in 1941. They were not ready to equalize teachers' salaries, were not prepared to let blacks vote, and were bent on using their political muscle in Congress to abolish the Fair Employment Practices Committee and defeat antilynching legislation. Indeed, in 1945 many blacks had looked forward to peacetime with apprehension, fearing a repetition of the "red summer" of 1919, with its many lynchings and race riots. A. P. Tureaud suspected that white state Home Guard units — he described them as "another Ku Klux Klan" — were being readied for use against blacks in such an eventuality.[9]

As 1946 unfolded it seemed that the NAACP's worst fears were coming true. Returning home through South Carolina by bus, Isaac Woodward, a black veteran still in uniform, exchanged words with a driver. The police chief of Batesburg hauled Woodward off the vehicle and beat him so badly that he lost his sight. This took place on February 13. Eleven days later, in Columbia, Tennessee, a fight between two veterans, one black and the other white, led to an armed confrontation between the police and the black community, with four officers suffering shotgun wounds as they entered Mink Slide, the black business district. Reinforced by five hundred National Guardsmen and seventy-five state troopers, the police went on a two-day sweep of Mink Slide, confiscating weapons, ransacking stores, and firing into buildings. More than one hundred blacks were arrested. Two were shot dead in jail. Twenty-six were put on trial for attempted murder. Worse soon followed. On July 25, four blacks were shot dead in Monroe, Georgia, and on August 8, a man was lynched near Minden, in Louisiana.[10]

These incidents attracted national notoriety. Less extreme examples of racist violence, however, were so commonplace that they usually passed without note save in the pages of the Negro press.

The files of the NAACP's national office were replete with complaints of police brutality from the Pelican State. In many instances, policemen simply picked on blacks, in a more or less arbitrary fashion, as a means of reestablishing the patterns of deference that had been upset by the war. On June 5, 1946, Mary Harris was driving through Louisiana with her two sons en route to Texas. State police stopped the car outside Bossier City. "Nigger, where are you coming from?" one of them asked the driver, Charles Harris. When he failed to "sir" the policeman with sufficient alacrity, he was hit across the head with a flashlight. The information that he was a musician from New York acted like a red flag to a bull. He ought to be in the fields chopping cotton, a policeman snarled. Harris and his mother were arrested and held overnight. "Let this be a lesson to you," a justice of the peace admonished them. "Remember you are not in the north now. This is the way we run the south and you stay in a nigger's place."[11]

Wealth, status, and education afforded no protection; indeed, some policemen delighted in humiliating blacks whom they perceived to be climbing above their proper station. Possession of a new car, for example, often attracted police attention. Roosevelt Hollingsworth, from San Francisco, was visiting Louisiana in May 1946 in his three-year-old Buick. State police arrested him at a gas station near Minden and accused him of driving a stolen vehicle. Refusing to believe that the Buick belonged to him, they held him for three days and confiscated the car. A few weeks later Johnnie A. Jones, a recently demobilized soldier who later became a prominent Baton Rouge attorney, was stopped by a state policeman as he drove toward New Orleans. "Without a word being said, he hit me . . . with his fist, knocked me down, kicked me several times, and grabbed me by the shirt," Jones complained. When J. K. Haynes, head of the LCTA, stopped at a gas station to drink some water, an attendant hit him over the head with a bottle. A policeman, looking on, drawled, "Son, don't you know better than to drink out of a white fountain?" Haynes got back in his car and drove off, knowing that to make an issue of it might cost him his life.[12]

Given this climate of intimidation, it is not surprising that the postwar years did not see the kind of mass direct action against racial segregation that characterized the civil rights movement of the 1960s. The repressive atmosphere of the Deep South seemed to preclude the methods of Gandhian nonviolence. In 1947 members of the Congress of Racial Equality and the Fellowship of Reconciliation challenged interstate bus segregation in a protest that anticipated the 1961 "freedom rides," but they confined their journey to the Upper South. Even there they were harassed, intimidated, and arrested; the protest failed to ignite mass support. The NAACP considered such tactics ill considered; it advised blacks traveling on trains and buses to abstain from "passive resistance" in view of the "well-known proclivities of southern trainmen and police officers to use excessive force" on blacks who refused to move on command.[13]

Even the most militant blacks and the most radical whites viewed segregation as invulnerable to direct action. Justifying an all-black fundraising event at the New Orleans Coliseum, Communist Party activist Oakley Johnson explained that "it *could not* be an interracial one and be the size it is, conducted under police surveillance and near-terrorism." When a party official in New York suggested that he organize a picket of the Louisiana Supreme Court, Johnson responded testily: "You know very well that no one would propose a picket line in Jackson, Mississippi, would they? Would *you* picket the Mississippi Supreme Court? Well, this city and state here — New Orleans and Louisiana — are in the South, and picket lines here would be slightly suicidal."[14]

Thus, even when segregation lacked the force of law, it was often sustained by the fear of violence. New Orleans, for example, had few segregation ordinances, but members of both races simply assumed that any violation of established custom would provoke a violent white reaction. As the superintendent of City Park put it, although no law barred blacks from the park, "there is a possibility of racial conflict where the two races gather together in large numbers on public property wherein it has not been the practice before." Custom could quickly become law, moreover, when segregation faced a direct challenge. When the Southern Conference for Human Welfare booked the Municipal Auditorium for its fourth annual convention in 1946, the building's governing body hastily adopted a rule mandating segregation.[15]

In politics, too, whites seemed determined to stifle black aspirations that had been heightened by the war and encouraged by the U.S. Supreme Court. The NAACP had hoped that the *Hall* v. *Nagel* decision, which the appeals court reaffirmed in May 1946, would break the back of disfranchisement in Louisiana. It did nothing of the kind: blacks faced the same hostility from parish registrars that they had encountered in 1944. Across the state black applicants, often led by uniformed veterans, told similar stories of rejection and intimidation. In Shreveport, the registrar insisted that two white voters "identify" each person; in Alexandria, registrars would not permit blacks to apply; in St. James Parish, "whenever Negroes presented themselves at the registration office . . . the Registrar of Voters was always ill." The registrar of Tangipahoa Parish warned that even if he allowed blacks to register, which he would not, any attempt to vote might have unfortunate consequences. "Things are so bad in this Parish," the NAACP reported, "that Negro papers are not allowed."[16]

In the majority-black parishes of the Mississippi Delta, local sheriffs employed rank intimidation. In May 1946, for example, Sheriff Matt Fowler of

East Carroll Parish summoned Rev. J. H. Scott, the president of the local NAACP branch. He understood that Daniel Byrd had arrived to address an NAACP branch meeting, Fowler explained: he did not like the idea of Byrd urging blacks to register. "You be damned sure and tell him don't say anything about voting." When Scott and another minister attempted to register, they found the door to the registrar's office locked. A voice from within told them to try the next door. It too was locked. "We gave up that time," Scott recalled.[17]

There were a few bright spots. In Lake Charles, all applicants were being registered. Similar reports came from St. Charles and Morehouse parishes. In Monroe and Lafayette, however, registrars accepted a few blacks only to become uncooperative after the first primary. In New Orleans, an energetic registration campaign netted 4,716 voters, but at least six out of ten applicants were rejected. "Veterans were continuously given the run-around for not having discharge certificates from their draft boards," reported the *Louisiana Weekly*. Then there was "that old 'mistake on your card' gag, with no explanation as to the mistake." The year 1946 saw the number of black voters increase by about 6,532 over the 1944 figure to the politically insignificant total of 7,561, 0.9 percent of the electorate.[18]

When blacks looked to Washington they saw a similar pattern: the promise of advancement followed by cruel disappointments. In June 1946 Congress killed the FEPC: blacks had to suffer blatant discrimination in employment for another twenty years. In December of that year, Truman appointed a President's Committee on Civil Rights, but none of its proposals became law. The enveloping Cold War then relegated the issue of racial discrimination to the back burner. As historian William C. Berman put it, "The postwar liberal tide was now receding, carrying with it the frustrated hopes of millions of American Negroes."[19]

In James A. Burran's view, black militancy quickly subsided after the end of the war. The violence of 1946, and the failure of the federal government to win convictions in the Minden and Monroe lynching cases, had a particularly demoralizing effect: such repression intimidated blacks, compelling them to either accept the status quo or leave the South altogether. Real change, according to Burran, had to await the upsurge of grassroots protest associated with the civil rights movement of the 1960s.[20]

But this view is far too sweeping. The most salient fact about white postwar violence was its *failure* to silence black protest. The NAACP not only consolidated its spectacular wartime expansion but continued to grow in peacetime. In 1946 it had thirty-three branches and about ten thousand members; between 1947 and 1950 twenty-five additional branches were either chartered or revived; by 1954, on the eve of the *Brown* decision, statewide membership stood at 12,500 and there were fifty active branches. The State Conference of Branches, which had been formed in 1943, brought about an unprecedented degree of coordination, particularly between New Orleans and the northern part of the state.[21]

Its response to the Minden lynching of 1946 exemplified both the NAACP's newfound confidence and the different climate created by federal involvement. The contrast between the way the NAACP investigated this lynching and the way Louisiana lynchings had been investigated in the 1930s is instructive. Back then, New York headquarters had taken the initiative, relying on whites like Howard Kester to visit the scenes of lynchings. Local NAACP branches, if they existed, were usually too frightened to openly investigate such cases; the New Orleans branch rarely ventured far from home and usually displayed a paralyzing caution. In 1946, by contrast, Dan Byrd headed straight for Minden and spent two days in the area questioning potential witnesses and obtaining the names of suspected lynchers. He then tracked down the surviving eyewitness and flew him to New York, whence his account of the lynching was flashed across the nation in dramatic headlines.

The Minden affair also illustrated the increasingly effective interplay between the NAACP and the federal government. NAACP pressure triggered an FBI investigation and a federal prosecution of the alleged lynchers — the first federal involvement in a Louisiana lynching. Together with publicity over racial violence elsewhere, it persuaded President Truman to appoint a Committee on Civil Rights, the first time since Reconstruction that the federal government had evinced any real concern over the discriminatory treatment of black people.[22]

The Minden lynching was a typical southern horror story, but it is a tale worth telling. John C. Jones was a 28-year-old veteran who had survived the Battle of the Bulge and earned the stripes of a corporal. Webster Parish, his home, was by no means a typical plantation area: a gigantic shell-loading plant had been sited near Minden, and numerous oil wells dotted the surrounding countryside. Jones's own grandfather owned oil-bearing land, and the old man, it seems, had been tricked into signing leases with the Premier Oil Company at absurdly low prices; in 1946 he received just $1.50 a month for the remaining active well. After his discharge from the army, Jones got a job with Premier and apparently raised awkward questions about the leases. He was also quite prepared to say "No" to a white man: when a neighbor expressed interest in his German pistol, Jones refused to part with the trophy save "over my dead body."[23]

On August 9, 1946, some men fishing for bass pulled Jones's body out of Dorcheat Bayou, about three miles north of Minden. Not until August 16, however, the day after Jones's burial, when newspapers reported the verdict of the local coronor's jury, did news of Jones's fate spread beyond Webster Parish. Dan Byrd, in Bogalusa at the time, knew instinctively that this was a lynching. After picking up A. P. Tureaud in New Orleans, he drove the three hundred miles to Minden, stopping only for gas. Accompanying the pair were three black journalists, John E. Rousseau, editor of the *New Orleans Sentinel,* and two reporters from the *Pittsburgh Courier.*

The following day, having "covered territory in Louisiana that we seriously doubt is on the map," Byrd wired a report from Shreveport, supplying Walter White in New York with the names of three suspected lynchers. Byrd also provided some gruesome details that enabled the NAACP to give a sensational twist to the story: according to a local embalmer, Jones's body had been burned and mutilated. Although subsequent testimony cast doubt on this claim, the NAACP's news releases told how Jones had been tortured with a blowtorch and hacked with a meat cleaver.[24] The head of the Shreveport NAACP, R. L. Williams, provided the names of six more suspected lynchers. Williams's main informant, a black café owner, claimed that the men, who included two sheriff's deputies, had celebrated in his barroom immediately after the lynching.[25]

The main witness to the lynching, however, had gone into hiding, and the NAACP spent a frantic week tracking him down, afraid that the lynchers or the Webster Parish sheriff might reach him first. Albert Harris Jr., Jones's seventeen-year-old cousin, had been beaten alongside Jones, but survived. He afterward fled to Texarkana with his father. As soon as the NAACP discovered their whereabouts Walter White tried to move them to Washington or New York. A Justice Department official suggested that the local sheriff take Harris into protective custody, but White pointed out that a man had been lynched in Texarkana just four years earlier. An Arkansas NAACP official arranged to put them on an eastbound plane on August 19, but the Harrises failed to appear. Four days later the pair showed up in Muskegon, a small town in Michigan, and revealed their identities to the local NAACP. After having the younger Harris examined by a doctor, who noted scars and abrasions about the head and body, the Detroit branch flew the Harrises to New York, where they appeared beside Walter White at a dramatic press conference.[26]

The Harrises told an extraordinary tale. On July 31, two sheriff's deputies, Oscar Haynes and Charles Edwards, picked up young Harris, who was known by the nickname "Sonnyman," and took him to jail. On the way they stopped by the home of Sam Maddry Jr., who accused Harris of loitering in his backyard and planning to attack his young, pregnant wife. After letting him sweat in jail for two days, deputy Haynes, the son of the sheriff, delivered Harris to a waiting car, whose white occupants drove him into some woods, tied him to an oil rig, placed a gunny sack over his head, and beat him. Thus tortured, Harris told the whites what they wanted to hear: that he had acted as a lookout while Jones, his cousin, prowled in the Maddry yard with the aim of raping Maddry's wife. (Daniel Byrd believed that Jones and Harris were taking a shortcut through the yard when they saw the woman undress through an unshaded window; as they paused to look, Mrs. Maddry recognized Harris.) When the badly beaten Harris staggered home, collapsing on the floor, his father drove him to Henderson, across the Texas state line.

The following day, Saturday, August 4, deputies Haynes and Edwards returned to the Harris home only to find "Sonnyman" conspicuously absent. Furious that the elder Harris tried to lie about his son's whereabouts, Edwards "backhanded" Harris across the face. Discovering the truth, the policemen ordered him to fetch "Sonnyman" at once. Harris and his wife drove to Henderson and delivered their son to Haynes at the Minden jail on August 5. He was placed in a cell across from Jones. On August 8, at about 8:30 in the evening, Haynes turned the pair over to a group of some ten white men who were waiting outside; Jones tried to make a run for it but was violently bundled into one of two cars. Disgorged from the vehicles about three miles north of Minden, Jones and Harris were stripped and beaten senseless, in Jones's case fatally.

When Harris recovered consciousness he made his way to Minden, where his uncle, Jones's stepfather, sheltered him. The next day a cousin arrived from Shreveport, thirty miles away, and took him by taxi to his mother in Cotton Valley, a hamlet not far from the Arkansas border. Harris and his father, Albert Harris Sr., then fled Louisiana. According to the later trial testimony of Minden police chief Benjamin Geary Gantt, deputy Haynes told him, "Those s.b.'s told me they wouldn't harm those negroes." It was the state's first old-style lynching since the killing of W. C. Williams near Ruston in 1938.[27]

When the Webster Parish grand jury refused to return any indictments, the Department of Justice instructed the U.S. Attorney for the Western District of Louisiana, Malcolm Lafargue, to institute federal proceedings under Sections 51 and 52, Title 18, of the U.S. Criminal Code. This Reconstruction-era statute specified penalties of up to ten years imprisonment for conspiracy to deprive people of their civil rights.

The government took no chances when the Harrises testified before the federal grand jury in Monroe on October 14, 1946. A U.S. deputy marshal and an armed guard accompanied them as they traveled by train and car from Chicago, with Edward Swan of the Detroit NAACP lending moral support. In Monroe, they were taken to the parish jail and placed in separate cells. In the early afternoon, however, when the U.S. attorney learned that Sheriff Haynes of Webster Parish had been nosing around the jail the previous night, he transferred the Harrises to the federal building, where deputy marshals kept an armed watch throughout the night. After appearing before the grand jury, the Harrises returned to Chicago under the same tight security. The grand jury indicted six men, among them Sam Maddry Sr., deputies Haynes and Edwards, and Chief of Police Gantt. The charges against Gantt were later dropped, reportedly because he cooperated with the federal authorities.[28]

The trial took place in Shreveport during the last week of February and the first few days of March 1947. Although not the first time the Justice Department had brought alleged lynchers to trial — there had been several such cases since 1942 — it was the first prosecution of its kind in Louisiana. It was the first time, too, that a Louisiana lynching had been investigated by the FBI, activity that engendered profound resentment among whites, intense irritation in J. Edgar Hoover, and angry criticism from Thurgood Marshall.[29]

Hoover thoroughly disliked civil rights investigations. After being ordered to take on the Minden lynching, in addition to the lynchings in Monroe, Georgia, he asked Tom Clark, now attorney general, to review the whole policy of using the FBI in such matters. "Rushing pell-mell" into these cases at the instance of "vociferous minority groups," Hoover argued, discouraged state action and focused criticism on the Justice Department when the prosecutions failed. Clark overruled him, insisting that the FBI investigate civil rights complaints regardless of the chances of successful prosecution. Hoover swallowed his defeat but liked it not one whit.

He liked even less a stinging attack on the FBI's performance by Thurgood Marshall. Writing to Tom Clark and Robert Carr, chief counsel to the President's Committee on Civil Rights, Marshall noted that "the FBI has established for itself an incomparable record for ferreting out persons violating our federal laws," from spies and kidnappers to "nondescript hoodlums who steal automobiles and drive them across state lines." Yet when it came to federal violations where Negroes were the victims, the Bureau had been unable to identify or bring to trial a single person. Marshall referred specifically to the Monroe and Minden cases.[30]

Hoover was livid. Marshall wanted to "embarrass" and "discredit" the FBI, he complained to Walter White. It was hardly the Bureau's fault if southern juries failed to indict or convict, or if federal civil rights statutes were too narrow. Clark publicly commended the Bureau for the thoroughness of its investigations, noting that in the Monroe case agents had interviewed 2,800 people and that in the Minden case its investigation had resulted in five indictments. "The mere naming of suspects," he told Marshall, "does not constitute a solution to the crime." Clark also echoed Hoover's complaint about lack of cooperation from the NAACP, especially from Marshall. Walter White advised Marshall to draft a "temperate and documented reply" so that they could meet Hoover in an effort to resolve the dispute. Hoover was not about to calm down, however. He agreed to meet White but refused to see Marshall, whom he accused of "gross misstatements and unfounded accusations." Marshall was unrepentant. "I . . . have no faith in Mr. Hoover or his investigators," he told White, "and there is no use in my saying so."[31]

Marshall's lack of faith extended to the prosecuting U.S. attorney. He and Malcolm Lafargue had crossed swords in 1943 during the rape trial of three black soldiers when, according to Marshall, Lafargue had betrayed "extreme prejudice against Negroes." Tom Clark turned down Marshall's request for a special federal prosecutor; as it turned out, Lafargue suppressed his white supremacist views and put in a creditable performance.[32]

Lafargue had an uphill task. The venue, Shreveport, was the least favorable in Louisiana, and the defense lawyers used their right of peremptory challenge to eliminate the sole Negro on the jury panel. When put on the witness stand, "Sonnyman" Harris failed to identify three of the five defendants as men who had beaten him on the night of August 8. One of the defendants he did recognize, Sam Maddry Sr., provided an alibi corroborated by four witnesses; the other, deputy Haynes, claimed to have released Jones and Harris at 6:30 P.M., after the younger Maddry and his wife declined to press charges. And although the government produced several witnesses who had seen or heard some sort of commotion outside the Minden jail, none would swear as to the identity of any of the whites. The only people who connected Haynes with the ruckus were black prisoners inside the jail, whose testimony the all-white jury would scarcely credit. Several black witnesses could not be persuaded to testify. Still, Hoover considered it the best civil rights case the FBI had made out: "we had clear-cut, uncontroverted evidence of conspiracy."

The defense strategy was predictable but effective. First, it sought to discredit Harris's testimony on two counts: by accusing him of having killed Jones himself and by linking him with the NAACP. It then implied that Jones had deserved his fate because he had attempted to rape Mrs. Maddry and had carried "lewd pictures and obscene poetry" in his wallet. Third, the defense tried to arouse indignation over the FBI investigation, asserting that witnesses had been intimidated by overzealous G-men. Finally, it characterized the prosecution as a case of politically motivated federal meddling that threatened the basis of white supremacy.

Judge Gaston Porterie was a model of fairness, and on several occasions he rebuked the defense lawyers for introducing irrelevant arguments and appealing to prejudice. On the second day of the trial he told them to stop insinuating that the government had brought the case for political reasons. A day later he overruled a question that invited the deputy coroner to speculate about "the character and physical makeup" of a man who carried lewd pictures in his wallet. Jones's sexual makeup was irrelevant, Porterie insisted, and any answer the coroner gave would only "arouse prejudice."

Lafargue did his best to counter the charge of outside interference. The federal government had been compelled to act because "the Webster Parish grand jury . . . didn't do a cockeyed thing. It was a whitewash." At stake was the rule of law, the right to a fair trial, "God-given rights." Complaining that Harris had been held in the Minden jail without being charged, Lafargue drew the damaging admission from a deputy sheriff that this was standard practice. Asked about the relevant Louisiana statute, the deputy admitted, "I never read it. I don't know." When defense attorney Harry V. Booth pointed out that holding people without charge had been "the custom throughout Louisiana for generation upon generation," Lafargue pounced. "That is exactly the basis of why we are here. I don't think custom can override the direct provisions of the Constitution, state or federal. It is the fundamental rights of civil liberties that we are prosecuting here." It was the U.S. Attorney's finest moment, and Judge Porterie backed him up. "No one," he agreed, "private citizen or officer, may take the law into his own hands." In the case of Jones and Harris, "due process" meant the right of Louisiana citizens to be tried in a state court.

In summing up, the four defense lawyers laid down the duty of the jurors, as southern white men, to teach the NAACP and the government a lesson. "We resent, and I will continue to resent, instruction [*sic*] of the federal government into our local affairs." The case would never have been brought "but for that negro uplift society in New York," part of a "vast movement . . . to exert influence of negro minority groups." As a result, "a veritable horde of FBI agents swept into this state like locusts of old." The prosecution impugned the integrity of Louisiana's courts and threatened to turn the federal courts into "a negro's court." Would the jury take the testimony of Harris alone "against all the white testimony in this case?" In a peroration that climaxed the defense, A. S. Drew pulled out all the stops, touching on political and sexual emotions that set white stomachs churning and white pulses racing.

> This is the most important case you jurors ever sat on. It will decide whether we people in the South can run our own business; . . . whether we are to set up a federal police court over here in Shreveport; whether we will be over here day after day to satisfy the whim of some organization up North. . . . There will be no co-mingling of white and black. They will always be treated well. No force in the world can bring us to co-mingling. I say that is being tried.

The jury acquitted all five defendants.[33]

The verdict, however, was of less significance than the prosecution itself.

Louisiana's first postwar lynching turned out to be its last. And across the South, even in Mississippi, the same trend prevailed. By the 1950s lynching had become so rare that each incident became the subject of national outrage and international opprobrium.

The eradication of lynching was, admittedly, an ambiguous triumph. Southern politicians and policemen had curbed the mobs by promising that black malefactors would be punished swiftly and severely — so swiftly and severely, it turned out, that the punishment often resembled lynching under cover of law. Where blacks were accused of capital crimes, the standards of justice in Louisiana courts were so minimal that many trials indeed merited the term "legal lynching."

Willie Francis, for example, went to the electric chair on May 9, 1947, at the age of eighteen. Charged with the killing of a white man two years earlier, his trial in St. Martinville lasted only two days; a jury of twelve white men pronounced him guilty and the judge imposed the mandatory death sentence. "It is impossible to know what actually transpired during the trial," write two students of the case. "No stenographic record was taken." Francis's two lawyers, appointed by the court just eight days before the trial, offered a defense that would be flattered by the term "perfunctory." They made no motion for a change of venue and no opening statement. They did not challenge the two written confessions, the longest only seventy-five words long, that formed the basis of the prosecution. They even failed to comment on the loss of the alleged murder weapon, a pistol, which mysteriously disappeared en route to the crime laboratory in Baton Rouge. In fact, the defense lawyers offered no evidence whatever on behalf of their client. Nor did they bother to file an appeal.

The only facet of the case that rescued it from obscurity was the execution. Or rather, the attempted execution, for when the executioner pulled the switch, a short circuit reduced the voltage. "I felt a burnin' in my head and my left leg and I jumped against the straps," Francis recalled. His lips swelled, his nose flattened against his face, and he jerked the chair about in his pain. When the frustrated executioner switched off the current, he cursed Francis and threatened to finish him off with a rock. A white observer confided that he had never witnessed such a disgraceful and inhumane exhibition: the two men in charge of the electric chair were so drunk that they hardly knew what they were doing.

A local white attorney, Bertrand DeBlanc, obtained a stay of execution from Justice Hugo L. Black, at whose urging the United States Supreme Court decided to review the case. Assisted by J. Skelly Wright (soon to be appointed to the federal bench) DeBlanc argued that a second attempt to execute Francis would be tantamount to cruel and unusual punishment. But in a five-to-four vote, the Court affirmed the sentence. Explaining his vote, Justice Felix Frankfurter argued that "this is purely a State question" and that the federal judiciary should judge state actions according to "the allowable consensus of opinion in the community" rather than their own personal conceptions of right and wrong. States should be allowed the widest possible latitude, Frankfurter believed; "Holmes used to express it by saying that he would not strike down State action unless the action of the State made him 'puke.'"

Privately, however, Francis's fate weighed so heavily on Frankfurter's conscience that he asked a friend in New Orleans, a prominent attorney, to urge the state authorities to commute Francis's sentence. "If Louisiana allows Francis to go to his death," the judge told his friend, "it will needlessly cast a cloud upon Louisiana for many years to come." Despite this extraordinary intercession, the Board of Pardons declined to exercise clemency. At the second attempt, the electric current flowed through Willie Francis unimpeded.[34]

The most vigorous challenge to "legal lynchings" came from the Civil Rights Congress, formed in 1946 from a merger of three Communist-controlled organizations. Led by William Patterson, veteran of the International Labor Defense, the CRC was constantly on the lookout for Scottsboro-type cases, and the defense of accused murderers and rapists became its specialty. Organized in 1948 by Dr. Oakley Johnson, a white professor of English at Dillard University and a veteran Communist, the Louisiana Civil Rights Congress fought for the lives of Milton Wilson, Ocie Jugger, and Paul Washington, but it lost all three to the electric chair.[35]

Milton Harold Wilson was accused of murdering a white couple, after raping the woman, in the pair's home in St. Charles Parish. At issue was an old question: had Wilson been tortured into confessing a crime of which he was innocent? He had been arrested on an unrelated charge and then interrogated over the killings between 11:30 P.M. and 5:00 A.M. "If ever a case in the annals of Louisiana jurisprudence showed undeniable evidence of police brutality and forced 'confessions'," wrote John Rousseau of the *Pittsburgh Courier*, this was the case. The first trial had to be called off because Wilson was urinating clots of blood. The case inspired such widespread anger that conservative businessmen Rivers Fredericks and Frederick Rhodes joined with union leaders Ernest Wright and Raymond Tillman in sponsoring a Milton Wilson Defense Committee. At the second trial, in January 1947, Wilson was convicted. However, the state supreme court ordered a new trial on the grounds that "there is not sufficient proof that the first confession was free and voluntary."

After the LCRC entered the case, the state supreme court upheld a second conviction. The Louisiana justices had now satisfied themselves that Wilson's confessions had indeed been voluntary. They found nothing objectionable in the fact that Wilson had been interrogated in the execution chamber. "The entire floor is painted green," the Court reasoned, "and unless one knows in advance that there is a trap door in the floor it would not be noticed." The CRC appealed the case to the U.S. Supreme Court, but with three justices dissenting, the Court let the verdict stand. Wilson was executed in July 1951.[36]

Paul Washington and Ocie Jugger were convicted of raping and robbing a white widow in her Metairie home. The pair had been implicated by a third man and then convicted on the basis of confessions. The accused did not sign the confessions for some two months. According to the Civil Rights Congress,

> The two men were dragged on a tour of police stations. . . . Their mouths were sealed with adhesive tape and they were handcuffed. Police and deputies beat them with blackjacks, choked them with garottes, slugged them with rubber hoses and chains, kicked, starved, denied them water, threatened them with shooting, gave them no sleep or medical attention — all during a period of weeks in which no one but officers were allowed near them.

Vincent North, who testified for the state, also claimed to have been beaten.[37]

After the Louisiana Supreme Court rejected the appeal, the LCRC battled on. Oakley Johnson reported that the defendants' lawyer suspected that Washington might in fact be guilty of the rape, but William Patterson brushed this aside as irrelevant. Both men, he told Johnson, were "historically innocent": three-quarters of all the blacks incarcerated in southern jails had never committed the crimes charged to them; as for the other quarter, "the responsibility lies with the State — for its destruction of their lives and its efforts to dehumanize and degrade them is the greatest crime of all."[38]

With Washington's execution scheduled for June 29 (Jugger had escaped from the Jefferson Parish jail) an LCRC delegation obtained an interview with Governor Earl Long. Long refused to see the black delegates, but he told Johnson and his wife that he would not intervene. The following day, CRC lawyers obtained a stay of execution from Justice William O. Douglas, which Sheriff Frank Clancy accepted with the utmost reluctance. He was "rather nasty," Johnson reported, "and said he wasn't going to stop no execution for no telephone call from someone he didn't know." The Clerk of the U.S. Supreme Court had to telephone the governor and the state attorney general before Clancy relented. Further appeals merely delayed the execution; in July 1952 Washington and Jugger, recaptured a year after his escape, were strapped into the electric chair. Reporting their deaths for the *Pittsburgh Courier*, John

Rouseau described an ironic "first": Negro deputies walked the deathwatch for the first time in Louisiana's history. As far as Louisiana's judicial system was concerned, however, little had changed.[39]

The killing by policemen of black prisoners and fleeing suspects illustrates the difficulty of distinguishing between "legal lynching" and normal police practice. In 1946, for example, police chief Beauregard H. Miller of Gretna shot Elliott Brooks for allegedly "resisting arrest." Local gossip held that Miller had killed seven blacks under similar circumstances. "The negroes of this section live in constant fear of great bodily harm and death at the hands of this supposed law-enforcement officer," a white resident informed Walter White. In another Gretna case, in February 1948, Roy Cyrus Brooks got into an altercation with a white bus driver. Brooks had sprung to the defense of a woman who had boarded the wrong bus and wanted her nickel back. Giving the woman his own nickel, Brooks told the driver that he would ride on the woman's fare. The driver ordered him from the bus and called a traffic cop. Patrolman Alvin Bladsacker pulled Brooks off the bus and marched him toward the Jefferson Parish courthouse. After walking about half a block, Bladsacker shot and killed him. The funeral of the forty-four-year-old victim drew two thousand people and halted traffic in Gretna for an hour. Thanks to a campaign by the Civil Rights Congress, the Jefferson Parish authorities placed the matter before a grand jury, which indicted Bladsacker for manslaughter. At the much-delayed trial, however, the jury deliberated for only seven minutes before acquitting the policeman.[40]

Complaints against police brutality reached a crescendo in the late 1940s, but the police remained a law unto themselves. In 1949 Father Joseph Fichter, a Jesuit priest, visited Superintendent Scheuring of the New Orleans Police Department to complain that a prisoner had been beaten. Scheuring examined the file and explained that according to three policemen the prisoner had fallen and hit his head on a vending machine. Recalled Fichter, "When I asked him for the rest of the testimony which might determine whether the truth was being told by the policemen or by the prisoner, he seemed amazed at such a request." Prisoners seemed to have a peculiar lack of balance: over the years the same vending machine cropped up repeatedly in accounts of prisoners "falling and hitting the head." Reports of brutality had little impact on Mayor Chep Morrison. The extraction of confessions from habitual criminals, he explained, required "a certain amount of coercion above and beyond normalcy." Coercion, however, sometimes became summary execution. In 1949 Frank Bates, a black longshoreman, was beaten to death in his New Orleans jail cell while awaiting trial for the murder of a Catholic priest. The same year a man died in the Gretna jail after being arrested and beaten by New Orleans and Jefferson Parish police.

A few whites did recognize the problem, and took desultory steps to mitigate it. Bernard Cocke, first as district attorney and then as a district court judge, tried to discourage police brutality, and during his brief tenure as U.S. attorney, Skelly Wright initiated several investigations. In 1949 two New Orleans policemen were discharged from the force after beating two black teenagers. Blacks, however, looked to the recruitment of Negro policemen as the only effective solution.[41]

Despite the continuing reality of police brutality, as well as more politically focused violence, blacks persisted in their efforts to become voters. The year 1947 saw the first attempts to register in Leander Perez's barony of Plaquemines Parish, generally regarded as one of the most repressive in Louisiana. It was a bizarre game of hide-and-seek that continued for the next six years. On November 28 Rev. Victor Ragas took a group of blacks across the Mississippi by boat to the parish courthouse at Pointe a la Hache. The intimidating presence of the sheriff, who hovered close by, caused some to abandon the attempt. The more stouthearted waited several hours, but the registrar, Frank Giordano, was nowhere to be seen. Three days later, when Ragas returned, Giordano showed up at 11:30 A.M., locked his office door, and then departed after a reclusive half hour. In neighboring St. Bernard, also under Perez control, blacks made three attempts in seven days. On the first occasion, the Clerk of Court told them it was "too late to register." A return visit found the registrar's office closed. On the third try a deputy sheriff bluntly informed them that "this is strictly a white primary" and "no colored people will be permitted to register." Ten months later thirty-six blacks, most of them fur trappers, made another attempt in St. Bernard. "Guns was flash on them," one reported, "and they were call every name that could be thought off and drove away like beast."[42]

By early 1948 black registration had edged up to twenty-two thousand, but that figure still represented only 2.4 percent of all registered voters. Thirty-one parishes had no black voters at all; many others had a mere handful. A few reported a single black voter, probably as the result of clerical errors, for these mysterious individuals never cast ballots and their identities were unknown to other blacks. Blacks accounted for more than 1 percent of the voters in only sixteen parishes, and they exceeded 2 percent in only eight.[43]

New Orleans provided some comfort. Thanks to energetic campaigns by the NAACP, the People's Defense League, the Knights of Peter Claver, the International Longshoreman's Association, and the Interdenominational Ministerial Alliance, registration in Orleans Parish had doubled. Together with the four thousand voters in neighboring Jefferson Parish, New Orleans accounted for at least half the state total. There were also significant increases in Monroe, Ruston, Jennings, Lake Charles, and the parishes of St. John the

Baptist and St. James. However, opposition to black voting remained the norm. The registrar of Iberia Parish rejected six blacks because they had no whites to "vouch" for them; the leader of the group, NAACP branch president Gus Baronne, left New Iberia after a spate of threatening phone calls. In Avoyelles Parish, "Sheriff Jeansonne was opposed to Negroes voting and therefore they did not go to the polls." Even when blacks managed to register, some election officials still barred them from the Democratic primaries. In Jonesboro and Lafayette registered voters were driven away from the polling stations; from Donaldsonville in Assumption Parish came reports of ballots being snatched from hands and of beatings.[44]

The perils and difficulties faced by black applicants remind us that it would be an error to dismiss the NAACP's "conventional" methods as overcautious and lacking in militancy. In much of Louisiana, and in much of the South, voter registration and litigation were tantamount to direct action. To act as a plaintiff in an equalization suit or to enter a parish courthouse to apply to vote meant directly confronting white authority and challenging the status quo. Such actions required a good deal of fortitude and could be extremely dangerous. They could also be effective. Judging by Louisiana, African-Americans in the South did not retreat pell-mell from their wartime militancy and become apathetic and quiescent. They continued to struggle, persistently and courageously.

St. Landry Parish makes an excellent case study of postwar black activism, a measure of both its bravery and its effectiveness. St. Landry represented white repression at its most brutal, yet by 1952 the unthinkable had become a reality: blacks were voting, and in large numbers, too. The parish exemplified the astonishing suddenness with which the climate of race relations changed in parts of Louisiana. It also reminds us that the repressive climate that SNCC workers faced in Mississippi in the 1960s confronted the NAACP throughout much of the South in the 1940s.

In contrast to the swamps and bayous further south, the countryside of St. Landry Parish is mostly open prairie, and the parish seat, Opelousas — the self-proclaimed sweet potato capital of America — looks more like a Texan town than a French colonial settlement. Culturally, however, St. Landry lies in the heart of Acadiana, the "Cajun" country of south Louisiana. The people are mostly Catholics. About half of them speak French, and a far greater proportion did so in the 1940s. Then, moreover, many spoke only French, and that was particularly true of blacks. With 78,000 souls, 44 percent of them African-Americans, St. Landry was a far cry from Protestant north Louisiana.

In the late 1940s, however, St. Landry seemed just as committed to white supremacy as the rest of the state, perhaps more so. In 1944, 1946, and 1948, blacks in most parishes made concerted attempts to register to vote. Not so in

St. Landry. When an NAACP official visited Opelousas in May 1946, a Catholic priest advised him that whites were "immovable" in their opposition to Negro voting, adding that "we would not want our boys to mix in politics." Joseph H. Jones, researching a master's thesis in sociology, found that the mulattoes of Frilot Cove "never try to vote because they would rather avoid the trouble which is sure to arise." When three blacks from Eunice, one of them a minister, tried to register on June 21, 1949, whites chased them away.[45]

The climate of fear was so pervasive that in 1949, when A. P. Tureaud drew up a suit against the St. Landry Parish school board, he could not persuade any of the plaintiffs to petition the board as a preliminary step. They were too afraid. The only way he managed to get up a petition was to have it signed by representatives of various Negro organizations. Tureaud regarded this procedure as legally unsound, but he reluctantly agreed to it "out of regard for the fears of the people in St. Landry."[46]

Those fears proved well founded: the parish authorities immediately exerted pressure on the plaintiffs. Louis Thierry, a bar owner, was arrested for violating the Sunday closing law and permitting gambling. After being beaten up by his Negro cellmates, he received a visit from the district attorney, J. Y. Fontenot, and his father, L. Austin Fontenot Sr., a political bigwig who had been an early ally of Huey Long. They asked Thierry to sign a document withdrawing from the equalization suit, warning that "any harm which may come to him will be due to his own folly." After he signed the proffered document, he was released straightaway.

Relating Thierry's plight to Thurgood Marshall, Tureaud reported that two other plaintiffs had been induced to withdraw. Three weeks later, when he met Assistant Attorney General Alex Campbell, Tureaud predicted that without immediate action from the Justice Department, "there would be few plaintiffs left in the case." A few days later, another plaintiff withdrew. By May 1950, Tureaud's pleas betrayed a note of desperation. Warning that if intimidation succeeded in St. Landry Parish it would set the pattern for the rest of the state, he urged a friend in Washington to lobby his Justice Department contacts "to bring down all the pressure possible on these Parish officials because they are not inclined to yield to persuasion."[47]

An extraordinary rape case involving a young black man by the name of Edward Honeycutt vividly illustrated the violent, repressive character of white control in St. Landry Parish. The Honeycutt case was a complex affair that produced internal conflicts within the NAACP as well as a clash between the NAACP and the left-wing Civil Rights Congress. Its most significant aspects, however, were an attempted lynching, a bold intervention by the NAACP, a dramatic second trial, and an effort to capitalize on the impact of the case by organizing a push for black voter registration. The results were explosive.

Edward Honeycutt was arrested near the town of Eunice on the afternoon of December 1, 1948, and charged with the aggravated rape of a white housewife. He had arrived in Eunice with his father after driving from their home in Farmerville, about 175 miles north, to deliver a truckload of lumber. Completing their task early that morning, they bought some beer and whiskey and proceeded to get drunk. Honeycutt then decided to take a bus to Lake Charles, but the clerk at the bus station, seeing his inebriated state, refused to sell him a ticket. When a commotion ensued, the clerk summoned the police, who conveyed Honeycutt to the town limits and told him not to return. Several hours later, still on the roadside, he was arrested.

According to his own account, the police took Honeycutt to the parish jail in Opelousas, where a deputy sheriff beat a false confession from him in front of two state troopers, two other deputies, and the sheriff of Evangeline Parish. The following morning, in the sheriff's office, he affixed his mark to a written confession, fearing another beating and possibly death if he refused.

On the night of March 6, 1949, three white men abducted Honeycutt from the jail, on the top floor of the three-story courthouse, and drove him to the banks of the Atchafalaya River. As his captors flipped a coin to pick the executioner, he managed to free his hands from the leather belt binding them. Jumping into the river, Honeycutt swam for his life, trying to stay underwater as the whites played a flashlight on the surface and fired into the bayou. Gaining the opposite bank, he evaded his captors but was too afraid and disoriented to make good his escape. The next morning, a fisherman found him hiding in a tree overhanging the river. The man rowed him back to his home and called the sheriff, who returned Honeycutt to jail. The would-be lynchers were identified in the newspapers as Edward Miller, a construction worker, Ariel Ledoux, a federal employee, and Maxie Savoy, a former deputy sheriff.

At his trial six weeks later, Honeycutt had no witnesses in his defense: his father was not allowed to testify and left Opelousas afraid to enter the courthouse. It was only at the end of the first day, after the jury had been sent out, that Honeycutt related how deputy sheriff Arthur Richard had whipped him and threatened to turn him over to a Eunice mob unless he signed a confession. Richard was waiting back at his cell with a gun and warned him to keep quiet about the beatings. In spite of this threat, Honeycutt repudiated his confession the next day and described the beating. "I was afraid to tell the truth," he explained. "I was scared to say." But the all-white jury found him guilty, and he was sentenced to death. His defense lawyers, who included L. Austin Fontenot Jr., brother of the prosecuting district attorney, filed an appeal. They argued that the confession had been made "under threats, force and duress," and that the trial judge had erred in restricting their questioning of prospective jurors, one of whom had already expressed an opinion on the case. Honeycutt, they noted, "was scared to death even on the witness stand in open court."

A group of white spectators formed the same opinion. The Reverend J. O. Dumas, a white Methodist minister, knew the Honeycutt family well — he and young Edward had grown up together — and journeyed from Farmerville to attend the trial. Four other whites, including the planter on whose land the Honeycutts lived, accompanied him, for the Honeycutt family was well regarded in Union Parish. They were appalled by the lynch-mob atmosphere and regarded the trial as a travesty of justice. Dumas also had some knowledge of the oppressive conditions of Honeycutt's incarceration: during visits to the jail he had been cursed and sometimes turned away. On December 13, Dumas drove to Natchitoches, the home of Dr. E. A. Johnson, the newly elected president of the NAACP State Conference of Branches. He implored Johnson to have the NAACP enter the case. As it was too close to the forthcoming appeal to take any action, Johnson asked attorney Louis Berry to observe the hearing. On January 9, 1950, the Louisiana Supreme Court ordered a new trial on the grounds that the prosecution had failed to rebut Honeycutt's allegation that he had been threatened and beaten. The following day, Johnson engaged Louis Berry and Edward Jackson to take over Honeycutt's defense.[48]

When an NAACP group tried to visit Honeycutt in early March, a surly deputy sheriff refused to let them see the prisoner. "I have never in my life experienced a more hostile situation," reported U. Simpson Tate, legal advisor to the NAACP's southwestern regional office. When Tate eventually interviewed Honeycutt, on April 13, he found him pleasant, friendly, articulate, and of "above average intelligence." As to his guilt or innocence, however, Tate was unsure. Asked point-blank if he had raped Mrs. Byrd, he repeatedly denied the crime. "But he could not look me in the eyes and say so. I asked him several times and watched him closely and his eyes were evasive."[49]

To Louis Berry, however, the question of Honeycutt's innocence was secondary. Here was an opportunity to press, in dramatic fashion, the constitutional issue of a Negro's right to a fair trial, specifically, the right to be tried by a jury upon which blacks had an equal opportunity to serve.[50]

Despite the U.S. Supreme Court's rulings in *Norris* v. *Alabama* (1935) and *Pierre* v. *Louisiana* (1939), black jurors were still a rarity in Louisiana. In two recent cases, both also involving black defendants accused of rape, Berry had argued that blacks had been arbitrarily and systematically excluded from jury service. In *State* v. *Perkins* (1947), the Louisiana Supreme Court dismissed the claim, pointing out that as the jury lists were compiled from the voter registration rolls, and as there were only 540 blacks registered to vote in East Baton Rouge Parish compared to 34,000 whites, it was only to be expected that the jury lists included only two blacks. In a revealing statement that bore no relation to reality, the court explained that this method of selecting juries could not discriminate against blacks because "Literate negroes are given the same right as white men to register as voters." It was a "laudable preference," moreover, to favor "those persons desirous of having a voice in government and willing to assume the responsibilities of citizenship." In 1948, however, Judge C. Iris Dupont sustained Berry's motion to quash the indictment of Edward Spriggs Jr. on the grounds that qualified blacks had never been called for duty in Iberville Parish. Spriggs was reindicted by a grand jury containing three blacks.[51]

When Louis Berry, Edward Jackson, and Vanue LaCour represented Edward Honeycutt at his second trial, they were the first black lawyers to appear in a criminal trial in St. Landry Parish. Given the history of the case and their experiences at the parish jail, they approached their task with trepidation. Fearful that there might be an attempt to lynch the lawyers en route, a delegation of blacks prevailed upon Governor Earl Long to provide police protection. State troopers in two cars escorted the lawyers as they drove from Baton Rouge to Opelousas; more troopers guarded each intersection along the road.[52]

Berry and his partners did not expect to win an acquittal, but they paved the way for an appeal by having the trial record show that the method of jury selection was loaded against blacks. The court and prosecution obviously anticipated this attack, because the grand jury panel that reindicted Honeycutt contained the names of four blacks, two of whom were drawn to serve. Moreover, although the trial jury was again all white, the panel from which it was chosen included eight blacks (two were disqualified, one excused, and the remainder excluded by the peremptory challenges of the prosecution). It was the first time that blacks had served on a grand jury and also the first time that black jurors presented themselves for trial duty.

In spite of their uphill task, the defense trained a revealing light on the method of jury selection. One jury commissioner admitted that he had not submitted the names of blacks: "I could not find none that was qualified." Another argued that while 95 percent of whites were fit for jury duty, only 10 percent of blacks, at most, were qualified. A third commissioner put the figure as low as 3 percent. Even so, they claimed, blacks were occasionally included on the general venire from which jury panels were chosen. Scrutinizing the jury list, the Clerk of Court recognized the name of "one of the best niggers in Opelousas." When LaCour objected to the word "nigger," the trial judge overruled him. "I don't think it is meant to be derogatory in any way. On the contrary, he was referring to the laudable characteristics of the person." In their appeal to the state supreme court — Honeycutt was again convicted —

the defense argued that the number of blacks selected for jury duty was negligible and that these few were handpicked from the personal acquaintances of the commissioners. The prosecution contended that most blacks were either illiterate or spoke only French.[53]

Unfortunately for Edward Honeycutt, his lawyers made procedural errors in framing the appeal, enabling the Louisiana Supreme Court to dismiss their motion for a new trial. The court also rejected their petition for a rehearing. On June 2, 1951, the Civil Rights Congress made a last-ditch attempt to save Honeycutt's life after the NAACP declined to appeal the case to the U.S. Supreme Court. It proved unavailing: on June 8 Honeycutt died in the electric chair, with his champion, Rev. J. O. Dumas, looking on.[54]

The case had a significance far beyond the fate of Edward Honeycutt or the issue of jury selection. In St. Landry Parish the Honeycutt case had become a black cause célèbre, and the arrival of black lawyers was an event of major importance. When the defense team arrived in Opelousas, the atmosphere turned out to be very different from the one it had anticipated. "To the astonishment of all observers," reported the *Louisiana Weekly,* "some 1,000 Negro spectators flocked to the court house, jamming the Negro balcony and overflowing into the corridors and upon the grounds, mingling freely with about an equal number of whites." Nearly thirty years later, Marion O. White, the president of the St. Landry branch of the NAACP in the 1960s, recalled attending the trial with his father and feeling thrilled to see black lawyers gamely quizzing pillars of the white community. For local blacks, the second trial was a psychological boost of major proportions.[55]

On Sunday, June 4, 1950, a few days after the second Honeycutt trial ended, a speaker from the Louisiana Progressive Voters League, Alvin H. Jones, addressed a civil rights rally in Lebeau, a small town seventeen miles from Opelousas. His message was simple, blacks must vote, and it had the blessing of Father B. R. Callaghan, pastor of Immaculate Conception Church, after whose founder, Pierre LeBeau, the community took its name. The following morning Jones took five blacks from Lebeau to the registrar of voters' office in the parish courthouse.[56]

When the group entered the registrar's office, some white men assaulted them. Two of the blacks immediately fled, but while fending off a pursuing white they were grabbed by a deputy sheriff. One broke away and escaped; the other, a sixty-seven-year-old, one-armed man, was thrown in jail. Meanwhile, inside the office, the rest of the group were being beaten. Jones recalled, "I was slugged with the butt of a gun and was pounded with a pair of brass knuckles. They left a hole in my head. I didn't stagger and they didn't knock me down. Neither did I run. Shortly afterwards I left the building. There were several other persons in the office at the time, several of which were white women. I heard one of them say to the officer, 'You shouldn't have done that — it's criminal.'" The following morning Frank and George Guillory, young black men, visited Opelousas to register for the draft. They asked a local lawyer, Edward Pavy, for directions. French speakers with an uncertain grasp of English, they wound up at the voter registration office by mistake. They were beaten and thrown in jail.[57]

The Justice Department knew all about the repressive character of St. Landry Parish, having been briefed by Tureaud in August 1949. They also received periodic proddings from Gustave Auzenne, a native of Frilot Cove then teaching at Howard University. The latest beatings made the argument for federal action unanswerable; as Auzenne wrote Tureaud, "We could not get a better case." Assistant Attorney General James M. McInerney ordered the FBI to make a full investigation.[58]

The G-men drew a blank. It soon became obvious to the FBI that the beatings had indeed occurred, that they were planned in advance, and that many whites must have knowledge of them. It was obvious, too, that many of the whites they spoke to were lying. After interviewing dozens of potential witnesses, however, including forty-four of the whites who registered to vote on the two days in question, they could not prove the identity of the attackers. The statement of George Blanchard, the registrar of voters, was typical. "He remembers that a commotion of some kind started in his office," the agents reported, "but stated he was busy registering voters at the time and did not notice any of the details of the commotion."[59]

In November 1951, Alvin Jones died at the age of fifty-one; like Leo Hardy, his death was hastened by the physical and psychological damage inflicted by a severe beating. Born in Napoleonville in Assumption Parish, he had degrees from Columbia University and the University of Pennsylvania. During a varied career he had been a high school principal in Houma, taught at Southern and Xavier Universities, and served as executive director of the New Orleans Urban League. White officials of the league had found him too militant for their liking. "He seems to have a constant chip on his shoulder," reported one. "He is admittedly angered by having to sit behind the screen in a bus, or by any insincere comment." Two months after his death the Department of Justice concluded that the case warranted no further action and advised the FBI to return Jones's bloodstained clothes.[60]

Some blacks in St. Landry Parish refused to be cowed, and they organized a parish branch of the NAACP. In October 1951, fifteen blacks visited the registrar's office. Finding it locked, Richard B. Millspaugh, a young black attorney who had recently set up practice in Opelousas, walked across the street to the office of the *Daily World* and inserted a notice reminding the registrar of his legal duty to keep regular office hours. Shortly afterwards Vanue LaCour filed a suit against the registrar on behalf of three plaintiffs. Days later, one of them, Lester L. Mitchell, a thirty-three-year-old insurance agent and war veteran, was shot dead by a deputy sheriff outside a tavern. The police described Mitchell as "rowdy and out of control." The two other plaintiffs fled St. Landry Parish for the comparative safety of Baton Rouge.[61]

Although the registration suit never came to trial, it was not abandoned under duress. Eleven months after Mitchell's slaying, Millspaugh received a phone call from "old man Fontenot" — L. Austin Fontenot Sr., the district attorney's father — informing him that blacks would be permitted to register. Millspaugh and three others became the first blacks to register in St. Landry Parish. Registrar Blanchard postdated their poll certificates to prevent them voting in the November 4 primaries. Within weeks, however, blacks were registering in droves. By 1956 the number of black voters exceeded thirteen thousand, more than 80 percent of the black voting age population and about 40 percent of the total electorate. These levels were among the highest, if not the highest, in Louisiana. White opposition to black voting had collapsed.[62]

Why this remarkable volte-face? On one level, the answer was simple: faced with a suit that they were bound to lose, embarrassed by negative publicity and an intrusive FBI probe, a few key white leaders, including Judge Lessley P. Gardner and L. Austin Fontenot Sr., decided to permit some blacks to vote. They were also, without doubt, reacting to a feeling of disgust shared by many St. Landry whites over the recent beatings and a sincere conviction that denying blacks the vote could no longer be justified.

The decision to encourage the *mass* registration of black voters, however, was taken by Sheriff D. J. "Cat" Doucet in 1952, and to be understood it must be placed in the context of the factionalism that characterized state and local politics. To Doucet, a veteran Long ally who had served as sheriff from 1936 to 1940 but had been out of office ever since, registering blacks offered a means of trouncing the opposition and assuring his own political future. Doucet had another reason to cultivate black votes. Under Earl Long's permissive regime, gambling and prostitution were rife in south Louisiana. Doucet ran a "wide-open" parish and took his cut from the vice interests; by creating a loyal black vote, he could fend off the "good government" elements who wanted to suppress these lucrative activities. Elected sheriff again in 1952, Doucet became a champion of black voting and its stout defender against all segregationist attacks. He remained sheriff until 1968, enjoying overwhelming black support until the end.[63]

What happened in St. Landry Parish illustrated, in rather dramatic fashion, what also happened to a greater or lesser extent in much of Louisiana. In parish after parish, registrars enrolled a handful of black voters and then very soon allowed mass registration. In some parishes, black registration soon exceeded 50, 60, and even 70 percent. By 1952, it had climbed to 107,000, and over the next four years the total increased by almost half as much again.

Part of this increase, without doubt, could be attributed to Earl Long. In 1948 Long received the endorsement of the Louisiana Progressive Voters League, an organization that was very much the NAACP in different clothes, and in return he gave a tacit commitment to foster black voter registration. Many blacks took it for granted that Long could work wonders when it came to influencing local registrars. When blacks were continually rejected in West Baton Rouge Parish, a colleague advised Tureaud to "get in touch with the Long Machine," since this was the "quickest way" to get blacks registered. The sharp rises in black registration in places like Monroe, Natchitoches, Alexandria, and Opelousas, plus the registration of at least some blacks in all but eleven parishes, indicated that this faith in Long was not entirely misplaced. As the *Louisiana Weekly* commented in 1952, "The average Negro citizen . . . feels that the Long administration is responsible, in some measure, for the fact that there are 95,000 or more registered Negroes on the rolls."[64]

In fact, the correlation between high black registration and Longism was imprecise. A much stronger correlation existed between high black registration and south Louisiana Catholicism. In November 1951 Bishop Jules Jeanmard of the Lafayette diocese issued a pastoral letter roundly condemning "the official who has recourse to subterfuge in order to rob a citizen, otherwise qualified, of his right to register and vote, because of the color of his skin." His intervention both encouraged blacks to apply and discouraged whites from continuing to reject them. Analyzing the registration statistics for 1956, John H. Fenton and Kenneth N. Vines found that in the twenty-five "French" parishes, where about 83 percent of the people were Catholics, the level of black registration was more than double the level in the overwhelmingly Protestant "Anglo-Saxon" parishes — 51 percent as opposed to 23 percent.[65]

If the Catholic Church encouraged them in their quest for the ballot, blacks also knew that the federal government was increasingly sympathetic to their cause. True, the white South still wielded formidable clout within the Democratic party: Louisiana's congressional delegation, voting as one, helped to defeat Truman's civil rights program. Yet the fact that a Democratic president proposed such measures in the first place — a permanent FEPC, abolition of the poll tax, a ban on segregation in interstate travel, and a stronger Justice Department with extensive powers to probe civil rights violations — was immensely heartening to black southerners. It showed that the southern wing of the party could no longer keep civil rights off the national party platform. Truman's 1948 election victory, won despite the defection of Louisiana, Mississippi, Alabama, and South Carolina, confirmed the South's declining influence within the Democratic party. Moreover, the Dixiecrat revolt enabled Truman to appoint federal judges from the loyal, more liberal wing of the party. In J. Skelly Wright and Herbert Christenberry, both of them nominated by the Longite faction, Louisiana gained two federal district judges who were sympathetic to the expanding national commitment to racial equality.

Judicial intervention was crucially important in advancing black voting rights. In a 1947 decision that had regional significance, Judge J. Waties Waring invalidated an attempt by the Democratic party in South Carolina to exclude blacks from the primaries, rejecting the party's claim that the repeal of state primary laws had the effect of exempting it from the *Smith* v. *Allwright* decision. When the Fourth Circuit Court of Appeals upheld Waring's judgment, further efforts to maintain the "white primary" became increasingly futile. As late as 1950, the registrar of Terrebonne Parish refused to permit blacks to register as Democrats. In 1951, however, Louisiana's Democratic State Central Committee bowed to the inevitable by expunging all references to race from its rules. An unconscionable time a-dying, the white primary had finally expired.[66]

Washington Parish, where it took William Bailey four years to become a voter, clearly illustrated the interplay between NAACP activism and judicial intervention. On his first attempt to register, in July 1946, the registrar had told Bailey to go away and learn the Constitution. One of his four companions quipped that they only wanted "to help you white folks out," whereupon the registrar shot back, "Well, we've don't need you niggers to help us. We've been getting along fine this long without you. We don't need you now." Letters to state and parish officials brought no satisfaction, the appointment of a new registrar made no difference, so blacks in Bogalusa formed a local branch of the NAACP and had attorney Louis Berry file a suit against the registrar, in the name of ten plaintiffs, in the federal district court in New Orleans. On July 19, 1950, Judge J. Skelly Wright permanently enjoined registrar Curtis Thomas from rejecting eligible blacks. Nine days later, Bailey became the first black voter in Washington Parish. About fifty others registered that same day.[67]

The first injunction of its kind in Louisiana, Wright's decision set an important precedent. Two years later, in 1952, Judge Gaston Porterie ordered Bossier Parish registrar Mary K. Brice to stop turning away black applicants on the grounds that she needed two white voters to "identify" each one. True, state law allowed the registrar to require such identification, but only if there were reasonable grounds for suspicion. In Bossier Parish, the law had been used as a "subterfuge for systematically excluding Negroes from the registration rolls," since the registrar had "failed to be able to establish the identity of a single colored person" during her thirty-one years of service. Porterie forbade Brice to discriminate on account of race or color.[68]

Blacks also filed suits in the parishes of St. Landry, Pointe Coupee, and Tangipahoa, but the registrars there began to enroll blacks rather than go to court. In some parishes the mere threat of litigation had the effect of getting blacks registered. FBI investigations also helped bring about black registration in St. Landry, St. Helena, and Franklin parishes.[69]

In the final analysis, the barriers to registration would not have been breached without the persistent efforts of blacks themselves. The historian is struck by the dogged determination of ordinary black men and women, who were prepared to suffer repeated humiliations, verbal threats, beatings, and even death in order to secure their democratic rights.

The NAACP played a vital role. When William Bailey and his companions were repeatedly rejected, they took their complaint to the Bogalusa city attorney, Jim W. Richardson. This young white lawyer, sympathetic to their plight, advised them to "get yourselves a national organization." It was sound advice. Blacks and whites both understood the power of the law: they knew that the registration battle was half won (or lost) as soon as blacks resorted to litigation. Richardson did not mention the NAACP by name, but the black delegation knew the "organization" he was referring to. The NAACP meant lawyers, *black* lawyers, and these were years when black lawyers were slayers of dragons, Davids who killed Goliaths. By 1950 there were more of them, too; that year saw the first two law students graduate from Southern University, doubling the number of black lawyers in Louisiana. As whites developed sophisticated legal strategies to evade court rulings, this almost mystical faith in lawyers and litigation declined. But for the moment this was a season of hope, a time, as the *Louisiana Weekly* put it, "of renewed faith in the promises of democracy and the great potentials of Louisiana."[70]

Chapter 6

RACE AND RED-BAITING

To be courted by white politicians was a novel and heady experience for black Louisianians. In 1946, to the pleasant surprise of all present, "both factions" showed up to canvass support during a dance being held in a Catholic church hall in St. Charles Parish. During the gubernatorial election the following year, A. P. Tureaud confided to a colleague: "I have . . . been approached for the various candidates who want my support." He confessed that he had a foot in the camp of each faction. A year later Donald Jones, the former New Orleans newspaperman who headed the NAACP's southwestern regional office, visited newly elected senators Lyndon Johnson and Russell Long in Washington. They were "honest and sincere," Jones reported. "Both voluntarily admitted that Negroes had voted overwhelmingly for them, and that therefore they recognized a peculiar obligation to Negroes." Jones was impressed by the fact that each senator gave at least an hour of his time.[1]

Exhilarating, too, was the discovery that black votes, although still relatively few, could make and break politicians. When Otto Passman defeated the incumbent congressman by 451 votes in 1946, black voters in the Monroe area congratulated themselves on having elected a "semi-liberal." They also helped to install John E. Coon as mayor of Monroe and keep him in office until 1956. In Alexandria the local black voters league, headed by Louis Berry, helped George Bowden to unseat Mayor Carl B. Close. In 1954 blacks in Opelousas celebrated the defeat of Mayor T. W. Huntington, during whose thirteen-year tenure "many atrocities, including murders, befell Negroes . . . who sought registration and other citizenship rights."[2]

Blacks still had a painful education ahead of them. Political neophytes, their training in politics had been limited to the Masonic lodge and the NAACP branch. True, it was sometimes said that if you could play politics in the NAACP, you could play politics anywhere — an observation that certainly applied to Ernest Morial, the first black mayor of New Orleans. Nothing, however, could adequately prepare blacks for the complex, cynical, and corrupt world of Louisiana politics, a world of shifting alliances and backdoor deals, in which duplicity was an art form and where nothing was ever quite what it seemed. White politicians moved adroitly to cultivate black leaders and became masters at persuading them that paltry crumbs represented honorable half-loaves. For blacks, the line between political realism and political naivete was exceedingly fine.[3]

Blacks very quickly found themselves enmeshed in a factional politics still monopolized by white politicians. Moreover, by strictly controlling the extent of black participation, whites both manipulated the black vote and preserved racial segregation. As black sociologist Daniel C. Thompson put it, "Negro political leaders have not been able to marshall enough Negro votes to present a serious challenge to the *status quo,* but they have been able to register just enough Negroes to ensure the political security of certain white supremacists."[4]

Had white radicals and liberals succeeded in recasting southern politics, black voters might well have chosen more constructive political alternatives. For two or three years after the war, it seemed that an overt challenge to white supremacy might actually take shape. Building on the political ferment encouraged by the New Deal and intensified by the war, groups like the Southern Conference for Human Welfare, the Catholic Committee of the South, and the Civil Rights Congress, as well as the unions of the CIO, pressed explicitly antiracist policies. Together, these progressive forces might have formed the basis, the "tangible nucleus," for a realignment within the Democratic party, fostering political opposition to segregation. Indeed, the very existence of such groups posed a challenge to white supremacy: the SCHW, for example, held nonsegregated meetings in New Orleans, as also, in a quiet way, did the CCS. Had these groups merely survived into the 1950s, they might have served, at the very least, as a rallying point for integrationist sentiment in the wake of the *Brown* decision.[5]

It was not to be. By 1947 the Cold War had thrust communism to the center of domestic politics, rudely displacing the liberal reform agenda of the New Deal. Encouraged by the Truman administration, anticommunism invaded civil liberties and mortally wounded Communist, radical, and even liberal organizations. Worse, by fostering a conservative political climate that stigmatized criticism of the established social order as "un-American," the Cold War enabled southern segregationists to link integration with subversion.

Red-baiting was not, of course, a new tactic for southern racists — the SCHW, for example, had been attacked as a Communist front ever since its inception in 1938 — but such attacks tended to emanate from archreactionaries and were widely dismissed as part of a right-wing attack on the New Deal. After 1945, however, the Truman administration gave new respectability to red-baiting through its federal loyalty program, its listing of subversive organizations, and its prosecution of the Communist Party leadership. Red-baiting came to be seen as a necessary political weapon to which no patriotic American could safely object.

There were anti-Communist liberals, to be sure, who deplored irresponsible and demagogic red-baiting of the kind popularized by Senator Joseph McCarthy. But the line between "responsible" anticommunism and "irresponsible" red-baiting was impossible to draw. In practice, few anti-Communist liberals were prepared to defend the targets of racist red-baiters; many liberals joined in these attacks. Thus southern racists, with the acquiescence of many liberals, harassed and silenced critics of white supremacy in the name of national security.

The demise of the Southern Conference for Human Welfare typified this fatal convergence of liberal anticommunism and reactionary red-baiting. Founded in 1938, the SCHW had lived a tenuous existence in Louisiana until November 1945, when Clark Foreman, the organization's chairman, assembled a group of twenty-five sympathizers in New Orleans. Foreman secured promises of support from, among others, A. P. Tureaud of the NAACP, Alvin Jones of the Urban League, Harold N. Lee of the Louisiana League for the Preservation of Constitutional Rights, and Hasket Derby, executive secretary of the Federation of Classroom Teachers. In April 1946, about a hundred people met in Alexandria to plan a statewide organization, and a follow-up meeting in Baton Rouge elected John W. Melton, a white Presbyterian minister, chairman of the SCHW's committee for Louisiana.

On paper, the Southern Conference brought together an impressive if motley array of social activists. They included veterans of the defunct socialist colony of New Llano, in Vernon Parish; the state heads of both the AFL and the CIO; white liberals of various hues; and a cross section of Louisiana's black leadership. In the same year, the Southern Conference moved its regional headquarters from Nashville to New Orleans. By 1947 the SCHW boasted nearly six hundred members in Louisiana.[6]

The SCHW's efforts to organize statewide, however, proved short-lived. Melton almost immediately resigned, a result, some suspected, of gentle persuasion by officials of the Southern Regional Council. Organized in 1944 as the successor to the Commission on Interracial Cooperation, the SRC was trying to set up interracial committees in each southern state, activity that brought it into direct competition with the SCHW. Tension between the two groups, despite an outwardly cordial relationship, also resulted from their differing political persuasions. While blacks tended to regard the SRC as insufficiently militant, especially in its refusal to oppose segregation, some white liberals saw it as a safer, less contentious alternative to the overtly political and even radical SCHW.[7]

Competition from the Southern Regional Council was a minor irritant compared with the barrage of accusations and innuendo that identified the SCHW with communism. The SCHW in Louisiana craved respectability. It counted on the backing of white liberals and mainstream black leaders; it hoped to receive support from such prestigious community pillars as Archbishop Rummel, philanthropist Edgar Stern, and Samuel Zemurray, president of the United Fruit Company. It invited the newly elected mayor of New Orleans, Chep Morrison, to greet the opening session of the fourth SCHW convention at the Municipal Auditorium. Its first postwar meeting aimed to establish the Southern Conference as a broad-based alliance of progressive forces that would become the legitimate opposition to the South's conservatives and white supremacists. "Things are percolating and the spirit is good," reported Georgia Mitchell, the SCHW's Louisiana coordinator.

But Mitchell and the leaders of the Southern Conference badly underestimated the extent to which its political ecumenicity, which allowed for the participation of Communists, had already damaged its reputation. They also misjudged the explosive nature of the segregation issue, which made it politically suicidal for any southern politician to identify with an avowedly integrationist group. Dave McGuire, Morrison's chief advisor, warned the mayor that the SCHW was widely regarded as pro-Communist and that they would make an issue of holding an unsegregated convention. "I suggest that City Hall and the Auditorium be extremely careful in any relations with this organization," he cautioned. Morrison decided not to greet the meeting after all, and the Municipal Auditorium adopted a formal policy of segregation that, in effect, excluded the SCHW. As a result, Georgia Mitchell complained, the SCHW found itself in a "completely embarrassing and demoralizing situation."[8]

Less overt, but equally damaging, was the suspicion and hostility of the Catholic Church. Liberal Catholics attended the SCHW's early meetings with the primary aim of preventing "communistic inroads." Reporting to Archbishop Rummel on the organization's 1942 convention, Father John F. Cronin dismissed charges of Communist domination and praised the bulk of SCHW supporters as "practical men and women." Nevertheless, the Catholic Committee of the South became increasingly loath to cooperate with the SCHW, arguing that the best way of combatting communism was to construct an explicitly Christian alternative. "Unless there is a Christian leadership, the radicals are going to take over," warned Paul D. Winter, the CCS's founder. Winter believed that Communists had tried to manipulate, with some success, earlier SCHW conventions.

By 1943 the CCS unit in New Orleans was sternly lecturing the black community on the dangers of communism. Fathers Jerome A. Drolet and Vincent O'Connell pointed accusing fingers at the ILWU and the Transport Workers Union. In November 1945 Father Cronin presented a report on communism to the Catholic bishops; based on material leaked by the FBI via the House Un-American Activities Committee (HUAC), it presented an alarming picture. CCS suspicion of the Southern Conference hardened, especially after Raymond Tillman and Ernest Scott, leaders of the Transport Workers Union in New Orleans and suspected Communists, became active in the organization. The possibility of formal cooperation ended.[9]

In June 1947, a HUAC report condemned the SCHW as a Communist front. Although it attracted widespread criticism, even ridicule, the report wounded its target. Despite the absence of credible evidence that Communists controlled the Southern Conference, the presence of a handful of concealed Communists became the organization's Achilles heel. The principled refusal of the SCHW to purge its ranks sapped support; it had already alienated tentative backers like Tureaud and Stern. Coming three months after President Truman's address to Congress in which he pledged America to the containment of communism, the HUAC report encouraged more people to quit the SCHW. "Tolerance of Communism is hamstringing the Conference," complained Bill Monroe Jr., an up-and-coming journalist. "We can't believe that issues of civil liberties, or unity, are real objections to the Conference taking *some* anti-Communist stand. Unless, of course, a large segment of Conference members *are* fellow-travellers." Besides Monroe, Isaac Heller, a lawyer and former member of the Orleans Parish school board, also resigned. So did Professor William Kolb of Tulane University, who established a local chapter of Americans for Democratic Action, a new organization of anti-Communist liberals that sought to undermine the SCHW.[10]

The issue of communism also prevented the SCHW from making common cause with "respectable" organizations such as the League of Women Voters. When Emily Blanchard, who was active in both organizations, proposed a joint program to encourage voter registration, she met with adamant opposition from Martha Robinson, head of the league, who made sure that the league's board of directors spurned the SCHW's overtures. The SCHW "bears all the marks of a Communist front group," Robinson explained. "Unfortunately, fine liberals like Mrs. Blanchard . . . often let their hearts govern their common sense." Blanchard wept inwardly at Robinson's "unjust cruel" attack. SCHW members were not "evangelists or martyrs," she told her friend, but good citizens who "did what they thought valuable in the day by day fight against the many headed dragons of ignorance and intolerance." In 1948 the board of the league refused to let Blanchard appear before it to defend the SCHW.[11]

The Southern Conference invited further attacks by aligning with the third-party presidential campaign of Henry Wallace, the former commerce secretary whom President Truman had fired for opposing his Cold War policies. While the SCHW did not formally endorse Wallace, enough prominent members campaigned for him to make a formal endorsement irrelevant. By involving itself in Wallace's Progressive Party, however, the SCHW committed suicide. The Wallace campaign split the membership, enhanced the influence of concealed Communists, and isolated the organization from the black mainstream. By the time of the election, whatever doubts blacks had harbored about Truman had been assuaged by the president's robust stand for civil rights and the ensuing defection of the Dixiecrats. Virtually every black leader in the state endorsed Truman. Wallace polled just 3,035 votes in Louisiana, less than 1 percent of the total. The SCHW went down with the Wallace ship, formally disbanding shortly after the election. It was survived by its tax-exempt auxiliary, the Southern Conference Educational Fund (SCEF), directed by Dr. James A. Dombrowski from New Orleans.[12]

The Progressive Party lingered on for about a year after Wallace's defeat. Its youth wing, Young Progressives of America (YPA), had a core of supporters in Tulane, Dillard, and Xavier Universities and became for a brief period the principal exemplar of interracialism in New Orleans. For this reason, it attracted police harassment that ranged from the absurd to the brutal. In February 1949, for example, police raided a party at the French Quarter apartment of Tulane student Arlene Stitch and arrested sixty-five people for disturbing the peace. In the municipal court, Lieutenant Thomas Fogerty admitted that the partygoers were merely dancing and talking but described seeing white females sitting on the laps of Negro males, and while the complaining neighbor acknowledged that the music had not been especially loud, "we all know," Fogerty explained, "that Negroes just normally have louder voices than other people." Judge Edwin Babylon imposed fines of five dollars on the defendants, all but two of whom pleaded not guilty and appealed. Four months later Judge Bernard Cocke reversed the convictions.

The French Quarter party affair had its comic aspects, but police attention did not always raise a laugh. In April, two policemen stopped at a YPA voter registration stall on Freret Street; their needling gibes soon turned ugly when a passerby, Samuel Spears, refused to move on with sufficient dispatch. Spears was arrested and, when he arrived at the Second Precinct station, beaten. By 1950 the Progressive Party had expired.[13]

Its rival, Americans for Democratic Action, the standard-bearer of liberal anticommunism, fared no better. ADA had absorbed a number of former SCHW members, including Harold N. Lee, Rabbi Emil Leipziger, and Albert Dent, but it never fulfilled its goal of becoming a mass organization that would "serve as leadership for both the negro and the worker." Overly sensitive to white fear of integration (it refused to hold an unsegregated dinner, for example) it neither inspired blacks nor impressed whites. Liberal faculty members at Tulane were apathetic, complained chapter head William Kolb, and labor leaders were "not too cooperative." In its first sally into local politics, an ADA-backed candidate was roundly thrashed by conservative New Orleans congressman F. Edward Hebert. The ADA vowed to challenge Hebert again in 1950, but by then the chapter had folded.[14]

Well before 1950 the Cold War had produced an ideological chilling effect that made criticism of the social order, so commonplace during the Roosevelt era, unfashionable, unpatriotic, and politically dangerous.

A relatively trivial example from New Orleans illustrated the hazards of expressing heterodox opinions. In 1948 a substitute teacher was fired from Alcee Fortier High School (a white school) after several pupils complained that they had been exposed to Communist propaganda. The complaints prompted Superintendent of Schools Lionel J. Bourgeois to send a questionnaire to the student body in an effort to expose further Communist influence. The results of the survey caused Bourgeois to admonish a white civics teacher, Sarah Towles Reed, for lack of "Americanism." Reed happened to be the principal founder of the New Orleans Classroom Teachers Federation and was a well-known political activist. Although only three out of 680 students complained about her, Bourgeois ordered Reed, who had taught at the school for twenty-five years, not to mention "Communism, Socialism, or other foreign 'isms.'" He added: "In any case where the American way of life is brought up in your class, it will be your bounded duty to extoll the merits of the American system." When the new school year began, every high school student received a copy of "One Hundred Things You Should Know about Communism," a gift from Congressman F. Edward Hebert.[15]

Blacks were alive to the danger that white supremacists like Hebert, a member of HUAC, would exploit anticommunism. As the *Louisiana Weekly* commented in an editorial opposing the Mundt-Nixon Bill, "Many reactionists . . . will hurl charges of 'Communism' at any effort to remove longstanding evils of discrimination."[16]

Soon, however, active anticommunism became the price of political, organizational, and personal survival. The Taft-Hartley Act, for example, required labor unions to file anti-Communist affidavits if they were to enjoy access to the National Labor Relations Board. The CIO expelled eleven unions that refused to comply, including the Marine Cooks and Stewards, the ILWU, and the Food, Tobacco and Agricultural Workers. Unions remaining in the CIO purged their ranks of Communists after bitter internal struggles. The Transport Workers Union, for example, removed Ernest Scott and Raymond Tillman from the leadership of Local 206 in New Orleans and expelled them from the union. The National Maritime Union ousted, among others, Hunter Pitts O'Dell, later to attract FBI-generated notoriety as a "Communist" colleague of Martin Luther King.

The drive against Communists in organized labor escalated to the level of state repression. In 1949 U.S. attorney J. Skelly Wright prosecuted seaman Robert E. Himmaugh, a member of the NMU, for concealing his Communist Party membership from a federal loyalty board. The NMU, Wright declaimed, was "nothing more than an arm of the Communist Party," which in the event of war would enable the Soviet Union to tie up shipping "from the East coast to the Gulf coast." Judge Herbert W. Christenberry sentenced Himmaugh to a two-year jail term.[17]

The attack on Communist-controlled unions destroyed or neutralized important forces of opposition to white supremacy. Unions like the Marine Cooks and Stewards and the ILWU were the most racially egalitarian elements of organized labor. As living examples of interracialism, they might have evolved and cohered into an important force for integration during the post-*Brown* years of the 1950s. Expelled from the CIO, however, the MCS closed its New Orleans office in 1950 and dissolved altogether in 1955. The ILWU survived its expulsion, but New Orleans Local 207 expired in 1957 after its president, Andrew Nelson, received a five-year jail sentence for violating the Taft-Hartley Act. Purged of the Communist-led left, the CIO lost its crusading zeal and in 1955 made peace with the more conservative and often blatantly racist AFL unions. Under the nominal leadership of Fred C. Pieper and his successor Victor S. Bussie, organized labor in Louisiana became allied to the Long faction; although for the most part a voice for racial moderation, it did little to actively promote integration.[18]

The Louisiana Civil Rights Congress became another casualty of the anti-

Communist inquisition when Oakley Johnson was forced to leave the state. Hailing originally from Michigan, Johnson had been a Socialist since 1912 and a Communist since 1919. In 1935–36 he taught at the Institute of Modern Languages in Moscow, and he spent most of the Second World War on the staff of the *Daily Worker*. In 1949 Johnson's past caught up with him. Hauled before a federal grand jury, he was quizzed by Skelly Wright about his political affiliations. When asked if he belonged to the Communist Party, Johnson sought refuge in the First and Fifth Amendments. By now he had become an embarrassment to Albert Dent, Dillard's president, and a serious annoyance to the university's board of trustees, which was headed by staunch anti-Communist Edgar B. Stern. On May 1, 1951, Johnson received a letter from Dent informing him that his contract would not be renewed. "I don't see any likelihood of the CRC here holding together very long after I leave," Johnson told William Patterson. He was right: by the end of 1951 the Louisiana Civil Rights Congress had folded.[19]

The leaders of the New Orleans NAACP were only too pleased to see the Civil Rights Congress disappear from the scene. Association stalwarts like A. P. Tureaud, Daniel Byrd, and Arthur Chapital were constantly on the alert for Communist "infiltration"; they regarded Oakley Johnson and the Congress as enemies, not allies. When Johnson began speaking up at New Orleans branch meetings, Daniel Byrd "spotted his intentions right off and immediately clipped his wings." In April 1949 Byrd warned that members of the LCRC, having been "run out" of the New Orleans branch, were trying to take over some of the rural branches near the city. Byrd prevented Johnson from addressing the Edgard branch. In the Jefferson Parish branch, Byrd lamented, LCRC infiltration was "almost complete." He vowed to "weed out" the infiltrators, including branch president Louis Brown. Tureaud advised Thurgood Marshall to shun Brown, explaining that "I have never been able to separate him from the influence of people connected with left-wing organizations."[20]

It was partly to expunge the influence of the Civil Rights Congress that the association's national leadership decided to purge the organization of Communist and left-wing members. With solid backing from the southern branches, the NAACP's 1950 convention voted 309 to 57 to investigate the activities of Communists and Communist sympathizers. "Do not become hysterical and make wild accusations," Walter White admonished the branches. "We do not want a witch-hunt." Nevertheless, individual members could now be reported to a "Committee on Political Domination" by branch presidents, secretaries, or other members. The board of directors was given sweeping powers to withdraw or deny memberships, as well as "suspend and reorganize, or lift the charter and expel any unit which . . . comes under Communist . . . control or domination."[21]

The resolution was ambiguous. Did it authorize branches to expel or deny membership to people simply because they were Communists or "fellow-travelers?" Thurgood Marshall, although strongly anti-Communist, vigorously opposed such a policy: it not only violated traditional NAACP principles but was also unworkable. The Communist Party had gone underground. How were Communists, let alone "fellow-travelers," to be identified? Marshall knew only too well the conservatism of many branches, particularly in the South. Some "have no conception of knowing what they should be doing and objectors to this who would be urging a more militant line could very easily be branded followers to the Communist line." In these branches, claimed Marshall, "I can conceive of some well-known Democrats, Republicans as well as Catholics who will be called Communists merely to keep them out of membership in the NAACP." People should be judged by their actions, not their political beliefs, and ought to be excluded only if they impeded or disrupted the work of the organization.[22]

The experience of Clarence Laws illustrates the ease with which a person could be falsely accused. An alumnus of the Federal Writers Project, former executive secretary of the New Orleans Urban League, and veteran of World War II, Laws held the post of publicity director for the *Louisiana Weekly*. In 1951, on the basis of allegations aired by Leander Perez, the army held a formal hearing to decide whether he should be discharged as a commissioned Reserve officer. The charges? That he had been a member of the Southern Conference for Human Welfare, that he had spoken at a meeting of the Southern Negro Youth Congress, that he had testified before the Committee Against Jim Crow in the Military Service, and that in 1950 "he maintained close association with known Communists" — in, of all places, the Orleans Parish Progressive Voters League. Thanks in part to the intercession of Archbishop Rummel (Laws was a Catholic) the board of inquiry cleared him. Four years later, however, the army discharged Laws as a security risk on the grounds that he had "failed to indicate association with the Southern Negro Youth Congress on his . . . Loyalty Certificate." It took nearly two years for the army to correct this injustice and give him an honorable discharge. Yet as late as 1960 A. P. Tureaud thought fit to raise the matter in an effort to keep Laws, then an NAACP field secretary, out of New Orleans during the school integration crisis.[23]

Thurgood Marshall may well have had New Orleans in mind when he warned against the danger of conservative branches overreacting to allegations of communism. In any case, Marshall lost the argument. The Korean War was raging and McCarthyism in full swing. Under the aggressive leadership of Alfred Baker Lewis, a majority of the NAACP's "Anti-Subversive Committee" decided that Communists should be rooted out. Indeed, Lewis took the view that people could be legitimately excluded from membership if they questioned the NAACP's support for President Truman's anti-Communist foreign policy. The number of actual expulsions in Louisiana was small, but the policy strengthened the conservatism of the New Orleans branch, which according to A. P. Tureaud made no effort to recruit white members because "we can't screen out white Communists." The branch annually refused to send James Dombrowski a membership card, despite receiving his dues each year without fail.[24]

The exclusion of Dombrowski from the New Orleans branch reflected a national NAACP policy to weaken and isolate the Southern Conference Education Fund. As early as 1947 Walter White deemed it wise to avoid associating with SCEF as "they are pretty well labelled now." NAACP officials tried to starve SCEF of funds by warning off potential supporters: as Roy Wilkins advised an inquirer, "The outfit is not wholly free of suspicion in some quarters, as we understand it." In March 1954 the Senate Internal Security Subcommittee, chaired by James O. Eastland of Mississippi, visited New Orleans to hold public hearings on SCEF. Despite the fact that the hearings amounted to a preemptive strike against the imminent *Brown* decision, the NAACP did not spring to SCEF's defense.[25]

Although not the first time that a congressional investigating committee explicitly linked a civil rights organization with communism, the Eastland hearings were the most ballyhooed. Two former-Communists-turned-informants testified that SCEF's deceased parent, the Southern Conference for Human Welfare, had been organized as a Communist front and alleged that SCEF's officers, especially Dombrowski, were Communist sympathizers or "dupes." In a ham-fisted way, the Eastland committee managed to obliquely attack liberal Supreme Court Justice Hugo Black by linking him with SCEF supporter Virginia Durr, his sister-in-law.

Despite the flimsiness of the committee's charges, the hearings nonetheless hampered SCEF's effectiveness, as liberals, either intimidated by the committee's attack or convinced that there was no smoke without fire, shunned the organization. Even many of SCEF's friends, including Rabbi Julian Feibelman, a board member, deserted it. The earliest and most consistent opponent of segregation in the South, SCEF continued to provide important support for the integration struggle: it gave financial backing to NAACP activist Amzie Moore in Cleveland, Mississippi, for example, and it encouraged the militant leadership of Rev. Fred Shuttlesworth in Birmingham, Alabama. It had been the most energetic exponent of interracialism in New Orleans, but red-baiting "relegated [it] to the sidelines" just as the *Brown* decision was thrusting the civil rights issue into the forefront of Southern politics. SCEF's influence would henceforth be felt mainly *outside* Louisiana.[26]

The Cold War ensured, for a brief period, the ascendancy of the NAACP within the struggle for civil rights. By putting its own house in order, the association safeguarded its reputation as a responsible, patriotic organization; by positively identifying with the liberal anticommunism of the Truman administration, it bolstered its position within the Democratic party. The association had foiled its radical and Communist-front rivals and by the early 1950s all but monopolized the civil rights field. Perhaps, as Steven F. Lawson and August Meier have suggested, civil rights and civil liberties functioned as independent variables: the cause of civil rights advanced even as anticommunism trampled on freedom of association and expression.[27]

Certainly, it would be an oversimplification to say that the political climate of the Cold War unambiguously favored the South's white supremacists. Liberals, as well as conservatives, invoked the Communist challenge, only in their case to inveigh *against* racial discrimination. Anticommunism also animated the teachings of such outspoken Catholic opponents of segregation as Father Jerome Drolet, pastor of St. Charles Parish in Thibodaux, Father Vincent O'Connell, chairman of the Catholic Committee of the South, and Louis J. Twomey, the Jesuit priest who headed Loyola University's Institute of Industrial Relations. Then again, Cold War exigencies helped persuade the federal government to repudiate the most blatant forms of racial discrimination, particularly legally sanctioned segregation. Thus, at the same time that it was creating loyalty boards and prosecuting Communists, the Truman administration was also integrating the armed forces, proposing civil rights legislation, and supporting the NAACP's brief against school segregation in the Supreme Court. Later, some of the very federal officials who had sternly extirpated communism in New Orleans, notably J. Skelly Wright, M. Hepburn Many, and Herbert W. Christenberry, became diligent upholders of black civil rights in the teeth of segregationist recalcitrance.[28]

On balance, however, the anticommunism of the early Cold War damaged the cause of racial equality far more than it helped it. When whites resisted the *Brown* decision, the organizations that might have rallied popular support for integration either no longer existed or had been rendered ineffective by red-baiting. Anticommunism succeeded in silencing virtually all the whites who had been involved in civil rights activities. Even in the universities, anticommunism stifled free debate and discouraged people who sympathized with the civil rights cause from making their views known. All faculty members and campus speakers were required to sign loyalty oaths. Professors identified as "integrationists" were hounded by legislative committees; some were fired. While McCarthyism subsided as a national force in the mid-1950s, in the South it continued to flourish for another ten years. Even in the early 1960s, any white person active in the civil rights movement aroused suspicion of being a Communist. McCarthyism thus made it that much easier for segregationists to defend white supremacy, that much more difficult for blacks to attack it.

The NAACP's anti-Communist stance enabled it to survive McCarthyism, but at a price. By insulating itself from the left it helped to undermine white support for its own integration policies. Moreover the destruction of organizations to the left made the NAACP increasingly isolated; when the ultra-segregationists launched a direct assault on the NAACP itself, the association found few defenders.

Perhaps the most profound effect of the anti-Communist fever, and also the one most difficult to measure, was the divorcing of the civil rights agenda from the labor-left agenda. In emphasizing "civil rights," that is, legal equality and the franchise, the black struggle neglected basic questions of poverty and economic disadvantage. As the economic radicalism of the New Deal era faded away, the scope of the struggle for racial equality narrowed. Few questioned the established economic order in the 1950s, and as a result, existing structural inequalities persisted and became in some respects even more pronounced.

It had been an article of faith among most New Deal reformers that economic modernization, and the passing of the old plantation-based, single-crop agriculture, would liberalize southern politics and undermine white supremacy. In fact, economic change was doing nothing of the sort. As the agricultural sector shrank at an unprecedented rate, displaced whites, scrambling for jobs alongside displaced blacks, succeeded in all but monopolizing the middle and upper reaches of the job hierarchy. As Louisiana became a predominantly urban state, whites clung to their occupational niches or carved out new ones, and the races became more physically separated than ever. White commitment to racial segregation showed few signs of weakening.

The speed and magnitude of Louisiana's economic metamorphosis were guaranteed to sharpen racial competition. Between 1940 and 1950 the state's farm population decreased by 286,000, during the 1950s it lost another 334,000, and by 1960 it stood at just over a quarter of its 1940 size. As a proportion of the total population it had declined from 36 percent in 1940 to 21 percent in 1950 and by 1960 it stood at only 7.2 percent, the lowest level in the South apart from Florida.

Black farmers left the land in particularly large proportions because the great majority operated small farms that they rented or sharecropped. Marginalized by the decline of cotton production (from two million acres in the 1930s to 352,000 acres in 1966) the number of tenant farmers and sharecroppers fell by more than 95,000, a decline of 89 percent. Between 1940 and 1960 the total number of farms in Louisiana decreased by about one-half and the number of black-owned farms declined by more than two-thirds. By 1960 black farms constituted only 23 percent of the total compared with nearly 40 percent in 1940. Farmers made up about a quarter of all workers in 1940, only 3.2 percent in 1960.

Many black sharecroppers became wage laborers, but mechanization was drastically reducing the demand for agricultural workers. In 1950 sugarcane was cut by hand and mechanical pickers harvested only 3 percent of the cotton crop. By 1960 machines harvested 96 percent of the cane, 60 percent of the cotton, and all of the rice. Between 1940 and 1960 the agricultural workforce declined from about a third of the state's labor force to 7.8 percent. "By the early or mid-1960s," writes Jay Mandle, "sharecropping . . . had passed into insignificance and so too had the southern plantation economy."[29]

The transformation of the South's black population from a rural peasantry into an urban proletariat represented, as Edgar Stern noted in 1945, "a social problem that approaches in size and gravity the question of displaced people in Europe today." Yet the federal government did virtually nothing to cushion the effects of this mass migration beyond funding the most rudimentary of welfare programs. Blacks had to compete in an ostensibly "free" job market in which white employers and unions colluded to rig the rules against them.[30]

The demise of the Fair Employment Practices Committee was a disaster of the first magnitude for blacks. True, the FEPC had always been hampered by tepid support from Roosevelt, but it had served notice on employers and unions that they were accountable to the federal government and that, if nothing else, the FEPC had the power to harass them. It had even compelled recalcitrant industries to accept some blacks in hitherto "white only" jobs.

By 1945, however, industrial employers were thumbing their noses at the FEPC in anticipation of its abolition. When victory brought the cancellation of wartime contracts, companies shed black labor and returned to their old ways. Smaller employers also vehemently opposed the FEPC. "In most of the state of Louisiana . . . the average white businessman is *not* going to mix negroes and whites together in his office and/or factory," a New Orleans engineer advised Senator Allen Ellender. The latter needed no prompting. The FEPC, he claimed, wanted to force employers to hire "so many Jews, so many colored people, so many Catholics, so many Protestants."[31]

White workers, fearful of a postwar recession, rejoiced over the FEPC's death and were determined to defend their privileged position within the job market. An incident at the Todd-Johnson shipyard in New Orleans exemplified that resolve. On the morning of September 24, 1947, hundreds of whites walked off the job to protest the hiring of two black supervisors. Blacks at that time comprised less than 1 percent of the yard's workforce. As the Urban League complained, the cracks opened up by the FEPC "never widened and . . . some of them were closed."[32]

The sluggish growth of the state's manufacturing sector reinforced the resolve of white workers to maintain job segregation. Between 1947 and 1962 Louisiana's rate of growth in manufacturing employment lagged well behind the national average; indeed, it remained one of the least industrialized states. Moreover, some industries stagnated or declined. Employment in shipbuilding, for example, decreased from a peak of 18,000 in 1943 to 6,628 in 1960. Other industries took advantage of technical improvements to reduce payrolls. Jobs in petroleum refining, for example, decreased by 16 percent between 1952 and 1960. Part of that decline, however, stemmed from the recession of 1957–58, which hit Louisiana particularly hard. Taking the decade as a whole, the total number of jobs in manufacturing fell from 145,000 to 142,000.

Blacks were especially vulnerable to layoffs: they were less educated and less skilled; equally important, managements acquiesced in the discriminatory policies of white-dominated unions. In the petroleum, paper, and shipbuilding industries the proportion of black workers diminished during the 1950s. When the Gaylord Corporation constructed a new bag plant in Bogalusa, it recruited an all-white workforce with the exception of one or two black porters.[33]

As Louisiana enjoyed the economic boom of the late 1940s and 1950s, buoyed by an oil bonanza that saw output increase from 131 million barrels in 1945 to 400 million in 1960, blacks had to make do with the crumbs. Even in industries in which they were relatively well represented, they remained almost exclusively in low-wage, "unskilled" jobs. A survey of Texas and Louisiana oil refineries conducted in the mid-1950s found that blacks made up about 12 percent of the refinery workers and 15 percent of the production workers. There were few black managers, professionals, technicians, or office workers, however; the survey counted only ten blacks in white-collar jobs, 0.2 percent of the total. It is doubtful that any of the ten were in Louisiana. The closely knit drilling crews, now found increasingly on offshore platforms, remained all-white, all-male preserves. It was a similar story in shipbuilding, where in 1960 blacks composed 15.6 percent of the total workforce but about four-fifths of the laborers. Although the proportion of black skilled workers increased during the 1950s, the boilermakers' union remained virtually all white. The shipyards employed no black clerical workers.[34]

In expanding employment sectors such as trade, financial services, and government, whites often succeeded in excluding blacks from the better-paid jobs. In 1950 blacks made up about a third of the New Orleans population but only 0.08 percent of the workers employed by NOPSI, the local utilities company, 0.015 percent of the phone company's workforce, and 0.054 percent of the workers in city government. There were no black firemen and only a handful of black policemen. In the private sector (with the obvious exception of black-owned businesses) clerks, stenographers, bank tellers, sales assistants, and transit drivers were all "white only" occupations. NOPSI did not hire its first black bus drivers until 1961. Many unions still excluded blacks as a matter of policy. The president of the United Steelworkers (AFL) reported in 1950 that his union had no Negro members "and the present membership does not wish to have any." Craft unions of plumbers, electrical workers, and machinists still barred black apprentices. There were one or two bright spots. In the Post Office the proportion of black clerks rose to almost a quarter after the Senate held hearings on discrimination in 1948. In education, the proportion of black teachers in the state remained about the same, but they doubled in number between 1940 and 1960, and pay improved dramatically.[35]

The President's Committee on Government Contract Compliance, created by Eisenhower, was a poor substitute for the FEPC. Although the Committee contained dedicated people, it had few teeth. It did laboriously document the extent of discrimination in several industries, and its investigation of the oil industry prodded the giant Esso refinery in Baton Rouge into adopting a fair employment program with the aim of promoting blacks into higher positions. Esso's commitment, however, amounted to little more than window dressing. As the plant's general manager privately conceded, "The company conformed with the customs of the community and was in no wise a crusader." The new policy, he added, would probably affect no more than one hundred black employees because, "with few exceptions, Negroes lacked native ability." The manager also confessed that the company's contract with the union could be interpreted so as to prevent blacks being promoted out of traditionally Negro jobs.[36]

Gene Sutherland of the American Friends Service Committee, who elicited these admissions, had the task of convincing local employers to adopt "employment on merit" programs. Opening an office in Baton Rouge in 1955, he found that old attitudes died hard. The assistant director of the Louisiana Department of Commerce "felt that from the mentality standpoint, Negroes were probably handicapped for the performance of complicated tasks." To his dismay, Sutherland found a union official, despite twenty years in the CIO, echoing the idea "that the Negro is a somewhat inferior race." Department store managers listened to the AFSC man politely, but "none were willing to be 'guinea pigs' and 'crusaders' . . . in changing employment policies." They only employed black sales clerks during the Christmas shopping season, the sole exception being the woman who operated a popcorn machine at Kresge.

One manager reported that he stopped using Negro boys to carry groceries to customers' cars after a "well-to-do woman" complained. The head of the local chamber of commerce told Sutherland he had no knowledge of discrimination and hoped that he had not come to Baton Rouge to stir up race riots.[37]

Thus most blacks stayed on the bottom of the occupational ladder while whites steadily ascended. In Baton Rouge, 86 percent of black workers held manual jobs in 1960, compared with 48 percent of whites; 22.7 percent of white families enjoyed an annual income of $10,000 or more compared with only 2.7 percent of black families. Here, in the heart of Louisiana's petrochemical industry, one of the most prosperous areas in the state, half of all blacks lived at or below the official poverty line, compared to a white level of 11 percent. In New Orleans, the proportion of white workers who were classified as "white-collar" increased from 32 percent to 55 percent between 1940 and 1960; the proportion of black workers in this middle-class category increased from 8 percent to 10 percent. Statewide, 57 percent of all black families were classified as "poor" in 1960, compared with 21 percent of white families.[38]

The result was that while Louisiana attracted white migrants from other states, particularly Mississippi, blacks were voting with their feet. Between 1940 and 1950 the black workforce declined by 46,000 while the number of white workers increased by 83,000. During the 1950s a net total of 92,000 blacks left the state while a net total of 42,000 whites arrived. Blacks were a diminishing proportion of the state's total population and an even faster shrinking component of the workforce. As Samuel Lubell observed in 1951, industrialization accompanied by pervasive job discrimination was marginalizing black labor in the South and shoring up white supremacy.[39]

White politicians were in no doubt as to where the overwhelmingly white electorate stood on the issue of racial segregation. In 1948 the militantly prosegregation States' Rights candidate, Strom Thurmond, carried Louisiana with 49 percent of the vote; President Truman came a poor second. True, one can put a gloss on this result that downplays its significance: Truman ran strongest in urban working-class areas; the turnout of 45 percent was exceptionally low; and Thurmond's possession of the "rooster," the symbol of Louisiana's Democratic party, gave him an automatic advantage. As Sindler comments, "the Dixiecrat movement was more a shrewdly managed coup by conservative leaders than a grass-roots rebellion." Of equal salience, however, are the facts that Truman's pro–civil rights candidacy aroused practically no organized support in the state and that Thurmond did, after all, win.[40]

When the race issue faded into the background, politicians like Earl Long and Chep Morrison could win handily without stressing appeals to racial prejudice. In 1950, for example, Morrison squelched the Dixiecrat candidate,

Alvin A. Cobb, while loftily condemning his opponent's anti-Negro rhetoric. But while liberals congratulated New Orleans for spurning racial hatred, Morrison did not read too much into his victory over a political nonentity like Cobb. As Morrison aide Dave McGuire explained to Carl Rowan, a young black reporter, "The mayor won last time because there were other issues. Next time there may not be those other issues and the bigots could win — strictly on the race question."[41]

In fact, as Morrison well knew, the race issue was political dynamite. The growth of the city's black population brought mounting pressure to improve housing and public services. At the same time whites, especially in the newer, middle-class neighborhoods, felt increasingly threatened by black encroachment. Morrison considered the maintenance of segregation essential to his continued political success.

Morrison reconciled these conflicting pressures by improving facilities for blacks in a manner that preserved and even strengthened segregation. His handling of the park question was typical. Under the direction of Lester J. Lautenschlaeger, the city's Recreational Department refurbished Shakespeare Park and constructed or improved several playgrounds, recreation centers, and swimming pools for blacks. These still did not suffice. In 1949 the city's black population of 182,000, still shut out of City and Audubon parks and with no legal access to the lakefront, was suffocating from lack of leisure space. Faced with the prospect of NAACP-backed suits for the integration of parks, Morrison decided to push ahead with the construction of a full-sized park solely for blacks.

The location of the park posed a thorny political problem. As his public relations advisor, Scott Wilson, pointed out, the difficulty lay in "finding a park area in a negro area so that the aggravating necessity of them passing through white sections will be forestalled." Morrison decided to build a municipal park and golf course on a 360-acre tract near the lakefront end of the Industrial Canal, pursuing the scheme in collaboration with an adjacent housing development, Pontchartrain Park Homes, a private subdivision promoted by Edgar Stern and Charles Keller with the aim of providing homes for middle-class blacks. When Pontchartrain Park opened in 1956 Morrison boasted that he had preserved segregation by providing truly "separate but equal" facilities that satisfied all but a handful of professional malcontents. Similarly, Morrison backed the development of a Negro beach by the Levee Board. Located along a remote section of Lake Pontchartrain fourteen miles from downtown Canal Street, "Lincoln Beach" opened in 1954, enabling the city to clamp down on unofficial bathing by blacks along the city's built-up lakefront, long a source of irritation to whites in that increasingly affluent part of the city.[42]

Even the apparent "integration" of the police force fit into Morrison's strategy of shoring up segregation. By 1950 New Orleans was the only large city in the South with no black policemen. Faced with court action initiated by a rejected black applicant who had achieved one of the highest test scores on record, Morrison agreed to the recruitment of two blacks, with the private understanding that they were to operate in Negro areas only. The men in question, moreover, were dressed in plainclothes and assigned to the juvenile bureau. As Morrison's biographer noted, "The cautious manipulation worked superbly. They were hardly noticed." In New Orleans, as in ultra-segregationist Shreveport and Monroe, the recruitment of black policemen did not signify any retreat from segregation. Few in number, they were accorded an inferior status, segregated within the organization, and utilized as a means of combatting black crime.[43]

During his fourteen years as mayor of New Orleans, Morrison demonstrated a flair for holding out the threat of a racist backlash as a reason for doing as little as possible. For years, for example, the NAACP urged Morrison to appoint a biracial committee. The mayor treated the suggestion sympathetically but proved adept at finding reasons for delay: he could not act until the next election was out of the way, or while the legislature was in session, or while emotions were still inflamed over the current integration crisis. But there was always an election in the offing; some integration issue — parks, buses, schools — was always present; the threat of legislative retribution continually hovered over the city. The result was inaction. Even so, many blacks found it hard to censure Morrison too severely. "He is not a bigoted race baiter," stated one. "He has tried to ameliorate conditions, but he is limited politically by his constituency."[44]

The NAACP's equalization strategy accorded with these political realities: equalization suits promised immediate improvements within the structure of segregation but stopped short of challenging segregation itself. In June 1950, however, at a two-day lawyers' conference in New York, the NAACP Legal Defense and Educational Fund decided to commence a frontal attack on segregation. Henceforth, instead of seeking to realize the "equal" part of the "separate but equal" doctrine, it would sue for the admission of blacks into all facilities, regardless of their racial designation. The goal was no longer equalization but integration — to overturn the *Plessy* decision that had controlled the law and helped to shape southern society for more than half a century.

This pivotal conference took place hard on the heels of two important Supreme Court decisions involving attempts by blacks to enroll in white universities. In *Sweatt* v. *Painter,* the more important of the two, the Court ordered the University of Texas Law School to admit Herman Sweatt, a qualified black applicant, despite the existence of a law school at all-black Texas Southern University. Crucially, the Court accepted the NAACP's contention that segregation, per se, amounted to unconstitutional discrimination. The Texas Southern law school was not only palpably inferior in its teaching and facilities, the Court reasoned, but also lacked "those qualities which are incapable of objective measurement but which make for greatness in a law school," such as "reputation of the faculty, experience of the administration, position and influence of the alumni, standing in the community, traditions and prestige." The shift in NAACP strategy from equalization to integration had been formally agreed upon in 1948, but the decision had been put on ice pending the *Sweatt* decision. When it came, it gave Marshall the confidence to go forward."[45]

The first Louisiana case in line with the new NAACP policy was a suit against Louisiana State University for admission to its law school. By the summer of 1950 J. K. Haynes had lined up a dozen suitable applicants; once they had been formally rejected the NAACP would have an airtight case. As always, however, success could never be taken for granted. The suit not only demanded skillful legal footwork but also some delicate diplomacy. It was important, for example, to secure the benevolent neutrality of Felton G. Clark, president of Southern University, who might regard the integration of LSU's law school as a threat to the law school at Southern. It was essential, too, to have the major NAACP players working in harmony, especially A. P. Tureaud and Dr. E. A. Johnson, whose arguments over the handling of legal cases had been accentuated by a clash of personalities.[46]

In July 1950, Thurgood Marshall arrived in Baton Rouge to go over tactics with the Louisiana NAACP leadership. Associated Press correspondent Warren Rogers, tipped off about the meeting, surprised the group as they sat at the rear of a fish restaurant in Scotlandville, the black neighborhood near Southern University. Reluctantly admitted to the conclave, Rogers joined Marshall and the others — Tureaud, Haynes, Johnson, Byrd, and two or three Baton Rouge leaders — as they sat over a tableful of catfish bones. Anxious to catch LSU off guard, Marshall extracted a promise from the reporter not to write anything before the attempt to register.

The next morning Rogers witnessed the scene at the registrar's office as twelve young black men applied for admission to the law school. "Tureaud, short and middle-aged . . . stood at the counter," Rogers recalled, "tight-lipped and silent." Days later, on July 28, LSU's board of supervisors denied admission "pursuant to the laws of Louisiana and the policies of this Board." That was all Marshall and Tureaud needed to bring suit on behalf of one of the rejected men, Roy S. Wilson. The rest was clear sailing: in October a three-judge federal court ordered Wilson's admission. J. Skelly Wright, appointed to the bench a year earlier at the age of thirty-eight (the youngest federal judge in the nation) wrote the opinion. He later recalled this, his first integration order, as a personal watershed. "Until that day I was just another Southern 'boy.' After it, there was no turning back."[47]

The only thing to take the shine off this signal victory was Tureaud's belated discovery that their plaintiff, Roy Wilson, had a number of skeletons in his closet and could not boast the kind of irreproachable character that the NAACP looked for in Negro "firsts." Marshall could not conceal his annoyance. "You sure pick some clients," he chided Tureaud. "There is no doubt in my mind that Wilson will be bounced out with much ceremony and . . . we will get a bad press on it." When the university authorities moved to expel Wilson, the NAACP refused to back him up, and LSU's first identifiable black student withdrew three months after his admission.[48]

Still, a legal barrier had been broken. The following year Lutrell Payne entered the School of Agriculture and completed his studies successfully. Eight blacks enrolled in the fall of 1952, twelve the following semester. In 1953 about one hundred blacks enrolled in the graduate, law, and medical schools, and Tureaud's son, A. P. Tureaud Jr., became LSU's first black undergraduate. In 1954 Ernest Morial, LSU's first black law graduate, was sworn in to the state bar. "I was inspired," he explained, "by the need for individuals . . . to fight for justice and equality in order that the principles of democracy become a part of our daily lives; so that all men may believe in the fatherhood of God and the brotherhood of man."[49]

The *Sweatt* decision, however, was narrow in scope. It applied only to universities, and then only to professional and graduate schools. At the undergraduate level, LSU continued to resist: the board of supervisors appealed Tureaud's admission and eventually cancelled his registration while the case was in litigation. By the time the federal appeals court confirmed his admission, young Tureaud, who felt lonely and isolated on the LSU campus, had transferred to Xavier University. Additional suits, moreover, were needed to integrate the half-dozen other state colleges and universities, not to mention the twenty or so trade schools. As the *Louisiana Weekly* cautioned, "The fight here will have to be waged from parish to parish . . . until victory is eventually won. It is an unfortunate fact that the Supreme Court moves very, very slowly and cautiously and frequently clothes its decisions in phrases which confuse more than clarify the issues in question."[50]

The struggle of LSU to exclude A. P. Tureaud Jr. gave the NAACP a mild foretaste of what to expect when blacks sued to integrate elementary and high schools. It was one thing to integrate universities, quite another to integrate schools. As Senator Russell Long told Donald Jones a year earlier, whites in Louisiana would eventually accept integration on the college and graduate levels — he himself favored it — but the sudden abolition of segregated schools would provoke a storm of opposition and have disastrous consequences.

For blacks, now familiar with the concept of equalization, integration was a leap in the dark. At the NAACP lawyers' conference of June 1950, "some of us," Tureaud reported, "expressed doubt about being able to get many cases." Plaintiffs would be difficult to find, they warned, because parents would be putting their children at risk; they would be especially reluctant to offer their elementary-school-age children as guinea pigs. Writing to Marshall the following year, Dan Byrd, now a field secretary for the "Inc. Fund," emphasized the need to educate the branches about the shift in policy. "This is something entirely new and the branches are uninformed."[51]

During the next four years Byrd crisscrossed the state — clocking up as much as 4,000 miles in a single month — to drum up support for the new policy, organize petitions to school boards, and sign up potential plaintiffs. On September 4, 1952, Tureaud filed suits against the school boards of Orleans and St. Helena parishes demanding the admission of black children to white schools. The fate of these actions now pivoted on the outcome of the *Brown* case shortly to be considered by the Supreme Court.[52]

The NAACP had embarked upon an uncharted and dangerous journey in a vessel of unproven seaworthiness: despite Byrd's upbeat reports, blacks did not flock to climb on board. Nevertheless, the reluctance of blacks to attack integration head-on could not disguise swelling discontent with the "Southern way of life."

In Louisiana, and across the South, blacks wanted dignity and opportunity, segregation or no. Clearly, they were prepared to challenge the status quo in the courts. They also, on occasion, resorted to protests that entailed direct action. In 1947, for example, the New Orleans branch of the NAACP instigated a boycott of four Canal Street department stores that refused to allow black women to try on hats. Blacks picketed the stores until suppressed by the police under a court injunction. In 1951 parents and children in Alexandria picketed the parish courthouse after the school board, at the behest of local planters, delayed the start of the school year until cotton picking was completed. In 1953 black children in Lafayette boycotted a newly opened high school because it failed to measure up to the facilities of the white high school. According to Byrd, over 90 percent of the students joined the protest.[53]

Three months later, in June 1953, blacks in Baton Rouge conducted a week-long boycott of city buses. Almost unnoticed at the time, this protest was a direct precursor of the Montgomery bus boycott and an event of major significance in the evolution of the civil rights movement.

Few practices evoked such widespread indignation among black southerners as segregated buses. Black passengers had to pay their fare at the front door but board at the back door; they then had to sit in the rear of the bus. The rear of the bus was more uncomfortable: the back rows were located above the motors, and their occupants had to endure the discomfort of, literally, hot seats; in the summer months the back of the bus was often enveloped in clouds of dust and dirt when the vehicle was in motion. In the middle rows, the driver was supposed to divide the seating on an ad hoc basis, according to the ratio of one race to the other, adjusting a moveable "screen" backwards or forwards. Thus passengers already seated could be asked to move or stand. Indeed, because the law forbade whites and blacks from sitting in the same row, several passengers might have to stand in order to accommodate a single member of the other race. Even if there were no white passengers, blacks were forbidden to occupy the front rows, and as blacks now composed a majority of the passengers in most southern cities, it was increasingly common for the front seats to be empty. This prohibition was especially galling when the buses wound their way through black neighborhoods. "In the heart of their own community," writes Aldon Morris, "blacks had to stand over vacant seats designated for white passengers."

Their feelings on the matter expressed far more than resentment over discomfort and inconvenience. Blacks knew perfectly well that whites accepted physical proximity when they were cooks, farmhands, nursemaids, and servants. Only when physical proximity implied equality of status did whites draw the line, and they drew that line in a way that emphasized the inferior station of blacks within a system designed and controlled by whites. The symbolism of being assigned the back of the bus rather than the front was unmistakable, and it sank in at a tender age. It was every young child's wish, for example, to sit up front and watch the driver in action; black children were denied this experience. Even if the rules were enforced impartially, the system clearly put blacks at a psychological disadvantage. The fact that the drivers were always whites made matters worse: they tended to be solicitous toward white passengers, indifferent or even hostile toward black ones. Blacks often complained about their brusque manner and threatening tone of voice, about their use of terms like "boy," "girl," "Auntie" and "nigger." When A. P. Tureaud tasked the Trailways company about drivers who addressed black men as "boys," an executive wrote back explaining that "boy" was an affectionate appellation. "I cannot see why this should be objectionable."

It was no accident that the phrase "back of the bus" became a synonym for racial discrimination. Segregation on trains was irksome, but few blacks traveled by rail with frequency. Buses, on the other hand, were part of everyday life; in the cities it was difficult to avoid them. And on buses blacks experienced segregation in its most public and humiliating form. Here, they were clearly separate and visibly unequal.[54]

Tension over buses and streetcars, exacerbated by chronic overcrowding, had reached the boiling point during the war years and, despite some reduction in friction, had simmered ever since. In November 1946 the East Carroll Parish branch of the NAACP reported that one of its members had been forcibly ejected from a bus "because he failed to stand back toward the rear of the bus as fast as the driver thought he should have." In 1948 an argument with a bus driver had led to the arrest and shooting of Roy Brooks, the incident that spurred the formation of the Louisiana Civil Rights Congress. By the early 1950s individual acts of defiance on the part of black passengers were so numerous that a pattern of defiance was emerging in many parts of the South. Most went unrecorded, but they sometimes showed up in court. In Richmond, Virginia, for example, during the early months of 1953, seven blacks were arrested for refusing to move further back on the command of the driver. On May 18 about a thousand people attended a meeting to protest the arrests.[55]

In several southern cities, blacks succeeded in alleviating the situation by persuading the bus companies to adopt a "first-come, first-served" system of segregated seating. Under this plan, "reserved" seats were abolished or drastically reduced: blacks simply filled the bus from the rear and whites from the front, with the proviso that members of the same race could not occupy the same seat. This arrangement at least mitigated the problem of blacks having to stand when reserved "white" seats were empty. The transit companies were generally amenable to this system, for it enabled them to fill seats that, given the declining proportion of white riders, were underutilized.

In March 1953 the Baton Rouge city council passed Ordinance 222 which authorized the "first-come, first-served" scheme. The exact provenance of this measure is unclear. In 1949 the city had outlawed the operation of about sixty independent, Negro-operated buses that were serving black neighborhoods but threatening the survival of the bus company. Backed up by the threat of a drivers' strike, the company demanded, and received, a monopoly franchise. In return, the company undertook to provide a "full and fair" service. That commitment was difficult to meet, however, when buses had to pass up black passengers when "white" seats were empty. In the summer of 1952, the company asked the city to relax the requirements of segregation in order to permit more efficient utilization of bus capacity. The bus drivers, however, later claimed that Ordinance 222 was enacted at the behest of the NAACP and accused Mayor Jesse L. Webb Jr. of promising to change the law in a bid for Negro votes. In all likelihood, both explanations are correct: the measure represented a convergence of interest between the bus company and local blacks. Certainly, the NAACP welcomed Ordinance 222 and took steps to publicize it within the black community.

The drivers, however, bitterly resented the revised rules. They had not been consulted about the changes, and the company, it seems, left them in ignorance. In early June, a black passenger refused to move back and asked a white to move forward instead; the driver made a beeline to the nearest police station and demanded the arrest of the Negro. When the latter mentioned the new ordinance, both the driver and the police were incredulous and had to call the parish clerk to confirm its existence. The drivers protested vigorously, arguing that Ordinance 222 undermined segregation. Faced with a strike, the company met Mayor Webb and proposed amending the ordinance to meet the drivers' objections. Webb refused, and the company ordered the drivers to enforce the new law. Meanwhile, the NAACP distributed handbills telling blacks what to do if challenged. "Do not resist arrest," it advised, "but take the officer's badge number so it can be reported to the proper authorities."

The drivers were disgusted. "That Negro outfit is . . . telling Negroes they have a right to sit anywhere they want and advising them not to move," complained the secretary of the drivers' union. On the morning of June 15, after two recalcitrant drivers were suspended, the men walked out. The sole issue, they insisted, was the maintenance of segregation. As the city, the company, and the drivers tried to negotiate a way out of the impasse, the author of Ordinance 222, councilwoman Mildred DuBois, began to receive abusive and threatening phone calls. On June 17, a contingent of drivers' wives paraded outside city hall.

On June 18 the state attorney general, Fred LeBlanc, came to the drivers' rescue with an opinion that Ordinance 222 conflicted with state law on segregation. The following morning the drivers returned to work, as the city council agreed to consider ways of amending the ordinance. Meanwhile, the drivers were told to follow the former policy of reserving the front seats for whites.

But on the evening of LeBlanc's ruling, Raymond Scott, secretary of a "United Defense League," made a radio appeal for blacks to stay off the buses. He promised that cars would be available at designated points to convey blacks to and from work. When the drivers went back on June 19, there were virtually no black riders.

The leadership of the United Defense League revealed itself at a mass meeting at Mt. Hebron Baptist Church that evening. Its organizational heart comprised a board of directors that included Fannie Washburn, a housewife; T. Roosevelt Smith, a refinery worker; Raymond Scott, a tailor; Acie Belton, another refinery worker; and Johnnie Jones, a lawyer. All were active in local voters leagues. Heading the UDL was the Reverend Theodore J. Jemison. Described as a "32-year-old, well-dressed, spectacled man," Jemison hailed from Selma, Alabama, where his father, Dr. D. V. Jemison, was a respected and influential pastor and also president of the National Baptist Convention, the largest black organization in the United States. The younger Jemison had moved to Baton Rouge in 1949 to succeed Gardner C. Taylor as pastor of Mt. Zion Baptist Church, one of the largest churches in the state. Since then, he had also served as president of the local NAACP. The main speaker at the June 19 rally, Jemison delivered an impassioned address. "It's illegal to boycott," he playfully noted at one point. "We're just not riding." A reporter was impressed by the "frequent and fervent 'amens'" that punctuated his oration.

The boycott was in full swing. A fleet of more than a hundred private vehicles, "ranging from a 1923 Dodge to an ambulance," sustained the protest, with three gas stations providing fuel at wholesale prices. Blacks "hooted and laughed," a local newspaper reported, "as nearly empty buses loafed through Negro sections." When a solitary black tried to board one bus, onlookers jeered until the man came off. White reporters were impressed by the efficiency of "Operation Free Lift," the UDL's improvised transportation system. "A steady stream of cars and trucks pass in front of the Old State Capitol picking up Negro passengers from the large crowd gathered there. Dispatchers facilitate the movement of the 'free ride' vehicles and passengers are grouped together according to their destinations. 'Keep 'em rolling, let's go, anybody for East Boulevard,' a dispatcher shouted, as the cars pulled up in file along the curb before improvised route signs." One car, its brakes having failed, crashed into the brand new Chevrolet of a bus company official. According to one estimate, each day of the boycott was costing the company $1,600.

About a thousand blacks attended a rally at McKinley Junior High School on June 20. Jemison, the keynote speaker again, proposed that the company employ Negro drivers on predominantly Negro routes and warned that blacks would ask for an independent franchise unless they obtained satisfactory seating.

> We are not going to pay 15 cents and stand up. . . . This is not the fight of an individual or a group of individuals, but this is the onward march of a people who desire to be free. We will not retreat one inch. We have sounded forth the trumpet and we shall not sound retreat. . . . We're going to drive cars until the Council satisfies us, and if our people stop driving, members of the executive board will drive until our cars' wheels fall off.

Jemison sat down to "wildly enthusiastic applause," the *Morning Advocate* told its readers, and the crowd "emptied their pockets" to the tune of $1,000. Negro clubs chipped in another $500. Rallies on the next two evenings drew an even larger turnout.

On June 23, however, Jemison called off the boycott. The council had agreed to adopt an "emergency" measure, Ordinance 251, which modified

Ordinance 222 to the extent of reserving the two short front seats for whites and the long rear seat for blacks. The practical impact of this change remained to be seen. According to the *Louisiana Weekly*, "Negroes will not have to move back towards the rear if other Negroes get off behind them and a white person boards the bus." This was an optimistic interpretation. But Jemison, who took the initiative to end the boycott, decided to accept Ordinance 251 as a temporary compromise while reserving the right to challenge it in court. The revised measure at least had the virtue of increasing the number of seats available to blacks. Formally ending the protest at a rally in Memorial Stadium that drew seven thousand people, Jemison tried to discourage the idea of attacking the principle of segregation. "You cannot change traditions and customs overnight. . . . If the good people of Baton Rouge don't want to sit beside us, we don't want to sit beside them." Many felt let down. "An echoing ovation of voices shouting, 'stay off, stay off' rose up after Jemison's statement," reported the *State-Times*.

The denouement turned out to be disappointing. Shortly afterward the UDL leaders filed suit in the state district court against the city of Baton Rouge. They challenged the attorney general's June 18 ruling, argued that Ordinance 251 was invalid, and sought to have Ordinance 222 reinstated. The case was eventually dismissed; it did not even reach the state supreme court. In 1957, shortly after the U.S. Supreme Court struck down bus segregation in Montgomery, Alabama, Jemison took his fight into the federal courts. It took another five years, however, to obtain a definitive ruling that desegregated buses in Baton Rouge.[56]

In light of the stupendous impact of the Montgomery bus boycott, it is tempting to view its precursor in Baton Rouge as a lost opportunity, a protest that, handled differently, might have become the historical turning point that Montgomery became. The similarities between the two boycotts are striking. In both cases, the leaders were young, educated Baptist ministers whose fathers were well-known clergymen; both had lived in their communities for a relatively short time; both had succeeded pastors who were well-known activists. As in Montgomery, NAACP members were prominent in the leadership of the boycott, but in both cities they formed a broad coalition, an "organization of organizations," to include every section of the black community. Like the Montgomery Improvement Association, the United Defense League used mass meetings to mobilize support, maintain enthusiasm, and raise money. Both Jemison and King used their preaching skills to great effect. Finally, both the MIA and the UDL started out with similar demands, asking for "first-come, first-served" segregated seating.

Why, then, did the Baton Rouge bus boycott have so little impact or effect? One could argue that the leaders of the UDL made a mistake in calling off the boycott so quickly and that they erred in challenging the law in the state courts rather than the federal courts. Some UDL leaders retrospectively criticized Jemison for being insufficiently militant. Certainly, he became increasingly conservative over the years and played little role in the civil rights movement of the 1960s. In Montgomery, on the other hand, the presence of several left-wing white and militant black activists — people who had links to SCEF and the Highlander Folk School — helped to push the bus boycott into a more uncompromising direction.

But there is a simpler explanation for the contrasting outcomes of the two boycotts. The Baton Rouge bus boycott ended because Ordinance 251, while falling short of what the protesters wanted, represented an improvement over the old arrangements. Had the MIA been offered a similar compromise during the early days of its protest, the Montgomery bus boycott might well have been equally short-lived. After all, at the outset the MIA leaders expected the boycott to last a week or so. Similarly, to say that Jemison was no King ignores the fact that King, too, was not a militant activist when he was tapped for the leadership of the MIA and that it took months for him to emerge as a dominant leader and nationally known figure. In short, it was the obduracy of the Montgomery city council that prolonged the boycott, reinforced its militancy, caused it to escalate its demands, allowed King to develop as a leader, and inadvertently accorded it great historical significance. In the final analysis, the main reason why the two boycotts turned out so differently might well have been timing: one took place before the *Brown* decision, the other afterward. In 1953, the Baton Rouge city council proved amenable to some sort of compromise. In 1955–56, when white hostility to *Brown* pervaded the political atmosphere, the Montgomery city council felt that compromise would be seen as capitulation.

In one vital respect, however, Baton Rouge was every bit as important as Montgomery. The Baton Rouge bus boycott showed that even in the Deep South blacks were ready to openly protest, en masse, against the segregated status quo. An entire community had been speedily mobilized and effectively organized.

The following year blacks in New Orleans came together in a similar exhibition of unity and mass action. Every May, the city's schoolchildren paraded in honor of John McDonogh, the slaveholder who had bequeathed his fortune to the public schools of Baltimore and New Orleans. In 1954, however, black teachers, parents, and principals formally protested against the continuation of a segregated parade in which black children marched at the rear of the procession. When the school board rejected a compromise worked out by schools superintendent James Redmond and black lawyer Revius Ortique, a proposal to boycott the event attracted swift and overwhelming approval. Organized by Ortique and by NAACP branch president Arthur J. Chapital, the protest united the city's black leadership. When the parade took place on May 8, only thirty-four black children participated. This "stunning display of solidarity," writes Kim Lacy Rogers, was "the first mass protest by New Orleans' Negro community." [57]

Nine days later, the Supreme Court of the United States ruled for the plaintiffs in *Brown* v. *Board of Education*. The decision was a triumph for the NAACP Legal Defense Fund. The white reaction to *Brown,* however, sharply revealed the limits of change through litigation. With no political support from within the state, the NAACP needed six years to integrate a single school. Blacks proved powerless to further the cause of integration through the ballot box. And the convergence of racism and red-baiting rendered white support for integration politically insignificant.

Chapter 7

THE IMPACT OF *BROWN*

On May 12, 1950, an audience of Shreveport Rotarians listened to Ben C. Dawkins Jr. speak on the future of the South. The son of a federal judge, and soon to become one himself, Dawkins would exercise great influence over the course of race relations in north Louisiana. "Educate our negroes," he exhorted the Rotary Club; give them better public health care, "eliminate the miserable negro slums," and provide blacks with "economic opportunities commensurate with their abilities." There was no questioning the speaker's sincerity. Violent racism repelled him: as a young boy in Monroe he had witnessed a horrific lynching. He won election to the Caddo Parish school board in 1949 committed to making drastic improvements to black public education. As president of the board he pushed through a $20 million bond issue, $11 million of it to build twenty-eight new black schools. For this and other efforts to assist blacks, *Look* magazine honored Shreveport as one of eleven "All-American Cities" of 1954.

Of his attachment to segregation, however, Dawkins left his audience in no doubt. Decrying the "politicians, social reformers, and starry-eyed do-gooders" who "harried" and "badgered" the South, he warned that the abolition of segregation "would only result in mongrelization of both races." Segregation, he insisted, was "our foundation stone . . . upon which we must stand forever."[1]

Even the most educated whites found it difficult to discuss integration calmly and rationally. In 1954, after becoming chairman of the board of Flint-Goodridge Hospital, a black institution owned by Dillard University, Rosa Keller tried to persuade the Orleans Parish Medical Society to admit black doctors to membership. When she first took this idea to the society's president, Dr. Alton Ochsner, the reaction of this world-famous surgeon reminded her of Captain Queeg in *The Caine Mutiny*. "His face began to twitch, his hands nervously moved things around on his desk, his eyes darted around quite strangely, and he mumbled incoherently." He then exploded, using language that made Keller blush. "I was utterly taken aback," she recalled, "and when I went home I went to my room and just broke into tears." Ochsner, surgeon to Latin American dictators, founder of Ochsner Hospital, and a man at the pinnacle of New Orleans's social elite, could not stomach the thought of associating with blacks as equals.[2]

However, like the "Kremlinologists" who once pored over the opaque officialese of Soviet leaders to discern the true meaning behind their strident dogma, politically astute blacks did not automatically accept segregationist rhetoric at face value. By the early 1950s many blacks believed that white attitudes were far more malleable than the evidence of public and political discourse would suggest. Recent southern history was littered with rhetorical "nevers" that had become obsolete soon after their utterance. Between 1944 and 1954 whites had, in fact, accepted a degree of change that would have been unthinkable fifty or even twenty years ealier. Many blacks felt optimistic that, despite oratorical saber rattling, southern whites would bow to judicial mandates and accept the gradual dismantling of racial segregation.

In April 1954, for example, Judges Wayne G. Borah, Edwin F. Hunter, and Ben C. Dawkins ordered the admission of four blacks to Southwest Louisiana Institute at Lafayette. Local state senator M. Eloi Girard opposed plans to build a black college in Lafayette, advising his constituents that "some form or degree of integration — like it or not — is coming sooner or later." By November, some eighty blacks had been admitted without any untoward incidents. "These Negroes have acted as ladies and gentlemen," reported Isom Guillory of the state board of education. The following December, Judge Hunter ruled that fifteen black applicants must be accepted by McNeese State College in Lake Charles. According to the historian of that institution, President Lether Frazar "called a meeting of male students as soon as he knew that integration was inevitable, and he told them that he was not going to have any trouble." None occurred. By the spring of 1955 Southeastern Louisiana College in Hammond had also been integrated; according to Daniel Byrd, the dean met the first black students and wished them well. "The white students are also adjusting quite nicely and appear much more relaxed and friendly."[3]

The integration of the New Orleans public libraries furnished another instance of white resistance to change collapsing virtually overnight. In 1953 Rosa Keller, a woman of strongly egalitarian instincts, used her appointment to the library board to press for the admission of blacks, who were then excluded from both the central library and all the main branches. A petition from the League of Classroom Teachers and an ecumenical delegation headed by Monsignor Henry C. Bezou, superintendent of the city's Catholic schools, argued the same case. The library board, however, vehemently opposed integration, causing a discouraged Keller, finding herself in a minority of one, to consider resigning. To her astonishment, Mayor Morrison urged her to stay and fight and promised to back her up. In 1954, after what Keller remembered as a "very ugly and difficult battle," blacks were quietly admitted to the branch libraries, and the new central library opened as an integrated institution.[4]

One could, of course, read too much into such integration victories. Like the admission of a few blacks to university graduate schools, the integration of public libraries involved institutions peripheral to the daily lives of most white people. Schools were a different matter.

Nonetheless, the NAACP radiated optimism. In March 1953, as the South awaited the Supreme Court's decision in the *Brown* cases, A. P. Tureaud and Daniel Byrd asked for an informal meeting with the St. Helena Parish school board, the defendant in one of the NAACP's integration suits. When the board agreed, a delighted Byrd told Thurgood Marshall that "with any luck we could come out with an agreement for a 'Consent Decree' and integration by September."

The meeting, however, did not go quite as Byrd anticipated. Hoping to preempt the NAACP's action, the superintendent of schools, J. L. Meadows, "converted the leading Negro minister and the Negro principal [to] separate but equal . . . saying that the Board will give the Negroes what they want." When the school board met some thirty parents, the minister, and the principal, Meadows offered immediate improvements that would leave segregation intact. But the NAACP delegation of Byrd, Tureaud, and J. K. Haynes refused to bite. For about ninety minutes, they argued the inevitability and desirability of integration. Byrd mentioned the potential financial savings, told the board how to desegregate without friction, and offered the services of the NAACP in working out a plan. After the meeting, Byrd was still optimistic. The board had listened quietly, and Meadows confided off the record "that he is looking for integration within the next three years."[5]

When the Supreme Court finally handed down its decision in the *Brown* cases on May 17, 1954, the NAACP was sanguine about the outlook for compliance. At a conference in Atlanta five days after the ruling, Thurgood Marshall asked for a state-by-state report from the organization's southern leaders. With the exception of Mississippi, all were guardedly optimistic. Resistance was predicted in the Black Belt areas, but most expected that a few well-aimed suits would break the back of it. In Arkansas, three counties were already moving towards integration. Summing up the situation in Louisiana, Dr. E. A. Johnson told the conclave that in Orleans and St. Helena parishes, where suits had already been filed, desegregation was an imminent possibility. "If we can succeed in building a climate of opinion favorable to immediate desegregation," the NAACP advised its branches, "legal action may not be necessary."[6]

In a tone of sorrowful resignation, many of the leading newspapers in Louisiana urged compliance. *Brown* was now the law of the land, the *New Orleans Item* reminded its readers. "Wisdom calls for calmness and moderation, for reflection and discussion of ways best to live with the decision." The *Times-Picayune* agreed. "All the South can do — all the states and localities can do," it reasoned, "is shoulder the burden the court has placed upon them." The *Baton Rouge State-Times* urged the "level-headed leaders of the two races to work the problem out with the least friction possible." Its sister paper, the *Morning Advocate,* pronounced the status quo "doomed."[7]

Even in Shreveport, that bastion of conservatism, Catholic pastor Joseph B. Gremillion felt that *Brown* would soon gain acceptance. "The whites are surprised," he wrote. "Some way or other they never thought this would happen, and then again they knew it was coming. . . . The mythical 'man in the street' doesn't like it one bit, but he is not over-wrought." The politicians and leading citizens would put on a show of resistance, he predicted, but it would be halfhearted. After two or three years of litigation, he felt that Shreveport, along with the rest of the state, would accept integration. Gremillion himself greeted *Brown* with joy and relief: "Truly a magnificent step forward in the realization of our ideal of a Christian society."[8]

Sanguine prognoses such as these profoundly underestimated whites' horror of integrated schools. The term "racist" has become devalued through overuse: it fails to prepare one for the depths of disgust, contempt, and condescension with which whites, to varying degrees, still regarded their black fellow citizens in the 1950s. When state senator William Rainach wrote that "we have the bedrock of human nature on our side," he stated his own bedrock belief in black inferiority. Few southern whites contested that belief. True, whites now tended to use sociological arguments to justify segregation, trotting out statistics on crime, illiteracy, illegitimacy, and disease. But such "proofs" simply reaffirmed the assumption of black inferiority. "I do not particularly like to quote venereal disease statistics about any group, or to cite crime rates," Senator Ellender informed a black correspondent. "But these are things we must recognize. . . . Your race is not perfect, that is something you must understand." Actually, Ellender loved to quote statistics on crime and venereal disease; he assiduously collected them for over thirty years.[9]

Allen J. Ellender, a Catholic from Houma, Terrebonne Parish, a United States senator for thirty-six years, was a true believer when it came to race. He first made his mark in the Senate with a twenty-seven-hour filibuster against the 1938 antilynching bill and, although he softened his rhetoric over the decades, he never abandoned the sentiments he expressed in that oratorical marathon. Ellender's basic anti–civil rights speech rested on the premise that "the Negro is inferior to the white man." All the other arguments simply elaborated that point, and the senator merely had to jot down a few notes in order to unlock his rich store of racial myth. The "habits" of Negroes "indicate inherent dishonesty, laziness, slothfulness, etc." As a "business and professional man, the Negro is sub-mediocre." The black soldier "is an inferior soldier." Blacks had no capacity for civilization and government — witness Liberia, Nigeria, Haiti, and Harlem. "Good Caucasian stock" had developed the United States, but progress in the South had been retarded because of the presence of blacks. "Any 'Negro' of notable ability owes success to white blood." Racial amalgamation, on the other hand, resulted in barbarity and backwardness: "Negro blood has degraded and ultimately destroyed every white civilization where allowed to mongrelize."[10]

The fear of "racial amalgamation" infused ultrasegregationist thinking and gave it a visceral passion that seemed to defy logic. "Fantastic as it may appear," Leander Perez divulged to the Young Men's Business Club of New Orleans, "the social aim" of integration "is a Negroid South." State senator William Rainach shared that conviction. "I have reluctantly been forced to the conclusion," he informed a Minden teacher, "that nothing short of the extinction of both the white and black races into a shade of brown will satisfy those who are attempting to uproot all our traditions and ways of life."[11]

The "amalgamation" theory viewed black males as actual and potential rapists or, at the very least, agents of sexual corruption. As Baton Rouge attorney Paul Borron warned Governor Robert Kennon, the "distressingly low moral standard of the Negro" made the prospect of having black teachers over white children unthinkable. Integration, another man predicted, "would cause either fornication or . . . intermarriage resulting in mulattoes by the millions." As Kim Lacy Rogers has noted "sex stewed at the center of the white man's terror and rage, joined to a blind, furious racial ignorance and sexual insecurity." That statement needs amplifying: many white women felt the same way. "What, pray God, is going to happen to the Psyche of genteelly raised white children, particularly little girls, . . . when deliberately thrown among those uninhibited, boisterous, undisciplined, unrestrained primitive aborigines?" a New Orleans woman wondered.[12]

Not all segregationists subscribed to the idea that integration would lead inexorably to racial amalgamation. Many simply regarded blacks as a disease-ridden, mentally inferior, and culturally backward people with whom they did not want to associate. "What the Negro is and the way he lives is the cause of his being segregated," wrote one father. "I have no desire to ever subject my-self or my family to their social companionship." Another parent pointed to "common-law concubinage, rapes, knifings, murders, thefts and assaults, irre-sponsibility and lawlessness in general" as reasons why "I couldn't be happy if I am compelled by law to raise my family" within an integrated society.[13]

The alleged cultural deficiencies of black children became a major justifica-tion for school segregation. "I am not qualified to know whether there is such a thing as an inferior or superior race," testified Clarence Scheps, president of the Orleans Parish school board and comptroller of Tulane University. He did know, however, that "the average Negro child" came from a "vastly inferior" environmental background and a "deprived home," many lacking "facilities of a sanitary nature almost taken for granted in the homes of the average white family." In an integrated situation, blacks would be unable to compete and whites would be held back. Mayor Morrison, while eventually prepared to concede "token" integration rather than close the public schools, believed it would be "calamitous" to "dilute our teaching facilities half and half with black and white mixed side by side."[14]

Louisiana's lawmakers trumpeted defiance of the Supreme Court. The state legislature responded immediately to the *Brown* decision by passing a raft of bills and resolutions to condemn and obstruct the ruling. With only three dis-senting votes in the house and one in the senate, the legislature labelled *Brown* "an unwarranted and unprecedented abuse of power" and branded racial inte-gration "intolerable, impractical, and in the ultimate sense unenforceable." Three bills designed to circumvent *Brown* became law after minimal debate: one restricted state support to all but segregated public schools; another em-powered local school boards to assign pupils to schools on an individual basis; a third mandated segregated schools under the "inherent police power of the state" as a means of preserving "public health, morals, better education, peace, and good order." Submitted to the voters as Constitutional Amendment 16, this act also empowered the legislature to amend the constitution at any time, rather than every other year.

A new Joint Legislative Committee to Maintain Segregation, chaired by state senator William M. Rainach of Claiborne Parish, assumed the task of drafting obstructionist laws and devising a broad strategy to forestall integration. Under the driving leadership of Rainach and assisted by the wily Leander Perez, the JLC rapidly became the spearhead of opposition to *Brown*. As part of a statewide campaign to whip up support for Amendment 16, Rainach blasted the NAACP in a fifteen-minute television commercial. "The arrogant, alien NAACP and its hirelings," he warned, proposed substituting "a foreign system of life that creates strife and confusion for an order of life under which our white and colored people are making progress."

When the votes were counted in November, Amendment 16 carried by a margin of more than five to one. "The pillars of strength," Rainach jubilantly noted, "are a crescent beginning at Concordia and extending north and west along the Arkansas border and then south along the Texas line to Sabine." Here, in the parishes with the highest black population, the amendment carried by margins of at least seven to one and in many cases over ten to one. Similar levels of support obtained in the Florida Parishes. Predictably, Plaquemines Parish, the fiefdom of Leander Perez, turned in the most lopsided margin of all, forty-eight to one.[15]

Differing constructions, it is true, could be placed on these political developments. Only 30 percent of the state's registered electors bothered to vote on Amendment 16, suggesting that most whites did not feel particularly strongly about *Brown*. The depth and durability of the legislature's opposition to *Brown* was also difficult to gauge. The legislature had a herdlike quality, as well as a tendency towards theatrics and buffoonery, and its show of defiance consisted of measures that legislators well knew would be knocked down by the federal courts. Governor Robert F. Kennon, moreover, seemed skeptical about efforts to frustrate *Brown* and declined to assume the leadership of the ultrasegregationists. Kennon, who had helped to swing Louisiana into the Republican column in 1952, entertained hopes of an appointment to the federal bench and did not want to antagonize President Eisenhower. "He supported us to the minimum extent," Rainach recalled.[16]

Yet white *support* for integration was all but invisible. At the beginning of 1955, the Louisiana Committee on Human Rights, an offshoot of the Southern Regional Council, held a meeting to assess white attitudes. The reports were almost uniformly pessimistic. In Baton Rouge, a Methodist minister who actively opposed Amendment 16 had been dismissed from his church. Regarding Thibodaux, Father Jerome Drolet detected no improvement in race relations since 1940. Southern liberals had not been prepared for *Brown,* the conferees agreed, and this was as true in Louisiana as elsewhere. "The decision came before these people were willing to come out publicly and say they were in favor of integration. Even if they feel that segregation is wrong, they cannot publicly say that and keep their face."[17]

The weakness of the LCHR itself obliquely reflected the continuing strength of segregationist sentiment. When the Second World War ended, the interracial movement was moribund in Louisiana, and attempts to revive it met with black skepticism and white hostility. In Baton Rouge Leo M. Favrot, a former Rosenwald Fund official, assembled a biracial committee in 1946. Favrot reported that blacks were wary of supporting the Southern Regional Council as long as it refused to squarely oppose segregation, and he also advised that a state interracial committee would likely founder on white opposition. By 1951, after Favrot's death, the Baton Rouge committee was reported to be "on its last legs," and soon thereafter it expired. The New Orleans Committee on Race Relations, originally formed in 1944 but only intermittently active, provided the basis for the Louisiana Committee on Human Rights, which by the early 1950s had gathered about 120 members. Despite the commitment of its chairman, Reverend Albert D'Orlando, a Boston-born Unitarian minister resident in New Orleans since 1950, the LCHR had a tenuous existence.[18]

The Catholic Church seemed to offer a beacon of hope. The church in Louisiana was already inching away from segregation. In 1948 two blacks entered Notre Dame Seminary in New Orleans. A year later Archbishop Rummel abandoned the practice whereby black parishioners marched at the rear of the annual Holy Name parade, and when the board of City Park refused to permit an integrated parade, he cancelled the event. Rummel also ordered the removal of all "white" and "colored" signs from the city's churches. In 1952 Loyola University admitted two black graduate students. The following year Bishop Jules Jeanmard of Lafayette ordained a black priest for the diocesan clergy, the first bishop in the Deep South to do so. In 1953 Archbishop Rummel ordained Aubrey Osborne, the first black priest in the archdiocese of New Orleans. In a pastoral letter that year, he urged a stop to the informal segregation that persisted within churches. "Let there be no further discrimination in the pews, at the Communion rail, at the confessional and in parish meetings, just as there will be no segregation in the kingdom of heaven."[19]

The Catholic hierarchy made clear its opposition to the obstructionist actions of the state legislature after the *Brown* decision. Thanks to Archbishop Rummel's intercession, a bill authorizing school boards to give financial assistance to children in private schools never came to a vote. And in a private, hand-delivered letter to Governor Kennon, Rummel registered a strong protest against the tenor of the segregation bills, endorsing an editorial in the archdiocesan newsletter that condemned them as reactionary and unconstitutional. Such prejudice "should have no place on the Statute Books of a democratic state or in the government of a free people."[20]

The church's own reaction to *Brown* seemed to augur a speedy desegregation of parochial schools. "We fully recognize and approve of the decision," stated Monsignor Henri Bezou, superintendent of schools for the Archdiocese of New Orleans. In September 1954 Father William Crandell, southern provincial of the Jesuits, issued a letter of guidance for the integration of Jesuit schools, parishes, and retreat houses. "We must say that race segregation, based solely on race, is seriously immoral and, therefore, may not be approved by a Catholic." A few months after *Brown II,* Archbishop Rummel stated that the integration of Catholic schools would begin "not before September 1956" and that "during the intervening year pastoral letters and other instructive communications will serve to prepare the way for the most propitious plan to be followed." Many assumed this to mean that integration would begin in 1956, and few doubted that the speedy integration of the 180-odd schools in the Archdiocese of New Orleans (over half of them in Orleans Parish, accounting for well over a third of the city's pupils) would render the maintenance of segregated public schools exceedingly difficult.[21]

It did not happen. An overwhelming majority of the laity bitterly opposed racial integration, and much of the priesthood silently sympathized with their views. Archbishop Rummel, old and frail, abandoned his half-promise of early integration, and the Catholic schools in Louisiana remained entirely segregated until 1962, two full years after the first public schools integrated. Instead of setting a moral and practical example to the public schools, the church set an example of procrastination and delay.

Father Joseph H. Fichter knew only too well the racism that pervaded clergy and laity. A trained sociologist with a doctorate from Harvard, Fichter joined the faculty of Loyola University in 1947. Displaying a passion for research that would land him in hot water on many occasions, he conceived the idea for a four-volume study of a southern parish that would lay bare the social roots of the Catholic Church in the South. He selected Mater Dolorosa, a "white" parish in a middle-class section of Carrollton, in uptown New Orleans. His methodology was simple: "Each major religious function of the parish is measured against the 'ideal' set forth in the teaching and legislation of the Catholic Church." During 1948, he and a team of student assistants put the congregation and clergy of Mater Dolorosa Parish under the microscope.

The results shattered Fichter's original hypothesis. As he later explained, "We looked for an internal social integration that would be manifested in daily human relations and that would be peculiarly Catholic and parochial.

We failed to find it." Solidarity among the parishioners was based not so much upon Catholic doctrine as upon class and, even more so, upon race. Moreover, in both belief and behavior, these in many ways typical white Catholics were "at considerable distance from the complete Christian ideology of the Catholic Church." This was especially true on the matter of race. In order to test the congruence of doctrine and belief, Fichter conducted a crude opinion poll. Asked "If the kindergartens of the parochial schools were opened to Catholic Negro children, would you allow your own children to attend them?" only 26 percent answered affirmatively. Asked if they favored the continuation of separate parishes for Negro Catholics, 88 percent answered yes. Fichter noticed that the dozen or so blacks who attended Mass at Mater Dolorosa always sat at the back of the church.

Father Joseph Pyzikiewicz, the parish priest, was a Polish immigrant in his mid-fifties who had pastored Mater Dolorosa since 1933. His political and racial attitudes reflected those of his parishioners. The word "nigger" came trippingly off his tongue, and he soon grew to resent Fichter's racial liberalism. "I don't want you emptying my church with your race sermons," he once told him. Fichter discovered that the subject of race was "so irritating to Father Joseph that he could not have an objective intelligent conversation about it." Indeed, the pastor became so displeased with Fichter's study that he persuaded the Jesuit authorities to suppress publication of the remaining three volumes.[22]

In his own endeavors on behalf of racial equality, Fichter was a whirlwind of energy and initiative. In consultation with Harvard sociologists Gordon Allport and Samuel Stouffer, he drew up a plan to desegregate Loyola University and, by way of preparation, organized two new interracial groups. The Catholic Commission on Human Rights (CCHR) became the New Orleans unit of the Catholic Committee of the South; its black participants included A. P. Tureaud and several faculty members from Xavier University. The Southeastern Regional Interracial Commission (SERINCO), a student group, drew members from Sacred Heart College in Grand Coteau, Spring Hill College in Mobile, and the colleges in New Orleans. Both groups met regularly, put out newsletters, and pressed for the wholesale integration of the church, including its schools, colleges, and hospitals. Fichter acted as their advisor and chaplain.[23]

Fichter struggled, however, against a powerful current of indifference, timidity, and downright hostility. Only two white parishes welcomed the CCHR's interracial services. With respect to his plan to desegregate Loyola, Fichter recalled, "the goodwill and cooperation of the administration and faculty . . . were not forthcoming." The board of directors tried to rein him in, complaining in November 1947 that "Father Fichter is moving entirely too fast in view of conditions here in the city." A few months later it criticized him for neglecting to secure official permission before inviting black speakers onto campus. "The Board felt that Father Fichter had pushed the matter of racial relations too far." Loyola was integrated at a snail's pace. In 1950 Father Thomas Shields, Loyola's president, allowed Louis Twomey to enroll twenty blacks in the Institute of Industrial Relations, a peripheral institution that offered noncredit courses to nonstudents. Twomey and Fichter were profoundly disappointed by Shields' failure to follow through: in 1951 the law school rejected an application from Richard Gumbel, "one of the all-time best products of Xavier University." In 1952, two years after LSU, Loyola Law School finally admitted two black students. However, ten more years elapsed before the undergraduate school accepted blacks.[24]

Derided by some fellow Jesuits as the "social salvation boys," Fichter and his principal ally, Louis Twomey, made a great moral impression on many students. If anything, Twomey had the greater influence, for while Fichter's researches took him away from Loyola for lengthy stretches, Twomey taught there continuously for more than twenty years. Among the young students who attended his classes on jurisprudence, with their strong emphasis upon social justice and God-given natural rights, were "Moon" Landrieu, a future mayor of New Orleans; William J. Guste Jr., a future attorney general of Louisiana; and John P. Nelson, who became a civil rights attorney and prominent Catholic layman.

Yet Loyola educated generations of committed segregationists. Indeed, Father Martin Burke, reputed to be one of Loyola's most eminent philosophers, vigorously defended racial segregation in his lectures and seminars. In truth, Fichter and Twomey, "the terrible Loyola twosome whose names stuck in the throats of the Loyola alumni," were mavericks. Archbishop Rummel tolerated and even encouraged their activities, but most of the Jesuits regarded them as a source of annoyance and embarrassment. Despite its official pronouncements, the southern province of the Society of Jesus did virtually nothing to promote integration. Its schools and retreat houses continued to exclude blacks, Twomey complained to Rome. "Our pulpits are practically silent on the race question." When the CCHR held a series of public lectures on school integration, the radio station owned by Loyola, WWL, declined to broadcast them. WWL did, however, air "Lifelines," a daily dose of ultra-right-wing political opinion paid for by Texas oil billionaire H. L. Hunt. Most Jesuits, Twomey believed, subscribed to white supremacy in one form or another. In the opinion of lawyer John P. Nelson, "The Catholic educational system was as conservative as the Citizens Council."[25]

In the sprawling diocese of Alexandria, which embraced the scattered Catholic population of north Louisiana, interracialism had a solitary outpost in Shreveport's Friendship House. The child of a Catholic lay movement based in Chicago, Friendship House opened its doors with the blessing of Bishop Charles P. Greco and the enthusiastic support of Father J. B. Gremillion, pastor of St. Joseph's Parish. Located in a small house in a black neighborhood and staffed by lay workers who practiced evangelic poverty, Friendship House extended a welcome to all and offered, in Gremillion's words, "a drawbridge of friendship across this moat of discrimination." Its regular symposia, featuring such speakers as A. P. Tureaud, Clarence Laws, and J. K. Haynes, attracted an interracial and ecumenical audience. White bigwigs were encouraged to attend: Friendship House believed that by associating whites and blacks "in a social and intellectual level" and by exploring "all the aspects of discrimination and segregation," such contact represented an effective way of "working for an integrated society."[26]

Shortly after it opened in October 1953, police raided Friendship House and arrested its two staff members, Anne Foley and Mary Dolan. They were held as prostitutes, then as suspected Communists, and finally released after Father Gremillion's intercession. In August 1954 a patrolman arrested Foley and two companions, a white man and a black woman, as they watched the sunset over Lake Cross from a parked car. "They were escorted to the city jail," wrote Gremillion, "fingerprinted and locked up with drunks and derelicts." Denied a phone call, they remained in jail overnight, "the butt of crudity and cursing."

On July 31, 1955, Friendship House closed after Bishop Greco withdrew his support. Three weeks earlier, the diocesan newsletter had revealed that a two-hundred-pupil Catholic high school to be constructed in Shreveport would "open its doors to students of all races." This was news to Shreveport whites, who had been told that the proposed school was for blacks. When Friendship House pointed out the discrepancy in the diocese's newsletter, it was denounced by the press and repudiated by Paul F. O'Brien, a wealthy businessman who had donated the land for the school and who happened to be Shreveport's most respected Catholic layman. Diocesan officials quickly backtracked. It would be "unlikely," they explained, that any white students would apply to the new school in the near future. Meanwhile, Friendship House was to be closed in the interests of "promoting human solidarity." As an irate parishioner remonstrated with Gremillion, "You're pushing this nigger business too far, Father. It's all right to give the nigger better wages and more schooling, but this business of social equality, no sir!"[27]

The church authorities frankly avowed a very specific and material reason for soft-pedaling integration. If the parochial schools admitted blacks before the public schools did, there might be a mass exodus of white children. The church also feared retaliation from the state legislature, which might cut off the subsidies it provided Catholic schools in the form of free textbooks, free lunches, and free bus transportation. It might even impose taxes on church property. Parochial schools were not merely the church's pride and joy, they were part of its lifeblood. An essential tool for perpetuating the faith, Catholic education was the principal attraction of that faith as far as many Catholics were concerned. To destroy or damage its schools would be to strike at the heart and soul of the church.

Because the Catholic Church formulated no regional response to *Brown,* the pace of change would be dictated by the individual bishops, and the bishops, neither seeking nor desiring unity, sought refuge in delay.

The Alexandria diocese provides an excellent example of the casuistical reasoning whereby the church endorsed the morality of integration but furnished multiple reasons for inaction. It ruled out a sweeping edict from Bishop Greco on the grounds that "an order from on top would result in an effective boycott of the schools." Thus the speed and means of integration would depend upon a variety of local factors, including the ratio of black to white, the economic status of the area and its people, the quality and effectiveness of its leaders, the willingness of people to make sacrifices, and the desire of the Negro to integrate — blacks, it asserted, were primarily interested in economic equality and presented "no solid front . . . as to just what they want this year, in this community, in these given circumstances." Finally, integration was contingent upon "the state of perfection in grace that a given community has reached. . . . The people of some parishes simply have a better grasp of the practical need for implementing the doctrine of the Mystical Body than others." [28]

Even *before* the segregationist resistance had built up steam, the bishops' response to white opposition was a characteristic, paralyzing caution. Their withdrawal of support from the Catholic Committee of the South was of a piece with the closure of Friendship House: enthusiastic interracialism had become an embarrassment. The CCS held what turned out to be its last convention in 1953. It "barely staggered through 1954," writes Katherine Anne Martensen, and "simply withered away" as the bishops "allowed it to die." In 1935 Archbishop Rummel had advised the Holy See that in the opinion of the southern episcopate public discussions of racial matters "are apt to do more harm than good" and that the race question "should be permitted to work itself out." This conviction still dominated the bishops' thinking twenty years later. [29]

Archbishop Rummel thought he had good reason to approach desegregation circumspectly. Experience had taught him not to overestimate the authority of his office, or that of the church generally, in matters temporal. In 1953, for example, he had thrown his full support behind an organizing drive among the sugarcane workers by the National Agricultural Workers Union. Parish priests like Harry Maloney, Jerome Drolet, and Roland Boudreaux offered advice, raised money, opened their churches, and, according to union leader H. L. Mitchell, did "everything except sign up the members and collect the dues." When NAWU called a strike, the archdiocese funnelled thousands of dollars to the union to help feed the strikers. Rummel's attempts to mediate, however, failed completely. Although most of the sugar growers were Catholics, they rejected his pleas to negotiate with the strikers: they were bent on breaking the strike, and break it they did. The following year, Rummel expressed unequivocal opposition to an antiunion "right-to-work" bill — introduced by Willie Rainach — being considered by the state legislature. But once again his intervention proved ineffective and the bill passed. These defeats brought home to Rummel the extent to which Catholics were prepared to oppose him when he addressed political issues.[30]

Like most Christians, Catholics tend to ignore the church's social teaching whenever it suits them, but this characteristic seemed to be especially pronounced in Louisiana. "We Catholics of French descent," Father Gremillion believed, "inherit Voltaire's world, a world without the spiritual, and Jansen's spiritual life, a life isolated from the taint of the world." Historically, too, Louisiana Catholics had a tendency to openly defy ecclesiastical authority, a reflection, some believed, of the anticlericalism that they inherited from the early colonists and which the French Revolution had accentuated. Archbishop Rummel was under no illusions that, if and when he ordered desegregation, the white laity would meekly submit. Fear of "another open break with the Catholic laity such as occurred during the 'right-to-work controversy,'" Louis Twomey believed, explained the Archbishop's refusal to act when the Knights of Columbus insisted on segregated seating during a basketball game at the new, officially nonsegregated Loyola field house.[31]

In New Orleans the full fury of Catholic ultrasegregationists had yet to be released, but by the end of 1955 Rummel was already worried by the first rumblings of revolt among the white laity. In September Rabbi Julian Feibelman had presented the Orleans Parish school board with a petition in support of integration bearing 179 signatures. This galvanized Emile Wagner, the only Catholic on the school board, into working up a prosegregation petition of more than 14,000 signatures, a campaign that launched the Citizens Council movement in New Orleans. Sensing which way the wind was blowing, Daniel Byrd warned Thurgood Marshall to expect more opposition. "The Archbishop has been vacillating . . . and I don't have too much hope in his having any undue influence over Wagner." Rummel began to apply the brakes. In October he wrote to the head of the Josephites to complain that their priests in New Orleans were pressing for "rather immediate integration." "It is my conviction that integration cannot be forced down the line on all fronts, especially at the present time when the controversy over integration in the schools is the subject of serious tension. Efforts to push for integration in parish societies, the Catholic Youth Organization, playground programs, etc. would only multiply our difficulties." Rummel doubted that black Catholics shared the Josephites' sense of urgency.[32]

An incident three weeks earlier had reinforced Rummel's caution. On October 1, Father Gerald Lewis, a priest from the Society of the Divine Word seminary in Bay St. Louis, Mississippi, journeyed to Plaquemines Parish to assist Father Clement Meyer with the Sunday services. The night before, Lewis, who was black, received an anonymous telephone call warning him to stay away. When he arrived at St. Cecelia's Chapel in Jesuit Bend, a group of white men barred him from entering the church; the ringleader was Leander Perez's brother.

Rummel, who had approved the assignment of Lewis, called upon the parishioners to repent. When they refused to submit, he closed the chapel. The Vatican praised the archbishop's courage. On December 12, however, Leander Perez himself disrupted a catechism class at Our Lady of Perpetual Help in Jesuit Bend, reportedly forcing the black children to the rear of the church at gunpoint and ejecting one child from the building. Twomey and Fichter urged Rummel to excommunicate Perez; after all, Bishop Jules Jeanmard of Lafayette had recently excommunicated several parishioners of Our Lady of Lourdes Church in Erath for a similar offense. But the archbishop, now approaching his eighth decade and with no stomach for a battle, let the matter pass. "The effect of this leniency," Fichter believed, "seemed to embolden the segregationists." Before the year was out Emile Wagner wrote to the archbishop and bluntly told him that "something more than the mere unsubstantiated declaration of any one man . . . is required to convince intelligent Catholics that they are guilty of sin when they espouse the cause of segregation." Only the Pope, he added, could pronounce on such matters. Rummel ignored this direct challenge to his authority.[33]

By the end of 1955 Father Louis Twomey, an outspoken supporter of integration, had become a regular recipient of segregationist manifestos from anxious and outraged Catholic parents. These missives conjured up a fearful stereotype of the sexually precocious, libidinous and lubricious Negro. "I cannot see my daughters intermingling with negro children," vowed a Chalmette father, "especially the negro boys, who are far in advance [sic] in their knowledge of sex because of their degraded home life." He had "nothing against the negro race," the man added. "I don't believe in mistreating them." According to one grandmother, "It is common among the negroes . . . that when a child reaches puberty it must be 'mated to keep it healthy.' " Confessing to "the shivers" when she imagined her grandaughters going to school with such people, she believed that Negro lack of chastity "is not necessarily because they are colored, but because they have no family pride, as how could they, the poor things." Such letters represented the milder end of the racist spectrum: others, often unsigned, comprised little more than vile epithets and obscenities. "Actually," Twomey admitted to a fellow priest, "I never thought that human beings could put into writing what I have received."[34]

For a while, blacks in Louisiana took heart from the fact that both Earl Long and Chep Morrison, the dominant political figures in the state, were racial moderates. Both men solicited black votes and eschewed racist appeals. By 1956, moreover, black registration had reached 160,000. Perhaps the black vote could influence white politicians to urge compliance with the *Brown* decision.

Their distaste for racial extremism, however, did not lead politicians like Morrison and Long actively to advocate acceptance of integration. They were racially moderate in a Deep South context, which, even in Louisiana, made support for segregation a sine qua non of political survival. Thus Long expressed his "billion percent" approval of segregation. Morrison offered a more modest "100 percent."

Although both Longs and anti-Longs sought black votes, moreover, they did so furtively and never missed an opportunity to attack opponents for pursuing the "bloc vote." Thus in 1948 the Regular Democratic Organization, Earl Long's New Orleans allies, faked a photograph of Mayor Morrison swimming with blacks. "Morrison betrays the white race!" another RDO leaflet proclaimed. "Mayor of New Orleans gives Negroes Equal Political and Social Rights! It is even reported that King Zulu will take Rex's place at the next Mardi Gras!" Morrison himself generally eschewed open appeals to racial prejudice. When pushed, however, he could race-bait with the best of them: in 1960, for example, during his second bid for the governorship, he accused opponent Jimmie Davis of operating an integrated nightclub, with mixed dancing, in Palm Springs.[35]

Blacks thus found themselves in an ambiguous if not contradictory position. On the one hand, they hated segregation and sympathized with the NAACP's platform of equal rights; on the other, they voted for white politicians who never ceased to proclaim their fealty to racial segregation. And while black leaders trumpeted the merits of political participation, they often discouraged members of their own race from running for public office.

Such tactics were defended, of course, with the time-honored arguments that politics is the art of the possible and that blacks had to make the best of things in an imperfect political world. As Republican leader Van Buren Harris put it, the black voter "cannot enjoy the privilege of voting for candidates on merit" but "must trade his vote for specific benefits," using "the old method of the horse trade." Such advice reflected political arithmetic. The low levels of black registration effectively barred blacks from political office. Unable to win election themselves, therefore, black "politicians" functioned primarily as go-betweens who "delivered" black votes to white political factions in return for whatever concessions they could negotiate. The fact that white politicians simultaneously cultivated black support while deploring the Negro "bloc vote" was accepted as part of the electoral game.[36]

Without a doubt, white politicians — the modifier "white" is really superfluous — tried to manipulate black leaders by keeping their expectations low. Private frankness could be quite disarming to people unaccustomed to having personal access to powerful whites. Tête-à-tête, many a politician confided that his public stand against civil rights did not represent his real position, that he had to go through certain motions lest a rabid race-baiter defeat him, and that he would assist blacks as much as he possibly could.[37]

That black voters had to choose between evils, therefore, did not obviate the need to choose, and in the context of postwar Louisiana politics Earl Long was plainly the lesser evil. First, although the division between "Longs" and "anti-Longs" continually shifted, as the civil rights issue became more prominent the most ardent white supremacists were increasingly to be found in the anti-Long camp. Long downplayed the race issue during his 1948 election campaign. Later in the year, most of his political opponents jumped on the Dixiecrat bandwagon, drumming up fear of civil rights legislation to award the "official" Democratic label to States' Rights presidential candidate Strom Thurmond. They even attempted to keep Truman's name from appearing on the ballot. Long, however, frustrated this ploy and remained loyal to the national Democratic party. As governor, moreover, he encouraged black voter registration.[38]

In the second place, blacks were attracted to Long's program of expanded public services. They had already benefited from some of the Longite reforms of the 1930s, particularly the institution of old age pensions and the rebuilding of Charity Hospital in New Orleans, measures passed after Huey's death for which Earl Long took, and deserved, much credit. When Long became governor again in 1948 he raised the state old age pension to $50 a month, paid hefty bonuses to returning war veterans, built hundreds of new schools, and not only increased but also equalized teachers' salaries. It was scarcely surprising that Long received the lion's share of the black vote. As governor, Long made himself accessible to blacks and formed personal relationships with, among others, J. K. Haynes, Dr. E. A. Johnson, Louis Berry, and Ernest Wright.[39]

Politics did not, however, offer a clearcut alternative between Longs and anti-Longs; things were never that simple. Furthermore, state and local politics were so intertwined, often bafflingly so, as to make clear choices extremely difficult.

In New Orleans, for example, most black voters supported Mayor Chep Morrison, who forged a strong alliance with the Orleans Parish Progressive Voters League (OPPVL), the most influential and broad-based black political organization in the city. Originating in a Committee to Re-Elect Truman, the OPPVL was formally organized in March 1949 and included many of the leading figures in the black community. Over the next decade, the OPPVL faithfully supported the Morrison ticket.[40]

Morrison and Long, however, soon became enemies. Morrison, ambitious to be governor, became a prominent anti-Longite; Long itched to secure Morrison's defeat and regain control of New Orleans. Thus the long-running enmity between Morrison and Long faced blacks with perplexing political choices. They could not simply support Morrison for mayor and Long for governor: they had to choose between rival tickets in every election. Caught in constant political crossfire made yet more complicated by backdoor deals both real and imagined, blacks found that maintaining a principled and consistent position became well-nigh impossible.

Long attempted to undercut Morrison's black support in south Louisiana by forming an alliance with Ernest Wright and the People's Defense League. In 1948 Wright resigned his position with the Amalgamated Clothing Workers Union and became a full-time political organizer. With Louis Berry, who acted as the PDL's legal adviser, Wright drummed up support for Long in and around New Orleans and tried to establish the PDL as a statewide organization. By 1950, the PDL claimed chapters in twenty-six parishes. In reality, it took root in only a handful; outside Orleans, it was strongest in Tangipahoa, where it formed an alliance with District Attorney Joe Arthur Sims, a close friend of Earl Long, and ended the ban on black voter registration. The PDL's loyalty to Long exceeded, if anything, the OPPVL's support for Morrison.[41]

The PDL's obeisance to the Long ticket, however, soon tarnished Wright's reputation, especially when he reportedly took payments from the Long camp in return for "delivering" black votes. The PDL's prestige also took a bad knock when Wright endorsed Longite candidate Charles A. Zatarain in the 1950 mayoral election. By then, Long had become extremely unpopular in New Orleans for stripping the city of its municipal independence in a vindictive attempt to destroy Morrison's power. Zatarain's supporters, moreover, made a clumsy attempt to exploit the race issue by distributing photographs of Morrison in the company of Ralph Bunche. Morrison swamped Zatarain with 64 percent of the vote. Nevertheless, the PDL carried on backing the

Long ticket, no matter how hopeless the cause or objectionable the candidate.[42]

The OPPVL's devotion to Morrison, however, also produced strained loyalties. In the 1950 U.S. Senate race, for example, Morrison backed the candidacy of Malcolm Lafargue, who was challenging Russell Long, the popular young incumbent and son of the late Huey Long. The OPPVL obediently endorsed Lafargue, but the decision caused a schism within the organization. Lafargue was a weak candidate, and blacks regarded him as an ardent white supremacist, notwithstanding his role as federal prosecutor in the Minden lynching trial of 1947. Lafargue won the backing of the state's leading "Dixiecrats," including Leander Perez, who had broken with Earl Long to become Louisiana's most strident opponent of civil rights. Blasting the OPPVL as "nothing but trained seals and the rubber-stamp men for Mayor Morrison," ILA president Dave Dennis resigned from the organization, as did Clarence Laws, C. C. Dejoie, and A. P. Tureaud. They all backed Russell Long — Tureaud even appeared on a radio spot with Ernest Wright — who crushed Lafargue. The hidden irony of this split was that Morrison reportedly made a deal with Earl Long before the election. Morrison agreed to do as little as was decently possible for Lafargue, the rumor went, and Long agreed to call off his dogs in the legislature and let New Orleans alone.[43]

Over the following years the number of black political organizations multiplied. Some of these organizations, as well as others that lasted no longer than the current election campaign, simply sold their support to the highest bidder. All but the most extreme segregationist could purchase the support of at least one of them.[44]

The issue of black candidates exemplified the dilemmas confronting black voters as well as the devious nature of Louisiana politics. Many argued that it was futile for blacks to run for political office because without white support, which was never forthcoming, they stood no chance of winning. Worse, black candidates split the Negro vote and damaged the chances of the more liberal white candidates. Others replied that black candidates were essential if blacks were to gain political experience: they stimulated black interest in politics, they spurred voter registration, and they contributed practical knowledge of elections and campaigning.

Lurking behind the debate was a widely held suspicion that certain white politicians — Earl Long was most often mentioned — sponsored black candidates in the hope of splitting the Negro vote and reducing the black support received by political opponents. In 1951 Daniel Byrd accused Ernest Wright of entering Negro candidates for the state legislature at Long's behest, a ploy to hurt the Morrison-backed candidates in Orleans Parish. The gubernatorial candidacy of Kermit A. Parker, a black New Orleans pharmacist who had well-known ties to Long, also evoked cynicism: many interpreted it as a Long strategem to diminish black support for Hale Boggs, who was backed by Morrison and the OPPVL. The OPPVL harbored similar suspicions about the perennial campaigns of Earl J. Amadee, whom the league refused to support.[45]

The reluctance to support black candidates also reflected a fear that assertive political tactics might exacerbate white fears of a Negro "bloc vote" and provoke a backlash against black registration. As political scientist Allan Sindler put it in 1956, "The Negro's entry into politics has been smoothed by the over-all moderation of his demands and by his failure to storm registrar's offices or to insist upon a pro rata'racial allotment of parish posts." But white control of the registration process put blacks in a cleft stick. On the one hand they sought to become a decisive factor in state and local elections; on the other, as Sindler pointed out, it was precisely because the relatively small black vote had *not* been decisive in state politics that whites accepted it with relative equanimity. However, should blacks push too hard, or should a unified black vote regularly hold the balance of power, then whites might well clamp down on black registration.[46]

Hence, while whites could not direct the black vote with any degree of certainty, they could exercise a fair amount of control by manipulating the registration process and trading on black political diffidence.

The most obvious way of manipulating the black vote was to restrict it. Many a politician encouraged black registration only to "freeze" it when safely elected. Further, while Louisiana's factional politics to some extent encouraged black registration by forcing candidates to compete for the black vote, politicians did not like to see high registration levels in their opponents' bailiwicks. "The only way I could persuade the governor [Earl Long] to pass the word to the registrar to let my people register," averred one black New Orleanian, "was by pledging him my loyalty and promising I would not intercede for any Negro who might vote for [other] candidates." By the same token, Long slowed down black registration in New Orleans after black voters there spurned his mayoral candidate, Charles Zatarain, in 1950. Likewise, although Mayor Chep Morrison cultivated the twenty-five to thirty thousand black voters of New Orleans, in the late 1950s he supported attempts to "purge" black voters outside the city after the latter preferred Long to him in the 1955–56 gubernatorial election.[47]

Long has been praised, and rightly so, for encouraging black registration. "As soon as he became governor in 1948," states the most authoritative biography, "Earl passed the word to parish registrars: sign up black voters." Long's role in facilitating black registration should not be exaggerated, however. For one thing, as governor he had only limited influence over local registrars who, with the important exception of Orleans Parish, were appointed by the parish police juries (county commissions). True, registrars could be removed by the Board of Registration, which comprised the governor, lieutenant governor, and speaker of the house, but this power was rarely invoked and was of limited utility in any case, because the local police jury nominated the new registrar. Registrars themselves were low-level functionaries, often women, who had no political weight. Thus local politicians, particularly the sheriff and the district attorney, determined the policy on black registration in any given parish. The idea that Long could dictate the level of black registration by virtue of his possessing a powerful political "machine" is therefore mistaken. Unlike his brother Huey, Long's power depended not so much on formal organization as on informal contacts. As one insider put it, "Earl had more alliances in Louisiana than Solomon had wives." Moreover, factional alignments continually shifted. A sheriff or district attorney might be in the Long camp one year, in the anti-Long camp the next.[48]

Even in parishes where the leading politicians were staunch Longites, there was no clear pattern of high black registration. Washington Parish, for example, a traditional Long stronghold, had only 27 percent black registration in 1956. Even in Winn Parish, Long's own home base, black registration stood at just 29 percent in 1952 and 57 percent in 1956. The most that can be said is that some Longite politicians encouraged high levels of black registration while others did not.

Nor did a high level of voter support for Long ensure a high level of black registration: many of the most pro-Long parishes had low levels; some of the most anti-Long ones had high levels. In the 1956 election, for example, Long failed to carry thirteen parishes in the first primary. In two of them, black registration was nil; in two more it was less than 1 percent; in one it stood at 10 percent; in five it ranged between 11 and 49 percent; and in three the level exceeded 50 percent.

There was no consistent correlation, therefore, between high black registration and support for Long by key local officials. It was true, however, that the strongest opponents of black voting tended to be vehemently anti-Long. Black registration was nil, for example, in the majority-black cotton parishes of Tensas, East Carroll, Madison, and West Feliciana, which fell within the jurisdiction of District Attorney Thompson Clarke, a vehement anti-Longite. In Claiborne Parish, home of Willie Rainach, the most conservative member of the Louisiana Senate, black registration was negligible. And only a few dozen blacks voted in Plaquemines Parish, satrapy of Leander H. Perez. As early as 1954 this trio began to consider ways of halting and reversing the rise in the black vote statewide.[49]

The large black urban vote is another reason for caution in attributing too much of the increase in black registration to Earl Long. In 1952 the parishes that contained Louisiana's three biggest cities, Orleans, Caddo, and East Baton Rouge, contained 38 percent of the state's black voters, despite a relatively low level of registration. Anti-Long politicians controlled all of them. True, Orleans Parish was a special case, being the only parish where the governor appointed the registrar of voters, but Long's direct control of the registration process in New Orleans did not lead to a high level of black registration: in 1952 it stood at only 22 percent. Had Long been committed to black voting as a matter of principle, one would expect the figure to be far higher. The slowdown in black registration in New Orleans that occurred after 1950 suggests that Long, like so many white politicians, encouraged black registration as long as the resulting votes were cast the "right way."[50]

Even very high levels of black registration disguised a kind of manipulation, for the arbitrary nature of the registration process made the vote a conditional favor rather than an inalienable right. What could be given could also be taken away, and black voters displayed understandable reluctance to oppose the sheriff who first enfranchised them. "Vote for the Sheriff who gave you school busses and the ballot," advised a 1951 election advertisement for Sheriff P. D. Hebert of St. John the Baptist Parish. It was an effective pitch. Hebert had allowed black registration to rise to about 70 percent; moreover, his opponents accused him of registering blacks too freely.

In Jefferson Parish, Sheriff Frank "King" Clancy enjoyed similar loyalty. One of the first politicians to encourage black registration (although never at very high levels), Clancy used Negro ministers to advise black voters, an arrangement that appeared to work well. In 1952, for example, while blacks elsewhere voted heavily for Carlos Spaht, the gubernatorial candidate backed by Earl Long, blacks in Jefferson Parish delivered an overwhelming vote for Robert Kennon, Clancy's preference. A similar situation prevailed in St. Landry Parish, where a local lawyer advised Chep Morrison that he could never get black support there without the say-so of Sheriff D. J. "Cat" Doucet.[51]

Loyalty to the local sheriff stemmed from fear as well as gratitude. The sheriff was a potent and all-seeing official, noted James M. Nabrit. "His goodwill is an enormous asset. He and his deputies know the county, its citizens, and what is going on." If black voters threatened to deviate, the sheriff could employ the stick as well as the carrot. Catholic priest Jerome Drolet reported that sugarcane workers in Lafourche Parish were sometimes intimidated, and in Iberia Parish threats by Sheriff Gerald Wattigny prompted the NAACP to lodge a formal complaint with the Justice Department.

Generally, however, whites simply assumed, often correctly, that blacks were sufficiently deferential to vote the "right way" with a little guidance. "They either would tell them how to vote," recalled Dr. James Henderson, a black dentist in New Iberia, "or they'd go to West End Park, where most of the blacks would gather, and give them a little hot-dog supper . . . and tell them, 'Now you vote for this person and that person.' Or if you worked for a white person, they would give you a list of names of who to vote for, and those people would vote for them." Ernesto Galarza, a union organizer among the sugarcane workers, explained that black voting took place in a context of dependence and deference. Few blacks started a conversation with whites "without prefacing it with the familiar 'Y'unnerstan' I ain't tryna be a smart nigger.'" While the plantation labor vote could not be "delivered" as a reliable bloc, Galarza believed that the local planter-politicians could "convey" it by using "the right doses of persuasion, vigilance, indoctrination, and small favors rightly timed." Throughout the state, the buying of votes was commonplace. The practice endures to this day.[52]

In the cities, of course, it was far more difficult to bring such direct influence to bear, a fact that helps to explain the much lower levels of black registration there. Successive governors, all of them from north Louisiana — Earl Long, Robert Kennon, and Jimmie Davis — used their power to appoint the Orleans Parish registrar as a means of restricting the black vote in New Orleans, thus reducing the gubernatorial prospects of Chep Morrison. But it probably suited Morrison, too, to have black registration stuck at around thirty thousand. In 1949 it was calculated that forty thousand black voters could hold a balance of power in every city primary election. Before the Voting Rights Act of 1965, however, black registration never exceeded thirty-five thousand. Better a small and pliable black vote than a large, unmanageable one.

Thus, whites tolerated black voting, but not to the extent that it could exert real influence or act as an independent "bloc vote." While the black vote could assist racial moderates such as Morrison and Long, it could not persuade these key political leaders, or *any* white political leaders, to break with the politics of segregation. White politicians might deplore vicious racism and oppose the more extreme segregationists, but they refused to support the *Brown* decision. The eventual result was that they surrendered the political initiative to the most ardent and well-organized opponents of integration.

In this context of political drift, time became the ally of the most determined and organized whites, the ultrasegregationists. Rainach recognized that the schools issue had not yet assumed great urgency among white voters. He also worried that support for segregation seemed soft in southwest Louisiana; in Lake Charles and Lafayette, for example, nearly a third of the voters opposed Amendment 16. Then again, would white opposition to integration stand up if it led to closure of the public schools? "Our whole cause will be lost," Rainach admitted privately, "if we are forced to abandon our public school system." Finally, Rainach knew that "we face ultimate defeat in the federal courts and all legal action is merely a delaying tactic." The skein of obstructionist laws drafted by the JLC and rubber-stamped by the legislature was simply a means of buying time while Rainach and his allies prepared an ambitious offensive to immobilize the NAACP and eradicate all political support for integration.[53]

The Supreme Court gave the Rainachs of the South all the time they needed. In deciding *Brown,* the Court delayed any consideration of implementation for a full year, expecting southern whites to use the time constructively and come up with plans to phase out segregation. Instead, ultrasegregationists like Rainach used this year of grace to consolidate opposition to integration and devise strategies of resistance. Moreover, *Brown II,* the implementation decree of May 17, 1955, virtually invited the South to engage in further delaying tactics. The decree contained no deadline for compliance, it failed to define what constituted compliance, and it suggested a host of factors that might be valid reasons for additional delay. The Court dumped the task of enforcement into the laps of the fifty-seven federal district judges of the South, with only the vaguest of guidelines as to how they should go about their task. They were merely instructed to proceed "with all deliberate speed," whatever that meant.

The NAACP put a brave face on *Brown II.* "All in all," wrote Thurgood Marshall and Robert Carter, "the net result should be more widespread voluntary desegregation than might have occurred had a more stringent order been issued." Whether they really believed that, however, is another matter. In Louisiana, A. P. Tureaud openly confessed his disappointment over the absence of a deadline "beyond which local school boards may not delay." The segregationists, by the same token, were delighted. "It was the mildest decree the Supreme Court possibly could have handed down," thought state representative John S. Garrett, Rainach's right-hand man on the JLC. "This is as much as we could have hoped for."[54]

The absence of any strong political pressure to enforce *Brown* compounded the inadequacies of *Brown II.* President Eisenhower, privately critical of *Brown,* declined to endorse the decision and made no effort to enforce it until southern defiance eventually forced his hand in the 1957 Little Rock crisis. The Congress, deadlocked between North and South, distracted by McCarthyism and partisan wrangling, also disclaimed any responsibility for *Brown.* Thus the burden of enforcement fell upon black plaintiffs, and because the federal courts treated each school district as a separate entity, hundreds of individual suits might have to be filed in order to create the necessary legal impetus.

"We must face the fact," Marshall wrote, "that in the deep South, with rare exceptions, desegregation will become a reality only if Negroes exhibit real militancy."

Although blacks in Louisiana had a reputation for being conservative and slow to move, expressions of rising militancy were not hard to detect. In May 1955, for the second year running, parents in New Orleans withheld their children from the segregated McDonogh Day ceremony, and this time the boycott achieved complete solidarity. A few months earlier in Baton Rouge, blacks had boycotted a talent show because its sponsor, the Junior Chamber of Commerce, held it in a whites-only auditorium. The Rev. T. J. Jemison, who banged the drum for that protest, also pulled two school bands out of the 1955 Boy Scout parade after the organizers placed them at the rear of the procession, behind some late-entered horses. In Shreveport, long the most repressive of Louisiana's cities, a group of women formed a "Committee on Stores" to press local merchants to exhibit greater courtesy and provide fitting rooms and toilets. The group conducted a quiet campaign of negotiation and gentle pressure — backed by hints of a boycott — and in June 1955 organized a mass meeting addressed by Jemison.[55]

In another sign of the times, in 1955 the *Louisiana Weekly* replaced its long-running "Do's and Don'ts" cartoon, which had advised blacks on socially correct behavior, with the humorous "Tan Topics." The new cartoon exposed the absurdities of racism and lampooned whites. A typical example: two shabby, bewhiskered, barefoot "crackers" are sitting in a broken-down shack and swigging from a jug of whisky. One says to the other, "Can y'all imagine nigrahs being equal?" Or, more poignantly: a young black child asks, "If you're a man, gran'pa — how come they call you 'boy'?"

The NAACP, however, had little idea how to harness this latent militancy. The NAACP's lawyers half anticipated a groundswell of black popular support for *Brown* that would somehow propel desegregation forward, but they had underestimated the ambivalence and hesitancy of black attitudes toward school integration. Such a groundswell failed to spontaneously arise, and the NAACP seemed unable to stimulate and organize an effective campaign of popular pressure.

Attempts to force the pace of integration through direct action quickly failed. At the beginning of the 1954–55 school year, for example, lawyers Alex Pitcher and Johnnie Jones accompanied about thirty black children to the gates of a white elementary school in Baton Rouge. Barred entry, they returned the next day. At the instance of Rainach and the JLC, Pitcher and Jones were promptly hauled before the Grievances and Ethics Committee of the Louisiana Bar Association. Not surprisingly, such demonstrations were rare, and the state and national officers of the NAACP did little to encourage them. The NAACP's leaders conceived of *Brown*'s implementation almost exclusively in terms of litigation. But when the NAACP's suits became bogged down in the courts they could offer no other strategy than further litigation.[56]

How well equipped was the NAACP for its Herculean task? Upon his appointment as executive secretary to the Louisiana State Conference of Branches, Leonard P. Avery, a Baton Rouge lawyer, wrote to each of the fifty-two branches. Only six replied. After a year in his job, Avery estimated that about half the branches were dormant. The Shreveport branch underwent yet another reorganization in 1940, but by 1949 was reported to be "practically dead." The NAACP remained weak, in fact, throughout most of northern Louisiana, the main exception being the new branch in Natchitoches, which under the leadership of Dr. E. A. Johnson grew to 765 members in little over a year. Statewide, the NAACP's membership stood at 12,764 in 1955, below its 1948 peak of 14,119.

Attempting to explain the local decline in membership, the secretary of the Baton Rouge branch pointed to an aging leadership: with a single exception, all the officers were over fifty. The death or retirement of elderly stalwarts, however, sometimes occasioned a branch's decline. The Monroe branch, for example, one of the strongest in the 1930s and early 1940s, lost much of its vigor after C. H. Myers stepped down. The Alexandria branch, also one of the strongest in the early 1940s, suffered from ennervating factionalism. Other branches lost popular support when less articulate members felt excluded by self-perpetuating leaders who manipulated nominations and elections. Membership figures, however, gave only a rough guide to the organization's vitality. Even the New Orleans branch, with 4,500 members, found it difficult to function: turnout at branch meetings was so poor and attendance at executive committee meetings so sparse that routine work sometimes could not be carried out. By the mid-1950s the burst of grassroots energy released by the enormous expansion of its membership during the war was clearly on the wane, despite the fillip of the *Brown* decision.[57]

Welding the fifty-odd branches into a coherent statewide force remained a problem. Travel had been eased by better highways and the expansion of car ownership, but illiteracy and organizational inexperience still handicapped branches in the rural areas. Between 1947 and 1952, moreover, the State Conference of Branches had no field secretary; the burden of correspondence fell upon the president, who, in A. P. Tureaud's case, not only had a private law practice but also litigated all the NAACP's education suits. Inevitably, some branches slipped through the net. "It would seem that you don't know anything about us," complained Rev. W. H. Samuel, president of the Leesville branch.[58]

Tureaud himself became the center of internal wrangling that for a time threatened to immobilize the LSC. By 1950 a new generation of black lawyers, most of them products of Southern University Law School, resented Tureaud's tight control over the NAACP's most important legal work. Tureaud, in fact, was quite willing to encourage younger lawyers — he established a strong working relationship with Jesse N. Stone, for example, a Southern University graduate who started a practice in Shreveport — but he expected respect and a demonstrable commitment to the NAACP. Criticism of Tureaud also emanated from Donald Jones, the NAACP's Dallas-based southwestern regional secretary. Jones regarded Tureaud as ineffective as president of the LSC, and also believed that Tureaud's position as the retained lawyer of the Louisiana Education Association (the black teachers' organization) excluded local branches from a crucial area of the NAACP's work. In October 1949, partly due to Jones's sub rosa intercession, Tureaud was replaced as LSC president by Dr. E. A. Johnson, head of the Natchitoches branch. Tureaud bitterly resented his defeat.[59]

Tensions over the handling of litigation came to a head with the NAACP's intervention in the Honeycutt rape case. At a meeting of the LSC's Legal Redress Committee in December 1949, Tureaud flatly refused to work with Louis Berry because of his involvement with the Civil Rights Congress; indeed, he refused to serve on the committee at all if Berry were part of it. Failing to win his point, he walked out of the meeting. It took a considerable effort of persuasion on the part of Dr. E. A. Johnson, the incoming LSC president, to make Tureaud accept the position of committee chairman. A month later, however, the row erupted again when Johnson decided to take up the Honeycutt case and, on the advice of U. S. Tate, legal advisor to the regional office, appointed Berry to conduct Honeycutt's defense. Tureaud argued that Honeycutt was guilty and that the case had no merit. He was also furious at being bypassed and appalled at the selection of Berry. Angry letters flew thick and fast, and Thurgood Marshall sprang to Tureaud's defense.[60]

While the row concerning the Honeycutt case blew over, Johnson and Tureaud continued to quarrel over control of the NAACP's litigation. In 1951 Johnson suggested that the Legal Redress Committee should be chaired by a nonlawyer, arguing that "a disinterested person . . . might use strategy in distributing the cases." John G. Lewis of Baton Rouge, grand master of the Prince Hall Masons in Louisiana, took over the position, but Lewis, a man of conservative disposition, was unlikely to challenge Tureaud or friend and fellow Mason Thurgood Marshall. Besides, Tureaud's relationship with the LEA ensured his continuing control over the all-important education cases. Johnson continued to champion the cause of younger lawyers, but he had lost the battle. When illness forced him to step down in 1954, the presidency of the LSC passed to Doretha A. Combre of the Lake Charles branch, who readily deferred to Tureaud. The "old guard" of Tureaud, Byrd, and Chapital was securely in control, and remained so for the next ten years.[61]

These were in one sense petty bureaucratic squabbles spiced by personal antagonisms, but they also had considerable significance in terms of the NAACP's evolution. Johnson was neither a radical nor a rabble-rouser; nevertheless, almost by inadvertence, he challenged the increasingly centralized control of strategy by Tureaud and Thurgood Marshall. He tried to open up the NAACP's decision making, create a broader role for the branches, bring in new faces, and encourage cooperation with other organizations. His championing of the Honeycutt case expressed a willingness to utilize the courtroom for the purposes of agitation and dramatic effect — a "political" approach to litigation that evoked the methods of the ILD and the Civil Rights Congress. Tureaud represented the growing concentration of decision making in the hands of Marshall's Legal Defense Fund, whose strictly "legal" approach to litigation insisted that the NAACP should take up only cases that could set judicial precedents. This aggregation of power reduced the role of the branches, left younger lawyers on the sidelines, and caused the NAACP to neglect the use of the courtroom as a means of mobilizing and organizing popular support.

As the NAACP's popular base atrophied, the ultrasegregationists assiduously recruited whites to their cause. During 1955, white resistance to *Brown* coalesced around two organizations. The Southern Gentlemen, founded in April, spread from Baton Rouge into the Florida Parishes and by November claimed fourteen local chapters. Meanwhile the Citizens Council movement, launched by Willie Rainach in Homer, Claiborne Parish, spread across a dozen parishes in northern Louisiana. The two organizations had the identical aim of preserving segregation but differed in one important respect. Headed by J. B. Easterly Sr., a Baton Rouge businessman, the Southern Gentlemen refused to divulge its membership and cultivated a Klan-like air of secrecy. The Citizens Councils, on the other hand, abjured secrecy and made no effort to conceal their membership.

One of the first efforts of the Southern Gentlemen was a furtive attack on the American Friends Service Committee, which opened an office in Baton Rouge in early 1955. AFSC worker Gene Sutherland had great difficulty renting office space and on one occasion found himself evicted after three days. He suspected, but could not prove, the fine hand of the Southern Gentlemen — as he also did when a shotgun blast shattered his office window. In October, the Southern Gentlemen tried to make an issue of "Operation Sage Brush," some impending Army maneuvers. Raising the specter of black troops on leave from Fort Polk flooding the state capital, it demanded that Baton Rouge be placed "off limits" to Negro soldiers. City officials flatly refused, local merchants being notably unenthusiastic about the prospect of losing lucrative customers. Nevertheless, pressure from the Southern Gentlemen persuaded some stores to reinstall segregated drinking fountains.[62]

In New Orleans, the Citizens Council enjoyed the advantage of having Emile Wagner, one its most energetic supporters, on the school board. In December, Wagner persuaded the board to deny use of the Rabouin high school auditorium to the Citizens Forum on Integration, a group headed by Rabbi Feibelman, on the grounds that the CFI's sponsors included an alleged Communist who headed a subversive organization, James Dombrowski of SCEF. Over Wagner's objections, however, the board decided to allow the citizens' group to use the auditorium if it disavowed SCEF. Feibelman reluctantly accepted this condition, reasoning that SCEF was "so completely identified with integration that whatever it or Dr. Dombrowski touched was doomed to failure." The public meetings went ahead. Wagner had further isolated SCEF but failed in his primary objective. Toward the end of 1955 a mysterious chain telephone campaign urged whites not to contribute to the United Fund because it gave money to the Urban League, an organization the callers described as both integrationist and subversive. The league had little doubt that the whispering campaign originated with the Citizens Council. It gradually died away before too much damage could be inflicted.[63]

In the rivalry for the leadership of the segregationist cause, the Citizens Councils enjoyed one inestimable advantage over the Southern Gentlemen: Willie Rainach. A dynamo of nervous energy who threw himself into the defense of segregation mind and soul, Rainach appreciated the importance of mass support. "The only real solution," he believed, "lies in organizing our people completely from the ground up." It was for this reason that he insisted that the Citizens Councils operate openly. The secrecy of the Southern Gentlemen gave that organization a sinister aura that attracted the sleazy and deterred the respectable. Rainach wanted to attract Louisiana's leading white citizens. "We know that we must stay within the law to win public approval," he argued. "Ours is a democratic leadership organization. It's not secret and not militaristic." As chairman of the Joint Legislative Committee on Segregation, moreover, Rainach gave the Citizens Councils the political clout that the Southern Gentlemen could not hope to match. He also enjoyed the backing of Leander Perez, who played an important role in organizing the Citizens Council of Greater New Orleans, which became, in terms of membership, by far the largest of the ultrasegregationist groups in Louisiana — perhaps in the entire South — and its affiliation with Rainach's movement proved decisive. Unable to dominate southern Louisiana and with no foothold in the northern part of the state, the Southern Gentlemen soon became an adjunct of the Citizens Councils.[64]

Although the ultrasegregationists were clearly a force to be reckoned with, they also suffered major political setbacks during 1955. In June Governor Kennon vetoed a measure sponsored by Rainach that would have allocated $33.5 million of tideland oil revenues to the equalization of black schools, a drastic proposal designed to avert integration. Kennon preferred to spend money on highways.[65]

Later in the year, both Rainach and the Southern Gentlemen tried to make segregation the dominant issue in the governor's race, but Kennon's reticence about segregation had kept the racial temperature down, and the absence of any impending court orders made it difficult for the ultrasegregationists to raise it, especially when the contest was dominated by two racial moderates, Chep Morrison and Earl Long, who both sought to maximize their black support. Segregation had to vie with gambling, the right-to-work law, state spending, and various other campaign issues. Although all five candidates affirmed their support for segregation, only one of them, James McLemore, bothered to attend a Southern Gentlemen rally in Hammond. McLemore distinguished himself from the pack by proclaiming himself the "white man's candidate" and running solely on the race issue. He finished last, with only thirteen thousand votes.

In one of the strongest performances in the state's history, Earl Long romped home with 51 percent of the vote and carried all but two parishes. "Uncle Earl," moreover, had made few direct appeals to racism, although Morrison advisor Dave McGuire alleged that Long had furtively subsidized McLemore's ailing campaign in order to "have others do . . . hatchet and smear work against Chep." To Rainach's frustration, the black vote, then at an all-time high of about 160,000, was cast in overwhelming proportions for Long, thus decisively contributing to his first-primary victory. Adding insult to injury, Long persuaded the Democratic State Central Committee to cancel the runoff primary for all the other statewide contests, not merely the governor's race, thus ensuring the election of the entire Long ticket. Fred LeBlanc, the incumbent attorney general and a key Rainach ally, was pitched out of office. The rout of the conservatives and Dixiecrats delighted blacks. The *Louisiana Weekly* rejoiced that "the political power of Leander Perez is broken."[66]

Reports of Perez's political death were greatly exaggerated. Throughout 1955 he and Rainach had been planning a counteroffensive that would smash the NAACP, decimate the black electorate, destroy the Long machine, and stop integration in its tracks. They designed their strategy with great thought, meticulously cementing political alliances and patiently waiting for the right moment to strike. To those who, like Shreveport lawyer W. Scott Wilkinson, anxiously urged him to "get on the offensive and put a few negroes in jail," Rainach cautioned against overhasty action. "In this fight we must be unusually deliberate," he explained, "since it is only through carefully planned action that we can hope to win." Three elements had to be in place before he moved: money from the state legislature to pay for lawyers to defend segregation, a statewide Citizens Council movement that would mount a sweeping "purge" of black voters, and the cooperation of the governor and the attorney general in prosecuting the NAACP.[67]

In June 1955 Rainach and Perez took charge of coordinating the defense in the St. Helena Parish case, one of the NAACP's two school integration suits. Reasoning that the best form of defense is offense, they engaged a private investigating agency to follow up the allegation of J. L. Meadows, the superintendent of schools, that some of the NAACP's plaintiffs had not consented to the suit. If true, they intended to prosecute the attorneys for violating the state's Unauthorized Practices law. Governor Kennon assented to this plan, and in July the legislature appropriated $100,000 to help pay for the legal defense of segregation. Attorney General Fred LeBlanc agreed to use this money to hire William Shaw, chief counsel of the JLC, as an assistant attorney general, and Sargent Pitcher Jr., a Baton Rouge attorney, as a special counsel. This would provide ample legal muscle for the St. Helena Parish school board. A. P. Tureaud filed a suit challenging the legality of the $100,000 appropriation.[68]

Meanwhile, in St. Helena Parish itself, the Southern Gentlemen unleashed a campaign of intimidation against the plaintiffs. According to Fred Overton, a prosperous farmer from one of the most respected black families in the parish, the head of the segregationist group asked him to withdraw from the suit and influence others to act likewise, accompanying his request with not-so-subtle threats. Superintendent Meadows visited other plaintiffs with the same purpose in mind. A member of the school board frankly warned Ellis Howard, president of the local NAACP, that the Southern Gentlemen had taken over the parish and were copying the pressure tactics of the Citizens Councils in Mississippi. Daniel Byrd assured Thurgood Marshall that at least seven of the plaintiffs would stick with the suit but added, "Some Negroes are in fear, great fear for their lives."[69]

Rainach's negotiations with Kennon and LeBlanc proved delicate and protracted. By November, however, everything was falling into place. Early that month, Rainach and his legal advisers sealed a political compact with Attorney General LeBlanc. As soon as Judge J. Coleman Lindsey dismissed the NAACP-backed suit against the state's $100,000 segregation defense fund—and the conferees obviously had prior knowledge of Lindsey's decision — LeBlanc would publicly accuse the NAACP of subversion and violation of Louisiana laws. Rainach would back him up and endorse LeBlanc for reelection. State police would then raid the NAACP's main offices and seize its files.

The ironic denouement: the state would indict and prosecute the NAACP's officers for failing to file membership lists with the secretary of state, a requirement of the Fuqua Ku Klux Klan law of 1924. At the end of November Rainach cleared the plan with Governor Kennon, who agreed to furnish the necessary state police.[70]

Two weeks later Rainach, Perez, and eight other men gathered in a Monroe hotel room to organize the Association of Citizens Councils of Louisiana. Formally launched in January 1956, it vowed "To protect and preserve, by all legal means, our historical Southern Social Institutions in all of their aspects; To marshal the economic resources of the good citizens of this state in combatting any attack upon these social institutions . . . [and] to fortify them to reject the assault which is constantly being waged upon our institutions by the Socialistic and Communistic forces in this country." During the early weeks of 1956 Citizens Councils sprouted all over northern Louisiana. Meanwhile, the Citizens Councils of Greater New Orleans kicked off a drive to sign up fifty thousand members.

Rainach's preparations were complete. In March 1956 he finally gave the signal, and in short order he and his allies suppressed the NAACP, wiped thousands of black voters from the registration rolls, and launched a relentless campaign to isolate, discredit, or destroy all critics and opponents. The gloves were off. The counterattack had begun.[71]

Chapter 8

COUNTERATTACK

T he segregationist onslaught stunned the NAACP. "For a while I thought Louisiana would remain dormant and be on the wait and see side," lamented Doretha A. Combre, president of the State Conference of Branches, "but now it seems that we are pulling for first place in the segregation issue." Overnight, the political climate darkened. Despite Earl Long's landslide election victory, the Citizens Councils rapidly became the dominant force in state politics, and when Long finally attempted to check their influence he suffered a crushing defeat. By 1960 the ultrasegregationists had so weakened the NAACP that only federal pressure and black determination prevented a complete stalemate in the battle for civil rights. Given the scale of the segregationist counterattack, it is a remarkable tribute to the courage, tenacity, and ingenuity of many blacks that organized protest endured at all.[1]

The state's attack on the NAACP came as a bolt from the blue; the organization scrambled to safeguard its cash and its records before the authorities seized them. Branch treasurers withdrew money from banks and sent it to New York. The New Orleans branch deposited its files in the law office of A. P. Tureaud for safekeeping. The gentlemanly Tureaud was appalled that Attorney General Fred LeBlanc, a man who had sought his political support in 1948, hauled the NAACP into court without giving him the courtesy of an advance warning.[2]

With ten NAACP officers summoned to appear in a state court on March 29, Tureaud and Robert L. Carter of the national office hurriedly filed a petition with Judge Skelly Wright to have the case removed to a federal court. Technically, the mere filing of the petition should have halted the state proceedings, but Judge J. Coleman Lindsey went ahead with the hearings regardless. The NAACP now had to show cause why it should not be enjoined for failing to file membership lists with the secretary of state. Robert Carter argued in court that the 1924 anti–Ku Klux Klan law (often referred to as the Fuqua law, after Governor Henry L. Fuqua) was not only "vague and indefinite" but also an unconstitutional abridgement of free speech and association. Moreover, he charged, the state had singled out the NAACP as part of "a major organized effort . . . to suppress all organized and individual opposition to racial segregation."

Carter's arguments did not prevail. Lindsey had been a member of the legislature that passed the Fuqua Act and was something of an expert on the Louisiana constitution. He enjoined the NAACP from "doing any business or acting as a corporation." On April 24 he made the injunction permanent. The NAACP could hold no further meetings until it produced its membership lists.[3]

As they suppressed the NAACP, Rainach and his allies opened a campaign to disfranchise blacks. In January 1956, the Citizens Council of Webster Parish complained that Winnie P. Clement, the registrar of voters, had accepted "unqualified" people by failing to require applicants to read, or in the case of illiterates understand, any section of the Louisiana or U.S. Constitution "and give a reasonable interpretation thereof." Throughout the state, in fact, this "interpretation" test had fallen into disuse, permitting large numbers of blacks, and illiterates of both races, to register and vote. Strictly but selectively enforced, however, it could be used to disfranchise virtually anyone. As one expert on state government averred, much of the Louisiana constitution would baffle the most erudite lawyers. The Citizens Councils intended to force parish registrars to apply this impossible standard to blacks as a means of freezing the black vote. Their opening gambit, however, did not go quite as planned. Explaining that "if the Negroes have to do it so do the white people, that's only being fair," Mrs. Clement proceeded to reject twenty-four whites in the space of two weeks. Forced to resign by the outgoing State Board of Registration, she was immediately reappointed by the incoming board, controlled by Governor Long.[4]

Unfazed, Rainach attacked black voting on another front. A 1940 law, passed by the "good government" faction headed by Governor Sam Jones, provided that two registered voters could challenge the registration of people they believed to be "illegally registered" by filing sworn affidavits with the registrar. Voters thus challenged had to produce a counteraffidavit signed by *three* registered voters in order to stay on the rolls. If they failed to furnish this document within ten days of receiving a mailed notice of challenge, the registrar automatically struck them off. The Citizens Councils planned to use this challenge procedure, originally designed as a safeguard against "floating" voters who flouted the residence requirements, to eliminate black voters en masse. Negro registration had passed "the danger point," Rainach warned, with the NAACP trading its large bloc vote "with one group of people and then another until no political faction feels it can be elected without the Negro support." Once "illegally registered" blacks had been cleared from the rolls — and Rainach had it in mind to reduce the black electorate by about nine-tenths — white politicians would be able to unite wholeheartedly behind segregation, as they already had done in Mississippi.[5]

The "purge" began in Monroe. In March, members of the newly formed Ouachita Parish Citizens Council prepared affidavits of challenge against the parish's 5,700 black voters. Registrar Mae Lucky then gave the purgers access to her office so they could pick out "mistakes" in the application forms of the challenged voters. Between April 16 and May 22, Lucky accepted challenges to 3,420 black voters, all of them residents of Wards 3 and 10 of the city of Monroe. Only twenty-three whites received challenges. Notified of the challenges by mail, hundreds of blacks descended on the registrar's office, the lines forming at six o'clock in the morning and soon winding back to the courthouse lawn. The registrars, idly chatting among themselves and vacantly staring out of windows, made no effort to expedite the proceedings, processing no more than fifty people a day. Moreover, they refused to allow blacks to vouch for challenged voters if they lived in a different precinct, if they had already vouched for somebody else, or if they themselves had been challenged.

Increasingly frustrated by having to wait outside the courthouse while the registrars twiddled their thumbs, the challenged voters concluded that they stood a much better chance of staying on the rolls if they had a white person vouch for them. After all, they had often seen whites come in to the registrar's office with "their Negro" and go straight to the head of the line. Henry Carroll, a black high school principal who had voted for more than twenty years, asked former Governor James A. Noe, who owned a Monroe television station, to assist them. Noe agreed to meet Carroll at the courthouse, and he asked the attorney general to send someone to clarify the situation. LeBlanc dispatched William Shaw, general counsel to the Joint Legislative Committee and executive secretary of the Association of Citizens Counsels.

When Carroll and Noe arrived at the registrar's office, Shaw, standing behind the counter, began to aggressively question Carroll. Local Citizens Council president Billy Adams, also behind the counter, interjected questions of his own. Appalled by their hectoring tone, Noe tried to intervene and asked Shaw if he belonged to the Citizens Councils. Admitting that he did, Shaw asked if Noe belonged to the NAACP. Now incensed, Noe angrily berated Shaw, and as the temperature rose the two men almost came to blows. Noe eventually forced a grudging admission from the attorney general that voters could vouch for any number of people. He also had 1,500 counteraffidavit forms printed when the registrar's office exhausted its supply. Time was running out, however. On May 12 the registrar's office closed. Henry Carroll managed to save his registration, but of an estimated 1,600 challenged voters who went to the courthouse over half were struck off. All told, the Citizens Council disfranchised over 3,000 blacks.[6]

Thoroughly alarmed, Daniel Byrd and J. K. Haynes alerted the NAACP's national leadership to the gravity of this sudden turn of events. "White Citizens Councils are rising in every nook and corner of the State," Haynes noted, and their leaders included school superintendents, doctors, lawyers, teachers, and businessmen. When a Citizens Council appeared, the lash of economic and social pressure soon followed. Black businessmen found their sales to whites fall off. "Negroes who would dare raise their voices in behalf of right" lost the social approval of whites who had previously helped and befriended them. In Madison Parish, black teachers reportedly had to list, under oath, all their memberships; in Bossier Parish, they were ordered to suppress all discussion of integration. Byrd endorsed Haynes's pessimistic analysis. "Make no mistake about it, the Citizens Councils are following the pattern instituted by the White South during Reconstruction. They are planning and planning well, planning systematically to hold the line and keep the NAACP out of Louisiana. . . . Unless we can stop them, in the next several months almost all Negroes will be disfranchised in Louisiana." Both men warned that the climate of growing intimidation threatened violence. "Tension . . . has increased with unbelievable rapidity."[7]

Meanwhile, the Citizens Council of Greater New Orleans began a simultaneous offensive on several fronts. Their first objective: to scotch tentative plans for the integration of Catholic schools. On February 15, Judge J. Skelly Wright struck down Constitutional Amendment 16, providing for the maintenance of segregation under the "police powers" of the state, and ordered the

Orleans Parish school board to prepare for desegregation "with all deliberate speed." The board intended to turn foot dragging into a fine art, and there was no immediate prospect of integration in the public schools. The parochial schools of the archdiocese, however, were another matter: beyond the jurisdiction of either state officials or federal courts, they could, in theory, be integrated by a simple order from the archbishop.

By 1956, lay opposition to Archbishop Rummel had become increasingly vocal. On January 10, for example, about one hundred people stalked out of a meeting of the parents club of Jesuit High School, the largest Catholic school in Louisiana, when the principal, the Reverend Claude J. Stallworth, refused to permit discussion of a resolution opposing integration. The Catholic segregation movement remained relatively inchoate, however, until Rummel provided a rallying point. That came in mid-February, when priests throughout New Orleans read a pastoral letter from the archbishop condemning racial segregation as "morally wrong and sinful" and insisting that "the alleged mental defects, moral and criminal propensities, economic shortcomings and social disabilities" attributed to blacks, far from proving the Negro's unfitness for integration, actually constituted "an indictment against continuing segregation." Such sentiments enraged white Catholics, who had, after all, been born and raised in a church that sanctioned and practiced racial segregation. Louis Twomey described the reaction of the laity — and of many priests as well — as "sullen at best and defiant at worst."[8]

Clarence Laws, the NAACP's Louisiana field secretary, attended Mass at St. James Major Church on the Sunday that Rummel's pastoral letter reached the ears of the faithful. The manner in which the Reverend Carl Schutten read the text and the comments he interjected appalled Laws, and he sent a letter of complaint to Rummel. In announcing that he had a long letter from the archbishop, Laws related, the priest "deliberately emphasized . . . the word 'long' in a manner hardly calculated to inspire respect for, or sympathy with, the views expressed in Your Excellency's letter." On at least three occasions, moreover, Schutten "made derogatory remarks concerning the health, morality, intelligence and resourcefulness of Negroes." According to Laws, the pastor also reassured his white parishioners that Rummel's letter was by no means the last word on the subject, adding, "I know what is on your minds, and I am in sympathy with you."[9]

Emile Wagner and his allies had everything to play for: Rummel's pastoral letter had failed to announce a date for the beginning of desegregation, stressing the need for "further consideration and study." The segregationists now concentrated their fire on Father Fichter and the Catholic Commission on Human Rights, which, with Rummel's blessing, organized a series of public lectures designed to dispel some of the racist myths that bedeviled rational discussion of integration. The CCHR received a grant from the Fund for the Republic to bring eight guest lecturers to New Orleans and mail over two hundred thousand items of prointegration literature. Fichter's effort immediately drew the wrath of Citizens Council stalwart Emile Wagner who, armed with a HUAC report obtained by Leander Perez, charged one of the guest lecturers, New York politician Hulan Jack, with being a Communist. Father Schutten, an active Citizens Council supporter, tried to persuade Father Patrick Donnelly, president of Loyola, to have the lecture cancelled.

Having failed to prevent Jack's appearance at Holy Name of Jesus School on February 26, Wagner instigated an open rebellion against the archbishop by organizing an avowedly segregationist "Association of Catholic Laymen." Rummel informed Wagner that he considered the organization "unnecessary, ill-advised and capable of causing much scandal, confusion and dissension among our Catholic people." His admonition had no effect. The following day, March 20, about eight thousand Confederate-flag-waving, "Dixie" singing whites derisively chanted Rummel's name during a Citizens Council rally at the Municipal Auditorium. A week later, the Association of Catholic Laymen openly solicited "Caucasian" members in the pages of the *Times-Picayune*. An appalled archbishop summoned the organization's ringleaders and pointed out the error of their ways. Wagner's delegation complained about the prointegration activities of the NAACP, the Urban League, and the CCHR. The archbishop defended the NAACP and advised the group to read Father Costello's *Moral Aspects of Segregation*. His warning had no effect: after another futile meeting, the association cheekily sent Rummel a list of thirty questions. Rummel declined to reply. "I am afraid of the mood of your organization," he stated. "It appears to be deeply prejudiced." Finally, on April 23, Rummel ordered the association to disband on pain of excommunication. It reluctantly obeyed.[10]

The dissolution of the Association of Catholic Laymen proved a barren victory. Catholics continued to play leading roles in the Citizens Council movement; indeed, Catholic opposition to Rummel did more to boost council membership than any other factor. "Archbishop Rummel . . . has helped us tremendously," boasted William Shaw, "by his opposition to our segregation stand." Emile Wagner, moreover, continued brazenly to oppose the archbishop. On May 17, segregationists rallied at the Pelican Ball Park and loudly booed Rummel's name. Twelve days later Wagner published an open letter that systematically contradicted the archbishop's pastoral letter on segregation and directly questioned his authority to make moral pronouncements on the subject. He later wrote to the Pope asking that Rummel be overruled. Twomey considered Wagner "articulate in his opposition and arrogant in his virtual defiance of the Archbishop."[11]

Integrationists suspected but could never prove that the threatening and harassing telephone calls they received originated from a Citizens Council telephone bank. Whatever the case, a vicious campaign of intimidation and abuse accompanied the council's public attacks. Rabbi Feibelman had experienced the telephone "treatment" the previous September. "These calls were denunciatory," he remembered, "with invectives, condemning slurs, and curses. 'Who der hell you think yer are?' 'How kin you get dat way?' 'Don't you know nothing what's going on?' 'You nigger lover. . . .'" Father Eugene McManus, a teacher at St. Augustine High School, received a telephone death threat after he spoke as a panelist at one of the CCHR's lectures. He tried to be both charitable and philosophical. "How [do we] explain the emotional surge that seems to have turned the fair minded people of our city into blinded, frenzied bigots? The answer is fear. . . . The sincere desire of parents to protect their children has been perverted into hatred for Negroes. Fair minded people have been told by questionably sincere doctors that Negroes in the classroom will transmit venereal diseases to their children." [12]

Although the ultrasegregationists failed to stop Fichter's lecture program, the Citizens Council did not let the CCHR out of its sights. Council president Emmett Lee Irwin challenged the Commission on Human Rights to file a membership list with the secretary of state; when it failed to do so he called on the FBI to investigate the group. In Washington, HUAC announced that it planned to investigate the Fund for the Republic for subversive influences. [13]

The council's efforts to link integration with communism received a timely assist from Senator Eastland, whose committee on internal security returned to New Orleans at the end of March for more hearings. The city's own "Red Squad" pitched in with enthusiasm. Mayor Morrison had appointed a former FBI agent, Guy Banister, to investigate corruption within the New Orleans Police Department but, eager to divert attention from this politically embarrassing subject, encouraged him to hunt for Communists. Banister, whose obsession with communism approached paranoia, appointed sergeant Hubert Badeaux to head an "Intelligence Division"; after a year of sleuthing, Badeaux had identified Hunter Pitts O'Dell, a former seaman then employed as a waiter, as an organizer for the Communist Party. A few days before Eastland opened his hearings, Badeaux raided O'Dell's apartment, seizing quantities of notes and documents.

The timing of Eastland's latest visitation may have been entirely fortuitous, but the senator's prominence in the Citizens Council movement and his friendship with Leander Perez make one disinclined to accept such a charitable explanation. The hearings could hardly have been better timed as far as the ultrasegregationists were concerned. After five days of hearings, Eastland claimed to have exposed "an active Communist underground" in New Orleans "that has sought to infiltrate labor unions, the churches, farmer organizations, parent-teacher associations, the channels of public opinion, and other streams of influence in our society." Although the committee did not explicitly link subversion with civil rights, the mere exposure of secret Communists gave credence to Citizens Council charges that the integration movement was bristling with Reds. Moreover, with political orthodoxy being defined by a right-wing Mississippi segregationist, discretion became the better part of valor for many people who might otherwise have endorsed integration. Finally, Eastland's hearings encouraged Banister and Badeaux, fervent segregationists both, to institute surveillance of civil rights activists. Badeaux opened dossiers on more than three hundred individuals and fed selected tidbits to Willie Rainach, with whom he forged a surreptitious political alliance.[14]

Father Fichter's status as a Jesuit priest immunized him from charges of communism, and being a combative man, he gave as good as he got in his exchanges with the Citizens Council. But the CCHR's educational campaign, in the context of Rummel's vacillation, inadvertently played into the hands of the segregationists by underlining the recalcitrance of clergy and laity. The CCHR could not, Fichter recalled, "find any pastor or principal of an elementary school in a white parish willing to allow an 'integration' forum on the premises." Few priests, nuns, or seminarians turned out for the lectures. The radio station owned by Loyola, WWL, declined to broadcast them — "too controversial," explained Father Donnelly — and the diocesan newsletter, *Catholic Action*, all but ignored them. Rummel's isolation became painfully obvious, and the CCHR found itself on a most precarious limb.[15]

The Citizens Councils itched to get their hands on the CCHR's membership lists, even trying to obtain them through Rummel, but Fichter remained adamant and gently chided the archbishop for his naivete. "Because of the viciousness and the kind of reprisals they visit on their opponents," he wrote the aging prelate, "I am completely unwilling that they know the names of members. . . . Please forgive me if I beg you also to be suspicious of the 'Catholic source of good standing' which is requesting this information." Nevertheless, the campaign of vilification and intimidation effectively silenced the CCHR. In June, thirty teachers resigned from the group after the legislature passed a law allowing the dismissal of teachers for "advocating or in any way performing any act toward bringing about integration of the races" in public schools or colleges. At the same time, the CCHR decided to issue no further public statements, reasoning that public controversy frightened members away. Fichter scolded the group for its timidity. "If the only point on which you can get complete agreement is the decision to do nothing, then, of course the decision is absurd and futile. . . . It may as well fold up in a dignified way."[16]

A month later, on July 31, 1956, Archbishop Rummel caved in. "Certain conditions and circumstances," he explained, had made it "inadvisable" to commence integration in the Catholic schools that year. In a curious sentence that had the Citizens Councils worrying that some schools had already been integrated on the sly, Rummel announced a postponement of integration "at least" until September 1957 "in schools in which it has not yet been effected." In fact, not a single Catholic school had been integrated. With this statement, Rummel began nearly seven years of procrastination, delay, and retreat. In 1957 the Catholic schools remained segregated. Indeed, the archbishop had nothing further to say on the subject until July 1959, when he promised integration "at the earliest opportunity and definitely not later than when the public schools are integrated." Even this definite-sounding commitment proved empty. Father Twomey implored the Vatican to issue an official response to Wagner's appeal to the Pope. Rumor had it, he complained, that Rome's silence meant that "the archbishop has been secretly instructed by the Holy See" to drop his plans for integration. The Vatican ignored Twomey's letters.[17]

In 1956 the rise of the Citizens Councils seemed irresistible. "Our organization is growing so rapidly," claimed William Shaw, "we cannot keep an accurate, up-to-the-minute count." He estimated a statewide membership of between fifty and a hundred thousand, with councils operating in twenty-two of Louisiana's sixty-four parishes. The movement claimed twenty-five thousand members in New Orleans alone.

This was no fringe group. True, members of the state's top economic elite generally stayed aloof from the movement, but the leadership of the councils had a distinctly middle-class, even upper middle-class, character. The president of the Citizens Councils of Greater New Orleans, Dr. Emmett L. Irwin, a physician, had served as president of both the Orleans Parish Medical Society and the Louisiana Medical Association; he had once headed the department of surgery at the LSU School of Medicine. Long active in right-wing causes, his courtly manner and white-linen suits added to his patrician air. Emile Wagner also exuded social respectability. A widower with five daughters, he worked as an attorney for a savings and loan association and served on the Orleans Parish school board. He had once headed the Loyola University alumni association. Another prominent council member, attorney Louis Porterie, was the son of a former Louisiana attorney general and federal district judge, Gaston L. Porterie. In the northern part of the state, the councils had a full complement of lawyers, sheriffs, school superintendents, small businessmen, and local politicians.[18]

In May 1956 the Citizens Councils launched an attack on the New Orleans Urban League, one of the last remaining vehicles of interracial cooperation.

Individual board members were attacked by name at a May 17 rally, causing several to resign. The council then threatened to boycott the United Fund if the Urban League continued to receive money from the citywide Community Chest. A majority of the league's board members adamantly opposed suggestions to voluntarily withdraw from the Community Chest; "There is no appeasing the Citizens Council," stated one. The Community Chest, however, voted to exclude the League from its 1957–58 fundraising campaign. "This whole business would never have happened," complained Chest chairman Clifford Favrot, "if the Supreme Court hadn't been silly enough to hand down that [Brown] decision." The tension at the crucial meeting was so great, reported one participant, "that no one even cracked a smile at the ridiculousness of the statement." Leagues in four other southern cities suffered similar exclusion.[19]

When the state legislature convened in May 1956, the influence of the councils could be seen in the fact that virtually every bill proposed by Rainach's Joint Legislative Committee became law. The legislature mandated segregated waiting rooms, toilets, eating facilities, and water fountains in train and bus stations. It also banned interracial participation in "any dancing, social functions, entertainment, athletic training, games, sports, and other such activities involving personal and social contacts." To shore up the defense of segregated schools, the legislature immunized school boards against suits, empowered itself to classify schools in New Orleans by race, and repealed the compulsory attendance law for schools ordered to integrate by court order. In an effort to rid LSU and other state colleges of black students, the legislature required applicants to obtain certificates of "eligibility and good moral character" from their high school principals. The catch was obvious: teachers who endorsed certificates for blacks seeking admission to "white" colleges rendered themselves liable to dismissal. In a swipe at the NAACP, teachers were prohibited from supporting organizations under injunction.[20]

The power of the Citizens Councils stemmed not only from their bourgeois leadership but also from their open expression of what most white Louisianians believed. The ultrasegregationists differed from other whites not so much in their racial views as in the intensity with which they held them, the extent to which they focused on race to the exclusion of other issues, and the lengths to which they would go to defend segregation. According to opinion polls a minority of whites, somewhere between a quarter and a third, professed a willingness to accept court-ordered integration rather than see the schools closed, probably more, in fact, than the number who preferred to close the schools rather than integrate them. However, very few whites indeed — in practical political terms, an infinitesimal number — advocated integration as a positive good.[21]

Herein lay the tactical advantage of the Citizens Councils: their opponents found it extremely difficult to argue against measures to defend segregation. Those inclined to do so could ponder the fate of New Orleans representatives Bernard T. Engert and Mrs. Bland Cox Bruns (the only woman in the legislature). Both had opposed Amendment 16 in 1954; both lost their seats in 1956. Legislators deemed it prudent to go along with Rainach's committee until such time as unqualified support for segregation threatened even worse alternatives to integration such as school closings, economic damage, and harm to their own political interests. Most of Rainach's bills met little or no opposition; a resolution asserting Louisiana's right of "interposition," in effect its right to defy federal authority, passed both houses without a dissenting vote.[22]

The Citizens Council movement represented a direct threat to the Long machine. Opponents of Long dominated the movement's leadership. They had tried to prevent Long's election by raising the specter of the "bloc vote," but white voters had been unimpressed. Even before Long took office, however, they had struck at his political base with the purge of black voters in Monroe. This attack paid off handsomely: in May 1956 Jack Howard, the Citizens Council candidate, beat Mayor John Coon, a Long supporter, by fewer than a thousand votes. As District Attorney Albin P. Lassiter later explained, the challenged voters had been registered by the Long faction "through force, cajolery, unkept promises, and, in general, political skullduggery."[23]

Long declined to openly oppose Rainach. One Longite politician approached A. P. Tureaud and told him that the governor wanted to knock out the ban on interracial sport; he would be willing to finance a suit. Tureaud refused to cooperate, reasoning that whites who opposed the measure should have the guts to say so in public. Long would not do so; while skeptical of the committee's bills and "tired of that colored bugaboo," he did not want to be accused of "courting the colored people." Besides, Long considered that he had bigger fish to fry. His legislative program included increases in the old age pension, pay raises for teachers, and the establishment of a branch of Louisiana State University in New Orleans. In fact, the legislature gave Long most of what he wanted on nonsegregation matters, including repeal of the anti-union "right-to-work" law. Long used up valuable political debts in the process, and he probably calculated that to challenge Rainach at this point would be seen by many of his supporters as tantamount to an endorsement of integration, a gesture that would prove both futile and politically costly. Thus Long signed every JLC-sponsored bill except one.[24]

When the legislators left Baton Rouge, the Citizens Councils stepped up their attack on the black vote. Council members resumed the "purge" in Monroe and before the year was out initiated mass challenges in nine other north

Louisiana parishes. In Bienville Parish, 552 of the 587 black voters were dis-qualified; in Red River Parish, only a dozen blacks remained on the rolls after the registrar accepted about fifteen hundred challenges. Most registrars re-fused to accept counteraffidavits. The registrar of Caldwell Parish insisted that supporting witnesses had to be identified by a law enforcement officer and a Citizens Council member. Other registrars simply rejected counteraffidavits out of hand. All told, the "purge" eliminated as many as nine thousand black voters.

The councils then pressured registrars to administer the "constitutional in-terpretation test" to new applicants. Some registrars adopted the test devised by Leander Perez for Plaquemines Parish: applicants selected one of twenty-five cards, each of which contained three questions. Others administered an oral test. Many simply rejected blacks on the basis of alleged errors in fill-ing out the standard application form. Recalcitrant registrars found their jobs in peril when the local Citizens Councils petitioned police juries for their removal. In north Louisiana, most eventually toed the council line. "I was real strict in 1957," recalled Winnie Clement of Webster Parish, "right after they did everything but shoot me." With a system of periodic registration in force, which required voters to reregister every four years, selective application of the interpretation "test" could slash the black electorate without the need for a purge; in Webster, for example, the number of black voters fell from 1,773 to 79. Other parishes, once purged, adopted a system of "permanent registra-tion," whereby those remaining on the rolls did *not* have to reregister. Whites were thus in effect exempted from the new interpretation test.[25]

In November the councils suffered a setback: voters rejected a constitu-tional amendment requiring rejected applicants to avail themselves of a series of complicated and time-consuming administrative appeals before resorting to federal court action. Drafted by Leander Perez and Thompson L. Clarke, district attorney for Madison, Tensas, and East Carroll parishes (where not a single black voted) the measure clearly aroused the opposition of many whites. Undaunted, Rainach announced plans to extend the "cleanup" of "illegally registered voters" to south Louisiana. He sent each parish registrar a Citi-zens Council pamphlet outlining the procedure for challenging and removing voters and, if no local council yet existed, offered to visit the parish to help organize one. "By this time next year," he predicted, "Louisiana will be a shining example to the nation on how to thwart the NAACP."[26]

During the last nine months of 1956 the NAACP in Louisiana remained paralyzed. Blacks could still support the national organization, however, and with little prompting they began to send money as soon as the ban came into effect. The state association of Negro dentists collected $100, the Alpha Phi

Alpha Fraternity $250. In New Orleans the United Clubs, a confederation of Mardi Gras clubs and a musicians' union, decided to organize a "blackout" of the 1957 Carnival season. Taking inspiration from the bus boycott then unfolding in Alabama, the clubs coined the slogan, "It is immoral for Negroes in New Orleans to dance while Negroes in Montgomery walk." By cancelling or scaling down their annual dances, they collected $60,000 for the national NAACP. Albert Dent, the president of Dillard University, carried the money to New York.[27]

Enjoined from holding meetings in the state, about fifty activists from Louisiana met in Houston on June 10, 1956, and with the encouragement of the national office resolved to set up shadow organizations to carry on the association's work. A Citizens Improvement Council came into being in Lake Charles; blacks in New Orleans organized the New Orleans Improvement League. Further north, in Monroe, the purge of black voters prompted the formation of the Guiding Voice, Inc., whose president, Dr. John I. Reddix, filed a suit in federal court against registrar of voters Mae Lucky. Prominent NAACP activists tended to stay in the background. For one thing, the new organizations relied heavily for leadership on doctors, dentists, ministers, businessmen, and other people relatively immune from white retaliation. The NAACP had to be careful, moreover, to keep an organizational distance from the new groups, ensuring that the old cadre of NAACP activists functioned as supporters rather than leaders and did nothing that might be construed as a violation of the injunction. The same consideration led the NAACP to close its New Orleans office and transfer Clarence Laws, its Louisiana field secretary, out of the state.[28]

A decision by the state appeals court in late November offered a glimmer of hope: a three-judge panel ruled that Judge Lindsey had erred in trying the NAACP after a removal petition had been filed. Only the U.S. district court had the competence to determine the validity of the case's removal; the state courts had no right to judge the NAACP's appeal. Assuming that the case had, in fact, been removed to the federal courts and that Lindsey's injunction had no validity, seventy-one NAACP activists met in Alexandria on December 9 to relaunch the organization. Three days later, a smaller group convened in New Orleans to make arrangements for a mass meeting early in the New Year that would mark the statewide kickoff of the 1957 membership drive. Two of A. P. Tureaud's young law partners, Ernest N. Morial and A. M. Trudeau, assured the group that the NAACP remained beyond the reach of the state courts until such time as a federal judge ruled on the removal petition.[29]

State attorney general Jack P. F. Gremillion immediately disabused the NAACP of its optimism. Lindsey's injunction still stood, he insisted, and to show he meant business, the diminutive attorney general dispatched state troopers to the Peter Claver building to prevent another meeting of the NAACP executive committee. Forced to execute a rapid about-face, Roy Wilkins wired branch leaders to hold no meetings until further notice.[30]

As 1956 drew to a close the NAACP faced a cruel dilemma. If branches filed membership lists in order to comply with the 1924 Fuqua law, the organization could operate openly once more. Compliance with the law, however, would drastically reduce the membership and probably kill off most of the branches: few people would renew their subscriptions because the Citizens Councils would obtain the membership lists, publicize their names, and expose them to reprisals. Moreover, unless the NAACP submitted lists by the end of the year, the 1,673 memberships collected before the injunction went into effect would all lapse. As John G. Lewis explained to Roy Wilkins, "It will be impossible for us to have any members in the state after January 1 because we will have been unable to conduct any membership campaign." Robert Carter of the national office instructed Tureaud and Laws to have the branches consult their members before filing lists.[31]

Unfortunately, there was not enough time for consultation. With Gremillion threatening further prosecution unless the state received lists by December 31, the NAACP had to bite the bullet. On the last day of 1956, Arthur Chapital deposited the membership list of the New Orleans branch with the secretary of state's office. Lake Charles and Shreveport were the only other branches to file lists. Throughout the state, confronted with the necessity to hand over membership lists, branch officers resigned. The letter that Doretha Combre received from C. W. Anderson of Jennings, Jefferson Davis Parish, was typical. "As of today I'm sending in my resignation as president of this branch," he wrote. "Please notify Mr. Clarence Laws and Mr. Wilkins at your earliest convenience because we don't know who [is] watching our mail. About to go underground. Hoping to come up some day fighting on the forefront."[32]

The NAACP was back in business. But the injunction, followed by compliance with the Fuqua law, decimated the organization. From 13,190 members and sixty-five branches in 1955, it was reduced to 1,698 and seven branches. Membership in New Orleans fell from 4,750 to 1,300. In the rest of the state, the few remaining branches limped along with a handful of members apiece.[33]

Improvised local organizations kept the flame of protest alive outside New Orleans, but they could not replace the NAACP. The proliferation of independent groups threatened a fragmentation of the coordinated, statewide setup that the NAACP had painstakingly built since the founding of the State Conference of Branches in 1943. Roy Wilkins, the NAACP's new executive secretary — Walter White died in 1955 — feared that the new "shadow" groups might develop an organizational momentum of their own that would make it difficult if not impossible for the NAACP to pick up the pieces.

NAACP leaders differed, however, as to how to go about reconstructing a statewide organization. When Roy Wilkins visited New Orleans in May 1957, he suggested concentrating on the six largest cities. Tureaud agreed, telling branch leaders from Houma and St. Helena Parish that it would be premature to reorganize yet. When Doretha Combre, Clarence Laws, and Arthur Chapital called a statewide meeting in Alexandria for September 21, Tureaud advised them to keep it small. "Our continued agitation for activation of branches in communities where we cannot effectively operate," he explained, "may result in our being called upon to defend the NAACP in needless litigation." Combre and Chapital disagreed, arguing that individual branches should decide for themselves whether or not to reactivate. Combre sent out one hundred invitations. "Having travelled over the state and remembering some of our strong leadership found in small communities I couldn't see how I could so well leave them out," she wrote Tureaud. In the event, however, only twenty-seven people showed up for the meeting. "Negro citizens are jittery," Roy Wilkins reported, "and many of them do not want to be caught up in lawsuits, so they hesitate to join the NAACP."[34]

Fear of economic reprisals acted as a powerful inhibition on NAACP membership, and that fear was well grounded. William Rainach obtained the membership lists from the secretary of state and forwarded them to local newspapers and Citizens Councils. The extent of reprisals is difficult to document, but there are enough examples to suggest that they were common, especially in north Louisiana. When Frank Davis, who operated a café in Coushatta, refused to drop out of the Red River Parish branch, the mayor ordered him to close his establishment at eight each evening; his landlord then increased the rent by $25 a month. Davis went out of business. In Shreveport, Sheriff J. Howell Flournoy received a phone call from William Rainach telling him that one of his Negro deputies had spoken in favor of integration. Flournoy fired the man. Teachers felt especially vulnerable. Technically, they could not be dismissed merely for membership in the NAACP, but they could lose tenure if they performed "some act" that reflected an intent to advocate or bring about integration in public schools and colleges. The distinction was too blurred to be of reassurance, and teachers and other public employees quit the NAACP in droves.[35]

Between 1957 and 1960 the NAACP struggled to stay alive outside New Orleans. In March 1958 Clarence Laws reported branch presidents refusing to call meetings and members issuing public denials that they held memberships in the organization. In one branch a minister announced that "if Negroes attend NAACP meetings and are beaten," it would not be his fault. A letter from the president of another branch summed up the demoralized state of the organization. "The local NAACP up here seem to be discouraged ever since the State required all members to register in the State office. I can't get any one to agree to register their name, in fact I can't get them to meet. It was a hard job to hold them before that law came out. They don't seem to be interested in doing their selves, but they love to hear of others doing." In 1959 the NAACP still did not have a single functioning branch in north Louisiana. The Shreveport branch, which in 1948 boasted a membership of fourteen hundred, now had only forty members, and according to branch president R. L. Williams only a handful showed up at meetings. The Friendship, Bienville Parish, branch saw its membership decline from sixty to seven.[36]

The chilling effect of the Fuqua law spurred the formation of more local "shadow" organizations, a development that received encouragement from the newly formed Southern Christian Leadership Conference (SCLC). Launched at a meeting in Atlanta in January 1957, SCLC comprised a loose alliance of the same kind of independent local groups, many of them fronted by ministers, that were sprouting up in Louisiana, and so offered an organized response to the banning of the NAACP in Alabama and its repression in other states. On February 14, 1957, at a meeting in New Zion Baptist Church in New Orleans, about one hundred people voted to establish SCLC as a permanent organization. A number of activists from Louisiana pledged to work with SCLC, among them Rev. T. J. Jemison of Baton Rouge, Dr. C. O. Simpkins of Shreveport, Clarence "Chink" Henry of the New Orleans longshoremen's union, and Rev. A. L. Davis, who hosted the meeting. Initially conceived as a means of capitalizing on the success of the Montgomery bus boycott (it started life as the "Southern Leadership Conference on Transportation and Nonviolent Integration") SCLC's founding gave a stimulus to protests against bus segregation in Louisiana.[37]

The Reverend Abraham Lincoln Davis emerged, somewhat unexpectedly, as the champion of bus integration in New Orleans. Widely recognized as the city's most influential black Protestant minister, Davis had helped to found the Interdenominational Ministerial Alliance, becoming the group's president in 1941 at the tender age of twenty-seven. He was also deeply immersed in politics: since the early 1940s he had campaigned vigorously for black voter registration and, as president of the Orleans Parish Progressive Voters League, became Mayor Morrison's most prominent and powerful black supporter. He enjoyed access to the mayor and, with Jackson V. Acox, the OPPVL's secretary, and Clarence "Chink" Henry, president of the ILA, shared in whatever patronage Morrison doled out to blacks. Never previously active in the NAACP, Davis had the reputation of a political wheeler-dealer rather than a civil rights leader. As Earl Long once noted, Morrison had a black preacher "who preaches nothing but Morrison."[38]

In March 1956 Davis began preaching a more militant sermon. Presiding over a mass meeting of 2,500 people at Union Bethel AME Church, he declared his opposition to segregation in no uncertain terms. Blacks in New Orleans had been "tired for years of sitting behind screens," he said, referring to the moveable boards that marked the racial dividing line on buses. With the NAACP about to be banned, he urged the churches to lead a popular struggle for integration. The Citizens Councils were seeking to recruit 50,000 whites, he noted. "I am issuing the call to 100,000 Negroes in this vicinity to rise up and let Perez and his followers realize that the time is out for segregation and for all that this evil monster stands for." The meeting collected $3,000 for the Montgomery bus boycott, then in its fourth month.[39]

Davis's new militancy dismayed Dave McGuire, Morrison's administrative aide and political advisor. "Two or three years ago," he sadly informed a Standard Fruit executive, Davis "would have said that the NAACP was doing a disservice to the community in its advocacy of immediate integration," but now he seemed to be threatening a bus boycott. Appearances to the contrary, however, Davis had not broken with Mayor Morrison and had no intention of instigating a boycott. Everybody knew that the widely dispersed black population in New Orleans would make a bus boycott difficult to organize. Davis also noted the reservations of Arthur Chapital and A. P. Tureaud, who doubted that a direct challenge to the bus segregation laws would generate a federal court case. Earlier that year, for example, a group of seventy-two Xavier students had boarded an empty bus and occupied all the seats, including the twelve reserved "white" ones in the front. The bus driver had them arrested, but charges of "disturbing the peace" were later dropped. During the remainder of 1956, Davis, the leaders of the outlawed NAACP, and the newly formed New Orleans Improvement League agreed to await the outcome of *Browder* v. *Gayle,* the Montgomery bus segregation case.[40]

In January 1957, shortly after the U.S. Supreme Court voided Alabama's bus segregation laws, George Dinwiddie, the president of New Orleans Public Service, Inc., rejected the idea of voluntarily desegregating the company's buses and trollies. Publicly, Morrison endorsed Dinwiddie's position. Privately, however, he promised Davis that he would guarantee peaceful implementation of a federal court order to integrate. On February 1, 1957, Davis filed suit against the mayor to stop him enforcing segregation. He also organized a series of mass meetings, including the one that brought Martin Luther King and SCLC to the city on February 14, to whip up popular enthusiasm and raise money for the legal costs. On May 24, Judge Skelly Wright ruled that all state laws requiring segregation on public transportation in New Orleans were "unconstitutional and therefore invalid." (Tureaud, it seems, received advance knowledge of the order through the interracial grapevine: Wright told his mother about it, his mother mentioned it to her maid, and the maid informed Tureaud.) During the twelve months that it took the Supreme Court to affirm Wright's judgment, buses remained segregated. As of 12:01 A.M. on May 31, 1958, however, bus and trolley segregation ceased.[41]

A burning cross graced Judge Wright's lawn that night, but no violence or disorder attended integration. The legislature passed a bill giving passengers the right to deny their adjacent seat to members of the other race, but even segregationists found fault with the measure. In New Orleans, one rider explained to Rainach, whites often boarded buses in which black passengers already occupied every window seat. Rainach's bill would merely "aid and solidify the present arrogance of the negroes" by confronting whites with the unpleasant alternatives of "asking permission to sit beside a negro or stand up." Earl Long vetoed the measure. "It's easy to say 'nigger' and scare everybody in the state," he explained. "I think you [should] have a kindly feeling toward the Negro."[42]

The most vigorous and sustained challenge to bus segregation took place in Shreveport under the auspices of the United Christian Movement (UCM), a loose organization formed in the spring of 1957 by a group of ministers and a dentist. On the morning of June 15 five of the ministers, including A. L. Scott, the UCM's executive secretary, boarded a trolley bus and occupied the front seats. During the forty-four-minute round trip the dark-suited clerics looked intently at their Bibles, undisturbed by the driver; a photographer from the *Shreveport Sun,* the city's black newspaper, softly whistled the refrain from "Battle Hymn of the Republic." White passengers reacted calmly. A mail carrier refused to board when he spied the ministers, but one young woman sat beside Scott "as if she didn't even notice the Negro passenger next to her." On the instructions of Mayor James Gardner, the police did not arrest the ministers.[43]

The June 15 trolley ride did not signal the end of segregation. Gardner and police chief Harvey Teasley sternly warned that they intended to enforce state segregation laws and that future violations would not be tolerated. The *Shreveport Journal,* an ardent champion of the Citizens Councils, applauded their tough stand and, in an editorial titled "No Room for Agitators," denounced the ministers' demonstration as a calculated threat to "the peaceful and friendly relations between Shreveport's white and Negro citizens." During the following year the UCM refrained from mounting any more direct challenges, but in December 1957 seven ministers filed suit in the federal district court to have the enforcement of segregation prohibited.[44]

When the state repealed its bus segregation laws after Skelly Wright's order in the New Orleans case, the president of Shreveport Transit Company, Ed Jacobs, announced that drivers would "no longer attempt to control the location as to where passengers are seated." Shortly thereafter, he moved for dismissal of the suit on the grounds that the segregation issue was now moot. The UCM took Jacobs at his word: in July 1958 Mrs. Dorothy Simpkins, Mrs. Eloise Demery, and Rev. C. Dorsey seated themselves at the front of a bus in order to "find out just how 'moot' the question really is." The driver did not challenge them, and on July 20 Dorothy Simpkins's husband, Dr. C. O. Simpkins, informed Tureaud that blacks were riding in the front of the bus without incident.[45]

Unwilling to accept defeat gracefully, however, city and company officials played a cat-and-mouse game with black riders in an effort to keep segregation substantially intact. The *Journal*'s defiant editorials set the tone. Trusting that "98 per cent of the citizens, both white and Negro, can be counted upon to continue segregated seating . . . as a matter of choice," the paper urged the city council to enact an ordinance empowering drivers to assign seats on an individual basis — the kind of law adopted in Tallahassee, Florida, for the purpose of perpetuating segregation by subterfuge. Echoing the "legislate and litigate" policy that was becoming the dominant theme of Louisiana's resistance to integration, the *Journal* made light of the constitutional question. "It does not matter that our socialistic Supreme Court might eventually declare such a law unconstitutional; much time would elapse and, in the interim, another statute could be prepared." Days later, on July 25, Mary and Princella Bender, two teenage girls, boarded a nearly full bus and took the last available seats, the ones directly behind the driver. When a white woman objected, the driver asked the pair to move back. They refused, whereupon he flagged down a motorcycle policeman who arrested the pair. Princella spent the night in the city jail, Mary in the juvenile jail, and they were charged with disturbing the peace.[46]

The city's efforts to avoid a definitive court ruling received an assist from Judge Ben C. Dawkins Jr. Elevated to the federal bench in 1953, Dawkins, unlike many of Eisenhower's southern judicial appointees, evinced little enthusiasm for advancing the civil rights of blacks and on occasion exhibited overt hostility to that cause. Dawkins regarded himself as a racial moderate, and by the standards of the *Journal* and the Citizens Councils, he was. Nevertheless, the young lawyer who eight years earlier had passionately affirmed his commitment to racial segregation still believed that "forced association . . . can not and will not work."[47] And while he realized that the judicial thrust toward integration inaugurated by *Brown* could not be reversed, he had no qualms about trying to slow it down. On August 29, 1958, three days after the city council enacted a bus seating ordinance clearly designed to preserve segregation, Dawkins granted a six-month continuance and advised the black plaintiffs to seek an interpretation of the new ordinance from the state courts. Federal courts, he explained, had been "much too hasty in issuing injunctions right and left, like a small boy on a gravel pit flinging rocks in all directions, with respect to state or local legislation." Dawkins implored the parties to preserve "the mutual respect which both races have had for each other, lo these many years."[48]

The cat-and-mouse game went on. In early October Dr. C. O. Simpkins, now president of the UCM, tested the status quo by sitting in the front with several black companions. The ride was uneventful, he wrote Tureaud. "They did not ask us to move even when one of the white riders objected to sitting behind Negroes." In one of its periodic "Trolley Reports," the UCM informed the black community that more and more Negro passengers were refusing to move to the rear when drivers ordered them back. On October 24, however, a driver stopped his trolley and hailed a policeman when a young woman, Lessie B. Harris, disobeyed an order to move back. Convicted of disturbing the peace, Harris had to return to jail when unable to pay her fine. The clearest indication that the city meant to enforce segregation came in January 1959, when a policeman arrested Dorothy Simpkins, who was riding with her eight-year-old daughter, after she refused to leave her front seat. During the following year the number of such arrests multiplied. Tureaud filed an amended complaint, but with Dawkins in no hurry to decide the case segregation lingered on. In 1962 Dawkins dismissed the suit for lack of prosecution, although the segregation issue had yet to be clearly settled. Shreveport illustrates how easily assertive black leadership could be frustrated by a hostile federal judge and an unyielding white community.[49]

Bus integration in Lake Charles underlined the importance of community attitudes and judicial sympathy. A mass meeting sponsored by the Lake Charles Citizens Committee on August 8, 1958, set the ball rolling, and in March 1959 local black attorney Leo F. McDaniel filed suit against city and bus company officials. Six months later Judge Edwin F. Hunter struck down the city's bus segregation ordinance and enjoined the defendants "from doing any acts or taking any action" to segregate passengers. Hunter did not equivocate. "The *Gayle* decision is binding upon us," he declared; "the *Morrison* decision is binding upon us."[50]

To some extent, of course, federal district judges reflected the political culture of their districts. The same age as Dawkins and appointed to the bench in the same year, Hunter was born in Alexandria, "the political navel of the state" where Protestant north met Catholic south, a city that lacked Shreveport's history of hard-edged racism and staunch anti-Long conservatism.[51]

Lake Charles also had a tradition of racial moderation. Southwest Louisiana had not been a major slaveholding area before the Civil War, and Lake Charles itself was a largely twentieth-century city that looked as much toward Houston as toward New Orleans. The *Lake Charles American* had been one of only three newspapers — all of them in southwest Louisiana — to oppose Amendment 16 in 1956, and the city's prosegregation vote for that measure had been the lowest in the state. Blacks voted freely there, much more freely than in Shreveport, and the Lake Charles branch of the NAACP was the largest in the state outside New Orleans. The Citizens Councils found Lake Charles inhospitable terrain. "Lake Charles . . . does not have enough Council members to influence the city officials there," a local racist lamented in 1960. As in New Orleans, city officials put up only token resistance to bus integration.[52]

The persistence of segregated buses in Baton Rouge is puzzling. The Baton Rouge branch of the NAACP had once been one of the strongest in Louisiana, and blacks there had shown remarkable unity during the week-long bus boycott in 1953. Moreover, Baton Rouge did not have a history of racial violence or a reputation for white extremism. Yet litigation over the buses dragged on for nine years, from 1953 to 1962, earning for Baton Rouge the dubious distinction of being, with cities like Shreveport, Birmingham, Augusta, and Macon, one of the last southern cities to integrate its public transportation. Why did it take so long? The answer to this riddle seems to lie in a combination of weak black leadership and the growing influence of ultrasegregationists in the city's politics.

It is a startling fact that the NAACP had no functioning branch in Louisiana's capital city between 1956 and 1962. The Baton Rouge branch failed to file a membership list by the end of 1956 and thus not only forfeited its right to operate legally but also lost all its members. Its failure to comply with the Fuqua law seemed to indicate a loss of nerve on the part of the branch's leading members. The gradual retirement of B. J. Stanley in the early 1950s and his death in January 1956 had deprived the branch of one of its mainstays. As the branch faced extinction, nobody stepped forward to provide the needed steadiness of purpose.

As the Baton Rouge branch became defunct, T. J. Jemison, the city's most prominent black minister and leader of the 1953 bus boycott, took the initiative in founding a "shadow" organization, the Baton Rouge Christian Movement. In February 1957, after a series of futile meetings with bus company executives, city officials, and the state attorney general, Jemison and several others sued in federal court for an end to bus segregation. The case lay dormant for over three years. Eventually, in April 1961, Judge Herbert W. Christenberry ruled for the plaintiffs, but another year passed before the court of appeals affirmed the judgment. During the five years that it took *Jemison* v. *Christian* to wind its way through the courts, blacks in Baton Rouge made no attempt to boycott the buses or otherwise directly challenge segregation. Lacking militant leadership, the Baton Rouge Christian Movement became little more than a name. Jemison soon dropped out of the new Southern Christian Leadership Conference, and the National Baptist Convention, which his father had once headed and which he aspired to lead, became the focus of his energy and ambition.[53]

Weak leadership both reflected and reinforced divisions within Baton Rouge's black community. Home to both Southern University and a sprawling Esso Standard Oil refinery, the city boasted a substantial black middle class and a much larger black population of blue-collar and service workers. Moreover, the faculty and staff of Southern, directly dependent on a state board of education controlled by white politicians, had a strong disincentive to involve themselves in civil rights protest. The geographical separation of black neighborhoods overlaid these class divisions. After studying the record of Baton Rouge's black leadership in the years after 1953, one student characterized it as "feeble and factionalized."[54]

An aggressive segregationist movement exploited black disunity and strengthened the city's resistance to black demands. Although ultrasegregationists never achieved the dominance in Baton Rouge that they established in Shreveport, they did become increasingly influential. In 1954, hard on the heels of the *Brown* decision, Baton Rouge gave birth to the Southern Gentlemen. Two years later it became the target of a school integration suit, only the third to be filed by the NAACP in Louisiana, which pushed segregationists to organize resistance. Fate also lent a hand when the racially moderate mayor, Jesse L. Webb Jr., died in a plane crash. Jack Christian, his successor, styled himself a staunch segregationist and lined up with the Rainach-Perez forces.

Well stocked with resourceful lawyer-lobbyists ready to utilize their talents in the cause of white supremacy, Baton Rouge became a focus of opposition to integration. District Attorney J. St. Clair Favrot consulted Rainach and Perez in devising a legal strategy for the parish school board. Favrot also employed a tactic that became a favorite weapon of Baton Rouge D.A.'s: the prosecution of civil rights activists on spurious or trivial charges. In 1957 he prosecuted black attorney Alex Pitcher on a "worthless check" charge, prompting A. P. Tureaud to demand Pitcher's withdrawal from all NAACP cases. Two years later Favrot convened a grand jury to investigate T. J. Jemison's administration of his church's finances. After Jemison admitted cashing a check for $100 and using the money to support candidates in the school board election, he was indicted and prosecuted for theft (the prosecution failed). Favrot's successor, Sargent Pitcher Jr., an ultrasegregationist and close ally of Rainach, continued the tradition, prosecuting a string of NAACP and CORE leaders on a variety of charges.[55]

As the bus cases made clear, the federal courts played a crucial role in sustaining the faltering movement for equal rights. Of Louisiana's federal judges, only Ben Dawkins felt out of sympathy with black aspirations; others did not hesitate to strike down segregationist artifices and apply the principles of *Brown*.

These judges were a mixed bag: no obvious common factor accounted for their support for equal rights. Like Wayne G. Borah, a Republican appointee who had served on the federal bench since the 1920s, Herbert W. Christenberry and Edwin F. Hunter saw themselves simply as conscientious jurists with a sense of fair play and a respect for the Supreme Court. Skelly Wright and John Minor Wisdom, on the other hand, developed a deep sense of the historic injustices inflicted upon blacks, and their legal thinking reflected a determination to right past wrongs. They came from both sides of Louisiana's political fence: Christenberry, for example, the son of Huey Long's secretary, had been a loyal Longite; Wisdom, a Republican party activist, had been staunchly anti-Long. With the exception of Hunter, who hailed from Alexandria, all the judges who supported black civil rights were New Orleanians.[56]

John Minor Wisdom deserves special mention. He was the only judge from Louisiana — and probably the only federal judge in the South — to have been actively involved in civil rights before his appointment to the bench. He had been a key member of the New Orleans Urban League and had served on the Committee on Government Contracts, an antidiscrimination watchdog chaired by Vice President Nixon. Nominated to the Court of Appeals for the Fifth Circuit in 1957, he became one of the most forthright and influential liberals on the southern bench.

Eisenhower did not consistently appoint racial liberals; he also appointed Ben Dawkins. As Robert Burk has noted, "Eisenhower's appointments to the federal bench in the South . . . owed more to partisan loyalty than to any guiding judicial philosophy." Nor did Republican judges have a monopoly on virtue when it came to civil rights; Christenberry and Wright, for example, were Truman appointees. Nevertheless, their party traditions and status as political outsiders made the southern Republicans, as a group, more disposed to racial and political change in their region. As "mavericks from Southern political orthodoxy," writes Burk, they were more detached "from the white supremacist traditions of Southern Democratic politics." A cynic might suppose that Republicans like Wisdom, the leader of Louisiana's Republican party as well as Eisenhower's southern campaign manager, had a political motive in supporting black civil rights. On the other hand, Wisdom's very Republicanism had stemmed, in part, from his detestation of Louisiana's corrupt and undemocratic one-party system. His desire to break down that system, with all its manifest injustices, transcended partisan politics.[57]

The importance of federal judges in sustaining the momentum of integration can scarcely be overstated. On February 15, 1956, Skelly Wright became the first district judge in the Fifth Circuit (covering Georgia, Florida, Alabama, Mississippi, Louisiana, and Texas) to hand down a school integration decree. Dismissing Amendment 16 and the 1954 Pupil Placement Act, he placed the Orleans Parish school board under the specific requirement of *Brown* to admit children on a nondiscriminatory basis "with all deliberate speed." While Wright allowed the school board time, his decision made it likely that New Orleans would be the first city in the Deep South to integrate its schools.[58]

In early 1957, Wright and Christenberry removed two other weapons from the segregationist arsenal, striking down the prohibition on teachers belonging to organizations advocating integration and voiding the requirement that applicants to state colleges and universities must furnish "certificates of eligibility and good moral character" signed by their high school principal. The year 1958 saw the court-ordered entry of the first black undergraduates to LSU, the integration of buses in New Orleans, and in another case decided by Wright, the integration of City Park. The LSU undergraduate suit dated from 1953, the City Park case from 1949.

Some federal judges learned to respond more quickly to segregationist delaying tactics. When the state board of education ruled that the LSU decision did not apply to the new branch of LSU in New Orleans (LSUNO), Christenberry granted the plaintiffs a speedy hearing and issued an injunction thirty minutes later. Two hundred blacks entered LSUNO when it opened in September 1958, making it "the first fully integrated public university in the Deep South." Before the year was out, Wisdom, Christenberry, and Wright voided the state's ban on interracial sports in a suit filed by boxer Joe Dorsey.[59]

Once described as "fifty-eight lonely men," the federal district judges of the South who followed the spirit of *Brown* often found themselves socially isolated and, in the mid-1950s, bereft of political support from either the president or Congress. In the sphere of civil rights, the federal government resembled a three-engine plane limping along on a single engine, the judiciary: the plane flew slowly and erratically and might crash at any moment. Clearly, the judges needed help.

In his State of the Union message of January 5, 1956, President Eisenhower went on record, for the first time, as favoring a civil rights bill. Over the following weeks Attorney General Herbert Brownell, the main advocate of legislation, drafted a proposal that included the creation of an independent, fact-finding commission on civil rights, the elevation of the Civil Rights Section of the Justice Department to full division status, and stronger powers for the Justice Department to protect voting rights. Brownell had to battle long and hard to secure administration backing. In addition to Eisenhower's lack of enthusiasm and the skepticism of other cabinet members, he faced strong opposition from J. Edgar Hoover, who in a briefing to the cabinet on March 9 implied that civil rights legislation would play into the hands of black extremists and the Communist Party. Having obtained only a lukewarm endorsement from Eisenhower, Brownell tried to build congressional support by focusing public attention on the continuing denial of the vote to blacks and, in particular, the related activities of the burgeoning Citizens Council movement.[60]

The purge of black voters in Monroe, probably the most blatant example of its kind in the South, gave the Justice Department a golden opportunity to dramatize the need for legislation. On October 10, in a statement to the Senate Subcommittee on Privileges and Elections, Assistant Attorney General Warren Olney III described the purge as "a problem of major concern to the whole Nation" for which "there is no adequate remedy available to the Department of Justice." After Eisenhower's reelection in November, Olney ordered the FBI to investigate the Monroe purge, as well as those reported in other north Louisiana parishes, with a view to prosecuting those responsible under the Reconstruction-era criminal conspiracy statute. In early December, with the Bureau providing details and numbers from ten parishes, the department empaneled a federal grand jury in Monroe.[61]

Inevitably, Justice's decision to utilize the FBI elicited cries of "foul" from ultrasegregationists. North Louisiana politicians wired protests to Washington denouncing the FBI's "fishing expeditions" and "witch hunts." The *Shreveport Journal* warned the Bureau that its reputation was at stake. "The FBI agents themselves . . . have shown by their actions — their courtesy and apologetic manner — that they have no stomach for the miserable mission of snitching and informing to which they have been committed. . . . But if the United States Justice Department continues to misuse the FBI, the American people will come to look upon it as a Hitlerian Gestapo and its Agents will be reduced to the status of Keystone Kops." William Rainach advised people that they did not have to answer the FBI's questions.[62]

The avalanche of criticism hit home: FBI agents loathed this assignment. They already felt profoundly uncomfortable conducting "discreet inquiries" into the Citizens Councils, an investigation started some months earlier at the insistence of the Justice Department. These were whites of their own social class, who shared their own political beliefs, and who were in many cases personal acquaintances and trusted sources of information. For months, the local agents contented themselves with passing on information gleaned from newspapers, an investigation so perfunctory that even Hoover, who shared their dislike of this task, registered his dissatisfaction. The object, he reminded the New Orleans office, was to ascertain the council's potential for violence. "Obviously this information cannot be obtained solely from articles appearing in the public press." Hoover instructed the agents to use "established reliable sources" to build up profiles of individual Citizens Council leaders. The agents balked. These were not subversive or violent organizations, New Orleans stressed. The councils comprised "the most prominent and influential people"; moreover, "practically all of the established sources who are normally contacted in these cases are in sympathy with the aims and purposes of the Citizens Councils."

The purge inquiry only intensified the agents' discomfort. New Orleans advised Hoover to drop the Citizens Council investigation. To continue it, warned SAC Chiles, "is tantamount to the seeking of information concerning prominent individuals throughout the States of Louisiana and Mississippi, and could result in adverse comments and response from the various communities affected." The Director, always eager to reduce the Bureau's civil rights case load, agreed. On December 26, 1956, he ordered all inquiries into the Citizens Councils discontinued.[63]

Soon afterward, the purge investigation fell flat on its face. On February 12, 1957, having deliberated for ten days and heard dozens of witnesses, including FBI agents, the federal grand jury in Monroe declined to return any indictments. There was a double victory for the Citizens Councils: the previous day, Judge Ben Dawkins found for the Ouachita Parish registrar of voters in the case of *Reddix* v. *Lucky*. Dawkins not only cleared Mae Lucky of discrimination in her handling of the mass challenges, but also went on to accuse the plaintiff, dentist John Reddix, of "bad faith" and "sheer stubborn vindictiveness" for having made no attempt to reregister since being disqualified. "He apparently prefers litigation to registration." Dawkins likewise dismissed a companion suit against Lucky filed by James Sharp, a black lawyer. Sharp claimed that his ability to practice law had been injured by Lucky's refusal to do business with him in her office, having placed all the registration cards of black voters in the police jury room, in the charge of an assistant. Dawkins could hardly conceal his scorn for this argument. By placing their cards in a separate office, the judge claimed, Lucky had been able to give challenged black voters better service. Dawkins sarcastically refused to enjoin "the segregation of inanimate objects."[64]

The segregationists' howls of protest turned into chortles of glee. On February 13 Jack Gremillion appeared before a subcommittee of the House Judiciary Committee to explain away the Monroe purge. "Do not pay any attention to that Monroe affair," he advised the committee. "That is strictly politics." They "did have some difficulty with respect to voting," he admitted, but it had been "more or less an exception." Besides, he told one congressman, "about 99 percent of them are back on the rolls." Gremillion denied any knowledge of the Citizens Councils. Making light of the constitutional interpretation test, he claimed that registrars "cannot say 'I want you to explain something' that is impossible to explain. [Applicants] have the right of choice insofar as concerns the section or phrase of the Constitution they wish to interpret." Gremillion's testimony was so disingenuous that the Justice Department supplied the committee with a point-by-point rebuttal.[65]

Although ostensibly a victory for the Citizens Councils, the Monroe investigation represented one of the opening shots in a long political battle over black disfranchisement that drew the federal government ever more deeply into the South's affairs and eventually culminated in the 1965 Voting Rights Act. More than principle was at stake. The growing black vote in the North and the sizeable, and potentially much larger, black vote in the South offered rich political pickings. In the mid-1950s Republican strategists sensed that Democratic divisions over civil rights gave their party an opportunity to recapture the loyalty of many black voters, who had switched en masse to the Democrats during the New Deal. As political analyst Samuel Lubell put it, "The South today is the greatest exposed flank of the Democratic party. Through it the Republicans can strike at the very core of the Democratic party in the Northern cities."[66]

The 1956 presidential election confirmed the Democrats' vulnerability. While Eisenhower's victory surprised no one, the extent of the Republican inroads into the Negro vote did. According to Lubell, black support for Eisenhower increased from 25 percent in 1952 to 36 percent in 1956, a far bigger shift than that of the electorate as a whole. The swing among black voters was even more pronounced in the South: the Republicans gained 19 percent, as opposed to 8 percent in the North.

Eisenhower carried Louisiana by 40,550 votes, and blacks may well have supplied his margin of victory. In Shreveport, the Democratic vote in black precincts fell by 27 percent, in New Orleans by 37 percent, and in Baton Rouge it slumped by 64 percent. Tureaud explained the figures as a protest against the segregationist legislature, which danced to Rainach's tune. The *Louisiana Weekly,* endorsing Eisenhower, reasoned that a vote for Adlai Stevenson meant a vote for the southern Democrats. "Without a question Ike has moved forward on the civil rights question." Digesting the bad news, Senator Hubert H. Humphrey complained that Democrats were "digging our own graves by inaction in the field of civil rights." Heightened competition for the black vote eased the passage of the administration civil rights bill, which became law on September 9, 1957 — the first civil rights law in eighty-two years. Two weeks later, his hand forced by Governor Orval Faubus's calculated defiance of a federal court order, President Eisenhower sent troops to Little Rock to oversee the integration of Central High School. "Well, that's it," Earl Long reportedly commented. "The feds are behind the niggers."[67]

The ultrasegregationists, however, had no intention of throwing in the towel. Congress's approval of the Civil Rights Act and Eisenhower's intervention in Little Rock gave 1957 the appearance of a turning point, but these actions had more symbolism than substance. The impact of the Civil Rights Act remained to be seen: the original bill had been so weakened that many regarded it as a tactical triumph for the South's senators. As for school integration, the administration still hewed to its policy of leaving the implementation of *Brown* to the federal district courts, using coercion to enforce court orders only as a last resort. Moreover, the result of the Little Rock crisis, the entry of nine black students into a formerly all-white high school, seemed a paltry gain in light of the massive force employed and the sum of political capital expended. It was hardly a resounding victory for integration, especially when Governor Faubus closed Little Rock's four high schools during the 1958–59 school year. The crisis also had disturbing political ramifications: Faubus easily won a second term in 1958, a result that further undercut racial moderates by showing that bitter-end resistance to integration paid electoral dividends. "The size of [Faubus's] victory *was* unexpected," Roy Wilkins told the NAACP's branch presidents. "We thought that he would win, but not by so wide a margin. We must recognize that the Faubus victory will have an effect far beyond the borders of Arkansas, but we must not be frightened by it."[68]

In Louisiana, Rainach and his allies stepped up their three-pronged campaign of harrassing the NAACP, reducing the black vote, and uniting whites behind an all-out defense of segregated schools.

No sooner had the crippled NAACP reemerged as a legal entity than it came under attack as a Communist front. In March 1957 Rainach's Joint Legislative Committee held three days of hearings on "Subversion in Racial Unrest" that featured two former party members, Manning Johnson and Joseph Zack Kornfeder, as the star witnesses. The NAACP, claimed Johnson, "is nothing more than the vehicle of the Communist Party, in which the Communists are colonizing for the purpose of inciting racial rebellion in the South, with the ultimate object, in the insane confusion, to seize power and take over the reins of government." Hubert Badeaux, Guy Banister, and Leander Perez testified along the same lines.

Even by the kangaroo-court standards of McCarthyism, it was a crude affair. The hearings consisted entirely of accusations. Kornfeder and Johnson, moreover, had a record of perjury that gave them little credibility — Johnson had once accused Ralph Bunche of being a Party member. Guy Banister cut a ludicrous figure. He warned the committee that a handful of dedicated saboteurs could "knock out a great city like New Orleans" by means of smuggled atom bombs or germ warfare. He speculated that Soviet germ warfare experiments might have caused recent outbreaks of hoof and mouth disease in Canada and "wheat stem rust" in Montana and the Dakotas. "An investigator must do many things," Banister confided. "He must go into many places he would not ordinarily go — even into the French Quarter after dark." Perez, who testified to the "subversive" background of NAACP field secretary Clarence Laws, was also a man who saw Communists everywhere, one who, according to the FBI, "is so completely engrossed in his own ideas and opinions that anyone or anything that is not in complete agreement with him is either a Communist or a Communist tool."[69]

Whether the hearings persuaded many whites is hard to say. Nevertheless, in the atmosphere of the 1950s accusations of communism, especially coming from official bodies, usually had some effect. Fear of "godless Communism" still hung over America like a pall, and real Communists were still being unearthed by Congressional committees. Just three weeks before Rainach opened his hearings (a nice coincidence, if coincidence it was) HUAC arrived in New Orleans and named twenty alleged Communists. One of them, the head of the ILWU, faced prosecution by the federal authorities for failing to declare his party membership. Shortly afterwards Hubert Badeaux, head of the NOPD's "intelligence division," filed charges of criminal anarchy and subversion against five alleged Communists, including Hunter Pitts O'Dell. Badeaux also sent HUAC a file on Unitarian minister Albert D'Orlando, with the comment, "I hope the bum gets out of line and gets cited for contempt."

D'Orlando's appearance before HUAC the following year provided a telling illustration of how segregationist red-baiting could still isolate and discredit white supporters of civil rights. Even liberal organizations like the Southern Regional Council required loyalty oaths. The SRC had reluctantly accepted D'Orlando's refusal to sign one when he became chairman of the Louisiana Council on Human Relations, but his silence in the face of questions from HUAC about his political activities before 1945 put him beyond the pale. D'Orlando returned to New Orleans under a cloud of suspicion. When he resisted pressure to resign from the LCCR, that body simply ceased to function. When he refused to quit the Urban League, the board of directors stopped notifying him of its meetings.[70]

The staunchly anti-Communist NAACP was an inconvenient target. Even the conservative New Orleans *Times-Picayune,* usually supportive of red-hunting inquisitions, found the Rainach hearings unconvincing. But for credulous whites — and Louisiana's whites were possibly the worst-educated in the nation — it did not require a great mental leap to believe that Communists were behind the integration movement and that, to quote the *Shreveport Journal*, "the CP in NAACP means Communist Party." The NAACP regarded charges of communism as sufficiently threatening to justify considerable energy and expense in their rebuttal. In March 1957, for example, Roy Wilkins wrote to George Shannon, the *Journal*'s ultrasegregationist editor, to protest one of his distorted editorials. The following year Wilkins helped the New Orleans branch present two half-hour television programs that answered the Citizens Councils' allegations. A Shreveport Citizens Council resolution attacking the NAACP as Communist-infiltrated evoked a lengthy reply, prepared by Clarence Laws and national publicity director Henry Lee Moon, that quoted J. Edgar Hoover's *Masters of Deceit* in the organization's defense.[71]

Red-baiting attacks were expensive and time-consuming distractions, but the NAACP could live with them. Act 260 of the state legislature, on the other hand, threatened once again to put the organization out of business. Passed in the summer of 1958, the law prohibited organizations from being affiliated with any out-of-state organizations that had any members or directors belonging to "Communist, Communist-front or subversive organizations." The law relied upon HUAC to define the forbidden category. It also required organizations to furnish non-Communist affidavits when they filed their membership lists. Robert Carter considered the statute "clearly unconstitutional" and advised branches to ignore it. When the New Orleans branch failed to file a membership list for 1958, however, Secretary of State Wade O. Martin began criminal proceedings. And when Shreveport branch president R. L. Williams courageously agreed to host the NAACP's 1959 statewide meeting when no other branch would, the authorities moved aggressively to stop the session from taking place. "The sheriff had Williams brought down to the station," writes Willie Burton, "where he was questioned for almost two hours by 13 or more state, parish and city officials." Williams refused to be intimidated and even advertised the meeting in the *Shreveport Journal,* but on October 10, at Rainach's request, a state court judge enjoined the Shreveport branch from holding any further meetings. Once again, the NAACP found itself paralyzed.[72]

A federal court finally rescued the beleaguered organization. On February 6, 1960, a panel comprising Judges Wisdom, Wright, and Christenberry exempted the NAACP from the Fuqua law, noting that the state had never enforced it until 1956. They also knocked down Act 260 because it "would require the impossible." The state never again seriously challenged the NAACP's right to operate. Nevertheless, the damage had been done; most branches remained dead or dormant. It took ten years for the NAACP to regain the ground it lost in 1956.[73]

As they continued harassing the NAACP, Rainach and his allies intensified their drive to whittle away the black vote. On September 4, 1958, Rainach and Shaw arrived in Winnfield, Earl Long's home town and, accompanied by members of the local Citizens Council, proceeded to methodically examine the registration cards of black voters.

The registrar, Mary C. Flournoy, deeply resented their presence. "I asked them to take the cards as they came and challenge the defects," she later recalled. "But they didn't want to do it like that. . . . Those people wanted to pick out the cards. . . . They brought a list along of the people they wanted to challenge." When they began correcting mistakes on the cards of white voters, Flournoy decided to act: Rainach and his confederates returned from lunch to find the registrar's office locked and Flournoy nowhere to be found. At 11 P.M., armed with subpoenas from a local judge and a warrant for the arrest of the assistant registrar, the purgers finally regained access to the office and stayed up until the early hours photographing records. Rainach then hauled Flournoy before the Joint Legislative Committee and extracted a promise to "comply strictly with the laws." They told her to adopt the constitutional interpretation test and, Flournoy recalled, "pull those hard cards on colored people." Mrs. Flournoy was not one to give in easily. "One thing, especially, I need advice on," she wrote Rainach. "How to cope with a fine Old Timer who has voted all his life and now finds the 'Younger Generation' refuses him the privileges he prizes most; the right to help or reject any local politician. Believe me. There's plenty of bitterness among them." Yet though she resisted applying the interpretation test, black registration in Winn Parish did decline.[74]

By 1958 the north Louisiana phase of the "voter cleanup" had been largely completed, and the Citizens Councils turned their attention to the Florida Parishes and south Louisiana. In East Feliciana Parish, a Citizens Council delegation confronted the registrar, Charles S. Kilbourne, about his refusal to employ an interpretation test and his policy of helping people fill out the application form. When Kilbourne refused to back down, the police jury had him replaced. The new registrar promptly accepted about 1,500 challenges; black registration plummeted from 1,276 to 50.[75]

Blacks had little success in reregistering, and complaining to the federal authorities could evoke vindictive reactions. In late 1957 M. M. Coleman ran into state senator Herman Jones on the streets of Minden. Coleman, a funeral director, headed the Webster Parish Better Citizenship League. He asked Jones when the registrar's office would be open to Negroes on an equitable basis. When Jones evaded his question, Coleman suggested that whites could avoid federal lawsuits by forming a biracial committee composed of the "better and more liberal people." The five-minute exchange was tense but polite. However, when FBI agents appeared at the registrar's office in March 1958, the local Citizens Council launched a counteroffensive. Jones alleged before a grand jury that Coleman had threatened him with federal intervention. The jury then indicted Coleman for "attempted intimidation of a public official."[76]

Emboldened by his success in the northern part of the state, and increasingly confident that he had Earl Long on the run, Rainach launched the second phase of the voter purge. Starting in December 1958, the Joint Legislative Committee held meetings in every corner of the state to brief registrars, sheriffs, district attorneys, and other officials on how to disfranchise blacks. JLC attorney William Shaw pressed registrars to administer a constitutional interpretation test using the "card system" devised by Leander Perez. Requiring applicants to interpret the Constitution would eliminate blacks, he explained, because it tested "native intelligence" rather than "book learning," and "most of our white people have this native intelligence while most Negroes do not." Perez outlined the procedure for challenging "illegally registered" voters, warning that registrars could be fined and even imprisoned for allowing such people onto the rolls. Rainach closed the meetings with a reminder that the Communists and the NAACP sought to mobilize the "Negro bloc vote" and that the fight for school integration had "shifted from the courts to the political arena, from legal moves to a fight for the votes of Negro masses." The presence of Douglas Fowler, director of the State Board of Registration, and Jack Gremillion, state attorney general, left the registrars in no doubt that Rainach's goal of reducing the black vote was tantamount to the official policy of the state.[77]

Everything went according to plan at first. In St. Helena Parish the Citizens Council forced one registrar to resign and compelled his successor to fail black applicants. The registrar of Washington Parish, Curtis Thomas, was made of sterner stuff and initially resisted the mass challenges filed by two Citizens Council members. Thomas ignored minor errors on the application forms and accepted challenges only on the basis of residence, thus enabling all but 16 of 157 challenged voters to save their registration. The Joint Legislative Committee arrived in Franklinton and proceeded to haul Thomas over the coals: Rainach accused him of "willful, malicious and deliberate violations of the law." Thomas asked the district court to enjoin the purgers, complaining that they interfered with his job, created a nuisance, and served "no useful purpose." District judge C. A. Barnett, however, rejected Thomas's request. It was time for people in Louisiana "to stand up and be counted," Barnett declared, for democracies could not tolerate "habitual and prolonged abuse of the elective franchise." The judge ordered Thomas to strike the 157 challenged voters from his rolls. Within weeks, three Citizens Council members had purged 85 percent of the parish's black voters, 1,377 people.[78]

Earl Long at last woke up to the political threat staring him in the face. Hitherto he had consistently deferred to the Joint Legislative Committee, allowing Rainach to retain the political initiative. Even after Rainach's brazen effort to purge black voters in Winn Parish — including an attempt to disfranchise Long's own cook — Long still hesitated to take Rainach on. "A lot of people are following you not because they agree with you," he admitted, "but because they are scared not to." But the spread of the purge to south Louisiana, with its much larger black vote, convinced Long that his political survival was at stake. Rainach intended to run for governor in 1959; the purge was a blatant ploy to increase his chances by eliminating pro-Long votes. Washington Parish was a Long stronghold. So was St. Landry Parish, Rainach's next target.[79]

Beginning in November 1958, the Civil Rights Commission in Washington received a "continuing stream" of affidavits from people who were denied the right to vote in Louisiana. Many came from Shreveport and were gathered by Ella J. Baker, the executive director of SCLC, working with C. O. Simpkins and the United Christian Movement. Earl Long also supplied the commission with evidence of voting discrimination, including documents detailing Rainach's purge. Thus armed, the commission made plans to hold hearings in Shreveport. In May 1959, Long finally came out into the open, introducing two bills aimed at halting the purges. One made it illegal to challenge voters who had been registered for a year or more, the other forbade the removal of voters for trivial mistakes on their application forms.

By now, however, Long had conceded so much political ground that his strength had been irreparably weakened. He could not get his voting bills passed. As one legislator put it, "We just couldn't be seen as soft on the nigger question." In a final effort to save the bills, Long entered the senate chamber and proceeded to orate to the legislators while swigging from a bottle of soda laced with whisky. He passionately defended the right of blacks to vote. "You got to recognize that niggers is human beings!" he shouted at Rainach. "There's no longer slavery!" It immediately became clear, however, that the strain of this confrontation had precipitated some kind of mental breakdown: Long was crude, rambling, abusive, profane, maudlin, incoherent, and generally out of control. The governor was evidently a very sick man, with an increasingly insecure grip on reality. His family had him committed to a mental institution in Texas.[80]

Rainach was jubilant. "I clashed head-on with the governor for the first time," he wrote a friend, "and we gave him the worst drubbing ever administered to the chief executive in the history of this state." Shortly afterwards, Rainach notched up another victory when Judge Dawkins enjoined the Civil Rights Commission from going ahead with its scheduled hearings in Shreveport. Rainach hurried to Opelousas to direct the purge of St. Landry Parish, the stronghold of Longite sheriff D. J. "Cat" Doucet and home to more black voters than any other parish except New Orleans.[81]

Long's highly publicized confrontation with Rainach, however, helped to mobilize opposition to the Citizens Councils. The local officeholders who depended on the black vote had no intention of allowing a north Louisiana reactionary to destroy a vital component of their power base. On May 26 Sheriff Doucet threw down the gauntlet. "I'm waiting for him in St. Landry. . . . If you knock them off the rolls, I'll put them back on." When three Citizens Council members arrived at her office to initiate the purge, registrar Ruby C. Rider subjected them to the kind of "slow-down" tactics that in other parishes were usually applied to blacks, accepting only twelve challenges a day. A week later Doucet appeared at a Citizens Council rally in Ville Platte and handed out copies of an "Open Letter to Senator Rainach" published in the June 30 edition of the *Franklin Banner-Tribune*. The editorial, written by editor-proprietor Robert Angers Jr., spoke of a black soldier who became a sergeant in World War Two and who happened to be illiterate. "The measure of a man's love for his country comes from his heart. No law is worth the paper it is written on that denies a free man the right to vote. If we lose the right to vote or to express our opinion at the ballot box, senator, this nation is doomed for you, for the sergeant and for me." "Cat" Doucet echoed these sentiments. "Even if a person can't read or write, he's an American citizen and taxpayer. Let everybody vote, this is America not Russia." Rainach had failed to dent the best-known symbol of black voting in Louisiana.[82]

Meanwhile, in Washington Parish, blacks decided to fight back. In April 1959 NAACP stalwart William Bailey Jr., who nine years earlier had been the parish's first black voter but who was now disfranchised for omitting the final "e" of "Pointe Coupee Parish," journeyed to New Orleans to seek help from U.S. attorney M. Hepburn Many. Many was appalled by Bailey's story and eager to prosecute the purgers. At Many's behest — and it was surely significant that Many asked Bailey to do this rather than the FBI — Bailey made a trip to the state capitol to procure the membership lists of the Ku Klux Klan, the Southern Gentlemen, and the Citizens Council.

It was unusual at that time for black people, other than janitors, to be seen in the grandiose, marble-lined capitol, and Bailey felt conspicuously out of place as he walked past the legislators, who had just adjourned, and asked the elevator operator to take him to the seventh floor. At the secretary of state's office, a startled secretary stared as a lanky, mild-mannered Negro requested to see the membership list of the Washington Parish Citizens Council, blurting out, "Are you a lawyer?" When Bailey perused the document, names leaped from the page. "I saw so many people that I knew so well," he recalled, neighbors, tradesmen with whom he did business, people he considered friends. "I was so amazed and shocked." He paid for two copies of the list. Convinced that they had a case of statewide importance, the NAACP backed Bailey to the hilt. "Hep" Many agreed. Armed with a copy of the Citizens Council membership list, he convinced the Justice Department to invoke the 1957 Civil Rights Act and enter the case as expeditiously as possible. It did so on June 29.[83]

Thus far the history of the Civil Rights Act had been, in the words of political scientist Donald Strong, "chiefly a tale of frustration." The two previous federal prosecutions had both failed. One case collapsed when the registrars of Macon County, Alabama, resigned, leaving the Justice Department with no one to sue. The other case, concerning Terrell County, Georgia, had been dismissed by a federal district judge who held the Civil Rights Act to be unconstitutional. The fact-finding agency created by the act, the U.S. Commission on Civil Rights, had also run into trouble: in July 1959 Judge Dawkins issued an injunction to stop the commission from holding hearings in Shreveport. "It's all part of the game," Dawkins commented, shrugging off criticism that his decision was political rather than legal. Blacks looked on in disgust and disbelief.[84]

Luckily for the government and the NAACP, they could not have found a more sympathetic arbiter than Judge J. Skelly Wright. In October, Wright denied a defense motion to dismiss Bailey's case. "In a democratic society," he explained, "there is no greater offense than illegally depriving a citizen of his right to vote. . . . Instead of challenging the constitutionality of the Civil Rights Act of 1957, these defendants should be searching their souls to see if this charge is well founded." Wright believed that it was. A random sample of white application forms revealed that sixty percent of them contained the same kind of errors and inconsistencies for which blacks had been successfully challenged. Registrar Curtis Thomas agreed that such errors could be found in at least half of the white forms. Yet only four whites had been purged. On January 11, 1960, Wright decided that the purge had been illegal because the law had been applied in a discriminatory fashion. He ordered Thomas to restore all 1,377 purged names within ten days. He further instructed Thomas to tell the court if, during any three-month period, more than 5 percent of the voters of either race were challenged.[85]

Thus, Rainach's voter purge ground to a halt in the face of an unlikely alliance of Cajun politicians, federal officials, and the NAACP. Parish registrars, however, still had virtually untrammeled power to reject black applicants, and the ultrasegregationists intended to legislate further pitfalls and obstacles. Moreover, while blacks had blunted the segregationist counterattack, Rainach's relentless campaign against integration had stirred up deep wells of racism and forced the issue of segregation to the top of the political agenda. By entering the governor's race, challenging favorites Jimmie Davis and Chep Morrison, Rainach intended to keep it there.

The impact of Rainach's racist appeals shocked Morrison's campaign managers. "Integration is an issue," reported one. "I told you four months ago that it wasn't. I want to correct my error. It is." Kenneth Walker, the editor of a Natchitoches newspaper, sent the same message. "This racial thing, since Little Rock, has become a tense, tight emotional thing with powerful influences." Heading up the campaign in north Louisiana, Vance Thompson advised that "there is no possible defense of integration in this section of the country." In New Orleans, Dave McGuire warned that support for Rainach seemed to be growing. "The feeling of some people [is] that you are 'soft' on segregation. Some women are rabid on this subject."[86]

The result of the first primary confirmed their worst fears. Although Morrison led the field, with Davis second, Rainach finished a strong third after a "rapid, heated, uncoordinated campaign" that concentrated entirely on the segregation issue. While he did best in north Louisiana, Rainach also won substantial support in the south, including 11 percent of the vote in New Orleans. Morrison's performance in north Louisiana, by contrast, was dismal; Rainach's support in New Orleans and its suburbs exceeded Morrison's total for all twenty-eight northern parishes.

The ticket of James A. Noe and Earl Long, running for governor and lieutenant governor respectively, offered a traditional Longite cornucopia of state spending and welfare programs. Beyond proclaiming their "one million percent" fealty to segregation, Noe and Long eschewed appeals to racism. "We do not wish to hold any of our underprivileged people up to ridicule or scorn." They came in a poor fourth, a result that indicated that Earl Long — who had managed to get himself released from a Louisiana mental hospital only to become, in the words of Glen Jeansonne, "an increasingly pathetic figure" — was finished as a force in state politics. In fact, Long astounded everyone by winning election to Congress the following year, just a week before he died. But he had ceased to be an effective force for racial moderation.[87]

With Rainach in a strong position to influence the outcome of the second primary, and with Jimmie Davis angling for Rainach's endorsement, the Morrison team urged their man to dispel the perception that, in Dave McGuire's words, he was "overly sympathetic to Negroes." Morrison needed little urging. Nothing if not an opportunist, he had tried earlier in the year to cut a deal with the ultrasegregationists, offering Rainach second place on his ticket and support for his purge of black voters. Now, with the Davis campaign accusing him of kowtowing to the "bloc vote," Morrison hit back in kind. Davis had "solicited colored votes," he charged, "and was, indeed, publicly supported by the State President of the NAACP." Noting that his opponent, a onetime professional country singer, had once owned a nightclub in Palm Springs, he wondered if the establishment had been segregated. "Or was mixing of the races permitted? And what kind of 'games' were played?" Boasting that he had been sued by the NAACP more often than any other official, Morrison offered a "firm, unqualified pledge to support and work to maintain segregation." By the end of the campaign his reputation as a racial moderate lay in tatters, and all to no avail. Endorsed by the unlikely alliance of Rainach, Perez, and Long, Davis trounced Morrison.[88]

Morrison's campaign appalled his liberal supporters. "I am absolutely heartsick over this turn of events," Rosa Keller told him. "These are very difficult times to be campaigning in the Deep South, but nothing is to be gained by the present tactics." Morrison was unrepentant. His "Negro friends" understood perfectly that he could not afford to be labelled "the Negro candidate." Davis had solicited black voters: his hypocrisy had to be exposed. Actually, many of Morrison's black supporters winced at his turn toward racism. Albert Dent thought that Morrison should have gone down gracefully and enhanced his national stature in the process. Instead, he became simply another loser, his reputation diminished.[89]

Above all, the 1959–60 gubernatorial campaign graphically revealed that blacks had become politically isolated. The level of black registration remained stuck at about 160,000 voters, fewer than in 1956; blacks made up only 15 percent of the total electorate. Rainach's achievement lay in mobilizing a hardcore segregationist vote that exceeded the black vote, even assuming that blacks voted as a solid bloc. Blacks could not act as a "balance of power" when both candidates, each trying to outdo the other as a defender of segregation, went all-out to win over the white vote.[90]

When the all-white state legislature met in the summer of 1960, Louisiana's solons treated blacks as a political cipher. With the new administration of Governor Jimmie Davis backed by the most extreme segregationists in the state, notably Rainach and Perez, a raft of blatantly racist bills swiftly became law.

The most egregiously vindictive were two measures that criminalized common-law marriage and made it a crime to have more than one child out of wedlock. "Heretofore we have put a bounty on illegitimacy," explained representative John Garrett. The intent of this new moral concern soon became evident: a companion measure directed the state to stop welfare payments to the parents of illegitimate children on the grounds that such people could not provide a "suitable home." By the end of July some 23,000 children, the vast majority of them children of color, had been dropped from Louisiana's Aid to Dependent Children Program. Another law disfranchised seven categories of people who were defined as "not of good character," including those in common-law marriages and the parents of illegitimate children. The same law, Act 613, also required prospective voters to take both a literacy test *and* a "constitutional interpretation" test, thus closing the loophole that had allowed illiterates to register. The amended application form asked prospective voters to answer statements that would baffle a lawyer. Submitted to the electorate as a constitutional amendment, and approved, the act represented the most drastic tightening of the official voter registration requirements in forty years.[91]

Blacks in Louisiana were locked into a political war of attrition, and they were losing. The movement for civil rights spearheaded by the NAACP now had to rely almost exclusively upon the federal courts. The New Orleans integration crisis of 1960 showed that the movement was nearing the point of exhaustion: new tactics and fresh forces were desperately needed.

Chapter 9

THE NEW ORLEANS SCHOOLS CRISIS

For ten years now, black parents in New Orleans had applied, petitioned, and litigated to have their children admitted to whites-only schools. Six years had elapsed since the *Brown* decision and four years since Judge Skelly Wright first ordered the Orleans Parish school board to prepare for integration. By 1960, however, the board had done absolutely nothing to comply with that injunction. On the contrary, it had appealed Wright's 1956 ruling up and down the federal courts, losing each decision but winning numerous delays. The board refused to concede that integration was inevitable, even imminent, or to prepare whites for that eventuality. And it completely discounted the wishes of the blacks who comprised a majority of the school population.[1]

On May 16, 1960, however, Judge Wright imposed an integration plan of his own. At the start of the next school year, he decreed, first-grade students would be permitted to enter either the nearest formerly all-white school or the nearest formerly all-Negro school, "at their option." The black spectators in the federal courtroom, about fifty in number, smiled. A. P. Tureaud, representing the plaintiffs, breathed a sigh of satisfaction that eight years of litigation was at last getting results. Wright had just handed down the first court-ordered integration plan ever.

Wright's order appalled the school board. If applied literally, the potential for racial mixing would be enormous. Black public school enrollment already exceeded white enrollment by nearly ten thousand, and the disparity was greatest in the first grade. Superintendent James Redmond estimated that in the next school year seven thousand Negroes would enroll in the first grade as opposed to four thousand whites. In the city's numerous racially mixed neighborhoods, children often had to walk past the nearest school to attend a "Negro" or "white" one: if children attended the nearest or next nearest school, almost two-thirds of the forty-eight white elementary schools might be integrated. Moreover, as virtually no whites would choose to attend black schools, the practical effect of Wright's plan might well be an uncontrolled influx of black children into some of the white schools, flooding them beyond capacity. Redmond predicted an administrative nightmare and classroom chaos.[2]

In all probability, Wright did not intend to let his sweeping order stand, but devised it as a means of prodding the school board into coming up with its own, less drastic alternative. While four of the five board members (the exception being Citizens Council stalwart Emile Wagner) began edging toward the uncomfortable conclusion that segregation was doomed, they were yet unwilling to be the instrument of integration. On June 20 the board asked Governor Jimmie Davis to block integration by invoking "interposition" — by, in effect, defying federal authority. It was a futile gesture: interposition was nothing more than a resurrection of the states' rights doctrine that had perished in the Civil War; it did not have a shred of constitutional legitimacy. By passing the buck to Davis, however, the board hoped to prepare whites for eventual integration. If Davis failed, as seemed likely, the alternatives would boil down to two: accepting some measure of integration or scrapping the public schools entirely.[3]

During the summer of 1960 the state legislature flirted with the possibility of abandoning Louisiana's school system. It had already authorized the governor to close integrated schools, but this option had been foreclosed by a decision of the federal courts arising from the Little Rock case. An act empowering Davis to shut schools threatened by violence or disorder aimed to accomplish the same end, but this, too, would not survive the test of the Little Rock decision. The courts had not yet, however, prohibited a state from abandoning its entire school system, and the legislature duly authorized Davis to close every school in the state if any one of them integrated.

Initially regarded by all but the most extreme segregationists as akin to the H-bomb, a deterrent that should never be used, the school closing option nonetheless picked up popular support as Wright's September 8 deadline approached. Encouraged by the Citizens Councils, some white parents began to form educational cooperatives with a view to starting private schools; by August, seventeen cooperatives had been chartered or were in the planning stage. Governor Davis insisted that he would keep the schools segregated *and* open, but he gave no indication of how this feat of squaring the circle could be accomplished. One possibility, however, lay in Act 496, which authorized the governor to supersede any school board facing court-ordered integration and to run the schools under his own authority until such time as the legislature adopted its own integration plan. If implemented, this scheme could certainly disrupt, and perhaps wreck, the public schools of New Orleans.[4]

With the New Orleans school system facing possible destruction, a group of white liberals started a campaign to rally opposition to school closing. Aided and abetted by the Southern Regional Council, which helped to organize a similar effort in Atlanta, they emerged in March 1960 as "Save Our Schools." Mary Sand served as president; John P. Nelson headed its public relations committee; Paul Rilling of the SRC acted as an outside adviser. Like the "HOPE" campaign in Atlanta, SOS concentrated on the single goal of keeping the public schools open, carefully avoiding, for obvious tactical reasons, "any public identification with frankly pro-desegregation forces." The same consideration explained the lack of black participation, a fact that black leaders understood and accepted. Albert Dent, president of Dillard University, raised substantial funds for SOS from black New Orleanians.

The modus operandi of SOS was frankly elitist. It aspired to recruit "persons of influence and prestige" with the aim of persuading the "community power structure" to support its goals, thereby heading off a full-blown crisis. As the deadline for integration approached, SOS mounted a sophisticated public relations campaign, financed by the Stern Family Fund and handled by a professional advertising agency, to influence public opinion. In addition to newspaper advertisements and television spots, SOS mailed out thirty thousand brochures, with different versions for businessmen, teachers, public officials, and politicians. In all its propaganda, SOS hammered away at one basic theme: school closing would inflict catastrophic damage on the economy and social fabric of New Orleans.[5]

SOS proved unable to attract the bigwigs that would have given it clout in the community. Instead, the organization revolved round a nucleus of well-known liberals, many of them already associated with the integration cause. Some, like Rosa Keller, Peggy Murvison, and Gladys Cahn, were active in the Urban League; others, like Father Joseph Fichter and John P. Nelson, were well-known Catholic integrationists. Although a few boasted impressive social connections — Betty Wisdom, for example, was the daughter of a prominent businessman and the niece of John Minor Wisdom — as a group they could be too easily dismissed as an unrepresentative group of Tulane professors, do-gooders, and "race-mixers." SOS also evoked anti-Semitism: it had too many Jews and liberals to be of any help, explained one school board member.[6]

In June 1960 a second citizens group appeared on the scene. Like SOS, the Committee for Public Education (COPE) lobbied to keep the schools open; like SOS, it received advice from the SRC and money from the Stern Fund. COPE, however, contained no known integrationists, and it deliberately distanced itself from SOS in order to enhance its image as a group of segregationist but law-abiding citizens. Despite their common goal, the two groups did not cooperate but instead, as Paul Rilling complained in August, "continue to backbite and squabble." Nevertheless, as Morton Inger has argued, both SOS and COPE played an important role in helping to shift the debate from integration versus segregation to the preservation of the public school system. The emergence of COPE had especial significance. Strongly backed by the four "moderate" members of the school board, its very lack of liberal credentials enabled whites to accept compliance with Judge Wright's order without being tarred as Communists or integrationists. As Inger put it, COPE functioned like "an advance motorcycle escort that guarantees the safety of the marchers in a parade through hostile territory." By August, the cause of open schools had been endorsed by the Tulane University Senate, the Junior Chamber of Commerce, the Central Labor Council, and all of the major religious denominations.[7]

This groundswell of moderate opinion encouraged the wavering school board to finally bite the bullet and prepare for some degree of integration at the start of the 1960–61 school year. On August 14, over the objections of Emile Wagner, the board heard a sobering report from Superintendent Redmond on the possible economic effects of a schools shutdown: even if teachers continued to be paid, the local economy would lose up to $8.7 million. All but Wagner agreed to fight for open schools and comply with the federal courts. "I believe there is absolutely nothing that the governor or the attorney general can do to maintain a segregated school system in Louisiana," averred school board president Lloyd Rittiner.

The board's attorney, Sam Rosenberg, began preparing a suit to challenge the state's school closing laws. He collaborated closely with COPE, which found the plaintiffs, with Lester Kabacoff, attorney for the Stern family, and with U.S. attorney Hepburn Many, who represented the Justice Department. Judge Wright knew of this effort and encouraged it. It finally saw the light of day on August 17, when attorney Charles Richards filed suit against Governor Davis on behalf of thirty-one white parents. "The strategy . . . was brilliant," write two legal scholars. "The white parents first publicly disassociated them-selves from the NAACP by asking Judge Wright to dissolve his injunction; then, knowing full well that such a request was fruitless, they asked . . . that the court enjoin state officials from interfering with the public schools." That same day Governor Davis signed an executive order declaring that he had "superseded" the school board and taken over "control, management and administration" of the New Orleans public schools. He appointed James Red-mond as his "agent," and ordered him to reopen the schools on September 8 on a segregated basis.[8]

Davis's action directly challenged Skelly Wright's integration order, and the judge responded in the swift and decisive fashion that became his hallmark. On August 26, in a courtroom packed with black spectators, a three-judge panel comprising Wright, Herbert Christenberry, and Richard Rives heard arguments on *Williams* v. *Davis,* the white parents' suit, now consolidated with the NAACP's eight-year-old *Bush* case. The proceedings had barely got-ten under way when state attorney general Gremillion, as one newspaper put it, "pulled a Gromyko": he stormed out of the chamber denouncing the court as a "den of iniquity" and told reporters outside that "Negroes are running the country." Shocked but composed, the three jurists concluded the hearings in the absence of anyone representing the State of Louisiana. The follow-ing day, in an opinion drafted by Wright, the court struck down the state's school closing laws, set aside a state court injunction against the school board, ordered Davis to relinquish control of the schools, and enjoined state officials from interfering with the school board's integration plans.[9]

This unequivocal decision, so it seemed, cleared the way for a smooth and speedy resolution of the controversy. Two days later the school board, minus Emile Wagner, met privately with Judge Wright to propose its own integra-tion plan, based on the state's pupil placement law, and pleaded for time to put this plan into effect. Wright accepted the board's proposal and extended his deadline by ten weeks. Although the new school year would begin as usual on September 8, integration would be effected in midterm, on Novem-ber 14. The school board was delighted, but the primary reason for Wright's postponement was his desire to secure a firm commitment from the Justice Department to enforce desegregation. He knew from U.S. attorney Hepburn Many that the Eisenhower administration did not wish to be confronted with an integration crisis before the presidential election, and he could not afford to ignore this political consideration. As he explained many years later, "I had to work with Washington . . . because I knew that I was going to be alone, totally and absolutely alone."[10]

The school board could now obey the court while keeping integration to an insignificant trickle. The pupil placement law gave them a powerful tool for preserving the substance of segregation. First, it placed the burden of integration upon blacks, for unless they applied for a transfer to a white school they would be automatically assigned to a black one. Second, it enabled the board to winnow out all but a handful of applicants. Devised by the state legislature as a "racially neutral" means of perpetuating segregation, the act laid down seventeen criteria to be considered in approving transfers, including intelligence, scholastic aptitude, home environment, "psychological effect upon the pupil," and other factors that were even more vague and subjective. Moreover, the labyrinthine administrative procedure for processing applications added further hurdles. Despite the obvious intent of these laws, however, the Supreme Court had approved their use as a method of achieving token integration.

Lloyd Rittiner predicted that "probably not more than a dozen" blacks would be admitted to white schools. In fact, after submitting to a battery of tests and running the school board's bureaucratic gauntlet, only five of the 137 applicants had their requests for transfer approved. Although the school board defended the placement procedure as rigorously objective, the result seemed foreordained: a handful of blacks would be transferred, all of them girls, and the only white seeking transfer to a Negro school had his application rejected.

The parents of the rejected children were mystified and angry. "As near as I can piece it together," Daniel Byrd informed Thurgood Marshall, "the children were given some pictures to match up. They were also given a picture of a cow cut-up, and they were asked to pick up the head, the tail, and the legs." John B. Furey, a white instructor at Dillard, warned Redmond that the selection of so few children spelled trouble. The five successful applicants "must be literally shaking in their boots," and their parents, he predicted, would face "a systematic program of embarrassment, humiliation, and harassment." To make matters worse, Wright agreed to drop one applicant when the school board discovered she was illegitimate. The burden of integration would fall upon the shoulders of four young girls.[11]

The month of September and much of October resembled a kind of "phony war," with both sides, the supporters of open schools and the die-hard segregationists, making frantic, behind-the-scenes efforts to marshal support for the inevitable outbreak of hostilities. In a ploy to exclude the obstructive and defiant Wagner from the board's deliberations, Lloyd Rittiner appointed himself and the three other moderates to a "committee" charged with "keeping Orleans Parish public schools open." Paul Rilling advised Mary Sand that SOS no longer needed to campaign against school closure, and that the group should avoid rocking the boat. Lester Kabacoff agreed, urging both SOS and COPE to lie low. "All has been done that can be done and . . . it is now in the lap of the gods or the Governor." Davis himself stuck to his position that the schools would stay "open and segregated" but gave no hints that he would interfere. When John Garrett told a Citizens Council rally that Davis would call the legislature into special session before November 14, Davis flatly disavowed any such intention. On September 8, the public schools reopened without incident. The FBI reported a "noticeable lack of tension." [12]

As the weeks drifted by, however, the school board looked forward to November 14 with mounting apprehension. Anxious for community support, Rittiner and his colleagues pleaded with influential whites to issue strong public statements in favor of open schools. They met continual rebuffs. In the news media, only WDSU radio and television campaigned vigorously against school closing, endorsing SOS and carrying more than fifty editorials on the subject of desegregation. The weightiest opinion maker, however, the *Times-Picayune*, did nothing to persuade whites to accept token integration. John F. Tims, the paper's publisher, was an ardent segregationist who considered the *Brown* decision disastrous; George W. Healy, the editor, shared his views and bitterly resented federal compulsion; associate editor Harold McCall believed that integrated schools would lead to "racial amalgamation." Deploring both "forced integration" and "school closing," the most influential newspaper in New Orleans refused to choose between either option, preferring to leave that distasteful task to "the people themselves." The *States-Item*, owned by the same company as the *Times-Picayune*, ran a series by Robert Kelso that incisively demolished the argument for abandoning the public schools, but the paper's editorial stance exhibited the same reticence as that of its stable-mate. "Public opinion in New Orleans is apathetic and complacent about the approaching crisis," complained Rilling of the SRC. [13]

No group seemed more indifferent to the prospect of crisis than the city's business community. In September, Lester Kabacoff persuaded some of the city's most prominent businessmen to meet Lloyd Rittiner over a private lunch. The small group included *Times-Picayune* publisher Tims, Darwin Fenner, chairman of the Merrill Lynch brokerage firm, and Richard Freeman, owner of the local Coca-Cola plant, chairman of Delta Airlines, and a man who did not permit his sister, Rosa Keller, to soften his segregationist convictions. Rittiner asked them to take out a newspaper advertisement opposing school closing and calling for "law and order." The men started quibbling: integrated schools should place boys and girls in separate classrooms; blacks and whites should use separate toilets. Pressed by Kabacoff, the board reluctantly agreed to single-sex classrooms, but it drew the line at integrated toilets. The advertisement failed to appear. Shortly afterward, these same businessmen visited Governor Davis and urged him not to call a special session of the legislature. All had been key Davis backers in the recent election, and they assumed that Davis would be cooperative. But they kept their visit a secret and maintained their public silence.[14]

In early November, barely a week before integration, Benjamin Muse, a newspaperman now working for the Southern Regional Council, stopped at the New Orleans Chamber of Commerce to impress upon its leaders Virginia's dismal experience with school closing. The chamber's two top officers greeted him with hostility and suspicion, and they became even more antagonistic when Muse tried to defend integration. Conceding that perhaps 90 percent of the chamber's members opposed school closing, the businessmen absolved the organization of any responsibility to take a public stand. "We're not going to do anything unless the situation gets critical."[15]

The school board's isolation became even more pronounced when it slowly emerged from a welter of confusing statements and rumors that the Catholic schools would remain completely segregated in 1960–61. Having promised to desegregate the parochial schools no later than the public schools, Archbishop Rummel divulged on June 17 that "no definite plan of integrating Catholic schools was at the moment anticipated." Two months later the prelate urged Catholics to pray for "an early solution of the race problem," and in a strongly worded pastoral letter he denounced plans to close the public schools in order to avoid integration. On August 31 Rummel announced that the parochial schools would reopen in September on a segregated basis but reaffirmed his intention to begin desegregation "no later than when the public schools will become actually desegregated." This meant, presumably, that some Catholic schools would be integrated in midterm, coinciding with the November 14 deadline toward which the Orleans Parish school board was working.

On October 9, however, just short of his eighty-fourth birthday, the archbishop fell and badly injured himself. Monsignor Henry Bezou, the archdiocesan superintendent of schools, described to Benjamin Muse the resulting consternation in the hierarchy. The ruling triumvirate agreed that Rummel could not possibly be burdened with a final decision on integration in his present condition; at the same time, they could not usurp the archbishop's authority and take that decision upon themselves. When Muse pointed out that the church had an opportunity to ease the problems of the public schools and improve the atmosphere generally, Bezou, "a rather gruff old administrator," dwelt on the need for prudence. The parochial school system was economically vulnerable. The withdrawal of tuition-paying white students and the loss of wealthy donors would be disastrous. There was also the possibility of violence and disorder. "With vigor unbecoming a layman," Muse stressed that integration was a Christian imperative. "In apparent spiritual pain," according to Muse, Bezou agreed. But no word came from the chancery until November 12, when Rummel declared, ambiguously but ominously, that Catholic schools would stay segregated until "public school integration has been effectively carried out." The church would let the public schools be the guinea pigs and then assess the result of the experiment.[16]

During these days of increasing uncertainty, the election campaign of Matthew Sutherland became a referendum on open schools. One of the four "moderates" on the school board and the only one up for reelection, Sutherland was an unrepentant segregationist, but he urged voters to "face the issues as they are" and swallow token integration. Backed by COPE, SOS, and the Independent Women's Organization (an influential group closely connected to Morrison) he faced a Citizens Council-backed candidate who warned of "the black cloud" hovering over New Orleans. More rumors that Governor Davis planned to call a special legislative session added to the tense atmosphere. "This war of nerves is getting us all down," complained Betty Wisdom of SOS. If Sutherland lost, she feared, "the White Citizens Council will have to make a desperation ploy." Toward the end of the campaign he picked up the endorsement of the *Times-Picayune* and a statement of support from a "business and professional men's committee" comprising one hundred members of the city's economic elite. In recommending Sutherland the businessmen resorted to the lowest common denominator of racial moderation: Cold War rhetoric. "Our struggle with the Soviet Union for leadership of the world," they explained, "makes it imperative that the education of our children not be interrupted or stopped."[17]

It was too little, too late. Although Sutherland won handily, Governor Davis had already summoned the legislature in a last-minute strategem to block integration. Davis played his cards close to his chest, refusing to divulge any details of the legislation being prepared by Perez, Rainach, Garrett, and Gremillion. Thus the school board and its supporters had little time to mobilize opposition and did not know precisely what to oppose until, on November 4, the first day of the special session, twenty-nine bills were placed before the legislators. Four days later the entire package became law. The key measures authorized an eight-man legislative committee to take over the Orleans Parish schools. On November 10, four days before integration day, members of the committee arrived at the school board offices with an escort of state police and announced that no transfers of pupils would take place. Furthermore, anyone attempting to implement integration, including federal officials, was liable to arrest and imprisonment under another new law.[18]

It would tax the reader's patience to give a blow-by-blow rendering of the fast-moving and repetitive legal duel between the state legislature and Judge J. Skelly Wright. During five consecutive special sessions Louisiana's solons engaged in what historians Frank Read and Lucy McGough aptly described as "a legislative carnival unique in the annals of American lawmaking." Breathing defiance in an atmosphere that sometimes approached hysteria, fire-eating segregationists rammed through one bill after another in an effort to block integration. No sooner did the bills become law, however, than Skelly Wright annulled them.[19]

Wright knew that he could count on unswerving support from the Department of Justice. Although criticized in hindsight for not exerting its authority soon enough for fear of jeopardizing Republican fortunes in the presidential election, the Eisenhower administration had made its position plain enough. As early as August, local U.S. Attorney Hepburn Many had vowed that "the court will use whatever force is necessary. The greater the resistance, the greater the force." On November 10, Many asked Wright to enjoin interference with federal officials. Wright obliged, issuing a restraining order that not only covered state police officials but also applied to every mayor, district attorney, police chief, and sheriff in Louisiana. Simultaneously, Wright restrained enforcement of the other segregation laws and ordered the legislative committee to stop interfering with the schools of New Orleans. On November 12 Attorney General William P. Rogers sent Davis a telegram warning him not to obstruct the court and promised Chep Morrison the government's full cooperation in preventing violence and disorder.[20]

The to-ing and fro-ing of bills and injunctions resembled a game of ping-pong. On November 12, state superintendent of schools Shelby Jackson declared November 14 to be a statewide school holiday. Wright swiftly cited Jackson for contempt of court, whereupon the legislature, hurriedly reconvening on Sunday, November 13, declared the school holiday in its own name. It also removed from office the four "moderate" school board members, fired superintendent James Redmond, and assumed direct control over Orleans Parish schools. Forty-five minutes later Skelly Wright enjoined Governor Davis and the entire legislature, commanding the school board to proceed with integration on Monday irrespective of what state officials said or did. His unprecedented action left ultrasegregationists seething with anger and gasping in disbelief. They had assumed, apparently, that the legislature would be beyond Wright's grasp. "He hasn't got the right," fumed one legislator, "it's unheard of." Continuing its game of brinkmanship, the legislature dispatched a contingent of state troopers to enforce the school holiday in New Orleans.[21]

Although the Department of Justice beefed up its force of U.S. marshals, Wright had to consider the possibility that state troopers, acting as "sergeants at arms" for the legislature, might physically block them. Early on the morning of November 14 Wright briefed the marshals charged with escorting the black first-graders into the formerly white schools. He handed each marshal a copy of a sternly worded decree addressed "to whom it may concern," each document embossed with a gold stamp and the seal of the court "to make it look more legal." If they met with obstruction, the marshals were to read the decree and press on, turning back only if somebody pulled a gun on them.

Because the destination of the four girls remained a closely guarded secret, the marshals enjoyed an element of surprise. The state troopers had to visit each of the city's forty-eight elementary schools in order to notify the principals of the legislature's school-holiday order. In every case, however, the principal obeyed school board instructions and kept the school open. Meanwhile federal marshals, driving in unmarked cars and wearing only a lapel badge and a gold armband to identify them, escorted three of the girls to McDonogh No. 19 school and the fourth to William J. Frantz school. White onlookers jeered and booed; blacks applauded and cheered. There were no demonstrations, no violence, no disorder. When state troopers arrived at the schools, they made no effort to get the black children to leave. "The worst is over," predicted Lloyd Rittiner. Whites would now "accept the inevitable."[22]

The mood of optimism soon evaporated. The next evening whites packed Municipal Auditorium to hear the stars of the Citizens Council movement. "Let's don't be cowed," Willie Rainach implored them. "Let's use the 'scorched earth' policy. Let's empty the classrooms where they are integrated." Winding up the three-hour rally, Leander Perez reviled Communists, "Zionist Jews," that "smart-alec mulatto lawyer" Thurgood Marshall, and the "weasel, snake-head mayor of yours." He urged the audience to march on the school board's offices the next day. "Don't wait for your daughter to be raped by these Congolese. Don't wait until the burr-heads are forced into your schools. Do something about it now." The following morning, hundreds of white high school students rampaged through the downtown civic center, assaulted blacks, and surged in and out of public buildings. Some raced into City Hall and pounded on the locked doors of the mayor's suite, with Morrison inside. The police finally quelled the crowds with fire hoses. That morning, the third day of integration, only nineteen white pupils remained at Frantz school and just two at McDonogh No 19.[23]

The state legislature did its best to maintain the fever pitch. It commended the boycotters "for their courageous stand" and had the resolution printed in the New Orleans newspapers on three consecutive days. No senators and only two representatives voted against it. The legislature then froze the school board's share of state funds, placing the money in a special legislative account, and warned banks and businesses to deal with the Orleans Parish school board at their peril, for the state refused to recognize that body as a legal entity.

Advocates of legality and compromise were ignored in the near hysterical atmosphere. State legislator Louis Michot of Lafayette wanted to introduce a bill accepting the status quo, warning that blood might flow in the streets of New Orleans if the segregationists kept up their fight. After an angry exchange with Wellborn Jack of Shreveport, Michot literally wept with frustration, sobbing loudly as he pounded his fists on the desk. When a group of Frantz and McDonogh parents staged a mock funeral for Skelly Wright, carrying a miniature coffin onto the floor of the legislature, "the House stood up and, with a long roll of applause, saluted the parents."[24]

But Wright was very much alive, and if the legislature believed that threats and defiance would intimidate him, they did not know their man. At the height of the crisis, journalist W. J. Weatherby interviewed Wright to ask what made him so firmly committed to integration. With revealing candor, the judge confessed that in many ways the traditional attitudes of the white Southerner lingered inside him. "When I shake hands with a Negro, I have a different feeling than when I shake hands with a white. . . . You don't erase a whole life in a few years. . . . I don't intend to associate personally with Negroes." As long as he lived in the South, Wright added, he would not invite them into his home. Asked if his religious views had influenced him, Wright replied "I'm a bad Catholic." Pressed by Weatherby, however, he then recounted an incident that symbolized his feelings about segregation. Once, looking out of his office window during a Christmas party, he saw that a party was also being held in the opposite building — two parties, in fact, blacks and whites in separate groups. He then realized that these were blind people. The futility and irrationality of segregation came crashing home to him. As he spoke, wrote Weatherby, Wright "was so moved that he could not complete the story for several minutes."[25]

Wright went through what must have been a personal hell. He was reviled, threatened, and socially ostracized, becoming a virtual outcast among white New Orleanians. The police guarded his house twenty-four hours a day. He accepted all this philosophically, understanding that he was merely "the vortex of an emotional situation." The charge of hypocrisy, however, did bother him. His son attended Country Day, a prestigious private school in suburban Metairie, and Wright knew that working-class whites angrily held that the advocates of integration seemed to be a well-heeled group who ensured that their own children would not experience it. Wright briefly considered transferring his son to a public school but decided against it on the grounds that it would place an intolerable burden on the boy. Nevertheless, he remained unshakable in his determination to see integration through.[26]

NAACP leaders like Arthur Chapital and A. P. Tureaud also received their share of hate and harassment. Crudely written postcards and letters spewed racial invective; they were filed and ignored. Abusive telephone calls were more difficult to deal with. "Well I'm going to tell you something," Tureaud told one caller. "I may be a son of a bitch, but I'm not a black son of a bitch." When racists called during the night, he used to drop the receiver on the floor. One civil court judge would blow hard on a whistle.[27]

Federal authority triumphed over threats and defiance, and the legislature could do little more than watch in impotent rage when, on November 30, judges Rives, Christenberry, and Wright knocked over the legislature's elaborate house of cards by invalidating the Act of Interposition. After that, writes Morton Inger, "the battle between the federal courts and the state of Louisiana was . . . utterly predictable." The legislature held five consecutive special sessions, but further attempts at obstruction triggered swift legal countermoves by the school board, the NAACP, and the Department of Justice, followed by forceful injunctions from Wright and his fellow judges.

The incoming Kennedy administration decided to vigorously prosecute the case. Although the legal situation was clear-cut, Justice Department lawyers considered it essential "for psychological reasons" that the government "do everything it can to uphold the orders of the district court." Especially noteworthy was the entry of the Justice Department into the *Bush* case as an amicus curiae, or friend of the court, not merely, as in the Little Rock case, to support motions by the NAACP-backed plaintiffs, but also to initiate actions in its own right, in this instance seeking to enjoin state officials. By accepting its intervention, the courts "established, for the first time apparently, the right of the Justice Department to assist in enforcing desegregation orders."

Lifting the legislature's crippling financial siege proved more difficult. Accustomed to securing annual bank loans totalling $12 million, money borrowed against property taxes collected by the city during the following year, the school board found banks unwilling to lend or even honor checks written against its own accounts. To make matters worse, the city refused to hand over tax revenues earmarked for the school board because of the tangled legal situation.

Every payday became a crisis. Each month, the legislature played a cat-and-mouse game with the school board, belatedly writing individual paychecks but refusing to pay the teachers at Frantz and McDonogh schools or Redmond and his administrative staff. Moreover, state funds met only about a third of the monthly payroll, forcing the board to scratch around for almost $2 million more. Paychecks arrived weeks late; many arrived months late. On December 21 the three-judge court ordered the city to turn over $200,000 in tax revenues and restrained four banks from refusing to honor the school board's checks. At the request of U.S. Attorney Many, the court also cited three state officials for contempt of court for their refusal to pay more than one hundred school board employees, including the Frantz and McDonogh teachers.

The ruling eased but did not solve the school board's financial predicament. Writing to Robert Kennedy, the new attorney general, Morrison likened the situation to the Berlin airlift. Still unable to negotiate a loan, the board on January 20 failed to pay a third of its employees, nineteen hundred people. The mayor appealed to New Orleanians to pay their property taxes early, and enough people responded to give the board sufficient money to make up the shortfall. The legislature still refused to pay teachers at the integrated schools, and Shelby Jackson held back some $350,000 in money earmarked for the school lunch and school milk programs. On February 16 the Justice Department instituted additional contempt actions against Jackson and two other state officials, compelling a reluctant legislature to grudgingly release $2 million in tax revenues to the city of New Orleans. The state of Louisiana had done its worst.[28]

At one point Daniel Byrd thought that "the Luzanna legislature will keep ignoring any and all court decisions until a number of them are jailed." When push came to shove, however, the ultrasegregationists lacked the courage of their convictions. Faced with jail for contempt, state officials caved in. Attorney General Gremillion sobbed for joy when Judge Edwin Hunter let him off with a suspended sentence. Superintendent of Schools Shelby Jackson meekly answered "No" when Judge Wright asked if he intended to interfere with the New Orleans schools. "Talk is cheap," noted James Redmond, "and the talk is brave on the floor of the legislature, but there's no overt action — they're pretty cautious about *that*." All the bluster about going to jail rather than obeying the courts turned out to be hot air. The legislature huffed and puffed, but it failed to blow down the Orleans Parish school board.[29]

Although legally integration was an accomplished fact, it was not a social reality. Hardly any white children remained in Frantz and McDonogh schools, and the Citizens Council organized a highly effective campaign of intimidation to maintain and solidify the boycott. The few white parents taking their children to school ran a twice-daily gauntlet of between forty and two hundred mothers, their faces contorted with rage, shrieking threats and obscenities.[30]

Belying their jolly nickname of "the cheerleaders," these poorly educated, working-class women vented an unvarnished racism that had rarely been seen before in public. Reporters, accustomed to polished and articulate Citizens Council types like Emile Wagner, were fascinated and repelled by them. Bill Monroe of WDSU once tried to engage them in debate. "In a minute or two," he recalled, "I was surrounded by a screaming, spitting, hysterical mob. . . .

I didn't enjoy the experience but I did learn something from it. I got an emotional understanding, a kind of understanding that goes deeper than the intellectual, of the depth and intensity of the feelings involved in this problem. Even though you've lived side by side with it, you cannot realize how fully these emotions can possess people until you've seen them come to the surface right before your eyes, raw and trembling." Writer John Steinbeck, observing the protesters outside Frantz school, was revolted by their raw hatred. "No newspaper had printed the words these women shouted. It was indicated that they were indelicate, some even said obscene. On television the sound track was made to blur or had crowd noises cut in to cover. But now I heard the words, bestial and filthy and degenerate."

Those who braved the boycott endured physical as well as verbal intimidation. On November 29, for example, "cheerleaders" blocked and shoved Lloyd A. Foreman, a Methodist minister, as he escorted his daughter to the Frantz kindergarten. Another parent found herself surrounded by demonstrators who pounded on the roof of her car before she could drive away. By the end of the month only two white children attended Frantz school; McDonogh No. 19 had no white pupils at all.[31]

For the four six-year-old black girls assigned to William J. Frantz and McDonogh No. 19, the experience of integration combined the bizarre and the hellish. Apart from the mobs and the threats, they faced a weird isolation within their new schools, the white teachers initially resenting their presence and not quite knowing what to do with them. During their first year at McDonogh No. 19, the three black girls were the only pupils in the school. They at least had each other for company. Ruby Bridges, the sole Negro at Frantz, found herself in a class of one, with her own teacher. At first she was kept apart from the few white children even at lunchtime. With the insouciance and adaptability of the very young, however, the children endured and even seemed to thrive in their violence-laden, pressure-cooker environment. In addition, Arthur Chapital of the NAACP organized a campaign to give the students encouragement and moral support. "Cards, letters, gifts, and small donations" arrived for the girls from across the United States.

Yet the children betrayed their anxiety in quiet, inadvertent ways. Robert Coles, a child psychiatrist who closely monitored her progress, noted that Ruby Bridges "slept well, studied well at school, [and] played regularly after school." Nevertheless, she displayed a distinct loss of appetite, a symptom that puzzled her parents. At school, too, Ruby ate little. When the school staff cleared out her locker at the end of term they found it full of the sandwiches her mother had given her for lunch. It slowly emerged that although Ruby seemed to shrug off the cacophony of profanity and abuse spewed out by the "cheerleaders," one particular threat, reiterated daily in a shrill, insistent voice, came to worry her obsessively, a woman's shout of, "We're going to poison you until you choke to death."[32]

SOS made a determined effort to crack the boycott of Frantz school. A "Back to School" committee leafletted 250 families, seventy of whom received telephone calls or personal visits from SOS workers. Police superintendent Joseph I. Giarusso advised the school board not to provide buses for returning children, reasoning that buses would be too easy a target for stones and other missiles, and he promised to give police escorts to private cars. So on December 1, SOS began a lift service for white parents and children. A week later, after the cars underwent considerable harassment from the "cheerleaders," U.S. marshals began escorting them. Prodded by Hepburn Many, the Justice Department ordered the FBI to identify hecklers and investigate any threats made against parents. Smarting from criticism over its lax performance, the police began taking a tougher line toward the demonstrators, pushing them back behind barricades a block away from the school. The campaign had an immediate tonic effect: by December 6, white attendance at Frantz had increased from two to twenty-three.[33]

But the back-to-school movement proved short lived. The ultrasegregationists shifted their tactics, leaving the streets and starting "a quiet neighborhood campaign of intimidation and terrorism through vandalism." White parents had their car tires slashed, rocks thrown through their windows, red paint splashed onto their porches. They became targets for stone-throwing teenagers when they ventured out to shop. Mysterious "officials" visited them at home, offering "protection" if they stopped sending their children to Frantz. And they received constant phone calls, day and night, abusive, silent, threatening, obscene. Hepburn Many arranged for unlisted numbers, but these soon became known to the Citizens Council. One morning a mimeographed list of the SOS drivers was distributed among the "cheerleaders." They too became subject to the telephone treatment. Betty Wisdom received incessant "silent crank calls"; she treated her tormentors to readings from the Constitution. The threats to Mary Sand, on the other hand, "got so specific" that she called the police. Only after a reporter phoned police headquarters, however, did help arrive. Police superintendent Giarusso promised round-the-clock protection for white parents, but the police could not stop the threats and vandalism.[34]

Anxious to prosecute the ringleaders, Hepburn Many pressed the FBI to expand its investigations, but the Bureau was loath to have its good name associated with "news stories concerning integration." It gave the U.S. attorney minimal cooperation. Eventually prodded into action by higher-ups in the Justice Department, Bureau agents turned up little in the way of evidence. It even botched the job of photographing the demonstrators, twice sending Washington blank or underexposed film.[35]

Neither the police nor the Justice Department could alleviate the economic pressure directed against white parents who defied the boycott. Jimmy Gabrielle, who refused to withdraw his daughter from Frantz school, quit his job as a city gas-meter reader when taunts from fellow workers made life intolerable. Unable to find another job, he moved to Rhode Island with his wife, Daisy, and their six children. At least three other Frantz parents lost their jobs. Most of the white children who returned in early December soon dropped out again. "Practically no progress is being made in getting children back to school," Betty Wisdom complained. "Everyone wants a herd of others to go back first. . . . At this rate, we'll be lucky to hold on to eight."

SOS had paid little attention to McDonogh No. 19, regarding the situation there as "hopeless for the time being." It was astonished and delighted, therefore, when on January 27, 1961, the nine-year-old son of John H. Thompson turned up at the school, the first white pupil since November 17. Another Thompson boy arrived the next day. Two days later, however, the Thompson family left New Orleans, having been told to vacate their apartment by a nervous landlady who did not want "any disturbance in the neighborhood." The McDonogh boycott was again complete.[36]

Integration could hardly have been implemented under worse conditions, and the school board could not have made a worse choice of schools to integrate. Both Redmond and the board insisted that the selection of Frantz and McDonogh No. 19 had been dictated by the objective criteria laid out in the pupil placement procedure, one of which decreed that the test scores of the black applicants should equal or exceed the median level of the white school to which they applied. However, as Inger points out, Redmond's selection committee overlooked, or chose to ignore, another of its own criteria: "the possibility of breach of peace or ill will or economic retaliation within the community." Some believe that the board took the line of least political resistance, imposing integration on the poorest and least influential area of the city. Others, like historian and NAACP activist Raphael Cassimere, suspect that the school board "maliciously calculated that if we start at the places where the tension is the greatest, then maybe we can defeat segregation by showing it just can't work." The board's choice seems even more perverse considering that the PTAs of two white uptown schools had stated their willingness to accept integration.[37]

Whatever the explanation for the selection of Frantz and McDonogh No. 19, it guaranteed disaster. By choosing two schools in the Ninth Ward, one of the poorest and most neglected areas of the city, the board placed the entire burden of accepting a hugely unpopular social change on badly educated members of the white working class, and it did virtually nothing to prepare them for that burden. Interpreting the selection as a victory for the affluent uptown whites who had greater political "pull," many Ninth Ward whites vented their anger on Morrison. Telephone calls from irate whites flooded the city hall switchboard. "Why don't Mayor Morrison integrate the schools where his children attend?" "Mayor Morrison never did like the Downtown area." These class and political resentments were music to the ears of the Citizens Council.

The fact that the Ninth Ward bordered St. Bernard Parish, controlled by Leander Perez, compounded the school board's error. Perez not only encouraged white parents to send their children to schools in St. Bernard, he even built an annex to Arabi elementary school to help accommodate them and provided bus service to and from the Ninth Ward. Of course, the proximity of the Ninth Ward also made it that much easier for Perez and the Citizens Council to orchestrate the campaign of intimidation.[38]

But if the school board committed egregious errors, it had good reason to feel bitter about the inaction and moral cowardice of influential whites. As James Redmond put it, "When the churches don't do a thing, when they sit mum and ignore the situation and worse yet, tuck in their tails and run; when civic groups won't touch this issue because it's 'too hot'; when business associations and chambers of commerce . . . turn their backs and say, 'Well, this hurts our pocketbook, we can't afford to take a side in this,' then you're subjecting your school system to destruction." For all his faults, Redmond added, Earl Long would never have allowed such a crisis to develop.[39]

Chep Morrison, on the other hand, did practically nothing to avert the crisis. Taking the line of least political resistance, he argued that the city's schools were out of his hands, content to let the school board carry the ball. Morrison's hands were tied, of course, by his strong segregationist stand in the recent gubernatorial campaign and by his political ambitions for the future, which included both reelection as mayor and another stab at the governorship. Throughout 1960, in fact, Morrison underlined his segregationist credentials, denying use of Municipal Auditorium to the NAACP, rejecting proposals for a biracial committee, and suppressing sit-ins and picketing. In August, he finally endorsed the school board's use of the pupil placement act on the grounds that it would keep "mixing to the barest minimum." While he declined to campaign for public acceptance of integration, Morrison considered Davis's promise to keep the public schools "open and segregated" an empty one. Nevertheless his political advisers strongly urged him to let Davis and the legislature mount their last-ditch stand. "It will either accomplish its purpose," wrote one advisor, "or will be conclusive evidence that nothing further can be done." Thus as late as September 16, Morrison was promising to "always cooperate with the Governor in any of his attempts to maintain segregation." When the legislature attempted to take over and then wreck the city's schools, he belatedly fought back in the name of "home rule." By then, however, he had already surrendered the initiative to the ultrasegregationists.[40]

Although Morrison had promised a tough approach to "law and order" regardless of his feelings about integration, his tepid actions actually encouraged the riots and demonstrations. Having banned the NAACP from Municipal Auditorium on the grounds that its meetings might be "emotionally arousing," he allowed the Citizens Council to rent the hall on November 15 for the purpose of inciting a riot. Having banned picketing in connection with sit-ins, he tolerated behavior from the "cheerleaders" that, on any interpretation, counted as breach of the peace, intimidation, and assault. He even blamed much of the disorder on the news media, claiming that irresponsible reporting encouraged the demonstrators and that in some instances film crews "set up" scenes of violence. Actually, as was shown when authorities finally did crack down, forceful policing could have nipped the demonstrations in the bud.

Morrison refused to praise or help the white parents who courageously defied the boycott. Asked to comment on the Gabrielle and Thompson families, who had been forced to leave the city, the mayor dismissed them as typical Ninth Ward " 'floaters' — they come and they go and they have no real roots in New Orleans, so their parting is of no great moment or importance to them."[41]

Morrison knew from the hundreds of letters he received that the unedifying spectacle of the "cheerleaders" had dragged the name of New Orleans into the mud. "I am sick — almost physically ill — after viewing the appalling sight and sound of American mothers trying to get their own little, confused children to join the booing of adults," a Miami woman wrote the mayor. "And who are they booing? A tiny bewildered little girl." Many letters also expressed anger. Wrote a German-born doctor from Long Island, "My family and I have given up the idea of visiting New Orleans this spring, having been a witness to history in 1933. The memories evoked by your fellow citizens are repugnant to me." Morrison's response to such criticism was characteristically evasive: he had two form replies prepared, one for friendly letters and the other for critical ones. "The less said in these answers the better," Dave McGuire told the letter drafter, for "the Mayor has never exactly spelled out his position in writing."[42]

The schools crisis dispelled once and for all any lingering hope that the Catholic Church might lead by example in the matter of integration. Appalled by the violence and demonstrations, Rummel shelved the integration of parochial schools indefinitely. Catholic integrationists were mortified. Through irresolution and fear, complained Louis Twomey, the church had surrendered its moral advantage and thrown away an opportunity for a "tremendous triumph of the Mystical Body in this Anglo-Saxon Protestant-dominated section of the United States." Even at this late stage, the integration of at least some Catholic schools would have bolstered the position of the school board. Now the entire weight of initiating integration had fallen upon the public schools, the Catholic schools following suit only when it seemed safe to do so. The hierarchy could not have appeared more feeble had it tried. Rummel had taken three different positions in sixty days, John Nelson noted; moreover, not one Catholic group tried to rally support for public school integration. As Father Twomey put it, "The situation of the Church in all this sorry mess is truly pathetic." [43]

Smarting from the international black eye that rioting teenagers and shrieking "cheerleaders" had inflicted on the face of New Orleans, the city's business leaders finally called for obedience to the courts, an end to demonstrations, and support for the school board. They even feted the four moderate school board members at a testimonial dinner held at the Roosevelt Hotel, a high-society affair attended by sixteen hundred people.

According to Morton Inger, however, the business elite, more than any other group or individual, had caused the isolation of the school board in the first place, as well as the breakdown of law and order that they now publicly deplored. Most of these men had backed Davis over Morrison, confident of their ability to control the hillbilly singer who preached "peace and harmony." Others had actively supported the Citizens Councils, appearing at public rallies alongside Leander Perez. The refusal of leading businessmen and professionals to prepare for integration played into the hands of ultrasegregationists, giving Davis "no alternative but to keep pressing his crusade against federal interference and racial mixing." The attitude of the city's businessmen, moreover, reinforced Morrison's inclination to say as little as possible. "Well, if those s.o.b.'s aren't going to do anything," the mayor reportedly commented, "I'll be damned if I'm going to stick my neck out!" In April 1961 Morrison narrowly failed to win the voters' approval for an amendment to the city charter that would have allowed him to run for a third term as mayor. Shortly afterward he accepted an appointment from President Kennedy as U.S. ambassador to the Organization of American States. The city council appointed one of its own, Victor H. Schiro, to serve out his term.

In Dallas and Atlanta, business leaders spearheaded successful campaigns to win community acceptance of peaceful integration. Those in New Orleans declined to do so. Crescent City businessmen were not necessarily more racist, Inger suggests, merely less progressive. He describes the city's business leaders as a closed elite, hostile to outsiders, anti-Semitic — a stagnant, inward-looking group that lacked civic consciousness and displayed more interest in prestige, tradition, and family than in economic development. Betty Wisdom, in a more impressionistic way, offered a similar viewpoint. Writing shortly before all hell broke loose in the Ninth Ward, she lamented "the deadly apathy toward progress in New Orleans. . . . This is one of the few American cities I know of in which the populace is still content with bread and circuses once a year and the aristocracy, having provided the free show, feels no obligation to provide anything further." The subsequent economic decline of New Orleans lends weight to this analysis.[44]

Nevertheless, businessmen were not so obtuse that they failed to see that continuing turmoil over integration would badly hurt the city's economy. Indeed, Louis Twomey believed that fear of losing the enormous NASA contract arising out of the Saturn Project, more than any other factor, finally convinced them that a repetition of 1960 had to be avoided at all costs.[45]

School integration in 1961 went without a hitch. In May 1961 the school board quietly sponsored the formation of Citizens for Public Schools. It had the same objective as COPE, "to maintain our public schools and to preserve law and order," and the membership of the two groups overlapped. Citizens for Public Schools, however, boasted more "heavyweights," notably Harry Kelleher, a well-connected corporation lawyer, and the group provided a bridge between the school board and the New Orleans business elite. A month before the start of the new school year, eight top members of that elite met in the plush surroundings of International House to discuss a statement that had been worked out by a committee of prominent men from all parts of the state, the intention being to head off any further interference from the legislature. Published as a full-page newspaper advertisement a week before classes began, the "Declaration of Principles relative to Our Urgent School Problem" affirmed that "public education in Louisiana must be preserved," that parishes should be free to obey the federal courts, and that "preservation of law and order . . . requires compliance with the final decisions of the United States Supreme Court." The statement trailed the names of 315 white New Orleanians, all of them prominent in some way, many of them paragons in their respective fields.[46]

With the great and the good of New Orleans, including his political backers, firmly behind him, Mayor Victor Schiro vowed that "law and order will be maintained at any cost." To carry out that pledge, police chief Giarusso prepared a sixteen-page plan to prevent possible disturbances. "We will have to meet demonstrators with sterner action than we did last year," he told his officers. "Generally, we will not allow crowds to gather and if they should gather we will move them out of the area." He assigned at least sixty men to each of the six integrated schools. In mid-August assistant attorney general Burke Marshall visited Schiro and Giarusso to coordinate the federal contribution. One hundred and fifty U.S. marshals were deployed. The FBI rented "stationary surveillance points" near the schools and equipped its agents with walkie-talkies, two-way radio transmitters, and cameras to both film and photograph any incidents. In selecting additional schools to integrate, the school board chose four uptown schools and, with Judge Wright's permission, ruled out two other schools "in rough neighborhoods in which desegregation would probably be difficult." Anxious not to inflame passions so close to the beginning of the new school year, Wright postponed hearings on an NAACP motion attacking the board's use of the pupil placement law.[47]

The FBI's summary of the first day of school came as a welcome anticlimax to all involved in this elaborate planning: "No spectators or demonstrators noted. No incidents." The first few days passed so quietly that on September 8, the fourth day of school, Wright released the U.S. marshals and Giarusso sharply reduced the police presence. By the end of the month the FBI had discontinued its "surveillance points" and even stopped making daily spot checks at each school.[48]

All could congratulate themselves on a job well done: the mayor, the school board, the police department, the business elite, and the Justice Department had all cooperated to head off trouble. Yet integration in 1961 amounted to twelve blacks attending six formerly all-white elementary schools, and five were at McDonogh No. 19, which had only four white pupils in its second year of integration. Once again, the school board had used the pupil placement law to screen out all but a handful of blacks. In 1961, moreover, fewer black parents applied for their children to transfer, and fewer still submitted their children for testing. As the NAACP so accurately pointed out, the pupil placement law functioned as a device to perpetuate segregation. It discriminated against blacks on its face, most obviously by insisting that black children should only be admitted to white schools if they achieved certain test scores, when there was no such entry requirement for white children. Other "factors" used to eliminate black applicants were equally transparent.

Skelly Wright had his reasons, of course, for letting the school board employ the pupil placement law. In the early years of integration, judges like Wright were more concerned with precedents than with numbers. He still had to establish that children of color could enter formerly white schools without incident, and he therefore approached the issue pragmatically, treating it as a social problem as much as a legal one. The disqualification of black applicants because their entry into particular white schools might cause disorder clearly violated the important *Cooper v. Aaron* decision, in which the Supreme Court ruled that white authorities could not use the threat or occurrence of disorder as an excuse to deny black plaintiffs their constitutional right to attend integrated schools. In light of the school board's experience with Frantz and McDonogh No. 19, however, Wright agreed that it was only prudent to let conditions in the Ninth Ward settle down before integrating additional schools there. Furthermore, when so much attention bore down on so few children, the board's elaborate screening procedure ensured that the surviving applicants were the best of the group, the ones most likely to cope with the pressures and succeed academically. Indeed, Wright was so concerned that the children should be as clean as the proverbial hound's tooth that he asked the FBI to conduct background checks of their parents; the Citizens Council would have a field day if it discovered any with "criminal records or subversive leanings."[49]

The integration of Catholic schools the following year went equally smoothly — Plaquemines Parish excepted — although it took determined pressure from a group of lay people to bring it about. When the public schools integrated peacefully in September 1961, the church finally ran out of excuses for further delay, but Archbishop Rummel, old, infirm, and increasingly senile, seemed incapable of making a decision. In March, about three hundred lay Catholics formed the Catholic Council on Human Relations with the primary aim of bringing about the integration of parochial schools. C. Ellis Henican, a lawyer, served as president; Henry Cabirac, a businessman, acted as executive director; and John Nelson, the prime mover in organizing the group, took the position of secretary. Biracial in nature, the council included prominent black Catholics such as Ernest Morial, Tureaud's law partner, and Dr. Leonard Burns, who served as a vice president. The council had no formal status within the Catholic hierarchy, but it did enjoy access to Rummel through its chaplain, Msgr. Charles Plauche, who happened to be the chancellor of the archdiocese.[50]

Throughout the summer of 1961, Cabirac solicited information from other dioceses about their experiences with school integration. Reports from Miami, St. Louis, San Antonio, Washington, D.C., and elsewhere exuded optimism: there had been no disorder, no boycotts, no sudden influx of blacks into formerly white schools. The comments of the chancellor of the Galveston-Houston diocese were typical. He had been "pleasantly surprised by the results of our school integration. . . . We have heard of absolutely no adverse effects." The one school that had failed to find "room" for colored children, he added, had been subsequently destroyed in a hurricane. In every case, the respondents advised that firm action, with a minimum of publicity, seemed to be the best policy. The council decided that instead of seeking to build up public support for integration in the Catholic community at large, it needed to concentrate its fire on the archbishop.[51]

When Cabirac and Henican met Rummel in August, they failed to pry a firm commitment from him. Part of his continuing procrastination, they surmised, stemmed from the opposition of Henry Bezou, superintendent of schools, who feared that integration might trigger retaliation from the legislature — the withholding of free textbooks, for example, or the taxation of church property. He also feared a boycott by white parents. In an effort to win over this key administrator, the council arranged for Bezou to meet Maurice "Moon" Landrieu, a state legislator from New Orleans who had voted against every one of the twenty-nine segregationist bills proposed in the first special session of 1960. Landrieu assured Bezou that the threat of punitive action by the legislature was receding. The people of New Orleans had united behind the public schools to beat back the state's efforts to close or disrupt them. In addition, Landrieu explained, the state did not wish to commit any act that might jeopardize the possibility of a favorable settlement of the Tidelands issue, a long-running dispute with the federal government over the ownership of offshore oil. Officially, of course, the dispute was in the lap of the Supreme Court, but the state would be foolish to antagonize the Kennedy administration when it had to negotiate over the disposition of oil revenues. Bezou was convinced. He agreed to support integration.[52]

With Bezou on board, the council finally secured a commitment from Rummel. At a meeting on November 29, the archbishop tentatively agreed that all eight grades of the Catholic elementary schools should be desegregated in the fall of 1962.[53]

The council had given careful thought to this plan, which appeared to have several advantages. Opening all elementary schools in the archdiocese to blacks and allowing the entry of, it was hoped, at least one hundred black children into formerly white schools would make it difficult for the ultra-segregationists to target individual schools for boycotts. With all eight grades desegregated at once, children of the same family would not need to attend two different schools. And by announcing the plan in March, after the mayoral election and shortly before registration for the following school year, the decision would have been thoroughly "talked out" and accepted by the following fall.[54]

The council underestimated Rummel's capacity for indecision, now accentuated by advancing senility. When the council's public relations committee met the archbishop on December 6, Rummel refused to make a final decision and insisted on the need for further study. Two months later, responding to the pleading of two Josephite priests, he voiced his fear that integration would mean "a deterioration of the Catholic school system." Father Eugene McManus, a teacher at St. Augustine High School and a strong civil rights advocate, replied that an increasing number of Negroes were contemplating leaving the faith "because of the discrepancy between what the Church teaches and what the Church does"; rather a few white children leave the schools than blacks leave the church. The exchange apparently had some effect, because Rummel shortly afterwards "just about agreed" to go ahead with the plan. He continued to fret about a possible economic boycott, however, and wanted to restrict integration to the first three grades. To further confuse the issue, Bishop John Cody had arrived in New Orleans as "Coadjutor" of the archdiocese. Imported to relieve the administrative burden of the increasingly feeble archbishop, his arrival seemed to encourage Rummel to abdicate responsibility for the integration issue. In February 1962 he had still not taken the final decision. Time was fast running out.[55]

The council mounted a diplomatic offensive to push Rummel off the fence. After meeting Burke Marshall, Cabirac assured the archbishop that the Justice Department would put political pressure on the state to maintain law and order and that the Tidelands issue gave the Davis administration good reason to heed the federal government. Cabirac also played down the threat of a boycott: in Raleigh, for example, fewer than 3 percent of the white children had left after integration, and many of those soon returned. Matthew Ahmann, executive director of the National Catholic Conference for Interracial Justice, joined the chorus. "I think a withdrawal of support is unlikely," he wrote Rummel, "if all your schools are desegregated at once and not just a few which would become targets for pressure."

In mid-February the council made a final push to "swing the eight grade deal," and two factors enabled them to finally prevail. The first was the active support of Cody, whose assignment to the archdiocese may well have been for the specific purpose of implementing integration. The second was an assurance that Judge Skelly Wright would shortly order the integration of the first six grades of the public elementary schools. Henican had suggested this to Wright in order to minimize the risk of parents transferring their children between the Catholic and public schools as a means of avoiding integration. Wright welcomed a chance to ease the integration of parochial schools and at the same time boost integration in the public schools.

On March 27, despite a plea from Bishop Tracy of Baton Rouge to postpone integration for another year, Rummel finally announced that all eight grades of Catholic elementary schools were to be integrated. In addition, black eighth graders would be permitted to apply for entry into formerly white high schools. The order affected, potentially, seventy schools and thirty-six thousand children in New Orleans alone, and few doubted that it would speed up the integration of Catholic schools in the rest of Louisiana and the Deep South. Burke Marshall offered Cabirac a public statement from President Kennedy congratulating Rummel. The Council turned the offer down.

An embarrassed Cabirac explained that in New Orleans, sadly, "the President of the United States's word is not looked upon with favor in such matters."[56]

Thanks largely to Cody, the church now began to act with uncharacteristic decisiveness. Three weeks after the integration order, Rummel excommunicated Citizens Council leaders Leander Perez and Jackson Ricau, as well as Mrs. B. J. Gaillot, a New Orleans housewife who formed her own ultrasegregationist group called "Save Our Nation." All three had publicly attacked Rummel's order and defied his orders to desist. While they continued to agitate against integration, the excommunications had a sobering effect upon white lay Catholics and showed that the hierarchy meant business. Shortly afterwards, Rummel ordered Msgr. Carl Schutten, pastor of St. James Major Church, to resign from the board of the New Orleans Education Foundation, a body created by Emile Wagner to set up private, all-white schools.[57]

On April 9, as the CCHR expected, Skelly Wright extended integration to the first six grades of the public schools. The following month, however, the plan to link public and parochial school integration came unstuck. Wright was "kicked upstairs" to the court of appeals in the District of Columbia — Senator Russell Long vetoed his appointment to the Fifth Circuit — and his successor, Frank B. Ellis, restricted integration to the first grade alone. Nevertheless, the school board and the church had a mutual interest in retaining their students, and they reached an informal agreement that each system would permit approximately the same degree of integration. Although the church had no pupil placement law to draw upon, it could determine the approximate number of transfers through informal screening; as Plauche put it, "unsuitable Negro youths" might be "deterred in private counselling." When the new school year began in September, 104 blacks attended twenty formerly all-white public schools, and 154 entered previously white parochial schools. The Catholic schools integrated with little overt resistance on the part of whites.[58]

Plaquemines Parish, inevitably, defied the trend. Months before, Msgr. Plauche had confided to Benjamin Muse that the church would not encourage blacks to apply to white schools in Plaquemines, knowing Leander Perez's dictatorial power there. Nevertheless, several black parents applied to have their children enrolled in Our Lady of Good Harbor elementary school in Buras, and the parish priest, a sincere integrationist, admitted them. The day before the school opened, Perez organized a rally in Buras and exhorted Catholics to boycott the school and ostracize any parents who allowed their children to attend.

In his biography of Perez, Glen Jeansonne describes the course of the boycott and some of the methods used to effect it. Five black and thirty-eight white children attended the first day of school on August 29. The following morning the five black children failed to appear and twelve fewer whites showed up. The day after that, bomb threats forced the church to temporarily close the school. When it reopened on September 4, white attendance was down to twelve and the black children had not returned. Perez then arranged to shut off all state aid to the school (textbooks, buses, lunch funds, milk funds) and ensured that at least one of the black parents, Marcus Prout, lost his job. As in the Frantz and McDonogh boycott, recalcitrant parents received visits from a pair of Citizens Council "heavies" who made veiled but sinister threats. This being Plaquemines Parish, a stronghold of voodoo and superstition, somebody scattered feathers from a white cock around the school grounds, a gris-gris warning of death. On a less exotic but more practical level, someone drained the school buses of their brake fluid. Many acts of violence and intimidation, of course, could never be traced directly to Perez, but few doubted that he was their ultimate source.

By September 7 the boycott was complete. Some of the black children forced out of Our Lady of Good Harbor went to the parochial school for mulattoes — such schools being another peculiarity of Plaquemines Parish — but their enrollment caused such fierce opposition from the mulattoes that the church had to temporarily close that school too. As for Our Lady of Good Harbor, the church let the empty school stand open for the remainder of the year, a mute symbol of defiance and hope, until in August 1963, at the start of another school year, a bomb damaged the building and the church closed it for good.[59]

The only other recorded case of retaliation occurred in Morgan City, St. Mary Parish, where a single black fourth-grader enrolled in Sacred Heart School. The absence of visible protest moved editor Bob Angers Jr. to congratulate the local population for handling the incident "calmly and with dignity." Soon afterwards, however, the girl's father lost his job when three firms threatened to boycott his employer. The Council for Human Relations helped to find him a new job with an insurance company.[60]

Throughout the rest of the archdiocese, integration went smoothly. Outside the city of New Orleans segregation in the public schools was total, and there the church led the way. Overall, parochial school enrollment declined by about 3 percent, but by the end of September attendance at the integrated schools was climbing.[61]

Beneath the surface, however, there was a good deal of covert resistance to integration, much of it difficult to detect. At Our Lady of Lourdes school on Napoleon Avenue, for example, parents were told to produce church certificates of marriage in order to register their children, a new requirement. In St. Maurice Church, where two prominent members of the Citizens Council attended, the pastor claimed that his school had "no room" for two black children who tried to register, although the assistant pastor confided that spare places existed. At some integrated schools, the parents' clubs voted to abandon all social activities, and many parish societies refused to accept blacks. "By and large," Ellis Henican told Cody, "the [white] parents have accepted desegregation reluctantly and are forbidding their children to become too friendly with the Negro children."[62]

Thus, by 1962 token integration had been achieved in both the public and Catholic schools of New Orleans. The threat of school closing and legislative retaliation receded. Having gone to the brink but stepped back, the Citizens Councils went steadily downhill; by the end of 1963 they had ceased to be a significant force. For a time, it appeared that the state might circumvent integration by financing private segregated schools through a system of tuition grants. By 1962–63 over seven thousand white children received state "grants-in-aid," including the 1,171 pupils of the Ninth Ward Cooperative School, which had been set up by Armand Duvio, a plumber, for the children who had quit McDonogh No. 19. Ultimately, however, tuition grants had only a marginal effect. Voters refused to fund a full-blown system of state aid to private schools, and in 1967 a federal court ruled that Louisiana's grants-in-aid program was illegal.[63]

The New Orleans integration crisis of 1960 has been endlessly analyzed, and the city's leaders have been roundly criticized for allowing the crisis to happen. In the final analysis, however, apportioning blame misses the point, as do comparisons with Dallas and Atlanta or with the peaceful integration of 1961. If the business leaders had shown more prescience, if Morrison had displayed more political courage, if the school board had made wiser choices, if Archbishop Rummel had not been so old and feeble, then perhaps the turmoil and violence might have been avoided. Even if integration had been as smooth as clockwork, however, the underlying obstacle to its long-term success remained: white New Orleanians were overwhelmingly and deeply opposed to it. A slick, Dallas-type public relations campaign backed by the corporate elite might have prevented boycotts and demonstrations, but it could not have removed that fundamental obstacle. By defining the issue as one of public order, wondering whether New Orleans could have avoided becoming "another Little Rock," it is easy to miss that more basic issue. True, even a meager police enforcement effort could easily have curbed the disorders, but the "cheerleaders" were merely symptoms of a problem, not the problem itself. Opposition to integration permeated every social class. The shrieking "cheerleaders" could be dismissed as ignorant white trash; the school board, the businessmen, the mayor, the governor, the legislature, and the Catholic Church could not.

To focus on the violence, therefore, is to underestimate the racism of the elite itself. The city's leaders did not fail to head off the crisis simply through miscalculation or lack of nerve. Nor were they merely barometers of white opinion. Although Morrison did not share the hard-line segregationist views of advisers like Dave McGuire, he gave a revealing glimpse of his belief in black inferiority in a private reply to a northern critic. White opposition to integration was "not a matter of civil rights," he explained; "rather, it is a matter of evolution of the cranium and subsequent capacity to learn." As for the Catholic Church, Louis Twomey believed that opposition from the priesthood rather than opposition from the laity repeatedly stayed Rummel's hand; "Possibly three-fourths of the priests would like to forget the whole thing." With regard to the city's business leaders, one can argue that they indeed *were* more prejudiced than their counterparts in more "progressive" cities. They "did not want to see blacks better their status," writes Arthur Selwyn Miller; they "liked the way things had been . . . and had no interest in 'progress' of any type. Unlike Atlanta, the elite wanted to preserve the *status quo*."[64]

The integration of Tulane University provided another telling example of how this white elite churlishly bowed to the inevitable while striving to preserve the marriage of wealth, class, and racial privilege that they personified.

According to the will of Paul Tulane, its nineteenth-century benefactor, Tulane University provided places for "young white persons in the city of New Orleans." Although the university had long admitted students from outside New Orleans, as well as nonwhites from Asia and India, it still excluded African-Americans. Tulane now faced the loss of a $6 million grant from the Ford Foundation if it continued to exclude blacks. Yet rather than simply admit them without further ado, a course that many faculty members had been advocating since 1954, the board of administrators invited a "friendly suit" on behalf of two black women who sought admission to the School of Social Work. Rosa Keller, who agreed to help finance the suit, hired John P. Nelson to handle the case.

A decorated war veteran and devout Catholic, Nelson was a rarity among the white lawyers of Louisiana: he was a passionate integrationist who counted Father Louis Twomey of Loyola as his friend and mentor. Rather than seek a judicial reinterpretation of Paul Tulane's will that would permit the board to admit blacks, the face-saving outcome preferred by the board itself, Nelson wanted blacks admitted as a matter of right. He therefore asked Judge Skelly Wright to declare this private university a public institution, one that stood guilty of racial discrimination under the Fourteenth Amendment.

In support of his contention, Nelson arrayed solid evidence showing that the state of Louisiana had assisted the university's birth, subsidized its growth, and still had a say in its affairs. Judge Wright agreed, deciding that there had been sufficient state involvement in the affairs of the university to bring it squarely within the reach of the Fourteenth Amendment. He enjoined the university to admit the two black plaintiffs. This was his last decision as a federal district judge in New Orleans. Nelson hoped that Tulane's board, seventeen of the wealthiest and most influential white men in New Orleans, would acquiesce in Wright's decision.

The board, however, reacted with outrage, accusing Keller, Wright, and the university faculty of conspiring to wreck the university by depriving it of its private status, and obtained a stay from Judge Frank B. Ellis, Wright's successor. Ellis eventually affirmed Tulane's status as a private institution while disallowing the racial restriction contained in the state charter of 1884. Thus Tulane was free to admit blacks but could not be compelled to do so. In February 1963 the university did, in fact, admit its first black student. Nelson suspected that a deal had been cut. "I'm convinced that the Board of Administrators got Ellis and said, 'Listen, if you give us our private image back, we'll take blacks in,' because Ellis gave them their private image back and, man, they didn't appeal. No way."

For Nelson, the suit turned out to be anything but "friendly." Instead, it had entailed "a year of bloody, bloody battles." As historian Kim Lacy Rogers notes, it "generated bitter, unswerving local hostility" and "destroyed whatever remaining chances John Nelson might have had for an elected judgeship or a political career." As for Skelly Wright, some believe that his Tulane judgment, as much as his schools decisions, made his position in New Orleans untenable. With Louisiana's senators blocking his advancement to the Fifth Circuit, he was elevated to the federal appeals court in Washington, D.C. He left New Orleans bitter at the abuse and social ostracism that he, his wife, and his son had suffered. "I'll never set foot in that town again to do anything public," he told Albert Dent, "unless those sons-of-bitches that ran me out of New Orleans invite me back."[65]

No court ruling could convince whites that integration was a good idea. The four "moderate" members of the school board, and then the city's businessmen, reluctantly accepted token integration as the price for saving the public schools, but they continued to stubbornly resist anything more than tokenism. Only in 1963 did the board adopt a desegregation plan of its own rather than one forced on it by the courts. Even then, the board fought over every inch of ground. Under pressure from the federal courts it eventually had to abandon the pupil placement law, abolish racial zoning, extend integration to the upper grades and the kindergartens, and integrate the Benjamin Franklin High School for gifted children. Nevertheless, its foot-dragging tactics proved remarkably effective: at the start of the 1964 school year integration still amounted to only 809 black children in thirty-one formerly all-white schools. As William G. McCall put it, the board demonstrated "that litigation could be prolonged almost indefinitely" and that "by the skilful use of delaying tactics, the process of school desegregation could be slowed to the point of almost imperceptible movement."

All the while, the school board congratulated itself on the magnitude of its break with the past while making plain its distaste for integration. "When you tell these people that Negroes are growing militant, they get angry," observed Betty Wisdom. "When you tell them that they are doing more damage than the racists, they get incredulously angry. . . . 'You can't expect us to like integration or make it easy; it goes against the grain,' how I wish I had a dollar for every time I've heard that."[66]

If the integration crisis of 1960 represented the turning point in the NAACP's attack on segregated schools in Louisiana, a growing number of blacks began to question, in the words of Southern University professor Adolph L. Reed, "the legalistic ritual of going through the local courts, all the way to the United States Supreme Court, and over and over again, with little, if anything changed." As Skelly Wright later argued, the very failure of the courts to implement *Brown* ultimately pushed the civil rights struggle to a higher level. The southern courtrooms became a theater that educated the nation about the "structure and the hate of white supremacy" as well as the "indifference of the Federal Government. It was this scandal dramatized in the Federal courtrooms of the South which created the civil rights movement of the 1960s as a potential political force. . . . A compelling moral principle, barred from the political system, was taken up by the Supreme Court and given formal legitimacy; then, when the political system refused the legal principle, as it had the moral one, the idea travelled back into the private sector, back to the people, and created a whole new politics." Sidelined by the NAACP's snail's-pace litigation, a younger generation decided to attack segregation directly, using their bodies and their lives.[67]

Chapter 10

NONVIOLENT DIRECT ACTION, 1960–1962

T he short ride through Baton Rouge from Louisiana State University to Southern University is a vivid lesson in the history of segregation. After LSU's spacious and stately campus, its columned and porticoed buildings speaking of wealth and privilege, Southern seems cramped and spartan, its library small, its structures sparely functional. The very air seems to underline the disparity between these institutions: LSU is located in one of the city's most salubrious areas; at Southern, on the northern edge of Baton Rouge, one can sometimes smell the vast Exxon refinery located nearby.

Yet generations of black Louisianians have retained a fierce pride in Southern University. Chartered by the state legislature in 1880 and relocated from New Orleans to Baton Rouge in 1914, Southern had grown into the largest black state college in the South by 1955, with some 3,300 students. It even claimed to be the largest Negro university in the world. For many blacks, Southern had been the only available means of acquiring a degree and climbing out of poverty, and its alumni formed a strong source of loyalty and support.

Nobody was more adept at cultivating that loyalty than Felton Grandison Clark, the university's president. Indeed, Clark and Southern were virtually synonymous. In 1938 he had inherited the presidency from his father, Joseph Samuel Clark, who lies buried on campus, his grave annually adorned with wreaths on Founders' Day. Between them, these two men all but created Southern University in Baton Rouge. In wheedling money from white politicians they had sometimes resembled the Uncle Tom-like college president satirized so mercilessly by Ralph Ellison in his novel *Invisible Man*. But they had gotten results. Blacks acclimatized to segregation accepted their racial diplomacy as a necessary evil.

By 1960 Felton Clark had been president for nearly twenty-two years, almost as long a tenure as his father's. A tall, dapper man with a trim moustache, Clark could be smooth and articulate, and he invariably charmed white visitors. "With all his qualities of intelligence, insight and graciousness," wrote one, "President Clark is quite a remarkable person." To black faculty members, however, Clark was a remote and dictatorial figure who treated Southern as his personal fiefdom, hiring and firing at will.

Lately, Clark's brow wore an increasingly troubled look. The NAACP's campaign against segregation and the resulting white counterattack not only threatened the university's long-term future but also made his own position increasingly uncomfortable. Clark responded to these pressures by disengaging himself from social activism and retreating into the president's office. Visiting him in December 1959, Wade Mackie of the American Friends Service Committee noted Clark's increasing isolation and self-absorption. "He is loaded down with administrative work and has far too little association with the faculty."[1]

Three months later the student sit-in movement hit Southern with the force of a tornado, threatening to destroy the university and bring Clark's tenure to a premature end.

On February 1, 1960, four black students sat down at the "white" lunch counter of a Woolworth's store in Greensboro, North Carolina, and asked for coffee. Their insistence on remaining seated when a flustered black waitress refused to serve them inspired college students throughout the South. Sit-ins spread like a brush fire. In Atlanta, Nashville, and a score of smaller cities, black students sat quietly at department store lunch counters, picketed the sidewalks outside, gathered for parades and rallies, and submitted to arrest and incarceration.

This spontaneous outburst of youthful idealism, and the students' dignity and discipline, impressed blacks and whites alike. The sit-ins crystallized great moral force and gave the civil rights movement fresh vitality. They mobilized a previously inert generation, spawned a new group of leaders, created new organizations, and fashioned novel and imaginative protest methods. And in winning the support of many white students, they also rekindled the flame of interracialism that had been snuffed out by McCarthyism. The *Louisiana Weekly* hailed the sit-ins as "the best thing that ever happened in the South."[2]

As the sit-ins exploded across Dixie, Shelby Jackson, Louisiana's superintendent of education, called in Felton Clark and other black college heads to discuss rumors that out-of-state organizers were on their campuses fomenting sit-ins. Clark agreed to investigate and keep Jackson informed.

The first ripples of the sit-in movement soon reached Louisiana. On March 7 the Reverend T. J. Jemison addressed an "unauthorized" student meeting in the Southern University auditorium; the following day about two hundred Dillard students marched outside their college campus in New Orleans, their placards calling for desegregation, human rights, freedom, and "Action without Violence." A week later the state board of education instructed the college heads under its jurisdiction to take the sternest measures possible against any students engaging in demonstrations.[3]

Well aware that something was afoot, Felton Clark tried desperately to head off sit-ins at Southern. On March 9 he called in the organizers of the Jemison meeting, Major Johns, Marvin Robinson, Donald Moss, Jo Ann Morris, and Janet Houston, and extracted an admission that they were considering sit-ins. He urged them to drop the idea, warning of dire consequences. On March 15, however, Johns wrote to the Congress of Racial Equality in New York asking for advice: his group planned demonstrations and "a letter from you may well serve as a booster to our morale." Replying for CORE, Gordon Carey stressed the importance of nonviolence and promised to have field secretary James T. McCain visit Baton Rouge. Meanwhile, as Johns consulted CORE, Felton Clark instructed his deans to contact as many students as possible, visiting dormitories as well as classrooms, in an effort to undercut the expected protests. After the appearance on campus of Dr. C. O. Simpkins of Shreveport, who interrupted a student dance to extol the sit-in movement, Clark summoned Marvin Robinson and told him "exceedingly firmly" that demonstrators could expect automatic expulsion. According to Clark, Robinson and his confederates agreed to accept that punishment gracefully.[4]

On the afternoon of March 28, 1960, having been assured by T. J. Jemison that the black community would raise their bail, seven students sat in at the lunch counter of the Kress store in downtown Baton Rouge and were swiftly arrested for "disturbing the peace." Released on bonds of $1,500, the seven returned to Southern University in a triumphal motorcade led by their attorney, Johnnie Jones, and Rev. Jemison. Addressing virtually the entire student body, Jemison lauded the sit-ins and asked each person present to contribute two dollars to a bail fund. The following day nine more students staged sit-ins, seven at Sitman's drug store and two at the Greyhound bus terminal. The police arrested both groups.

The arrests electrified both the students at Southern and the Baton Rouge black community. On the evening of March 29 Jemison introduced four of the original sit-in participants to a packed meeting at Mount Zion Baptist Church. "The crowd roared with laughter and applauded throughout his two-hour marathon," wrote a reporter, and heartened to Jemison's suggestion that blacks stage a boycott of downtown stores over Easter. The next morning Southern students walked out of their classes en masse, piled into buses taking them downtown, and marched to the state capitol. There, in the shadow of Huey Long's statue, they held an hour-long "prayer meeting" featuring Major Johns as principal speaker.

Late in the afternoon, after a day of tense discussion behind closed doors, President Clark announced that Johns and the sixteen arrested students had been "suspended indefinitely." By his own lights, Clark was making the best of a bad situation. He took it upon himself to soften the board of education's directive, meting out indefinite suspension rather than outright expulsion in the hope of reinstating the students "when things had quieted down." More-over, the nine students arrested in the second round of sit-ins, who remained in jail, were suspended "pending further investigation," a hint that they might be readmitted quite soon.

As far as the seventeen were concerned, however, the university had ex-pelled them, and they exhorted Southern students to boycott classes until they were readmitted. The students responded with enthusiasm, and the class-rooms stayed empty. Barred from campus, Major Johns and Marvin Robin-son made twice-daily appearances at a house overlooking the railroad tracks bounding Southern, speaking to the students through a loudspeaker. With teaching at a standstill, students began to leave the university, some taken home by anxious parents.

With his world collapsing about him, Felton Clark summoned up all his au-thority and powers of persuasion to stem the flow. On the evening of March 31 and into the early hours of the next morning he visited campus dormitories, urging students to reject "ill-meaning advisers" who were out to destroy the university. At a faculty meeting on April 1 he made it clear that every staff member was expected to assist in ending the student boycott: their jobs were on the line. Later, he met a hastily assembled "citizens committee," headed by Robert Tucker and T. J. Jemison, which pressed Clark to readmit the expelled students, or at least show some flexibility. Clark insisted that the board of education had allowed him no room for maneuver, but he did agree to meet the students.

The next day the student boycott began to collapse. Shortly before midnight, having talked with Clark for four and a half hours, eight of the expelled students announced that they accepted their expulsions and wanted to end the protest. Their decision stupefied the three thousand students who had sat in front of the administration building excitedly awaiting the outcome of the meeting. "This is a scene I shall never forget," wrote Jim McCain. "Students began crying, both boys and girls, yelling that they would leave also, but one by one the students' leaders appealed to them that this was their decision. . . . 'We ask that you listen to us again.'" The next morning, however, Major Johns and Marvin Robinson called for a resumption of the boycott, claiming that Clark had violated his agreement with them by expelling another student. Clark, addressing about fifteen hundred students and alumni in the university gymnasium, hinted that Communists were at work behind the demonstrations and warned that anyone using force or intimidation against students who wished to attend class would be promptly arrested.

By now, the students did not know whether they were coming or going. Hundreds had gone home for the weekend unsure of whether to return. Hundreds more had left the campus but lacked the money for their fare home. Meanwhile, the citizens committee dithered. After hearing Clark's impassioned pleas to save Southern, however, the committee agreed that its bail fund should not be used to support the boycott. With no means of getting home, students began to drift back to campus. By the beginning of May Southern was returning to normal. About seven hundred students quit the university, but most returned to classes. Fifteen of the suspended students applied for readmission, and all but three were accepted.[5]

McCain of CORE attributed the debacle to lack of support from Baton Rouge's black community: by heeding Clark's entreaties and withholding money for train and bus fares, the citizens committee undermined the boycott. "This is a mighty pathetic group of people," he told the New York office, "especially the suppose[d] leaders." Wade Mackie of the AFSC rendered a similar judgment, describing the city's Negro community as "about as poorly prepared for constructive action as one could imagine." Jemison had stepped into the leadership vacuum but then mishandled the bail fund and compounded the confusion by failing to help the students who were milling about the lobby of the city's black hotel wishing to go home. J. K. Haynes and John G. Lewis had had to clear up the mess.

But Mackie also noted that the students who instigated the sit-ins erred in failing to apprise the black community of their plans. In urging a boycott of classes, moreover, the student leaders abruptly changed the issue from that of gaining service at white-only lunch counters, the original object of the sit-ins, to that of a fight with the university administration that threatened to destroy Southern itself. When Jim McCain avowed that the fate of Southern should be subordinated to the larger objective of striking at segregation, the citizens committee balked.[6]

Praised by the board of education for the "outstanding manner" in which he handled the demonstrations, Clark was reviled by many blacks and white liberals. Speaking in New Orleans, Thurgood Marshall stoutly defended the student protests and demanded that black college presidents like Clark "stand up and be counted." The *Louisiana Weekly* castigated Clark for failing to show a jot of sympathy for the students; instead of carrying out the dictates of the board of education, he should have resigned.

In his public statements, Clark adopted the lofty position that duty impelled him to take unpopular decisions, however painful they might be, for the greater good of furthering educational opportunity for blacks. "A Negro president of a university in the South must be battling all the time," he explained. "He is between the fire of Negro people and elected officials, who happen, most of the time, to be white. And without losing one's integrity one must walk a straight and narrow path." In a private letter to some of his critics, however, he betrayed pettiness, self-pity, and a narrowness of vision that showed complete lack of comprehension as to the significance of the new student militancy. For Clark, the protests had been nothing more than a personal attack on himself, inspired by jealousy of Southern. "*Somebody* got to the students," he explained. "Somebody . . . who was just plain mean, viscious [*sic*], and out to destroy the president of Southern University, or . . . his nearest symbol, that is, the University itself." That attack, he believed, had been encouraged by "known enemies of Southern," especially the alumni of other black colleges, most of them from New Orleans, who were jealous of his institution. "Like my father before me, who literally gave his life for Southern," he concluded, "I put holding Southern together before I did my own personal happiness."[7]

Ultimately, loyalty to Southern proved to be Felton Clark's trump card; as Jim McCain conceded, "I was not a native of Louisiana, neither was I an alumnus of Southern, therefore I didn't have the love for the school that others had." Indeed, Clark received letters of praise from many Southern alumni around the country. "Yesteryear," wrote a sympathetic Los Angeles high school principal, "many decisions were made which seemed undesirable and spineless. As we grow older . . . we can see why these things were done and at what a high cost to the individuals who were noble and strong enough to make them."

It is tempting to dismiss Clark and his supporters as elderly conservatives whom history had cast in the role of Uncle Toms. But even the NAACP, which made integration its talisman, was ambivalent about the abolition of black colleges. In 1959 Arthur Chapital had organized a petition drive against the establishment of a branch of Southern University in New Orleans, an unsuccessful fight that helps to explain Felton Clark's paranoia about black leaders in New Orleans. A. P. Tureaud, on the other hand, did not favor an attack on the dual college system. Eventually, in 1969, Chapital persuaded the NAACP to file suit against Louisiana's segregated state colleges; by then, however, an upsurge of black nationalism had brought black institutions back into vogue, and strong black opposition to the NAACP, much of it from students, helped to frustrate its objective. Despite federal court decisions calling for the merger of segregated state colleges, Southern still endures as an overwhelmingly black institution, both a symbol of racial segregation and a monument to black achievement. Thus the clash over Southern's future that helped to undermine the sit-in movement in 1960 exposed deep ambivalence in the black community over integration, foreshadowing a struggle that continues to this day.[8]

If the 1960 student protests flopped, leaving many blacks in Baton Rouge with a lasting distrust of CORE, they also did little to persuade whites that segregation should go. If conditions in Louisiana dissatisfied them, quipped lame-duck governor Earl Long, then the Southern students should go back to their "native Africa." A front-page editorial in the *Baton Rouge Morning Advocate,* published at the height of the Southern uproar, expressed the same sentiment in more refined language. Condemning the demonstrations as "immature" and warning that boycotts "can bring retaliation," the paper advised blacks that only "time and orderly evolution can bring progress." Three days later the *New Orleans Times-Picayune* echoed this line. The sit-ins produced nothing but "hatred, fear and violence," earning the students "only the contempt of the majority." About the only sympathetic view came from Bill Monroe in a news editorial on WDSU, the most liberal of New Orleans's television stations. Praising the conduct and sincerity of the students, Monroe pointed out an obvious but often-ignored fact: the sit-ins showed that "the feeling among Southern Negroes against segregation is more widespread than some officials like to admit." He urged whites not to get alarmed by them or try to suppress them.

The Louisiana legislature, however, aimed to throttle the sit-in movement by stiffening the penalties for such "catch-all" offenses as disorderly conduct, criminal mischief, and criminal trespass. At the heart of its anti-sit-in package was Act 70, which redefined disturbing the peace to include any act that did, or might "forseeably," disturb or alarm the public. To make it crystal clear that this legal blunderbuss was aimed at black demonstrators, the legis-lature explicitly exempted picketing and "lawful assembly" by labor unions. In New Orleans, at the urging of Dave McGuire, Mayor Morrison ordered the police to make careful contingency plans to deal with possible sit-ins and demonstrations.[9]

On the surface, the campus scene in New Orleans seemed quiet. In their college newspaper, students at Xavier questioned the need for sit-ins. No pro-tests took place on the newly opened campus of Southern, located near Lake Pontchartrain on a remote fringe of the city. Even the Dillard students who paraded on March 8 had punctiliously observed college regulations and stayed within the law. But the spread of the sit-in movement, and the dramatic events at nearby Southern, had an effect. Some students became impatient for direct action and began to cast about for a means of expressing their militancy. The Congress of Racial Equality, which added Major Johns and Marvin Robinson to its staff, eyed New Orleans as a promising base for nonviolent protests in the Deep South.

The Consumers League of Greater New Orleans provided many students with their initial experience of direct action. Organized in the winter of 1959 with the goal of increasing black retail employment, it targeted stores in predominantly black neighborhoods, many of which refused to employ Negro checkout clerks. In April 1960 the league launched a boycott of several white-owned establishments on Dryades Street, then a major shopping artery patronized almost exclusively by blacks. The volunteer pickets included Rudy Lombard, a Xavier student, Oretha Castle, a student at Southern in New Orleans, Hugh Murray, a white graduate student studying history at Tulane, and Jerome Smith, who had recently quit Southern University. A young black lawyer, Lolis Elie, provided legal advice, and Dr. Raymond B. Floyd, a Xavier instructor, headed the league. A throwback to the "Don't Buy Where You Can't Work" campaigns of the 1930s, the boycott also enjoyed the backing of older preacher-politicians like Avery Alexander and A. L. Davis. The boycott soon began to bite: one supermarket, which refused to consider hiring a black cashier on the grounds that a Negro might antagonize white customers, saw its weekly turnover decline by $3,000.

Prior to the Consumers League boycott, Jim McCain had made two un-successful attempts to set up a CORE group in New Orleans. By the summer, however, the Dryades Street campaign had assembled a group of young activ-ists who, having cut their teeth on picket lines — now temporarily halted by a state court injunction — itched for more assertive and risky protests. During a Consumers League meeting at A. L. Davis's church they spoke with Marvin Robinson, now a CORE field secretary, after he and four other expelled Southern students dramatically entered the church to the acclamation of the audience. On July 28, meeting with McCain and Robinson at the Dryades Street YMCA, about twenty students discussed setting up a CORE chapter. Robinson urged the national office to give them all the help they needed. "The climate in New Orleans is ripe and ready for an 'action group' like CORE."[10]

The lassitude of the NAACP enhanced CORE's opportunity. The NAACP in Louisiana was suffering from a deep malaise. It had only just reestablished its right to operate freely, and its four-year fight for survival had left it enervated and to some extent demoralized. Victory in the federal courts did not spark a sudden revival of branch activity: at the end of 1960 statewide membership reached only 5,456. The fourteen branches outside New Orleans had just 1,236 members between them, and only Lake Charles had more than one hundred. Many former activists remained fearful. "The Branch officers have refused to act now that the courts have ruled in our favor," reported a member from St. John the Baptist Parish. "Some of the officers I have contacted have no desire to open the Branch again."[11]

The reaction of the New Orleans branch to the sit-in movement typified the organization's inability to capitalize on the spread of direct action: it set up a committee. Meeting on April 3, the group recommended a boycott of five variety-store chains but recommended picketing only "if we can be assured of police protection." It then appointed a subcommittee to meet the police chief in a futile effort to obtain such an assurance. Months passed and the branch still took no action. It then appointed another committee to consider a legal challenge to the legislature's anti-sit-in laws. After this committee reported, the branch instructed A. P. Tureaud to immediately file suit against Acts 70 and 80. Four months later, however, Tureaud explained that such action was "not practical."

Branch leaders, in fact, were ambivalent about direct action. Although Tureaud was skeptical, and also had a continuing fear of infiltration by white leftists, the newly revived Youth Council was enthusiastic. In 1958 the Youth Council in Oklahoma City had carried out successful lunch counter sit-ins; although they failed to have the impact of the Greensboro sit-ins, they did stimulate the formation or revival of Youth Councils elsewhere, including New Orleans. Branch president Arthur Chapital recognized the value of more militant action and was growing impatient with the timidity of the organization's national leadership. As an experienced labor organizer, however, Chapital believed in careful preparation and planning. Pleading for a full-time field secretary, he explained that a sit-in campaign required the kind of expertise and leadership that the New Orleans branch simply did not possess.[12]

This was precisely the expertise in which the Congress of Racial Equality specialized: it had been founded to foster nonviolent direct action. In August, as the NAACP tried to set up negotiations with Woolworth and other variety stores, six members of the New Orleans CORE group made the long drive to Miami to attend a CORE Action Institute. There, for three weeks, they lived, studied, protested, and played as members of an interracial community committed to racial justice and equality.

During the first few days, CORE staff members led discussions of nonviolence. While some of these "workshops" focused on nonviolence as a philosophy asserting that love could conquer hate, a notion some found unconvincing, other sessions taught practical lessons in nonviolence as a direct-action technique. Hugh Murray, a white history student at Tulane University and the son of a New Orleans longshoreman, remembered how "we learned how to huddle on the ground to provide maximum protection without fighting back. We had practice sessions in which some of us would pretend to be enraged racists harassing the others in our group who carried CORE picket signs. . . . It was anti-assertiveness training so that we could be assertive in protest; it was anti-assertive for our egos, so that we could become assertive for our cause. And the cause was justice and integration." As the participants gained confidence, they put these techniques to the test: twenty were arrested trying to integrate a Miami supermarket cafeteria; others picketed the establishment and visited black churches to whip up support for a boycott.

The young activists also learned to overcome their racial self-consciousness. Hugh Murray recalled that as he relaxed with the others in their motel swimming pool, "I had to think of the fact that someone was not White. I would be talking to people not consciously aware of their color. It was the first time that had ever happened to me." [13]

When the group returned to New Orleans they found the other CORE members already preparing for a sit-in. By then an NAACP request for negotiations with the variety store managers was beginning to bear fruit. City officials had held separate meetings with the merchants and the NAACP, and a joint meeting was in the offing. Indeed, Mayor Morrison felt so confident that he had the situation under control that he brushed off Dave McGuire's warning to postpone a trip to Washington scheduled for Friday, September 9, lest CORE launch sit-ins. Albert Dent had assured him that CORE would postpone its plans, he told McGuire. "So quit worrying." But CORE, ignoring a plea from the NAACP to give the negotiations a fair chance, refused to delay any longer. [14]

When James McCain arrived in New Orleans on the afternoon of September 9, he found seven CORE members, five blacks and two whites, sitting at the lunch counter of one of the Woolworth stores on Canal Street. A rope barrier erected by the police cordoned them off from the rest of the store. They had been there for about four hours. Shortly afterward the police arrested the group and charged all seven with criminal mischief. The following day, a Saturday, members of the NAACP Youth Council picketed both of Canal Street's Woolworth stores.

CORE had not anticipated arrests; Woolworth's policy laid down that store managers should not call in the police. But Chep Morrison, backed up by Dave McGuire and District Attorney Richard Dowling, was bent on suppressing black demonstrations, and on September 12 he announced that he had instructed the police to prevent further sit-ins and "so-called peaceful picketing." The next day Morrison tried to get the negotiations back on track, urging black leaders to desist from demonstrating while he arranged a meeting with the by now seriously annoyed store managers. Most of the blacks were amenable, but Rudy Lombard, representing CORE, refused to give Morrison the assurance he wanted. When Lombard reported that the meeting had been a waste of time, the CORE group voted to challenge the mayor's proclamation by stepping up its protests. They immediately set to work making placards.

On September 16 seven pickets, including CORE field secretary Jim McCain, took up positions in the shopping area of a predominantly black section of Claiborne Avenue. After an hour, in front of hundreds of curious spectators, the police took them away in a paddy wagon. The next morning Rudy Lombard and three other CORE members sat in at McCrory's on Canal Street. When they refused to leave, the restaurant manager closed the lunch counter, removing the stools and switching off the light. Summoned by the store manager, the police took them to jail.

Although CORE's protests derailed the negotiations, they delighted and to a remarkable extent united the black community. Visiting churches, union halls, and Masonic temples, the group quickly raised hundreds of dollars from cheering audiences. On September 18 about three hundred people, including several ministers, prayed and sang hymns in a playground outside the Orleans Parish jail. The next day some three thousand people met at the ILA hall on Claiborne Avenue to hear a succession of speakers, including longtime Morrison supporters like Rev. A. L. Davis and longshoremen's leader Clarence Henry, applaud the CORE "jailbirds." The support of the Consumers League was especially gratifying, for it provided CORE with a strong link to the city's older black leadership, helping to frustrate white efforts to isolate the group. The Reverend Avery Alexander and four other members of the league went to jail with Jim McCain. League stalwart A. L. Davis, the city's most influential black minister, opened his church to CORE's workshops.[15]

The sit-ins added a new dimension to the civil rights struggle in Louisiana. Youth and élan invigorated what had become a tired campaign presided over by elderly men. With no ties to the established political factions, the CORE activists spurned debilitating compromises and paralyzing delays. They did not always plan carefully, but their sense of urgency, taste for action, and obvious bravery more than compensated for occasional rashness. By coolly defying the law they threatened to neutralize two of the most potent weapons in the segregationist arsenal: fear of the police and the threat of jail. Finally, they provided CORE with an organizational foothold in Louisiana. "If we are successful in New Orleans," Gordon Carey assured Rudy Lombard, "this will be one of the first times that interracial direct action has penetrated so far into the deep South on a consistent planned basis." [16]

Whether the CORE group would survive, however, was still an open question in late 1960: the chapter remained small, its ability to mount additional sit-ins limited. Moreover, the city maintained the ban on picketing, making it difficult for CORE to tighten its boycott of Woolworth's and McCrory's. CORE and the Consumers League distributed some forty-three thousand leaflets, but the police soon began to clamp down on street leafletting. The district attorney was reportedly bent on suppressing CORE, McCain told New York. "We must prove to the authorities that we are in this area to stay." By the end of the year, however, CORE's campaign petered out as the school integration crisis riveted national attention on New Orleans and almost tore the city apart. [17]

The white mobs that rampaged through the central business district on November 15, the shrieking "cheerleaders" who spewed profanity outside Frantz and McDonogh No. 19, and the vindictive, ranting legislators who cast about for scapegoats — all combined to produce an intimidating tension that temporarily cowed the black community and immobilized CORE. A two-week program of workshops, campus visits, and mass meetings coincided with the first two weeks of integration; it proved a complete flop.

Sidelined by the crisis and frustrated by their inability to influence events, the small group of CORE stalwarts became increasingly gloomy and their meetings accomplished little. On December 10, eight CORE members were arrested on Canal Street as they handed out leaflets calling for a boycott, but the chapter then lapsed back into torpor. Yet thanks to a trickle of new members, including some white students from Tulane, the chapter survived. The easygoing chairmanship of Rudy Lombard helped to keep the group intact. Described by Hugh Murray as "tall, strong, slow to speak and rambling once he had begun," Lombard provided "a flexible practical leadership which encouraged 'participatory democracy' before the phrase became popular. A different leader might have failed." [18]

The "chilling effect" of the schools crisis proved short-lived. Indeed, by revealing the courage of the four girls, underlining the determination of the federal government, and focusing an international spotlight on New Orleans, the white boycott helped to forge black solidarity and heighten popular awareness of the civil rights issue. By its very nature, the NAACP's involvement in the schools issue limited decision making and active participation to a handful of lawyers. Still, the integration crisis accelerated the thrust toward united black action over related issues, most notably the welfare cutoff and voter registration.[19]

The state's mean-spirited welfare cutoff was not directly related to the schools issue, but it was most assuredly part of the legislature's overall strategy of resistance to integration. The plight of the children excluded from the Aid to Dependent Children program, five thousand in New Orleans and twenty-three thousand across the state, led to some pitiful sights. "It is not uncommon," wrote J. Harvey Kerns, the head of the Urban League, "to observe small children tugging at their mother's dress, crying, 'Mama, I'm hungry.'" Blacks were incensed. "Our recent legislature will, without a shadow of a doubt, go down in history as one of the most thoughtless, unjust, unprincipled, and hateful bodies ever to serve in its capacity as lawmakers," stated an uncharacteristically outspoken editorial in the LEA Journal.

Widely reported abroad, particularly in Britain, the cutoff prompted journalist A. J. Liebling to write that "the Great State minus Earl" had finally achieved "the international prominence of the Union of South Africa." Blacks in New Orleans united around "Operation Feed the Babies," a relief effort coordinated by the Urban League; donations also poured in from around the country and even from overseas. The national outcry enabled the Urban League to mobilize an intensive lobbying effort directed at the federal government. It was no means clear that Louisiana's "suitable home" rule could be overturned on the basis of racial discrimination; some two dozen other states, most of them outside the South, had a similar rule. After hearings in Washington, however, the Department of Health, Education, and Welfare adopted a new policy that forbade applications of the "suitable home" test. The state legislature repealed the vindictive statute of 1960. In February 1961 Kerns reported that the vast majority of the children had been readmitted to the ADC program. The outcome of the dispute was a significant expansion of welfare rights that had national importance.[20]

The schools crisis also gave impetus to the search for unity around the goal of political power. The Coordinating Committee of Greater New Orleans, which evolved in 1961–62, was the brainchild of Dr. Daniel C. Thompson, the Dillard sociologist whose study of the city's black leadership revealed all too clearly its political impotence and fragmented organization. The committee attempted to harness the city's disparate black organizations to a voter registration drive with the aim of decisively influencing the 1962 mayoral election. It cast its net as widely as possible, embracing not only the mainline civil rights groups but also social clubs, prominent ministers, political freelancers, university professors, barbers and beauticians. Crucially, it had the blessing of the Catholic Church and the active support of the Josephite Fathers. Just as in 1956 the United Clubs cancelled their Carnival balls to raise money for the NAACP, in 1961 the same group instigated a "blackout" of Carnival to help finance the committee. Blacks responded magnificently, although the refusal of the Zulu Social Aid and Pleasure Club to cancel its Mardi Gras parade, partly due to Mayor Morrison's personal intercession, created a false impression of normalcy. The *Louisiana Weekly* blasted the Zulus as "smiling and shuffling Uncle Toms" and urged blacks to exact political revenge on Morrison.[21]

During 1961 the New Orleans CORE chapter gradually revived and the impetus of direct action intensified. In March, after the Canal Street merchants failed to agree on desegregation, CORE began picketing Woolworth, McCrory, and other chain stores. At the same time the Consumer's League, which coordinated its moves with CORE, began picketing on St. Claude Avenue, a working-class neighborhood below the French Quarter. The police responded by arresting pickets for disturbing the peace and obstructing public passageways. Picketing and sit-ins continued, sporadically, throughout the summer and fall. The Consumers League also threatened to boycott NOPSI, the city's privately owned public utilities company, over its failure to employ black bus drivers.[22]

The increasingly confident CORE group now set the pace for black protest in New Orleans, its growing assertiveness bolstered by the snowballing of direct action across the South. In particular, the daring Freedom Rides — CORE's own project — gave the national organization the kind of publicity that hitherto it had only dreamed of. "For the first time," write Meier and Rudwick, "the mass media recognized CORE as a major race relations organization." As well as encouraging an influx of donations and new members, the Freedom Rides also gave CORE a new sense of identity and cohesion, an esprit de corps fueled by shared danger and common purpose. Moreover, because the Freedom Rides terminated in New Orleans, the Crescent City chapter played an especially important part in the project, providing food and shelter throughout the summer of 1961. Police harassment of incoming Freedom Riders, far from intimidating the group, encouraged greater defiance. In the most blatant incident, police arrested three Freedom Riders in a private home, beat them up, and then charged them with vagrancy, battery, and attempted escape. In a protest against police brutality, CORE members staged sit-ins at the mayor's office and at a district police station; fifteen of them were arrested.[23]

The very experience of direct action encouraged greater militancy. Being assaulted on a picket line or incarcerated in the parish jail often turned out to be less harrowing than imagined, and many were amazed by their self-possession under stress. Connie Bradford, a Tulane student from Birmingham, described how, picketing McCrory's on Canal Street, she was abused and hit by a white woman. "I thought that it would be very difficult to be non-violent in a situation like this. However, all I had time to think about . . . was keeping on my feet and keeping my arms down. I had no time to strike back, either in anger or in self-defense. . . . I hope that the people in the crowd were affected in some way by the sight of a non-violent CORE member being roughed up by a screaming, nearly hysterical woman." The belief of this young white student in the redemptive power of nonviolence might seem, in retrospect, naively idealistic, but such incidents helped to convince CORE members that nonviolence was, indeed, a practical method. Once their fear of the unknown had been dispelled, many returned to the picket line, and to jail, time and time again. Moreover, for members like Jerome Smith and Doris Jean Castle, who had traveled on the early, most dangerous Freedom Rides and served time in Mississippi's notorious Parchman penitentiary, New Orleans seemed tame.[24]

CORE's loose, decentralized structure also contributed to the dynamism of the New Orleans chapter. An action-oriented organization that encouraged local initiatives, CORE attracted young people who chafed under the aging, "top-down" leadership of the NAACP. The NAACP Youth Council in New Orleans, for example, came into continual conflict with the adult branch, whose elderly leaders were far more cautious and deliberate. The Young Turks of 1940 were now the Old Guard of 1960, and their most prominent member, longtime branch president Arthur J. Chapital, tried doggedly to exert his authority over a new generation of Young Turks led by Llewellyn Soniat and Raphael Cassimere. The disputes between the branch and the Youth Council eventually became so intractable that they had to be arbitrated by New York. In CORE, on the other hand, young activists were free to make their own decisions and act upon them; there was no divided authority to confuse matters and no old guard to restrain them.

The role of lawyers in the two organizations provided another contrast. Within the NAACP, lawyers often exercised a controlling influence on strategy and tactics; for example, it was on the advice of its lawyers, notably A. P. Tureaud, that the New Orleans branch refrained from conducting sit-ins. In CORE, on the other hand, lawyers normally played second fiddle. This is not to say that lawyers were peripheral. The black law firm of Robert F. Collins, Nils R. Douglas, and Lolis E. Elie, founded in 1960, became a central part of CORE, both in New Orleans and the state, and later became a dynamic political force in its own right. Yet while Collins, Douglas, and Elie rendered advice and representation, and sometimes helped to formulate strategy, they did not dominate decision making or possess the power to veto direct action. This relative freedom from legalistic restraint and adult supervision exercised great appeal for many young people, and CORE was able to recruit more than a few bored and frustrated members of the NAACP Youth Council.

The increasing salience of civil rights as a national political issue also nourished CORE's militancy. Faced with growing black insurgency in the South, the federal courts and the Kennedy administration attempted to limit the power of white authorities to enforce segregation. The Freedom Rides, for example, compelled the Kennedy administration to ban segregation and discrimination in interstate travel as of November 1, 1961. Six weeks later, in *Garner* v. *Louisiana,* its first decision concerning lunch counter sit-ins, the Supreme Court invalidated the convictions of the Southern University students arrested in Baton Rouge in 1960. The state had produced no evidence whatever, the Court concluded, to substantiate the charge of disturbing the peace. Although the decision did nothing to stop the police from continuing to arrest sit-in demonstrators, the latter now knew that there was a fair chance that their convictions would be set aside by the federal courts.[25]

Even Louisiana's state courts began, in some instances, to affirm the right to peaceful public protest. In 1962 the state supreme court reversed the convictions of Jerome Smith, Dave Dennis, Connie Bradford, and Julia Aaron, who had been arrested for "obstructing public passages" while handing out leaflets on Canal Street. By then, the police in New Orleans had given up trying to suppress picketing, and for the next few years pickets on Canal became, if not a permanent fixture, at least a familiar sight. Occasionally, when state judges had little choice but to convict, they framed their judgments so as to facilitate reversal. For example, *Lombard* v. *Louisiana,* the first case to arise out of the New Orleans sit-ins, fell to civil district judge Bernard Cocke. A former district attorney who detested police brutality and other egregious forms of racial discrimination, Cocke deliberately set his sentences high enough so as to give the U.S. Supreme Court jurisdiction. In 1963 that Court duly set aside the convictions on the grounds that the arrests, in conjunction with Mayor Morrison's declared intention to quash sit-ins, constituted state action to enforce segregation, a clear violation of the Fourteenth Amendment.[26]

By then businessmen in New Orleans had already quietly desegregated their lunch counters. A notable victory, lunch counter integration was also a rather surprising one, for it took place under a new mayor whose attitude toward blacks ranged from indifference to hostility. Victor H. Schiro, a veteran council member, rejected Chep Morrison's middle-of-the-road approach in favor of a harder segregationist stance. Campaigning for election in his own right he courted the Citizens Council, smiled for the cameras at the dedication of the Ninth Ward cooperative school (created as a refuge for those boycotting Frantz and McDonogh No. 19), and studiously ignored the black vote. In February 1962 he roundly defeated Adrian Duplantier, a racial moderate. Having backed the wrong horse, Duplantier, blacks found themselves out in the political cold.[27]

In truth, the black vote remained far too weak to exert much influence on city politics, especially when the segregation issue tended to polarize voting according to race. Moreover, despite the best efforts of the Coordinating Council — and its voter registration drive in the fall of 1961 reached into more than two hundred schools, churches, barbershops, beauty parlors, and pool halls — the black vote did not increase. Governor Davis appointed a new registrar of voters, A. P. Gallinghouse, who was charged with implementing the new state policy of freezing the black electorate. Gallinghouse ensured that his staff rejected most black applicants for alleged "errors" when filling out the voter application form. Moreover, periodic purges of voters who had moved or failed to vote almost exactly counterbalanced the number of new voters. At thirty-six thousand, about 27 percent of black adults and only 17 percent of the total electorate, the black vote had scarcely grown since 1950. Under the current rules, which were carefully and cunningly designed to discriminate against blacks, voter registration drives became exercises in futility and frustration.[28]

It was scarcely surprising, then, that Schiro, who possessed reasonably sensitive political antennas, saw little point in cultivating black support. One of the most mild-mannered of men personally, he was obnoxious to blacks politically. One of his first acts as mayor was to sack A. L. Davis, whom Morrison, having procrastinated for years over creating a biracial committee, had appointed as his "race relations advisor" in the closing days of his administration. While Schiro could be forgiven for removing a stalwart Morrison man like Davis, blacks saw his refusal to name a replacement as a deliberate snub. Ironically, whereas Morrison's soothing approach had tended to discourage black militancy, Schiro's obvious hostility had the opposite effect, even though little of substance separated the two when it came to dealing with racial questions. Just as Morrison had denied Municipal Auditorium to the NAACP when he learned that Thurgood Marshall was speaking, so Schiro denied it to the Consumers League when he discovered that Martin Luther King was the star attraction. Schiro's action incensed blacks far more than Morrison's identical act of the previous year.

Yet Schiro's segregationist orthodoxy was misleading: in practice the mayor was a flexible pragmatist. A man with no political ambitions beyond New Orleans, he readily deferred to the judgment of businessmen like Darwin Fenner, Clifford Favrot, Richard Freeman, and Ashton Phelps. And these men, however much they loathed integration, had come to the realization that whites must perforce give ground, even if they only conceded it inch by inch. The formation of CABL (the Committee for a Better Louisiana) in June 1962 testified to their profound concern over the state's continuing economic malaise. Measured against virtually every index of growth, Louisiana was falling further behind other southern states — even Mississippi had a better record in creating industrial employment. The economic vitality of New Orleans, in particular, was closely linked to the civil rights issue. The health of the tourist industry, the award of federal contracts for the space program, and the ability to attract private industry all depended upon ensuring orderly change and, above all, avoiding the kind of public disorder of which the schools crisis had been the most damaging example. In 1961 the business leaders began to play a much more active role in overseeing racial change. They saw to it that Schiro prepared for the second year of school integration much more carefully than Morrison had done in 1960. They also influenced the decision of NOPSI to hire its first black bus drivers rather than face a possible consumer boycott.[29]

The decision by this same group of men to countenance lunch counter integration followed the same civic and economic logic. Put simply, the protests initiated by CORE in September 1960 had become more than an inconvenience: they had reached a point where they threatened the viability of Canal Street as a major retailing artery. On December 16, 1961, after a typically inspirational visit by Martin Luther King, CORE launched a new campaign of sit-ins in cooperation with the Consumers League, the NAACP Youth Council, and the Interdenominational Ministerial Alliance. This time, noted Betty Wisdom, they seemed to mean business. "The withdrawal of the Auditorium permit [for the King meeting] seems to have been the last straw for some Negro leaders. . . . I have never seen such determination in the Negro community before. They'll get their rights or die trying." [30]

It was not the first time that black organizations had acted in concert. Yet three weeks after the renewal of the Canal Street campaign, NAACP branch president Arthur J. Chapital received a stinging rebuke from Roy Wilkins for cooperating with CORE. "The organization that you are going out of your way to help has members who are busy creating the impression that your Association is no good," wrote Wilkins, "and they are spreading this so well that some people who usually give money to us are not doing so." Why, he asked, had Chapital permitted the NAACP in New Orleans to play a secondary role in the campaign, allowing CORE to carry out the sit-ins and reap the resulting credit? If the black community supported the idea of sit-ins, why had the NAACP failed to respond? When Chapital replied that the branch had abstained from sit-ins on the advice of its lawyers, he received a further reprimand.

If NAACP branches, composed of cautious adults, and if NAACP local legal advisors, conservative and anxious to maintain a local reputation, are going to hold our branches back in the face of the demands of the times, then we will see other groups stepping in and taking over while the NAACP dies a slow death. . . . While you are "holding back" CORE and other groups are coming forward and picking up the energy, imagination and daring among our young people that we are carelessly throwing to one side. . . . You, as the leader of the NAACP in New Orleans, are far behind the sentiments of your own community.

The national office, he sniffily added, had never advocated "such super caution."[31]

This was an astonishing about-face for Wilkins. Having for years privately disparaged nonviolent direct action as little more than "blowing off steam," he now attacked NAACP stalwarts like Chapital and Tureaud for being wedded to the NAACP's traditional methods, the very methods that Wilkins himself had stoutly defended as superior to boycotts and demonstrations. Now, almost overnight, he wanted to inject the NAACP with youthful militancy. In February he sent Gloster Current, the NAACP's director of branches, to drum a sense of urgency into the New Orleans NAACP. The association was losing members, Current warned, and it had to adopt a more aggressive stance. Why, for example, had the branch failed to take prompt legal action against the Municipal Auditorium commission, which had barred NAACP meetings while allowing Citizens Council ones? Current also tried to strengthen the autonomy of the Youth Council, which continually resisted the branch's attempts to restrict its freedom of action. "The youth are the future of our movement and we must not throttle them," he reminded Chapital during one dispute. Privately, Current considered Chapital something of an obstacle to strengthening the NAACP. "We must act at once," he told Wilkins, "to give the people of Louisiana an opportunity to elect younger leaders." Accordingly, Current engaged in some behind-the-scenes politicking to stop Chapital assuming the presidency of the State Conference of Branches upon the death of Doretha Combre.[32]

The pressure to treat CORE as a mortal threat, however, came almost wholly from the top, from the association's national officials; at the local level, most NAACP members viewed CORE as a welcome ally. There were tensions and rivalries, to be sure, but the two organizations continued to cooperate under the auspices of the Coordinating Council. With CORE providing the sit-in demonstrators, the NAACP and others supplying pickets and moral support, the intensified boycott of Canal Street launched in December 1961 soon began to bite. The manager of the McCrory's restaurant was particularly belligerent. "If these places are spoiled for the shopping public by the blight of integration," he believed, "then Canal Street . . . is doomed." On one occasion the appearance of "communist-led CORE radicals" prompted him to pull out a gun. In February 1962, however, the merchants sued for peace, and Joseph Simon, the president of the chamber of commerce, asked Lolis Elie to assemble a committee of black leaders with whom a committee of merchants could negotiate.

When the two sides held their first meeting — surely an historic occasion — they agreed to a timetable whereby all segregation by custom, not law, would be phased out. As a sign of good faith, stores in the midcity area quietly removed racial signs from toilets and drinking fountains. CORE, for its part, agreed to remain passive until the negotiations came to fruition. After innumerable delays, exacerbated by the merchants' concern for secrecy (they feared that the Citizens Council might boycott individual stores) and the usual reluctance to act while the state legislature was in session, the whites agreed to desegregate lunch counters throughout the city. In early September, carefully planned "tests" took place in selected stores. The news media agreed to hush up the story and the tests passed off without incident. Meanwhile, the negotiators moved on to discuss the issue of black employment on Canal Street above the mop-and-broom level.[33]

By 1962 New Orleans no longer presented a face of die-hard racism. Lunch counter integration coincided with the first year of Catholic school integration and the second year in which a handful of integrated public schools opened peacefully. A few months later, Tulane University admitted its first black students. New Orleans was reverting to the pattern that characterized the Morrison years of the 1950s: the grudging acceptance of inevitable change. The city's business elite was determined to live down the ugliness of the 1960 schools crisis.

These were men, however, of small compromises rather than strategic vision. Collectively, they wielded great power. Judge John Minor Wisdom, who knew them intimately, described them as a kind of "interlocking directorate" or "closed corporation," for the same people could be found on the governing bodies of the Hibernia and Whitney banks, Tulane University, NOPSI, the Orleans Parish Levee Board, and the Board of Liquidation of the City Debt. Many belonged to the same social clubs (Boston and Pelican), sent their children to the same private schools (Newman and Country Day), and masked in the same Mardi Gras krewes (Rex, Comus, Momus, and Proteus). This concentration of old wealth made New Orleans one of the most conservative cities in the South. More exclusive and tradition-bound than wealthy whites in other southern cities, such people were slow to embrace change and, in Wisdom's view, "never did really assert themselves in favor of desegregation."[34]

Shunning blacks in their social lives, rarely meeting them in their professional lives, they kept the word "nigger" very much a part of their everyday vocabulary. Newsman Bill Monroe captured this reflexive racism when he described an incident he witnessed in a downtown barbershop involving a "well-to-do, well-known" businessman. As the man rose to leave, "The Negro shoeshine boy came up with his coat and started to help him on with it. The man told him, 'I don't want any help from you, nigger. You're one of those smart niggers.' The shoeshine boy made some amiable remark designed to save face. . . . The man said, 'You talk too much, nigger.' The shoeshine boy fell silent." Historian Numan V. Bartley considered the leading businessmen of New Orleans "profoundly reactionary." Sociologist Morton Inger thought they had "strong anti-Negro feelings." When they acceded to change they were, to quote journalist Ralph McGill, "more influenced by the slowing of the cash register than by morality."[35]

Yet the incremental integration of New Orleans compared favorably with the glacial state of race relations in Shreveport, at that time the state's second biggest city. Indeed, beside Shreveport, the Crescent City was a haven of liberalism. Since 1954, when it had basked in the accolade bestowed upon it by *Look* magazine as an exemplar of good race relations, Shreveport had become, along with Birmingham, Alabama, the most oppressive city in the South for critics of white supremacy. As a Catholic priest wrote in 1961, with heavy irony, "This is Shreveport, U.S.S.R., with a police state and thought control, and the rule of the White [Citizens] Councils."[36]

Connections, rather than numbers, made the Citizens Council movement in Shreveport so potent. Even when, after 1960, the movement declined and disintegrated in the rest of the state, the Shreveport-based Citizens Councils of Louisiana remained a force to be reckoned with, despite its increasingly fascistic character. "Its raucous Negrophobia, excessive even by Deep South standards, its apparent obsession with the 'internal Red menace,' and its unblushing anti-semitism marked it as an extremist organization akin to the Ku Klux Klan," wrote Neil R. McMillen in his history of the Citizens Councils.[37]

The political context of the area, however, gave such extremism powerful resonance and influence. In other cities, blacks tended to exaggerate the coherence and authority of the white elite; not so in Shreveport. As a white lawyer who grew up there affirmed, "There truly is a white power structure in Shreveport, the real McCoy."[38] Throughout the 1950s and on into the 1960s a dozen people—bankers, utilities executives, newspaper proprietors, oil and gas executives—dominated both the economic and political life of the city. This "small group of powerful men," recalled former mayor James Gardner, molded the direction of Shreveport's economic growth, discouraging any rapid expansion in manufacturing, for example, in order to limit the influence of organized labor. They also exercised a strong voice in local politics, often handpicking key elected officials such as mayor, sheriff, and commissioner of public safety.[39]

Shreveport's geographical position, perched on the northwestern border of the state, magnified the conservative influence of this white elite. "Shreveport is hermetically sealed," stated attorney John R. Martzell. "No ideas get in or out." Whites in Shreveport found it difficult to identify with the rest of Louisiana; they considered themselves part of "Ark-La-Tex" rather than the Pelican State. Residents were far more likely to visit Dallas than New Orleans, and even after New Orleans got its own NFL franchise, the local television station carried the games of the Dallas Cowboys. But unlike Dallas, another city dominated by oil money, Shreveport had Old South roots that reinforced its attachment to white supremacy. The city lay within the historic Black Belt that stretched from the Mississippi Delta across northern Louisiana and southern Arkansas. The result was a peculiar kind of isolation that made it one of the most conservative cities in the South. Although, in the opinion of NAACP official Harvey Britton, Shreveport "was not that representative . . . of the entire state," the city and its hinterland had given Louisiana many of its most influential conservative leaders, including governors Robert Kennon and Jimmie Davis and Citizens Council founder William Rainach. In Shreveport, Britton recalled, "you had the true die-hards as an institution."[40]

The *Brown* decision marked the beginning of a relentless campaign by Shreveport's ultrasegregationists to silence the heresy of interracialism. With the acquiescence of the power structure, the active assistance of the police, and the shrill support of the *Shreveport Journal* and the even more reactionary *Shreveport Times,* the Citizens Councils subjected white moderates to intimidation and coercion. Two particular targets were the former supporters of Friendship House, which had closed in 1955, and liberal faculty members at Centenary College, a small, private institution affiliated with the Methodist Church. Such people found themselves under constant surveillance by the police and sometimes awoke to burning crosses in front of their homes. In 1959 an official of the American Friends Service Committee reported that Centenary had abandoned its integrated international clubs, campus dances no longer hired Negro bands, and the college president had become a "tortured soul."[41]

The ordeal of Ethel and Joe Daniell illustrates the lengths to which the Citizens Councils would go. This elderly couple were not outspoken integrationists, but they had been among the founders of Friendship House and over the years had continued to support, in a quiet way, the Catholic interracial movement. Joe Daniell, moreover, had made himself unpopular within the American Legion's Forty and Eight club by objecting to its exclusion of blacks. Social ostracism followed swiftly: forced out of the 40 and 8, he also lost his commission as a deputy sheriff.

One night in July 1961, the Daniells found a burning cross outside their house with a pencilled note that read, "Nigger lover you had better change your ways." Police Chief Harvey Teasley declined to investigate the incident, suggesting that they contact the fire department. The Daniells then discovered that their battery and oxygen-supply business, which they had founded in 1930, was the subject of an economic boycott. The Caddo Parish school board cancelled its contract; pressure from the local auto mechanics' association, many of whose members belonged to the Ku Klux Klan, caused nearly all the garages in the Shreveport area to do likewise. Company trucks were sabotaged; two truck drivers attempting to deliver to small garages were attacked. The Daniells discovered that one of their employees was a police informer and that they both had thick police files identifying them as Communists and subversives. "The Citizens Councils pulled no punches," they told Burke Marshall of the Justice Department. "They wanted us out of business. George Shannon [editor of the *Shreveport Journal*] said he would give us a story when we got out. Bill Shaw [of the Citizens Council] said we had to go." When the largest supplier of oxygen in north Louisiana told them that he had been threatened with a cross-burning unless he ceased trading with them, the Daniells admitted defeat. In October 1961 they sold their company for $77,000, a fraction of its worth, and moved to California. Burke Marshall told them, regretfully, that he saw no basis for federal action.[42]

Shreveport's repressive climate made protest action by blacks fitful and fragmented. The state's injunction against the NAACP in 1956 had led to the dissolution of the local branch and the formation of the United Christian Movement. However, the UCM's affiliation with the Southern Christian Leadership Conference made its relationship to the NAACP problematic. The UCM retained A. P. Tureaud to handle its bus and trade-school integration suits, but neither Tureaud nor Dr. C. O. Simpkins, the UCM's president, found their collaboration satisfactory. Tureaud deplored Simpkins's public criticism of Judge Ben Dawkins; Simpkins complained about Tureaud's slowness in pressing the suits and his failure to keep the UCM informed. In 1961 the two cases still languished in legal limbo. Many blacks felt disillusioned, and both the UCM and the newly reorganized NAACP branch received unjustified blame for Tureaud's supercaution.[43]

At Simpkins's urging, SCLC made Shreveport one of its earliest priorities.

In 1960 it hired Harry Blake, a young Baptist minister and Shreveport native, as its first full-time field secretary. In October SCLC held its annual convention in Shreveport. As Blake drove home after the three-day meeting, a car pulled alongside and a bullet showered him with shattered glass.[44]

In 1961 Freedom Riders came to Shreveport. One of them, Dave Dennis, had grown up in the city before moving to Lafayette; now a leading member of New Orleans CORE — his sit-in activities having forced him to drop out of Dillard University — he helped to put together a Shreveport CORE chapter. Attempts to use the bus station facilities soon revealed Shreveport's recalcitrance. Bus riders were mobbed and arrested. When James Farmer addressed a mass meeting in August, the police harassed blacks and allowed about one hundred whites to picket the church.

Signing on as a full-time CORE field secretary, Dennis tried to set up a program of direct action, beginning with testing of the bus stations when the Interstate Commerce Commission's desegregation ruling came into effect on November 1. Upon leaving a church meeting on October 24, however, sixteen members of the fledgling CORE chapter were arrested by waiting police and charged with vagrancy and loitering. Although Jesse Stone managed to bail them all out within two days, their experience in jail was thoroughly unpleasant and stunted the chapter almost before birth. Police intimidation, Dennis informed Gordon Carey, "has frightened away some of our members and some of us are confronted with charges that are not directly related to the race problem." As for the bus station, the police continued to enforce segregation; the mayor simply ignored letters from assistant attorney general Burke Marshall. Not until 1962, after a successful prosecution by the Department of Justice, did city officials comply with the ICC ruling. Shreveport was probably the last city in the South to do so. Even then, the FBI told Harry Blake that it would be unwise to actually use the desegregated facilities.[45]

Shreveport now had three civil rights organizations: CORE, SCLC, and the NAACP. The repressive climate made competition a luxury, and they tried their best to cooperate, a process aided by the fact that Harry Blake was active in all three. Their semi-united front, however, soon ground to a halt in the face of police intimidation, Klan violence, and neglect by their parent organizations. Like the Birmingham police department under "Bull" Connor, the Shreveport police kept up continuous surveillance of civil rights activities through informants, wiretaps, electronic "bugs," and the "tailing" of individuals. Through harassing arrests — vagrancy was a favorite charge — the police played a kind of cat-and-mouse game. (Lawyer Jesse Stone recalled that every time a friend from California, a preacher, visited Shreveport, the police arrested the man without fail, simply because he sported a SNCC badge showing a white hand clasping a black hand.) A rash of Klan bombings, however, had a far more serious effect. In 1961 and 1962 the Klan dynamited a black Masonic lodge, threw firebombs into a church during a CORE meeting, blew up a new home being built for C. O. Simpkins, and set a fire at Simpkins's summer cottage.[46]

On June 8, 1962, Harry Blake called SCLC in Atlanta to warn of threats against Martin Luther King's life. King ignored them and flew in to kick off a voter registration drive. Finding the meeting place, the Little Union Baptist Church, picketed by members of the Citizens Council, Wyatt Walker, SCLC's executive director, tried to negotiate with the police for their removal. The police thereupon arrested him and Blake for "loitering." The pair were held in the Caddo Parish jail for two days; prison officials even subjected them to a psychiatric examination, ostensibly to determine their sanity. By the end of 1962 Simpkins had quit Shreveport to set up a dental practice on Long Island. The UCM disintegrated and Blake, to quote SCLC official Andrew Young, was "pretty much at the end of his rope." By early 1963 the CORE chapter, led by Lavert Taylor and Joseph Russell, had become moribund. Only a weak NAACP branch survived, and Blake, after resigning from SCLC, gamely took over its presidency. Lack of participation by black ministers plagued all three organizations. So did insufficient support from New York and Atlanta; other cities always seemed to have a stronger claim on their resources. Once again, blacks felt let down, and with each disappointment it became increasingly difficult to revive their enthusiasm.[47]

CORE had more success in reviving direct action in Baton Rouge. In October 1961 a group of students led by Ronnie Moore, Weldon Rougeau, and Patricia Ann Tate organized a CORE chapter at Southern University with a view to launching a new wave of sit-ins. They proceeded covertly, with members of New Orleans CORE — Dave Dennis, Doris Castle, Jerome Smith, and Julia Aaron — sneaking into the dormitories to proselytize among the students. Felton Clark, however, was aware of these secret meetings, thanks to his security officer, William Pass, who received a steady stream of information from student informers. Clark also knew that this time, unlike 1960, the students had lined up promises of bond money and other financial support from the local communities of Scotlandville, Southern Heights, and Zion City. They also had the backing of FOCUS, a new black voters league headed by Raymond Scott, a tailor, and Acie Belton, a refinery worker. On December 8, CORE initiated the routine preliminaries to direct action: letters to the merchants requesting negotiations, the distribution of leaflets calling for a boycott of twelve downtown stores, and a two-day workshop on nonviolence.

On December 11, the day of the Supreme Court's *Garner* decision, CORE members held sit-ins at two variety stores. Two days later, when CORE set up picket lines, the police moved in and arrested twenty-three people, including

Dave Dennis and Weldon Rogeau. That evening, about thirty-five hundred students assembled to hear Ronnie Moore, chairman of Baton Rouge CORE, and the Reverend B. Elton Cox, a visiting CORE field secretary. Many of them turned out the following morning for a five-mile march to the parish courthouse in downtown Baton Rouge.[48]

However, December 15 started badly and ended disastrously. As about two thousand students streamed off the campus, the police arrested Ronnie Moore and four companions in their sound truck. As the demonstrators formed into a dense crowd outside the castellated Victorian gothic building that once housed the state capitol, the police asked Elton Cox to disperse the gathering. Cox refused, insisting that they march to the courthouse and conduct a peaceful protest. Police officials reluctantly acquiesced. When they reached the courthouse, two blocks away, police chief Wingate White told Cox to confine the demonstration to the sidewalk on the west side of the street, about one hundred feet from the courthouse steps. Rain fell on the students, lined up five deep, as they sang "God Bless America" and "We Shall Overcome." Rippling cheers and applause rose from the throng when they heard the refrain echoing from the jail cells of the courthouse. Cox then spoke, concluding with an invitation to eat lunch at the twelve stores that CORE had targeted. If they still failed to get service at the lunch counters, Cox added, they should sit in for one hour.

The police then panicked. Sheriff Bryan Clemmons told the students to disperse immediately. Cox's response signalled defiance, and when the demonstrators failed to move, two sheriff's deputies started to shove some students. One policeman then set off a tear gas canister; dozens more exploded, forcing the students to flee. When they reassembled outside the state capitol, the police again teargassed them, and a K-9 squad waded in with German shepherds. As Cox and others sought refuge in a church, the police arrested him. Forty-nine students, also arrested that day, joined him in jail.[49]

With most of CORE's leaders incarcerated, leadership devolved on D'Army Bailey, who rallied the students that evening and led a march to the campus residence of Felton Clark. Faced with some three thousand angry students, Clark assured them that sooner than expel any of the student demonstrators, he would resign his position as president of Southern. Somewhat mollified, the students dispersed. The following day the state board of education ordered the presidents of state universities to ban student demonstrations, both on and off campus, and to automatically suspend any students who were arrested. Felton Clark closed Southern University four days early. Many of the arrested students spent Christmas in jail; Moore and Rougeau were not bailed out until January 4. On the day of their release U.S. district judge

E. Gordon West issued a temporary restraining order against CORE, banning demonstrations and virtually all other protest activities.

When students returned to campus in the second week of January, they were still in a rebellious mood, and Bailey fomented the discontent. On January 17, upon learning that Clark had expelled seven students, the CORE leaders, about one thousand students held a vigil outside Clark's residence. Clark refused to address them. At a special convocation of faculty the next day, he denounced the students in the most hostile terms, describing them as hoodlums, anarchists, and "culturally void." He also pointedly reminded the assembled professors not to act like "the dog that bit the hand that fed it." The next day Clark closed the campus and required all students to register anew for the spring semester; the name of D'Army Bailey was added to the list of those expelled. When Ronnie Moore and Weldon Rougeau returned to the campus to collect their belongings, the police arrested them for trespassing. Students returned on January 25 to a campus patrolled by state police. Forty more students found that they would not be readmitted. "We at Southern," Clark explained, "are interested in education, and nothing else."

For Adolph L. Reed, a member of the history and political science department, it was all too much, and he sent Clark a scorching, ten-page letter of resignation. Likening Clark's defense of his actions to that of Nazi war criminal Adolph Eichmann — he was only obeying orders — Reed asked, "Can 'education' exist in the abstract? Can there be 'education' that exists apart from people and issues?" The sight of policemen on the campus, he added, was a "disgusting spectacle." After quitting the university Reed publicly lambasted Clark in the pages of *Nation* magazine, and historian C. Vann Woodward, writing in *Harper's*, heaped more opprobrium on the man. Yet once again Clark had triumphed. Despite the censure of the American Association of University Professors, his autocratic control over Southern was intact, his ability to fire recalcitrant faculty members unimpaired. Not until 1969 would Southern experience student protests on anything like the scale of 1960 and 1961.[50]

CORE's hopes to "break Louisiana wide open" wilted under a barrage of injunctions and prosecutions. The state's legal onslaught hinged upon the demonstration of December 15, and Elton Cox bore its brunt. In the words of the Louisiana Supreme Court, Cox's "inflammatory" speech had turned the protest into a "disorderly and seething mob" that "intended to storm the courthouse." Concluding that "a riot was inevitable," the court upheld Cox's conviction for disturbing the peace, obstructing public passageways, and picketing a courthouse. Judge Fred LeBlanc meted out a sentence of twenty-one months.[51]

But that was only the beginning. While in jail, Cox heard rumors that district attorney Sargent Pitcher had shared bribes with trial judge LeBlanc. Out on bond pending his appeal, he mentioned the allegation in an NAACP meeting. Such charges were the common stuff of Louisiana politics, but when news of Cox's speech got back to him, Pitcher promptly indicted Cox for defaming him and LeBlanc. The relevant criminal libel statute outlawed "anything which tends to expose any person to hatred, contempt or ridicule or to deprive him of the benefit of public confidence or social intercourse." If it were to be enforced, half the population of Louisiana, including every politician in the state, would face indictment. Nevertheless, on November 30, 1962, Cox was convicted and sentenced to an additional two years. By the time he left jail on bond in February 1963 he had served a total of 107 days.[52]

Collins, Douglas, and Elie implored CORE to make the persecution of Cox a national cause célèbre. Here was a "True Horror Story," they assured Marvin Rich, a "tremendous constitutional case" that merited "total saturation." CORE did put forth considerable efforts to publicize the Baton Rouge situation, including hearings before a "Committee of Inquiry" in Washington graced by the likes of Eleanor Roosevelt, Norman Thomas, and Walter Reuther. But the Cox case received little national attention. The news media simply lacked the capacity to focus on more than one civil rights story at a time, and in 1962 it was concentrating on the exploits of Martin Luther King Jr. in Albany, Georgia. CORE also had problems coordinating its legal defense in Louisiana: Baton Rouge lawyer Johnnie Jones angrily withdrew from all CORE cases, demanding over $7,000 in unpaid fees; the young and inexperienced Murphy Bell stepped into the breach.

Even when it mustered its best legal talent, however, CORE could do little about the law's interminable delays. It was not until the end of 1964, when the U.S. Supreme Court invalidated Louisiana's criminal libel statute, that Pitcher dropped the defamation charges against Cox. In 1965 CORE's lawyers finally overturned Cox's original conviction when the Supreme Court held that the December 15 demonstration had been orderly, that the Baton Rouge police had permitted it to proceed, and that Louisiana's law against picketing near a courthouse had been improperly applied. By then, however, the damage had been done: Cox had been put out of action. Even in 1965, moreover, Pitcher refused to let go: he promptly reindicted Cox on the charge of "attempting" to obstruct justice, a prosecution halted by the Fifth Circuit Court of Appeals on the grounds that its "transparent purpose is to harass and punish [Cox] for his leadership in the civil rights movement."[53]

It was a similar story with Judge West's injunction against CORE. Writing to Eleanor Roosevelt, CORE general counsel Carl Rachlin described it as "one of the broadest and . . . most unconstitutional injunctions I have seen in many a day." Eventually, the Fifth Circuit Court of Appeals overruled West on the grounds that the original complaint against the December 15 demonstration involved no federal issue. At most, Judge Wisdom acidly noted, the demonstrators had blocked traffic and caused a heavy police presence: "A similar situation exists every year at Mardi Gras." By the time West dissolved the injunction, however, it had been in force for two full years, banning CORE from picketing, sit-ins, and demonstrations, and even from advocating these activities during 1961 and 1962.[54]

CORE could count itself unlucky in the combination of enemies it faced: not only an unbending black university president but also a vindictive district attorney, a segregationist state judge, and a federal judge who was utterly out of sympathy with the civil rights cause. Sargent Pitcher Jr. had been a charter member of the Citizens Councils of Louisiana, and as district attorney for East Baton Rouge Parish he harassed and prosecuted militant black leaders throughout the 1960s. In his former incarnation as Louisiana's attorney general, Fred LeBlanc had been a key conspirator in Pitcher and Rainach's attack on the NAACP in 1956; as a state judge he set sky-high bail for civil rights activists and imposed stiff sentences. Although born in Massachussetts, U.S. district judge E. Gordon West was another unabashed segregationist. He considered *Brown* v. *Board of Education* "one of the truly regrettable decisions of all time" and did his utmost to delay its implementation. These key officials made an unbeatable trio: CORE could not withstand the hostility of both the state and the federal judiciary.[55]

There was no countervailing power, moreover, coming from the Kennedy administration, which remained unmoved by pleas for intervention. "May I inform you about the pathetic situation in Baton Rouge, Louisiana?" one Southern University student wrote the president. "The Baton Rouge police force cursed us; they threw tear gas bombs on us, at us, and everywhere. They even put dogs on us. Is that justice, Mr. President?" This plaintive letter wound up on the desk of Harris Wofford, Kennedy's increasingly isolated and ineffectual civil rights advisor. The Justice Department had looked into the allegations of police brutality, he wrote back, but the investigation had disclosed "no violation of federal law." (Wofford, tired of being used to "buffer" Kennedy from his critics, was shortly to quit the White House staff.) Privately, Burke Marshall expressed disquiet over the "grossly excessive" bail in the Baton Rouge cases and asked Justice Department attorneys if anything could be done about it. Apparently they replied in the negative.[56]

By the summer of 1962 the tide of nonviolent direct action ebbed throughout the South as "defeat and sheer exhaustion," to quote Meier and Rudwick, exacted their toll. CORE-led campaigns in Huntsville, Alabama, and Rock Hill, South Carolina, also ended in failure, as did the better-known SNCC-

SCLC campaign in Albany, Georgia, led by Martin Luther King. The segregationist strategy of legal repression through court injunctions and prosecutions was proving far more effective in stymieing the civil rights movement than raw violence. The abstention of the federal government from local conflicts such as Baton Rouge and Albany underlined the lesson of the Freedom Rides: southern officials needed to fear only direct federal intervention in the case of egregious police brutality or unrestrained mob violence. Blacks could not depend on the federal government to guarantee the right to demonstrate, they could only look to the federal courts. And in Baton Rouge that meant E. Gordon West, a recent Kennedy appointee.[57] Blacks could be forgiven for questioning the depth of the new administration's commitment to racial equality.

Nevertheless, civil rights organizations seized the opportunity to participate in the Voter Education Project, despite their awareness that the Kennedy administration was encouraging this initiative with the intention of diverting the energies of the movement away from demonstrations and toward voter registration. Funded by the Field, Taconic, and Stern foundations and administered by the Southern Regional Council as a "research project" (a ploy to facilitate tax-exempt status), the VEP disbursed $888,000 for voter registration drives between April 1962 and December 1964. For CORE in Baton Rouge, reeling from the defeat of its direct action campaign, VEP money provided a lifeline. CORE employed Ronnie Moore as a full-time field secretary and took on expelled Southern students as subsistence workers. In August 1962 they embarked upon CORE's first voter registration drive in Louisiana.[58]

It was not a success. CORE now paid the price of its previous failures in the form of increasing isolation from the city's black community. Wade Mackie believed that CORE's demonstrations had "upset the Negro community and split it into factions, leaving very little for CORE to work with after things simmered down." The CORE canvassers met apathy and sometimes outright hostility. "You must be prepared to leave a home at any time," reported Jim McCain. "Some persons we have visited will not cooperate in any form. You feel like giving up at times." In Scotlandville, black ministers refused to let CORE use their churches. Support from the NAACP was minimal.[59]

As 1962 drew to a close, CORE stood at the threshold of a major reorientation. Direct action had chalked up some gains in New Orleans but had foundered in Shreveport and failed, twice, in Baton Rouge. Now, following the example of SNCC, where field workers had already started working in rural counties in Mississippi and Georgia, CORE in Louisiana began to look outside the big cities.

Voter registration in the rural areas offered a number of attractions. It could give CORE the kind of continuity and stability that nonviolent direct action, by its sporadic nature, could not. Here was an activity that could be carried out on a year-round basis, that reached down into the grass roots of the black population, and in which there would be few, if any, competing organizations. Further, the prospect of working in some of Louisiana's "worst" parishes represented the kind of challenge that CORE, with its ethos of confrontation, relished. Finally, there was a straightforward financial incentive: the VEP agreed to fund voter registration drives in six rural parishes around Baton Rouge.

The decline of CORE in New Orleans reinforced this new direction. In February 1962 a bitter internal row erupted within the New Orleans CORE chapter, resulting in the expulsion of fifteen members, most of them whites, and the withdrawal of many more. It would be an overstatement, perhaps, to see this purge as a "move from integration to black nationalism," which is how Hugh Murray later described it, yet it did prefigure the interracial tensions that became increasingly marked within CORE (and SNCC) as more whites became involved in their activities.

The reason for the expulsions and the manner of their execution were bizarre. At the regular meeting of New Orleans CORE on February 1, 1962, chair Oretha Castle read aloud an article that had appeared in the *Louisiana Weekly* criticizing CORE members for interracial social activities. Then the membership committee, in a prearranged coup, entered the room and suspended the white males and black females deemed responsible for provoking such criticism. Uproar ensued. The victims of the purge, a group led by vice chair Ed Clark, a white Tulane student from Tennessee, protested vigorously. CORE dispatched Richard Haley to mediate the dispute, and in March Jim McCain ordered the suspensions lifted. After a number of acrimonious meetings, however, the Clark faction decided to withdraw from CORE, leaving the chapter all black.

In light of CORE's commitment to interracialism, it was an extraordinary episode. The suspended members stood accused of endangering CORE's support within the black community by fraternizing across the color line. As one CORE official put it, while "interracial social exchange is an essential part of CORE discipline," members should not "leap too far or too quickly beyond current general acceptance." Recalling the row years later, Oretha Castle put the matter more bluntly, asserting that white Tulane students had joined CORE with the primary aim of dating black women, having heard that "the CORE chapter was where you could come into contact with black women without any problems." That was not the kind of public image that CORE wished to project, Castle explained, and it was also uncomfortably redolent of the way in which white men had traditionally exploited black women for sexual gratification.

Others, however, believed that interracial dating was simply a pretext for what amounted to a straightforward faction fight. During the first year of its existence the chapter had comprised, in the words of Carlene Smith, a "small group of committed actionists (almost all of them Negroes), bound together in close personal association by the experience of the Freedom Rides." Beginning in the fall of 1961, however, the chapter saw an influx of new members, including many students from Southern University in New Orleans and also a fair number of white students from Tulane and LSUNO. Accustomed to making decisions within a small, intimate group of veteran activists, the chapter's original nucleus found itself ill equipped to deal with a larger membership, one lacking the esprit de corps and cameraderie shared by the founding members. The newcomers, for their part, began to question the reluctance of the original CORE circle to open up decision making beyond, as they saw it, "a small clique of favored individuals." To Carlene Smith, a black member since 1960, the assertion that white students joined CORE to pick up black women was absurd. Consensual dating, especially within the context of a CORE chapter, could hardly be considered sexual exploitation. All of the suspended members, moreover, were dedicated activists who had proven by their deeds "that their integrationism is not a pose." Smith regarded the purge of whites as a highly questionable maneuver by an entrenched old guard to retain control of the chapter.

The reassertion of black control came at a cost. The founding members in effect turned their backs on the possibility of converting CORE into a mass membership organization. After the purge, and partly because of it, the New Orleans chapter lost much of its dynamism. Dominated by Oretha Castle and a small circle of friends, it failed to grow and expand, becoming simply one of several organizations operating within a broad coalition. The chapter's prestige further declined when, in the summer of 1963, it ended its boycott of Canal Street, leaving the NAACP Youth Council to picket alone when the white merchants reneged on their promises of fair employment. New Orleans CORE never again spearheaded the civil rights movement in the way it had done between 1960 and 1962. Henceforth voter registration became CORE's central thrust in Louisiana. CORE moved out of the relative safety of the cities and into the countryside, where blacks and civil rights workers were far more exposed and vulnerable.[60]

Chapter 11

THE MOVEMENT, 1963–1964

The young volunteers who assembled in Plaquemine in July 1963 inaugurated a new phase of the civil rights struggle in Louisiana. During three successive summers, CORE "task force" workers proselytized the black population and, directed by a staff of full-time field secretaries, spread the gospel of militancy in ever-widening circles. Working in some of the most repressive areas of the state, they turned hot, dusty streets into symbolic battlefields where two ideas, racism and equality, openly confronted each other. By persuading blacks to demand the ballot and by mobilizing them to protest in the streets and public places, they made an incalculable contribution to the demise of Jim Crow, fomenting insurrection within the South and increasing the pressure from without.

In one sense, CORE's paid field workers and summer volunteers filled the leadership vacuum left by the repression of the NAACP, a void that existed throughout much of rural Louisiana and which was particularly stark in the northern half of the state. In fact, CORE did much more than that:

it furnished a level of help in the form of field workers and lawyers that the NAACP, even at its functioning best, had never been able to offer. The strength of the NAACP lay in its local branches, but too often those branches were left to fend for themselves as the national organization concentrated its resources in New York and Washington, and the Legal Defense Fund carefully nurtured a handful of strategic lawsuits. For an organization with a mass membership of half a million, the NAACP's field staff was tiny. In Louisiana, for example, the combined staff of the NAACP and the Legal Defense Fund comprised two people: Clarence Laws, the state field secretary, and Daniel Byrd, who worked on school integration under Thurgood Marshall's direction. Since 1957, moreover, the NAACP and the Inc. Fund had functioned as separate organizations, a situation that enhanced the power of the latter at the expense of the former. The NAACP, admittedly, was obliged to spread its staff thinly so as to cover the entire country; groups like SNCC, CORE, and SCLC maintained roving staffs, which they concentrated in certain states, SCLC in Alabama, SNCC in Mississippi, CORE in Louisiana.

More importantly, the large staffs fielded by the NAACP's rivals also derived from different concepts of organization. As David J. Garrow has argued, SNCC's 1961 decision to create a cadre of full-time workers who could devote themselves exclusively to grass-roots organizing in the Black Belt was a crucial innovation, marking "the first time that indigenous blacks in many areas of the rural Deep South had such day-to-day organizational assistance available to them." SNCC's field workers, as exemplified in the pioneering work of Bob Moses in Mississippi, lived and worked among the rural poor, making an open-ended commitment to community organizing that often stretched into years.[1]

With its emphasis on developing chapters that would affiliate with the national body, CORE had somewhat different organizing methods. Over time, however, chapter development became a lesser priority and CORE, like SNCC, concentrated on getting staff in the field. By expecting their field workers to work for a pittance and by recruiting self-financing summer volunteers from the North, SNCC and CORE both established the kind of solid physical presence that enabled local black communities to break out of their mental and geographical isolation. Together with the attorneys of the Lawyers Constitutional Defense Committee, a group formed at CORE's instigation in 1964, SNCC and CORE created an infrastructure that summoned forth and sustained a movement for civil rights outside the South's big cities.

Most of the full-time field secretaries were African-Americans and native Louisianians: Marvin Robinson, Ronnie Moore, and Weldon Rougeau from Southern University; Dave Dennis, Ike Reynolds, and Oretha Castle, veterans of the New Orleans CORE chapter; Spiver Gordon from the movement in

Plaquemine. Yet they also performed the catalytic function of "outside agitators." As an organization, CORE paid little attention to state boundaries; staff members were mobile resources to be deployed where necessity and opportunity demanded. A Louisianian like Dave Dennis might serve in Mississippi; a North Carolinian such as Bruce Baines might be assigned to Louisiana. Moreover, when they remained within their own state, field secretaries rarely stayed exclusively in one community. Whatever their precise track record, field secretaries soon acquired sufficient experience and sophistication to be able to enter an unknown community and quickly size up the situation — survey the "white power structure," locate the black influentials, assess the prospects for nonviolent protest. Their evaluations were sometimes superficial: no two communities were the same, and that was especially true in Louisiana; to a native of south Louisiana like Spiver Gordon, north Louisiana was terra incognita. Nevertheless, their rough-and-ready judgments usually contained enough insight to provide a basis for effective action.

Until 1965 most of the summer task-force workers were white northerners, middle-class college students aged nineteen to twenty-three. The role of whites in the movement produced tensions within CORE, as it did within SNCC. White volunteers could expect to have their motives questioned and their effectiveness disparaged by black staff members. The typical volunteer, it was often alleged, treated the movement as a vehicle for personal growth, a romantic interlude, a summer adventure, or a chance to act out missionary fantasies. Some were obsessed with "proving themselves" by getting beaten and arrested, regardless of the risk to others or the damage to their project. Others, according to a CORE discussion paper, tried to demonstrate their sincerity only to inspire mistrust. "They will eat red beans and rice, suddenly begin using bad grammar, exclaim at the quaintness of outhouses." Some held that color, culture, and class prevented whites, however well intentioned, from truly identifying with the black community. By 1964 many black staff members were freely stating that northern whites did not belong in the civil rights movement; by 1965 the question had become so heated as to be a continual source of dissension. A decision about whites should be made one way or another, complained one volunteer, "as some of the whites who were not prepared for this sort of conflict found the emotional strain of constantly having to justify their being there to the Southern Negro Task Force members unduly harsh."

Sexual tensions complicated and sometimes bedevilled the working relationship between black and white staff members. To many black men in the movement, white female volunteers represented sexual challenges of the most tantalizing kind, and the latter became the constant objects of sexual advances wanted and unwanted. Such attentions placed these women in an unenviable position: if they formed sexual relationships with black coworkers they risked compromising their effectiveness and scandalizing local Negro communities. If, on the other hand, they rejected would-be partners they risked insult and abuse of the most wounding kind. "Sex became the metaphor for racial tension, hostility and aggression," writes a student of the 1964 Freedom Summer in Mississippi. "Nearly every project had real problems with interracial sex." Such problems were less acute in Louisiana, but they were nonetheless present. Sexual tensions in the Monroe Freedom House had almost produced an "explosion," Spiver Gordon reported in late 1964. "It is my suggestion that men and women working for CORE shouldn't be housed in the same house."[2]

Yet on balance, CORE's interracialism was a great asset to the movement. Undoubtedly, some whites went South for the wrong reasons, lacked real commitment, harbored romantic illusions, displayed political naivete, betrayed paternalistic attitudes, and exhibited cultural insensitivity. However, the charge that northern whites were ineffective organizers in many cases disguised black resentment of "the basic organizational skills that most of the volunteers had," the fact that they were in reality *effective* organizers. The best of them were dedicated activists who had already demonstrated their commitment before coming to Louisiana, and some stayed on beyond the summer to become valued project directors. Miriam Feingold, a Swarthmore student from Brooklyn, was a veteran of the Freedom Rides who had served time in Mississippi's Parchman penitentiary. Mike Lesser joined the CORE chapter at Syracuse University at its inception in the fall of 1961 and had taken part in marches, sit-ins, picketing, canvassing, and virtually every other phase of its activity. William Yates, a rarity for being in his late thirties, was a veteran of Boston CORE. Living among black families, many established strong bonds with local activists and learned to overcome their "whiteness." Ordinary blacks evinced little hostility toward them and sometimes specifically requested them, recognizing that the arrival of white field workers was a certain harbinger of change.[3]

To white southerners, the appearance of these "outside agitators" acted as a red flag to a bull. Rabid segregationists reserved their most venomous hatred for the Yankee "Christers," "communists," and "white niggers" who made common cause with southern blacks. In becoming targets for aggression, however, the white volunteers served a useful function: acting as lightning rods for racist violence, they helped to crystallize black insurgency by furnishing the first overt, dramatic acts of defiance against white supremacy. The assignment of Gary Craven to Tallulah helped spark the first demonstrations in Madison Parish; the appearance of Bill Yates and Steve Miller provided the stimulus for the formation of the Bogalusa movement. Despite their concern that whites were unduly prominent on CORE's staff, black field secretaries recognized their utility. "I think it would be a good idea if at least one white stayed in Jackson Parish," Fred Brooks recommended, noting that the "movement spirit" had picked up again when white staffers moved back into Jonesboro.[4]

White racists were not only incensed by the appearance of white "traitors." The mere fact of CORE's integrated staff posed a direct challenge to Jim Crow. Segregationists knew full well that the survival of white supremacy depended upon white solidarity. White division meant defeat; the color line had therefore to be absolute and inflexible. Even isolated acts of racial egalitarianism threatened segregation: hence the violent repression that had snuffed out the effort to organize black and white farmers in the late 1930s; hence the virulent red-baiting that had extinguished the relatively weak interracial movement of the 1940s and early 1950s. Visible examples of interracialism contradicted and subverted the ideology of white supremacy; they also emboldened others to resist. In the context of a rigid caste system, it was a radical act for blacks and whites to live together and work together on a basis of mutual respect.

White supremacy had also survived since Reconstruction because southern whites had persuaded northern whites not to interfere with the South's "Negro problem." Cut off from northern political support, black communities had been easily intimidated, especially in the small towns and rural areas. With the arrival of northern civil rights workers, isolated communities that had lived in fear of the local sheriff now had a lifeline to the outside world. The presence of northern whites made it easier to attract the attention of the news media, and CORE's national office churned out a steady flow of publicity to prick the consciences and loosen the purse strings of Americans above the Mason-Dixon line. The families and friends of the northern volunteers also functioned as important support networks, and some of the volunteers could exert political influence by sheer virtue of their family connections. The daughter of U.N. diplomat Ralph Bunche and the son of former Secretary of the Interior Harold Ickes both served on CORE's Louisiana task force. The presence of northerners helped to breach the white South's political defenses.

Many of the white northerners on CORE's first summer task force experienced culture shock. Miriam Feingold was appalled by the poverty and squalid housing conditions she encountered. In an unincorporated area of Plaquemine — one of two black neighborhoods deliberately gerrymandered out of that town's boundaries — people had to draw their water from pumps and relieve themselves in outhouses or in the woods. Around Clinton, in East Feliciana Parish, she saw people living in dilapidated wooden shacks with no fireplaces and no glass in the windows, where "the wall boards in some places don't reach the floor because they've been eaten away by the weather." Mothers and children went barefoot in midwinter. Feingold also found the slow and easygoing pace of life in the South, where blacks joshed each other about "colored people's time," a little frustrating at first. "*Nothing* proceeds here according to schedule," she complained in a letter to her parents. "In these small, hot towns, I really don't think people feel the pressing urgency of anything — we ask them to come to the clinic at 12:00 — they show up at 1:00 or later if not at all."

Police harassment also proved unnerving at first. CORE workers and the blacks who associated with them became perpetual objects of unfriendly police attention. To be tailed, questioned, verbally abused, and occasionally arrested soon became part of the everyday routine. To be assaulted by local whites and even shot at from passing cars constituted real risks, and few male CORE workers escaped at least one beating of varying severity. "I'm sure this isn't Mississippi," commented Feingold, "but the white people are still pretty mean."[5]

Plaquemine, CORE's base, was a town of about eight thousand people on the west bank of the Mississippi, south of Baton Rouge. A Plaquemine schoolteacher, W. W. Harleaux, had asked for CORE's help, pointing out that no blacks had succeeded in registering to vote in Iberville Parish since 1960.

Like seventy-two thousand other black Louisianians, Bill Harleaux was a veteran of the Second World War. A light-skinned man in his mid-fifties, he had been active in the civil rights struggle for twenty years and was a rare example of a militant schoolteacher. In the 1940s he had been the driving force behind the fight to equalize teachers' salaries in Iberville Parish, the most bitter and protracted equalization fight in Louisiana. A familiar figure within the NAACP until the legislature forced teachers to resign from the organization, he now headed the Iberville Parish Industrial Voters League. Since 1953 he had worked as the principal of a Plaquemine elementary school. Kenny Johnson, a former pupil, recalled that portraits of black heroes adorned the school's corridors and classrooms and that Harleaux taught black history all the year round, not merely during Negro History Week.

Ronnie Moore could hardly fail to be impressed by the man. Harleaux's request for CORE assistance, moreover, had the backing of three other pillars of the black community: Tolbert Harris, a retired Army captain, Bertrand Tyson, a young physician, and Jetson Davis, a Baptist minister who was the brother of Rev. A. L. Davis of New Orleans. Moore agreed to move CORE's state office from Baton Rouge to Plaquemine. There he planned to organize voter registration drives throughout Louisiana's sixth congressional district.[6]

The sixth congressional district in many ways represented a microcosm of

Louisiana. It included predominantly Catholic parishes west of the Mississippi River (some of the oldest plantation areas in the state) and the mainly Protestant "Florida Parishes," which lay east of the river and north of Lake Pontchartrain. The Florida Parishes themselves exhibited great contrasts. Parishes like St. Helena contained no towns of any size, and the scattered houses, a mixture of traditional wooden "dogtrots" and modern brick bungalows, testified to a southern upland culture dominated by yeoman farmers. East and West Feliciana, on the other hand, were typical of the South's Black Belt cotton counties; here large plantations still held sway. Tangipahoa Parish contained the college town of Hammond, Washington Parish the paper-mill town of Bogalusa, two urban centers that exerted very different cultural influences.

The black voter registration statistics reflected this diversity. In the Catholic parish of Ascension, for example, black registration stood at 56 percent; the Protestant parish of West Feliciana, on the other hand, did not have a single black voter (one of only four in the state, all of them majority-black cotton parishes, that still maintained total disfranchisement). Overall, blacks composed a higher proportion of the total electorate than in any other district with the exception of the seventh, the heartland of Acadiana. The local congressman, James H. Morrison, first elected in 1942, had compiled a liberal voting record and tried to avoid the segregation issue.[7]

Despite the relatively high level of black registration, the number of black voters had not increased since 1956; in this, too, the sixth district was typical of Louisiana. Two parishes, Washington and East Feliciana, had been the targets of Citizens Council "purges," and although Judge Skelly Wright had restored those stricken from the rolls in Washington Parish, the situation in East Feliciana had still not been redressed. There, black registration numbered only 80, down from 1,276 in 1958. In East Feliciana, the Citizens Councils succeeded in removing a relatively liberal registrar and installing their own man. In other parishes, such as St. Helena, the councils exerted such pressure on the registrars that black registration came to a virtual standstill.[8]

In the plantation areas, economic dependency underlined the fear of white authority. In West Feliciana, for example, over 80 percent of black farmers were tenants or sharecroppers (Ronnie Moore could locate only nine independent farmers) and many could still remember the suppression of the Louisiana Farmers Union in 1937, the last organized challenge to planter control. Here, where no blacks had voted since 1922, Sheriff Teddy Martin and a handful of white families had dominated local politics for decades. When Ronnie Moore first visited the parish in the winter of 1962–63 he considered it too dangerous to stay overnight; no blacks would house him, and one elderly sharecropper waved Moore off his farm at the point of a shotgun. In Tunica, near the notorious Angola state penitentiary, he was ordered out of a ministers' meeting "because the local people feared for their lives." In twenty-six days of canvassing he failed to persuade a single person to visit the registrar's office.[9]

Eventually, Moore penetrated West Feliciana via the neighboring, somewhat less hostile parish of East Feliciana. This sparsely populated rural area presented CORE workers Ed Vickery and Miriam Feingold with the challenge of developing indigenous leadership where, in contrast to Plaquemine, there was no voters' league, no NAACP branch, no strong individual of the caliber of Bill Harleaux, no history of any kind of civil rights activity. The existing Negro "leaders," Vickery noted, "functioned by and large as message carriers between the white power structure and the Negro community and consisted of preachers, school principals and a Negro mortician." His analysis could have come straight from Gunnar Myrdal's *American Dilemma,* so little had changed since the 1930s. Black ministers initially shunned them, Feingold reported, and many blacks, refusing to house them, expressed "general incomprehension as to why I'm here."

The CORE workers eventually found two elderly women who were prepared to provide lodging, and one of them, seventy-four-year-old Josephine "Mama Jo" Holmes, allowed her home to be used for voter registration clinics. Ronnie Moore described her as a "very militant, very courageous woman," and her local knowledge proved invaluable. The other woman, Charlotte Greenup, then in her eighties, had spent thirty-eight years in Chicago, nine of them working as a secretary to Oscar DePriest, the city's first black congressman. With a toehold in Clinton, the CORE workers acted as a catalyst for the emergence of local leaders. Corrie Collins, a recently discharged Army veteran, agreed to head a CORE chapter, and its meetings were soon attracting twenty to forty people. The police took a keen interest in these activities: one day they set up a roadblock near the voter registration clinic, questioning all Negroes and noting details of their cars. When Mike Lesser accompanied two applicants to the courthouse on August 2, a deputy sheriff arrested him. He spent three weeks in jail. Compared to Mississippi, however, the repression was mild; there was no police brutality and little private violence.

At first, local activists were heavily dependent on the task force workers, and many were hesitant in their support. It was difficult, Vickery confided, to find local people with the time, the skills, and the commitment to undertake the kind of militant work demanded by CORE: only four people could be really depended on. Yet the movement gradually developed a momentum of its own. High school students became involved; several ministers opened up their churches; and by August Feingold could report that even some teachers, "the most Uncle Tom group around," had expressed interest in the movement. One young teacher, Hazel Matthews, joined CORE in defiance of her principal: "I tell him if getting me fired will add another star to his Crown do so." Ten years later Miriam Feingold remembered how she was "repeatedly impressed with how many able people were willing to take on leadership roles at considerable risk to themselves and their families."[10]

With a small but firm base in East Feliciana, CORE could now penetrate the neighboring parish. Visiting West Feliciana by day and arranging meetings in East Feliciana at night, Ronnie Moore succeeded, after months of work, in persuading two ministers to make an attempt at registering. On August 10, 1963, in great trepidation, Joseph Carter and Rudolph Davis entered the courthouse in St. Francisville, a graceful town noted for its antebellum houses. To Carter the silent corridors seemed forbidding and labyrinthine: "We didn't see nobody, no way, no how." They finally encountered the registrar, Fletcher Harvey, as he emerged from his office and locked the door behind him. Harvey told them they needed to bring two voters from their ward for the purposes of identification. "Well, the High Sher'ff knows me," Davis averred, "and not only that — all of you knows me here." Harvey resisted the obvious, saying, "Yes, I know they call you Rudolph Davis, but I couldn't swear to it." As this Kafkaesque dialogue petered out, Sheriff W. C. Percy turned up and had Carter arrested. Bailed out by CORE worker Rudy Lombard, he filed suit against Percy for wrongful arrest.

His wife threatened to leave him if he went back to the courthouse and his neighbors begged him not to return, but Carter, a fifty-five-year old man whose education had stopped at the fifth grade, persevered. In a Masonic hall in Laurel Hill, fifteen black ministers from West Feliciana met to consider another attempt to register. When Carter asked for volunteers, all but one of the ministers stood up. By the end of September more than one hundred people had attended CORE's voter registration clinic. Finally, on October 17, Ronnie Moore accompanied a busload of applicants, forty-three in number, to the courthouse in St. Francisville, where they sweated inside the bus as the registrar dawdled over some white applicants and then went off for his lunch hour. Eventually Carter walked past three FBI men, who stood with their backs turned to a crowd of braying whites, to enter the courthouse. Harvey and another white man, Joe Cutrer (whom Carter had known since childhood), then quizzed him as to his identity. "Ain't a damn thing wrong with this," Cutrer admitted, after scrutinizing Carter's documents — driver's license, social security card, pastor's card — for what seemed like an eternity.

Thirty-five minutes after he entered the office, Carter emerged as the first black voter in West Feliciana Parish. As CORE workers congratulated him and took photographs, Carter overheard a white man comment, "Yeah, take the dumb SOB's picture, because that's the last one you'll get of him." But despite a smattering of threats and a few shots fired into the home of the man who had driven the bus, the white response was relatively muted. Carter himself went unmolested, although he carefully avoided white stores and traveled to Baton Rouge to shop. Within a few days five more blacks succeeded in registering.[11]

With the registration of fifteen blacks in Tensas Parish in January 1964, the last parish in Louisiana to maintain total disfranchisement capitulated. The other two holdouts, East Carroll and Madison, fell in 1962 and 1963 respectively, when Judge Ben Dawkins found the registrars guilty of racial discrimination in consistently rejecting all black applicants. The breakthroughs here represented the culmination of decades of struggle by small groups of dedicated activists. In Madison Parish the men behind the successful suit — Zelma Wyche, Harrison Brown, Moses Williams, and others — had been pursuing their goal since 1947. The plaintiffs in East Carroll Parish had first attempted to vote in 1946. In both Madison and East Carroll, the principal black activists were longtime members of the NAACP; John Henry Scott had been president of the Lake Providence branch since 1938.

Few of the NAACP's state and regional officials, however, ventured into this northeastern corner of Louisiana, and blacks faced the greatest difficulty challenging white officialdom. Tensas, East Carroll, and Madison were majority-black cotton parishes that bordered Mississippi. Here whites had maintained a policy of total opposition to black voting long after the rest of Louisiana had conceded at least token black registration; here, too, intimidation had been much more oppressive than in most other parishes. In 1954, for example, Sheriff C. E. Hester of Madison Parish browbeat and threatened black attorney James Sharp, representing a group of blacks who had filed suit against the registrar of voters. Sharp never set foot in the parish again and the suit never came to trial. Seven years passed before blacks made another attempt to register.

As Sharp's story indicates, blacks in this remote corner of the state suffered from inadequate and unreliable legal assistance. The plaintiffs in East Carroll Parish experienced a similar letdown. Impatient with the overcautious Tureaud, John Henry Scott drove all the way to New Orleans so that Louis Berry, assigned to the case by the state NAACP, could file a complaint against the registrar. When Judge Ben Dawkins dismissed the suit in 1954 on patently erroneous grounds, Berry failed to appeal the decision, proposing instead an approach to Governor Earl Long to have the registrar removed. This idea failed to bear fruit, and when Berry moved his practice to California the East Carroll Parish suit lapsed.[12]

In these areas of maximum white resistance and weak black organization, assistance from the Justice Department proved crucial. The Kennedy administration stepped up the department's voting rights litigation, filing suits against many of the South's most resistant registrars. Cooperating with black plaintiffs and meticulously compiling overwhelming evidence of discrimination, Justice Department lawyers won the suits in East Carroll, West Feliciana, and Madison parishes that led to the registration of the first black voters. Government suits in Bienville, Jackson, Red River, and Washington parishes reinstated thousands of black voters who had been "purged" by the Citizens Councils.[13]

Federal intervention also inhibited white violence and intimidation. In East Carroll Parish, for example, the Justice Department wielded the threat of prosecution to compel white merchants to end an economic boycott of Joseph Atlas, a black cotton farmer who, after testifying before the Civil Rights Commission in New Orleans, had been unable to sell his soybean crop, get his cotton ginned, or buy butane gas. The Justice Department also initiated an investigation of the Lake Providence police, and a federal grand jury indicted several officers for brutality to prisoners. The activities of the FBI in such cases, although much criticized by the civil rights movement, helped to discourage the more egregious forms of state-sponsored violence and coercion. When the police jailed one of the court-registered plaintiffs the night before an election, the FBI secured his release. As official violence declined, however, private terrorism increased. When a shotgun blast wounded John Henry Scott in August 1962, the FBI investigated the incident but could not bring the culprit to justice. Shootings and arson soon became commonplace.[14]

Federal action, moreover, was still far too tentative to have much effect on black registration statewide. The registration system continued to disfranchise the bulk of the black voting-age population. Indeed, wily segregationists like Leander Perez had long argued that the registration of *some* blacks was an effective defense against the charge of discrimination. Although Rainach's plan to "purge" the bulk of the black vote failed, the election of Governor Jimmie Davis in 1960 gave the ultrasegregationists a chance to implement their fallback strategy of freezing the black electorate at current levels. Between 1960 and 1962 the legislature made voter registration fiendishly difficult for black applicants. One act elaborated on the vague "good character" clause of the 1922 constitution by adding six definitions of "bad character"; they included common-law marriage and the parenting of illegitimate children. Applicants were required to own up to "bad character" by striking the appropriate "have (have not)" against six statements couched in pseudolegal gobbledygook.

The legislature added other mystifying questions to the application form. Applicants now had not only to name the parish, precinct, and ward where they lived, but also swear that they had lived there "continuously" since a certain date. They were also asked to identify "the householder at my present address"; put down their color, sex, and occupation; remember the ward, precinct, and parish of their *last* registration; and denote the party they were "now affiliated with." In 1962 the legislature permitted registrars to jumble the order of the questions so as to further confuse black applicants. Orleans Parish, for example, prepared five different versions of the application form, with the order of the blanks to be filled in, and the sequence of the "have (have not)" statements to be struck out, different on each one. Nearly two-thirds of all black applicants were rejected on the basis of alleged mistakes in filling out this form. In East Feliciana, the registrar failed three black applicants in four for the same reason. Even in relatively liberal Tangipahoa, half of all black applicants failed to complete the form to the registrar's satisfaction.

As if the application form were not a sufficient barrier, the legislature erected another hurdle in the form of the "citizenship test." The 1922 constitution had enabled illiterates to register if they could "understand and give a reasonable interpretation" of any section (chosen by the registrar, of course) of either the U.S. or the Louisiana constitution. In practice, however, few registrars had ever enforced this "interpretation test" until the Citizens Council-inspired clampdown on black registration in the late 1950s. In 1960 the legislature tried to make registrars throughout the state quiz black voters on the Constitution by making the interpretation test an addition to, rather than an alternative to, the literacy test. However, even the ultrasegregationists recognized that allowing registrars to pick out *any* section of either constitution was open to such obvious abuse that the interpretation test, as it then stood, would not withstand a challenge in the federal courts. The state board of registration therefore adopted a variant of the system devised by Leander Perez for use in Plaquemines Parish: an ostensibly objective "citizenship test" in which registrars employed standardized questions with multiple-choice answers. Applicants had to get four out of six questions right.

The questions themselves demanded the most arcane knowledge. Applicants could be asked to give the precise number of presidential electors from Louisiana or identify the Articles of Confederation; they might have to display detailed knowledge of the procedure for impeaching the president. Some questions, moreover, had no clearly correct answer: faced with the question, "Our form of government, in which we elect officers to act for us is called a _____" applicants had to choose between "representative form of government," "limited form of government," and "congressional form of government." Others involved the kind of philosophical conundrums that provoke endless debate among political scientists. Did the votes of "the few," "the majority," or "male citizens" "usually decide public questions in the U.S."? A respectable case could be made for any of these answers.[15]

The registration process was thus an elaborate charade, a tiresome and infuriating cat-and-mouse game that for most blacks made applying to register an exercise in futility. In a typical week in Iberville Parish, reported Miriam Feingold, "I contact 150 people, train 60, send 18 to the registrar's office, and have 9 of them get registered." Most of those attending the registration classes could barely write their own names, she noted; they were "overcome by the forms. They clam up, and can't write anything until I point to a line and say, 'Write your name there.'" Inside the registrar's office, however, applicants were on their own. They were not permitted to refer to notes, not even when, for example, they had to calculate their age in years, months, and days. "It is pathetic," wrote Feingold, "that some of the most enthusiastic people are the ones who have common law spouses, which automatically disqualifies them." For most blacks, the process of applying to register was intimidating and humiliating. Small wonder that many, when confronted by CORE canvassers, lied and claimed to be already registered.[16]

Not all registrars made a habit of tripping up black applicants, and some even helped them. Thus in Lake Charles the NAACP could mount a highly productive registration campaign, with a success rate of over 90 percent. Lafayette and St. Landry parishes also put few barriers in the way of black registration. The overall pattern, however, remained static, gains in southwestern Louisiana being offset by losses elsewhere. In Shreveport, for example, a typical registration drive contacted forty-six people and instructed nineteen, of whom nine actually applied and only six passed. Results were especially disappointing in New Orleans, where well-organized and well-funded drives produced no overall increase. "I would estimate that one of every four we teach actually apply," reported Yvonne Minor of the Coordinating Council; long waits, surly policemen, hostile registrars, and, of course, the experience of previous rejections, put most people off. On one day black applicants were rejected at the ratio of ten to one.[17]

Judged in terms of numbers, therefore, two years of VEP-sponsored voter registration drives yielded the most meager results. The 4,677 new voters CORE helped to register between 1962 and 1964 represented a poor return for an effort that involved dozens of summer "task force" workers and hundreds of local volunteers. Moreover, most if not all of this increase was wiped out by the periodic "purges" whereby registrars dropped people from the rolls if they had failed to vote during the preceding two years or because they had neglected to notify the registrar of a change of address. Such purges were a particular bane in New Orleans. Other parishes periodically cleared their rolls and required a complete reregistration of all voters, another opportunity to fail black applicants.[18]

Thus the net increase in black voters was negligible, and many parishes showed no increase at all. Measuring black registration as a proportion of the total electorate, the results were even less impressive: in the twelve parishes composing the sixth congressional district, for example, the black electorate grew in only two. One was West Feliciana, where the twenty-one black voters, all of them registered since 1963, made up less than 2 percent of the electorate; the other was Iberville, the parish CORE had worked most intensively, where the black electorate grew from 25.9 percent to 28.7 percent of all voters. In some parishes, the black electorate remained far below its 1956 peak, in both absolute and relative terms. Two years of work in East Feliciana, for example, increased the black electorate from 80 to 180, a far cry from the 1,361 who could vote in 1956. CORE added 743 voters in Ouachita Parish (Monroe), but in 1964 there were still 4,038 fewer black voters than in 1956.[19]

Such dismal statistics persuaded the Justice Department to broaden its attack on voting discrimination. In 1963 the government won a signal victory in *U.S. v. Louisiana,* one of two statewide suits (the other being *U.S. v. Mississippi*) that challenged the application of constitutional interpretation tests. Written by John Minor Wisdom in sparkling and impassioned prose, *U.S. v. Louisiana* amounted to an historical treatise on the disfranchisement of black voters in Louisiana, an achievement that reflected both the thoroughness of the Justice Department's brief and also Wisdom's own considerable knowledge of, and passion for, history. Forming a continuous narrative that began with Reconstruction and finished with the rise of the Citizens Councils, Wisdom's opinion left no room for doubt that the interpretation test was conceived and implemented as a device to systematically disfranchise blacks — "the highest, best-guarded, most effective barrier to Negro voting in Louisiana." The district court enjoined its use. As Justice Hugo Black put it, in a Supreme Court opinion affirming the decision, "This is not a test but a trap, sufficient to stop even the most brilliant man on his way to the voting booth." The district court also suspended the successor to the interpretation test, the new "citizenship test," until such time as *all* voters were required to reregister and take the test. This was the doctrine of "freezing relief," pioneered by Judge Frank M. Johnson in Alabama, which stated that tighter registration standards discriminated against blacks if most whites had already registered under looser standards. The order affected twenty-one parishes.[20]

However, these court decisions added very few black voters, either directly or indirectly. If the Justice Department had been able to effectively harness the personnel and investigate zeal of the FBI, it might have been able to blanket the Deep South with voting rights suits. But as civil rights workers discovered at the time, and as Kenneth O'Reilly has amply documented from the Bureau's own files, J. Edgar Hoover "tried on every front to impede the implementation of the voting litigation campaign," waging a war of "bureaucratic resistance" that the Kennedy administration lacked the political will to overcome. As a result, the Justice Department virtually wrote off the FBI, forcing the lawyers of the Civil Rights Division to personally conduct their own investigations. With a legal staff of only fifty-three, this do-it-yourself strategy compelled the department to concentrate its resources on a small number of "bad" counties and parishes. Progress proceeded at a snail's pace and was virtually imperceptible. Justice Department lawyers had to accumulate mountains of evidence merely to document the obvious; tens of thousands of voter applications had to be copied and analyzed; each suit took months, sometimes years of preparation. The effect could be likened to a series of pinpricks on the hide of an elephant.[21]

Even when its painstaking research resulted in evidentiary overkill, moreover, the Justice Department could not count on winning its day in court. While Louisiana's federal bench did not boast an ultrasegregationist as extreme as Harold Cox, the Mississippi judge who consistently obstructed the department, it did have Benjamin Dawkins and E. Gordon West, both of whom were distinctly unsympathetic to the civil rights cause. Indeed, West, the more blatantly segregationist of the two, had been appointed by President Kennedy, one of half a dozen Kennedy appointees who became thorns in the side of the Justice Department. Dawkins, an Eisenhower appointee, was less consistently hostile, and the Justice Department liked to think that the thoroughness of its briefs made an impression on him. In the Bienville Parish case, Dawkins had been initially unsympathetic, but after hearing the government's witnesses he rendered a favorable verdict, citing the "veritable parade of . . . negroes, holding bachelor's and master's degrees, who, since 1956, have been denied the right to register."[22]

Yet while Dawkins was open to persuasion, his civil rights sympathies only went so far. He refused to enjoin use of the "citizenship test," describing it as "simple and fair," and defended the right of states to tighten their voting qualifications. In 1965 he threw out a government suit against Mae Lucky, the registrar of Ouachita Parish, on the grounds that she rejected white as well as black applicants. Similarly, he refused to reinstate the blacks who had been purged in the mass challenge of 1956, arguing that whites had been challenged as well and claiming that the challengers, although members of the Citizens Council, had not acted as "agents of the Citizens Council." Ironically, Dawkins later displayed great concern for ensuring that blacks received fair political representation. Before the passage of the Voting Rights Act, however, he seemed to regard blacks as politically immature. "We deplore the Negro practice of 'bloc voting,'" he averred, and hoped that in future Negroes would vote "according to the best interests of their State and Nation rather than for their own selfish or venal purposes."[23]

Even sympathetic federal judges were cautious about using the power to directly register voters, vested in them by the 1960 Civil Rights Act, and were reluctant to set aside the stringent tests required by state law. In July 1962 Judge Edwin F. Hunter registered twenty-eight blacks in East Carroll Parish (the first judge to use this power) but only after they passed a written test. Twenty-five others failed it. According to David J. Garrow's estimate, federal judges directly registered only about a thousand black voters throughout the entire South. "Only two [federal] referees appear to have ever been appointed," Garrow adds, "and they recommended the registration of no more than several hundred more."[24]

Perhaps the fundamental weakness of the litigation strategy was its assumption that the existing voter registration requirements could be made to operate fairly. Voting rights suits thus tended to attack the administration of stringent registration laws, not the concept of such laws. This gave southern legislatures ample scope to concoct new tests and requirements when older ones came under legal attack, hence the new "citizenship test" that replaced the former "interpretation test." Judges like John Minor Wisdom recognized that even if fairly applied, such tests would tend to produce "a small, elite electorate," but he could not bring himself to take the decisive step of rejecting such tests altogether and implied that a strict test, if fairly applied, might be constitutional, however unfortunate the results. Moreover, registrars had ample scope for rejecting blacks even without the interpretation or citizenship test. Six months after the decision in *U.S. v. Louisiana*, Ronnie Moore saw "no significant change": registrars could still reject blacks because of alleged errors in filling out the application form. Indeed, this remained the most common excuse for failing black applicants. In New Orleans the rate of rejection averaged 64 percent.[25]

In October 1963 the Justice Department attacked the standard application form as a blatant disfranchising device. As always, the government brief was meticulous: it analyzed the single-sheet application form in two hundred devastating pages, with several hundred pages more of historical and statistical documentation. Research for the brief included analyses of voter registration in every parish since 1942; a detailed study of the state's public school system, with a breakdown of per capita spending by race since the 1930s; and interviews with virtually every registrar in the state. As things transpired, by the time the suit was decided the issue had been overtaken by historical events — Selma and the Voting Rights Act — which rendered the entire litigation strategy irrelevant. Knocking out the application form, however, would merely have invited registrars to resort to other excuses for rejecting blacks. As John Minor Wisdom noted, the root cause of black disfranchisement lay in the "raw power vested in the registrar" by the state, which led to manifold forms of "discriminatory and arbitrary conduct." Without a drastic extension of federal power over the registration process itself there was little that Wisdom and other sympathetic judges could do to enfranchise blacks. A registrar's scope for discriminating against black applicants was virtually limitless; federal litigation merely attacked the most obvious abuses.[26]

It was hardly surprising, then, that CORE workers expressed profound exasperation at the Justice Department's litigation strategy. Ronnie Moore, the Louisiana project director, expressed that frustration loud and clear in his reports to New York. "Are these complaints doing any good at your end?" he wrote Jim McCain in April 1963. "The Justice Department ain't doing a d—— thing on my end. . . . If we don't stop these denials, voter registration in Louisiana will come to a standstill and our rolls will decrease." In September 1963, Moore gloomily summarized the results of CORE's first summer of voter registration work. "When you look at the total picture, in one place we find apathy, in another fear, and yet another illiteracy. In every parish it is discrimination by nature in Louisiana's voter registration system. . . . In short, we are doing our best, but unless this damn system is obliterated, the task of developing the Negro voter potential in Louisiana is a lost cause." Small wonder, then, that CORE workers had great difficulty in persuading blacks to apply to register, when, as Ed Vickery reported from East Feliciana, "so many travel so far so often to fail."[27]

Judged by numbers, CORE's efforts in 1964 were similarly fruitless, and voter registration in northern Louisiana proved even more difficult and dangerous. In December 1963 CORE opened an office in Monroe, a beachhead for its intended expansion into the northern parishes. By comparison, Catholic south Louisiana came to seem like heaven. "Monroe is hell," wrote Mike Lesser, a white staff member. "More harassment than I have ever found in any community. . . . I have been picked up three times in the last three days, and I am surprised that I don't have [a cop] sleeping in my bed at night — they follow us so closely." Lesser and his colleagues found local blacks weary of voter registration drives: they had seen Dr. John Reddix and the NAACP fight for eight years to restore those purged in 1956 and get nowhere. CORE managed to involve about twenty high school students in its canvassing drives, but few adults became involved. Indeed, as CORE's efforts floundered, the police realized that they had little need to harass the CORE workers as long as they stuck to voter registration. "The white folks don't bother us," reported Spiver Gordon, "since we are not directly painting their little castle black."[28]

In West Monroe, the adjoining town on the opposite bank of the Ouachita River, the police were not so cynically obliging. During a five-day registration drive in June 1964, they stopped and threatened local volunteers, parked outside black churches holding registration clinics, in one case recording the proceedings, and arrested two white CORE workers for vagrancy (later changed to "disturbing the peace"), introducing them to the inmates of the city hall jail as "nigger lovers." Integrated canvassing teams were considered fair game: as police chief Johnny Mitchell explained, "When you go in there in a mixed group, you are going to be arrested." Peter Teachout, a Harvard law student, reckoned that the aim of such harassment was not so much to intimidate the CORE workers as to scare off local blacks. And, he believed, such applications of "Louisiana underlaw" served their purpose quite effectively. "The Negro community respects the police power in the sense that they could be easily intimidated by any indication that cooperation with CORE will result in trouble with the cops. The police established the situation early in the game, and . . . the arrests did our drive serious damage." Of the hundreds canvassed during the five-day effort, more than one hundred had volunteered to register, but fewer than twenty actually applied, of whom less than half passed.[29]

Jonesboro, a small paper-mill town in Jackson Parish, raised the problem of harassment in a particularly stark form. CORE worker Fred Brooks, veteran of the Nashville student movement, was arrested for drinking from a "white" water fountain as he accompanied black applicants to the courthouse. Sheriff Newt Loe threatened to "peel his damn head." Two weeks later Loe told a white task-force worker from Ohio to be out of Jonesboro by the morning "for his own good." Driving toward Monroe on July 4, Ronnie Moore and Mike Lesser found themselves boxed in by three cars, forcing them to race back to Jonesboro at ninety miles an hour, the whites "in hot pursuit." Moore was arrested for "reckless driving" and released on a bond of $750. A week later four CORE workers and a local volunteer were stopped on the highway and questioned for two hours by sheriff's deputies. The police impounded their car.[30]

CORE made no headway whatever in its plans for registration drives in rural north Louisiana. The most promising parish was Madison, where blacks clearly outnumbered whites and where the local voters league, headed by barber Zelma Wyche, sought CORE's assistance. When Mike Lesser arrived in Tallulah on February 23, however, police chief Jimmy Rogan promptly clapped him in jail and charged him with "disturbing the peace." The following morning, after receiving a suspended sentence of twenty-five days, Lesser and his companion, Bill Brown, were escorted out of town by the police "and told never to return."[31]

Even in the parishes that had been worked since the previous year, CORE's 1964 summer task force found the going tough. In East Feliciana, Mimi Feingold reported, "We still lack the support of all the teachers and most of the ministers"; in neighboring West Feliciana "fear is all-pervading." In St. Helena

Parish, the registrar used the "slowdown" technique: "He allows each applicant 45 minutes to complete the test, then talks to them an additional 15 or 20 minutes." Even in relatively liberal Tangipahoa Parish, low-level police harassment and scattered incidents of minor violence handicapped CORE's efforts. "People have grown increasingly reluctant to come to clinics, attempt to register, or have anything to do with CORE," wrote Loria Davis. In Plaquemine, reported Spiver Gordon, voter registration drives had reached the point of diminishing returns; the area had been worked and reworked, and people were no longer very interested.

State laws that kept the registration offices closed for much of the summer hardly helped matters. CORE used that time to collect the signatures of would-be voters, a "freedom registration" modeled on the work of the Council of Federated Organizations (COFO) in Mississippi. The petitions cut no ice with the registrars and had limited propaganda value. "I don't really see the need for mock registration," Marvin Rich told Ronnie Moore. "It seems to me that now is the time for *real* registration drives in Louisiana." Even when the books were open, however, CORE managed to add only 1,070 new voters. "One of our failures," Moore lamented, "is that we have not developed approaches in our voter registration program in order to keep the people interested and active."[32]

Political ultracaution sometimes reinforced a widespread unwillingness to attempt to register: many could still not make the mental leap required to envisage a politics in which blacks voted by right. Moreover, CORE's militancy and propensity for confrontation alarmed some older black leaders, who feared that if black registration increased much beyond its current levels, whites might react adversely.

Jack Minnis, the VEP's director of research, came across numerous instances of black political deference during the course of his visit to Louisiana in the summer of 1963. In Baton Rouge, for example, the leader of a voters' league told him that voter registration should be conducted quietly, without fuss and publicity, lest the registrar "become tougher and tougher under pressure from the Citizens Council." Minnis became convinced that in most parishes the registrars placed a ceiling on black registration and then used the alleged threat of the Citizens Council to help justify that ceiling to blacks. Sympathizing with the registrar's supposed "dilemma," many blacks accepted the ceiling on black voting as "one of the given obstacles, the presence of which one simply acknowledged and then ignored." In some cases, Minnis suspected, black leaders did not wish to imperil their access to white politicians by seeing the black vote grow beyond their ability to influence it. Jack Brady, Minnis's old mentor on the *Lake Charles Beacon,* put the matter rather more bluntly. "The evidence is overwhelming that among the older generation of Negroes, the politician's money, prestige, and small favors from the status quo has infiltrated the ranks with 'Uncle Toms.'"[33]

Yet what was sometimes facilely called "apathy" on the part of blacks often amounted to a shrewd and rational judgment that under the current rigged rules they were effectively excluded from political participation. In a pungent footnote in *U.S.* v. *Louisiana,* John Minor Wisdom described "apathy" as an "unctuous, self-excusing word" that whites used to justify low black registration. "There was no apathy in the Negro electorate in 1897," he noted, "when Negro registration equalled white registration in Louisiana. And it is a fair inference that Negro interest in voting . . . is no less in 1963 than it was in 1897." The copious affidavits documenting the rejection of black applicants, supplied to the Justice Department by CORE and other civil rights groups, eloquently contradicted the notion of black "apathy." The wonder is not that so few applied to register, but that so many did. However few passed the registrar's hurdles, the figures demonstrated "the remarkable persistence of people who would continue to try to register despite such adversity."

Hence CORE's voter registration work, like that of the movement as a whole, should not be judged by mere numbers. As Steven F. Lawson put it, although civil rights workers "failed to destroy the tyranny of the registrars, they did loosen the mental knot keeping blacks away from citizenship." The meager numerical gains induced frustration, yes, but they also generated a sense of great accomplishment. "That nine people actually succeeded in registering," explained one CORE worker, "out of one hundred and fifty contacted, sixty given instructions, and eighteen sent to the registrar's office, was seen as a morale-boosting achievement by the community as well as by us." Decades later, former civil rights workers often cited the same luminous memory as their happiest recollection of those days: seeing the face of an elderly black woman light up with pride when they pinned to her dress a button saying "I am a registered voter."[34]

Moreover, CORE viewed voter registration as political action in the broadest and most profound sense. Summer volunteers who naively regarded the movement as a philanthropic or missionary activity whereby whites helped southern blacks to attain their "rights" were sometimes surprised at CORE's radical edge and overtly "political" objectives. However, as a briefing paper for summer volunteers made plain, CORE saw itself as part of a "massive and important movement to change a political, social, economic, and educational structure that is Bad." The goal of voter registration was not merely the election of black politicians but "total social Change." Voter registration imparted a sense of possibility and self-worth to a people inured by oppression to resignation and powerlessness. As Richard King has argued, the movement's rhetoric of "freedom" involved more than inspirational sloganeering. Participation in the movement entailed acts of defiance, courage, and commitment that led to self-discovery and psychological transformation. A "new sense of personhood emerged from the process of overcoming personal nullity and acting with others to create a political community." Voter registration drives, insisted Miriam Feingold, left previously somnolent communities "with a legacy of organizational skills, higher expectations, and, most importantly, the sense that they could take positive action to change their own lives."[35]

Nevertheless, the unpalatable truth was that despite the voter registration drives of CORE and other civil rights groups, the numerical strength of the black electorate actually declined in Louisiana from 15 percent of all voters in 1956 to less than 14 percent in 1964. The state that once had the highest proportion of black voters now had one of the lowest. In absolute numerical gains, the VEP results in Louisiana were only marginally better than those in Mississippi, the worst state in the South. Moreover, when ranked according to percentage increase, Louisiana stood at the bottom of the table, with the worst record by far.[36]

Ultimately, it took SCLC's dramatic protests in Selma, Alabama, to force a drastic solution to the problem of black disfranchisement in the form of the 1965 Voting Rights Act. Bypassing the federal courts altogether, this act automatically suspended all registration "tests and devices," including literacy and interpretation tests, in states and counties where fewer than half the voting-age population had gone to the polls in the presidential election of 1964. Equally important, the act empowered the attorney general to appoint federal registrars without first obtaining a federal court order. It was a complete departure from the laborious and ineffective litigation strategy.

The Voting Rights Act, as David Garrow has argued, testified to the abject failure of that strategy. Yet right-to-vote litigation had served a constructive purpose over and above the fact that its very failure had demonstrated the need for a different approach.[37]

The Voting Rights Act could only dispense with the need to prove discrimination because years of work by the Justice Department, involving dozens of lawsuits and vanloads of evidence, had demonstrated the ubiquity and tenacity of racial discrimination to the satisfaction of all but the most die-hard segregationist. As a process of education in the stateways and folkways of southern racism it was costly, frustrating, and, for blacks and civil rights workers, painful. But it was necessary. The government would never have proposed, and the Congress would never have passed, such a radical measure as the Voting Rights Act had not the South's registration system been so thoroughly and convincingly discredited.

The Civil Rights Commission, too, played an important part in amassing and displaying the evidence that helped to damn the South's public officials. The Kennedy administration regarded the commission as a political nuisance and repeatedly hampered its work. At Chep Morrison's request, for example, Robert Kennedy delayed the commission's Louisiana hearings until an amendment to the city charter allowing Morrison to run for a third term as mayor had been submitted to the voters of New Orleans. When the hearings were eventually held, however, they presented the most thorough exhibition to date of discrimination in voting. A parade of black witnesses related their personal experiences of being disfranchised. The proceedings also offered the spectacle of Mary Ethel Fox, the registrar of Plaquemines Parish, failing to calculate her age to the correct number of years, months, and days, a common excuse for rejecting black applicants.[38]

It was the Justice Department, however, armed with the power of subpoena and forced to meet the exacting standards of the federal courtroom, that made the case against southern registrars watertight and irrefutable. The most damning testimony, moreover, often came from the mouths of the registrars themselves: by interviewing them and then comparing their statements, the lawyers of the Civil Rights Division exposed their unfair, arbitrary, and inconsistent standards. The quotations were cited to particular effect in *U.S. v. Board of Registration of Louisiana,* the government's suit against the voter application form. "You know the [form] is like a lottery ticket," admitted the deputy registrar of Orleans Parish. "There's various ways that people answer a card, and you have to determine from their answers just whether or not they're right or wrong." He had never discussed with the twenty-one other deputies what standards should be employed in judging the answers on the cards. The result was that each registrar accepted or rejected applications according to his or her own notion of what a correct form should look like. When there was, literally, no "correct" way to fill out the card, the system invited and encouraged the most blatant discrimination. Most whites passed because registrars assisted them and overlooked "errors." Most blacks failed because registrars wanted them to fail.[39]

The Justice Department's briefs could never persuade segregationist judges like Gordon West or Harold Cox, but they did make the majority of judges on the Fifth Circuit Court of Appeals increasingly impatient with recalcitrant registrars. Even more important, its experience of litigating voting rights suits exerted a profound influence on the Justice Department itself: the more it discovered about the South's registration system, the closer it moved toward an out-and-out attack on that system itself. The statewide suits and the doctrine of "freezing relief" were steps in that direction. So was the contention, articulated in *U.S. v. Board of Registration,* that complicated forms and tests discriminated against blacks "because of the inferior educational opportunities afforded them by the State of Louisiana." By the time that Martin Luther King launched his Selma campaign in early 1965, the Johnson administration had already privately acknowledged that the South's registration system would never operate fairly without stringent federal legislation.[40]

It would be erroneous, of course, to suppose that the Justice Department's litigation strategy led, ineluctably, to the more radical Voting Rights Act. Although the department built up a formidable legal case against southern registration practices, only pressure from the civil rights movement forced the issue into the national consciousness, eventually compelling the federal government to resolve it. The problem was not so much lack of evidence to convict the South as it was lack of political will to put the South in the dock and render a verdict. For all its stated good intentions, the litigation strategy betrayed the reluctance of the Kennedy administration to alienate the South's Democratic solons by pursuing an aggressive civil rights policy. The civil rights movement itself, through its escalating protests, transformed the political atmosphere and made strong civil rights legislation feasible. The 1965 Voting Rights Act would have been unthinkable had not the landmark Civil Rights Act of 1964 already advanced the limits of the politically possible. And that breakthrough derived, in large part, from the impact of Birmingham.

The Birmingham protests of early 1963 forcefully dispelled the notion that the civil rights movement would be content to collaborate with the Kennedy administration in nibbling away at white supremacy through voter registration campaigns alone. Indeed, Birmingham transformed the entire context of the civil rights struggle. King's audacious demonstrations, staged in the South's most notorious citadel of segregation, not only forced Kennedy to propose a radical civil rights bill but also inspired an upsurge of direct action throughout the South. The shock waves of Birmingham traveled upward to the federal government and downward to the grass roots of black America. They also jolted the corporation board rooms and chambers of commerce, reverberated through local, state, and national politics, and provoked a complex interplay of white reactions ranging from violent resistance to a reluctant acceptance that segregation was a lost cause.

The demonstrations that swept through southern towns and cities during the summer of 1963 illustrate the futility of analyzing events at the state level in isolation from regional and national trends. Local protest movements articulated local goals and affected the climate of state politics, but they could rarely, except in a few cities, move local authorities determined to resist them. As part of a regional movement, however, local protests helped to focus a spotlight on the hidden recesses of southern racism and make civil rights a compelling national issue. That spotlight burned brightest at Birmingham, but the hundreds of lesser-known movements across the South, among them Plaquemine and Clinton and Jonesboro and Monroe, kept the light of protest alive and, to quote CORE's historians, "aroused northern white sentiment and thus paved the way for the 1964 Civil Rights Act." The Civil Rights Act, in turn, resonated back across the South, spurring blacks to assert their demands more audaciously and according new legitimacy and protection to black protest. Thus the divergence, alleged by some, between the goals of local black movements and those of national civil rights organizations was more apparent than real. As Steven F. Lawson notes, although local movements and national groups experienced frictions and differences, more often than not they were mutually dependent and shared common goals. The local, regional, and national spheres of the civil rights struggle overlapped and were mutually reinforcing.

CORE played a central role in encouraging black insurgency outside Louisiana's big cities. In most of the communities it touched, CORE worked with some form of established black leadership. In one town the contact might be a veteran NAACP activist, in another a local voters' league, in a third a civic organization that perhaps owed its existence to the dissolution of the local NAACP branch in 1956. Yet CORE's role consisted of more than advising, strengthening, and assisting local leadership: in virtually every instance CORE's entry into a community *precipitated* local protest campaigns, stimulating the kind of militant direct action that local blacks had previously shied away from. In many communities, too, CORE had to create militant local leadership where none had existed before, sometimes by fostering splits within the existing leadership (CORE's very appearance in a community often caused such splits) and sometimes by seeking out courageous individuals and knitting them together into some kind of cohesive group. Thus CORE's field staff helped to empower local blacks and acted, in Garrow's words, as the "actual human catalysts of the movement."[41]

The status of CORE workers as "outsiders," whether blacks or whites, enhanced their ability to foment black militancy. Local people, by themselves, could be picked off, bought off, intimidated, and otherwise silenced, but CORE workers were impervious to economic pressure and, as short-term visitors, rarely had to consider the long-term necessity of "getting on with the white folks." Moreover, while individual CORE workers could be beaten — and even, in Mississippi, murdered — they could also be replaced. The constant turnover of volunteers kept the level of enthusiasm high; few stayed long enough to put down the roots — property, family, jobs — that tended to dilute militancy. With little at stake in the community, they had little to lose. Because of their youth, they were unburdened as well by that long-term perspective that often became, for the aging leadership of the NAACP, an inhibiting caution. Although often blissfully ignorant of what an older generation had achieved, and far too prone to facilely dismiss people as "Uncle Toms," the CORE workers' disdain for gradualism imparted a sense of possibility that proved psychologically liberating for many black southerners. CORE, like SNCC and SCLC, developed a quality of "unstoppability" that enabled it to carry the movement into many of the most repressive areas of the South.

Of all the civil rights organizations, CORE was the one most committed to nonviolence as a method of social action: sit-ins, boycotts, picket lines, and marches were standard weapons in its arsenal. Sometimes depicted as an alternative strategy to voter registration, nonviolent direct action actually went hand-in-hand with voter registration. Indeed, as Miriam Feingold stressed, "For those of us who worked on voter registration as part of CORE's task force in Louisiana, there was virtually no distinction between the two: both involved enormous risks for the local people and for ourselves, and this feeling was shared by all other civil rights groups working in the South."[42]

VEP money was not supposed to finance demonstrations. However, voter registration proved difficult to sustain for more than a few weeks at a time; canvassing soon reached a point of diminishing returns, especially when rejection by the registrar remained the most common outcome. In many communities, moreover, blacks were initially loath to support CORE for fear of the consequences. Thus CORE workers utilized nonviolent protests as another means of challenging, arousing, and politicizing the black population, especially its young people.

Direct action chipped away at the wall of intimidation that underpinned white supremacy, the fear that kept blacks "in their place." For as long as blacks could remember, jail was a hell hole and the sheriff a man with a gun whose badge gave him a license to kill. Demonstrations helped to dispel this paralyzing fear of "the law." The experience of jail was rarely as terrifying as the threat of it, and the "high sheriff" lost his aura of omnipotence the first time marchers defied his order to disperse. The effects of direct action, moreover, were cumulative. As sit-ins and demonstrations spread across the South the fear of white retribution diminished correspondingly, and the scale and pace of the nonviolent insurrection in turn intensified. By the fall of 1963 demonstrations had become so commonplace that white supremacy lost the sense of "normality" that once persuaded blacks to reluctantly acquiesce in their own subordination.

Escalating black protests produced a divided white response. Although ultrasegregationists appeared to retain the political ascendancy in state politics during 1963 and 1964, white unity over the defense of segregation, already precarious, was crumbling. The integration of schools in New Orleans had inflicted a major blow to the ultrasegregationist cause. School closing had been exposed as an empty threat and Governor Jimmie Davis had drawn back from the brink in his confrontation with the federal courts. Davis himself, while an unabashed segregationist, was not cut out to be a racist demagogue in the mold of Orval Faubus or George Wallace. He proved a weak governor with scant interest in administration and little sense of political strategy. An inept legislator, he failed to win a sales-tax increase aimed at financing a comprehensive system of private, segregated schools through state tuition grants. The remainder of his second administration was noteworthy chiefly for incompetence and scandal. The failure of ultrasegregationists to agree upon a central strategy was also reflected in the retirement of William Rainach and the rapid decline of the Citizens Councils. Rainach became estranged from Davis after the latter failed to deliver on a promise to create a State Sovereignty Commission with wide-ranging powers; in 1961 Rainach retired from politics, and the movement he had been instrumental in creating soon disintegrated. By 1963 most of the Citizens Councils had collapsed, and the few that survived had lost most of their members and wielded little political influence.[43]

The passing of the "massive resistance" phase of segregationist opposition allowed the forces of racial moderation more room for expression and maneuver. The demonstrations of 1963 and the introduction of the Civil Rights Bill persuaded many whites that segregation was a lost cause and that communities should acquiesce in the inevitable lest further resistance aggravate social turmoil and inflict economic damage. Thus in Baton Rouge, Hammond, and New Orleans influential whites sought to avoid demonstrations by negotiating with black leaders. The progress of voluntary desegregation here, as well as in southwest Louisiana cities like Lake Charles and Lafayette, smoothed the way for the generally peaceful implementation of the public accommodations section of the Civil Rights Act. In addition, after the trauma of the New Orleans schools crisis of 1960–61, few whites had the stomach for further street disorders. The third year of school integration in New Orleans was peaceful, as was the first year of integration in Baton Rouge (1963) and in St. Helena Parish (1964).

Black militancy, however, tended to polarize white opinion, reinforcing the will of many whites — perhaps most — to defend segregation. In addition, the interventionist policies of the federal government enabled whites to personalize their anger. After he introduced the Civil Rights Bill in June 1963, John Kennedy's popularity plummeted throughout the South, Louisiana being no exception. To judge by the behavior of the state legislature, most whites remained as intransigent as ever: in a 1963 special session legislators passed another raft of anti-sit-in bills and approved a resolution commending Governor George Wallace of Alabama. Governor Jimmie Davis lacked

Wallace's aggressiveness, but his own view of the civil rights movement was clouded by the myopia of racism. Colored people in Louisiana were happy, he assured President Kennedy. "People don't know how good a relationship we do have among most of them; it's so fine. I have one managing my own farm, you know. . . . A colored man runs it. He sells my cows." If the federal courts failed to stop the marches and demonstrations, he warned, "It's going to be the bloodiest thing. It's going to be a civil war." Davis failed to provide strong leadership on the race issue, but he did nothing to restrain ultrasegregationist politicians and officials.[44]

Thus the absence of a coherent strategy at the state level presaged a decentralization rather than a diminution of segregationist resistance. Moreover, in some ways this decentralized resistance proved more effective than high-profile confrontations with federal authority, which tended to be self-defeating. It was far more difficult to exert federal power against a plethora of sheriffs, police chiefs, and state officials than it was against a single central authority like a governor. Even the decline of the Citizens Council movement proved a mixed blessing, for many former supporters turned to the Ku Klux Klan, a far more violent and dangerous organization.

The most aggressive act of state repression after 1960 occurred on October 4, 1963, when police in New Orleans struck at the Southern Conference Education Fund (SCEF). In addition to raiding SCEF's headquarters and carting away its records, they searched the homes of James Dombrowski, SCEF's executive director, Ben Smith, the organization's treasurer, and Bruce Walzer, Smith's law partner. State troopers turned SCEF's records over to the Senate Internal Security Subcommittee, chaired by Mississippi Senator James O. Eastland. Instigated by Leander Perez and executed on the orders of Louisiana's "little HUAC," the Joint Legislative Un-American Activities Committee, "Operation Tip Top" led to the arrest and indictment of Dombrowski, Smith, and Walzer on charges of subversion, charges that carried jail penalties ranging from ten to thirty years. The raid also provided grist for the segregationist propaganda mill, in the form of thousands of confiscated documents. In a series of hearings that would have made Senator McCarthy blush, LUAC portrayed SCEF as a Communist front and tarred the entire civil rights movement as a subversive enterprise emanating from the Kremlin.[45]

The SCEF raid represented a final phase in the recrudescence of red-baiting that accompanied the rise of the civil rights movement in the early 1960s. Ultrasegregationists had long appropriated anticommunism to attack organizations working for racial equality; during the Davis administration such efforts became a matter of state policy. In 1960 the Louisiana legislature created its Joint Un-American Activities Committee, which immediately proceeded to hound Dr. Waldo F. McNeir, a professor of English at Louisiana

State University who had had the temerity to write to politicians saying that "segregation is wrong" and that the legislature's efforts to block integration were "a disgrace and a national scandal." The university forced him to resign. The same legislature required schools to teach a six-week course on "Americanism" that propounded as truths such statements as "The destruction of America is the number one aim of international Communism" and "Whether we like it or not, Russia is at war with America." Universities had to teach a compulsory course on "Americanism vs. Communism." (LSU got away with substituting a two-semester course in U.S. history, "the greatest success story the world had ever known.") The State Sovereignty Commission, also created in 1960, distributed a booklet that likened the NAACP to Hitler, Khrushchev, Castro, and Communists in general. In 1962 the legislature reenacted its Communist Control Law, which in 1958 had been invalidated by the state supreme court. The 1963 raid on SCEF was the first time that Louisiana invoked this law against a civil rights organization.[46]

By the early 1960s, however, allegations of communism were not as effective as they had been in earlier years, especially when they emanated from ultrasegregationists. The rump of the Citizens Councils had become tainted with anti-Semitism and now occupied the fringes of the radical right. Leander Perez, the brains behind the SCEF raid, had inhabited the lunatic fringe for years; even the FBI considered him a monomaniac on the subject of communism. The Catholic Church, too, was far less inclined to endorse automatically charges of communism. As Father Louis Twomey of Loyola University put it, such charges were often "quite blatantly based on a cold calculated effort to undermine the human rights of Negroes." Once a fire-eating anti-Communist himself, Twomey was now "exceedingly weary of the anti-communists. . . . These people fail to realize that Communism arises out of our failures." Archbishop Rummel's excommunication of Perez in 1962 symbolized the church's evolution away from the reflexive, conservative anticommunism of the past.[47]

At the time, however, the attack on SCEF posed the most serious threat to the civil rights movement in Louisiana since the state's injunction against the NAACP seven years earlier. If the Communist Control Act could be used to prosecute SCEF, then it could be wielded against all and sundry, for the law defined as a "Communist front" any organization that had been cited by HUAC or other congressional committees. The indictments also represented an attack on the National Lawyers Guild, for Smith and Walzer were charged with being members of that "Communist front" too. The raid's timing, in fact, was no accident: it coincided with a National Lawyers Guild workshop in New Orleans devoted to civil rights law.

When Dombrowski and SCEF appealed to the federal district court, judges Frank B. Ellis and E. Gordon West refused to stay the prosecutions, arguing that the validity of the Communist Control Law should be a question left to the state courts. "Can we deny the State the basic right of self-preservation: the right to protect itself?" asked Ellis. "If so, truly this would be a massive emasculation of the last vestige of the dignity of sovereignty." John Minor Wisdom vigorously dissented, insisting that federal courts had a duty to decide if a state were "abusing its laws by punishing the plaintiffs for their advocacy of civil rights for Negroes." The "crowning glory" of American federalism was not states' rights but the constitutional protection afforded to individual citizens "against *all* wrongful governmental invasion of fundamental rights and privileges."

The Supreme Court's decision in *Dombrowski* v. *Pfister* (1965), which invalidated much of the Communist Control Law and reversed the judgment of the district court, was therefore enormously significant. Had the Court endorsed the principle of abstention, the Communist Control Law might have become a devastating weapon in the state's efforts to harass and weaken the civil rights movement. Moreover, even if the state courts had halted the prosecutions, the indictments would still have produced a "chilling effect" by temporarily paralyzing SCEF and intimidating other activists. The *Dombrowski* case clearly revealed the crucial importance of the federal judiciary in offsetting or at least mitigating state repression. The decision also critically weakened segregationist red-baiting. Fear of being tarred as a Communist had silenced all but a few whites who might be sympathetic to the civil rights movement. Even in the universities, loyalty oaths and red-baiting had created an intimidating atmosphere that made academics afraid to express dissent. This fear now began to dissipate.[48]

Dombrowski illustrated how the machinery and procedures of the law itself had become a vital resource for the civil rights movement. One aim of the attack on SCEF and the National Lawyers Guild was, quite simply, to diminish the legal representation available to civil rights plaintiffs. When there were only ten black lawyers in the entire state, and only a handful of white ones who would take on civil rights work, the significance of the attack can be readily grasped. This was not the first time that segregationists had tried to put civil rights lawyers out of business, nor would it be the last.

More was at stake than the mere number of lawyers. The National Lawyers Guild was important not only for the representation it provided but also for its pioneering legal tactics. At the New Orleans workshop, for example, Arthur Kinoy described a procedure for keeping civil rights cases before the federal courts. According to a Reconstruction law he dusted off, plaintiffs could appeal to higher courts if federal district judges remanded civil rights cases to the state courts. When CORE lawyers tried out this argument, the Fifth Circuit Court of Appeals proved receptive; it began to stay state prosecutions while considering such appeals. Without this mechanism for appeal-ing remand orders, legal harassment might well have crippled the civil rights movement. The successful prosecution of two or three hundred key activ-ists, Lolis Elie believed, would have stopped the Louisiana movement dead in its tracks. However, the Inc. Fund, hostile to the leftist orientation of the Lawyers Guild, doubted the efficacy of the removal tactic and rarely used it.[49]

The writ of the federal courts, moreover, did not always run in backwoods Louisiana. Indeed, in the first Louisiana case involving the appeal of a re-mand order, state district judge John R. Rarick simply ignored a stay order issued by the Fifth Circuit Court of Appeals. Rarick had enjoined CORE in East Feliciana Parish from picketing, demonstrating, and "congregating with others on public streets and highways and upon public sidewalks and in and around any free entrance to any place of business or public buildings." When Collins, Douglas, and Elie removed the case to the federal court, Judge Gordon West promptly remanded it, and the authorities in East Feliciana pro-ceeded to prosecute two dozen CORE activists for illegal picketing. The day before the trial, the three lawyers went to the home of John Minor Wisdom to ask for a stay while they appealed West's remand order. A sympathetic Wis-dom issued the stay, and Robert Collins, in Clinton for the trial, informed the court that it no longer had jurisdiction over the case. "They were all flabber-gasted," he remembered, "including the judge and the district attorney."

Ten days later, however, Rarick opened the trial in defiance of the federal appeals court. "The purported stay of that Court," he fulminated, "is without warrant in law and is an absolute nullity, and is entitled to no more respect in this Court than any other act of officious intermeddling designed to obstruct justice." For the next several months, Rarick kept renewing his injunction every ten days. A transplanted northerner and ultrasegregationist, Rarick once took Lolis Elie aside and pointed to a tree outside the courthouse. "He said, 'See that tree? . . . Well, the last black sheriff we had up here, he was hanged from that tree.'"[50]

East Feliciana Parish presented a flagrant but by no means isolated case of the "legal" repression of civil rights activity. When CORE's voter regis-tration drive ran out of steam, the local chapter tried to maintain interest in the movement by petitioning the mayor of Clinton for a biracial committee, "in order to avoid civil domestic disturbance of racial tension." District attor-ney Richard Kilbourne promptly indicted the twelve signatories for "public intimidations by the use of threats." In October, when CORE organized a boycott of white merchants, the police arrested twenty-five pickets, all but three of them schoolchildren, for various offenses including disturbing the peace and contributing to the delinquency of a minor. The three adults spent a month in jail, the juveniles almost a week. Put on probation until they reached the age of twenty-one, the youths were effectively barred from further picketing. As if this were not enough, the city of Clinton conveyed the ownership of the sidewalks to the merchants themselves, enabling the police to arrest pickets for trespass. By the spring of 1964 the boycott had faded away.[51]

Without a doubt, the locality most impervious to federal authority, and where the most egregious violations of civil liberties occurred, was Plaquemines Parish, still under the heel of Leander Perez. "Blacks considered 'uppity' were tried before local courts on trumped-up charges and invariably received stiff sentences," writes Perez's biographer. Such victims rarely enjoyed legal representation. There were no black lawyers in the parish and those in New Orleans tended to avoid the place. In 1961 Earl Amadee and A. M. Trudeau had arrived at the courthouse in Pointe a La Hache to find that their clients had already been tried, convicted, and sentenced. Perez then personally threatened them, ordering the two lawyers to leave the parish forthwith.

The Perez-bossed parish council wove a web of repressive regulations that strangled the First Amendment. Public assemblies of more than fourteen people required a permit from the council; so did the use of public facilities for meetings; even private gatherings such as church dinners and sewing circles had to be approved. When Secretary of Defense Robert McNamara directed the commanders of military camps to monitor and report off-base racial discrimination, the council retaliated by prohibiting bars and restaurants from serving uniformed servicemen and by declaring Callender Naval Air Station off-limits to civilians. Such was the atmosphere of intimidation that the Plaquemines Parish NAACP, organized in 1961, initially met in New Orleans. Arthur Chapital upbraided New York for inadvertently mailing copies of *The Crisis* to members' home addresses, an action that jeopardized not only their jobs "but also their lives."[52]

The fact that it was the most repressive parish in the state made Plaquemines an attractive target for CORE, at least in theory. Leander Perez was probably the most powerful ultrasegregationist in Louisiana, and "if something could be done to break his hold and to destroy his image," Robert Collins believed, "this would mean something to the entire movement." In 1963 Mary Hamilton made contacts in the parish with a view to launching a voter registration drive. Learning of her activity, however, Perez ordered a crackdown. The police set up barricades on the West Bank highway, stopping and searching all cars driven by Negroes; a man discovered with CORE material in his car was arrested for carrying a concealed weapon, a penknife. Robert Collins thought it best if the man were not represented in court, reasoning that the appearance of a civil rights lawyer would do him more harm than good. Mary Hamilton dared not return to the parish "because our contacts there said . . . I would be immediately arrested." Perez let it be known that anyone arrested for demonstrating would be incarcerated in Fort St. Philip, an ancient edifice surrounded by an electric fence, a moat, and a snake-infested swamp. CORE failed to establish a foothold in the parish and its ambitious plans came to nothing.[53]

Elsewhere, CORE demonstrations ran into both legal repression and police violence. The most forceful expression of this combination took place in Plaquemine, Iberville Parish, CORE's principal base in Louisiana. In June 1963 blacks presented city officials with a package of demands that included fair employment, desegregation, a biracial committee, and the annexation of two black neighborhoods that currently received no municipal services. After a march to city hall went off without incident on August 15, 1963, black leaders threatened more demonstrations if they received no reply within twenty-four hours. Disclaiming any power to negotiate, mayor Charles Schnebelen told blacks to submit their demands to the city council in the usual manner.

Deciding to turn Plaquemine into a Birmingham-style confrontation, CORE imported James Farmer for its biggest demonstration yet. On August 19 more than a thousand blacks marched to city hall; they found thirty-eight police officers lined up in front of the building. After a tense silence lasting two or three minutes, somebody began singing "We Shall Overcome," and other marchers soon joined the refrain. When the four march leaders refused to stop the singing, police chief Dennis Songy arrested them. The police then forcibly dispersed the demonstration, arresting more than two hundred people. James Farmer spent ten days in the Ascension Parish jail in Donaldsonville, missing the March on Washington. CORE's aim of filling the jails came awry, however, when sixty prisoners came out on bail and the rest were dispersed to adjoining parishes. City officials, moreover, remained obdurate, telling Bill Harleaux and Rudy Lombard that they could promise nothing until the city council met on August 29. According to Mayor Schnebelen, one of the blacks warned, "There won't be a Plaquemine by August 29." CORE was temporarily stymied, however, when Judge Gordon West enjoined further demonstrations. When the protests resumed on August 31, after CORE obtained a stay of West's order, mounted policemen roughly dispersed about two hundred young people as they marched toward the home of the sheriff.

The black community was so outraged over this incident that even the town's ministers, only one of whom had supported the protests, united behind the campaign. On the morning of September 1, after a strategy meeting that lasted until dawn, the ministers led their congregations to the Plymouth Rock Baptist Church of Rev. Jetson Davis. After a thunderous rally punctuated by prayers, speeches, and freedom songs, about five hundred people prepared to set off on a silent march to protest the previous night's brutality. In the meantime, however, Gordon West, ignoring the stay order of the appeals court, reissued his injunction. As the marchers were lining up in twos a U.S. marshal served copies of the restraining order on Tolbert Harris, Ronnie Moore, Bill Harleaux, Jetson Davis, and James Farmer. They decided to march regardless.

After proceeding six blocks, the ministers were arrested and the rest of the marchers chased, teargassed, cattle-prodded, and billy-clubbed back to Plymouth Rock Baptist Church. The police then used tear gas and fire hoses to flush the blacks out, whereupon mounted policemen and state troopers drove them off the streets. Some sought refuge in Reverend Davis's house, where Mimi Feingold saw "injured women kicking and screaming on the beds, everyone crying and screaming." After the police lobbed tear gas inside, they fled in all directions. Feingold hid in a shed behind the church, a panic-stricken girl clinging to her. After a terrifying hour listening to the sounds of the carnage, she was discovered and arrested.

About three hundred blacks, including James Farmer, sheltered inside a funeral home. Flushed with the spirit of the chase and egged on by white onlookers, the police, who included hastily deputized civilians, many of them half-drunk, went on a rampage. CORE worker Spiver Gordon, mistaken for the bulky Farmer, was dragged from a house and beaten. Only the intervention of a state trooper, he believed, saved him from serious injury. As red-faced troopers kicked in the door of the funeral home baying for his blood, Farmer "felt like a modern Oedipus who, unaware, brought down a plague upon the city." Dissuaded from giving himself up, Farmer, accompanied by two former marines with guns, escaped to New Orleans hidden inside a hearse.[54]

CORE had achieved the confrontation it wanted, but to little immediate good. Although four hundred people were arrested, most were only too glad to be quickly bailed. "Things are pretty unbearable," wrote one girl, a high school student, from the Port Allen jail.

> They have locked our windows and given us dry bread to eat. . . . Some of the kids are worried about school. We can't stand it sure enough since no one has been here to give us an encouraging message. Most of us want out as soon as possible. . . . Last night they brought two drunks and put one in each of our cells. The one in our cell pull us out of bed, and vomit all over the place.

Once again, CORE's Gandhian strategy of "filling the jails" collided with harsh reality.[55]

With CORE still under injunction, sixteen-year-old Kenny Johnson organized a boycott of the cafeteria at the local Negro high school after the school board fired a lunch worker because her children had been in the demonstrations. When thirty-five students were suspended, their peers started picketing the white high school to dramatize their demand for integration. On October 7 the police used tear gas to drive away the students, and Johnson found himself in the State Reform School for Colored Youth for violating his parole. He faced detention until the age of twenty-one. Only a threat by CORE to file suit to integrate the institution induced the state to release him, by which time he had served three months, "the worst and most frightening experience" of his life. The picketing of white merchants continued through the winter, but in early 1964 Spiver Gordon reported that the boycott was only 65 percent effective and that black ministers were no longer supporting the movement. The campaign of direct action gradually sputtered out. As Meier and Rudwick noted, unlike Birmingham it "neither received much publicity nor galvanized the White House to intervene."[56]

In Shreveport police repression was a fact of everyday life, making the black community slow to respond to calls for direct action. Civil rights workers were continually picked up by the police — vagrancy was a favorite charge — and the newly elected commissioner of public safety, a former member of the sheriff's department named George D'Artois, made it unequivocally clear that he would not tolerate demonstrations. July saw stepped-up civil rights activity, with Charles Evers, brother of the slain NAACP official from Mississippi, addressing a mass meeting, a prelude to lunch counter sit-ins conducted by a reorganized CORE chapter. But prompt arrests quickly throttled these new protests, and poor cooperation between the different organizations — CORE, SCLC, and the NAACP — bedevilled efforts to mount further demonstrations.[57]

There seemed, for a fleeting moment, a chance that the city's merchants might negotiate desegregation when the leading members of the chamber of commerce tentatively agreed to biracial talks. But the attitude of the city's two leading newspapers made moderation a vice and extremism a virtue. The *Journal* gave a "voice to every hate peddler that comes along," complained one white moderate, while the *Times* condoned "even the most reactionary influences." Right-wing radio programs added to the supercharged atmosphere, comprising a volatile mixture of racism and anticommunism. By the summer of 1963, recalled former mayor James Gardner, a large proportion of the white population fervently believed that Communists had taken over the mainstream churches and that "the Russians had just passed through Belcher on the way to Shreveport." According to one journalist, Shreveport contained "more hate per square acre than any city in the United States." An exaggeration, perhaps, but the vehement conservatism of the city's influential whites was real enough. Proposals for a biracial committee collapsed at the first whiff of hostile publicity, and behind-the-scenes negotiations over lunch counter integration led nowhere.[58]

If George D'Artois reminded many of Bull Connor, it was fitting, perhaps, that the Birmingham church bombing of September 15, 1963, occasioned his most flagrant Bull Connor tactics. In the wake of that horrific event, the NAACP and the Interdenominational Ministerial Alliance planned a memorial parade for the four dead girls, marching from one church to another. The proposed route covered only six blocks and lay well away from the downtown business district. D'Artois denied them a parade permit, promising to "enforce the laws of the city and state regardless of a few individuals who want to destroy our American way of life." Black determination to march increased D'Artois's own determination to foil the protest. In the days leading up to the scheduled march and service, the police arrested both Clarence Laws, the NAACP's regional representative, and Harry Blake, the branch president, for alleged motoring offenses. Blake was arrested twice in two days.

On September 22 about two hundred police cordoned off the Thirteenth District Baptist Auditorium, the starting point of the march. Evading the police and walking singly or in small groups, about eighty blacks managed to reach the Little Union Baptist Church, where about four hundred people had gathered for the two-hour memorial service. Outside, riot squads and mounted police moved a large crowd out of the cordoned-off area. Afraid that this increasingly ugly atmosphere would end in police violence, black attorney Jesse Stone asked D'Artois to let the people in the church leave the building one at a time, thus avoiding any appearance of a parade. What happened next is a matter of dispute: either scuffles broke out, with youths tossing stones, or the police, unprovoked, drew their guns and pressed the crowd back. All accounts agree, however, that moments later several policemen grabbed Harry Blake, dragged him out of the church, and began beating him with their billy clubs; D'Artois himself joined in. Mounted police then broke up the crowd, at one point riding up the steps of the church. After a local black doctor treated his head wound, Blake was driven to a hospital in Dallas.

The following day, about two hundred students at Booker T. Washington high school, acting on their own initiative, attempted to march downtown. Police stopped them two blocks from the school, firing tear gas when they refused to disband. Driving them back, the police found another five hundred children outside the school gates and attempted to force them inside, prodding, punching, and kicking them. When principal Raleigh Brown tried to intervene, a policeman knocked him to the ground. The students then pelted the officers with any object that came to hand; they retreated inside when the riot squad arrived, "but each time the front door was opened," a reporter noted, "[the police] were met with a barrage of bottles and other objects." The Reverend J. W. Spellman eventually persuaded D'Artois to pull his men back. The principal then released the students one class at a time. A day later, D'Artois had his men surround J. S. Clark Junior High School, where about seven hundred students held a lunchtime rally. When the young people jeered the police and yelled "freedom," some of them lobbing rocks over the fence, he sent men into the schoolyard to silence the protest.[59]

The chilling effect of this police repression proved devastating. Despite the concern of the NAACP's national officials about the beating of Blake and the denial of a parade permit, the local branch evinced little enthusiasm for further demonstrations. The branch leadership, moreover, became increasingly ineffective. Blake himself, embittered by the failure of blacks who witnessed his beating to testify against the police, became much less active than before. The second most influential person in the branch, beautician Ann Brewster, committed suicide in November 1963, burdened by financial debts incurred through her activism and saddened by the apathy she saw in the black community. CORE sent a succession of field secretaries to Shreveport in an effort to revive support for direct action. None of them succeeded, and the national office abandoned its long-running goal of making Shreveport a major CORE project. SCLC also pulled out of the city, ending a seven-year involvement in the area. Between 1964 and 1968 Shreveport saw little in the way of public protest by blacks.[60]

In other Louisiana cities, however, whites opted for negotiation rather than outright repression. In Baton Rouge, Lake Charles, and Hammond, lunch counters were quietly desegregated. In New Orleans, renewed talks brought about further integration. The circumstances varied in each of these cities, but the broad impetus that led whites to make concessions was the same: fear of demonstrations, actual or threatened, fear of becoming "another Birmingham."[61]

Baton Rouge formed the state's first biracial committee in May 1963. In December 1962 Wade Mackie of the American Friends Service Committee asked the newly elected president of the chamber of commerce, newspaper and television proprietor Douglas L. Manship, to meet with a group of about a dozen black leaders. Initially reluctant, Manship eventually conferred with the group in February 1963, the first of several unpublicized meetings. In early May this informal committee found itself confronting a community crisis that demanded immediate action: the school board sent out assignment letters that allowed parents a little over a month to apply for transfers on behalf of their children for the following school year. Plainly designed to preempt Judge West's forthcoming ruling, the letters incensed the black community; virtually no black parents applied to transfer their children to a white school. Coming at precisely the time that the Birmingham crisis came to a head, Mackie struck while the iron was hot. Describing the mood of the Negro community as explosive, he called Manship on May 13 and asked if he wanted "to spend his time building a bomb shelter." The alternative, he suggested, was to calm the situation by means of an official biracial committee. Manship asked for two days' grace before blacks started demonstrating. By May 15, he and his allies had persuaded the mayor and the city council; by May 29 the committee had been appointed.[62]

Resentment of state interference in the city's public schools also facilitated the biracial accord. In 1961 Governor Jimmie Davis, empowered by a compliant legislature, had appointed three archsegregationists to the East Baton Rouge Parish school board in an obvious effort to stymie the NAACP's integration suit; the following year all three were defeated by candidates committed to keeping the schools open. In April 1963, as the board pondered submitting a desegregation plan in advance of an impending court decision by Judge E. Gordon West, four hundred whites put their names to a public declaration in which they urged compliance with the courts and the maintenance of law and order. The instigator of the statement, attorney B. B. Taylor Jr., deliberately excluded ministers and identifiable racial liberals: as Wade Mackie put it, "These people were not in favor of desegregation or integration. They were just opposed to disintegration."

A peculiarity of the biracial negotiations in Baton Rouge was the exclusion of the NAACP, usually central in such situations. The local branch had collapsed in 1956 and was only reorganized in 1962; even then it failed to attract broad support.

An important reason for the NAACP's weakness and isolation was the continuing fragmentation of black leadership in Baton Rouge. Two predominantly middle-class groups, the Frontiers Club and FOCUS, concerned themselves with voter registration and were loath to surrender the civil rights field to the NAACP. Another source of leadership, the administrators of Southern University, were beholden to an archsegregationist state administration and eschewed any hint of racial militancy. The most influential black minister in the city, T. J. Jemison, had set his sights on the presidency of the National Baptist Convention, then led by the Reverend J. H. Jackson, a foe of civil rights militancy in general and of Martin Luther King Jr. in particular. In the case of at least one prominent figure, it was rumored that whites were able to exert undue influence by holding past indiscretions over his head.

The character of the man leading the revived branch reinforced the disinclination of many blacks to support the NAACP. The Reverend Arthur Jelks, a fifty-year-old AME minister, was, according to Gloster Current, "a loose-tongue individual, impetuous, overly sensitive, and difficult." The fact that he was neither well educated nor a longtime resident of Baton Rouge made him even less acceptable to the city's black elite. The breach between the two widened when Jelks, even before the biracial committee had been named, blasted its putative black members as Uncle Toms and threatened demonstrations if the city failed to act on his demands. Clarence Laws summoned the branch officials to New Orleans in an effort to restrain Jelks. Middle-class blacks, however, still withheld their support, rendering Jelks's militancy a case of ineffectual posturing. A. P. Tureaud considered Jelks impossible to work with.

Having seen the bus boycott fail and CORE-inspired demonstrations end in shambles, middle-class blacks in Baton Rouge wished to avoid direct action at all costs. "The Negro power structure is passive," complained Gloster Current, the NAACP's director of branches, "and openly attempting to thwart any militant activity." Of the fifteen blacks appointed to the biracial committee, only one, dentist Dupuy Anderson, was active in the NAACP.

It was scarcely surprising, then, that some disparaged the biracial committee as an empty symbol. CORE's Ronnie Moore saw it as a means of discouraging black political mobilization, especially as some of its members had close ties to white political factions. Even Wade Mackie nursed doubts about the committee's effectiveness. None of the whites, he noted, could be described as community leaders, and some had "characteristics which were of doubtful value to say the least." The committee could claim some accomplishments, notably the desegregation of public buildings and the hiring of four black policemen, but even these, Mackie admitted, were things "we had already been pushing for and had some form of prior commitment in unofficial ways." The most visible change, the integration of department store lunch counters, had been the work of the Merchants Association rather than the biracial committee.[63]

Peaceful school integration in 1963 likewise owed nothing to the biracial committee and little to the city's supposed progress toward racial moderation. True, Baton Rouge was the second city in Louisiana to begin desegregation, but by 1963 the absence of public disorder was unremarkable; even ardent segregationists wished to avoid the miserable experience of New Orleans. Wade Mackie considered the school board's plan "the worst possible plan that could survive the scrutiny of the federal district judge," in this case E. Gordon West. Moreover, West vented his hostility to the *Brown* decision ("one of the truly regrettable decisions of all time," he had called it) by giving the board ample scope to discourage and eliminate black applicants for transfer. Indeed, West's order of July 18 virtually invited the board to restrict integration to the absolute minimum. "There is no law, nor is there any decision of any court which *requires* integration of public schools. The only requirement is that *forced segregation* of the public school system be abolished."

The fact that such a large number of black children, twenty-eight in all, entered formerly all-white schools in September said less about the school board's commitment to integration than about the success of the American Friends Service Committee in encouraging blacks to apply for transfer. The AFSC first mailed literature to students and then made personal calls. "The most effective item in the mailing list," Mackie reported, "was Martin Luther King's *Letter from Birmingham City Jail*." The AFSC's role in promoting integration made it the bête noire of local segregationists: a wiretap on its office phone was traced to state senator Wendell Harris, who in 1960 had defeated the liberal J. D. DeBlieux. Harris was indicted for illegal wiretapping and subsequently lost his senate seat to DeBlieux.[64]

Over the following years, Baton Rouge would sometimes be cited as an exemplar of good race relations and interracial cooperation. That reputation, however, obscured a growing chasm between the black elite and the black poor. In the absence of either a strong NAACP branch or a vigorous CORE chapter, there was no effective articulation or representation of black discontent. The biracial committee itself was so secretive as to be almost invisible. The result was explosive frustration: by 1967 Baton Rouge had become the Louisiana city considered most likely to "blow."[65]

New Orleans presented a somewhat different picture. Although the city refused to appoint an official biracial committee, the balance of forces was such that blacks possessed considerably more bargaining power than they did in Baton Rouge. For one thing, blacks in New Orleans presented a united front at the negotiating table in the form of the Citizens Committee, formed in 1962. If the coalition that composed the committee was wide rather than deep, it nonetheless included every significant civil rights–related organization in the city; it was in a broad sense representative of the black population. Moreover, the committee could do more than talk: the pickets of the NAACP Youth Council sometimes embarrassed the black negotiators, but they also proved highly useful to them. Most black leaders in New Orleans regarded demonstrations as a last resort, but they did not, as in Baton Rouge, seek to avoid them entirely.

The judicial climate in New Orleans was also much more favorable to the civil rights cause, and this in turn influenced both the pace of black protest and the political response to it. Starting with bus integration in 1958, NAACP suits had chalked up several notable successes, thanks in part to swift and favorable rulings by judges like Skelly Wright and Herbert Christenberry. In July 1963, for example, a three-judge panel ordered the New Orleans Recreation Department (NORD) to desegregate parks, playgrounds, and all other facilities. In the same month the Municipal Auditorium was ordered to abandon segregation in a decision written by John Minor Wisdom that mixed firmness and impatience. "Cities may as well face up to the facts of life: New

Orleans, here and now, must adjust to the reality of having to operate desegregated public facilities. Time has run out. There is no defense left. There is
no excuse left. . . . There is not even that last ditch, token desegregation." In
Baton Rouge, by contrast, Gordon West regarded delay as a judicial virtue
when it came to integration suits.[66]

Jobs and City Hall dominated the civil rights agenda in 1963. In March,
under the threat of an Easter boycott, Canal Street merchants undertook
to hire seventy-five blacks as sales clerks or in other jobs above the menial
level. When the NAACP Youth Council carried out a survey in July, however, it found only sixty-three jobs, and of those, it claimed, only twenty-two
were above the "mop-and-broom" or "dummy-dresser" level. Members of the
council thereupon picketed six of the negligent stores, much to the irritation
of some members of the Citizens Committee who contested the council's figures and feared that picketing would hamper the continuing negotiations. At
one point Harry Kelleher, one of the principal white negotiators, was told
that the protests had been called off; when he looked out of the window to
scan Canal Street with his binoculars he saw Raphael Cassimere and Llewellyn
Soniat, Youth Council stalwarts both, picketing a department store. Despite
some harsh criticisms from within and without the NAACP, the Youth Council, which had pointedly declined to sit on the Citizens Committee, refused
to back down. "After serious and lengthy debate," the adult branch agreed
to support the picketing. The Youth Council kept up its "selective buying
campaign" for more than two years.[67]

There was never much "mass" in nonviolent direct action in New Orleans.
By the end of 1963 the Youth Council's picket line averaged about twenty
people, and on some days it numbered one or two. Thus the constantly reiterated threat of "mass demonstrations" combined bluff and brinkmanship in
approximately equal proportions. Still, after Birmingham and the subsequent
explosion of direct action across the South, it undoubtedly enhanced black
bargaining power. The city's dependence on tourism made white businessmen in New Orleans peculiarly sensitive to the threat of disruption on Canal
Street.

Biracial groups like the Catholic Council on Human Relations, the Urban
League, and the Community Relations Council, an unofficial body organized
at the end of 1962, amplified the threat of demonstrations. Presenting themselves as responsible moderates who were resisting mounting pressure from
irresponsible firebrands, NAACP activists like Leonard Burns and Ernest
Morial could count on the white members of these groups (whose membership to some extent overlapped) to convey the demonstration threat to white
leaders in the starkest terms. "We are absolutely convinced that the negroes . . .
are determined to commence demonstrations almost at any moment," the

CCHR's white president warned Archbishop Cody on July 24. "The negro is not going to refrain much longer from asserting himself, even at the risk of what might conceivably happen as a result of public demonstrations."[68]

On August 9, four days before demonstrations were set to commence, Mayor Schiro finally agreed to some of the black demands: as of August 12 all racial signs would be removed from City Hall, black garbagemen and firemen would be hired within thirty days, and the city would not delay integration by appealing federal court orders. Lolis Elie, the principal black negotiator, was struck by the fact that the city's leading white businessmen, not the mayor, seemed to be making all the crucial decisions. "After we agreed," he later recalled, "I remember Darwin Fenner got on the phone to Vic Schiro, and he says, 'Vic, this is Darwin. Come on over here. I want to see you.' And in five minutes, here comes Vic. This agreement is shoved in his face and he signs it and leaves." By 1963 civil rights activists everywhere suspected that a "white power structure" exercised a dominating influence in virtually every community. Nobody did more to popularize this assumption than Jack Minnis, SNCC's director of research, who painstakingly laid bare the connections between politicians, the civic elite, and financial institutions. He had first developed this kind of analysis as a writer for the *Lake Charles Beacon* in the late 1950s, when he alleged that the political machine of Sheriff Henry "Hamm" Reid depended on a corrupt alliance with downtown businesses. In New Orleans, he believed, a small group of white businessmen represented a concentration of economic power that no mayor could ignore.[69]

The extended war of nerves over demonstrations did not, however, result in a clear-cut victory for the civil rights movement in New Orleans. For the most part disfranchised, blacks still possessed little political clout, and Mayor Schiro, closely attuned to the racist sentiments of the predominantly white electorate, dragged his feet over implementing the August 9 agreement. Indeed, in September blacks claimed that Schiro had reneged on his end of the bargain by failing to hire black firemen and failing to integrate the cafeteria in City Hall. After the Birmingham church bombing of September 15, pressure for some kind of demonstration, after months of threats, became irresistible.

The march that took place on September 30, 1963, was the largest and most visible expression yet of black unity. Mayor Schiro, however, still refused to appoint a biracial committee, and Darwin Fenner, whose opposition to such a body proved decisive, threatened to pull out of all biracial negotiations in the event of further mass demonstrations. City Hall remained a bone of contention. The cafeteria's refusal to serve blacks prompted several sit-ins in the fall and winter of 1963 that attracted a large number of white students from Tulane University. Federal district judge Herbert Christenberry eventually ordered the facility integrated, and he chastised the police for dragging Rev.

Avery Alexander up some steps by his ankles, a disgraceful incident that Chief of Police Joseph Giarusso later admitted had been a "mistake." All in all, city officials conceded as little as they could get away with and with visible lack of enthusiasm. Ostensibly integrated toilets that were locked and labeled "out of service" typified this mean-spirited approach.[70]

Still, white responses to the civil rights movement in 1963 revealed a widening breach between moderate segregationists, who were prepared to countenance change, and the ultras, who still proposed to fight integration every inch of the way. To some extent this breach reflected the cultural and political divergence between northern and southern Louisiana, a divide that had been very much in evidence during the 1959–60 gubernatorial election and which was again apparent in the 1963–64 election. Indeed, the 1963–64 election was almost a repeat of the race four years earlier. Chep Morrison again carried most of south Louisiana and won virtually all the black vote, but lost to John J. McKeithen who, like Jimmie Davis, received huge majorities from white voters in the northern parishes and won the Florida Parishes comfortably.

Although race was not the only issue in the election, it hurt Morrison. In the first primary two of the candidates, superintendent of education Shelby Jackson and former governor Robert Kennon, campaigned almost solely on the segregation question, with Kennon throwing in vituperative attacks on the Kennedy administration. Morrison, until recently Kennedy's ambassador to the Organization of American States, did not at first realize just how politically damaging his association with the administration was. As one advisor told him, his mention of his government service did not go down well in Shreveport. "The less said about President Kennedy and Bobby Kennedy and your connections with them, the better you will be." Whether Kennedy's assassination helped Morrison is difficult to say. What is certain, however, is that many whites refused to mourn the president's death. Indeed, as Henry Cabirac sadly noted, "There seem to be quite a few who are actually elated."

Once again, Morrison found himself on the defensive over race, and this time around he defended segregation with even less relish and conviction than four years earlier. "I support the rule of reason," he explained. "Segregation is no longer an issue — it is a problem." He was all for segregation, he elaborated, but it was "a fundamental truth that industry will not locate in a community with mobs in the streets or nights marked by bombings and violence." Accused by McKeithen of courting the "bloc vote" (read the black vote), Morrison adopted tougher language during the second primary, attacking the Civil Rights Bill and deploring "racial mixing." But McKeithen, like Davis in 1960, easily outflanked Morrison on segregation. One McKeithen flyer showed a photograph of Morrison with Ralph Bunche and claimed that "Morrison has

consistently received the support of the Negro suffrage and Negro revolu-
tionist movement in Louisiana." Another depicted Morrison with a beaming
A. L. Davis, underlined by the stirring message: "White voters! The Issue is
clear! It's 'sho-nuff' up to you!" The fact that he lost in the runoff by only
forty thousand votes suggests that a substantial number of whites shared Morrison's racial moderation, but it also confirmed the historical pattern detected
by Glen Jeansonne: whenever race constituted the main campaign issue, most
of Louisiana's white voters opposed change.[71]

Thanks to Catholic voters in south Louisiana, Kennedy had carried the
state in 1960. Given the unpopularity of the Civil Rights Act, however, President Johnson knew that he had a fight on his hands when he visited New
Orleans on October 9, 1964. "Goldwater sentiment is . . . anti-integrationist
in tone and that tone is loud and clear," counseled one aide. "The less said
about civil rights the better." Others echoed this advice.

Yet when Johnson spoke at the Jung Hotel, he departed from his prepared
text to underline his commitment to the cause of civil rights. Acknowledging
his admiration for Huey Long, Johnson deplored the fact that race still dominated southern politics. A former senator, he went on, had once complained
to Sam Rayburn that the South remained economically backward, its people
exploited by outside interests, because of that obsession.

> Wistfully, the old senator told Rayburn, "Sammy, I just wish I felt a little
> better. I would like to go back to ole" — and I won't call the name of the
> state; it wasn't Louisiana and it wasn't Texas — "I would like to go back
> down there and make them one more Democratic speech. The poor old
> state, they haven't heard a Democratic speech in thirty years. All they ever
> hear at election time is 'Negro, Negro, Negro.'"

These extemporized words showed Johnson at his principled best. They did
little, however, to reconcile whites to integration: in the presidential election 57 percent of Louisiana's voters cast ballots for Barry Goldwater, a vocal
opponent of the Civil Rights Act.[72]

It would take years, in fact, before the integration of public accommodations became a universal reality in Louisiana. In the weeks following the
passage of the Civil Rights Act newspapers reported myriad incidents of
white resistance and evasion. In Plaquemine, a café owner blocked the entry
of Spiver Gordon and Tolbert Harris with the words, "The first black . . . that
steps in here, I'll knock his brains out." In the basement of the state capitol,
whites jeered Rev. Arthur Jelks as he and two women NAACP members ate
at the "white" section of the cafeteria; with Leander Perez egging him on,
one white man punched Jelks on the nose as he left under a barrage of abuse.
A few blocks away white waitresses quit work and picketed their hotel after

the first blacks were served in the dining room. At LSU, white barbers walked off the job when told that they had to give haircuts to black customers. In Opelousas, the president of the local NAACP was arrested for disturbing the peace when he sought service at a motel. In Gretna, across the river from New Orleans, one café closed its dining room and converted to a drive-in. A café in New Roads told blacks that hamburgers cost twenty dollars apiece. Schwegmann's, a chain of giant supermarkets in the New Orleans area, still refused to serve blacks at its lunch counters. Restaurants throughout the state became "private clubs." In the Shreveport area, for example, about one hundred eating places formed the "Northwest Louisiana Restaurant Club," which only served people with membership cards (that is, whites).[73]

A few weeks after the act came into operation things began to settle down and a pattern emerged. In south Louisiana much of the white resistance turned out to be half-hearted, and in the cities of Alexandria, Baton Rouge, New Orleans, Hammond, Lake Charles, and Lafayette, blacks usually had little trouble using lunch counters, restaurants, movie theaters, and motels. In the rural areas, however, blacks were more cautious in testing their rights and desegregation was patchy. North Louisiana proved even more resistant, and in small towns like Tallulah, Ferriday, and Homer segregation remained the norm. All over Louisiana bars remained segregated, and even in New Orleans few blacks tried to cross the color line. When four members of the Free Southern Theater, three blacks and a white, entered a French Quarter bar in the spring of 1965 they were arrested for vagrancy. Integration was equally absent in other spheres of public activity. New Orleans and Baton Rouge closed their swimming pools rather than desegregate them. Public schools remained segregated with the exception of New Orleans and Baton Rouge, where a combined total of 857 blacks attended formerly all-white schools. About 250 black children attended integrated Catholic schools. Hospitals everywhere carried on segregating black patients in separate wards or, in private and Catholic hospitals, excluding them entirely. With the exception of Flint-Goodridge Hospital, none of the hospitals in New Orleans allowed black doctors to attend or operate on patients.[74]

As segregationists were pushed onto the legal defensive, the most extreme among them resorted to terrorism in an effort to destroy the civil rights movement. The Ku Klux Klan, that shadowy, amorphous, and faction-ridden entity, experienced a huge accession of popular support after the summer of 1963. As the debate over the Civil Rights Bill droned on in Congress, Klan rallies were reported in Rayville, Vidalia, Bastrop, Bogalusa, and Denham Springs. On April 19, 1964, reporter Robert Wagner had the misfortune to be captured by klansmen while photographing their barnlike meeting place in Jackson, East Feliciana Parish. "The place had the appearance of a guerilla camp," he wrote. "Everybody I saw had a gun. Some carried a shotgun in their hands and had, additionally, a revolver strapped around their waist." Wagner was eventually released after being flogged, imprisoned in a dog kennel, and warned not to report what he had seen on pain of death. FBI agents observed the meeting from a discreet distance.[75]

How much of the violence directed against the civil rights movement stemmed from the Klan is impossible to establish. The FBI's files on the Klan in Louisiana run to thousands of pages, but only a minute fraction has been declassified, and those pages that have been released are frustratingly uninformative. The Klan's membership is also a matter of guesswork. It is nonetheless clear that in 1964 the Klan initiated a campaign of terror that included arson, harassment, intimidation, and even murder. In East Carroll Parish blacks who voted found blazing crosses in front of their homes; three churches, a Masonic hall, and a Baptist center were burned to the ground. The wife and daughter of Rev. J. H. Scott received vile, threatening telephone calls. "My life was threatened to my daughter," Scott told Roy Wilkins. "They called again and told my wife they were going to kill me and rape her." The Klan presence was especially blatant in Jonesboro, where whites in "redneck cadillacs," Chevy pickup trucks with guns in rear-window racks, chased CORE workers and cruised menacingly outside the Freedom House. On July 14 about thirty cars, each containing three or four hooded klansmen, drove slowly through the "Quarters," the town's Negro section, a sheriff's patrol car heading the caravan. A few months later two churches went up in flames.[76]

The Klan organizations in Louisiana and Mississippi were closely connected, and the most ruthless klansmen were to be found in parishes that adjoined the Mississippi state line. Louisiana's Original Knights of the Ku Klux Klan actually started life in Natchez, Mississippi, and spread to the nearby Louisiana towns of Vidalia and Ferriday. Mississippi's White Knights of the Ku Klux Klan, which murdered three civil rights workers in Neshoba County, the most infamous Klan atrocity of the period, was an offshoot of the Original Knights, and its leader, Samuel H. Bowers, was a native of Louisiana and a graduate of Tulane University.[77]

The growth of the Ku Klux Klan, the complicity of many law enforcement officials, and the refusal of the federal government to assume responsibility for curbing racist violence sounded a death knell for the philosophy of nonviolence that had once infused CORE with optimism and idealism. By 1963 all but a handful of CORE workers had been rudely disabused of the notion that nonviolence could transform the racial attitudes of southern whites. As a discussion paper for summer volunteers insisted, "The concept that we are going to go South and, through love and patience, change the hearts and minds of the Southern whites should be totally discarded." CORE workers came to regard Martin Luther King with cynicism: the mere mention of his name was "apt to bring sneers and laughs."[78]

CORE workers soon discovered, moreover, that many ordinary blacks regarded strict nonviolence as nonsensical. In rural Louisiana the ownership of guns was commonplace, and here, where blacks were isolated and most vulnerable, guns were often seen as the *only* deterrent to white violence. In East Carroll Parish John Henry Scott dusted off his shotgun and began target practice after enduring "four or five years of horrible life like a buck with open season on him." In West Feliciana, CORE workers were only too glad to see black men bring weapons to their voter registration clinics. "Let me tell you," wrote Mike Lesser "those 15–20 shotguns guarding our meetings are very reassuring." Klan atrocities outside the state reinforced skepticism about nonviolence: the Birmingham church bombing and the murders of Schwerner, Chaney, and Goodman evoked anguished talk of armed self-defense and even violent retaliation. The Kennedy assassination evoked a similar emotional response. "[The] feeling of everyone here is that the time is almost here that guns will be necessary," Miriam Feingold noted in her diary during a meeting of CORE's southern staff in New Orleans two days after Kennedy's death. "How much more can [the] human body take? . . . Jim McCain says CORE can't afford to advocate retaliation. But Dave Dennis, Jerome Smith say to hell with CORE, we're with the people."[79]

Such sentiments troubled some senior staff members. "We must at all times advocate nonviolence," Ronnie Moore told the 1964 summer task force. "CORE workers *cannot* carry guns or knives. . . . Be *very* careful in advocating self-defense in [the] community. . . . Urge people *not* to carry guns." This advice, however, was fast being overtaken by events, for blacks were already, on their own initiative, beginning to arm themselves on an organized basis.[80]

In July 1964, after the Klan paraded through the Quarters, about a dozen blacks in Jonesboro formed an armed group called the Deacons for Defense and Justice. The group only admitted men over the age of twenty-one and many were in their thirties and forties. Several had served in World War Two and the Korean War. A tightly disciplined and secretive organization, the Deacons insisted that they shared the same aims as CORE, differing from other civil rights groups only in their readiness to use weapons to protect the black community from attack. Using CB radios and walkie-talkies to coordinate their movements, the Deacons posted guards at the CORE Freedom House, patrolled the Negro section at night, protected mass meetings, and provided escorts for civil rights workers entering and leaving town.[81]

The CORE workers in Jonesboro welcomed the Deacons' protection: without it, they believed, some of them would have been killed. Charles Fenton, the young white project director, kept in constant touch with the Deacons' patrols and was assigned his own personal bodyguard, a former army sergeant. Some of the summer volunteers were amazed by the ubiquity of guns on CORE projects in north Louisiana. "For many, [nonviolence] stops at the end of a demonstration or when the day's work is thru," wrote one. "Most accept self-defense at night for granted." Some CORE workers even began carrying guns themselves, especially when driving between towns in north Louisiana. "I had a .38 and a .357," recalled Ike Reynolds. "So I went prepared." Richard Haley, director of CORE's southern regional office, sent staff members a memo directing them to cease carrying weapons or resign from CORE, but he turned a blind eye to the practice.[82]

On December 10, 1964, a group of klansmen from the Natchez area poured gasoline into a shoe-repair shop in Ferriday and set it, and its black owner, alight. The victim, fifty-one-year-old Frank Morris, died of his burns three days later. Morris was unable to identify his assailants, and the FBI investigation ran into a wall of silence. When CORE workers entered Ferriday they found the black community paralyzed by fear. The murder of Frank Morris brutally epitomized the multifaceted crisis brought about by the resurgent Ku Klux Klan. Such terrorism challenged the federal government and threatened to nullify the Civil Rights Act. It also challenged the authority of Governor John McKeithen and threatened to discredit the state authorities. Above all, it challenged the civil rights movement and threatened to stifle its activities in parts of the state.[83]

In Bogalusa, in 1965, CORE and the Deacons clashed with the Klan head-on. The confrontation created a crisis of such magnitude that neither the state nor the federal government could afford to look the other way.

Chapter 12

NORTH TO BOGALUSA

Louisiana is a truly southern state in its attitude toward race relations. . . .
Louisiana, however, is not Mississippi. — Loria Davis, Mimi Feingold, and
Howard Messing, "Louisiana in Brief," 1964

I f CORE workers agreed that Louisiana was not Mississippi, Bogalusa was about as close to Mississippi as one could get. Situated in Washington Parish, the only part of Louisiana to adjoin Mississippi on two sides, Bogalusa lies just west of the Pearl River, which separates the two states. A short drive across the state line brings one to Poplarville, which attained international notoriety in 1959 when whites seized and murdered a black prisoner, Mack Parker, and dumped his body in the Pearl River.

If Bogalusa lay on Mississippi's doorstep, culturally, too, it seemed closer to its easterly neighbor than to Louisiana. The town lacked the relative antiquity of other Louisiana cities and had nothing of the Gallic flavor that characterized southern Louisiana. Founded in 1906 by the Great Southern Lumber Company in an area peopled, but sparsely, by small farmers, Bogalusa drew most of its workforce from the Florida Parishes and southern Mississippi. It attracted few immigrants, and New Orleanians looked askance at the place that touted itself as Louisiana's "Magic City." (A light opera playing in New Orleans offered one its characters, a condemned man, the choice between death and exile in Bogalusa; the man chose death.) Bogalusa remained overwhelmingly Protestant and non-Creole. British names predominated, and the town's official publications (ignoring blacks) boasted about its Anglo-Saxon homogeneity.[1] Finally, Bogalusa resembled Mississippi in the sheer violence of its response to the civil rights movement. By 1965 it boasted the largest and most powerful Klan organization in Louisiana, committed to perpetuating segregation through harassment, boycotts, beatings, and murder.

Yet if Bogalusa outwardly resembled a Mississippi town, its location in Louisiana was more than a geographical irrelevance: it provided a political context that profoundly influenced the events of 1965. It is difficult to imagine that a black movement as militant as the one in Bogalusa, arguably the most militant in the entire South, could have emerged in the repressive climate of Mississippi. And it is equally improbable that, had such a crisis occurred in Mississippi, it would have been tackled with the same combination of constructive mediation from the governor, resolute intervention by the Department of Justice, and vigorous action on the part of the federal district judge.

The Bogalusa crisis was one of only two occasions (the other being the New Orleans schools crisis of 1960–61) when the state's racial conflicts commanded international attention. It proved to be a landmark, a turning point even, in Louisiana's civil rights movement. The Bogalusa movement represented a new level of black militancy. Emphatically rejecting the self-sacrificing ethic, but not the assertive tactics, of nonviolent protest, it practiced armed self-defense in a visible and highly effective manner. However, the emergence of the gun-toting Deacons for Defense and Justice, regarded by many at the time as a harbinger of deadly armed conflict throughout the South, turned out to be less important than it first seemed. Contrary to exaggerated press reports, the Deacons never grew into a statewide, let alone a southwide, organization, and by 1967 it was defunct.

The most significant aspect of the Bogalusa crisis was the challenge it presented to both the state and the federal government. Bogalusa forced Governor McKeithen and the state's leading businessmen to confront the implications of the 1964 Civil Rights Act; it helped persuade them to assist rather than resist the birth of the postsegregation order. Bogalusa also became a major test of the federal government's determination to put muscle into the Civil Rights Act in the teeth of violent resistance from recalcitrant whites. The Department of Justice saw Bogalusa as a challenge that it had to confront head-on: it instituted a crackdown against the Ku Klux Klan, filed suits to desegregate schools and public accommodations, and prosecuted Crown-Zellerbach Corporation and the paperworkers' unions to ensure fair employment and representation in the town's paper mills. The Department's legal barrage also included a suit against the Bogalusa police force that, in effect, placed the police under the control of the federal district court, an action of unprecedented scope.

The Bogalusa crisis secured great legal victories for the civil rights movement, but it also sharply exposed the economic dimension of the racial conflict: the struggle for desegregation was fought against the backdrop of the giant Crown-Zellerbach plant, where black and white workers competed for a shrinking number of jobs and promotions. The decline in manufacturing employment demonstrated just how hard it would be for blacks to turn legal equality into economic advancement.

Still towering over the center of Bogalusa, the Crown-Zellerbach complex is the direct descendant of the world's largest sawmill, constructed between 1906 and 1908 to exploit the vast forests of yellow leaf pine that blanketed the area. The town grew up around that sawmill and became one of the most complete and self-sufficient company towns in the region. Through the Great Southern Lumber Company, the Goodyear brothers of Pennsylvania founded it, named it, and owned it. They built schools, houses, hotels, a hospital, and a giant store. They employed the police force, owned the banks, and supplied the electricity. They even patented the word "Bogalusa," using it as a brand name. The company's general manager, William Henry Sullivan, held the post of mayor from the town's incorporation in 1914 until his death in 1929. Sullivan's "control over Bogalusa," writes one authority, with only a little poetic license, "was as complete as any ante-bellum master over his plantation." In 1938, after the last virgin timber was felled, the sawmill closed down, its metal exported to Japan as scrap. However, thanks to a reforestation program started in 1922, Bogalusa survived. The Gaylord Container Corporation bought Great Southern and opened a new pulp and paper mill in 1942. By 1957, after Gaylord merged with the Crown-Zellerbach Corporation, the papermaking operation had expanded into a complex comprising three main plants. Few complained about the stench that pervaded the town; as a federal judge once commented, "People like to smell that, because that means good economy up there."[2]

Bogalusa grew up in an area where people were independent, clannish, suspicious of strangers, and prone to take the law into their own hands. In a rough, violent, frontier environment that made the Wild West seem tame, black lives were cheap. It was commonly accepted hearsay, wrote C. W. Goodyear in his 1950 history of Bogalusa, "that no white man in Washington Parish ever was convicted of the murder of a Negro until the twentieth century." Lynching was commonplace. In 1903, for example, a Negro suspected of murdering a white woman was tied to a tree and burned. His killers then ambushed a church meeting, leaving fifteen blacks dead. A few years later, a black man was lynched in Bogalusa itself. The Franklinton lynching of 1935, when a lynching party abducted Jerome Wilson from jail, underlined the lawless character of the area.

The northern capitalists who built and ran Bogalusa were acutely aware of the potential for racial violence in a town that quickly became 40 percent black. They coped with the problem through a combination of firmness and deference to white prejudice. The town was laid out so that the sawmill and log pond separated the white and Negro sections. General manager Sullivan instructed his force of deputy sheriffs that, rather than acquiesce in lynchings, they should utilize bloodhounds in order to identify black suspects. "When a fugitive was apprehended," explained Goodyear, "he was lined up with several other colored men. The bloodhounds were released. Invariably, they rushed toward the suspect as if to tear him to pieces. The identification was acceptable as court evidence and as a just basis for a jury's pronouncement of guilt." It was an improvement over lynch law only in that it saved such unfortunates from the mob. In 1919, however, company officials organized a mob of their own in order to suppress the IWW, which had committed the egregious offense of organizing blacks alongside whites. Assisted by the town's deputy sheriffs, the mob attacked the labor hall and killed the union's president. The IWW collapsed and its black organizer disappeared without a trace.[3]

One might have expected the area's history of racist violence to have produced a cowed and submissive black population, but such was not the case. For one thing, Washington Parish differed from the landlord-dominated counties of the Black Belt: most black farmers here owned their own land, growing beans, okra, greens, and a little cotton. They were self-sufficient and sturdily independent. Although local whites jealously guarded their monopoly over dairy farming and excluded them from their union (an affiliate of the old Southern Tenant Farmers Union, now part of the Amalgamated Meat Cutters) blacks had their own farmers' league. Black farmers also voted in the local elections held under the Federal Agricultural Stabilization Conservation Program (ASC).[4]

In the second place, blacks in Washington Parish were to some extent politically organized. With the assistance of the NAACP they had opened up the registration rolls in 1950 and ten years later defeated the Citizens Council's attempt to purge black voters. Although black registration languished in the early 1960s it still composed about one-tenth of the total electorate. Blacks tried to influence elections through the Bogalusa Voters and Civic League, an organization created in 1956 after the state's injunction paralyzed the NAACP. Led successively by Joe Dean, William Bailey Jr., and Andrew Moses, the league made political endorsements and attempted to negotiate concessions from the mayor and city council.[5]

The Crown-Zellerbach plants gave blacks another source of solidarity and strength. The complex had been unionized in 1939 and remained so in 1965; workers belonged to the United Papermakers and Paperworkers. Although the union maintained segregated locals, it enabled blacks to develop organizational skills and a capacity for collective action. The local civil rights movement that emerged in 1965 drew most of its strength from black union members; its leaders were longtime union activists, and it met in the union's hall.

Outwardly, Bogalusa lacked the perfervidly racist atmosphere of Mississippi. Even by Louisiana standards, it had not been noted for racial extremism. Washington Parish had for many years been a Longite stronghold: its state senator, B. B. "Sixty" Rayburn, was Earl Long's close ally; Curt Siegelin, Bogalusa's former mayor, served in Long's final administration. The local congressman, James H. "Jimmie" Morrison, was a racial moderate. So too was the current mayor, Jesse Cutrer. Since 1950 the registrar of voters, Curtis Thomas, had earned the respect of blacks for his impartiality; in 1959 he had actually brought a suit against the Citizens Council in an attempt to stop their purge of black voters. "The whites here were somewhat fair, under segregated conditions," conceded A. Z. Young, militant leader of the Bogalusa movement.[6]

But there lay the rub. As long as Bogalusa remained, in the words of Judge John Minor Wisdom, "segregated from cradle to coffin," outward calm and civility could prevail. As long as local blacks did not aggressively press for equality, the city's political leaders could mollify those whites who felt threatened by integration. By 1964, however, integration was no longer a distant enemy that could be kept at bay indefinitely through legal tactics. With the tide of the civil rights movement lapping at their door, whites in Bogalusa began to join the Ku Klux Klan.[7]

The Original Knights of the Ku Klux Klan (OKKK) spread to southern Louisiana at the beginning of 1964, and the Florida Parishes, the most rural and Anglo-Saxon portion, proved to be its most fertile soil. On January 18, six days after klansmen had met in a Baton Rouge lodge hall to launch their organizing drive, flaming crosses were seen throughout the area. On May 30 Bogalusa witnessed its first Klan rally. Guarded by white-hooded horsemen equipped with walkie-talkies, about eight hundred people, nearly half of them wearing robes and hoods, gathered at a vacant lot inside the city limits to hear vitriolic speeches and watch two thirty-foot-high crosses go up in flames. Bogalusa had an antimasking ordinance modeled after the state's anti-Klan law. City officials, however, decided to allow the "klonklave"; indeed, city policemen cooperated with the Klan marshals. Apprised of the event by local NAACP members, A. P. Tureaud sent a letter of protest to Mayor Cutrer. He also alerted the Justice Department.[8]

Crown-Zellerbach inadvertently swelled the Klan's ranks. During the 1950s Crown's expansion had brought prosperity to Bogalusa, and the white workers had reaped disproportionate benefits. A bag plant opened in 1957 had been staffed entirely by whites with the exception of a few black porters; Crown employed several hundred white women but not a single black one. In 1960, however, Crown embarked upon a program of plant modernization that entailed drastic reductions in the workforce affecting whites as well as blacks. The union fought back, and in August 1961 a strike halted production. Although on the surface the strike seemed an expression of interracial solidarity, black workers had voted against it. Underrepresented in the workforce and holding the lower-paid jobs, they felt that white workers were primarily interested in defending their own privileged position. Outvoted by the white local, they supported the strike, but without enthusiasm. The outcome of the seven-month struggle merely deepened the latent split between the black and white workers. The layoffs went ahead, and about five hundred Crown employees found themselves out of a job and assigned to the "Extra Board," a reserve labor pool whose members had first call on any vacancies that arose. By 1964 the workforce had been cut to twenty-nine hundred, of whom fewer than four hundred were black.[9]

As blacks began pressing for more and better jobs, whites felt doubly threatened. Hitherto the Crown complex had been thoroughly segregated: separate "lines of progression" ensured that whites rose higher and faster, received better pay, and did not work under blacks. For obvious reasons, the white-dominated paperworkers' union strenuously opposed any tampering with this complex seniority system. Acutely aware of the union's power, Crown showed no inclination, in the words of company chairman Reed O. Hunt, "to alter the accepted pattern of race relations in the community." Pressed by the federal government, however, Crown had to do something; therefore in 1963 it instituted a new policy of testing applicants for promotion. Then, in May 1964, Crown integrated the Extra Board, allowing blacks to bid for jobs in the "white" lines of progression.[10]

Neither of these changes had any real impact upon the pattern of segregation. Assignments were based upon job seniority rather than length of service in the mill. Unemployed blacks on the Extra Board therefore found it impossible to compete for vacancies in the "white" lines of progression when so many qualified whites were bidding for those same jobs. Moreover, unemployed workers placed on the Extra Board enjoyed "recall rights" whereby they had the first call on their old job should a vacancy occur. Blacks could, in theory, seek transfer to a "white" line of progression, but this required an applicant to leave his current position, join the Extra Board, wait for a vacancy, and then pass a test that whites had not had to take in the past. If he won the promotion he would enter the new line at the bottom rung, and because seniority in his old job did not count in the new line of progression, he would be the first to go in the event of layoffs. By the end of 1964 only four blacks had entered "white" lines of progression. The rest of the 340 black employees worked as porters or, in the case of the box factory, as loaders in a separate, dead-end line of progression.

Although Crown's largely cosmetic reforms failed to benefit blacks, they thoroughly alarmed whites. "The integration of the Extra Board . . . was the nightmare of Negro competition come true," wrote Vera Rony. The atmosphere within the Crown plants became increasingly tense. In the multi-wall bag factory, the sole Negro in the white line of progression decided to return to his old portering job after white employees threw bolts at him. Whites stopped patronizing the cafeteria when the company abolished separate black seating; it closed. When Crown desegregated the showers in the box plant, whites went home unwashed. Toilets were integrated by cutting a door in the partition separating the two facilities. Blacks did not venture through the doorway, believing that "the first black head that goes through it won't come back." Crown boasted a Klan unit of at least one hundred members and probably many more.[11]

City and Crown officials knew that they were sitting on a powder keg. Desperate to prevent demonstrations, especially during Bogalusa's Golden Jubilee celebrations in July 1964, Mayor Cutrer invited a group of blacks to serve on a twenty-one-member biracial committee. These men made up the city's most prominent black names, including railroad worker William Bailey Jr., the longtime NAACP president, minister and insurance salesman Andrew Moses, president of the Bogalusa Voters League, and L. C. Dawson, president of Local 189A, United Paperworkers. Later chastised as Uncle Toms, they calculated that by wielding the threat of CORE-led demonstrations they would be able to extract concessions in the form of black policemen, lunch counter desegregation, and improved municipal services. When three CORE workers "scouted" Bogalusa in the spring of 1964, the black group argued that the biracial committee should be given time; if the negotiations failed to produce results by the summer, they would then welcome CORE's help. Particularly impressed by the articulate and persuasive Moses, the CORE team went along with this strategem. "White people here are really afraid of CORE and demonstrations," Mimi Feingold reported. "They'll do almost anything to keep CORE out."[12]

Manipulation, however, was a game that two could play. Mayor Cutrer followed a policy of negotiation without desegregation, using the rising Klan threat as a means of persuading the black group to abstain from demonstrations. In July, with the expiration of CORE's pledge to stay out, Cutrer prevailed upon Moses and three others to visit CORE's state headquarters in Plaquemine and ask for another six months of grace. Ronnie Moore promised Cutrer that CORE would "stay neutral" until the end of the year. Further negotiations yielded nothing of consequence, however: restaurants and lunch counters behaved as if the Civil Rights Act had not been passed; the city's parks remained off-limits to blacks. Although the city undertook to let blacks take the civil service test for the police, the Bogalusa force remained all white. So did the fire service (the fire station, facing city hall, was a known Klan haunt).[13]

In the meantime, the Klan became increasingly aggressive. A white Tulane student who had taken part in a New Orleans sit-in was beaten. A family accused of associating with blacks left the city after threats and harassment. Five hooded klansmen abducted James Spears, a Crown-Zellerbach worker, and whipped him with a belt, punishment for allegedly inviting blacks to his house to play folk music.[14]

The *Daily News* roundly condemned these incidents and urged Bogalusans not to be intimidated by "these hooded saviors of the world." The Klan responded by burning crosses in front of the *News* building and the home of editor Lou Major, part of a blitz that saw eighteen crosses planted in Bogalusa and more than one hundred across the state. The Klan followed this up with a leaflet denouncing Major as a "dastardly, two-bit, little coward" and calling upon whites to "squeeze this type character out of your city." Enclosing a copy of the leaflet, Congressman Jimmie Morrison asked the FBI for a "complete investigation so that the violators of the law can be apprehended and dealt with." However, the Bureau's analysis of the leaflet drew a blank. Pressed by the Justice Department for more information, the Bureau compiled a two-hundred-page report on the Louisiana Klan that included a list of known members running to sixteen pages. In December, New Orleans reported that three factions had split off from the OKKK, among them the Bogalusa-area Klan. The constant splintering that characterized the Klan was an FBI man's dream. "They pose no intelligence problem," claimed one agent. "We know everything about them. The main concern is that the Klans create the climate for violence. Klavern meetings are filled with talks about dynamiting, guns and violence."[15]

Klan menaces thwarted Mayor Cutrer's efforts to persuade local businesses to desegregate; six months after its passage, the Civil Rights Act remained a nullity in Bogalusa. Indeed, the Klan's presence had become so pervasive that Cutrer was effectively isolated. With a membership of at least eight hundred, the Klan included a good slice of the city's white population, including Crown-Zellerbach workers, city employees, and a substantial number of small businessmen. The Klan had members on the parish policy jury and the city housing authority. The brother of a city judge joined, as did the city attorney, Robert Rester. Cutrer's own next-door neighbor was a member; he employed a klansman in his ice cream business. With the Klan breathing down his neck, sometimes literally, Cutrer's overwhelming concern became keeping the lid on an explosive situation. In the opinion of LeRoy Collins, the former Florida governor who now served as Lyndon Johnson's racial troubleshooter, Cutrer appeared "more interested in conciliating the Ku Klux Klan than in enforcing the Civil Rights Act." [16]

Depairing of leadership from the town's politicians, lawyer Bascom D. Talley Jr., a member of the National Citizens Committee for Community Relations, recently appointed by President Johnson, sought Collins's advice. Collins headed the Community Relations Service, a federal agency created by the Civil Rights Act for the specific purpose of helping southern communities comply with the public accommodations section of the Civil Rights Act. In mid-November he dispatched two staff members to Bogalusa, where they met Talley and several other white moderates, men who were anxious to head off a racial crisis and prevent the kind of violence that had engulfed McComb, Mississippi, another Klan-dominated community only fifty miles away. Out of these secretive talks came the idea of inviting Brooks Hays to address an interracial dinner. A former Arkansas congressman, whose opposition to Faubus had cost him his seat, Hays was a well-known racial moderate who now chaired the CRS's national citizens committee. Hays would explain the experience of other southern cities in complying with the Civil Rights Act. As a southerner and a prominent Baptist layman, he seemed an inoffensive choice. He would speak at a dinner in honor of the town's most respected citizen, Vertrees Young, an Ohio-born man who until recently headed the Gaylord Container Corporation, the division of Crown-Zellerbach that ran the Bogalusa paper plant. The meeting, by invitation only, was arranged for January 7, in the parish hall of St. Matthews Episcopal Church.

The Klan promptly mobilized to stop this meeting. Within days, it distributed a leaflet attacking the Hays visit as an attempt to persuade whites "that you should help intergration [sic] by sitting in Church with the black man, hiring more of them in your businesses, serving and eating with them in your cafes, and allowing your children to sit by filty [sic], runny-nosed, ragged, ugly little niggers in your public schools." The leaflet named the nine men who had invited Hays and warned that anyone attending the meeting "will be dealt with accordingly by the Knights of the KU KLUX KLAN." It concluded with a scurrilous attack, couched in doggerel, on lawyer Bascom Talley.

The sponsors of the meeting immediately felt the heat. They received threatening phone calls and found burning crosses in front of their homes. Cars drove back and forth outside their houses and "grim-looking men in work clothes" kept up a constant watch. One of the signatories, Ralph Blumberg, who operated a country music radio station, had his sponsors call up to cancel their advertising. A native of St. Louis who had lived in Bogalusa only four years, Blumberg was astonished by the backlash. "You wake up in the morning and say, 'Is this real?'" he told *New York Times* reporter John Herbers. Blumberg was sufficiently convinced by the threats to send his wife and two children to live in St. Louis. A man stopped the Reverend Bruce Shepherd in the street and told him, "Feeling is hot here and if you don't withdraw you'll find yourself dead." Shepherd's bishop ordered him not to venture out at night. Lou Major acquired a pistol; Bascom Talley kept a loaded shotgun nearby when he opened his front door. The Klan also put the screws on Mayor Cutrer. Summoned to a Klan meeting at the end of December he walked into a hall full of robed and hooded men. "All I could see was eyes," he later recalled. "You can't be too comfortable when you're talking to a bunch of eyes." Cutrer promised to try and stop the Hays meeting.

The Klan's campaign succeeded. The St. Matthews vestry, warned that the church might be bombed if the Hays meeting went ahead, voted to deny use of the parish hall; Vertrees Young, the man due to be honored, voted to cancel. Faced with finding another venue at the last minute, the sponsors asked for the use of city hall. Cutrer refused. On January 5 they abandoned the meeting. "We didn't want to give up to the Klan," explained Shepherd, "and we did a lot of soul-searching before we withdrew the invitation. But we had no one with us. We didn't have labor, business, city officials, the law. . . . We were just six guys bucking the whole darn town." Announcing their decision, the six moderates publicly lamented the fact that "fear should so engulf our community that it strangles free speech and the right of peaceful assembly and makes a mockery of democracy." [17]

The cancellation of the Hays meeting made national news and destroyed Bogalusa's image of racial moderation. Cutrer tried to retrieve the situation by arranging for the peaceful desegregation of public accommodations; he persuaded the city's merchants, or a majority of them, to serve blacks on a prearranged day. Cutrer then made a deal with the Bogalusa Voters League: CORE workers would be welcome to organize tests as long as they left immediately afterward. Assured that neither testers nor CORE people would be molested, the leaders of the BVL agreed. With the BVL apparently under control, Cutrer prevailed upon the Klan to keep out of sight and let the tests proceed unhindered. It was a dangerous game. As Bascom Talley told one of the CRS men, Cutrer was carrying water on both shoulders and did not seem to realize that both pots were boiling.

With a green light, finally, from the BVL, Ronnie Moore sent two experienced CORE workers to Bogalusa: Steve Miller, an Antioch student from San Francisco, and Bill Yates, a former professor of English at Cornell University. On January 28, 1965, blacks were served at eight restaurants, gained admittance to two movie theaters, and used the public library without incident. Seven restaurants or lunch counters turned blacks away. John Griffin of the CRS saw gangs of klansmen cruising the streets and learned that both Bascom Talley and Lou Major received death threats that night. Still, the tests passed off without violence and might be counted a partial success.

Cutrer's desegregation plan was an elaborate charade, however, and it soon unraveled. The Klan had no intention of permitting integration and had only tolerated the January 18 tests after Cutrer assured them that on January 19, CORE having departed, life would return to segregated business as usual. Moreover, having originally told the BVL that testing could be staggered over three days, he told the Klan and the city council that CORE would be in town for just one day. The BVL leadership had agreed to the truncated testing, but CORE regarded a single day as totally inadequate. Although Yates and Miller left Bogalusa on the night of January 28, they returned three days later to attend a mass meeting of the BVL.

In the packed labor hall the atmosphere was electric. The BVL's leaders, their position made more tenuous by the Brooks Hays fiasco, faced angry criticism over their dealings with Cutrer. Challenged by Yates and Miller to resume the testing and stage marches, Andrew Moses defended his leadership. Then someone from the floor charged that Cutrer had paid off the BVL's leaders in order to keep CORE out of Bogalusa. Pandemonium ensued. Jeers and shouts drowned Moses's reply. After a raucous debate — one participant called it "the noisiest meeting I've ever seen in Bogalusa" — Moses resigned in favor of McClurie Sampson. A few days later, however, Sampson also resigned.

The BVL's new president was A. Z. Young, a forty-two-year-old Crown-Zellerbach worker and a veteran of World War II.

> Mr. Young demanded to know from his audience where they stood: "Will you let your sons and daughters be hit by billy clubs, have live snakes thrown at them, have cigarettes put out on their bodies, and be chased by police dogs on picket lines and marches, while you stay at home? They are risking their lives; are you risking yours?" . . .

If there was any question regarding the status of the previous moderate leadership, Young settled it, "I am your leader; you are my followers." Deafening applause followed. . . . A mass popular movement was born before our eyes. Smiles, handshakes-"yes, man" "set the record straight" shouted the audience.

In the months and years to come, many whites came to view Young as an irresponsible firebrand. In Bogalusa he was already a recognized figure, having led the black local of the Pulp and Sulphite Workers for a decade. Robert Hicks, another Crown worker a few years Young's junior, became vice president. Gayle Jenkins, a hospital meals worker in her mid-thirties whose husband worked for Crown, became secretary. Her son, Don Expose, headed a new youth section.

Shortly before midnight on February 1, as klansmen gathered on Columbia Street, police chief Claxton Knight visited the home of Robert Hicks, where Yates and Miller were spending the night. Divulging that a lynch mob was after them, he advised the CORE workers to leave town forthwith and offered a police escort. After a tense discussion, Yates and Miller decided to take their chances in Bogalusa. "We didn't even have to remember Chaney, Schwerner, and Goodman," Hicks later recalled. "We just knew that if Yates and Miller left our house at that moment, we would never see them alive again." After Knight refused to provide police protection — "We have better things to do than protect people who aren't wanted here" — Hicks summoned help from neighbors and friends. Fifteen armed black men soon stood watch over the house. Meanwhile, Yates and Miller utilized the Hickses' telephone to awaken the CORE grapevine; the wires were soon humming with calls and telegrams to AP, UPI, the Justice Department, the FBI, Governor McKeithen, and the Crown headquarters in San Francisco. The CORE network even reached Jesse Cutrer and Claxton Knight. At four the next morning policemen returned to the Hicks home. Yates and Miller returned to New Orleans after a harrowing night. The latest issue of *Nation* carried an article by Paul Good entitled "Klantown, USA." Bogalusa, wrote Good, "has more Klansmen per square foot than this writer has ever encountered or heard of anywhere in the South."[18]

The Klan was not through with Yates and Miller. On February 2, Jesse Cutrer received a visit from Charles Christmas and Saxon Farmer, respectively Grand Titan and Grand Dragon (leader and second-in-command) of the Ku Klux Klan. They demanded that the two CORE workers stay out of Bogalusa. Cutrer assured the klansmen that he disliked their presence as much as anyone, but he had no legal authority to keep them out. (Months later, in federal court, he contended that he had not known that Christmas and Farmer were klansmen.) The pair left him in little doubt that they were deadly serious. The lives of the CORE workers were in grave danger. When the pair returned to Bogalusa on February 3, klansmen chased them in cars as they left the union hall. Screeching to a halt, they made a run for Andrey's, a black-owned café. Shaking himself free of pursuing whites, Miller barely made it through the door. Yates was not so fortunate: the whites kicked and punched him, breaking his hand, before a group of blacks forced the whites to back off and bundled him into the café. As klansmen lurked outside, menacing the café, policemen nonchalantly chatted with them. At sunset the police disappeared. Telephones went dead. After several hours of this siegelike situation, armed blacks moved the CORE workers to a private home where they could be more effectively defended. Eventually, FBI agent Frank Sass arranged for their safe exit: four police cars and Sass himself accompanied them to the city limits; state patrol cars then escorted them to Baton Rouge.

On February 15 the Klan transmuted itself into the "Anti-Communist Christian Association," filing a charter with the state authorities. City attorney Robert Rester helped draft the document and, with Charles Christmas, put his name down as the ACCA's legal agent. The formation of the ACCA did not mean that the Klan had repudiated clandestine violence. Quite the reverse: the assumption of a legal cover testified to the Klan's increasing confidence that it could operate brazenly and with impunity. On the same day that the Klan adopted its official alias, club-brandishing klansmen forced a group of blacks to leave a restaurant.

The Klan lost all restraint in its drive to expel CORE and throttle the BVL. Klansmen hurled bricks and bottles from car windows at black pedestrians; they assaulted blacks in cafés and gas stations; they flagged down cars and attacked their occupants. Car chases of ninety miles an hour and more became common. Meanwhile, the Klan's campaign to isolate white moderates continued unrelentingly; the sponsors of the Hays dinner were still marked men. They became used to sweeping tacks from their driveways. Telephone death threats were routine. Another Klan leaflet made a scurrilous attack on Bruce Shepherd and affirmed its boycott of the *Daily News* and Ralph Blumberg's radio station WBOX. Blumberg saw his monthly income reduced from $4,000 to $300 as all but one of his local sponsors quit. (He could still chuckle over the irony of the fact that 90 percent of the Klan were probably still listening to his country music.) Before the year was out, however, Blumberg had left Bogalusa, his business in ruins. Shepherd also departed.[19]

Bogalusa was, to all intents and purposes, without effective law enforcement; many police officers sympathized with the Klan and some, very likely, were members. Although the escalating violence profoundly troubled Mayor Cutrer, his control over the police was weak: under Bogalusa's commission council system, chief of police Claxton Knight answered to Arnold Spiers, the commissioner of public safety. Neither Spiers nor Knight showed any disposition to rein in the Klan. Moreover, Cutrer himself was loath to even acknowledge the Klan's existence. Their town descending into anarchy, Cutrer and the city council chose to look the other way. When Ralph Blumberg broadcast an editorial blasting the Klan, Cutrer accused him of "blacken[ing] our city's good name." As LeRoy Collins told Vice President Humphrey, "The Mayor and the police seem to feel that the way to avoid violence and maintain law and order is for Negro citizens not to seek to exercise their constitutional rights."[20]

This was the context in which the Deacons for Defense and Justice appeared on the scene. In one sense, the Deacons in Bogalusa were born on February 1, 1965, when Robert Hicks organized an armed guard for Bill Yates and Steve Miller, an improvised, ad hoc response to a specific threat. As guns became a fact of everyday life, however, Bill Yates realized that somebody needed to explain the mechanics of organizing a regular armed self-defense group that could provide reliable, round-the-clock protection. He arranged for two members of the Jonesboro Deacons, plus white CORE worker Charles Fenton, to visit Bogalusa.

Speaking to a small, closed meeting at the labor hall on February 21, Ernest Thomas and F. D. Kirkpatrick stressed the need to be well armed and well organized. Roving patrols should scout the Negro areas after dark: walkie-talkies and citizens band radios facilitated effective deployment and speedy response. In Jonesboro, said Thomas, "we have groups patrolling each street. We guardin' intersections, and every time a white man comes in, an automatic radio call is dispatched to a car to stop him and ask him his business." The police, too, had to be monitored and, if necessary, confronted. "When the policeman come around, we right on him too — we patrol him. You got to let him know that as taxpayers, you the ones that send him to the commode, you the ones that buy his air conditioners, and those big cigars he smokes, and that dirty hat he wears." Thomas warned against relying on the cheap, .22-caliber rifles that blacks tended to buy. "That's no weapon — you need high-powered rifles. If you're gonna use a pistol, use a .38. A shotgun is good to have for close-distance firing." If they standardized their weaponry, he added, they could buy ammunition by the case, ensuring a plentiful supply for everyday use. "If you got only three or four bullets, you're out of the fight before it starts. Keep plenty of ammo at your house, in your car, wherever you are. I carry with me most all the time a hundred rounds." The Deacons had a defensive purpose, Thomas stressed, but they had to be equipped and ready to repel Klan attacks. "It takes violent blacks to combat these violent whites. It takes nonviolent whites and nonviolent Negroes to sit down and bargain whenever the thing is over — and iron it out. I ain't about to. We're gonna be ready for 'em. We're gonna have to be ready to survive." Ten members of the BVL, including Robert Hicks and A. Z. Young, listened intently to the presentation. They needed little convincing, and at the end of the meeting set up a Bogalusa chapter of the Deacons.

Their first test was not long in coming. When Yates, Miller, and Fenton set off for New Orleans after the meeting, two Deacons rode in their car and a third, Royan Burris, drove behind them. Tailed by a car full of whites, they covered the journey to Covington in record time, at one point clocking up 110 miles per hour. As he turned round to drive back to Bogalusa, Burris was forced to stop by a Corvette driven by two whites. "Next time, nigger," they told him, "we'll kill you."

The following night, addressing a mass meeting attended by about four hundred people, Robert Hicks announced that the Deacons for Defense were in business. They would protect civil rights workers and make sure that no white people entered Negro areas at night.

> We're gonna patrol. And, like policemen who are running you down and say, "You speedin'," then we pull up to them and say, "What's the matter," and the policemen say, "He's speedin'." And we say, "We didn't see him speed," and when the policemen see we armed just like they is — a white man's just like anybody else — they gonna let you go when they see you gonna attack them back.

As the audience cheered and clapped, blacks with guns guarded the union hall.[21]

The Bogalusa Deacons soon became a legend in the civil rights movement and an object of worried fascination to whites. To the northern news media, accustomed to perceiving southern Negroes as long-suffering and all forgiving, the sight of black men openly sporting pistols, rifles and shotguns seemed at best incongruous and at worst terrifying. Who were these people? Focusing on Deacons president Charles Sims, a rough-hewn insurance salesman with a reputation for barroom brawling (he had eighteen arrests to his name, most of them for assault and carrying concealed weapons, and had once been shot and almost killed by his girlfriend), some reporters saw them as a disreputable collection of roughnecks and jailbirds. Others viewed them in a more sinister light, detecting the beginning of a terrorist group or guerrilla army. The air of mystery that the Deacons deliberately cultivated fueled such speculations and encouraged wild guesses as to their true strength. In June the press reported that the Deacons had fifty chapters in three states and a membership of up to fifteen thousand and that the organization was bent on acquiring machine guns and hand grenades. The possibility of a full-blown race war seemed all too real. To J. Edgar Hoover, ever alert to the remotest threat of revolution, the Deacons seemed eminently worthy of FBI attention. He ordered his men to investigate the group for "subversive and/or outside influences," and to personally warn the Deacons against carrying or firing guns.[22]

Ironically, it was the FBI that gave the Deacons a clean bill of health, disputing the exaggerated estimates of their strength and confirming their essentially law-abiding nature. Speaking off the record to local agents, some Deacons readily admitted that they deliberately inflated their numbers and weapons for the purpose of deterring the Klan. Such exaggeration was hardly surprising, noted the head of Domestic Intelligence, and it showed the danger of accepting the Deacons' public statements at face value. As agents' reports flowed in from across the South, the Bureau completed a jigsaw puzzle that revealed a gigantic hoax. The Deacons' membership probably numbered in the dozens rather than the hundreds, and certainly not in the thousands. Instead of fifty chapters they had but three, all of them in Louisiana. They had no grenades or machine guns. True, the Deacons were heavily armed, but local agents reminded Washington that in the rural South "the carrying of rifles and pistols are commonplace by the citizenry, both white and Negro." Moreover, Louisiana law permitted the carrying of weapons as long as they were not concealed on the person. In short, the Deacons were nothing to get alarmed about. They were strictly defensive and showed no signs of being tainted by left-wing or black nationalist ideas.[23]

Still, if the Bogalusa Deacons were few in number, probably no more than two dozen, they meant business. Cars bristling with guns escorted CORE staff members in and out of the city, often driving all the way to Baton Rouge or Covington. Armed sentries patrolled the labor hall during mass meetings. In the evening and throughout the night, the Deacons patrolled the four main black neighborhoods, enforcing a strict curfew. "Any Negro on the streets after the curfew is ordered to go to their homes immediately," the FBI reported. Cars failing to give the right signal to Deacon patrols — a blink of the headlights off and back on — were liable to be stopped and questioned. Men with rifles perched on the rooftop of CORE's headquarters, a barbershop owned by Deacons vice president Royan Burris. A stand of shotguns formed part of Robert Hicks's arsenal, and he fired them at klansmen on at least one occasion. Hicks and Young were convinced that they could well be dead but for the Deacons, and they steadfastly resisted attempts to make them disband or disarm. When Governor McKeithen ordered state troopers to confiscate guns, the Deacons refused to yield them up. If blood flowed in the streets, retorted A. Z. Young, it would be shed from whites as well as blacks. Although heavily outnumbered by the Klan and the police, the Deacons enabled the Bogalusa movement to hang on.[24]

Bill Yates, among others, appreciated the possible dangers if the Deacons became too prominent. They "should definitely be kept in the background," he recommended, "as they are not a civil rights organization and they tend to put the concern for protection first and the actual issues second." But whatever their individual feelings about nonviolence, CORE workers had few qualms about accepting the Deacons' protection. Bogalusa was terrifying enough with it; without it, they would not have been able to set foot in the town. Moreover, the CORE people could witness how the Deacons prevented the town's black community from being completely paralyzed by fear of the Klan, how they inspired a growing band of people to join the movement. Lawyer Lolis Elie marvelled at the sheer bravery of the Deacons, at their complete refusal to be intimidated.

The formation of the Deacons seemed at first only to heighten the tension in and around Bogalusa. The Klan monitored the police radio frequencies to ascertain the time and whereabouts of BVL picketing. The Deacons listened in so they could track police movements and respond to harassing arrests. The police returned the Deacons' gaze with ill-concealed hostility. "My men are watching them closely," warned Claxton Knight. "If one of them makes the wrong move he's gonna get his head blown off." The FBI, which commandeered a motel to house dozens of agents assigned to the town, tried to shadow all three groups. Meanwhile Bogalusa became an armed camp. One reporter entered a general store and saw "an integrated line of fifteen customers" waiting to buy revolvers and rifles. In a seedy bar patronized by whites, another newsman saw a woman open her purse to reveal a full-size pistol. "Them integrationists ain't gonna get me." [25]

With the situation in Bogalusa at a dangerous impasse, CORE looked to Crown-Zellerbach to move things forward. In San Francisco, the company's national headquarters, the local CORE chapter formed a Committee for Concern to mobilize pressure; it bombarded the company with letters, phone calls, and telegrams asking Crown to publicly oppose the Klan, support the BVL's demands, and intercede with city, state, and federal officials. Committee chairman Wilfred Ussery sought a meeting with Crown's top officials. [26]

With a local payroll of more than $18 million, Crown still dominated Bogalusa's economy. But the days when the Great Southern Lumber Company had run the town with a paternalistic glove and an iron fist were long gone. By the 1930s company towns had become politically unpopular and economically burdensome, and when Gaylord acquired Bogalusa it applied the latest principles of business efficiency. Between 1950 and 1953 it sold five hundred company-owned houses, persuaded Louisiana Power and Light to buy the city's electric system, and turned Sullivan Hospital over to a nonprofit corporation. As it sloughed off its civic and welfare functions, Gaylord adopted a stance of noninterference in local politics. Crown inherited Gaylord's hands-off policy and had seen no reason to change it.[27]

CORE was initially optimistic that Crown's top executives would treat the aspirations of Bogalusa's blacks with sympathy and sensitivity. Crown was reputed to be a socially concerned corporation. James P. Mitchell, one of its senior vice presidents and a former Secretary of Labor under Eisenhower, had led a blue-ribbon commission to study Negro unemployment in the Bay Area; he also helped organize San Francisco's Human Relations Commission. The position Crown eventually adopted, after initial confusion and some internal debate, gave CORE and the BVL no cause for satisfaction, however. The company decided to snub the Committee for Concern and spurn the kind of activist role that CORE asked of it. Crown chairman Reed Hunt defined the crisis as a local problem that should be handled by plant manager Roy Ferguson, and Ferguson believed in nonintervention. "We don't believe in trying to run a town," he stated; Crown could not promote "social reform" or "lay down the law to Bogalusa." Nor would he undertake to rid the Crown plant of klansmen, explaining that "an employee's private life is his own." Besides, he saw no evidence of Klan activity — opposition to civil rights seemed to come from "an anti-Communist White Citizens Council." In the sphere of Crown's direct responsibility, the plant itself, Ferguson insisted that the company had clean hands: it was committed to fair employment and in compliance with the Civil Rights Act.

CORE greeted this last claim with disgust and disbelief. As Bill Yates told the Committee for Concern, "The worst segregated conditions in Bogalusa are inside the plant, and here they have full and complete jurisdiction." Like U.S. Steel's laissez-faire attitude during the 1963 Birmingham crisis, Crown's position contradicted the notion that northern-based big business acted as a positive force for desegregation. "Crown-Zellerbach's vaunted liberalism failed to materialize," writes Steven M. Gelber. "At precisely the time that Mitchell was exhorting his colleagues in the Bay area to go the second mile, Crown-Zellerbach was trying to turn its back on the racial problems of Bogalusa."[28]

That assessment was a little unfair: Crown executives were very much concerned about the Bogalusa situation. Ferguson wholeheartedly backed Cutrer's efforts to bring about voluntary desegregation, and in February he helped to organize a twenty-four-person Community Affairs Committee to advise the mayor and city council. Six Crown officials eventually sat on the committee. But voluntary desegregation again foundered on the rock of Klan intimidation. When testing resumed on February 21, not a single restaurant, café, or lunch counter would serve blacks. "Each time a Negro enters an establishment," CORE reported, "the manager says that he can neither serve nor protect them. Then he makes a phone call and within five minutes a mob comes in and forces them to leave." Any businesses that served blacks and whites on an integrated basis, even gas stations that let blacks use the toilets, found themselves on the Klan boycott list. The Klan set up a "wrecking crew" to "wreck" members who broke the boycott. Throughout March, as the protests led by Martin Luther King in Selma, Alabama, seized the attention of the world, overshadowing events in Bogalusa, this state of affairs continued. Cutrer and Ferguson seemed to believe that by ignoring the BVL, by ignoring the Klan, calm would return and CORE go away. Meanwhile, policemen and sheriff's deputies harassed the Deacons, arresting and beating three of them.[29]

CORE decided to up the ante, hoping that a buildup of outside support and more militant tactics would elicit state and federal intervention, forcing Cutrer to change his position. It started picketing stores on Columbia Street to force the employment of Negro clerks. On April 4 a group of students from Kansas State University arrived in Bogalusa to conduct a voter registration drive. A few days later CORE national director James Farmer flew in to lead a march to the city hall.

CORE's big push brought the Klan out in force. Three whites tried to grab Bill Yates as he left the Hicks residence on the morning of April 7; Yates put his car into a fast reverse and managed to escape. About sixty klansmen later met near the union hall where a voter registration class was in progress. They left two coffins, one bearing Yates's name, outside the hall, illuminated by floodlights. Shortly after midnight, klansmen returned to the Hicks home, firing two volleys as they drove by. During their second pass Robert Hicks fired back. The following morning the Kansas State students canvassed a black neighborhood in the northern part of town, but had to be pulled out when four carloads of klansmen chased them.

By the time Farmer arrived on the afternoon of April 8, Bogalusa was in a state of high tension and excitement. The Crown plant was shut, downtown stores had been closed all day, and the entire downtown area was cordoned off by police barricades. The police had turned back four hundred high school students who had tried marching to City Hall.

The next morning Farmer and Ronnie Moore left the union hall at the head of five hundred marchers, walking at a fast clip in sweltering heat, hearts in mouths, silent. About one hundred policemen were on hand to separate them from the klansmen along the two-mile route. It was not enough. Klansmen darted out from behind parked cars and struck marchers. One, Randle Pounds, grabbed Farmer from behind and raised a blackjack over his head before being wrestled to the ground and arrested. When a police car knocked down another klansman who suddenly ran toward the marchers, the whites turned their fury upon nearby reporters and photographers. Cameras were smashed and newsmen roughed up; even an FBI man was beaten. The march halted and returned to the union hall. Six hours later, on their second attempt, the marchers finally reached City Hall. Cutrer met them on the steps and insisted that all their demands could be settled at the conference table. He had earlier tried to calm three hundred whites whom he coyly described as "our real conservative residents." [30]

With a crisis of Selma-like dimensions on their hands, Cutrer and the city council came under intense pressure to negotiate. Agents of the Community Relations Service urged the town's merchants to meet with the BVL to discuss desegregation, warning that the Justice Department was prepared to prosecute if they failed to comply with the Civil Rights Act. Vice President Humphrey, who had earned a master's degree at LSU, expressed a personal interest in the Bogalusa situation, and he told Governor McKeithen of his concern during a visit to Baton Rouge on the day of the Farmer march.

It took weeks of Byzantine diplomacy, however, before Cutrer agreed to sit at the table with Robert Hicks and A. Z. Young. Cutrer had hitherto consistently refused to negotiate with the BVL, a stand fully supported by McKeithen and Crown-Zellerbach. Compelled of necessity to modify his position, Cutrer now insisted that the United Civic League, a hastily assembled group of conservative blacks, sit alongside the BVL in any negotiations. The BVL countered by proposing a "superconference" that would include the state's top businessmen and political leaders. McKeithen rejected the idea. Negotiations almost got under way on April 20, but fell through again when Cutrer insisted on excluding Gayle Jenkins, the BVL's secretary. Cutrer then announced that he would commission a "survey" of the town's black population to identify its authentic leaders, asserting that "CORE and the voters league are a small group of self-styled leaders who do not represent the Negro community." The BVL countered by swiftly gathering two thousand signatures of support. As the sparring went on, the BVL continued to picket stores and restaurants, sometimes shadowed by Klan counterpickets. James Farmer led another four-mile trek from the union hall to City Hall and back. Shortly thereafter the Justice Department filed suit against six segregated restaurants, its first legal intervention in Bogalusa and its first suit to integrate public accommodations in Louisiana.[31]

John Martzell helped to persuade Jesse Cutrer to negotiate with the BVL. Retained by the mayor on the recommendation of federal district judge Frank B. Ellis, Martzell was a young white lawyer with a private practice in New Orleans. He now found himself representing the City of Bogalusa in every phase of its entanglement with the civil rights movement. Martzell hailed from Shreveport but was no segregationist; he had recently been a law clerk to Skelly Wright. He believed that the city's problems had to be resolved through negotiation, and he made a point of getting to know the other side. On a vacation trip to New York, he made a spur-of-the-moment decision to call up CORE headquarters and invite himself over. Upon meeting James Farmer, he recalled, "It was as clear as a bell to me that CORE didn't know zip about what was going on down there [in Bogalusa]. . . . They didn't know about the thing, they were unfamiliar with it, they clearly had no control over it, and it was what it appeared to be, which was a grassroots operation." Returning to Bogalusa, Martzell disabused Cutrer of the notion that "outside agitators" from New York were causing the trouble. If he wanted to address the city's problems, Martzell added, Cutrer had to deal with Young and Hicks. Martzell met Lolis Elie, who represented the BVL, to set up a meeting between the two sides.[32]

Governor McKeithen also wanted to resolve the conflict, and he prevailed upon Victor Bussie, Camille Gravel, and Michael O'Keeffe to act as mediators. It was a shrewdly chosen triumvirate. O'Keeffe, a young state senator, was the scion of a distinguished political family that included a mayor of New Orleans. Gravel, an Alexandria lawyer, had been a close ally of Earl Long and a Democratic National Committee member. Bussie headed the Louisiana AFL-CIO, had also been close to Earl Long, and was the most powerful labor leader in the state's history. All three were racial liberals; all three had political clout. Anticipating an explosion of Klan fury when negotiations commenced, McKeithen assigned another three hundred state police to Bogalusa. He also dissuaded Leander Perez and Sheriff Jim Clark of Selma, Alabama, from attending a rally organized by the "United Conservatives of Bogalusa." Even so, three thousand whites turned out to hear Klan leader Saxon Farmer and assorted Citizens Council speakers.

The intercession of the triumvirate delighted the Bogalusa Voters League. Lolis Elie, however, was skeptical. When the three men visited Martzell's law office in downtown New Orleans, Elie voiced that skepticism in such an abrasive manner that they walked out. "They were all insulted at the suggestion that they might not be absolutely liberal," Martzell recalled. The triumvirate helped to legitimate negotiations in the eyes of the Bogalusa city council, but its role was largely ceremonial. Elie and Martzell served as the principal facilitators. Drawing up elaborate ground rules for the talks, including an insistence on courtesy titles, the two men developed a close rapport.[33]

Concerned that they should not be overawed and outmaneuvered by the whites, the BVL team spent long, hot Sunday afternoons honing their negotiating skills in the law office of Collins, Douglas and Elie. With Jack Nelson and his white friends taking the roles of Cutrer, the police chief, and the city commissioners, the blacks learned what to expect from the opposition — time-wasting, agenda-stuffing, buck-passing — and how to react. "We'd teach them how to negotiate," Nelson recalled.[34]

On May 16 ten members of the BVL finally met Cutrer and the city council, the triumvirate sitting in to ensure fair play. As the talks proceeded, Martzell recalled,

> We'd start taking breaks, because it was desperately hot. And we'd all go over to the Coke machine. And they began to — you know, Americans are gregarious, southerners even more so — they began to see each other as human beings. And finally, I'll never forget one of the great moments when Jesse Cutrer said, "Mr. Young, I have to tell you, because you've got to understand my problem, the people of this city are just about ready to lynch me." And A. Z. Young said, "Let me tell you, Mr. Mayor, that I have a similar problem, because as I sit here I keep waiting to hear in the distance a march coming down . . . singing 'We Shall Overcome.' That's my problem."

The exchange marked a turning point of sorts, especially for the whites. As pickup trucks driven by klansmen slowly circled City Hall, Cutrer and his colleagues steeled themselves to make concessions.

The discussions yielded a number of commitments by the city. The council undertook to repeal its segregation ordinances and to integrate all public facilities. It promised to improve lighting, sewerage, and paving in Negro neighborhoods and to enforce housing codes more rigorously. It promised to hire black policemen and consider the employment of blacks in other city departments. Although the council refused to repeal the emergency ordinance enacted on April 7 that limited picketing to two people, it indicated willingness to reconsider the law's draconian definition of "disturbing the peace." Two days after the meeting, Cutrer announced the agreement in a radio speech. "The time has come to try to find solutions to our problems and recognize the rights and responsibilities of all our citizens."

An uncharitable critic might judge the agreement no more than a rehash of old promises and a grudging bow to the inevitable. Such an appraisal would be overly harsh. By putting these commitments in writing the council pledged itself to action, not just words. For example, the city had long ago stated that blacks would be permitted to take the civil service test for entry into the police force, but no blacks had ever taken the test, and it was widely assumed, even by blacks, that no black candidate would ever score high enough. Now, with a behind-the-scenes assist from Victor Bussie, the city saw to it that two blacks took the test and passed with flying colors, achieving the highest test scores ever. The council's acceptance of integration had equal significance, for it indicated, in effect, that it would no longer tolerate the Klan dictating to the community. And that took physical and political nerve. Lolis Elie considered Jesse Cutrer "a courageous man who loved his town more than his political career."[35]

A leaflet entitled "Who Bought Jesse Cutrer?" flooded the town. It provided a list of public officials who "should be tarred and feathered," including Cutrer, McKeithen, and Sheriff Dorman Crowe. The list did not include Arnold Spiers, the commissioner of public safety, or Chief of Police Claxton Knight. The meaning of these omissions was not too difficult to fathom in light of the violence that erupted in Cassidy Park.[36]

On the afternoon of May 19, Sam Barnes and Robert Hicks led a convoy of cars to Cassidy Park, a facility hitherto barred to blacks but now presumed to be integrated by virtue of Mayor Cutrer's agreement. The BVL telephoned the FBI and the city police well ahead of time to inform them of the test.

As a group of black children headed for the play area, fifteen to twenty white men, who were chatting with police officers, started toward them. Some brandished sticks; others wrapped belts around their fists. An uneven free-for-all erupted as the whites cursed, slapped, and chased the black testers. After five minutes about a dozen city policemen, sheriff's deputies, and state troopers waded into the melee, ordering the blacks to leave the park. As the blacks retreated to their cars, a police dog sank its teeth into the leg of fifteen-year-old Gregory Hicks. Deputy sheriff Vertrees Adams spotted Sam Barnes's pistol and arrested him for carrying a concealed weapon. Luckily for Barnes, two FBI agents followed the police station wagon between Bogalusa and Franklinton. Upon his arrival at the parish jail, however, Barnes was beaten up by three black convicts, one holding him, two hitting him.

About five hundred whites congregated at Cassidy Park the next day. When no blacks appeared, they beat up a photographer for the *Times-Picayune*, Terry Friedman, knocking him down half a dozen times in plain view of nearby policemen. Friedman shouted for help at the top of his voice, but the police only sauntered over when he played dead. They were "very nasty and belligerent," Friedman recalled, assistant police chief L. C. Terrell telling him to "get out of town." The bruised and shaken newsman drove out of Bogalusa with a state police escort, only to double back when the occupant of a passing car trained a gun on him. Friedman's camera ended up in a canal.[37]

The efforts of Cutrer and McKeithen to establish calm in Bogalusa quickly unraveled. The mayor's commitment to desegregate municipal facilities was rendered meaningless by his decision to close the city's parks. And the delinquent behavior of the police at Cassidy Park exposed the continuing power of the Klan to intimidate blacks and dictate to City Hall.

CORE, however, thrived on confrontation, and the Cassidy Park debacle prompted it to resume and intensify its picketing and plan further marches to City Hall. On May 29, a busy Saturday, the BVL sent out a handful of pickets shortly after stores opened. After each serious clash with white onlookers, the pickets withdrew to the Burris barbershop — only to reappear soon afterwards in twice the strength. This tactic continued for about six hours, to the fury of white shoppers and onlookers. By midafternoon, hundreds of whites roamed Columbia Street in crowds, heckling and assaulting the pickets. Fighting reached such a pitch that police and state troopers moved in "shoulder to shoulder, like a Roman phalanx," forming a human barricade in front of the Burris barbershop, the BVL's picketing headquarters. Major Tom Bradley of the state police persuaded A. Z. Young and Charles Sims to end the picketing. The confrontation resumed the following Monday, and 125 state troopers and 34 city police were hard pressed to keep order. "Crowds of whites remained on the streets . . . until the stores closed," noted one reporter. On June 1, Cutrer banned all marches.

The next day two black Washington Parish sheriff's deputies, O'Neal Moore and Creed Rogers, were patrolling near the hamlet of Varnado, a few miles north of Bogalusa, when gunshots rang out from a passing pickup truck. One of the shots wounded Rogers in the shoulder; the other struck Moore in the head, killing him instantly. About an hour later a police roadblock across the Mississippi state line stopped a vehicle that matched the one described by Rogers. It was driven by Ernest Ray McElveen, a forty-one-year old Crown-Zellerbach laboratory technician who sported membership cards in the National States' Rights Party and the Citizens Council of Greater New Orleans. Although McElveen was arrested and charged with Moore's murder, the case against him eventually collapsed for lack of evidence. Moore's killers (police believed that three men took part in the crime) escaped justice.[38]

The conflict now shifted to the federal courthouse in New Orleans. On June 25 Nils Douglas filed *Hicks* v. *Knight,* an action to compel the police to protect black demonstrators instead of harassing them, beating them, arresting them, and leaving them at the mercy of white mobs.

Judge Herbert W. Christenberry had a rather fearsome reputation as a tough, plainspoken, no-nonsense judge who did not like to be trifled with. The first to admit that he was "no swinging liberal" (in 1954 he issued an injunction that effectively destroyed the strawberry growers union), he had nonetheless compiled a record in civil rights cases that reflected abhorrence of racial discrimination and support for federal law. Lolis Elie, who had heard Christenberry teach law, respected the judge and anticipated a sympathetic hearing. Christenberry did not disappoint him.

The incident at Cassidy Park formed the centerpiece of the BVL's case, and Alvin Bronstein, chief staff counsel for the Lawyers Constitutional Defense

Committee, put Gregory Hicks on the stand to describe what had transpired on May 19, including how he had been bitten by a police dog. Having been warned that Christenberry was a rather stuffy, straightlaced judge who did not take kindly to courtroom stunts, Bronstein decided not to ask young Gregory, the fifteen-year-old son of Robert Hicks, to show the scar. As Hicks left the witness stand, however, Christenberry leaned over the bench and asked him to roll up his trouser leg to reveal the red gash above his knee. Years later, Bronstein could remember the stunned silence in the courtroom at that moment. "The judge looked at [Gregory Hicks], looked over at the table where the police chief and the sheriff and the deputies were sitting, sort of with a fierce look and then said, 'All right son, you can go now.'" On that dramatic note the first day of hearings ended.

Christenberry's skepticism of the police testimony soon became apparent. When Major Bradley stubbornly insisted that he had never heard policemen or white onlookers curse demonstrators, the disbelieving judge quipped, "You hear all right?" Captain Haynes "Twister" Wascom of the city police force suggested that the police dog had bitten Gregory Hicks either by accident or because Hicks had kicked at the animal. Christenberry was incredulous. "Do you want me to believe that boy . . . in the presence of a police officer, that he would kick at a police dog? Well I don't."

Early in the hearings, Christenberry made plain his view that the police had it within their power to protect demonstrators. "I am going to say for the record that . . . in a community the size of Bogalusa — and I know something about that country, I lived in St. Tammany for a long time — when the police decide they are going to enforce the law equally, they can do it, if they want to." On July 10 he ordered the city and parish police to protect the plaintiffs' rights to picket and assemble peacefully. His toughly worded injunction commanded the police to refrain from treating the plaintiffs with violence, harassment, intimidation, verbal abuse, unnecessary force, and unlawful arrests.[39]

By the time Christenberry issued his injunction, the atmosphere in Bogalusa had once again reached the boiling point. During a BVL march on July 8, Hattie Mae Hill, a black teenager, had been struck on the head by a rock; when two Deacons, Milton Johnson and Henry Austin, tried to drive her to safety, a crowd of whites attacked their car. Other whites spotted Gardner Compton, a freelance photographer from New York. "He's a white CORE nigger!" a woman yelled. "Kill him!" The bearded photographer found himself being furiously assailed "by a woman with a squeaky voice." Meanwhile, a white man, Alton Crowe, had pulled Milton Johnson out of the car and, with several others, proceeded to pummel him. Other whites threw punches at

Henry Austin through the car window. After failing to push the whites away and rescue his friend, Austin shot and seriously wounded Alton Crowe.[40]

The shooting, and Christenberry's order two days later, intensified, if that were possible, the fury of local ultrasegregationists. Thousands of whites turned out to hear J. B. Stoner and Connie Lynch, leaders of the Atlanta-based National States' Rights Party. "The nigger is not a human being," Stoner railed. "He is somewhere between the white man and the ape. . . . What the nigger really wants is our white women." The crowd lapped it up and returned the following evening for another dose of invective. Vertrees Young, angrily shaking his head, sought to mount the platform and speak in rebuttal; the ranting klansmen turned him away. Once Bogalusa's most respected and influential citizen, Young wept with frustration when Mayor Cutrer advised him that he, Young, could do nothing to help. Cutrer's own popularity had plummeted: over three thousand whites signed a recall petition, and only a technicality (the signatures were on the wrong form) prevented his opponents from forcing a special election.[41]

With the situation spiraling out of control, Cutrer and other city officials journeyed to Baton Rouge to ask McKeithen to send in the National Guard. While they debated the pros and cons, Vice President Humphrey phoned McKeithen and warned that if he committed the National Guard, it would be extremely difficult to extricate them. McKeithen sat on the steps of the governor's mansion beside Cutrer and Martzell. "No, mayor," he decided, "I think you've got to handle this situation yourself." But he assured Cutrer that he would send in enough state troopers to ensure order.

McKeithen also made a personal attempt to broker a pact, and on July 12 sent his personal plane to fly Robert Hicks and A. Z. Young to the governor's mansion. When the towering figure of Young, well over six feet tall, walked through the door McKeithen could not contain his laughter. "You're the guy they're going to push around up there?" he asked. McKeithen proposed a thirty-day "cooling-off" period; in return, he promised to set up more negotiations and see to it that Connie Lynch and J. B. Stoner left Bogalusa. "If we don't find answers in thirty days," he promised, "you can start demonstrating again." Young and Hicks agreed to place his proposal before the BVL. After a long debate, however, the league's executive committee rejected the moratorium. The skepticism of CORE workers and the opposition of Lolis Elie influenced the outcome. So did a passionate speech by black author Louis Lomax, who had become enamored of the Deacons for Defense after Charles Sims appeared on his television talk show in Los Angeles.

McKeithen refused to give up so easily, and the following day he flew to Bogalusa to meet the BVL's leaders. "Why don't you all give me a chance?"

he asked. "You've been demonstrating for sixty days and what did it get you?" When Charles Sims retorted, "It got you here, didn't it?" it became apparent that the famous McKeithen charm had met its match. During the ninety-minute meeting, held at the local airport, a combative Louis Lomax did much of the talking; reporters, witnessing the exchange through a glass partition, saw the two men shaking their fingers at each other. McKeithen was hugely impressed by Lomax and later went out of his way to talk with the black writer in private. The governor failed to move the BVL, however. To Roy Reed of the *New York Times,* the BVL's refusal to be sweet-talked marked a "milestone in the Southern Negro's campaign for effective political power." Here was a "brand new interest group in Louisiana politics — a group of non-professional, non-middle class and until recently non-political Negroes." There were still plenty of other blacks, however, who were willing, eager even, to sit down at the table with a Louisiana governor. The day after his abortive mission to Bogalusa, McKeithen met twenty prominent blacks in Baton Rouge to discuss the creation of a statewide biracial commission. He made no secret of his desire to use such a commission to head off demonstrations and undercut CORE. Despite this intent — or possibly because of it — the NAACP and most older black leaders welcomed McKeithen's plan.[42]

After the failure of McKeithen's mediation effort, Cutrer and A. Z. Young appealed to President Johnson for federal intervention. Johnson responded by sending assistant attorney general John Doar, the government's most experienced racial troubleshooter.[43]

During his four days in Bogalusa, Doar was appalled by how the Klan still roamed the streets and continued to assault civil rights demonstrators. The police faced, it must be said, a public order nightmare. Klansmen had a remarkable facility for blending in with the milling white onlookers, darting out to strike demonstrators and then darting back to the crowded sidewalks. On July 11, for example, an FBI agent saw forty to fifty young white men moving toward a BVL march; when a contingent of state troopers approached, they "seemed to melt into the crowd and the clubs, sticks, and ballbats . . . seemed to disappear." On other occasions, troopers were lured away from the marches by false reports of nearby altercations; "when they ran off to investigate, members of the Klan . . . coming from the opposite direction would throw punches or flail away with clubs at the unprotected marchers."[44]

Colonel Thomas D. Burbank, who commanded the state troopers, was a highly competent professional who wanted to avoid any repetition of the August 1963 incident in Plaquemine, when, in his absence, state police and local lawmen had run amok and attacked a civil rights march. Some of his men, however, approached the distasteful task of protecting demonstrators with distinct lack of enthusiasm. His commander in Ruston had bluntly warned that troopers from north Louisiana might prove unreliable and that he could not even guarantee his own behavior. By and large, however, the state troopers performed their unenviable job with discipline and efficiency.[45]

The same could not be said of the city and parish police, however, who were all but ignoring Christenberry's injunction. On July 16, for example, Doar saw whites attack pickets at the Pine Tree Plaza shopping center; the next day a barber drenched two white pickets with a hose and smeared soap on their arms and shoulders, commenting, "You pickets smell like niggers and need a bath." During the first incident, the police were conspicuously absent when the attacks took place; when they finally arrived on the scene they arrested two of the beaten pickets. During the second incident, policemen stood by laughing.[46]

Doar had seen enough. He decided to make Bogalusa a test case of the government's ability to enforce the 1964 Civil Rights Act. The Justice Department intervened in the *Hicks* case to seek a judgment of criminal and civil contempt against local police officials Arnold Spiers and Claxton Knight. It also charged deputy sheriff Vertrees Adams of the Washington Parish canine squad with four counts of brutality. A third suit sought to integrate three Bogalusa restaurants. Finally, the government sought an injunction against the Original Knights of the Ku Klux Klan and thirty-five individual klansmen. "The aim of such legal saturation," the department told presidential aide Bill Moyers, "is to bring the force of federal law into play in an unusually tough mill town."[47]

When he learned how the police had flouted his July 10 injunction, Herbert Christenberry was outraged. During a two-day hearing in New Orleans, the judge "watched in anger" when he saw a film of pickets being assaulted and "shook his head in astonishment" as a string of witnesses related tales of police indifference and brutality. On July 30 he found Spiers and Knight guilty of civil contempt and ordered them to devise a plan, in consultation with the Justice Department, to implement his previous order. Such a plan, he insisted, must include the instruction and training of police officers, written statements of compliance from every officer, and regular reports to the court on police performance. Spiers and Knight would be subject to jail and a fine of $100 for each day of continued noncompliance. In effect, the United States District Court had taken over control of the Bogalusa police department. It was an astonishing and novel assertion of judicial power.[48]

The Justice Department's civil action against the Klan, although not unprecedented, was the first instance of its kind in Louisiana and only the third in the South. It required considerable legal ingenuity and a massive investment of FBI resources. The Justice Department had to decide, for example, on what basis to seek the protection of pickets. Historically, the courts had treated the right to picket as a rather "weak" First Amendment right compared to freedom of speech and freedom of the press. Doar therefore framed the issue another way: in attacking demonstrators who picketed stores, he argued, klansmen were seeking to deny the pickets equal employment opportunities, thus violating the 1964 Civil Rights Act. Doar asked the FBI to ascertain whether the establishments being picketed were engaged in interstate commerce and employed over one hundred people, thus bringing them within the purview of the act. Doar also asked the Bureau to assemble newspaper photographs and television news film showing pickets being assaulted: although pictures merely supplemented the agents' reports, they had a dramatic impact when exhibited in court. The FBI was further charged with assembling Klan literature. Doar specifically wanted to know whether Klan leaflets had been prepared on city attorney Robert Rester's typewriter.[49]

In one sense, the hearings on the Klan before Judges Herbert Christenberry, Robert Ainsworth, and John Minor Wisdom proved anticlimactic. The government subpoenaed over one hundred witnesses, hoping to expose the Klan to the withering air of publicity. However, because the defendants admitted most of the complaint, only a few witnesses testified and the Klan managed to avoid extended scrutiny. Charles Christmas, a businessman from Amite, in Tangipahoa Parish, proved a slippery witness, calmly denying any connection between the Anti-Communist Christian Association, which he admitted heading, and the Ku Klux Klan, which he claimed had dissolved four months earlier. Saxon Farmer, the number two klansman, was more obsequious but no more forthcoming. Johnny Magee, the Klan's treasurer, told the court that the organization's financial records had been destroyed and that he could not recall who controlled the Klan's finances. "This court will not be trifled with," Wisdom warned, and when threatened with contempt Christmas and Farmer produced the names of 87 "former Klansmen." The FBI obtained another list, purloined by a white truck driver, containing 151 additional names. Given the strength of the Klan in the area, however, most klansmen managed to avoid being named in court.[50]

Nevertheless, the government had demonstrated its case to the satisfaction of the court. In a judgment graced with the historical insight, literary style, and moral principle that characterized his civil rights decisions, John Minor Wisdom described the Klan as "ignorant bullies, callous of the harm they know they are doing." Whether "cloaked and hooded as members of the Original Knights of the Ku Klux Klan, or skulking in anonymity as members of a sham organization, the 'Anti-Communist Christian Association,' or brazenly resorting to violence on the open streets of Bogalusa," klansmen had the same purpose and used the same methods. Exploiting hate, ignorance, and prejudice, they relied on "systematic economic coercion, varieties of intimidation, and physical violence in attempting to frustrate the national policy expressed in civil rights legislation." The three judges enjoined the defendants from engaging in threats, violence, and intimidation. For the next three years, Charles Christmas had to file monthly reports of compliance, including membership records and the time and place of Klan meetings, with the federal court. The publicity punctured the Klan's mystique and eroded its power to intimidate. As Jesse Cutrer put it, "When we discovered that the Klan were the guys on Columbia Road who had been holding up the parking meters for the last twenty years, it suddenly put them in a new perspective."[51]

By the summer of 1965 the Klan had become a powerful force in Louisiana, its acts of violence increasingly reckless. Although it was never proved, few doubted that klansmen carried out the murder of deputy sheriff O'Neal Moore or that the Klan lay behind the bombing campaign that resulted in a dozen explosions in New Orleans between March and July (targets included the church of Reverend Albert D'Orlando and the law offices of Collins, Douglas and Elie). Its ability to attract open public support enhanced the Klan's influence; Klan meetings advertised under cover names such as the "United Conservatives" drew thousands of enthusiasts. On July 4, for example, about five thousand people attended a rally in front of the state capitol in Baton Rouge to hear that faded hero of the ultraright, retired General Edwin A. Walker. On September 6, on the eve of the federal hearings on New Orleans, some three thousand whites rallied in support of the Klan at the Bogalusa airport; driving from downtown, their carcade stretched for three miles. The Klan could also count on sympathy and sometimes overt support from some politicians. Under the pretext of "investigating" it, the state legislature's Un-American Activities Committee issued a report on the Klan that amounted to a virtual endorsement. Civil district judge John R. Rarick, one of the most extreme and politically ambitious segregationists in the state, assiduously cultivated Klan support.[52]

An inspector in the FBI's New Orleans office considered the injunction hearings to have been a highly effective weapon against the Klan. "Stripping this veil of security by exposing to public censure the loutish types who thrive in Klandom's concealment will go far in reducing the volume of crimes which have confronted us in recent years." The FBI also used some highly imaginative techniques to infiltrate, destabilize, and discredit the Klan, the kind of covert tactics previously reserved for the Communist Party and other left-wing groups. The extent and effectiveness of this undercover campaign will probably never be known, for the FBI has refused to release the bulk of its files on the Klan, and its own account is highly self-serving. But it doubtless exacted a toll. The FBI, responding to pressure from President Johnson, had blanketed Bogalusa: at one point there were 120 agents in and around the town. "They tried to blend in by dressing like thugs," recalled John Martzell, but they could always be spotted "because they were the only guys with short-sleeve plaid shirts that were pressed. And they were the only guys who wore khaki pants with a crease in them."

If the Justice Department's attack weakened the Klan as an organization, however, the Klan spirit lived on. On March 10, 1966, for example, Thomas Bennett tried to make a phone call at a Bogalusa gas station, only to find a black Army officer, Donald R. Sims, at the call box. When he returned shortly afterward to discover the phone still occupied, Bennett went home to fetch a rifle and shot Sims three times in the back. Two months later, a group of whites attacked Fletcher Anderson after he left a café that had been integrated by federal court order. Even in 1967, three years after the Civil Rights Act, blacks did not enter restaurants without protection from the Deacons and without first alerting the police. After the schools integrated in the fall of 1965, the harassment of black children in the formerly white schools continued year after year. As Gayle Jenkins noted in 1967, the klansmen "don't care too much about the injunction." The Klan remained a menacing presence in Bogalusa.[53]

The federal judgment in *Hicks* v. *Knight* turned out to be similarly indecisive. Even after Christenberry's tough contempt order, the right to demonstrate remained fragile and dangerous. In October 1965 the city banned all marches from 6 P.M. to 8 A.M. That same month, when black children began a school boycott, the school board obtained an injunction against six leaders of the BVL and had them arrested for contributing to the delinquency of minors. Alvin Bronstein tried to have the case removed to federal court, but Judge E. Gordon West rejected his petition after delivering an extended monologue on the evils of communism. The events that followed caused October 20 to become known as "Bloody Wednesday." Two children's marches that day resulted in dozens of arrests, and blacks gathered outside the labor hall in the evening clamoring for a march to City Hall. Unwilling to violate the city's ban on night marches, Robert Hicks told the people to disperse. The police then chased them off the streets, snatching people from cars and pursuing them into bars and cafés. "I'll show you who rules this town," vowed Claxton Knight as he stormed into the Bamboo Bar to arrest Henry Austin. Willie Hughes, frail and elderly, was told to clear his pool hall; the police then shoved him onto a bus and took him to jail. A minister who bailed out his son-in-law at two in the morning was tailed by two sheriff's deputies, arrested for carrying a pocket knife, bundled facedown onto the floor of a police car, and taken to jail. In all, the police arrested nineteen people, all but one of whom received beatings of varying severity.[54]

During further contempt hearings in December, in which the Justice Department again intervened to support the plaintiffs, Christenberry expressed outrage over the police rampage. "I think the record shows that this was a deliberate scheme to harass these people, confuse them, and throw them in jail, in as wild a manner as possible." After hearing a parade of black witnesses, he flatly disbelieved the policemen who testified they had used only reasonable force.

> I have seen the scars, the abrasions, the photographs of these Negroes. They speak eloquently of what happened, and I know I couldn't have tried this case from its inception without knowing what the reputation of some of these officers is among the Negroes in that community for their violent conduct in handling Negroes. And I can't believe that some of these people would have offered the resistance that these officers would pretend that they did. I can't believe that a seventeen year old boy was going to put up a terrific fight against three police officers who had billies in their hands and guns on their hips. I believe I have had enough experience to know that these are not reasonable statements.

In one respect, he noted, the situation in Bogalusa had actually deteriorated: having curbed the white mobs, "the police and the sheriff are taking up where the citizenry left off. They are committing the violence themselves."[55]

Despite these stern words, however, Christenberry postponed any further action in the case pending the trial of deputy sheriff Vertrees Adams and "other developments." But in 1966 Adams, the only officer to stand trial on criminal charges, was acquitted of beating prisoners in jail and of paying prisoners to beat up Sam Barnes. Movement lawyers did manage to have the state court injunction against the BVL leaders lifted, but only in exchange for dropping the *Hicks* v. *Knight* contempt charges. In November 1966 Christenberry refused to allow contempt proceedings against Haynes "Twister" Wascom, who injured Jeffrey Horton, a white CORE worker, with a blow to the head from a billy club. In 1969 the judge finally declared the issues in *Hicks* v. *Knight* moot. None of the four defendants cited for contempt after "Bloody Wednesday" incurred any punishment.[56]

On the political front, the Bogalusa Voters League still faced an uphill struggle. By asking the "triumvirate" to intervene, Governor McKeithen had legitimized the idea of direct negotiations between the BVL and City Hall. But while further talks took place in August, Jesse Cutrer's days as mayor were numbered. In 1966 he suffered defeat at the hands of former mayor Curt Siegelin. Siegelin was not an ultrasegregationist, but he was attuned to the mood of the white majority and had no enthusiasm for dealing with the BVL. Indeed, Siegelin tried to avoid dealing with blacks at all. For example, after refusing to appoint a black member to the city housing authority, the mayor set up a "citizens advisory committee" that supposedly included three blacks, but this committee existed only on paper: it never met and its black members remained oblivious of their appointment. When compelled to allow for black participation in its Head Start program, the city ensured that conservatives effectively shut out the BVL. It could afford to snub the BVL because the latter lacked political clout. A year after the Voting Rights Act, blacks made up a third of the population of Washington Parish but only a sixth of the voters. In 1966 blacks in Bogalusa still had to make a twenty-one mile trip to the parish courthouse in Franklinton in order to register to vote.[57]

Two steps forward and one step back: the victories of the Bogalusa Voters League came slowly, equivocally, and at great cost. Federal intervention was no magic wand. It could not transform race relations overnight. It could not reconcile whites to integration and loss of status.

Yet the victories should not be discounted. With bitter reluctance the police curbed their predilection for beating, or allowing others to beat, people who marched or picketed on the streets of Bogalusa. "Yesterday was history in the Bogalusa City Court," wrote lawyer Harris David in October 1965, after Saxon Farmer was convicted for carrying a concealed weapon and failing to move on. In April 1966, police discovered Farmer haranguing about fifty young white men near a black high school. His audience melted away when the police reminded them that the federal injunction against the Klan applied to them as well as Farmer. A few months later, the police arrested Farmer's brother when, during another confrontation outside a high school, he aimed a shotgun at A. Z. Young. In 1967, after almost two years, the BVL persuaded a federal judge to overturn the city's ban on night marches. A BVL march from Bogalusa to Baton Rouge that year helped to bring about the employment of the first black state troopers. In 1968 Robert Hicks obtained an injunction against the Bogalusa Housing Authority and HUD to prevent the location of new public housing units in all-black neighborhoods.[58]

The movement's most clear-cut triumph involved Crown-Zellerbach. In July 1965 company officials finally assented to talks with the BVL. During a four-hour session on July 15, A. Z. Young, Robert Hicks, and Gayle Jenkins pressed for the hiring of black women and fairer promotion procedures. The trio proved articulate and determined, appealing in turn to the company's self-interest and its sense of fair play. They pleaded for a special effort to promote blacks according to length of service, arguing that past discrimination, inferior schools, and irrelevant tests all put blacks at an unfair disadvantage. "I am just as sharp as either one of those [white] boys they put over me," asserted Young. "Everybody down there knows it. . . . The Negro in this community at last has said 'I'm tired.' Everything he puts his hand to he's got to pick it up with his muscles. . . . I want to use my mind." Gayle Jenkins made plant manager Ferguson squirm by repeatedly challenging him to defend the existing transfer procedures. Ferguson could not, admitting "this is a problem."[59]

Following the negotiations, Crown merged its segregated lines of progression and decreed that applicants for transfer would not have to quit their current job. However, the company's freedom of action was severely restricted by its contracts with the white-dominated unions. Thus promotion was still based on job seniority rather than length of service, and blacks found themselves locked into the lower-paid jobs that they already held, with little or no chance of advancement. When further negotiations revealed the company's unwillingness to confront the unions, Robert Hicks filed a complaint of discrimination against Crown in federal court. The Department of Justice intervened to support it.[60]

In 1968, U.S. district judge Frederick J. R. Heebe ordered Crown to abolish its system of "job seniority" and replace it by a system of "mill seniority." He enjoined the paper unions when they called a strike aimed at preventing the new system from being implemented. Two years later, Heebe ordered Crown to stop using the testing program it had instituted in 1963: testing blacks for jobs which whites had previously acquired without taking tests constituted "the boldest form of discrimination." (Heebe also noted that blacks had been disadvantaged by segregated schools and that the tests were in any case irrelevant to the jobs at the mill.) It was game, set, and match for the BVL. Robert Hicks received a well-deserved promotion. In the coming years, however, the decline of Crown-Zellerbach's workforce took some of the shine off this stellar victory: by the 1980s the plant had shed two-thirds of its workforce and Bogalusa had lost over one quarter of its 1960 population.[61]

Why was federal intervention in Bogalusa so extensive and forceful? Federal concern over civil rights reached its zenith in the spring and summer of 1965, following the Selma protests led by Martin Luther King. This was precisely when the conflict in Bogalusa unfolded. The Bogalusa Voters League was thus a beneficiary of the Selma crisis, which peaked in March 1965 and sparked unprecedentedly strong federal action. In Alabama, Judge Frank Johnson had set a new standard in federal protection of the right to demonstrate, authorizing a fifty-mile march from Selma to Montgomery. Judge Christenberry's injunction against the Bogalusa police is impossible to imagine without such a precedent. Similarly, the Justice Department's injunction proceedings against the Original Knights of the Ku Klux Klan came at a time when the murder of Viola Liuzzo during the Selma protests had provoked a wave of revulsion against Klan violence, moving President Johnson to declare "war on the Klan." Selma also helped the Bogalusa movement by encouraging a fresh influx of northern sympathizers into the South.

Bogalusa illustrated the critical importance of the 1964 Civil Rights Act in both stimulating black militancy and bringing forth federal intervention. Presidents Kennedy and Johnson had hoped that the act would get blacks "off the streets and into the courts" by providing legal remedies for discrimination, but its effect was to get blacks into the courts *and* into the streets. The Civil Rights Act gave blacks a powerful incentive to demonstrate when, as in the case of Bogalusa, whites sought to preserve the racial status quo. They now demonstrated in the knowledge that the law was on their side and that the federal government was their active ally. Litigation did not preempt direct action; rather, direct action stimulated litigation.

The Civil Rights Act also gave the federal government powerful legal cover for directly intervening in the heart of the South's social, economic, and political affairs. Before the act, when demonstrators were jailed or beaten, as in Plaquemine in 1963, the Kennedy administration had usually turned the other way, disclaiming any legal grounds for action. With no formal mechanism for intervention, the government had relied upon persuasion and informal mediation when confronted with southern racial crises, employing coercion only if whites brazenly flouted important federal court orders. In general, it had followed a policy of the least possible intervention consistent with maintaining the integrity of the federal judiciary. It had followed the courts, not led them. With the Civil Rights Act the government caught up with the courts and in some respects overtook them; it now initiated rather than merely reacted. Virtually none of the actions of the federal government in Bogalusa would have been possible before 1964. Without the Civil Rights Act it could not have sued to integrate public accommodations, integrate public schools, or integrate the Crown-Zellerbach plant. Without the Civil Rights Act it could not have maintained a team of full-time mediators in the town in the form of the Community Relations Service. And without the Civil Rights Act it would not have sought injunctions against the Klan and the Bogalusa police force.

The Bogalusa Voters League could claim another, albeit indirect, accomplishment: Governor McKeithen's creation of a statewide biracial commission, the "Commission on Human Relations, Rights, and Responsibilities." Having personally intervened in two racial trouble spots — Jonesboro, with some success, and Bogalusa, to no avail — McKeithen needed some means of insulating himself from local crises of this kind. Personal intervention not only carried a diminishing chance of success with each instance but also threatened to tarnish his reputation, especially among white voters. A "nonpolitical," blue-ribbon commission, operating quietly in the background to defuse racial confrontations, provided an excellent buffer between McKeithen and irate whites who might feel threatened and betrayed by any concessions made to blacks. And, of course, by packing the commission with lawyers, ministers, NAACP moderates, and other "establishment" types, McKeithen hoped, in his own words, "to keep down disorders with the sheer weight of the prominent people backing the commission." Thus the CORE-inspired contagion of Bogalusa (as McKeithen saw it) might be prevented from spreading across the state.[62]

The advent of the state commission also signaled an important shift in the thinking of Louisiana's business community. McKeithen formed the commission at the instance of the Committee for a Better Louisiana (CABL), to whom he turned for ideas in the spring of 1965 as the crisis in Bogalusa succeeded the one in Jonesboro. Created in 1962, CABL was a powerful business lobby aimed at influencing state government; it included executives from virtually every important economic enterprise in Louisiana. Its mission was to improve the dismal statistics that placed Louisiana at or near the bottom of virtually every economic league table. At its inception, CABL did not even entertain the notion that racial discrimination, and racial tension, might be a cause of the state's deteriorating economic performance. Race had not been mentioned at its organizational meeting.

In 1963, however, as the shock waves of the Birmingham crisis rippled through the state, businessmen awakened to the fact that racial violence and racial disorder acted as a powerful brake on economic growth. Businessmen took the lead in setting up quasi-official biracial committees in Hammond, Baton Rouge, and Lafayette. By 1965 the state's leading businessmen were ready to recommend a statewide biracial body even when, as in New Orleans and Shreveport, they drew back from supporting biracial committees in their own local communities — for these men, too, the commission served as a useful political buffer. Edward Steimel, CABL's executive director, drafted the detailed plans for the commission. Fittingly, Vertrees Young, former head of Crown-Zellerbach's Bogalusa plant, helped to swing CABL's conservative membership behind the idea in his role as president of the organization.[63]

But the ultimate author of McKeithen's statewide commission was the 1964 Civil Rights Act. The fact that a Louisiana governor, and one from north Louisiana at that, could form such a body testified to the profound impact of federal legislation upon the thinking of southern segregationists. Whites in Louisiana did not like integration one whit, but they could now swallow some degree of integration, albeit with a grimace of distaste, because it had the force of national law behind it. The Civil Rights Act gave integration a legitimacy that, to white southerners, the judge-made law of *Brown* v. *Board of Education* had conspicuously lacked.

Nobody typified this change in attitude more than General Troy H. Middleton, the man whom McKeithen tapped to chair the commission. As president of LSU during the 1950s, Middleton had resisted the more extreme pressures of ultrasegregationists like William Rainach. Nevertheless, he had remained a convinced segregationist himself, fighting integration every step of the way in the courts and doing little to make LSU's few black students feel welcome. The Civil Rights Act caused Middleton to reexamine his position. "I took an oath in 1910 to defend my country, obey the laws, support the president, and in short to be a law-abiding citizen," he explained. "The Civil Rights Act is a law; to violate it would be to violate my oath. I shall never do that." Like a good soldier obeying his commanding officer, and with something of the convert's zeal, the "former country boy from Mississippi" devoted his retirement years to promoting racial equality. If ever a man changed, noted commission vice chairman Albert Dent, that man was Troy Middleton.[64]

Thus the biracial commission was more than a political conjuring trick by John McKeithen. Comprising an equal number of blacks and whites, the commission implied a political recognition of the state's black population that had immense symbolic and practical significance. Before 1963, whites did not negotiate with blacks in any context that implied equality. Now the business and political leaders of the state put their combined weight behind that concept of equality.

There is still something rather mysterious about the Bogalusa movement. What accounted for its raw militancy and remarkable staying power? Perhaps it was the town's history as a lumber and paper mill town, a tough industry located in a tough part of the South. Perhaps it was the history of union organization and labor-management conflict. Perhaps the very newness of Bogalusa made it easier for a militant black leadership to emerge — a leadership in which black ministers played no role. Lolis Elie believed that Bogalusa, almost fortuitously, boasted a handful of blacks who possessed remarkable courage.

But it would be a mistake to regard Bogalusa as unique or anomalous. The Bogalusa Voters League typified, and pioneered, a transition between the civil rights movement of the early 1960s and the more hard-headed black protest that came to dominate the latter half of the decade. This was not a transition, however, between a mild movement and a militant one, or between nonviolence and Black Power. It was a transition, rather, between a movement that had been struggling for recognition and one that had just achieved a political breakthrough. Far from declining, the struggle for racial equality intensified as blacks sought to capitalize on growing national success and growing federal intervention.

A. P. Tureaud as a young man. The dean of Louisiana civil rights lawyers, Tureaud fought racial discrimination over a period of fifty years. Courtesy Amistad Research Center, Tulane University.

Class at Valena C. Jones School in New Orleans, 1930. The teacher at the back of the room, Veronica B. Hill, was a longtime union activist and civil rights supporter. Courtesy Archives and Manuscripts/ Special Collections, Earl K. Long Library, University of New Orleans.

The absence of blacks among these school children photographed with Governor
Huey P. Long at Bogalusa in 1930 reflects the racial segregation of the state's schools.
Although Long did little to improve the status of black Louisianians, many viewed his
leadership as a change for the better. Courtesy Louisiana and Lower Mississippi Valley
Collections, LSU Libraries, Baton Rouge.

The people of Louisiana, white and black, were the worst educated in the nation.
Before 1940, few blacks in rural areas attended high school, and many did not attend
elementary school. In this home, where newspaper substitutes for wallpaper, a parent
struggles to teach basic literacy. Transylvania, East Carroll Parish, 1939. Photo by Russell
Lee, courtesy State Library of Louisiana.

Although the New Deal treated blacks and whites unevenly and failed to attack racial
segregation, it did give blacks vital economic assistance during the Great Depression. In
1936 black workers employed by the WPA built a whites-only swimming pool in the
town of Mansfield, De Soto Parish. Courtesy State Library of Louisiana.

Even the best-intentioned of the New Deal agricultural programs gave little succor to black farmers. In 1939 in Transylvania, East Carroll Parish, the Farm Security Administration compelled 250 black families to leave their farms to make way for a resettlement project for whites. Photo by Russell Lee, courtesy State Library of Louisiana.

[*above*]
Cane cutters being taken to the fields in south Louisiana during the cutting season, late 1930s. Sugar cane workers were among the poorest and most dependent of all agricultural workers. Their efforts to form unions in the late 1930s and early 1950s met with severe opposition.

[*below*]
The strawberry farms of Tangipahoa Parish were an important source of seasonal work for agricultural workers like this young strawberry picker, pictured at his home near Hammond, 1939. Photo by Russell Lee. Photos on this page courtesy State Library of Louisiana.

MASS MEETING

Sponsored by

THE N. A. A. C. P.

THE ISSUE !!!!

How Can The Negro Obtain His Civil Liberties In New Orleans?

HEAR THE LATEST DEVELOPMENT
IN THE NEGRO'S FIGHT FOR THE
MUNICIPAL AUDITORIUM

TIME:

SUNDAY, MAY 14th, 1939

3:30 P. M.

PLACE:

GREATER TULANE BAPTIST CHURCH

214 N. Johnson St., between Iberville & Bienville Sts.

ALL INVITED

Public Forum Led by the Following Speakers:
PROF. MAURICE PREVOST
MISS MYRTLE R. BANKS
MRS. BELLE DOUGLAS
PROF. B. D. PARKER, of Dillard University

☛ Don't Miss This Interesting Meeting!

The New Orleans branch of the NAACP challenged the city's refusal to let blacks hire the Municipal Auditorium. Loss of the suit in federal court prompted a group of younger blacks to contest the branch leadership. Courtesy Archives and Manuscripts/Special Collections, Earl K. Long Library, University of New Orleans.

[*opposite top*]
Soldiers in training in Louisiana, early 1940s. Black participation in the armed services had a tonic effect on the struggle for equality. Returning veterans spearheaded the push for the ballot after 1945. Courtesy Louisiana Division, New Orleans Public Library.

[*opposite bottom*]
Black NCOs relax in a recreation center in north Louisiana during World War II. In Alexandria and elsewhere the NAACP had to campaign for the establishment of USO centers for black servicemen. Courtesy Louisiana Division, New Orleans Public Library.

[*above*]
Sit-ins exploded across the South in the spring and summer of 1960. Police are shown arresting Southern University students who staged a sit-in at the whites-only lunch counter at Kress in downtown Baton Rouge, March 28, 1960. Courtesy *The Advocate* (Baton Rouge).

[*opposite top*]
States' Righters protest integration of New Orleans public schools on November 14, 1960. The political slogans reflect the influence of Leander Perez, who helped to orchestrate the demonstrations. Photo by Jack Barham, courtesy Department of Archives and Special Collections, Noel Memorial Library, LSU Shreveport.

[*opposite bottom*]
Whites opposed to court-ordered integration taunt police in front of City Hall in New Orleans two days after the integration of public schools, November 16, 1960. Courtesy Amistad Research Center, Tulane University.

[*opposite top*]
The first Freedom Riders arrive in Shreveport, July 22, 1961. Police were on hand at the Trailways bus station to enforce the state's segregation laws. Photo by Jack Barham.
[*opposite bottom*]
Helmeted police converge on the Little Union Baptist Church in Shreveport, September 22, 1963. Blacks had gathered at the church for a memorial service for four black girls killed in the bombing of a Birmingham church a few days before. Moments later police beat up the Reverend Harry Black, a local NAACP leader. Photo by Langston McEachern.
[*above*]
Students at Booker T. Washington High School in Shreveport flee as a tear gas bomb explodes in their midst, September 23, 1963. Police stopped a student march two blocks from the school. Photo by Lloyd Stilley. Photos on this page and opposite page courtesy Department of Archives and Special Collections, Noel Memorial Library, LSU Shreveport.

The Ku Klux Klan reached the height of its power during the Bogalusa movement of 1965. On July 4, Klansmen openly demonstrated in front of the governor's mansion following a rally on the steps of the state capitol. Courtesy *The Advocate* (Baton Rouge).

[*above*]
Governor John McKeithen, left, talks with aides prior to a rally staged by civil rights activists and a second by the Ku Klux Klan on the steps of the state capitol, August 19, 1967.

[*below*]
Civil rights leader A. Z. Young speaking on the steps of the capitol at a rally marking the end of the Bogalusa Voters League march from Bogalusa to Baton Rouge, August 19, 1967. Photos on this page courtesy *The Advocate* (Baton Rouge).

Marchers are flanked by state troopers and Louisiana National Guardsmen as they cross the Amite River bridge from Livingston Parish into East Baton Rouge Parish on the last leg of their journey from Bogalusa to the state capitol, August 18, 1967. Courtesy *The Advocate* (Baton Rouge).

NAACP march up North Boulevard to the Municipal Building in Baton Rouge, 1969. The protest march followed the shooting death of a young black man by a Baton Rouge police officer late in July. Courtesy *The Advocate* (Baton Rouge).

With registration of black voters came election of blacks to public office. Zelma C. Wyche, an Army veteran of World War II and civil rights activist, was elected chief of police at Tallulah in 1969. He later served as mayor. Courtesy Zelma C. Wyche.

Ernest "Dutch" Morial, Louisiana's first black state representative in the twentieth century, with his sons Marc and Jacques in 1968. A protégé of A. P. Tureaud, Morial became the first black mayor of New Orleans. His son Marc was elected to the office in 1994. Courtesy Amistad Research Center, Tulane University.

Chapter 13

MAKING RIGHTS REAL

Less than a year after the Voting Rights Act, arguably its greatest triumph, the civil rights movement split apart when two of the most dynamic organizations raised the banner of "Black Power." Sparking furious debate as to its precise meaning, Black Power fundamentally altered the character of SNCC and CORE, its principal proponents: they abandoned integration, repudiated nonviolence, and rid their ranks of white people. By the end of 1966, however, both organizations were in headlong decline, and the days of the "freedom summers," when hundreds of idealistic whites had gone South to work in "the movement," were fading into the romantic mists of a bygone era. In Louisiana, as elsewhere in the South, CORE was soon reduced to a shadow of its former self; by the summer of 1966 it had only five staff members left in the state. With black leaders at each other's throats, with Vietnam fast becoming the dominant political issue, and with white perceptions of race now colored by burning ghettos and the incendiary rhetoric of black nationalism, many commentators pronounced the civil rights movement dead.

Some CORE veterans felt profoundly alienated by their organization's embrace of black nationalism, and they resented CORE's takeover by people who had little or no experience in the southern movement. Ronnie Moore decided that CORE's idealistic spirit had died. That spirit had been grievously wounded when committed staff members like Jim Peck, Jerome Smith, Rudy Lombard, Dave Dennis, and Richard Haley were fired by the national office or else quit out of disillusionment. It expired altogether when, in the name of a shallow slogan, CORE disowned its most fundamental principle, nonviolence.

> I am and always have been in favor of self-defense of one's home, but I have always held that direct action which includes picketing, mass demonstrations, etc., must be non-violent. Not only for philosophical reasons must this exist, but it must exist for practical reasons. I know the reality of nonviolence because I have worked in the South and I have inhaled tear gas. I have witnessed police brutality; I have ducked bullets, therefore, I know when it was wise to pick up guns and when it was wise to be non-violent. And a man who says shoot at all times is either an idiot or a damn fool.

Moore, along with several other seasoned staff members, went to work for CORE's Scholarship, Education, and Defense Fund for Racial Equality (SEDFRE) which remained wedded to interracialism.[1]

Still, the cry of "Black Power" touched an emotional and intellectual chord among black Americans. It intensified racial pride, discarded the word "Negro" to the dustbin of linguistic history, and ushered in radically different styles of militancy. Black Power made the ideals of nonviolence seem anachronistic and mawkish. Dreams of a "beloved community" gave way to calls for black unity; the vision of a "salt-and-pepper" society faded before an insistence on "blackness." And a cult of the gun displaced the pacifist orientation of the civil rights movement. Nonviolence, it is true, had always hinted at the possibility of violence, but Black Power positively relished that possibility. The language of violence — ominous threats of retaliation, blood-curdling calls for revolution, grim predictions that this or that city was "about to blow" — soon became common argot in the black community.

Throughout Louisiana blacks appeared more assertive, at times even aggressive. Boycotts were often accompanied by intimidation, demonstrations sometimes degenerated into battles against the police, and by the end of the decade riots were breaking out in the most unlikely places — even in Lake Providence, a repressive north Louisiana town where black violence would have been unthinkable a few years earlier. When a new generation of black college students initiated a wave of protests between 1969 and 1972, the symbols of black nationalism and the language of insurrection permeated their rhetoric. High school students invoked Malcolm X and called for the teaching of black history even as they entered newly integrated schools. Not even the NAACP could insulate itself from Black Power insurgency: by 1968 the association was in turmoil at the national level, and sometimes at the local level too, over demands that it abandon interracialism and change the words in its title from "Colored People" to "Black People."

Some aspects of Black Power ran against the grain of Louisiana's Creole heritage. In Acadiana, for example, where white priests ministered to black Catholics and where white and black families sometimes openly acknowledged their blood relationships, notions of black separatism usually fell on stony ground. In St. Mary Parish, for example, black candidates garnered white support and even ran on integrated tickets. In the area around Opelousas, CORE worker John Zippert succeeded in organizing a farmers' marketing cooperative that counted thirty-five whites among its two hundred members. Some NAACP branches in southern Louisiana began to attract a significant number of white members.[2]

Yet the term "black" also had particular resonance in Louisiana, where Negroes had traditionally been highly sensitive to variations in skin color, and where the Creoles of New Orleans, generally lighter in complexion than the rest of the Negro population, still remained a distinctive and self-conscious group. Stokely Carmichael's celebration of black skin, thick lips, and "nappy hair" — African rather than European physiognomy — praised precisely those features that were disdained by many Creoles. Indeed, "Black Power" challenged the very concept of "Creoleness." It even sometimes implied that the old "lighter is better" standard should be replaced by a "blacker is better" ideal. However, the issue was less skin color than racial identity. The dilemma of the "tragic mulatto" caught between the black and white worlds had long been a literary cliché; Black Power now challenged light-skinned Creoles to abandon their alleged social exclusivism once and for all and to identify with the black struggle unambiguously.[3]

The extent to which Black Power traumatized Creoles and transmuted the Creole self-image can easily be exaggerated. Most Creoles had long ago identified themselves as "Negroes"; indeed, Creoles like A. P. Tureaud, Arthur J. Chapital, and Ernest N. Morial had led the civil rights struggle. Moreover, the civil rights movement of the early 1960s had already heightened racial solidarity, acting, in the words of historian Arnold Hirsch, as "an ethnic crucible melding black New Orleanians into a single whole." Resentment of Creoles persisted, but it had more to do with class than with color: many viewed Creoles as a pushy and clannish elite that tended to dominate black leadership. "The friction was there," recalled NAACP field secretary Harvey Britton, "but it was a subtle friction within the black community that made things difficult in terms of cohesiveness on issues, because it was always deciding which group called out the particular troops at a given point in time."[4]

It would also be an error to draw too sharp a distinction between the activism of the "civil rights era" and that of the "Black Power era." If the civil rights movement disintegrated as a coherent national force, it survived, albeit in an attenuated form, in the states, cities, and rural areas, where blacks continued to struggle for jobs, integrated schools, and political representation. Indeed, the evidence of Louisiana contradicts the notion that the civil rights movement suddenly collapsed after Black Power supposedly split it asunder.

Local activism did not grind to a halt when the SNCC and CORE workers departed. For one thing, many independent local movements survived and prospered because they continued to receive support from various sources. The Southern Regional Council launched a third Voter Education Project in 1967, channeling more registration grants to local voters leagues. The Lawyers Constitutional Defense Committee continued to represent local movements in court, with Richard Sobol and Alvin Bronstein covering Louisiana from offices in, respectively, New Orleans and Jackson, Mississippi. The Scholarship, Education, and Defense Fund, which in 1967 split from CORE to become an independent organization, directed a leadership training program that instructed thousands of local activists in politics and government. Finally, the federal government itself gave sustenance to local movements. The machinery set up to enforce the 1964 Civil Rights Act encouraged complaints against employment discrimination, and it helped blacks to desegregate schools, hospitals, and public accommodations. The Voting Rights Act led to the appointment of federal registrars, invited complaints against unfair electoral practices, and generated a flood of reapportionment suits. Finally, the government's "War on Poverty" funded community organizations and, by creating jobs that were thinly disguised patronage, facilitated political mobilization. Thus outside help did not dry up.[5]

The impact of CORE's demise, moreover, was mitigated by the NAACP's revival. Indeed, the association consciously took advantage of its rival's organizational collapse, sharpening its appeal to black youth who, fired by the rhetoric of Black Power, often had nowhere else to go but the NAACP's Youth Councils. The NAACP's growth was particularly marked in those towns and cities where blacks, either through apathy or fear or a combination of the two, had been previously quiescent. In New Iberia, Lake Charles, Opelousas, New Roads, Baton Rouge, and Shreveport vigorous NAACP branches attacked police brutality, employment discrimination, and school segregation. To a great extent, of course, the NAACP had recourse to litigation, exploiting new avenues of legal redress opened up by civil rights law. Yet the NAACP of the late 1960s also displayed a hard-hitting edge that had been largely absent in the early 1960s: it was more militant, more confrontational, and more oriented towards direct action. Somewhat paradoxically, the NAACP also benefited from the tendency of white leaders to treat the association as their preferred channel of communication with the black community. Governor McKeithen's creation of a biracial commission in 1965 typified this new, conciliatory attitude, for the commission was heavily loaded with NAACP stalwarts.

If reports of the civil rights movement's death proved greatly exaggerated, the influence of black nationalism was similarly overstated. An inspirational slogan rather than a coherent ideology, Black Power operated on the level of culture and rhetoric rather than as a programmatic commitment to violence or racial separatism. Black Power meant all things to all people: therein lay both its popularity and its weakness. As a rallying cry for black unity it exercised great appeal, but it provided no clear strategy and failed to provide strong alternative, let alone revolutionary, leadership.

Black Power verbalized threats and articulated anger, but activists tended to utilize such oratory as a means of enhancing their bargaining power rather than encouraging violence. In fact, Black Power rhetoric frequently *implied* violence rather than explicitly threatened it. When, for example, A. Z. Young led a march from Bogalusa to Franklinton in 1966, FBI agents carefully monitored the fiery speeches at the concluding rally, but reported that "no mention was made of violence as an answer to problems." A year later, listening to a mass meeting in Bogalusa, Miriam Feingold noted how

> the movement combines country-style Negro religion with black power rhetoric. Meetings here start with several long prayers and . . . a hymn or two, and even "We Shall Overcome" sounds like a Negro hymn! Then the president of the [Bogalusa Voters] League gives a rousing speech, sprinkled with anti-white sentiments. . . . There's even violent, riot-like talk, but just as quickly people condemn looting and burning, realizing, they say, that the wrong people get killed.

By and large, advocacy of violence remained at the level of symbol rather than serious intention. Threats of armed insurrection were accorded spurious credibility by "long, hot summers" of riots and the white press's fawning, credulous coverage of self-styled black revolutionaries. It is a striking fact that the Deacons for Defense faded away at precisely the time that the rhetoric of armed struggle was intensifying. More to the point, the avowedly revolutionary Black Panther Party, which established a presence in New Orleans in 1970, failed to attract much support. Only when it became the object of police repression did blacks spring to its defense.[6]

Moreover, just as SNCC, CORE, and SCLC had often used demonstrations as a form of political drama, gearing their tactics towards the news media, there was a conscious element of "street theater" in how local activists deployed the symbols of Black Power. National figures like Stokely Carmichael and H. Rap Brown were useful "bogeymen" to dangle in front of appalled whites: blacks could revel in their firebrand declamations without subscribing to their revolutionary messages. John Martzell recalled entering a barbershop in Tallulah, Madison Parish, and unexpectedly encountering Ron Karenga, inventor of the Kwaanza celebration and one of the foremost black nationalists of the day. "He had a dashiki, and a big leather belt, and a .357 Magnum, sitting there in the barber chair, with his hands across his chest and his eyes closed." By then, however, Martzell understood "the subtle theater" of such situations. "I wasn't overly impressed, and I couldn't really picture Ron Karenga spending a whole lot of time in Tallulah." Such cynicism could be dangerous, but it contained some insight: at the state and local level the civil rights struggle continued as before; the style changed, but the substance remained much the same.[7]

The late 1960s, to be sure, saw much less emphasis upon integration and much more upon the development of community institutions. This shift, however, was a natural transition rather than an abrupt change. Certainly, much of the idealism surrounding integration faded, and interracialism as an end in itself became far less prominent. Yet blacks continued to press for integration in the broad sense of access to public accommodations, public services, employment, and government. The struggle for school integration, far from being abandoned, actually intensified in the late 1960s and came to a head in 1970, a year often seen as the high-water mark of black separatism. Likewise, Black Power's emphasis on institution building was a development of a long historical tradition, one that went back to the Reconstruction era, and in some communities still further, rather than a novel concept. To some extent, of course, institution building represented a departure from the integrationism of the period 1954–65. The NAACP's goal of integrating higher education evoked widespread opposition from people who did not wish to see Louisiana's black colleges lose their identity by being absorbed into a unitary system. Similarly, black teachers were deeply divided over whether the LEA should merge with the LTA, the white teachers' association.

Yet in many cases blacks were not so much opposing integration as the manner in which integration was implemented, particularly if it meant the destruction of community institutions. Thus blacks often supported school integration while at the same time opposing the closure of black schools and the sacking of black principals. In fact, the NAACP's dogmatic integrationism had always aroused misgivings, and most southern blacks, it is fair to say, regarded integration as a means to an end rather than an end in itself.

Hence Black Power, as many observers noted at the time, provided ideological cover for some fairly conservative and traditional attitudes. It is doubtful that the popularity of the Black Power slogan indicated a fundamental change in how blacks in the South viewed their goals. As Clayborne Carson has argued, "Rather than claiming that a black power movement displaced the civil rights movement," historians should stress the underlying continuities between the two periods.[8]

The most obvious continuity was political action. In a much discussed article published in 1965, Bayard Rustin argued that the civil rights movement should abandon direct action and redirect its energies "from protest to politics." Such a shift, facilitated by the Voting Rights Act, did indeed take place, but it was neither abrupt nor complete. Political action had been a central thread of black protest for more than twenty years, and universal suffrage had been a major goal of the civil rights movement. Black political participation massively increased in the wake of the Voting Rights Act, but it built upon a solid foundation of methods, leaders, and organizations. The other side of the coin was a continuing readiness to employ direct action when the occasion demanded it. If, in the late 1960s, politics and litigation became the major vehicles of black activism, that was because they overtook, rather than displaced, the direct action methods of earlier years. Blacks never discarded direct action entirely, and the years 1966 to 1970 saw a resurgence of boycotts and demonstrations around such issues as employment, school integration, police brutality, and student autonomy.[9]

The persistence of "protest" alongside the growth of "politics" had a great deal to do with the simple fact that whites continued to resist black demands for equality. White racism did not suddenly disappear with the passage of civil rights laws. Such laws declared blacks to be legally and politically equal, but they were not self-implementing. Blacks still had to struggle against white recalcitrance, utilizing whatever method or combination of methods — political action, direct action, litigation — seemed most appropriate. Indeed, the struggle to translate the Civil Rights Act and the Voting Rights Act into tangible equality continues to this day and shows no sign of coming to an end.

The Voting Rights Act dealt a severe blow to Louisiana's racial order, but it did not usher in the political millenium. White resistance to black voting did not evaporate overnight. In New Orleans, the number of black voters increased by thirteen thousand between August and October 1965, but the registrars showed no hurry to process the applicants, keeping thousands "waiting patiently under a blazing sun or in drizzling rain." The Reverend A. L. Davis filed suit against the Orleans Parish registrar, accusing him of deliberate delaying tactics, but Judge Frank Ellis rejected the complaint. In Shreveport, registrars continued to be infuriatingly inconsistent over identification: during the weeks following the Voting Rights Act they rejected 337 black applicants for inadequate identification, but only 15 white applicants. In the five parishes that received federal examiners, black registration shot up. However, all five local registrars refused at first to accept the federally registered voters, and state judges actually enjoined the registrars from enrolling them.

In parishes without federal examiners, rises in black registration showed extreme variations. For example, Madison saw a dramatic increase, while Morehouse and West Carroll saw the number of black voters, already small, actually decline. Most parishes witnessed steady but not spectacular growth. Even when they registered, blacks could still face obstacles casting a ballot. In Washington Parish, some complained of being barred from the Democratic primaries because the registrar had listed their party affiliation as "none." Throughout the state, but especially in north Louisiana, illiterate voters were refused assistance at the polls.[10]

Local registrars fell into line, however, when they saw the futility of continuing to reject black applicants. Although the Justice Department appointed federal examiners sparingly — much to the disappointment of civil rights organizations — the threat of being circumvented did have the desired effect on most parish registrars. The federal courts, moreover, swiftly disposed of challenges to the Voting Rights Act and, in *U.S.* v. *Louisiana,* ordered local election commissioners to aid illiterate voters. In 1967, under pressure from the Justice Department, the state told registrars not to apply the "good character" tests enacted in 1960. Finally, Governor John McKeithen had no desire to see federal examiners sent to Louisiana, and he prodded recalcitrant parish authorities to mend their ways.[11]

Across Louisiana, James McCain reported in 1967, "registration is not a serious obstacle anymore." Even Leander Perez, who in 1967 stormed into the office of the federal examiners and spewed a stream of vitriolic abuse, proved powerless to prevent blacks from voting in Plaquemines Parish. Five years after the passage of the Voting Rights Act the number of black voters had almost doubled, and the proportion of blacks who were registered grew from 30 to 60 percent. That represented a net increase of about 154,000.[12]

Faced with the sudden enlargement of the black electorate, white politicians faced a dilemma. Should they exploit racial polarization in order to solidify the white vote? Or should they reach out to black voters and abandon the politics of segregation?

The alternatives, of course, were rarely that simple. For one thing, the black vote was not an undifferentiated "bloc"; most black communities boasted at least two rival political factions, and new ones were appearing all the time. Then again, white politicians could tone down, but few were willing to entirely abandon, appeals to white racism: southern whites still enjoyed a privileged position vis-à-vis blacks and many, feeling no sense of guilt over past discrimination, wished to retain as much of the status quo as possible. Moreover, as blacks pushed against the barriers of segregation and discrimination, social and economic conflict intensified. Competition for jobs, for example, was becoming more direct and more intense, with whites fearful that black advances would come at their expense. In the cities, residential segregation was becoming increasingly pronounced, as whites moved out of older, mixed neighborhoods to the newer, racially exclusive suburbs. Above all, the great majority of whites never reconciled themselves to school integration, an issue that by 1970 affected virtually every family in the state. Underlying such specific issues was a general feeling among most whites, ranging from mild uneasiness to pronounced fear, that a secure racial order had given way to a world in which blacks did not know their place, were threatening, dangerous, out of control.

How a politician balanced the often competing demands of black and white voters depended on many factors. Politicians had to consider the local electoral arithmetic. That candidates could win election with only a minority of the white votes was not an entirely new circumstance in Louisiana. Now, however, many could win with an even smaller minority if they won the greatly expanded black vote. As Watters and Cleghorn noted in 1967, "When a politician knows he can afford to lose 62 per cent of the old electorate, a figure which usually had been regarded as a landslide, his political bearings are suddenly shifted." Indeed, seeing the writing on the wall, almost a third of the South's congressmen supported the Voting Rights Bill. All those from the Deep South already had large black constituencies and, seeing that passage was inevitable, recognized that their future survival depended on black votes. It was no coincidence that the two Louisiana congressmen in favor of the bill, Hale Boggs and Jimmie Morrison, represented the congressional districts with the highest proportion of black voters. Without minimizing their political courage in casting "yes" votes — Jimmie Morrison's may well have cost him his seat in Congress — calculated self-interest clearly influenced their decision.[13]

The extent of a politician's ambition also influenced how he responded to black and white constituents: the desire for higher office tomorrow, for example, might well affect how he acted today. In the case of Chep Morrison, the desire to be governor had led to a more robust defense of segregation than he might otherwise have espoused. In John McKeithen's case, national aspirations had the reverse effect: the governor's racial moderation after 1964 owed at least something to his ambition to become the Democratic vice presidential candidate in 1968. When McKeithen failed to achieve this goal, he had to focus his sights on state politics once again, and his subsequent opposition to school integration could be explained, in part, by the need to shore up his support among segregation-minded whites.[14]

Some politicians stubbornly rejected the idea of courting the black electorate. "I won't stoop to entice these niggers," vowed representative Vail M. Deloney of East Carroll Parish. "They either vote for me or they don't." Some went still further and contemptuously spurned "the illiterate bloc vote." John R. Rarick, challenging Congressman Jimmie Morrison in 1966, made a virtue of the fact that he received practically no black support: "Morrison gets nearly 200 Negro votes to one for his opponent." Enjoying the enthusiastic backing of the Klan (some believed that he was a Klan member himself) Rarick terminated Morrison's twenty-four-year congressional career in the most overtly racist campaign since Willie Rainach's bid for governor. Morrison's fate showed the danger of a "white backlash." Candidates had to be careful not to court black voters so ardently as to alienate too many whites, who in 1970 still made up nearly four-fifths of Louisiana's electorate. Indeed, white registration increased by a quarter of a million between 1965 and 1970, rising to 80 percent of its potential. Hence while blacks made up over a third of the voting-age population in 1970, they still accounted for only 21 percent of the voters.[15]

Most white politicians, however, quickly softened their segregationist rhetoric and wooed blacks with shameless abandon. McKeithen led the way. Having alienated black voters almost to a person in his campaign against Chep Morrison, McKeithen had a keen appreciation of the Voting Rights Act's import. "Every time I'd go and ask him to do something," Jesse Stone remembered, "he'd say, 'How many people are registered to vote up there?' So I had to carry . . . the numbers and information in my pocket all the time." In 1965 McKeithen wanted black support for a constitutional amendment that would allow him to succeed himself in office. In creating the state biracial commission and urging compliance with the Civil Rights Act, McKeithen shed his segregationist clothes and donned the garb of racial moderate. Blacks not only voted for the constitutional amendment but also overwhelmingly backed McKeithen in 1967, when he crushed John Rarick to win a second term as governor, enjoying "the greatest margin of victory in modern Louisiana history."[16]

Even some vehement opponents of the civil rights movement managed to cling to office by forging alliances with newly influential black leaders. In Shreveport, for example, George D'Artois, the hard-nosed commissioner of public safety, gained the backing of both Alphonse Jackson, president of the LEA and Shreveport's first black legislator, and Jesse Stone, Shreveport's most prominent black lawyer. In his last campaign in 1972 D'Artois received a good percentage of the black vote. Similarly the right-wing, ultrasegregationist district attorney for Baton Rouge, Sargent Pitcher, attracted not a few black votes with the help of allies like Acie Belton, longtime leader of the Second Ward Voters League.[17]

That blacks voted for the likes of George D'Artois seems incongruous, to say the least, but such choices had less to do with venality or gullibility than with hard-headed political calculation. Unless they could muster the voting strength to elect black candidates, blacks had to vote, as they had done in the past, on a "lesser of two evils" basis. And often the devil you knew, especially the one already in power, was better than the devil you did not. The personal factor also came into the equation. It was almost a cliché among blacks in the South that the racist you could trust was preferable to the liberal you could not. Although D'Artois was a hard man, Jesse Stone explained, when he made a promise he always kept it. Similar logic influenced the choice of some blacks to support Victor Schiro when he ran for reelection in 1965. A segregationist, albeit a genial one, Schiro's record as mayor of New Orleans was hardly such as to endear him to black hearts. Moreover, his opponent, councilman Jimmy Fitzmorris, clearly outbid Schiro when it came to making specific promises to blacks. Yet Schiro received the endorsement of A. P. Tureaud, Rev. A. L. Davis, and Rev. Avery Alexander, who helped to deliver between a third and a quarter of the black vote. Politics in Louisiana, of course, had always been notable for opportunism and a readiness to switch sides: political alliances were governed as much by political horse-trading as by declarations of principle. Even newer and ostensibly more militant organizations like SOUL tended to play by the old rules. As SOUL founder Nils R. Douglas put it, explaining his dealings with a segregationist politician, "I am willing to make a compact with the devil if we had the remotest chance of securing our goal."[18]

Faced with a choice of lackluster white candidates — in the 1965 mayoral race, for example, between two former segregationists of doubtful sincerity — it is perhaps not surprising that black voters in New Orleans failed to speak with a united voice. In the absence of exciting elections and attractive candidates, moreover, a large pool of potential voters showed little interest in politics: by 1966 fewer than half of those eligible had registered. These nonvoters were disproportionately poor; many lived in the city's public housing projects. Reporting on an NAACP registration drive in the Ninth Ward, which contained two of the largest and most rundown projects, Wilfred Aubert explained the difficulty of motivating such people.

These are people who have suffered many years of deprivation, neglect and misery because the city administration has failed to keep its democratic promise to all its citizens. Therefore, they look upon everyone with suspicion and mistrust. . . . Poverty and fear have caused them to become indif-

ferent and they live a life of despair. Progress in this area is very slow. . . .
We must reach their natural leaders, such as the ministers, the barbers . . .
the barkeepers and other persons whom they trust.

Given something positive to vote for, however, the ghetto poor would indeed register, and black voters would prove capable of remarkable solidarity.
A large and solid black vote elected Maurice "Moon" Landrieu, a white racial
liberal who succeeded Victor Schiro in 1970, and Ernest "Dutch" Morial, who
became the city's first black mayor eight years later. Until black registration
reached a critical mass of about 30 percent of the total electorate, however,
the black vote in New Orleans remained, to quote Arnold Hirsch, "neither
sufficient nor independent enough to strike out on its own."[19]

In some of the rural parishes, the electoral arithmetic began to favor blacks
very soon after the Voting Rights Act, making the election of black candidates a real possibility. Old patterns of deference, however, did not die overnight, and blacks often went down to defeat because black voters failed to
back them. In some cases, white candidates simply bought votes for $5 or $10
apiece — a timeworn practice that continues to this day — and paid blacks $25
to $50 to act as campaign workers. But not a few blacks continued to support whites simply out of habit and ultracaution. "Many said that the time
was not right [for black candidates]," Ernest Middleton recalled of his 1966
campaign in St. Mary Parish. "Still others argued that the candidates were
not the right people or were not qualified. . . . Still others felt that Negroes
couldn't help Negroes." Black ministers, Middleton thought, were especially
negative. Moreover, religious sectarianism sometimes lurked beneath the surface in south Louisiana, further hampering black unity. In St. Mary Parish,
for example, a white Catholic priest, Father Frank Ecimovich, played a key
role in encouraging black candidates. However, Baptist and Methodist ministers felt threatened by Ecimovich's popularity and viewed his efforts "as an
attempt of the Catholic Church to take over the town."[20]

Perhaps the most remarkable example of black voters failing to support
black candidates occurred in the town of Lake Providence, in East Carroll
Parish, in the election of 1970. Although blacks composed about two-thirds
of the voters, whites were elected to the posts of mayor and town marshal — a
result that caused some disappointed blacks to smash the windows of downtown stores in anger and frustration. Yet NAACP field secretary Harvey Britton disbelieved charges that whites had rigged the vote, arguing that "the
Negroes lost because the black community did not support them."[21]

The fractured black vote sometimes reflected divisions within the local
black leadership, which, as James McCain lamented in 1967, "is partially split
in a few parishes." Factionalism was especially prevalent where CORE-backed

groups clashed with NAACP branches and other established organizations, or else challenged the right of certain individuals, usually teachers and ministers, to represent the black community.[22]

The War on Poverty sometimes exacerbated these quarrels, although its divisive effects should not be overstated. While conflicts over control of community action programs (CAPs) could be extremely bitter, the overall effect of the antipoverty program was to stimulate black political action. Many civil rights activists found secure niches in CAPs, employment that enabled them to bridge the transition from the civil rights movement to electoral politics. The War on Poverty also provided patronage jobs that nourished and sustained black political organizations. The classic example was Total Community Action (TCA), the poverty program in New Orleans, which gave employment to any number of political activists, especially those connected with the newer groups like SOUL, COUP, and BOLD. These organizations supported Moon Landrieu in his successful bid for mayor and garnered a further rich crop of patronage in return. Not coincidentally, Landrieu had exercised considerable influence in the selection of TCA's board members.[23]

Yet the War on Poverty also occasioned acrimonious disputes within some black communities, especially when rival groups vied for representation on the CAP boards and competed to win sponsorship of the preschool educational program, Head Start. CORE workers viewed the War on Poverty, with its provision for "maximum feasible participation" by the poor themselves, as a vehicle for radicalizing the poor in an overtly political way. The Southern Consumers' Education Fund, on the other hand, wished to downplay the connection between the War on Poverty and the civil rights movement, stressing the need to create efficiently run programs that would be immune from political attack. Founded and headed by Father Albert McKnight, a black Catholic priest born in Brooklyn and now living in Lafayette, this organization became the funding agent for the Head Start program in half a dozen parishes, and it soon found itself opposing CORE's demands in Shreveport and elsewhere. In Bogalusa the antipoverty program became a bone of contention between three organizations, with the Bogalusa Voters League, the Louisiana Education Association, and the NAACP all vying for representation on the board of the CAP. When the BVL failed to gain control, its representative resigned from the board, denouncing the remaining blacks as "Uncle Toms."[24]

CORE liked to depict such rows as conflicts between the black poor and the black middle class, but the issue was rarely that simple. In reality, CORE's claim to represent the black proletariat rested on shallow ground: as CORE workers sometimes conceded in private, the local groups that it backed often had little solid support and, far from being "independent," were heavily dependent on CORE for political guidance. Moreover, the terms "middle class" and "Uncle Tom" were not accurate descriptions but infinitely elastic terms of abuse. Thus interorganizational rivalries over the poverty program in many cases bore little relationship to class stratification within the black community.

It is nonetheless clear that white politicians exploited such rivalries by including some blacks and excluding others, with the obvious intention of controlling the poverty program as tightly as possible. In some cases this meant favoring the NAACP over CORE-backed groups; in others it meant selecting teachers and shutting out the NAACP. But black teachers were not always docile mouthpieces of the "white power structure." In St. Mary Parish, for example, teachers associated with the LEA successfully challenged a CAP board that had been handpicked by the local sheriff.[25]

Even a coherent black vote, however, could not guarantee the election of black candidates, for strenuous political mobilization by blacks often led to equally vigorous countermobilization on the part of whites. The 1967 results in Iberville Parish were especially disappointing, for the Iberville Industrial Voters League had confidently expected to be "the first group to make a major political breakthrough" in Louisiana. Over the years the voters league had received more support from CORE, SEDFRE, and the VEP than any other group in the state; by 1967 black registration exceeded 80 percent and composed 40 percent of the total electorate. In the first big test of black voting strength, however, all twenty-four black candidates lost. Here, as elsewhere, the requirement to gain an outright majority of the votes proved the bane of black candidates, who invariably led in the first primary only to lose in the runoff.[26]

Blacks also faced efforts by white officials to dilute the black vote by manipulating the electoral system. The most common device, employed throughout the South, was to substitute unitary electoral districts for ward-based ones. In 1968 the state legislature permitted such "at-large" elections for police juries and school boards, a system that militated against the election of blacks in all but a handful of majority-black parishes. The result was that five years after the Voting Rights Act blacks composed only a miniscule proportion of the state's elected officials, fewer than 1 percent. Only after 1970, when litigation by blacks and intervention by the Justice Department produced a more equitable electoral system, did the situation change markedly for the better.[27]

Nevertheless, if blacks failed to gain anything like a fair share of the political offices in Louisiana, the fact that they began to win even a few had great symbolic significance. In many parishes and cities people of color held office for the first time since Reconstruction. The astonishing transformation wrought by federal reform of the South's voting system was especially striking in the majority-black cotton parishes along the Mississippi River. In Madison Parish, for example, no blacks had voted before December 1962; less than seven years later Zelma Wyche, jailed half a dozen times for his civil rights activities, was elected police chief of Tallulah.[28]

Madison Parish was a textbook example of how the civil rights struggle persisted at the local level. The same men who had petitioned for the vote in the 1940s and sued for the vote in the 1950s and early 1960s now organized the black vote to win a share of political power. They also wielded direct action to integrate public accommodations and break the color line in employment. The decline of the civil rights movement as a national force did not slow them down. The advent of Black Power did not alter their goals, deter them from accepting white help, or persuade them that the federal government was an enemy. And rather than abruptly shifting "from protest to politics," they utilized demonstrations alongside litigation and political action.

CORE worker Cathy Cortez was not overly impressed by the leaders of the Madison Parish Voters League. These men were too timid, she thought, too trusting in the "good white folks." It had taken them fifteen months to finally accept CORE's help, and even then they were reluctant to embark upon direct action.[29]

But the nucleus of the Voters League, eight or ten men in their fifties and sixties, were a determined group of people. They went back a long way: some were veterans of the East Carroll Parish resettlement fight of 1938–39; some were veterans of the Second World War. Since 1947, when they founded the Voters League, they had stuck together through thick and thin. "There were lean years when we didn't do anything," one recalled. "But we were constantly trying to do something." Doggedly pursuing right-to-vote suits, their patience finally paid off in 1962: they won a federal injunction against Katherine Ward, the registrar of voters. By then they had become a tightly knit group that had firmly established its leadership credentials. Moreover, being the only civil rights organization in the parish (there was no NAACP branch) the league did not have to contend with the factionalism and disunity that sometimes prevailed in other communities.

As in Bogalusa, the arrival of white CORE workers to organize the testing of public accommodations — still off-limits to blacks nearly a year after the Civil Rights Act — provided blacks with the inspiration to confront the white authorities. The beating of white CORE worker Gary Craven on the streets of Tallulah galvanized the black community and, in the words of Zelma C. Wyche, led blacks to follow through with "every kind of 'in' you could mention." Sixty-one people were arrested testing the Post Inn Café, and it took only ten hours for the black community to raise sufficient cash to have them bailed out. In 1966 the league supported a student boycott of a new but unfinished and allegedly dangerous high school; in September two hundred blacks marched to the offices of the school board to protest against the maintenance of segregated school buses.

The league also instituted a boycott of Tallulah businesses that refused to hire black sales clerks. It was "probably the most successful boycott ever held in the state of Louisiana," thought John Martzell. "When the boycott was going on you could have shot a shotgun down Main Street and not hit anyone — empty, bare." Seventeen businesses closed their doors rather than succumb to the pressure. The A & P supermarket endured 111 days of boycotting and picketing before acceding to the league's demands. By the end of 1965 the league had the support of sixteen black ministers; the weekly mass meetings rotated among the various churches. In the meantime the league intensified its voter registration efforts; assisted by the federal examiners, black registration soon overtook white.[30]

Faced with black political control of both Tallulah and Madison Parish, whites stared into the future with horror. "All the white officials are implacable segregationists," an LCDC lawyer discovered. "Judge [Cliff] Adams explained that the whites are in a minority and have to fight back." Fight back they did. In October 1965 the leaders of the Voters League suffered a rash of fires: Moses Williams saw his tire shop go up in flames; Rev. Willie Haynes saw his church razed; the arsonists also struck at several homes. Few doubted that the Klan was setting the fires. But blacks were not intimidated. "Seems like every time they did something mean to one of us," Rev. Haynes told a reporter, "all the rest of us just pushed harder."[31]

As the number of black voters steadily mounted, white officials resorted to some devious strategems. Harrison Brown beat an incumbent school board member in the Democratic primary, but the clerk of elections, Jerome K. Post, gathered 510 absentee ballots for a hastily entered "write-in" candidate. These absentee ballots accounted for a quarter of the total white vote and caused Brown's defeat in the general election. It transpired that Post and his deputies had traveled to plantations and nursing homes, not only soliciting votes from the old and the infirm, but also allowing able-bodied people who had no intention of being out of the parish on election day to vote in their own homes. Post did not, needless to say, display similar diligence in securing absentee ballots from blacks. Judge Ben C. Dawkins ordered a new election, but the registrar of voters then disqualified 479 people, the majority of them blacks drawn from a list of "felons" obligingly supplied by the sheriff.

When Zelma Wyche ran for the office of town marshal in 1967 after Jimmy Rogan died in a car crash, he narrowly lost because his name had been disconnected from the Democratic lever on the voting machines. Throughout his campaign Wyche had urged blacks to vote the straight Democratic ticket, and over 500 people did just that, failing to record a vote for Wyche because they did not realize they were required to pull a separate lever for the marshal's race. A white candidate coasted to victory. Wyche only learned of the change on the morning of the election and he challenged the result. When Dawkins ordered a new election, he won. Even then, however, he had to file another lawsuit before receiving his commission. In 1970 blacks again went to court after the registrar purged a large number of blacks, but only a handful of whites, for failing to report changes of address. Once more Dawkins insisted on new elections.[32]

A veteran of World War Two who made his living as a barber, Wyche had long nurtured an ambition to become Tallulah's police chief. A tall, bespectacled, heavyset man in his late forties, Wyche inspired local blacks through force of personality and sheer guts. A natural leader who could only find his true potential once CORE had defied the white authorities and raised the sights of the black community, Wyche soon became the dominant figure in the Voters League. He displayed amazing coolness in the face of white threats. On several occasions whites levelled shotguns at him; he did not flinch.

Wyche's courage and audacity were conspicuously displayed on July 28, 1966, when he entered a truck stop on Highway 80, a notorious Klan haunt, to demand service. A white employee had closed the restaurant "to keep down trouble," locking the door and wedging a chair against the handle. Wyche forced his way in and demanded to see the manager. After he left, a white logger appeared in the doorway, aimed a gun, and threatened to "blow his brains out." Everyone else took cover (about fifty blacks had gathered outside the restaurant) but Wyche stood his ground, calmly facing the man until the police arrived. The incident cost Wyche a conviction for battery and a four-month jail sentence. "Get out of my face, man," Wyche had told his alleged victim, a white doctor. "We're not working on this nonviolence deal no more."[33]

Such statements seemed to resonate with the militancy of "Black Power." After the Klan arson attacks of October 1965 the Voters League made it abundantly clear that it would not take white violence lying down. Shouting through a bullhorn after the burning of Moses Williams's tire shop, Wyche warned, "You burn us one more time and we're gonna burn you right back. You hurt one of us and we're going to hurt the first white person we run across." The Voters League did not form an armed self-defense group along the lines of the Deacons, but neither did it discourage certain members from carrying guns. The influence of "Black Power" could also be seen in the league's decision to field all-black tickets, a departure from its earlier insistence on supporting white candidates as well as black ones. CORE worker Bruce Baines had returned to Tallulah from the Meredith March convinced that dogmatic adherence to CORE's interracial idealism would only slow black political advance. After initial resistance, the league accepted Baines's logic. Since 1966, Wyche explained, "It's been our objective to take every seat that we could take — and when it all boils down, we're gonna take *every seat* in the village *and* the parish."

If Wyche found the rhetoric and symbolism of Black Power useful, he had little sympathy for its separatist tendencies or clarion call for violent revolution. Like A. Z. Young and Robert Hicks, the leaders of the Bogalusa Voters League, Zelma Wyche personified a new assertiveness, even aggressiveness, that characterized the southern civil rights movement during the second half of the 1960s. But like Hicks and Young, he articulated goals that remained basically assimilationist or integrationist. Blacks in Madison Parish wanted equity within the American system: decent schools and public services, effective political representation, an end to segregation and police brutality, a fair share of the economic pie. Living in a majority-black parish where whites fought them every inch of the way, the Voters League was an all-black movement. But its decision to field all-black tickets did not entail a rejection of white allies or a repudiation of interracialism: it merely reflected political reality. "We found . . . that the whites in this community did *not* want black people in office," said Wyche, "even though we were trying to be fair." [34]

Far from adopting the "go-it-alone" policy advocated by SNCC, Wyche and the Voters League welcomed outside help, black and white. It regarded the federal government as an ally, and with good reason: the Justice Department appointed federal examiners in 1966 and two years later intervened on behalf of Wyche in his suit against the clerk of elections. In 1970 the government again sued the registrar of voters when 159 blacks were stricken from the rolls. Although white civil rights workers were no longer needed once local blacks had gained sufficient self-confidence, the Voters League continued to rely on white lawyers from the LCDC. The league also called upon SEDFRE to provide political education and training. Upon his election as police chief in 1969, SEDFRE staff members helped Wyche develop a police community relations program. Five years later it sent a team of experts to advise Adell Williams, Tallulah's first black mayor.[35]

A long-established nucleus of activists and a towering individual leader gave blacks in Tallulah cohesion and strength. In Ferriday, Concordia Parish, by contrast, organizational rivalries and the absence of effective leadership fostered weakness and disunity. The result was a fragmented movement that failed to achieve the dynamism of either the Madison Parish Voters League or the Bogalusa Voters League. The Ferriday movement failed, too, to attract the kind of vigorous federal intervention that had so helped blacks in Tallulah and Bogalusa. The absence of a history of black organization and leadership helps to explain this contrast: Ferriday had no NAACP branch, no strong union local, no active voters league, no leaders of the caliber of A. Z. Young, Robert Hicks, Gayle Jenkins, or Zelma Wyche. Yet Ferriday presents a not atypical example of a relatively weak local insurgency that, thanks to the impetus attained by the wider civil rights movement, still managed to change the status quo.

The slowness of indigenous black leadership to emerge owed something to the character of Ferriday itself, a sawmill town close to important oil fields. Loggers and roustabouts were tough men, and Ferriday, the boyhood home of Jerry Lee Lewis and Jimmy Swaggart, offered them the kind of entertainment that gave it the reputation of a "wide open" town. According to John Martzell, "In a state filled with mean towns . . . Ferriday is the meanest." Ferriday also lay within the economic hinterland of Natchez, Mississippi, and the Natchez area boasted one of the most murderous Klan units in the South. In December 1964 members of this group killed Frank Morris by torching his shoe repair shop; in August 1965 an explosion destroyed Hope Well Baptist Church; in November a bomb blew out the windows of Robert Lewis's home. (Lewis, leader of the new NAACP branch, was then arrested for "aggravated assault" when he stood outside with a shotgun). At the end of the year a black-owned Esso service station was burnt to the ground. In Natchez itself the president of the NAACP was seriously injured in a bomb attack. In 1967 the branch treasurer, Wharlest Jackson, died in a car explosion.[36]

So if blacks in Ferriday seemed more fear-stricken than those in Bogalusa, despite the fact that they composed a majority of the town's population, they had reason to be. "Bogalusa was a picnic compared to Ferriday," according to one FBI agent. When CORE workers arrived in the town in July 1965, they found a community "paralyzed, unable to act for fear of reprisals or terrorism." No minister would let them hold meetings in his church. Not a soul would house them: they had to commute from Alexandria through seventy miles of dangerous countryside. When the board of the NAACP state conference met in Ferriday, it began its deliberations well before noon "so that we can be out of Ferriday before dark for safety's sake." The CORE workers eventually found accommodation in the town, but they felt it prudent to change their address every few days. Molotov cocktails hurled from passing cars were an everyday occurrence.

When it became clear that the CORE team would not be intimidated, however, a local movement began to crystallize. At first the Ferriday Freedom Movement comprised students from the Negro high school, but in time a few adults lent support. As happened in Bogalusa and Tallulah, the beating of white CORE workers in broad daylight electrified the black community, prompting the first civil rights march in the town's history. "The Negro community feels guilty about letting 2 beatings occur in their neighborhood," wrote Meldon Acheson, a white summer volunteer, "so I walk around with my black eye and people can't get involved fast enough!"

Members of the Ferriday Freedom Movement integrated the lunch counter at Walgreen's drugstore and obtained cards from the public library. Several applied for admission to the local trade school, and in February 1966 three young children integrated a white elementary school. The movement called upon blacks to boycott the Arcade Theater, a movie house that still made blacks enter through a separate door and sit in the balcony. "I think they've started to move," Acheson reported, "and it's only a matter of time before they get their 'first-class' citizenship. . . . The determination of the youth, and their example of overcoming fear, has begun to catch hold of their parents." In the spring of 1966 black youths responded to a Klan circular by distributing a leaflet of their own in white neighborhoods. It consisted of a poem and contained the following lines:

> As I lay asleep in my bed
> The KU KLUX KLAN put a letter at my head.
> As I began to read it my anger grew bigger,
> Because the first line read, "Dear Nigger." . . .
> They've scared the people and have them upset.
> But I'll get one of those peckerwoods yet.
> They still think that I'm scared of ghosts,
> But I'll send them to hell with the DEVIL as their host.
> When things are good and going on alright
> PECKERWOOD stay from around my house at night.
> Because after reading the FIREY CROSS,
> I'M still the boss.
> To find out who's best you need a good distinguisher,
> So I hope you understand — THE FIREY CROSS EXTINGUISHER.

These sentiments were a far cry from the nonviolent gospel that CORE had tried to spread in the early 1960s.[37]

Meldon Acheson, a native of Iowa then attending the University of Arizona, had been an idealistic member of the Tucson CORE group. The ubiquity of guns in the black community and the matter-of-fact way in which the other CORE workers accepted their presence shocked him at first, but he soon learned to live with guns. "Most projects here in the dangerous areas have arms in the house to 'protect' against night attacks," he explained to his parents. But the klansmen "are as afraid of us as we are of them," he reassured them; the guns were never likely to be fired in anger. To David Whatley, the twenty-year-old leader of the Ferriday Freedom Movement, the threat of the

Klan was all too real and guns an absolute necessity. "Only by the Grace of God and the tiresome and lonely Gardshifts that we are undergoing every night from six o'clock until six thirty A.M. and later" had he survived a winter of Klan attacks. Whatley became the first and only African-American in Ferriday's previously all-white high school. "He goes through a lot each day," a CORE worker reported. "Books spit on, clothes wet when in gym, and the usual heckling."

As CORE's presence faded in 1966, a newly formed NAACP branch took up some of the slack. At first it had to meet in a vacant lot but eventually, by subjecting ministers to pressure and persuasion, it obtained the use of a church. In August 1966, after the bombing of a member's home, the branch announced a boycott of virtually all the town's white-owned businesses. The protest was inspired, in part, by the highly effective boycotts across the Mississippi River in Natchez and Port Gibson, both of them also organized by the NAACP. Rudy Shields, who directed the Natchez boycott, advised the Ferriday NAACP on how to conduct the campaign. The instigation of the boycott heightened tension considerably: the Natchez boycott had diverted much trade to the town, and Ferriday's white merchants now faced the prospect of ruin. During one of his visits Shields was arrested for "molesting a customer"; when NAACP president Robert Lewis led a protest march to the city hall he was met by twenty policemen and Mayor L. W. Davis, submachine gun in hand.[38]

By the end of 1966, however, the boycott was increasingly ineffective, and the movement no nearer its goal of forcing the city into face-to-face negotiations. Part of the problem lay in weak and fragmented leadership. The Ferriday Freedom Movement coexisted uneasily with the NAACP; the NAACP youth council was at odds with the elderly branch president; a Civic League organized by Father August Thompson was trying to promote biracial talks; and a shadowy Deacons for Defense group lurked in the background. In addition, a group of young blacks calling themselves "the Spirits" took it upon themselves to enforce the boycott through intimidation; their activities threatened to discredit the movement. Gloster Current sent Harvey Britton to resolve the impasse, and Britton recalled his shock upon first encountering the Spirits.

> [The NAACP] had a church meeting and a young man got up and talked about a couple of teachers who had broken the boycott, and the fact that the Spirits had visited them, and that they now understood. And my first thought was, "Here I am in a religious setting. I have a highly motivated group of young people in the church. . . . And faith is the thing that is moving them." And then the young man said, "And when all the windows in the cars were broken out, they understood."

Britton denounced such activities in no uncertain terms. Years later, he laughed at the naive stereotype that he, as someone born and bred in the North, had held of black southerners.³⁹

Britton's decision to lift the boycott, and the waning of Klan influence under FBI pressure and public disapproval, paved the way for a rapprochement between the "white power structure" and representatives of the black community. Various outside parties had tried their hand as mediators, including the federal Community Relations Service and the Louisiana biracial commission, but Father Thompson was the key individual in bringing the two sides together. A black Catholic priest who had lived in Ferriday since 1962, he made valiant and ultimately successful efforts to unite the black community behind a list of negotiable demands. In April 1967 the city finally set up a biracial committee, black voters electing seven people and the mayor selecting five of them. It was hardly the millenium, but it did constitute a victory for the black people of Ferriday.

Political power, however, proved elusive. When Father Thompson appealed to Governor McKeithen to use his influence on the whites, the governor, always the practical politician, told the priest that blacks should concentrate on voter registration. "You can have all the civil rights marches you want, but put your energies into getting people to vote. And I'll make sure that no-one screws around with you." But in 1966 the city council prescribed runoff elections, which ended the "first past the post" system. It also prohibited "single-shot" voting, which prevented blacks from concentrating their ballots on favored candidates. Together with the system of at-large elections, these rules enabled whites to translate their bare majority in voter registration into complete control of municipal government.⁴⁰

When black organizations competed for leadership, as in Ferriday, the establishment of a united front was always difficult. It was made yet more difficult by the position of the national NAACP, whose officers had always been extremely wary of cooperation with other groups. Now, more than ever, they wished to discourage local coalitions, fearing that NAACP branches might become tainted by association with the likes of SNCC and CORE, whose move toward black separatism created an ideological breach that they regarded as unbridgeable. At the NAACP's national convention in July 1966, Roy Wilkins denounced Black Power in the most forceful terms he could muster, characterizing it as "a reverse Mississippi, a reverse Hitler, a reverse Ku Klux Klan." But organizational self-interest, as much as doctrinal purity, dictated New York's distrust of other groups. As always, competition for publicity and money militated against coalitions in which the NAACP might become submerged. Now, moreover, New York calculated that the growth of black nationalism in SNCC and CORE would give the NAACP an opportunity, in the words of director of branches Gloster Current, to pick up "mature and balanced young people" from the "defections in their ranks."[41]

Local NAACP members did not necessarily share New York's hostility to other groups and sometimes expressed impatience with the sectarianism of Wilkins and Current. "I don't care who does the job in northeast Louisiana," wrote the head of the Ferriday branch, "just as long as the black man becomes a free man in this society." Mary Jamieson, appointed to the post of Louisiana field director at the start of 1966, shared these sentiments. A young white woman from Long Island, Jamieson had become active in the NAACP while a teacher at Holy Rosary, a black Catholic high school in Lafayette. She subsequently became the first white student at Grambling College. Jamieson recognized CORE's dominance in certain areas and tried to work closely with the local organizations that CORE had sponsored. In Ferriday, for example, she facilitated the election of David Whatley, head of the Ferriday Freedom Movement, to the vice presidency of the NAACP youth council. In Bogalusa, she wanted to revitalize the weak branch by harnessing the strength of the Bogalusa Voters League; NAACP lawyer Marion Overton White collected over one hundred memberships when he addressed a BVL meeting in August 1966.[42]

Jamieson's ecumenical approach, however, soon earned her reprimands from Gloster Current. Refusing to accept the memberships sent in by White, he warned her to avoid associating with the Deacons for Defense. That meant steering clear of the BVL. He also reproached her for issuing a joint press statement with CORE worker John Zippert. "It is best for the NAACP to proceed independently," insisted Current, even if that meant organizing some communities later rather than sooner. "We should organize slowly," he explained, "and as our movement is strengthened, some of the people who used to work with us are undoubtedly going to return." In October 1966 Current fired Jamieson.[43]

Harvey R. H. Britton, Jamieson's successor, was much more sensitive to the concerns of the national office, and he developed a close rapport with Current. A native of New York City, Britton had trained as a radio and television repairman before serving three years in the Army. He then attended a college in West Virginia, first as a preministerial student, then as a sociology major. Graduating in 1966, he joined the association as a temporary field director assigned to New Haven, Connecticut. After organizing a successful membership drive, Current sent him to Louisiana on a six-month posting. When Britton arrived to take up the post in January 1967, his knowledge of Louisiana was virtually nil. Twenty-six at the time, with a shock of wavy hair that accentuated his youthful appearance, Britton ended up serving as the state field director for nine years.[44]

He found the NAACP in a parlous condition. Of the fifty or so branches, half had fewer than one hundred members; a dozen had failed to meet for at least five years. Much of Britton's incessant traveling was wasted, for many branch officers had no idea how to respond to his requests for information. The association had still not fully recovered from the "chilling effect" of the 1956 injunction: in 1967 there were barely eight thousand members in Louisiana, fewer than in 1955. Schoolteachers were still very reluctant to take out memberships. Ministers, too, rarely supported the NAACP, and the preachers who headed branches tended to be old and incapable. Perhaps the most startling evidence of the organization's weakness was its lack of success in reestablishing strong branches in some of the biggest cities. Branches in Shreveport and Baton Rouge barely limped along; the Monroe and Lafayette branches were all but defunct; the Alexandria branch was in "constant decay."

With the exception of Lake Charles and the small branch in Lake Providence (which the Reverend John Henry Scott had led for almost thirty years) only the New Orleans branch had a record of stability. With a membership of more than three thousand, and with experienced officers whose service to the organization went back, in some cases, twenty, thirty, and forty years, the New Orleans branch provided a core of leadership in the state. But the prominence of the Crescent City branch, Britton thought, had a disadvantage: its leaders tended to dominate the state organization, deterring less experienced, less educated, and less articulate branch presidents from attending and participating. Hence the rural branches, which composed the bulk of the membership, had little contact with or influence within the Louisiana State Conference of Branches (LSC). The large membership of the New Orleans branch, moreover, belied its factionalism and general torpidity. In Britton's view only five branches in the entire state, all of them rural, functioned effectively.[45]

Yet Louisiana, Britton discovered, was the quintessential NAACP state, regardless of whatever other groups were popular at a particular moment. The NAACP's comparatively small membership was misleading, he later explained; "our members were more members-at-large, members in faith, members in that vein, as opposed to financial contributors or people who came to meetings." With deep roots in local communities, the NAACP had the prestige and the connections to mobilize support around gut issues.

Gut issues were never in short supply, but it took leaders to articulate them. One or two dedicated and able activists could transform a moribund branch into a vigorous campaigning organization. And that could happen virtually anywhere, irrespective of the community or its history of race relations. Conversely, with the retirement or departure of key individuals a branch could just as swiftly lapse into inertia. The four strongest branches of the mid and late

1960s, Opelousas, New Roads, New Iberia, and Shreveport, illustrate this life cycle of birth, spectacular growth, and then decline.

Charles E. Bryant and Marion O. White organized the St. Landry Parish branch in August 1963, and it soon became the second largest in the state. Bryant, a schoolteacher, and White, a lawyer, challenged the cozy modus vivendi that had existed since the early 1950s, when whites permitted black voter registration only to co-opt the black vote through a combination of vote buying, petty patronage, and alliances with Negro ministers. Sheriff D. J. "Cat" Doucet, regularly reelected by a strong black vote, personified this paternalistic style of politics. Attacking segregation head-on, in short order the NAACP integrated buses, lunch counters, restaurants, and the court-house. White filed over thirty lawsuits in the field of public accommodations, and the branch orchestrated dozens of sit-ins. Bryant himself was repeatedly arrested — according to one tally, over forty times. When restaurants evaded integration by becoming "private clubs," white NAACP supporters and light-skinned mulattos obtained membership cards. The city fathers "pretended to be nice," White recalled, creating a biracial committee and asking him and Bryant to serve. They assented, but made it clear that they would not be de-flected from their NAACP work. In 1965 Bryant came within a whisker of being elected to the city council; two years later he ran for sheriff and, by chipping away at Doucet's black support, helped a white candidate to end the remarkable career of "The Cat."[46]

In the small town of New Roads, in Pointe Coupee Parish, the NAACP underwent a transformation under the leadership of Emmitt J. Douglas, a barber and businessman. In 1966 the branch instigated a boycott of selected white merchants, maintaining daily picketing for several months. One of the targets, a pharmacist, sued Douglas for $450,000 in damages and had thir-teen pickets arrested on a complaint of intimidation. The dispute climaxed in a march of two thousand people, and it ultimately wrested some jobs from the grudging merchants. In 1967 the branch organized a boycott of local schools to protest the survival of segregation under a so-called freedom of choice plan. An impetuous man and a rousing public speaker, Douglas went on to serve as president of the state conference of branches, bringing to that position the kind of assertive leadership that it had not seen since Dr. E. A. Johnson held the post in the early 1950s. Working with younger activists like Llew-ellyn Soniat and Raphael Cassimere, both of whom had risen through the New Orleans Youth Council, Douglas gave the NAACP high visibility across the state and bucked up underperforming branches. His flamboyant person-ality and tendency to shoot from the hip landed him in trouble with both friends and foes. He managed to offend both Gloster Current and Charles

Bryant, and in 1969 the Baton Rouge district attorney indicted him for inciting a riot. But he gave the state organization a much-needed shot in the arm.[47]

New Iberia provided the most striking example of a branch that came out of nowhere. Defunct since the state's injunction in 1956, it was rechartered in 1964 on the intiative of Dr. James H. Henderson, Lester Scurlock, and T. A. Bolden. "We were determined that we were going to do something," recalled Henderson, a native of North Carolina who had practiced dentistry in the town since the mid-1950s. "And we got out and we talked. We went to all of the churches, we went to the P.T.A. meetings. . . . And I guess we showed sincerity in what we were after, and I remember people just fell into line, and when someone came up and tried to block us, we rode right over him." Franzella Volter, secretary of the branch twenty years earlier when J. Leo Hardy had been beaten and run out of town, became secretary once more. The fastest-growing branch in the state, it soon boasted about a thousand members, an impressive number for a town of thirty thousand where blacks made up only a quarter of the population. Few teachers joined, and fewer ministers; the bulk of the members, according to Henderson, were working class. Numbers, however, told only part of the story. Under Henderson's leadership, the branch picketed downtown stores and outlying shopping centers, forcing the hiring of black clerks. It also utilized the 1964 Civil Rights Act by filing over sixty complaints with the Equal Employment Opportunity Commission; targets included the famous McIlhenny Company, purveyor of Tabasco sauce to the world. Henderson and Volter served on the board of the LSC and helped to organize branches in Lafayette and St. Martinville.[48]

The rapid rise, and equally rapid decline, of the Shreveport branch provided a good illustration of how the fortunes of the NAACP often depended upon one or two individuals. At the time of Martin Luther King's death Shreveport was still a monument to segregation and still maintained one of the most repressive racial orders in the South. George D'Artois, the commissioner of public safety, had squelched attempted demonstrations in Séptember 1963, and he had kept up a blanket ban on all forms of direct action, including picketing, ever since then. The most influential politician in the city, he had the entire community, white and black, cowed. By the end of 1968, however, a young writer and actor, B. J. Mason, had revived the branch, defied D'Artois, and dispelled some of the fear that had immobilized blacks.

B. J. Mason was a twenty-four-year-old graduate of Grambling College and a gifted writer who worked part-time on the *Shreveport Sun*, Louisiana's oldest black newspaper. With Harvey Britton's encouragement, he took over the branch in May 1968 and made plans to challenge the ban on picketing. Mason presided over his first mass meeting in a church that stood opposite the police station; on May 27 he personally handed D'Artois a ten-point plan for improving police-community relations. Instead of rejecting the proposals out of hand, the commissioner, no doubt with an eye on the growing black vote, listened politely and agreed to institute some changes. On June 9, Mason and three others picketed Stan's Record Shop, a store that catered to blacks but stocked racist titles ("Kajun Ku Klux Klan") and employed no Negroes. The police did not arrest them — the first time blacks in Shreveport had been allowed to picket. Soon, as Mason described the scene, "students, ministers, mothers, and common laborers were to be seen marching quietly and slowly in eighty-plus degree temperatures. . . . One old shabbily-dressed black woman laugh[ed] hysterically amid cries of 'Thank God! Thank God! Thank God!'" After a nineteen-day boycott the proprietor agreed to hire five blacks. Other stores were singled out for "selective buying" campaigns, and pickets sauntering up and down the sidewalks became a common sight.

Mason then organized a Youth Council and installed one of the most enthusiastic pickets, Larry N. Cooper, as its president. Cooper called for the teaching of black history and was arrested for "disturbing the peace" while picketing a white high school. On September 18 he led a three-mile march, attended by several thousand youths, from Booker T. Washington High to the offices of the school board. Known to all as "Boogaloo," Cooper was a born orator, and he employed the rhetoric of "Black Power" to great effect. His brand of militancy also appealed to the not-so-young. "The Youth Council . . . had men in there 45 and 50 years of age," Harvey Britton recalled.

Faced with the fastest-growing NAACP branch in the state, which in December 1968 announced a "Black Christmas," a boycott of the downtown shopping area, D'Artois made a determined effort to break up the Youth Council. Police stopped and questioned everyone entering Cooper's apartment; they trailed cars and bugged meetings; they booked drivers for nonexistent traffic offenses; they arrested Cooper himself eighteen times. Determined to go through with the boycott, the NAACP scheduled a march through the downtown business district for December 14. D'Artois denied them a permit and deployed two hundred police — virtually the entire force — to stop it. About 250 people, led by Mason, Britton, and four ministers, covered a block before being halted by the police phalanx. After a tense confrontation, they turned around and regrouped at the church. The branch officers decided to try again the following week.

In any other southern city, the protest would be judged a failure, but in the context of Shreveport it represented at least a partial victory. The marchers had not been intimidated, nor had they been arrested. The boycott was holding. The NAACP had not exactly clipped D'Artois' wings, but it had stood up to him. "For the first time," Britton told Gloster Current, "meaningful restraints have been placed upon the Safety Commissioner; and the fear of many Negroes . . . has been removed. In Shreveport, one of the strongholds of racism in northern Louisiana, long supported and enforced by city officials, the stage has been set for meaningful change." It seemed an overoptimistic assessment: on December 21 the police arrested Mason and thirty-five others when they attempted to hold another march. Soon afterward, internal wrangling paralyzed the NAACP: Larry Cooper was expelled; Mason suddenly quit as branch president. Shreveport remained a tough city and D'Artois was still firmly ensconced in power. Yet blacks had breached a psychological barrier and now massed the votes to attack a political one.[49]

By the second half of the 1960s the NAACP had acquired a certain legitimacy in the eyes of many influential whites; they viewed it as a useful point of contact and communication. "The black and white antagonists always maintained a relationship with one another, always spoke to each other," Harvey Britton recalled. "So the NAACP was seen as a legitimate vehicle by the white community to transmit information to the black community, even though it may not have been as receptive to the information coming *back* through the NAACP." Only rarely was there no communication at all: usually, Britton stressed, "You see them on the street, and you say, 'How're you doing?' 'What y'all gonna do next?' That kind of stuff." Sometimes, too, whites accepted the NAACP as the bargaining agent for the black community. It was a striking contrast to the late 1950s, when the state had attempted to destroy the organization. By 1965, however, key people of influence in the state finally admitted that black insurgency would not go away, and they preferred to deal with the NAACP rather than CORE. Governor John McKeithen's decision to create a statewide biracial commission typified this realization, and the recognition he accorded the NAACP through the commission was a rather blatant attempt to isolate CORE. The personal rapport between McKeithen and Emmitt Douglas helped to cement the state-NAACP relationship: both men were born politicians of the joke-telling, back-slapping variety.

Significantly, McKeithen tapped Jesse N. Stone Jr. to help organize the commission's black representation. Like McKeithen, Stone came from north Louisiana and had been raised in a hard school of race relations; although firmly identified with the NAACP, he was used to dealing with white segregationists in a friendly and diplomatic way. Yet McKeithen almost torpedoed his own initiative by insisting on personally selecting some of the commission's black members, something that even the NAACP moderates balked at. They were dissuaded from boycotting the commission when Stone told them that however many members McKeithen named, the governor had agreed that he, Stone, would be able to name twice as many. To nobody's surprise, the black members of the commission included some fairly conservative people by the standards of 1965 black militancy, but they also included a fair cross section of the NAACP's leadership.[50]

Through the biracial commission McKeithen established personal contacts with many of Louisiana's NAACP-oriented black leaders, and he made himself accessible to them. Tall, funny, and personable, the governor resembled Lyndon Johnson in both his skill in dealing with people in a "one-to-one" situation and his appreciation of the growing black vote. Men like Emmitt Douglas and Harvey Britton got to know him well. They even grew to like him. His metamorphosis from segregationist to racial moderate had a calming influence on race relations during the second half of the 1960s.

McKeithen relished the considerable power of Louisiana's governorship and, in contrast to Jimmie Davis, did not hesitate to exercise it. Harvey Britton remembered calling on the governor and asking him to appoint the first black person to a draft board, pointing out that a vacancy existed in Shreveport. McKeithen picked up the phone and ordered the appointment made. A few minutes later the phone rang and, apparently, someone in Shreveport questioned the order. "Yes, yes! Me! The governor!" McKeithen barked. "That's who said put him on the board! Me! The governor! I said put him on the board!" Slamming the phone down he turned to Britton and said, "They don't understand sometimes. I'm the governor!"[51]

The commission's staff members, John Martzell and Jesse Stone, could draw upon McKeithen's authority to defuse racial conflicts. In May 1969, for example, police in Leesville arrested eighteen members of the NAACP State Conference who, having heard that black servicemen from Fort Polk were experiencing off-base discrimination, had set up an improvised "military complaints center" in a tent. The mayor of Leesville, "Fatty" Fertita, had vowed to keep the NAACP out of his city, and he did not appreciate McKeithen's friendly suggestion that he release the prisoners. Told to mind his own business and stay out of Leesville's affairs, McKeithen exploded. "As long as I'm governor of the state," he told Fertita, "you do what *I* say or you move that damn city to Texas." He then vowed to send in the state police and the National Guard, placing the city under martial law, unless the prisoners were set free. "At which point," Harvey Britton remembered, "the town of Leesville turned around and said to us, 'Out. Look, y'all gotta go.'" After being incarcerated in a filthy jail for two days, the prisoners were released on bond. Many years later, asked about this incident, McKeithen denied having threatened Fertita. Yet two weeks after their "very friendly" telephone conversation, the governor sent a large contingent of state police to Leesville to ensure that the city did not interfere with an NAACP mass rally.[52]

The biracial commission could only formally mediate a dispute if local white officials asked for its assistance, but when it did intervene, it often got results. In one north Louisiana town, for example, Jesse Stone persuaded a white family business, the target of a boycott, to talk with the Reverend Elijah Brass, their hated antagonist. When he first entered the family store to encounter "a group of white men seated round a pot-bellied stove," the outlook for brokering the dispute seemed unpropitious: the head of the family started the conversation by saying that Brass ought to be shot. In this case, however, as in many others, all it took was an outside mediator, backed by the authority of the governor, to bring the two sides together. Here, too, such mediation was a godsend to the black protagonists, who were desperate to settle before their protests collapsed. "I'm so glad to see you; I don't know what to do," Brass told Stone. "I've been to the cemetery today and I was praying to my dead father because I've got these people out here and we can't stay out and I just don't know what to do." To Stone, getting blacks out of the streets was often the best thing that could happen: "They were tired and ready to come home." [53]

Sometimes it only took one phone call from the governor to defuse an apparently trivial dispute that, in the increasingly hysterical atmosphere of the late 1960s, might have had tragic consequences if left to fester or approached in a ham-fisted way.

The student strike at Grambling College was one such instance. Founded in 1901 as a private high school, converted into a junior college in 1928, and by 1967 a four-year college with about four thousand black students and six white ones, Grambling was the personal fiefdom of Ralph Waldo Emerson Jones. Like many presidents of state-funded black colleges, Jones wielded autocratic power and, as long as he obeyed the dictates of the state board of education, could count on staying in his post until he chose to retire. "A simple, quiet Negro village in the scrub-pine obscurity of the Deep South," Grambling had scarcely been touched by the civil rights movement, or by any of the other cultural and political currents of the 1960s. The college made a fetish of athletics: it boasted more graduates who played professional football than any other college except for Notre Dame; Grambling's baseball team was coached by President Jones himself. The college's rules were not merely paternalistic but oppressive: students had to eat breakfast at 6:00 A.M. underneath signs telling them to "Take bite-size mouthfuls." Women were not allowed to wear slacks, drive cars, or smoke in the student union. Off-campus dating was forbidden; dormitories were locked at 10 P.M. [54]

In the spring of 1967 Jones agreed to liberalize the rules after a student protest. By October, however, the changes had not been implemented, and students instituted a boycott of classes. Contending that Grambling's ethos elevated the sports field over the classroom, the protesters attacked the preferential treatment received by athletes and argued that Jones should resign as college president if he continued to coach the baseball team. Over half the student body boycotted classes; about a quarter threatened to withdraw from college. Students blocked the entrances to the administration building and demanded action on their grievances.[55]

McKeithen dispatched Martzell and Stone to sort out the mess. They arrived at Grambling on October 27, the day of the Grambling–Texas Southern football game, to find that the students had effectively taken over the university. "Dr. Jones lived not unlike a Balkan prince," Martzell discovered. "We sat down to dinner, and they brought in . . . an incredible layout of food — you wouldn't believe it." Perusing the students' list of demands, Martzell could hardly believe that any college still maintained such trivial and onerous rules. Apprised of the situation by phone, McKeithen agreed: "If that's what's going on, I'd [expletive] revolt myself!" As gently as they could, Stone and Martzell told Jones that the governor thought he should concede the demands. Jones meekly agreed. The National Guard arrived on the campus, a few students were expelled, and the boycott collapsed.[56]

Much of the commission's work remained invisible. It organized area committees, for example, that could be quickly contacted by the commission's staff. When the unlikely figure of Rev. Avery Alexander appeared in north Louisiana to lead a march from Haynesville to Jonesboro, a route that led through the racist bastion of Homer, John Martzell quietly alerted influential whites and asked them to ensure the marchers' safety. He also persuaded the sheriff of Claiborne Parish to release Alexander after his arrest for parading without a permit. "They were protected and marched to their heart's content," Martzell recalled. According to Troy Middleton, the press followed a deliberate policy of not reporting the commission's interventions, "to prevent offering opportunities to rabble-rousers to come in and preach their hate doctrines."

During the five years of its existence, the statewide commission inspired and facilitated biracial negotiations in many Louisiana communities. Indeed, biracial committees — the bêtes noires of segregationists in the early 1960s — became all the rage during the second half of the decade. Alexandria created one in 1967; Mayor Victor Schiro of New Orleans appointed one in the same year. They already existed in Baton Rouge, Lake Charles, Lafayette, Hammond, Jonesboro, Opelousas, and New Iberia. Of all the major cities in the state, only Shreveport bucked the trend.[57]

Yet Jesse Stone expressed skepticism about the value of biracial committees. Too often, he believed, blacks made the establishment of a BRC the centerpiece of their demands. They then entered negotiations only to be fobbed off with vague promises, token concessions, or inaction.

The biracial committee, I thought, occupied too prominent a place in what they were trying to do. But there was this real desire on the part of black people to sit at the table and talk things out on a "man-to-man" basis when we really had no experience in bargaining and dealing with the white man. . . . And every time blacks and whites sat down at the bargaining table, blacks lost. We would proceed by telling the white people off, feeling good, but with them shaking their head and saying "this is a good meeting," you know, with nothing accomplished.

The setting up of a biracial committee tended to become an end in itself, rather than simply one means to an end. And this was in some measure true, he feared, of the state commission. Assessing the commission's accomplishments many years later, Stone confessed to some disappointment.[58]

For the whites on the state commission, getting to know Louisiana's black leadership, or at least an important segment of it, was an important learning experience. John Martzell was convinced that the frank discussions helped erode the ignorance that resulted in racial stereotypes. "One of the best ways to break down the myths about two groups is to put the groups together, and they laugh, and say, 'You mean you believe that!'" Yet most of the black members were worldly wise in dealing with whites and had little need of such education. And they became increasingly suspicious that the commission was being used to damp down racial fires rather than produce tangible improvements in the lives of Louisiana's black citizens.[59]

McKeithen's response to the Bogalusa-to-Baton Rouge march of August 1967 provided a typical example of the commission's basically reactive role. This march was also an excellent example of how local activists combined the traditional tactics of the civil rights movement with the new rhetoric of Black Power to successfully induce near-panic in the federal and state authorities.

The Bogalusa-to-Baton Rouge march had many bizarre and even comic aspects, not the least of which were its origins. In July 1967 A. Z. Young wrote to McKeithen requesting a meeting with the biracial commission to discuss the "steadily worsening" situation in Bogalusa. Due to what John Martzell described as a "bureaucratic foul-up," the letter was filed away without ever coming to McKeithen's attention. When he failed to receive a reply, Young thought he had been deliberately snubbed, and he announced that the Bogalusa Voters League would march on the state capitol. A hastily improvised list of demands focused on the lack of Negroes in state employment, drawing particular attention to the absence of a single black state policeman.

The scenario had all the ingredients of a political Molotov cocktail. The route of the march ran through the predominantly white portion of the Florida Parishes, an area populated by "tough, Mississippi-type rednecks," a good many of whom belonged to the Klan. During the Selma-to-Montgomery march of 1965 the presence of thousands of troops had not prevented the Klan from murdering Viola Liuzzo, a white woman. The possibility of klansmen attacking and even killing marchers during the 106-mile trek — twice the length of the Selma-to-Montgomery march — was all too real. The worst potential flashpoint was Denham Springs, in Livingston Parish, which Martzell characterized as "the Klan country of all Klan country."

Equally worrying, the march took place during the worst "long, hot summer" of the 1960s, in the immediate aftermath of devastating and bloody riots in Newark and Detroit. Every city in the country was trembling with tension. Baton Rouge, the march's destination, was widely regarded as the Louisiana city most likely to blow up, with a poorly organized black community almost at the boiling point over police brutality. The 271-man Baton Rouge police force had only twelve black officers, and these men were still in effect segregated on the job, traveling in separate patrol cars. When Mayor W. W. Dumas ordered the force to pair the black officers with whites, he had to rescind the directive when the whites threatened to strike. To cap it all, H. Rap Brown, the chairman of SNCC, was due to speak to the marchers from the capitol steps. Brown had recently been arrested for inciting a riot in Cambridge, Maryland, and had described the riots as "just dress rehearsals for revolution." The fact that Brown had grown up in Baton Rouge would give his visit further incendiary potential.[60]

The nine-day march passed without serious violence, but it produced some nasty moments. After dozens of whites tried to break through police lines to get at the marchers as they entered Livingston Parish, the head of the state police, Colonel Thomas Burbank, persuaded the Klan to leave the marchers alone as long as they went clear through the parish the next day. But when A. Z. Young insisted that they rest a day before resuming the march, the Klan repudiated the agreement, and Burbank, incensed that Young had broken his word, threatened to withdraw the state police. "The federal government went absolutely bonkers," recalled Martzell, threatening to send in paratroopers if the state failed to provide adequate protection. McKeithen ordered Burbank to continue guarding the marchers and, in addition, called up more than eight hundred National Guardsmen. Deploying the part-time soldiers was a shrewd move. "Those crazy rednecks out there," McKeithen explained, "they'll jump on a policeman but they'll never jump on an American soldier. They're so patriotic they'll just never do it." When he learned that the adjutant general proposed leading the march atop a tank and wanted his men to carry loaded rifles, the governor could barely contain himself with laughter. "These guys are the National Guard," he told Martzell. "I'm not going to give those guys any bullets!"

As the marchers passed through Denham Springs, soldiers flanking them on both sides, white onlookers jeered but kept their distance. Moreover, by the time the marchers arrived in Baton Rouge, "Rap" Brown had been arrested for carrying a gun onto a plane (the FBI had had him under close surveillance and nabbed him in New York). Police with shotguns patrolled Baton Rouge's black neighborhoods and fifteen hundred National Guardsmen stood at the ready. The feared riot did not take place.[61]

If the march proved a law enforcement triumph, it left the black members of the biracial commission seething with frustration. Only when A. Z. Young vowed to repeat the protest, threatening simultaneous marches that would converge on Baton Rouge from "the four corners of the state," did McKeithen convene the commission to discuss the question of state employment. The governor was especially embarrassed by the fact that Colonel Burbank had recently hired 150 state policemen, all of them whites. His explanation for this state of affairs, that sacrosanct civil service rules were to blame, did not impress the black members, who also questioned his claim to have improved the lot of blacks in state employment generally. Only the threat of demonstrations, complained Rev. T. J. Jemison, had moved the governor to address the problem. "The Commission will not receive one ounce of credit. The Bogalusa march will be the cause of a [black] state trooper, not the Human Relations Commission. . . . I regret that we have pussyfooted so long." Henry Carroll of Monroe put the matter more bluntly: "We are serving as Uncle Toms." A few months later, civil service rules having been bent, the state police hired two black troopers. As Jemison commented acerbically, "If white men want to do it, it is done."[62]

Some blacks had opposed the commission from the outset. To CORE lawyer Nils Douglas, it was a "do-nothing committee" that merely testified to the governor's fancy political footwork, his attempt to be all things to all men while remaining, at heart, a white segregationist. McKeithen certainly had the ability, as Camille Gravel noted, to mix political oil and water. Gravel once visited the governor's mansion to find him holding simultaneous meetings with blacks and klansmen, each group oblivious of the other's presence in the building. The biracial commission enabled McKeithen to institutionalize this policy of playing both ends against the middle. According to a 1966 survey of racial attitudes in Louisiana, whites expected the commission "to act as a kind of safety valve which will keep the lid on the situation and maintain as much of the status quo as possible." Blacks, on the other hand, wanted the commission to be a vehicle "for solid accomplishment." Judged solely in political terms, McKeithen walked this tightrope with great success: in 1967 he romped home to a second term, garnering 82 percent of the total vote and an even greater percentage of the black vote. This lopsided vote, however, overstated black enthusiasm for McKeithen: the governor was running against Congressman John Rarick, the Klan-backed candidate of the far right. Perhaps the most common opinion was that of James Henderson, the commission member from New Iberia. "I think he was as sincere as any white man in this state could have been at that time — but that doesn't mean that politically he didn't try to use us."[63]

By 1967 Stone and Martzell had become frustrated by McKeithen's use of them and the commission for crisis management. "Louisiana is doomed to future discord," they warned, "if the Commission's principal function in the public eye is 'keeping the lid on.'" Poverty and unemployment were now the biggest problems facing blacks, and they demanded urgent action. "Viewed in the coldest light the fact is that, by and large, Negro Louisianans are the State's poorest producers; and, by and large, white Louisianans are to blame. The question is what can be done about it." They believed that the biracial commission, in its present form, could do little. Even its chairman, Troy Middleton, agreed that the commission had exhausted its usefulness as an advisory body.[64]

The commission's inability to substantially improve the position of blacks in state and municipal employment underscored their point. Between 1964 and 1971 the number of black people employed by the state increased by about 4 percent. According to one careful study, however, this increase "did not improve the occupational position of the Negro state employee." To be sure, visitors to state government offices in Baton Rouge could now see a few black typists and secretaries where before there had been none. But black clerical workers numbered only fourteen out of nearly twenty-five hundred. The majority of black state employees remained in the lowest occupational category, that of unskilled laborer. Very few indeed were hired in supervisory, technical, and professional positions. For example, the one thousand or so examiners, inspectors, and investigators employed by state agencies included only seven blacks. The situation in city government was little better. A 1967 survey of Baton Rouge showed that blacks held 16 percent of the municipal jobs but made up 65 percent of the laborers. The fire department was over 97 percent white, a handful of black firemen serving in one "Negro" station. In Shreveport the disparities were even more pronounced: 82 percent of black city employees were classified as "service maintenance" compared with 13 percent of white employees.[65]

The stagnating economic position of the black population testified to the magnitude of the so-called crisis of victory confronting the civil rights movement. The goals of civil and political equality under the law had largely been accomplished: public accommodations had been desegregated, the battle for the vote had been won, discriminatory statutes based on race had been erased.

But if the civil rights movement had toppled the legal scaffolding of white supremacy, the edifice itself remained largely intact. Civil rights legislation had so far had singularly little effect on the distribution of wealth and the structure of the employment market; indeed, the individualistic ethic implicit in the Fourteenth Amendment and the 1964 Civil Rights Act reflected a deeply rooted ideological commitment to free market capitalism, to the belief that the removal of artificial racial barriers would enable blacks to enter the economic mainstream under their own efforts.

Some blacks subscribed to this optimistic faith. Revius Ortique, chairman of the New Orleans Community Relations Council, saw "an unparalleled era of opportunity in employment" for blacks; J. Harvey Kerns, secretary of the New Orleans Urban League, agreed that "never before have the opportunities for competent Negroes been so great." Others offered a more pessimistic assessment. The NAACP's Arthur Chapital warned that the language of equal opportunity would ring hollow if decent jobs were not available, and employers would not create jobs for blacks by displacing whites. Even in a theoretically "color blind" job market, he added, blacks, worse educated and worse trained than whites, would find it difficult to compete. Harvey Britton's experience in trying to secure secretarial help for the NAACP office in New Orleans exemplified this problem: most applicants lacked basic skills, he complained; those hired proved to be poor workers.

The explosion of riots in the urban ghettos of the North and West underlined the failure of the civil rights movement to bring tangible economic improvements to the lives of most black people. Politicized by the rhetoric of freedom and equality, the black poor felt massively disappointed when so little changed after the great legislative victories of the movement. The failure of the War on Poverty to alleviate their economic plight — especially when hopes had been raised so high by President Johnson's grandiose promises of a "Great Society" — added to that sense of disillusionment. In the wake of Watts, Chicago, Newark, and Detroit, black leaders gradually woke up to the fact that the urban poor constituted social dynamite and that the mainstream civil rights organizations had made virtually no effort to organize them. As Nils R. Douglas pointed out, the movement had owed its success to strategy and leadership rather than weight of number; "The crucial masses remain substantially untouched."[66]

The NAACP's failure to relate to those masses derived partly from the association's predominantly middle-class leadership, which found it difficult to identify and communicate with the ghetto poor. It also derived from the NAACP's basic orientation, the product of a long history of focusing on discriminatory laws and practices. "They lacked imagination outside of the civil rights movement," he recalled of the New Orleans branch leaders. "Anything

that did not speak literally to 'I see civil rights,' they couldn't deal with."
The legacy of Cold War anticommunism, when the NAACP had deliberately
divorced itself from the labor-left agenda, nurtured a lingering suspicion of
anything that hinted at socialism or economic radicalism. The war in Vietnam,
moreover, reinforced fear of communism among the older leaders. In New
Orleans, the Youth Council's wish to endorse Martin Luther King's criticisms
of the war evoked strong opposition from the branch.

The NAACP's shortcomings should not be judged too severely. In truth,
the social and economic problems of the black ghettos were of overwhelming
magnitude and complexity. If they defeated the best efforts of the federal government, with all its poverty experts and billions of dollars, it is scarcely to
be wondered that the NAACP — for all its prestige, a shoestring operation,
with a small staff and modest funds — did not know where to begin. Besides,
the NAACP always found that more immediate and more emotional issues
needed addressing. Much of the time it found itself reacting to specific incidents and situations; long-range planning remained an unaffordable luxury.
"There just wasn't time for that," Britton recalled. "It was still a time for access — 'you've got to get in here, you've got to get in there, you've got to stop
police brutality.' "[67]

The ghetto riots made "police brutality" an issue of searing urgency. The
term covered a multitude of sins: threatening, abusive, and racist language;
harassment and entrapment of homosexuals; sexual exploitation of black
women; the beating of prisoners; and, most controversially, the unnecessary
use of lethal force. It was a complex issue made yet more complex by other
overlapping problems, including inadequate law enforcement in black neighborhoods, the quality of justice available to blacks in the courts, and the
employment and use of black policemen.

The phrase "police brutality" became such a hackneyed cliché in the 1960s
that a cynic might suspect it had been so stretched through overuse as to
be emptied of meaning. Indeed, one would suppose that police brutality declined in the late 1960s, for the growth of the black vote would, logically,
make elected law enforcement officials more sensitive to the black community.
There is some evidence that police brutality did in fact diminish. Contrite law
enforcement officials sometimes apologized for past brutalities and pledged to
mend their ways. Jesse Stone extracted an apology from George D'Artois for
the 1963 beating of Harry Blake: "He said 'I'm sorry I did it. And I promise it
won't ever happen again.'" The Rev. J. H. Scott reported that the police chief
of Lake Providence, four of whose men were indicted by a federal grand jury
for beating Negro prisoners, "actually begged me forgiveness for the things
he had done." When blacks mounted a boycott of certain grocery stores in
Franklin, St. Mary Parish, the local police chief ordered his men to protect

the black pickets. Police brutality "became a thing of the past," averred one activist. In Tallulah, police chief Jimmy Rogan befriended the leaders of the voters league and tried to calm the town's racial tensions. "Back in the old days," he explained to John Martzell, "when we had some black fellow that gave us trouble we'd just take him into the back and bend him over a barrel and take a razor-strap and whip him a few licks and that was it. But you can't do that anymore. Times change."[68]

Hence the frequency with which blacks voiced the charge of brutality probably reflected heightened sensitivity to the issue rather than a general intensification of the problem. Nevertheless, the reality was harsh enough. Part of that reality was documented in *Police Handling of Arrestees,* a research project supervised by Father Joseph H. Fichter of Loyola University. This study came to the unequivocal conclusion that in New Orleans "tactics of terror are used by some policemen. . . . People who are ready to submit are punched senseless; people who are helplessly handcuffed are hit with clubs; people who are surrounded by policemen in a jail or show-up are cuffed and abused." The researchers' informants — lawyers, judges, witnesses, policemen, and a sample of two hundred arrestees — also provided evidence of deliberate false arrests. "The majority of arrests are 'bum raps,'" a former cop explained: if police felt that their arrest record fell below par, they would pick up men for vagrancy and loitering or go into bars and arrest women for prostitution. "They arrest many people for nothing at all, especially Negroes," one judge confirmed. "Have *you* ever been stopped and asked for an ID card, or have to show a dollar in your pocket?" Excoriated by Mayor Schiro and Superintendent Giarrusso as a tissue of lies, the meticulously researched report should not have surprised anyone with the least familiarity with the NOPD.[69]

Police misbehavior would occasionally so outrage blacks that a community rose up in protest. This happened in New Iberia, where on April 18, 1967, a distressed black woman, Rose Mary Harris, told James Henderson and Franzella Volter that the previous day an officer had raped her in the backseat of a police car. The branch officials had no doubt whatsoever about the veracity of her statement: there had long been rumors that the officer in question, Lt. Henry Dorsey, had sexually abused black women; here was firsthand evidence. The NAACP demanded the officer's indefinite suspension pending his prosecution for rape. NAACP delegations held long, tense meetings with city officials; blacks marched to city hall and demanded justice. Yet the case slipped away. The city's civil service commission first suspended Dorsey, then reinstated him. The city at first charged him with rape, then substituted the lesser charge of simple battery. When a jury acquitted him, Dorsey sued the NAACP for $1.5 million in damages. A judge dismissed the suit, but

Dorsey continued to serve on the New Iberia force until his retirement many years later.[70]

For Britton, the Dorsey case typified the inability of blacks to obtain justice in a judicial and law enforcement system that remained virtually lily-white. "Local officials absolutely refuse to accept major charges against whites when filed by Negroes," he reported. "In most parishes police officials still consider their main responsibility as that of protecting white citizens by 'keeping Negroes in their place.'" In a town on the west bank of St. James Parish, for example, a white bartender killed a Negro customer for making a pass at a white waitress. Police cruised the black neighborhood to stop blacks holding a protest march; the bartender was never prosecuted. The federal government offered little succor in such cases. The FBI treated blacks so dismissively, Britton complained, that he found it hard to persuade people to go to the Bureau. Ruby Hurley, head of the NAACP's southeastern regional office, told Britton that his experiences of the FBI were "par for the course"; she had been voicing the same criticisms herself for twenty years.[71]

If blacks could rarely bring whites to justice, they could expect scant leniency if they themselves wound up in the dock. A quarter of a century had passed since the Supreme Court first set aside a Louisiana verdict because blacks had been systematically excluded from juries. Yet such exclusion persisted into the 1960s. In 1966, for example, the federal appeals court had to quash a state court verdict because no blacks had ever served as jurors in Livingston Parish, even though blacks constituted 15 percent of the population. (The trial judge had justified their exclusion by pointing to "the well known fact that the moral standards of Livingston Parish Negroes are rather low.") Other cases revealed that blacks were conspicuously absent from juries in Acadia and Tangipahoa parishes. Not-so-subtle discrimination had kept blacks off grand juries in New Orleans by disqualifying, as a matter of policy, all "daily wage earners." This elastic category included manual laborers, domestic and service workers, truck drivers, carpenters, painters, mechanics, shipfitters, boilermakers, and plasterers, the very jobs that blacks were most likely to hold. "The system was neutral, principled, and — foolproof," noted John Minor Wisdom. "No Negro ever sat on a grand jury in Orleans Parish." A federal law of 1968 laid down that voter registration lists should form the basis for jury selection; yet before and even after that date, blacks were still being sentenced to death for capital crimes, including rape, by all-white juries.[72]

The ability of blacks to defend themselves in court had improved since the 1940s, when A. P. Tureaud and Louis Berry had been the only black lawyers in the state. But it had not improved that much. The Louisiana bar included only about twenty black attorneys, and many of them were poorly trained products of the segregated and inferior law school at Southern University. A plethora of white lawyers were quite willing to represent blacks in run-of-the-mill litigation, including the gamut of criminal cases. When it came to anything that smacked of civil rights, however, they refused to become involved. Civil rights cases were unremunerative; they also exposed lawyers to the censure of the white community. In addition, with rare exceptions such as John P. Nelson, Benjamin E. Smith, and Herman L. Midlo, white lawyers had no sympathy with the civil rights movement and no desire to represent it. Even the most "liberal" of them steered clear of cases involving CORE and the local groups associated with them. When Zelma Wyche, for example, approached two white attorneys in Tallulah, both refused to defend him. One explained that representing Wyche would kill his practice; the other said that local whites would lynch him. Were it not for the dozen competent black attorneys in the state, the services of the NAACP, and the out-of-state white lawyers working with the LCDC, many blacks would have gone into the courtroom quite literally defenseless.[73]

In 1967, moreover, even that thin line of defense threatened to crumble. On February 21 a deputy sheriff arrested Richard Sobol, the LCDC's chief counsel in Louisiana, when he visited the courthouse in Plaquemines Parish to represent a black client. Leander Perez then had Sobol prosecuted for violating state law by practicing without a Louisiana license. The Louisiana state bar association supported the prosecution, claiming that blacks did not need out-of-state lawyers like Sobol to represent them: Louisiana had "a large reservoir of white attorneys . . . willing to and capable of handling civil rights cases of any kind." To this mendaciously inaccurate claim, the bar association added the equally misleading assertion that the paucity of black lawyers was due to the "disinclination of negroes to enter the profession." If successful, the prosecution would drive the LCDC out of the state. Since its organization in 1964, LCDC lawyers had handled hundreds of cases in Louisiana. Many of them, moreover, were products of the finest law schools in the country and could run rings around the average southern attorney.[74]

The fact that no clear line distinguished "civil rights" cases from "ordinary" cases underlined the necessity for such lawyers. White officials were past masters at prosecuting civil rights activists on trumped-up charges and selectively applying the law to harass and intimidate. When black children boycotted segregated schools, for example, parents were prosecuted for "contributing to the delinquency of a minor," a charge never applied to parents of white children boycotting integrated schools. Other charges beloved of segregation-minded district attorneys included assault and battery, disturbing the peace, and passing worthless checks.

The case of Gary Duncan, the young black man whom Sobol had sought to represent, offers a perfect illustration of such harassment. Duncan was not a civil rights activist, but his cousin and nephew attended one of the first integrated schools in Plaquemines Parish. Leaving school one day, the children were cursed and threatened by a group of whites; when Duncan drove by in his car he stopped, intervened, and whisked the students away. During this brief confrontation he touched or slapped — the testimony conflicted — a white boy. Either way, the boy did not suffer a bruise, let alone a serious injury. Yet Duncan was arrested four times, convicted of battery, and sentenced to a jail term. Because his offense was classed as a misdemeanor, state law denied him the right to a jury trial. The judge who sentenced Duncan denied that the case had any bearing on civil rights.

To Louisiana's white attorneys, blacks like Duncan were not civil rights martyrs but common lawbreakers. As Bogalusa lawyer Bascom Talley attested during Sobol's appeal, he did not wish to represent the likes of A. Z. Young or Robert Hicks because "they were just as lawless as some of the whites." Another white attorney, asked about a theoretical case in which blacks were arrested for trying to integrate the drinking fountains at Pointe a la Hache courthouse, replied that he would not defend such people. "I am a white man first and foremost."[75]

To the immense relief of the LCDC, a three-judge panel of the federal appeals court enjoined Sobol's prosecution, terming it a plain attempt to harass civil rights lawyers and intimidate Plaquemines Parish Negroes. The Department of Justice supplied a strongly argued brief on Sobol's behalf and government attorney Owen Fiss helped argue the case. *Sobol* v. *Perez* frustrated the Perez-inspired attempt to render LCDC ineffective. And in a related case, the U.S. Supreme Court overturned Gary Duncan's conviction on the grounds that the denial of a jury trial had been unconstitutional. Federal district judge Fred Cassibry enjoined further prosecution of Duncan, accusing the parish authorities of bad faith and harassment.[76]

The killing of blacks by policemen presented the most egregious examples of alleged police brutality. These were also the cases most likely to move blacks to violent anger and least likely to incur legal retribution. In many cases, of course, policemen had to tackle armed and resisting suspects, situations that sometimes necessitated the use of lethal force. Often, however, police shot and killed suspects who presented no physical threat, using flight or the slightest degree of resistance as a pretext for opening fire. "In this state," Harvey Britton noted, "the mere suspicion that a Negro has committed a crime has proven to be sufficient reason for arresting officers to inflict bodily harm, and in many cases death." Actually, such grotesque overreaction was peculiar neither to Louisiana nor to the South. Members of the Los Angeles Police Department, for example, routinely shot at fleeing suspects, killing and maiming dozens of people every year. Moreover, white politicians sanctioned such methods. As Baton Rouge district attorney Sargent Pitcher put it, "I have always maintained that officers . . . are acting within the law when they have been forced to shoot a fleeing felon." Most whites, North and South, would heartily have endorsed this view. Juries everywhere were notoriously reluctant to indict or convict policemen accused of killing suspects, even if the latter turned out to be unarmed and innocent. The fact that policemen were far more likely to shoot blacks than whites underscored the belief, shared by virtually all black people, that the police placed little value on black lives and operated a double standard of justice.[77]

Some killings had so little justification that they occasionally shocked whites as well. A manager at a Shreveport steelworks witnessed the slaying of Ira Mason, a mentally disturbed black employee. "I would like . . . to join you," he wrote the local NAACP, "in bringing pressure on our Police Department to train and educate its members on how to handle situations such as these. I cannot in any way feel that Ira Mason had to be shot in order to subdue him." In Lafayette, a ringing burglar alarm brought police to a nightclub; battering the front door down, they killed the owner, Norbert "Baba" Landry, mistaking him for an intruder. A number of whites joined the NAACP in protesting the slaying. In New Orleans, the staff of the Human Relations Committee complained that the city's police department continued to ignore suspect killings.

> One particular policeman — according to the City Attorney's office — has killed six people in a year and a half. Two of the people were killed while the officer was off duty. Again, according to the City Attorney's office, the last shooting was outright murder. . . . Any time an officer's record reveals four or five complaints within twelve to eighteen months, we can reasonably suspect something is amiss.

The committee recommended that a doctor annually review the physical and mental health of every officer.[78]

In the summer of 1969 blacks in Baton Rouge could no longer contain their anger at what amounted to summary executions by the police. On July 25, two policemen chased a robbery suspect, James Olivey, onto a high school athletic field. The seventeen-year-old black youth turned and slashed at one of his pursuers with a knife, whereupon Officer Ray Breaux shot him dead. Less than three weeks earlier, police had killed another black youth in similar circumstances. When it transpired that Olivey, like the earlier victim, had been shot in the back, some blacks vented their anger by setting fires, breaking windows, beating white people, and shooting at buses. "We want an eye for an eye, a life for a life," Emmitt Douglas told a protest rally. Mayor W. W. Dumas imposed a curfew and Governor McKeithen deployed 250 National Guardsmen.

With Baton Rouge teetering on the brink of a full-scale riot, the NAACP sought to allay the tension, and at the mayor's request Douglas went on the radio to plead for calm. He also obtained a commitment from Dumas to have Officer Breaux suspended, pending an investigation of the fatal shooting. The NAACP demanded specific measures to combat police brutality, including more black officers and the integration of patrol cars. Dr. D'Orsay Bryant, head of the city's NAACP branch, announced a boycott of downtown stores to channel black anger into constructive protest. But Breaux remained on the force and was quickly exonerated by a local grand jury. A furious Douglas accused the mayor of breaking his word, but Dumas, claiming that civil service rules had tied his hand, now adopted a hard line. "We will back you 100 per cent," he told the assembled police. "Police officers will no longer take abuse and vilification from anyone." District attorney Sargent Pitcher then indicted Douglas for incitement to riot under a new state law that had been modeled on the antiriot clause — the "Rap Brown amendment" — of the 1968 Civil Rights Act. A few weeks later Pitcher suggested to police chief Eddie Bauer that his men use their guns "only in extreme emergencies." He added that the credit for this new policy should be attributed to "reputable black leaders" like Rev. T. J. Jemison, not to "agitators" like Douglas and Bryant.[79]

Policemen had hair-trigger fingers, however, because they understood that to shoot first and ask questions afterward had become tantamount to a national policy. In the context of endemic urban rioting, the employment of lethal force against blacks provoked little white dissent. Now, moreover, police violence became increasingly "political" as the distinction between legitimate protest and criminal behavior blurred. Black militants were apt to find themselves, literally, in the firing line, as their incendiary rhetoric and provocative tactics added up to riotous behavior in the eyes of policemen who were often straining at the leash. Two weeks before Martin Luther King's assassination, Patricia B. Miller, the director of Louisiana's Human Relations Council, predicted "wholesale slaughter" if students at Southern University engaged in demonstrations. The police, she warned, "have arsenals stored at strategic points to combat riots and are anxious for activity." On the national scene the shooting of university students soon became the most striking manifestation of police overreaction: between 1967 and 1970 blacks were gunned down on campuses in Orangeburg, South Carolina, Greensboro, North Carolina, and Jackson, Mississippi. In 1972 death finally came to Southern University: an unidentified sheriff's deputy killed two fleeing students with a shotgun blast.[80]

The Black Panther Party for Self-Defense attempted to organize nation-wide resistance to the police. Founded in Oakland, California, in 1966, the Panthers first made a name for themselves by striding into the state capitol with rifles in their hands. Likening the police to an army of occupation, they shadowed patrol cars and aggressively challenged officers who, in their eyes, wrongfully arrested or mistreated blacks. Their willingness to engage the police in armed confrontations — shootouts soon claimed the lives of both Panthers and policemen — fired the imagination of many young blacks. Attired in a fashion-conscious "uniform" of black beret, black sunglasses, and black leather jacket, the Panthers exuded charisma. They personified black racial pride, but they also eschewed the simplistic racial chauvinism of "Black Power," calling instead for black liberation within the context of a Marxist-Leninist-Maoist revolution that would unite the "lumpenproletariat" of both races. White radicals, and even some liberals, fell under the Panthers' spell. Helped by a news industry that found them fascinating in a frightening way, the Panthers grew by leaps and bounds, rapidly spreading to virtually every big city in the land.

Yet the Panthers' tactics proved disastrous. Far from weakening police authority within the ghetto, they actually enhanced the police's quasi-military and quasi-political power vis-à-vis black America. Assisted by an FBI intent on destroying black radicalism and encouraged by a national administration that branded the Panthers a "bunch of thugs" (the words of Attorney General John Mitchell) police forces across the country targeted the Panthers as criminals and revolutionaries. In city after city, Panthers were harassed, arrested, shot, and killed.[81]

The response of the New Orleans authorities to the arrival of a group of Black Panthers in the summer of 1970 was more restrained than that of police forces in Philadelphia, Chicago, and elsewhere. But Chief of Police Joseph I. Giarusso had no doubt that the Panthers represented a threat to society. He grew even more alarmed when the Panthers moved their headquarters to the Desire project in the lower Ninth Ward, the poorest and most neglected area of the city. "Steps should be taken immediately to neutralize these people," he advised Mayor "Moon" Landrieu, for their propaganda was "reaching an alarming number of people and indoctrinating them in the Panther philosophy which is communistic in nature and advocates guerilla warfare and revolution." He added that the Panthers openly advocated the murder of police officers, as expressed in their slogans "Off the Pig" and "Kill a Cop," and were stockpiling weapons in their headquarters. Giarusso conceded that they were few in number and that their principal activity consisted of providing free breakfasts to ghetto children. But he argued that the free breakfast program might be more insidious than open attacks on policemen, for it poisoned the minds of children with hatred of authority and hatred of white people. As for the small numbers, Giarusso reminded Landrieu that confining the leadership to a small, hard core derived from classic revolutionary tactics first promulgated by Lenin.[82]

In reality, as FBI wiretaps revealed, the small Panther group in New Orleans wished to avoid a confrontation with the police. But their violent rhetoric and thuggish behavior made a confrontation inevitable. On September 14 the Panthers discovered that two of their number were policemen who had infiltrated the group; thrown onto the "revolutionary justice" of "the people," the undercover cops were badly beaten before managing to escape. When the police finally moved in on them, the Panthers defended their apartment with grim determination: only after an all-night siege and a shootout lasting thirty-two minutes did the fourteen Panthers give themselves up. Incredibly, no one was killed. Later that day, however, police shot and killed a black man, Kenneth Borden, as he and a group of companions attempted to firebomb a grocery store where the undercover cops had taken refuge.[83]

Two months later, the police again entered the Desire project, two hundred strong and with an armored car in tow. Over two thousand blacks massed in front of the apartment building that housed the Panther headquarters, defying the police and physically preventing them from entering. Giarusso decided to withdraw his men rather than risk a bloodbath. Six days later, however, the police arrested twenty-nine Panthers and supporters as they left New Orleans in four rented cars. They finally ousted the six remaining Panthers from their apartment after a brief exchange of gunfire. "The backbone of this chapter has been broken," the resident FBI agent crowed to J. Edgar Hoover, "with almost 100% of its leadership presently incarcerated."[84]

To a good number of the eleven thousand residents of Desire, the Panthers were heroes. Many other blacks bitterly resented the zeal with which the authorities had harassed and persecuted them — arresting them for putting up posters, selling newspapers, "improperly securing" garbage cans, illegal parking, and the like. The manner in which the police finally gained entry into the Panthers' apartment — policemen dressed up as a Catholic priest accompanied by black "militants" — also evoked considerable anger. And few blacks could have failed to note the contrast between the repressive measures deployed against the Panthers, including massive police firepower, with the kid-gloved treatment accorded far more dangerous white terrorist groups. A young Vietnam veteran watched in anger as the police forced their Panther prisoners to lie on the ground. "There's an old organization known as the Ku Klux Klan," he told a newsman. "How come they don't do this to them? Why is it always the blacks?"[85]

Yet the suppression of the Panthers produced comparatively little political fallout for Mayor Landrieu. Indeed, the black leadership of New Orleans on the whole shunned the Panthers; some even praised the mayor and chief of police for employing restraint in their use of force. Lack of support for the Panthers did not mean that blacks approved of the way in which the police went about their everyday business. Quite the reverse: according to a survey of community leaders conducted shortly before the Panthers' arrival, blacks in New Orleans placed police harassment and overreaction above all other grievances. Feelings on the subject were so strong, in fact, that the researchers had difficulty in getting their respondents to change the subject.[86]

To many blacks, however, the Panthers' tactics made no sense. Four years earlier, Roy Wilkins had warned that a high-profile posture of armed confrontation would only "stir counter-planning, counteraction, and possible conflict." It also risked a "broader, more indiscriminate crackdown by law enforcement officers under the ready-made excuse of restoring law and order." The fate of the Panthers underlined the sagacity of that analysis. The Panthers violated the cardinal rule of revolutionaries by refusing to adopt the clandestine structure of, for example, the Bolsheviks or the Irish Republican Army. "They don't attempt to go underground," noted one black city official. "They denounce the system publicly and are willing to take the consequences. That is obviously a suicidal tendency." It was apt that Huey P. Newton, the Panthers' "Minister of Defense," should call his autobiography *Revolutionary Suicide*. (Newton, ironically, had been named by his father, a migrant from Louisiana, after Huey Long.) The Panthers evoked sympathy and admiration, but little political support.[87]

The Panthers, of course, posed no revolutionary threat; white officialdom, from President to patrolman, used an extraordinarily large sledgehammer to crush a nut of puny proportions. Commenting on such repression, historian William Chafe argued that the massive overreaction to such trivial threats reflected a white mood of "near paranoia." White leaders seemed incapable of distinguishing rhetoric from reality, taking the braggadocio of a few young blacks at face value, seizing "any evidence of radicalism to create a picture of black insurgency that warranted all-out retaliation." Perhaps, Chafe suggests, white repression of this stripe "can be seen as a ritual acting out of the need to destroy an enemy who challenged one's most dearly held values."[88]

Yet the Panthers' own actions could be interpreted in a similar light: they acted out their own need to destroy the enemy by courting ritualistic confrontations with the police. They could not, of course, physically destroy that enemy, but the firing of bullets represented a symbolic annihilation of the "pig" state's political authority. If the Panthers did not precipitate the police raid in the sense of firing the first shots, their words and actions made a violent police reaction all but inevitable. It is hard to see how the city authorities could have indefinitely tolerated the activities of the Panthers: they employed intimidation, they openly encouraged people to "kill pigs," they stockpiled weapons and turned their headquarters into a fortress. The Panthers thrived on violent confrontations because such clashes provided martyrs, confirmed their revolutionary credentials, and proved that America was evolving into a fascist state.

But the Panthers' supposition that a revolutionary situation existed was fantastic, and most blacks recognized it as such. By 1970, in fact, blacks in New Orleans were more committed to electoral politics than ever. The election of "Moon" Landrieu as mayor with only a minority of the white vote ushered in a new political era, one in which blacks were partners rather than clients, participants rather than passive spectators. Owing his success to solid black support, Landrieu ended the white near monopoly of City Hall jobs by making a large number of black appointments. Under Mayor Victor Schiro, City Hall had been virtually "lily-white," with no black holding a position higher than that of clerk. Landrieu placed blacks in charge of city departments, selected a black executive assistant, and appointed a black chief administrative officer. During his eight years as mayor the total number of blacks working in municipal government rose from 10 percent to 40 percent. Landrieu also ensured that his black allies received patronage jobs, as well as opportunities to prosper from contracts and "sweetheart deals." By 1973 the alliance between the white mayor and the black politicos was so firm that Landrieu coasted home to a second term of office.[89]

The isolation of the Black Panthers also reflected a profound desire, felt by many leaders of both races, to avoid the kind of violence that had wracked other cities. Blacks as well as whites were nervous about urban rioting and the possible destruction of their communities. In contrast to most other cities, blacks in New Orleans did not feel the sense of alienation so common among recent migrants. Members of the oldest urban black community in America, they had a sense of belonging. This helps to explain why New Orleans was the only big city that did not experience a major riot during the 1960s.

Ever since the school integration crisis, an informal biracial coalition had sought to alleviate, or at least contain, racial tensions. Biracial negotiations had continued at one level or another throughout the 1960s, with the city's white business elite circumventing Mayor Victor Schiro and dealing directly with black leaders. Through the Citizens Committee, formed in 1962, Canal Street had been desegregated. Through the Metropolitan Area Committee, formed in 1966, jobs had been created and recreation programs set up during successive "long, hot summers." In 1967 the city council created the Human Relations Committee; initially appointed by Mayor Schiro (on the day that Martin Luther King died in Memphis), it was eventually elected by popular vote, with blacks and whites each choosing half the members. The committee had a full-time staff headed by black newspaperman John Pecoul.

One of the committee's first tasks was to integrate the city's bars and taverns, which still routinely refused to serve blacks. Such discrimination was costing the city's economy dear. In 1965 twenty-one black players had walked out of the American Football League's all-star team after they were denied service on Bourbon Street. The all-star game subsequently had to be transferred when key black players said they would refuse to appear in New Orleans. Discrimination had caused the International Jazz Festival to close shop, and several national conventions had deleted New Orleans from their list of venues. In 1969 the city council finally enacted a public accommodations ordinance; it became law in the last days of Victor Shiro's tenure as mayor.[90]

As the 1960s drew to a close, many blacks dismissed the achievement of the civil rights movement as illusory. They felt alienated from government and cynical about American values. Yet the Voting Rights Act was proving to be a powerful agent of political integration. In the North, blacks had already discovered that the vote did not eliminate poverty and discrimination. Blacks in the South had still to learn that lesson; denied the ballot for so long, their faith in democratic politics remained buoyant. Moreover, despite the advent of a national administration that cared little for the problems of black people, the federal courts kept the momentum of the civil rights movement alive. In 1970, the year the Black Panthers were suppressed, the Supreme Court finally tackled a major item of unfinished business, ordering the immediate integration of the South's public schools. It proved a messy and incomplete operation. Blacks themselves watched the results with decidedly mixed feelings. Yet if school integration revealed the complexity and ambiguity of black attitudes, it also helped to bind the black population more closely to the political system. As the civil rights era petered out in the early 1970s, it became clear that a complex pattern of segregation and integration would persist into the foreseeable future.

Chapter 14

THE PROMISE AND THE REALITY OF

SCHOOL INTEGRATION

On April 2, 1969, a group of students at the New Orleans campus of Southern University (SUNO) approached the flagpole in front of the administration building. They carefully lowered the Stars and Stripes and, in its place, hauled up a flag of black, green, and red. Later that day, hundreds of students gathered in a lecture hall and chanted in unison: "I pledge allegiance to the Black Liberation Flag and to the cause for which it stands — Black People together, indivisible for liberation, self-defense, self-determination. I am prepared to give my life in its defense."[1]

When panicked officials located John Martzell to inform him of the student revolt, the governor's racial troubleshooter asked to know the precise details of the flag incident. Upon learning that the Stars and Stripes had been handed to a Vietnam veteran, who had then carefully folded it, Martzell instinctively knew what to advise: take the black flag of liberation down and put the American flag back up. "The minute I heard that they had a Vietnam veteran to fold the flag, the American flag, I knew what we were dealing with," he recalled. "We weren't dealing with people who were going to cause a great deal of trouble. They made their point. Having made their point, they take their flag down and put the American flag back up." The following day the Stars and Stripes were again flying in front of the administration building after police hauled down the black flag.[2]

The matter might have ended there had not the chief of police, Joseph Giarusso, decided to exploit the flag incident and provoke a confrontation. Generally respected as an honest and efficient cop, Giarusso nursed political ambitions and knew that nobody ever lost votes defending the Stars and Stripes. Condemning the "desecration of the flag," he criticized the dean of SUNO, Emmett W. Bashfull, for not disciplining the culprits. Mayor Vic Schiro joined the chorus of condemnation. Bashfull dutifully warned against any further tampering with the American flag.

The Afro-American Association had issued a list of demands several days before the flag incident. Most of them were so eminently reasonable that any university administration with an ounce of sense would have made concessions to the students. But now the flag itself became the focal point of the conflict, eclipsing the "non-negotiable" demands that formed the initial basis of the dispute. Having been publicly challenged — Giarusso virtually dared them to touch the flag when they held their next rally — the dissident students reacted in a predictable fashion. On the morning of April 9, half a dozen of them pushed aside some campus security guards and again raised the black liberation flag; hundreds of students watched and cheered. Dozens of policemen, who had arrived on campus before dawn, cleared a path to the flagpole and lowered the black flag. Scuffles broke out; several students were clubbed and more than twenty were arrested.[3]

Left to itself, the administration of Southern University might have quietly resolved the dispute. The intervention of the white police chief, however, made that outcome an impossibility. The sight of nine policemen ringing the flagpole protecting the Stars and Stripes was like a red flag to a bull. Over the following weeks students boycotted classes; they occupied the dean's office; they held marches and rallies. In May the protests spread to the main Southern campus at Baton Rouge, where students occupied the office of President Leon G. Netterville. Eventually, Governor McKeithen ordered the National Guard to occupy both campuses. A few students were suspended, six SUNO faculty members were fired, and one professor was deported. With the onset of final exams, the protests ended as suddenly as they had begun.[4]

A cynic might view the great Southern rebellion of 1969 as a tempest in a teapot rather than a harbinger of revolution. Campuses across Europe and North America were wracked by student unrest; black students from New York to San Francisco were brandishing guns and demanding courses in Black Studies; any number of southern black colleges were patrolled by soldiers during this period; on some campuses black students were shot dead. Viewed in this context, the protests at Southern were small beer. Indeed, it is striking how moderate were the students' demands and how easily Governor McKeithen managed to defuse the crisis. Campus-oriented issues — petty regulations, inadequate library facilities, increased tuition fees, an unresponsive administration — dominated the students' agenda, and McKeithen, instead of adopting the hard-line of confrontation adopted by police chief Giarusso, chose to reason with the students and make concessions.

Addressing a packed student gathering at SUNO on April 21, the governor turned on the charm and soon had his audience eating out of his hand. After persuading the students to remove the black flag, he pleaded with them to respect the Stars and Stripes. Hugh Murray, a white history professor and outspoken radical, could not help but admire the governor's nimble verbal footwork: when his use of the word "Negroes" prompted shouts of "Blacks!" he replied, "I'll call you black Americans." He evoked mirth when he said, "Please don't lock your dean in the closet anymore," and he elicited more chuckles when he described a stagnant, fetid pool of water, a persistent cause of complaint, as a "crawfish pond." He promised to have it filled in. Visiting the main Southern campus at Baton Rouge three weeks later, McKeithen held talks with student president William Jefferson (later to become Louisiana's first black congressman since Reconstruction) and undertook to carry out similar campus improvements.[5]

Murray was amazed at how easily a "white racist southern governor" could talk the students into calling off their protests. But the students' revolutionary pretensions, he had to admit, were hollow.

> All of the speeches about guns notwithstanding, the SUNO movement was essentially non-violent. Weapons were displayed but never engaged. Words were hurled but never bombs. The black students did not beg — they demanded. And they threatened should their demands be ignored. But the State of Louisiana called their bluff, and the students did nothing. Despite much talk the students chose not to fight.

Like so much of the overheated rhetoric spawned by Black Power, the language of threats and "non-negotiable demands" disguised a position of black powerlessness that had not changed, in its essence, since the student protests of 1960.[6]

In 1969, the Southern University system was governed in much the same way as ten years earlier. Unlike Louisiana State University, which enjoyed a large degree of autonomy under an independent board, Southern still came under the control of the state board of education, a body composed of white politicians. The authoritarian nature of Southern's internal administration, moreover, had not diminished. Felton Clark retired in 1968, but his protégé and successor, Leon Netterville, enjoyed similar latitude in the hiring and firing of faculty and the making of student regulations. Faculty members had no say in university decision making, and even department chairs exercised little independent authority. The administration of SUNO was delegated to Dean Emmett W. Bashfull, but Bashfull answered directly to Netterville. The practice of retaining teachers on one-year contracts reinforced Netterville's power and produced, in the words of the American Association of University Professors, "an atmosphere that is not conducive to acceptable standards of academic freedom." Indeed, after visiting Southern and talking with faculty members, the AAUP reported in 1968 that "an air of uncertainty, if not actual fear, hung over the campus."[7]

Southern was in theory an integrated university, but although its faculty included a sprinkling of whites, the student body was virtually all black. SUNO, for example, had one white student out of a total of eighteen hundred. The state authorities had not only failed to make any effort to integrate its system of higher education, it had extended segregation by creating new campuses of LSU (white) and SU (black) in Shreveport and Alexandria. The branch campuses of Southern, moreover, offered only non-degree courses lasting two years. Hugh Murray described SUNO as "an academic disaster area." Isolated from the city, starved of land and money, a more blatant example of discrimination would have been hard to find. "Nowhere," writes Raphael Cassimere, "not even in other southern states, was duality so clear, so unequal, so planned."[8]

It was hardly surprising, therefore, that the sit-in movement of 1960 and the student protests of 1969 displayed striking similarities. Once again, students found themselves in conflict with an insensitive, authoritarian administration that still cravenly did the bidding of the segregationist board of education. Once again, a campus revolt signaled a generational shift that brought black youths into conflict with the older leadership of the NAACP. And, once again, the reluctance of older blacks to imperil the existence of Southern University contributed to the movement's collapse.

Yet the contrasts between 1960 and 1969 were even more striking. The student sit-ins had articulated clear goals, yielded tangible results, and produced a structured movement in the form of SNCC and CORE. The protests of 1969 were confused in their aims, achieved nothing of substance, and left no organizational legacy of any enduring strength. The sit-in movement had been widely admired by blacks, promoting a high degree of unity across the lines of class and generation. The student strike of 1969 aroused little outside sympathy, leaving the wider black community unmoved and even offended. Above all, in 1960 the students had placed themselves in the radical vanguard of the civil rights movement, showing up the conservatism of the NAACP. In 1969, by contrast, the students had become the conservatives, and the NAACP, by adhering to its traditional ideals, now represented the cutting edge of change.

The separatist rhetoric of the late 1960s and early 1970s reflected the basic vagueness and ambiguity of the Black Power concept. Like attempts to define "Black Power," therefore, generalizations about "black militancy" or "black separatism" are exercises in futility. Its very slipperiness, however, made separatist discourse vulnerable to a racial chauvinism that was, at bottom, fundamentally conservative. Hugh Murray noted how the language of blackness was appropriated by opponents of change at SUNO: conservative black faculty members made racist appeals to the students in an effort to discredit George Haggar, an Arab-American political science professor whose fiery denunciations of "Fascist niggers, house niggers, black bourgeois masochists, [and] white liberals" had given him notoriety and influence. By manipulating separatist rhetoric, black supporters of the status quo caused the handful of genuine radicals to become isolated from the main student body. When push came to shove, and SUNO fired Haggar, Murray, and other white "ringleaders," their departure evoked no wave of protest from either students or faculty.

Reflecting on the SUNO strike several years later, Murray speculated that the growth of black nationalism reflected "an ongoing struggle within the black community leadership — a struggle between extremely racist conservatives and not very racist radicals." The latter utilized antiwhite rhetoric, he surmised, both to "outflank the conservative black opposition" and to press the attack on white racism.[9]

Yet even the self-professed radicals were not interested in attacking segregation; the "black flag of liberation" symbolized a new generation's rejection of the integrationist ideals of 1960. An ideology of black cultural nationalism permeated the students' language. They framed their demands around the aim of making SUNO "a relevant school for the needs of Black People," and much of what they sought had specific nationalist content, for example, a Black Studies department, a course on "Black Liberation." Their embrace of separatism placed the Southern students further than ever from the NAACP, which did not waver in its belief that state-sponsored black institutions simply perpetuated Jim Crow. As the Southern students rallied around the black flag, the architect of the NAACP's integrationist strategy, Thurgood Marshall, now a member of the U.S. Supreme Court, denounced black separatism in a speech at Dillard University. Marshall pointedly refused to give up the word "Negro."[10]

The NAACP did not maintain its commitment to integration without a considerable internal struggle, for the separatist undercurrents of Black Power had made waves aplenty within the association's ranks. The NAACP's 1968 national convention had been consumed by a challenge to the national leadership from a group of Young Turks, who wished to reorient the association in the direction of black separatism. They objected to the role of whites on the national board and proposed to change the organization's name to "National Association for the Advancement of Black People." After a bitter struggle, the old guard prevailed. Later in the year, however, a white staff attorney, Lewis Steel, published a stinging attack on the Supreme Court entitled the "Nine Men in Black Who Think White." When an outraged Roy Wilkins fired him, the association's longtime general counsel, Robert L. Carter, resigned in protest. The rest of the national legal staff, six attorneys, resigned alongside him. "The national office is now operating under considerable tension," Wilkins admitted, but he refused to reconsider Steel's dismissal and blasted the departed lawyers for fostering a "psychology of separatism."[11]

Separatist thinking at the NAACP's grass roots proved more difficult to expunge, although some activists so overreached themselves that they invited their own expulsion. Such was the case with Larry "Boogaloo" Cooper, president of the NAACP Youth Council in Shreveport. During a public meeting in February 1969, Cooper and several other Youth Council members tried to shout down Alfred Baker Lewis, a longtime white member of the NAACP's national board. Cooper accused the blacks on the association's board of being manipulated by the ten white board members. He then denounced Roy Wilkins as an "Uncle Tom" who, through his support for integration, was seeking to deny black youth a quality education. After Lewis was "repeatedly interrupted, noisily, rudely, and without provocation," the group finally stalked out. Harvey Britton suspended Cooper's membership and he played no more part in the NAACP.[12]

Elsewhere, however, antiwhite, antiestablishment thinking so permeated the mental outlook of young NAACP members that, in the absence of such flagrant behavior as Cooper's, Britton could only reason with them. A few days after Cooper's expulsion, the Youth Council in Lake Charles voted to withdraw from the NAACP. Britton tried to talk them out of it, arguing that slogans like "Uncle Tom," "Black Power," and "fighting the white man" were wholly negative and would lead to nothing but frustration. Britton had to chide the Youth Council in New Orleans for referring to policemen as "pigs" and for engaging in threatening behavior on the picket line.[13]

If black enthusiasm for the ideal of integration was ebbing, especially among younger blacks, it is not difficult to see why. The generation that came of age in 1969 was the first post-*Brown* generation of black southerners, yet the overwhelming majority had spent their entire educational experience within segregated, all-black schools. During their most formative years they had seen white Louisianians resist desegregation tooth-and-nail, leaving them in no doubt whatever that whites viewed them with condescension and contempt. Those few who had entered majority-white schools endured hostility, harassment, discrimination, and even violence.

When in 1969–70 desegregation finally became a widespread reality in Louisiana, racial attitudes had become so polarized that the ideals of integration were smothered in chaos, conflict, and mutual antagonism. Even after they had decisively lost the legal battle, moreover, whites continued to resist integration by voting with their feet. School integration promoted "white flight" from city to suburb, where the population, and the public schools, remained overwhelmingly white. And in the rural parishes, especially those with large black populations, many white parents took their children out of the public schools altogether, placing them in hastily created private schools, so-called segregation academies. Thus many school systems desegregated only to "resegregate."

Wholesale desegregation, moreover, came at an enormous cost to blacks. Maintaining a dual school system had been economically wasteful; a unitary system required fewer teachers and fewer buildings. White school boards, especially in the rural areas, addressed the problem of surplus capacity by closing black schools, demoting black principals, and firing black teachers. To add to the disillusionment, the much-touted educational advantages of desegregation proved elusive. When black children were at last placed in integrated classrooms, they found themselves struggling to keep up. Alarming numbers failed, dropped out, or were classified "educable mentally retarded" and assigned to special classes. Large numbers were suspended for infractions of discipline. Small wonder that many blacks regarded school integration as a Pyhrric victory.

To analyze the path of school integration between 1964 and 1969 is to arrive at an inescapable conclusion: unrelenting white opposition meant that schools were integrated under the worst possible circumstances. "The opposition to integration went all the way up," noted the *New Orleans Times-Picayune*, "from the poorest parent to the highest politician. It didn't have a fighting chance." [14]

Before 1964 the burden of initiating integration had fallen upon black parents. It entailed a lengthy path through the federal courts and meant, in effect, that the spread of integration was limited by the legal resources available to the NAACP, which had to confine its efforts to a handful of school districts.

Thus, ten years after *Brown*, NAACP suits had started the process of integration in New Orleans, Baton Rouge, and St. Helena Parish. Since 1962 school boards had no longer been able to use the Pupil Placement Act to winnow out black applicants for transfer. Even so, the percentage of black children attending majority-white schools was negligible.[15]

The Civil Rights Act of 1964 transformed the role of the federal government in the integration process. It empowered the Justice Department to initiate desegregation suits, and it authorized the Department of Health, Education and Welfare to withhold federal funds from school districts that failed to submit desegregation plans. It took years, however, for federal pressure to make itself felt to any great effect. Between 1964 and 1969 the snail's pace of desegregation barely accelerated.

Whites in Louisiana, as in much of the South, had accepted the desegregation of public accommodations, as well as the mass enfranchisement of blacks, with remarkably little resistance once Congress had acted decisively. School integration, however, was a different matter entirely. In 1965, when HEW issued its first set of compliance guidelines, most school boards simply refused to submit plans, preferring to wait until they were hauled into federal court. There, they calculated, sympathetic judges like Gordon West and Ben Dawkins would accept the most tenuous of commitments to desegregation.[16]

Gordon West's treatment of the St. Helena Parish case sent an unambiguous message to Louisiana school boards: here was a judge who would do his utmost to frustrate integration. By 1964 the NAACP's integration suit was already twelve years old: even A. P. Tureaud, that most patient of men, "respectfully submit[ted] that the defendants have had ample time to submit a plan." Finally, after the Fifth Circuit Court of Appeals rapped him over the knuckles for displaying a "startling, if not shocking, lack of appreciation for the clear pronouncements of the Supreme Court," West ordered the school board to come up with a desegregation plan. Even then, he tried to avoid imposing it by inviting the Community Relations Service to sort out the mess. The CRS could do nothing, and this attempt to dump the problem in the lap of the federal government failed. At the end of the summer West held his nose and entered an integration decree. The plan he accepted covered the top two grades only, and it gave black parents but a few days to request transfers for their children. Fear of violence and economic retaliation deterred all but nine children, or rather their parents, from requesting transfers to white schools. Only three of the children stuck it out and showed up at Greensburg High School on the first day of term.[17]

Given the fact that St. Helena Parish adjoined Mississippi and was regarded as a stronghold of the Ku Klux Klan, the narrowness of West's order was perhaps understandable. One school board member told the judge that "we'll never be integrated . . . until there are a lot of dead niggers around." Yet if West rationalized his procrastination as a desire to avert violence, he made no attempt to disguise his distaste for integration. "I personally regard the 1954 holding of the United States Supreme Court in the *Brown* case as one of the truly regrettable decisions of all times. . . . As far as I can determine, its only real accomplishment has been to bring discontent and chaos to many previously peaceful communities, without bringing any real attendant benefits to anyone."[18]

No other judge in Louisiana was as flagrantly contemptuous of *Brown* as Gordon West, but the judges of the Western District, under whose jurisdiction most of Louisiana's sixty-seven school districts fell, could hardly be described as enthusiasts for integration. They could be relied upon to give school boards an easier ride than HEW. By the end of 1965 only five Louisiana school boards had submitted voluntary plans, fewer than any other state. Over thirty simply failed to take any steps toward integration at all. In Shreveport, for example, the board told Jesse Stone that its "sole function" was to provide all children with "the best education possible." As it was already doing this, it could not be discriminating against blacks. More than twenty boards, however, sought court orders. The ability of school boards to use the federal courts as a refuge, moreover, compelled HEW to water down its initial guidelines, demanding little more in the way of compliance than the "freedom of choice" plans that federal district judges were endorsing. Southern politicians, in turn, cited the court plans to argue that the five complying districts were being treated unfairly. The tightening of HEW's guidelines in 1966 evoked further howls of protest and another exodus of school boards to the courts. By 1967 forty-five boards had chosen court orders over voluntary plans, the highest proportion in the South.[19]

The freedom-of-choice plans that became the norm between 1965 and 1967 presented parents with a theoretical right to send their children to either a previously all-white or a previously all-black school. But this right meant that the burden of integration remained on the shoulders of black parents. The effects of freedom-of-choice in rural Louisiana soon became clear: hardly any black children applied for transfers to white schools; no whites wanted to transfer to black schools.

Had HEW seriously expected a rush of black children to transfer, as some officials later claimed? It seems unlikely. As Gary Orfield has argued, the 1964 Civil Rights Act affected "large areas of the South where a rigid caste system was untouched by the civil rights movement." Federal officials were all too aware that school integration, however limited, might elicit a violent white backlash. In the case of St. Helena Parish, fear of violence reached all the way to the White House and prompted a heavy presence of federal marshals, FBI agents, and Louisiana state troopers during the first weeks of integration. But the South contained hundreds of counties like St. Helena; federal protection could not possibly stretch to cover more than a few. The federal government thus accepted freedom-of-choice as a means of achieving tokenism in these areas of hard-core racist resistance. "For the present," Orfield noted, "little change was demanded."[20]

Their acceptance of tokenism, moreover, did not mean that whites had relented in their opposition to integration. Many school boards did their utmost to frustrate the exercise of "free choice" by hedging it with administrative restrictions. It required extensive litigation to ensure, for example, that parents received choice forms in the mail and had enough time to return them. The harassment of parents who wished to transfer their children was a much more serious problem. The names of these people soon escaped from the files of the school board office; in some communities lists were passed around. Parents received threatening telephone calls, had crosses burned outside their homes, heard shots ring out from passing cars. Some lost their jobs, some their homes. Black principals often tried to dissuade them from taking their children out of the Negro schools. In Plaquemines Parish, the school board did not receive a single application asking for a black child to be assigned to a white school.

Those few black children who entered white schools had a miserable time. It would be wrong to assume that white teachers were uniformly hostile to the newcomers; many were kind and friendly, some surprisingly so. By and large, however, the black transferees were treated as lepers, with white children shunning them and the teachers trying to keep the two groups as separate as possible. The black children were usually assigned desks at the back or side of the classroom and sat at separate tables in the cafeteria. They played by themselves at recess and rode home on separate buses. In some places the school buses simply passed them by. They rarely took part in school sports; clubs and societies either met in the homes of white parents or ceased meeting altogether. Parent-teacher associations became inactive. School faculties remained segregated.

Some of the federal judges in Louisiana's Eastern District pushed school boards much harder. Frederick J. R. Heebe and Herbert W. Christenberry, for example, applied tough rulings to Bogalusa and Plaquemines Parish. But even they felt constrained by the freedom-of-choice concept, which had gained the status of official federal policy. By 1967 only 6 percent of Louisiana's black children attended school alongside whites. The movement of white children to predominantly black schools was statistically insignificant.[21]

Judge John Minor Wisdom decided to end what he regarded as an intolerable deadlock. Without scrapping freedom-of-choice altogether (a compromise to win over his fellow judges) he formulated an opinion that compelled the lower courts to apply uniform standards — much tougher standards — laid down by the Fifth Circuit Court of Appeals. In *U.S. v. Jefferson County Board of Education,* handed down at the end of 1966, Wisdom declared that school boards had an "affirmative duty" to bring about integration and that integration meant a "unitary school system in which there are no Negro schools and no white schools — just schools." He thus repudiated the distinction between "desegregation" and "integration," a distinction used by some judges to claim that *Brown* required the former but not the latter. Hence the presence of a handful of blacks in formerly all-white schools, mere tokenism, would no longer be tolerated. District judges, moreover, would be expected to accord great weight to HEW's guidelines. Wisdom appended a Model Decree, based on the HEW guidelines, to be applied by the district courts. These represented *minimum* standards, Wisdom emphasized. Freedom-of-choice could still be used, but it was no longer sacrosanct; indeed, he suggested other measures — the pairing of schools, geographic attendance zones — that might also be employed. "The only school desegregation plan that meets Constitutional standards is one that works."[22]

Years later, Wisdom gladly confessed that in *Jefferson* he was, in effect, legislating. "But it was a case of having to act," he explained; neither the Congress nor the Supreme Court would grasp the nettle. *Jefferson* articulated his belief that the appeals courts were the most important bodies in upholding national policy and protecting constitutional rights. It also expressed his passionate conviction that ending discrimination required more than paper remedies. "Affirmative action," he insisted, "is the proper action to take because of the nature of the wrong done to blacks."[23]

It took some time for the full implications of *Jefferson* to sink in, partly because it did not expressly forbid "freedom of choice." Indeed, the start of the 1968–69 school year brought only a modest advance in integration, with 28,000 black children, about 9 percent of the total, attending previously all-white schools, and a total of 241 white children, most of them in New Orleans, attending schools that were predominantly black. "School desegregation in Louisiana is neither a hope nor a promise," lamented Harvey Britton of the NAACP. Such statistics, however, convinced the Supreme Court to accept Wisdom's contention that freedom-of-choice should be abandoned if it failed to produce a unitary school system. In May 1968 the Court struck down a Virginia freedom-of-choice plan and ordered the school board to adopt a plan that "promises realistically to work *now*." Racial discrimination must be eliminated "root and branch." The Court had decisively rejected tokenism and made it clear that they expected substantial integration; they would judge school districts by numbers and percentages. They also demanded faculty integration and an end to discrimination in all school activities. Whites now faced the prospect of large numbers of black children entering predominantly white schools. Even worse, from their point of view, large numbers of white children might be assigned to previously all-Negro schools, and white teachers could find themselves teaching classes that were mainly or entirely black.[24]

Whites responded to the impending demise of "freedom-of-choice" with dire predictions. Rather than send their children to majority-black schools, many white parents would withdraw their children and either send them to private schools or educate them at home. Inside the schools, black and white children would fight each other; "moral standards" would decline; white teachers would resign; educational standards would plummet. With little support from white taxpayers, the public schools would go to wrack and ruin.[25]

The judges of the Western District, however, engaged in what one historian described as a "sophisticated foot-dragging episode" that kept freedom-of-choice alive for another year. In a November 1968 decision affecting thirty parishes in northern and western Louisiana, Richard Putnam, Edwin Hunter, and Ben Dawkins ignored the Supreme Court and threw freedom-of-choice a lifeline. "We are not today going to jeopardize the success already achieved," said Dawkins, "by casting aside something that is working and reach blindly into an experimental 'grab-bag.'" Gordon West, needless to say, rendered a similar judgment in respect to St. Helena and four other parishes.

In May 1969, however, the Fifth Circuit delivered the coup de grace. In twenty-nine of the districts under consideration, the court pointed out, over 90 percent of the black children still attended all-Negro schools; apart from one in Shreveport and one in Bossier City, no white children attended anything other than all-white schools. "We do not abdicate our judicial role to statistics," wrote Judge John Godbold. "But when figures speak, we must listen." The court ordered school boards to prepare new plans within thirty days, telling them to pay close attention to HEW's recommendations.[26]

During the summer of 1969 teams from HEW drew up plans for each school district; they included whatever combination of methods — busing, zoning, "pairing" — they calculated would effect the most extensive integration of students and faculties. HEW's staff was particularly intent on eliminating as many single-race schools, especially all-black schools, as possible.

Experienced educators recognized that the courts had finally breached the last line of defense surrounding segregated schools. "We are of the opinion that the legislative, judicial, and executive branches of the government will continue to support the demands of minorities throughout the United States," advised Donald L. Kennedy, the schools superintendent of Shreveport. It would be futile, he told the school board, to believe that freedom-of-choice could be perpetuated. Moreover, if the board refused to submit a new plan, the court would automatically accept HEW's proposals. The resignation of the board would have the same effect.

This was not, however, the message that school boards wished to hear, and they reacted to the Fifth Circuit's ruling with anguish and disbelief. The response of the Caddo Parish school board was typical: it unanimously rejected the HEW proposals and attempted to salvage an element of freedom-of-choice. "The HEW plan was even worse than most believed possible," the board stated. "The theme of the plan was to integrate and mix at all costs," regardless of "hardships to children or parents, community relations, future financing or possibility of violence." During long, vehement, and anguished meetings, the board members denounced the HEW people as fanatical ideologues who put racial mixing for its own sake before the educational needs of the children concerned. "They were blind to everything except color," the board complained, with unconscious irony. "They honestly believe that a white child who did not attend school with black children was deprived." The board adopted an "open enrollment" plan that assigned children to the school of their choice within geographic zones; it amounted to freedom-of-choice in another guise. The board's plan also ensured that "no child of either race will be forced . . . to attend a school in which the opposite race is in the majority." The Lake Charles school board adopted the same escape clause. In Bogalusa, the board attempted to justify the retention of all-black schools by arguing that they provided "a base of security for a portion of the Negro students who have difficulty scholastically . . . in competing in the integrated environment."[27]

Whites now looked to the Nixon administration, and the Supreme Court, to stave off the impending catastrophe. In campaigning for the presidency, Nixon had courted the white South and constructed a strong alliance with Senator Strom Thurmond of South Carolina, an archsegregationist. Strong hints that a Republican administration would slow the pace of desegregation, and a promise to appoint a southern conservative to the Supreme Court, fuelled white hopes that Nixon might be their savior. Like the rest of the Deep South, Louisiana had gone for George Wallace in 1968, but whites were not bereft of political influence with the White House. North Louisiana, especially the Shreveport area, was a center of Republican strength, and Charlton H. Lyons, the grand old man of Pelican State Republicans, pressed HEW secretary Robert Finch to ease the desegregation guidelines. Reporting on his lobbying efforts, he told the Caddo Parish school board that the prospect of the Supreme Court repudiating freedom-of-choice was "unthinkable." Shreveport area congressman Joe D. Wagonner became a key intermediary between panic-stricken whites and the Republican administration. Technically a Democrat, Waggoner's voting record aligned him firmly on the side of the Republican party, and it was through Waggoner that Nixon aide Harry Dent informed Judge Ben Dawkins that HEW would be seeking to delay the full implementation of integration plans.[28]

When Robert Finch made his much-anticipated announcement on July 3, 1969, Dawkins was delighted. In an extraordinarily polemical public statement to the *Shreveport Times,* the judge lauded Waggoner, praised the "obvious compassion" of Nixon and Finch, and excoriated the "militants," "liberals," and "Socialists" who decried the new guidelines. The latter were a "tiny, tiny fragment" of the population, he believed, compared with those he described, invoking Nixon's famous catchphrase, as "the Great Silent Majority." Dawkins condemned the old guidelines as "outrageous, utterly unrealistic or totally impossible economically" and promised that "we judges will not — the words are WILL NOT — accept or approve them." He ordered the HEW officials to negotiate new plans with local school boards, plans that did not require "substantial busing of students, or unreasonable assignments to other schools, simply to achieve a racial balance." Judges Edwin Hunter and Richard Putnam shared Dawkins' sentiments. Criticizing HEW's plan for Lake Charles, Hunter warned a federal official that "when you allow children of a tender age to be used in an experiment, you are fooling with danger." The judges knew full well, however, that there could be no return to freedom-of-choice; while they rejected HEW's proposals, they prodded school boards to meet HEW halfway. Thus the plans they eventually approved, while falling short of what HEW wanted, would still effect a drastic erosion of segregation.[29]

John McKeithen now decided to fan the flames of popular resistance to integration. The banning of freedom-of-choice, he warned, would result in "massive civil disobedience by tens of thousand of white parents." And if parents kept their children out of school, he added, the state authorities would make no attempt to enforce the compulsory attendance law. Local officials promised that they, too, would turn a blind eye. "I'm famous for dismissals," said Lake Charles district attorney Frank Salter, "and if anyone files charges against a parent, I'll dismiss them." A Citizens Committee for Quality Education (an offshoot of George Wallace's American Independence Party) sprang up to encourage white protests. Freedom-of-choice, which ten years earlier had been condemned by die-hard segregationists as the road to "mongrelization of the races," now became a white rallying cry. About twelve thousand whites attended a "freedom-of-choice" rally in Lake Charles; "shotguns and rifles," observed one resident, "were prominently displayed in pickup trucks and cars." Smaller demonstrations took place in Baton Rouge, New Iberia, Lafayette, and Ville Platte.[30]

When the new school year started in late August, white opposition had reached fever pitch. A few days earlier, Robert Finch had sent a hand-delivered letter to Judge John R. Brown, chief judge of the Fifth Circuit Court of Appeals. Finch asked the court to delay the implementation of *Alexander* v. *Holmes County Board of Education*, a case affecting thirty-three school districts in Mississippi. If forced to integrate in August 1969, Finch warned, the result would be "chaos, confusion and a catastrophic educational setback." Brown was astonished by this extraordinary intervention. Nevertheless, much against his better judgment he assented to the delay. By giving the school boards until December 1 to submit new plans, the court was in effect postponing integration until August 1970.

The delay applied only to Mississippi, but many whites in Louisiana convinced themselves that political pressure was paying off and that the Supreme Court might still uphold freedom-of-choice. The opening of schools did indeed bring chaos, as the predicted boycott finally materialized. An estimated twenty-seven thousand children failed to return to school. In St. Landry and St. Evangeline parishes the schools failed to open at all; in West Baton Rouge Parish they opened but then closed. Bus drivers in Ascension Parish refused to transport children because of threats. In Washington Parish six black teachers were refused admittance to a white school. Encouraging the white boycott, McKeithen declared October 13 "Freedom of Choice Day." Two weeks later, addressing four thousand whites in Opelousas, he vowed that if HEW's plans came into effect, the legislature would not "vote a dime for public education."

The Supreme Court, however, soon dashed the hope that integration could be further diluted or delayed. On October 29 it ordered the Fifth Circuit Court of Appeals to issue an order, "effective immediately," for school districts to "terminate dual school systems at once." In December the Court refused to hear the appeal of thirty-four Louisiana school districts against court-ordered integration plans, and in January it reversed the Fifth Circuit a second time after the appeals court allowed districts to integrate in two further stages. When it said "immediately," the Supreme Court affirmed, it meant just that: school systems were to complete the integration process at once, in the middle of the current school year.[31]

As in 1960 during the New Orleans integration crisis, the governor shook his fist and the legislature huffed and puffed. But their gestures of defiance rang hollow. Called into special session by McKeithen, the legislators passed a "freedom-of-choice" law that, everyone knew, would not withstand the scrutiny of the federal courts. They also appropriated $10 million to assist private schools, a measure that failed to get past even the Louisiana supreme court.[32]

McKeithen's antics dismayed people who had admired the governor's metamorphosis from racist to racial moderate. "Maybe he has been a segregationist at heart and it has finally come out now," speculated Troy Middleton, chairman of the biracial commission. Commission staff member Jesse Stone saw McKeithen's volte-face as pure politics: "He'll do anything that he thinks is in his interest to do." His national ambitions at an end, his gubernatorial career almost over, McKeithen had his eye on a Senate seat and was trying to shore up his popularity with the white voters. Whatever his motive, it earned him the enmity of black voters, who in 1971 exacted their revenge by defeating his bid for the Senate.[33]

McKeithen's bluster, in fact, attracted a good deal of criticism from people who believed that further resistance to the courts would damage the public school system and damage the state. "Over and over again," the *Times-Picayune* editorialized, "private school systems have proven poor and even hopeless substitutes for public schools." The *States-Item* was more blunt. "For Louisiana to skid back into the politics of racism or fall into a new era of racial animosity would be disaster compounded. . . . Decades of dual school systems built on a foundation of racism have brought us to the present terrible tangle." How many whites accepted such a judgment is impossible to say, probably only a small minority. Many more, however, recognized the futility of fighting the courts. When Gordon West told the Association of School Boards that "substantial mixing of the races" and "complete integration of faculties" could no longer be avoided, all but the most unreconstructed segregationist had to pause. "Even a so-called conservative like myself has got to admit that we've got an integrated school system," said Lieutenant Governor C. C. "Taddy" Aycock, "and we might as well make up our minds to live with it."[34]

February 1970 witnessed the biggest educational upheaval of the twentieth century, with integration becoming a social reality for the first time since the *Brown* decision sixteen years earlier. When the dust had settled, about a third of Louisiana's black children were attending majority-white schools. A far smaller proportion of white students, about five percent, attended majority-black schools. A significant number of all-white schools and a much larger number of all-black schools remained, but compared with the situation that prevailed before 1969, the public school system had been transformed. When the 1970–71 school year began, the proportion of children in integrated schools — schools where the minority race composed at least one-tenth of the enrollment — had risen to 63 percent.[35]

In parts of Louisiana, especially those rural parishes where they were a minority, whites spoke as if their world was coming to an end. "Integration for any area with sixty per cent Negro and forty per cent white just simply cannot survive," the superintendent of DeSoto Parish wrote Ben Dawkins.

> If we continue our present course DeSoto Parish will become an all Negro parish and the economy will be completely destroyed. I in no way mean this as a threat, it is just a positive reality which is being made by the white people of this parish. The buying and selling is at an all time low. . . . Seemingly DeSoto Parish will be integrated northern style, that is, it will become a Negro ghetto and white people will move away.

Dawkins circulated the letter to every judge of the Fifth Circuit Court of Appeals. Federal district judges, he complained, had been placed "in the position of The Charge of the Light Brigade where it was said 'Theirs is not to reason why, but to do or die.'" He was at the end of his tether, the judge added. "All of this has exhausted me both physically and emotionally."

Hastily improvised private schools sprang up to cater to white children withdrawing from the public schools. In Madison Parish, where two such schools appeared, 800 of 1,100 white children left the public schools, as did twenty-five of seventy white teachers. Usually located in church buildings and named "Christian Academies," these schools received indirect state subsidies in the form of textbooks and bus transportation. In some parishes school boards gave the "segregation academies" desks and chairs and allowed them to lease buildings for nominal rents or buy them at bargain basement prices. The private school movement was especially marked in north Louisiana, where Concordia, Tensas, East Carroll, Shreveport, Monroe, and Claiborne all registered a sharp decline in white public school enrollment. But some south Louisiana parishes such as Pointe Coupee, St. Landry, and Evangeline also lost substantial numbers of white students to new private schools.[36]

The public school system showed remarkable resilience: across the state as a whole the white outflow was relatively small. Of the estimated 27,000 children who boycotted the beginning of the 1969–70 school year, about half had returned by October 1970. By 1971, moreover, total enrollment in white private schools declined by a further 5,000; by 1975 it was down another 4,000. The number of private schools declined in proportion. Moreover, only a minority of the 450 private schools could be termed "segregation academies"; the majority were Catholic schools of long standing. Even if all the parochial schools are included, the 134,000 white children attending private schools in the mid-1970s represented only one-fifth of total white school enrollment. If the state had been able to provide substantial subsidies, many more private schools might have been organized. The federal courts, however, whittled away the amount of help that private schools received from the state. Tuition grants had been outlawed in 1967. In 1975 the department of education was enjoined from supplying textbooks, school materials, and funds for transportation. All-white schools that continued to discriminate also lost their exemption from federal taxation.[37]

For blacks, however, school integration was a massive disappointment, a painful, bewildering, and sometimes frightening experience that caused widespread disillusionment with the twenty-year-old goal of the NAACP. Throughout the state, but especially in the rural parishes, the creation of unitary school systems entailed the closure of black schools, the demotion of black principals, and the dismissal of black teachers.

Some of this was unavoidable, but the manner in which it was implemented reflected the gross imbalance of political power that still prevailed throughout Louisiana. Only a handful of school boards contained black elected members, and not a single one had a black majority; every school superintendent was white. That school boards showed favoritism toward white schools and white teachers flowed, inevitably, from the fact that blacks had no political influence over school administrators. The relative oversupply of white teachers in many school districts exacerbated the problem. White schools generally had lower staff-student ratios, and the merging of segregated systems created a surplus of white teachers. The loss of black schools, the dismissal of black teachers, and the assignment of white teachers to previously all-black schools all cushioned white teachers from the effects of rationalizing the grossly wasteful dual system. They also minimized the number of white children assigned to majority-black schools. As much as they dreaded the entry of large numbers of blacks into predominantly white schools, whites regarded the prospect of entering previously all-black schools as far worse. Having to attend a school named after Booker T. Washington, located in the heart of a black neighborhood, entailed an intolerable social stigma in the eyes of the white community.

Some black teachers lost their jobs because of alleged incompetence; others because they failed the National Teachers' Examination, a requirement that school administrators had rarely imposed before 1969. The educational attainments of many black teachers, of course, left much to be desired — a consequence of the segregated educational system. Indeed, the process of integration revealed just how bad some of those teachers were. Yet the weeding out of incompetent teachers reflected the racial bias of a lily-white school administration. As a black lawyer put it: "The whites have the power. The power to call black teachers what they want to call them. And in a lot of cases they call them incompetent. Now I'm not saying that 100 per cent of black teachers who come through this office are competent. But it sure is strange that I haven't heard of any white teachers being displaced because of incompetency." How many black teachers lost their jobs is difficult to determine. Without doubt, many left the profession to take advantage of new employment opportunities. Yet between 1966 and 1971 the number of white teachers employed in the public schools increased by well over 4,000, while the number of black teachers increased by only 650.

The demotion of black principals caused particular anger. High school principals found themselves assistant principals serving under whites. Sometimes they were phased down along with their schools. High schools became junior highs; junior high school principals found themselves in charge of elementary schools; elementary school principals wound up as ordinary classroom teachers. In many cases administrators softened the blow by giving former principals grand-sounding titles for jobs that carried few important duties and little responsibility: "coordinating principal," "teacher assistant," "federal program coordinator," "supervisor of child welfare and attendance." Between 1966 and 1971 the number of black principals declined from 513 to 362. The number of white principals increased from 941 to 1,057. Black principals were *never* assigned to majority-white schools; white principals, on the other hand, were often placed in charge of majority-black and even all-black schools.[38]

For black teachers assigned to predominantly white schools, integration often proved traumatic and humiliating. A white teacher in Arabi, just outside New Orleans, described a foretaste of what lay ahead of them.

> One day a couple of colored teachers showed up for a meeting in our school, and the results were unbelievable. The students in the next class I went into were all banging on their desks and shouting together: "Two, four, six, eight, we don't want to integrate." It was only after they were assured that no "niggers" were coming to their school, that they settled down.

The first black teachers to be assigned to a previously all-white school in Washington Parish were greeted by jeering white pickets, who kept them out of the school for three days. Judge Heebe had to assign federal marshals to escort them. Extreme examples, no doubt: Arabi lay within St. Bernard Parish, part of Leander Perez's political domain; Washington Parish comprised the hinterland of Bogalusa, "Klantown, USA." Yet children who had been brought up on a diet of racism, who had been taught to view blacks with contempt and to regard integration with dread, would hardly view black teachers with respect. A study group from the National Education Association, comprising twenty people, spent a week in Louisiana investigating the effects of integration. In many schools, they reported, "humiliation is heaped upon black teachers from all sides — from the students who say their parents have told them 'not to listen to no nigger'; from the principal who addresses them only by their first name; from school board members and superintendents who, openly and in their presence, have announced that no parents would send their children to a 'nigger' school."[39]

For black students the benefits of integration seemed elusive. Entering predominantly white schools for the first time, they complained of coldness, hostility, and discrimination both inside and outside the classroom. White teachers and principals applied a double standard, they complained. Some "change the tone of their voice from a friendly, cordial one when speaking to white students to an unfriendly and hostile one when speaking to black students." Many, they believed, disciplined black students more severely than whites, punishing them for the slightest infractions and meting out draconian punishments. In sports and social activities, they claimed, blacks suffered discrimination: white band directors rarely selected blacks; the homecoming queen was always a white girl. Even dress codes, they complained, discriminated against black students by forbidding "Afro" or "bush" hairstyles and by proscribing blue jeans and African-style "dashikis."

The suspension of black students very quickly became a burning issue, and the NAACP received a stream of complaints alleging unfair treatment. "Blacks are being put out of school in great numbers," reported Robert Lee Lewis from Vidalia in Concordia Parish, "while no whites are being put out at all." The "Concerned Parents of Rayne" wrote that "the principal and assistant principal continue to suspend the children . . . for little or nothing." True, black students were not always blameless: altercations and free-for-alls involving black and white students flared up with depressing frequency. But blacks complained that the white culprits got off more lightly, while the blacks found themselves suspended or expelled. In some school systems, the suspension of black students reached epidemic proportions. In Shreveport, for example, eighteen hundred blacks found themselves banned from school; blacks made up 40 percent of the school population but accounted for 70 percent of the suspensions. Figures from the Bogalusa schools revealed similar disparities. Black students themselves had no doubt where to pin the blame: they were being "harassed, insulted, nagged, and discouraged as a device to have them drop out or transfer rather than treating them as other non-black students."[40]

Most bewildering of all, especially to parents, was the frequency with which black students received failing grades. From across the state, anxious and irate parents reported that children who had done well in all-black schools had suddenly fallen behind and were often struggling to stay in school. "They were performing well at Armstrong, honor students etc.," a Rayne parent claimed. "Now even the honor students are failing." She and many others convinced themselves that their children were being victimized by a discriminatory grading system. They also suspected that the disproportionate number of black children assigned to classes for the "educable mentally retarded" indicated a not-so-subtle attempt to resegregate children within supposedly integrated schools.[41]

To view black students solely as victims of racist teachers, however, would be to oversimplify a situation of enormous complexity. The historical legacy of racism in some way informed every interaction between black and white, yet that legacy ensured that even whites of good will, who were ready to make a sincere effort to accept black students, found themselves poorly prepared to cope with problems that had as much to do with class, culture, and politics as they had to do with color. Black students, for their part, were just as ill prepared to adapt to majority-white schools. Problems and conflicts that they attributed solely to "white racism" often had much more complicated explanations.

In fact, much of the friction between black students and white teachers should be seen in the context of class rather than race. Teachers everywhere were having to adapt their teaching methods to a generation of children accustomed to looser parental discipline and greater personal freedom. By the 1970s the traditional method of standing at the front of the classroom and lecturing had become increasingly ineffective. Black children, however, often presented a particular challenge: usually poorer, sometimes ill fed, they tended to be more unruly than middle-class white children. White teachers, who tended to take their authority for granted, frequently found themselves out of their depth when faced with noisy, ill-disciplined children who could not keep still, had short attention spans, and defied them at the drop of a hat. The husband of a white teacher assigned to an all-black school in a poor neighborhood of New Orleans complained that the students "daily mock, deride and revile her, using vulgar words and epithets. . . . Maintaining order and discipline is impossible." The woman resigned. As another white teacher put it, "Only those with the heart and mind of a Peace Corpsman" should be assigned to schools in the poorer areas of the city.[42]

The cultural divide between the races also hampered white teachers. If whites and blacks spoke the same language, they used different dialects, each with their own grammatical and phonic peculiarities. In a time before scholars had explored the linguistic subtleties of "Black English," whites had difficulty understanding, let alone appreciating, a speech pattern that struck them as crude and unlettered. Blacks, for their part, encountered similar difficulties understanding their white teachers. The room for misunderstanding and miscommunication was vast.

If white attitudes presented a problem within integrated schools, black attitudes sometimes compounded the problem. In 1969–70, when black children first entered white schools in substantial numbers, they had been sensitized to racism by a decade-old civil rights movement. They had also just witnessed, through television at least, four successive years of urban rioting. Since 1966 they had absorbed the rhetoric of "Black Power," and their outlook reflected the belligerency and sense of cultural nationalism associated with that concept. They did not enter integrated schools with meekness or deference; they did not feel any need to "earn" white acceptance. They still wanted integration, but on their own terms. They demanded equal treatment and full participation, but they also wanted to nurture their racial identity, and they expected the schools to recognize that identity. They were assertive, politically aware, sensitive to insults, and quick to defy white authority. As Harvey Britton put it, "Black students, seeing themselves as educational freedom fighters, often enter desegregated schools with a view of disciplining the instructor." This contentiousness, he believed, contributed to the wave of suspensions and expulsions that marked the early years of mass integration.[43]

The 1969 troubles at Alcee Fortier High, a formerly all-white school near Tulane University, foreshadowed some of the conflicts that spread across the state the following year. The first school system to be desegregated by court order, New Orleans boasted the first schools that could be described, in terms of numbers at least, as truly integrated: by 1968–69 blacks composed a third of Alcee Fortier's student body. The administration made little attempt, however, to prepare white teachers for potential problems or encourage black students to feel at home. Nor were the white students welcoming. Black students had a difficult time adjusting, and many fell afoul of white teachers who, unaccustomed to having their authority challenged and without a formal grievance procedure to fall back on, acted in an authoritarian manner. Blacks soon accounted for over half of the total suspensions. In January 1969 a group of black students tried to petition the principal for a more equitable discipline code and the establishment of a "Black Student Union." The principal flatly refused to negotiate, prompting the students to announce a boycott of the school and begin picketing the various entrances. The demonstrations became noisy and disruptive, and on January 20, at the principal's request, the police intervened and arrested eighty demonstrators. The protests eventually fizzled out, those arrested were released, and the protesting students returned to school.[44]

As racial crises go, it was a small one. But the Fortier High affair exhibited in microcosm many of the disturbing elements that afflicted integrated schools. Black students, reacting against an insensitive principal, poorly prepared teachers, and unfriendly white students, found no means of redress other than open rebellion and self-segregation, actions that widened the racial divide and increased their isolation.

The following year, as integration spread to the rest of Louisiana, such conflicts erupted across the state, sometimes with the additional aggravating factor of black resentment over closed schools, demoted principals, and dismissed teachers. In Iberia Parish, fighting erupted at Jeanerette High School on the first day of the new school year. Three days later, after a black girl was expelled for striking a white teacher, blacks quit the school and tried to march to their old school, which had been downgraded to a junior high. The police erected road blocks in an effort to stop them. The students and the police exchanged rocks and tear gas; the mayor imposed a curfew; fifty state troopers arrived to help restore order. In Plaquemine, students demanded the reinstatement of their former high school principal, whom the school board had named a "coordinating principal" and replaced with a white man. Encouraged by William H. Samuels, president of the local NAACP, they boycotted the schools for three months and held marches and demonstrations that, to quote Harvey Britton, were "marred by fire bombings, rioting and other acts of civil disorder requiring the calling out of the National Guard." At the request of the Justice Department, which viewed the boycott as an interference with desegregation, Judge Gordon West issued an injunction against the protesters.[45]

Elsewhere, seemingly trivial disputes between black and white students sparked serious disturbances. In October 1969 blacks walked out of Bogalusa High School after no blacks were elected to the homecoming court. Judge Heebe ordered the students back to school and chided them for refusing to accept the result of a democratic vote. "Maybe I'm getting old," he added, "but I recollect . . . in my high school and college days, the homecoming court didn't excite me too much." In May 1970 he assigned U.S. marshals to the school, which had again been disrupted by fighting among students. The following September an altercation during a football game, which resulted in the expulsion of several blacks, led to more racial confrontations. On one occasion about six hundred students engaged in a free-for-all during recess; police in riot gear were rushed to the campus. A few days later, about one hundred students refused to return to class, blacks and whites facing each other in the schoolyard and engaging in a tense "staring contest." Teachers separated the groups, but as the students left school they hurled rocks at each other over the heads of policemen. Heebe had to issue another injunction to prohibit student walkouts.[46]

Not all schools experienced such serious or prolonged disruption. Racial clashes often turned out to be a passing phenomenon, the product of the initial shock and strangeness of integration. Moreover, the tendency to label every clash between a white and a black student as "racial" sometimes led people to exaggerate the significance of each incident.

Still, few schools escaped racial conflict, and the beginning of the 1971–72 school year brought little respite. Another dispute over homecoming caused a walkout by black students in Abbeville, Vermilion Parish, in October 1971, followed by a "riot" two months later. "It could best be described as a free for all," Daniel Byrd reported, "with everyone swinging and whites committing assaults and batteries on Negroes, and Negroes assaulting and battering whites." A year later blacks challenged the election of a white homecoming queen at Jeanerette High in Iberia Parish; the principal suspended forty black students, some of them for four years. In 1972 fighting erupted at Destrehan High in St. Charles Parish, and it continued intermittently for several years. In 1974 a black student shot and killed a white student, leading to the arrest and conviction — a wrongful conviction, many believe — of Gary Tyler. The Tyler case generates controversy to this day.[47]

The breakdown of discipline sometimes became so severe that it compelled school boards to address the problem directly, belatedly adopting measures that ought to have been, but rarely were, part of the preparation for integration. "There was an incredible amount of racial unrest," recalled the deputy superintendent of the New Orleans school system. The school board created a "conflict intervention team" that could respond swiftly to racial problems. Without such an effort, he believed, the conflicts "would have exploded beyond all belief." Other school boards set up biracial committees; sometimes federal judges ordered them to do so.[48]

The efforts of Shreveport's biracial committee were a model of their kind. Appointed by Judge Nauman S. Scott to bring about further integration of Caddo Parish schools, the committee was equally divided between blacks and whites and met under the chairmanship of Charles T. Beaird, a philosophy professor at Centenary College who also happened to be the millionaire owner of a thriving metalworks. The plan it came up with included the appointments of an assistant superintendent for community affairs, a director of human relations, and a director of student affairs. These specialist staff members developed sensitive policies for ironing out racial misunderstandings and educating white teachers. Racial conflicts, they emphasized, often arose because whites did not consider the cultural and class differences between black and white students. They paid particular attention to the problems associated with integrating blacks into sports and social activities, issuing detailed advice covering interracial dating, the selection of cheerleaders, and the encouragement of black interest in athletics. Happily, Shreveport's school system soon became one of the more trouble free in the state.[49]

In many schools, however, racial problems were allowed to fester. By 1973, Daniel Byrd noticed, blacks were becoming disillusioned with integration, often manifesting their alienation through aggressiveness toward white students and pressure on other blacks not to associate with them. "The dislike and hatred of young blacks against whites has reached an excessive proportion," Byrd reported from Ponchatoula, Tangipahoa Parish, "resulting in fights between students . . . and rebellion in the classroom." In Lafourche Parish, he noted, "Racism and animosity has polarized to the extent that Negro students isolate themselves and cluster around each other where they feel secure. In fact black racism is so pronounced that if one of them makes the honor roll he is called a 'hunky' lover by other sisters and brothers." Byrd had to revise his view that the expulsion and suspension of blacks was solely a result of racist teachers. Sadly, he admitted, "Negro students are not innocent of all the charges against them"; profanity, disruptive behavior, belligerent attitudes, and physical assaults against teachers accounted for many of the suspensions.[50]

The most stark and depressing evidence of integration's failure was the "re-segregation" of schools in New Orleans as whites moved out of Orleans Parish into suburban Jefferson Parish to the west. The extent to which racial tensions within integrated schools contributed to this exodus is impossible to say. The movement from city to suburb had started well before 1960 and would have continued regardless of school integration. Yet it is also true that the vast majority of whites consistently opposed integration and, given the chance, sought to avoid it. Conditions within individual schools, however, seem to have been a less decisive factor than the numerical balance between black and white. "Given a too unfavorable racial balance," noted schools superintendent Carl Dolce, "the white students will flee the schools." All the evidence pointed to the fact that once black students exceeded 30 percent of a given student body, the chances of preserving meaningful integration rapidly diminished. "Maintaining racial balance is a complex activity," Dolce explained. "The process is somewhat akin to a game of checkers: move one piece and the effect upon the entire game might be significant."

In New Orleans, however, black students already made up 67 percent of the public school population in 1968–69, and the proportion grew year by year. "Each time the system loses a school to a resegregated all-Negro pattern," Dolce noted, "neighborhoods change and it becomes increasingly difficult to house those remaining whites in acceptably racially balanced school situations." Pushing to extend integration became counterproductive: whites simply left when whites became, or believed they were about to become, a minority. In 1972, for example, black parents at McDonogh 40 elementary school won a court order pairing the school with predominantly white Abrams elementary school. The object was to use busing to achieve a black-white ratio of 57:43 in each school. Within two years, however, white enrollment at Abrams dropped from 53 percent to 20 percent. Dr. Mack Spears, the first black to be elected to the Orleans Parish school board, admitted that integration had reached a point of diminishing returns. The system did not have "enough white bodies to go around."[51]

Through the use of busing, the scope of integration could probably have been extended in Shreveport, Baton Rouge, and several smaller cities. Black enthusiasm for integration had waned to such an extent, however, that the NAACP could muster little support for its proposals to integrate more all-black schools. Many communities, in fact, mourned the loss of black high schools and wished to preserve those that remained. Dan Byrd's report from Natchitoches Parish in December 1972 typified an attitude that was becoming, if not prevalent, increasingly common.

> In the past, this has been a parish favorable to the program of the [NAACP]. At the present, you won't find a dozen people who will speak in favor of integrated public schools. Downgrading of Negro schools, dis-placement of teachers and principals and the widespread suspensions and expulsions of Negro students . . . are probably the reasons for this change in attitude. One Negro principal is reported to have said he doesn't want any white students in *his school*.

Reflecting on the NAACP's integration strategy a few years later, Constance Baker Motley recognized that the lawyers of the Legal Defense Fund had failed to appreciate the extent to which blacks in the South prized black schools as community institutions and regarded their black teachers and prin-cipals as role models for black children. Black teachers themselves angrily charged that integration had been implemented at their expense. Indeed, by the early 1970s, they had become so disenchanted that the thirty-year-old alliance between the LEA and the NAACP threatened to end in acrimony.[52]

The NAACP had long been aware of the vulnerable position of black teach-ers in the South. In 1955, as part of its strategy for implementing *Brown*, it encouraged them to form the National Conference of State Teachers Asso-ciations (NCOSTA), which included the LEA and twelve other southern and border-state groups. Through a complicated banking arrangement designed to guarantee the anonymity of contributors, NCOSTA funded a new De-partment of Teacher Information and Security within the NAACP's Legal Defense Fund. Daniel Byrd worked as one of the department's three staff members. When school boards across Louisiana began sending out dismissal notices, the LEA appealed to the Legal Defense Fund for help. The LDF could only protect the jobs of black teachers, however, if HEW and the fed-eral courts insisted that desegregation plans contain appropriate safeguards, and except in a handful of cases, they failed to do so.

Black teachers felt betrayed. Some members of the LEA, notably J. K. Haynes, its veteran executive secretary, accused the LDF of abdicating its re-sponsibility to the black teaching profession. Relations between the LEA and the LDF had worsened after Jack Greenberg replaced Thurgood Marshall in

1961 upon the latter's appointment to the federal bench. Greenberg, a white man and a Jew, born and raised in Brooklyn, lacked Marshall's knowledge of the South and his extensive network of personal contacts and friendships. Moreover, whereas Marshall had been as much an activist and organizer as a lawyer, Greenberg approached his job in strictly lawyerly terms. After A. P. Tureaud died in early 1972, relations between the LDF and LEA became even more strained.[53]

The unsympathetic attitude toward black teachers sometimes displayed by the NAACP — not the LDF — exacerbated the tension. Both branch officers and full-time officials had long complained of lack of support from black teachers. Black principals, in particular, had rarely backed the civil rights movement, and many of them had actively impeded it, not least by discouraging the participation of black teachers. The demotion of black principals, therefore, evoked a pronounced lack of sympathy within the NAACP. Indeed, some saw a certain poetic justice in their plight. As Harvey Britton put it in a letter to the president of the Haynesville branch, "It is regrettable that all the Negro principals were lost, but their own failure to stand up for their rights is probably the reason why. Many teachers will find themselves likewise without jobs unless they become more involved with their own problems."

For many in the NAACP, black principals and teachers who had curried favor with the school boards and shunned the civil rights movement were not worth fighting for. Britton cited the example of one black principal who, when the "Afro" or "bush" hairstyle became popular,

> adopted a policy at his school that you can only have an "American haircut." . . . And the reason that he did that was to appease the school board and the power structure down there — they never told him he had to do this. But that was his way of saying, "Hey, look fellas, I'm still part of the system. I'm going to look after your interests in the black community." So when people like that became jeopardized in terms of their job standings, the community reacted because they said, "That's our principal" or "That's our teacher." But in retrospect they really weren't . . . because they had already sold out the black community.

Marion Overton White of the St. Landry Parish NAACP tried to persuade demoted high school principals to take posts as administrators within the integrated schools, but most of them opted to head black elementary schools instead. To White, such men were weak, incompetent "Uncle Toms." Until recently, he pointed out, 99 percent of black principals "wouldn't be seen dead inside the NAACP."

The NAACP also had the temerity to state that many black teachers were bad at their jobs and that these, too, were not worth saving. A few teachers privately admitted as much and accepted that not every dismissed teacher ought to be defended. As future LEA president Basile Miller put it in 1967, if black teachers wanted the civil rights movement to help them, they would have to weed out the incompetents from their own ranks. Blacks "only wanted honest teaching in our classrooms, which they had *not* been having." The LEA needed to "brutally remove, or at least censure, teachers known by everybody not to be willing or able to teach." Such views, however, had to contend with the growing association of racial pride with black institutions. Many blacks became increasingly resistant to any measures that appeared to weaken them or threaten their existence.[54]

The future of the remaining all-black schools widened the rift between the NAACP and the LEA. It first came to the fore in Bogalusa, where Judge Heebe ordered the abolition of all single-race schools at the start of the 1969 school year. The LEA strongly opposed the school board's plan to close the two remaining all-black schools, arguing that the board wanted to get rid of them — two of the newest and best — simply to prevent whites having to travel to black neighborhoods and attend formerly all-black schools. Such a scheme, the LEA argued, stigmatized black schools and black teachers. Heebe rejected this argument, ruling that "it does not imprint the stigma of inferiority on the Negro race to close all-Negro schools."[55]

As the full effects of integration became clear, black opposition to the closure of all-black schools hardened. LDF proposals for further integration in the wake of the Supreme Court's 1970 decision in *Swann* v. *Charlotte-Mecklenburg,* which approved the use of citywide busing, found little favor among blacks in Louisiana — or rather, as Daniel Byrd put it, among "the blacks that are talking."[56]

Whites were not slow to exploit black loss of faith in integration. In February 1970, for example, the segregationist mayor of Monroe, W. L. Howard, addressed the student body of all-black Carroll Senior High School and urged the students who had been reassigned to white schools not to go. Such blatant interference with court orders, however, was rare. A much more subtle and effective manipulation of black racial pride could be seen in the deliberations of the biracial committee appointed by the court to further integration in Shreveport. The black members initially demanded a 50:50 racial balance in each and every school. They eventually settled, however, for a plan that allowed for 90:10 ratios in the high schools and the preservation of single-race elementary schools. As part of the trade-off, blacks won a 50:50 faculty ratio. Committee chairman Charles Beaird explained how black sentiment for the "neighborhood school," traditionally a concept favored by segregation-minded whites, came to be accepted by the blacks. "The black leaders were in a spot because they couldn't admit that the black schools were bad because this was a blow to black pride and black self-esteem."[57]

By the mid-1970s the process of school integration was running out of steam. Defined in terms of blacks and whites attending the same school in approximately equal numbers, it was a very patchy affair. Integration worked best in rural areas and in small cities where blacks composed a minority of the school population (ironically, Bogalusa and Plaquemines Parish arrived at two of the best-integrated systems in Louisiana). It has also succeeded, statistically at least, in some of the suburbs of New Orleans. In Jefferson Parish, for example, only one of eighty-one public schools is more than 90 percent single-race.

Integration has worked least well in the big cities. Of 108 public schools in New Orleans, twenty are entirely black; fifty-nine others are more than 90 percent black. In fifty-three of the seventy-five schools in Shreveport, children of the "other race" composed fewer than 10 percent of the student body. Even when the 1973 desegregation plan was implemented, eleven schools remained all black and nine all white. One-fifth of Baton Rouge's 108 schools were entirely white or entirely black. In 1981 the federal district court found that the city's school board was still unwilling "to actually desegregate the public schools." Ordering a more rigorous plan that closed twenty-two single-race elementary schools, the court bemoaned the "failure of leadership, courage and wisdom on the part of local officials."[58]

Black disillusionment with integration became so widespread within the teaching profession that the proposed merger of the LEA with its white counterpart, the LTA, evoked widespread opposition. "I am certain that I could not accept the ramming down the throats that white people are accustomed to when Negro principals and teachers are concerned," wrote a St. Landry Parish teacher. Without adequate safeguards, many feared, the interests of blacks would lose out every time in a white-dominated organization. The fact that most white teachers adamantly opposed forming an integrated organization made the case for merger even more difficult to sell. Whites "neither welcome us nor want our company," admitted one merger advocate. In 1967 the National Education Association instructed segregated state associations to negotiate mergers on pain of suspension and ultimate expulsion. Two years later, the LTA and the LEA being as far apart as ever, the NEA suspended both organizations and put forward its own merger plan.[59]

It took five years, however, to persuade the two associations to come together, and until the very end, it remained touch-and-go as to whether the LEA's membership would approve the plan. J. K. Haynes, the LEA's executive secretary of thirty-years standing, led the opposition to the merger. In the estimation of former LEA president Alphonse Jackson, Haynes "saw LEA as a source of strength for black people and poor people." Indeed, just how much strength the LEA wielded is often overlooked; NEA official Samuel B. Etheridge was astonished at the extent of its political influence.

> It enjoyed patronage undreamed of by an education association. When the State Department of Education refused to operate the Head Start program because it did not want to integrate, LEA operated the Head Start program; LEA leaders were able to use the governor's plane for important out-of-state trips and were able to successfully nominate important state officials. That kind of power is difficult to give up.

The NAACP, however, had no interest in the institutional survival of the LEA; it would not fight to preserve Haynes's job or the jobs of other black administrators. It would be an error, however, to dismiss Haynes's opposition to merger as merely self-serving. Haynes had become profoundly disillusioned with school integration because of the manner in which whites had implemented it. Across the state, he complained to Daniel Byrd, the schools had lost 3,000 black teachers and 120 black principals. Furthermore, he claimed, black children had reaped no educational advantage from integration. "Black youngsters are dropping out, copping out, rebelling and being driven out of school. The teaching-learning is poorer today than two decades ago."

By 1975 Haynes's opposition to stated LEA policy to accept merger had become so intemperate that some considered it counterproductive, and when the decisive vote was taken in November of that year the membership endorsed merger. During a six-year transition period, blacks were guaranteed 40 percent of the executive council seats, equal membership on some committees, and the presidency of the new organization in alternate years. In 1978 the LEA passed into history. Haynes fought merger to the bitter end. If black teachers accepted "consolidation with dignity," they did so in large part because, in the end, they had little choice in the matter. Merger reflected no great enthusiasm for integration.[60]

Loss of faith in integration manifested itself even more starkly in the storm of protest that followed the NAACP's proposal to abolish Louisiana's segregated university system. Strongly advocated by Arthur Chapital before his death in 1969, the issue of university integration had been taken up by Leon Panetta, director of HEW's civil rights office in the new Nixon administration. In 1970, after six years of inaction, HEW asked ten southern states to devise plans for integrating their state college systems.

State officials not only refused to submit a plan (Louisiana was the only state that failed to do so) but also made it clear that they intended to undermine black support for integration by threatening black colleges with closure.

As one McKeithen advisor told Panetta, "Leon, we've got you over a barrel and you know it . . . if you keep pushing we'll submit a plan that will provide for the closing of Southern and you'll have the blacks all over you . . . yep, it'll be desegregation all right, but you and I know it would never happen." The matter dropped from HEW's agenda after Panetta lost his job.

When the issue resurfaced in 1971 in the form of a resolution by the Louisiana State Conference of Branches, it opened up a hornet's nest. Opposition from the black colleges was overwhelming. Black students who had just witnessed the phasing-out of black high schools, the demotion of black principals, and the loss of black coaches argued that integration had deprived black children of positive black role models and an environment free of racism. To them, school integration was a cautionary tale, not an example to imitate. The Student Government Association of Grambling accused the NAACP in bitter terms.

> How can you expect anyone to join an organization which is out to subject them to the grave injustices of the past, out to make them jobless, out to submerge our recent struggle for identity, and most of all, out to help the white man implement his program to keep blacks uneducated. . . . Did you not learn from the previous mistake (our Black high schools)? Or, is it just that you want to keep looking good to the white man and live in luxury off his donations, while keeping your black counterparts in white-made ghettos? . . . We will unite all Black colleges against merging.

Other black colleges lodged equally forceful protests.

NAACP state president Emmitt Douglas set up a special committee on higher education that included representatives from Southern and Grambling. The committee was so badly divided, however, that it could not agree on a report. The chairman, Raphael Cassimere Jr., had been among the first blacks to attend the University of New Orleans, and he later joined UNO's history faculty. Submitting a chairman's report, he produced a ringing endorsement of integration that quoted the response of W. E. B. Du Bois to the *Brown* decision. Blacks must accept integration, Du Bois had written, "in justice to generations to come, white and black. They must eventually surrender race 'solidarity' and the idea of American Negro culture to the concept of world humanity, above race and nation. This is the price of liberty." The committee refused to accept his report and Cassimere resigned. Douglas had to disband the committee and replace it with an all-NAACP group. "Sharp debate ensued even there," Cassimere recalled, "amid charges that the NAACP was trying to destroy black institutions." The new committee eventually called for the merger of the Southern and LSU systems under a state board of higher education on which blacks enjoyed proportional representation. As long as the black colleges remained under a lily-white board, it argued, "white officials can single out and isolate blacks within a segregated system [and] they will always be tempted to short-change and ignore them."[61]

The protests then wracking Southern University added a pathetic coda to that conclusion. A renewed bout of student unrest had erupted in October 1972. Calling for the heads of President Netterville and other top officials, students marched to the state board of education and boycotted classes. The students' demands were almost identical to those of the 1969 SUNO protest: better housing, better food, more books in the library, courses in "Black Awareness," permission to fly the "Black Flag of Liberation." Now, however, the students appeared much more uncompromising and aggressive: they hectored and insulted; they used threats and intimidation; they not only boycotted classes but also disrupted them. State officials, including Governor Edwin W. Edwards, expressed sympathy with many of their demands but found it impossible to negotiate with them in a calm and rational manner. On November 16 about one hundred students occupied Netterville's office; shortly afterwards, at Netterville's request, fifty-five sheriff's deputies and thirty state troopers arrived on the campus. Most of the students then left the administration building, but a few only did so after the police fired tear gas. As they fled from the gas, two students, Leonard Brown and Denver Smith, were killed by a shotgun round. Southern University closed for the rest of the term.

An official investigation into the deaths found no evidence that students had possessed firearms or other weapons. They had not held anyone hostage when they occupied the administration building; they had not inflicted any real damage to the building or to Netterville's office. As state attorney general William J. Guste put it, "Yes, the students were impeding the use of the building; yes, they were preventing ready ingress and egress; yes, they were disrupting the activities at the university and in particular at that building. But . . . none of those acts is justification for the killing of two students." An unidentified sheriff's deputy, the report concluded, had fired the fatal shot.[62]

It took nine more years for even a partial resolution of the higher education question to emerge. In 1974, after the NAACP took HEW to court, the federal government finally sued to desegregate the dual university systems of Louisiana and other southern states. The plans accepted by HEW, however, left segregation largely intact: by 1978 whites composed only 1.4 percent of Southern University's student body, blacks only 4.7 percent of LSU's. In 1977 the NAACP again took HEW to court, resulting in stronger court-ordered requirements. In 1981 the Justice Department and the state entered into a consent decree that laid down specific policies and targets. The plan stopped well short of outright merger, however, and at the end of the 1980s, despite an increase in "other race" enrollment, LSU and Southern-Grambling remained substantially segregated. While the old white colleges now have a sizeable black enrollment (amounting to about one-fifth of the student body at UNO, for example), the old black colleges remain overwhelmingly black. Southern University has survived the civil rights movement and shows every sign of reaching the twenty-first century alive if not well.[63]

In Louisiana's public schools, too, segregation endures, despite a system that is, in theory, unitary. By 1993 white enrollment in the Orleans Parish schools had declined to 8 percent of the total, making integration, in the sense of a racial mix that reflected the city's population, impossible to achieve. And even that statistic understates the extent of segregation within the system, for a large proportion of the white children are concentrated in the "magnet" schools for gifted children and in predominantly white schools in affluent white areas of the city. Thus, despite the persistence of a few racially mixed neighborhoods, the pattern in New Orleans reflects that of big cities across the nation: resegregation of urban school systems as whites move to the suburbs or place their children in private schools. The figures all told a similar story: in Memphis, the proportion of black children in the public schools increased from half to three-quarters; in Richmond, from 56 percent to 88 percent; in Boston, from 40 percent to 74 percent. Even so, resegregation has been especially marked in New Orleans. Only in Detroit and Atlanta did the decline in white enrollment exceed that of New Orleans, and only Atlanta and Washington, D.C., now have a greater degree of segregation within their public schools.[64]

Even when blacks and whites attended the same schools and sat in the same classrooms, integration fell far short of the ideals of the civil rights movement. Physical proximity may have helped to erode the more egregious stereotypes that children held of the other race, but interracial friendship remained elusive. In Plaquemines Parish, for example — by the 1980s a model of integration — a school bus driver was reprimanded because she practiced a pattern of segregated seating. "White mothers didn't want white children to sit with black children," she explained, "and black mothers didn't want black children to sit with white children." In Bogalusa, too, the statistics indicated a successfully integrated school system, yet children and parents still avoided mixing with the other race. "Students attend separate high school proms, class reunions and parties," the *Times-Picayune* reported. "Children play in separate little leagues." The election of homecoming queens was still in abeyance, having been dropped fifteen years earlier when it became a divisive racial issue. Yet Bogalusa was no worse than other cities: everywhere, black and white students tended to keep to themselves in classrooms, cafeterias, and playgrounds. Even faculty integration, which in New Orleans went relatively smoothly, rarely led to interracial friendships.[65]

The most telling indicator of social integration, interracial marriage, told a similar story. Legalized in Louisiana by a 1967 U.S. Supreme Court decision, it remained a relative rarity: ten years later interracial weddings accounted for 0.7 percent of the total. The dream of an integrated "salt and pepper" society, Martin Luther King's dream of a "beloved community," had faded. "It's really kind of funny," mused NAACP stalwart and UNO historian Raphael Cassimere. "We thought a lot of these problems in race relations would be behind us by now. Instead, society has been resegregated." One white liberal sadly commented, "If you had told me back in the 60's that we would have made so little progress in racial integration and understanding . . . I would have laughed at you." By the end of the 1980s, however, a resurgence of overt white racism, symbolized by the rise to political prominence of David Duke, the former Grand Wizard of the Ku Klux Klan, showed that racial divisions were no laughing matter.[66]

Chapter 15

STRUGGLE WITHOUT END

I n 1991 a gubernatorial campaign in Louisiana riveted the nation's attention. David Duke, a Nazi sympathizer and a former leader of the Ku Klux Klan, had won the Republican nomination for governor. Finishing second in Louisiana's "open" primary election and beating Charles "Buddy" Roemer, the incumbent, into third place, he stood a real chance of becoming the state's chief executive. That bizarre and alarming prospect drew a question mark against the supposed achievements of the civil rights movement.

Duke's message could not have been simpler: blacks were backward, lazy, violent, and immoral; far from being treated unfairly, they were so pampered by "affirmative action" and welfare handouts that whites were the real victims of racial discrimination. Head of a "National Association for the Advancement of White People," which he founded in 1981, Duke made little effort to disavow his Klan and Nazi credentials beyond bland admissions of "dabbling in far-right politics as a teenager." However, despite vague assertions that he now "reject[ed] categorically racial or religious intolerance," Duke continued to espouse Nazi racial doctrines, argued that the Holocaust was an historical myth, and sold Nazi and racist literature from his NAAWP headquarters. In 1989 he won a seat in the state legislature. In 1990 he garnered over two-thirds of the white vote in his race for the U.S. Senate. And in November 1991, in a bid for the governor's office, he again received the endorsement of a clear majority of Louisiana's white voters.[1]

The reemergence of race as the dominant issue in two state elections was an astonishing development. With the collapse of legalized segregation and the ending of the white monopoly on political power, race had long ceased to be, outwardly at least, the primary organizing principle of state politics. Indeed, it had become conventional wisdom that although politicians might make subtle appeal to racial prejudice, to openly inject the race issue into a political campaign was the height of folly. By the early 1970s the strength of the black vote had become so obvious that white candidates risked alienating it at their peril.

The 1971 election of Governor Edwin W. Edwards demonstrated, for the first time, the decisive influence of the black vote on the state level. To be sure, Edwards, a French-speaking Cajun, also benefited from the relative growth of south Louisiana and the consequent muting of the religious issue: by 1980 the southern parishes accounted for 68 percent of the state's population; Louisiana was ready for a Cajun and a Catholic. Equally important, Edwards had no segregationist past to live down. "Race means nothing to him," thought Camille Gravel. "Never has." Ever since his election to the city council of Crowley in the 1950s — the first council in the state to have black members — Edwards had been accustomed to treating blacks as significant political players. In 1971 he gathered black support with unselfconscious ease. With the backing of SOUL in New Orleans and the support of Jesse Stone and Alphonse Jackson in Shreveport, Edwards garnered more than two-thirds of the black vote in the 1971 Democratic primary, narrowly winning a tight contest against state senator J. Bennett Johnston. And in the general election against Republican Dave Treen, Edwards's black support surpassed 90 percent.[2]

Politicians of all stripes quickly adjusted to the realities of biracial politics. When J. Bennett Johnston ran for the U.S. Senate in 1971, mounting a campaign devoid of racist appeals, black voters rewarded him with solid and decisive support. In backing Johnston, blacks also punished John McKeithen, who stood as an independent, for his raucous defense of school segregation during his second term as governor. Even die-hard segregationists could understand the new electoral demography. Otto Passman, congressman from the Monroe area since 1946, had long boasted the most conservative and prosegregation voting record in the state. In 1973, however, after surviving a serious challenge in a district where blacks constituted a third of the voters, he earned an approval rating of 39 percent from the Congressional Black Caucus, a higher score than any congressmen from Alabama or Mississippi. State representative Risley Triche underwent a similar metamorphosis. The Assumption Parish legislator had been a loyal henchman of Leander Perez; in 1960 he fought tooth-and-nail to stop the integration of schools in New Orleans. In 1972, however, he supported two bills designed to outlaw job discrimination. "We now find that we were wrong," he explained, referring to his stand on segregation in 1960. "I want my family and my citizens and my friends and my constituents . . . to grow out of racism and bigotry." The price of refusing to change was illustrated by the fate of Congressman John Rarick. First elected in 1966 as the favored candidate of the Ku Klux Klan, he lost the 1974 primary, and hence his seat, to a racial liberal.[3]

It seemed, for a time, that white politicians were prepared to make amends for Louisiana's racist past, and that something like a consensus on racial equality might soon emerge. In 1969 the New Orleans city council enacted a public accommodations ordinance that finally integrated the city's bars. In 1972 the state legislature abolished the state sovereignty commission, whose sole purpose had been the defense of segregation. The legislature also repealed eleven segregation laws, a symbolic act of reconciliation (the statutes had already been nullified by the federal courts) all the more significant for being initiated by Dorothy Mae Taylor, the first black woman to be elected a state representative. A new state constitution fashioned in 1973 incorporated a "Right to Individual Dignity" that forbids discrimination because of race, religion, idea, belief, and political affiliation.[4]

The passing of the old racial order was most dramatically illustrated, perhaps, in the collapse of the Perez dynasty in Plaquemines Parish. This mineral-rich area had been, for all practical purposes, the personal fiefdom of Leander Perez, whose fierce racism and unscrupulous methods ensured that political opponents were powerless and the black population so cowed that dissidents feared for their lives. After the death of the patriarch in 1969, power passed to two sons, Chalin and Lea, who continued to hold sway for another ten years. In 1979, however, fourteen years after the Justice Department sent federal registrars into the parish, a black man was elected to the parish council. In the same year three black oystermen, angered by the curtailment of their fishing rights by a new state law, organized the Fishermen and Concerned Citizens Association. The FCCA openly challenged the commission council, and for the first time in living memory blacks demonstrated outside the parish courthouse, demanding the removal of council president Chalin Perez.

The following year the vice president of the council, Luke Petrovich, rebelled against the Perez brothers (who by now were engaged in a bitter feud) and initiated an investigation of parish finances.

As Lea and Chalin continued their fratricide, Petrovich waged a relentless campaign to uncover the way in which the Perez family had, over a period of fifty years, enriched themselves from mineral revenues that rightly belonged to the parish. When the sordid details of this massive fraud finally came to light, the name Perez had turned to mud. In 1983 the parish council cancelled the annual public holiday that marked Leander Perez's birthday, and in 1987 it renamed Judge Perez Drive and Lake Judge Perez. Anxious to avoid a trial in the state courts, the Perez family eventually agreed to relinquish control of 60,000 acres of land and pay the parish $10 million in back royalties. The settlement involved a mere fraction of the estimated $78 million in illegal profits that the family had siphoned off since 1936, but it represented a damning admission of guilt and drove a final nail into the Perez political coffin. For decades, Plaquemines Parish had voted the way Leander Perez had wanted it to, turning in the most fraudulent results in the state. But in 1991 the parish recorded a majority for Edwin Edwards, a result that would have been unthinkable when Perez was alive. Perez's shadow shortened even more when River Oaks Academy, one of five private schools he had set up in 1966 to avoid integration, closed its doors because of falling rolls. The other four "segregation academies" had already gone out of existence.[5]

By the 1980s the segregationist redoubts of old had crumbled. West Feliciana Parish, which in 1963 did not have a single black voter, became the only parish in Louisiana to record a majority for George McGovern in the 1972 presidential election. In 1979 William Bailey, longtime head of the Washington Parish NAACP, became president of the Bogalusa city council. By 1993 black mayors were serving in twenty towns and cities, including Ferriday, Lake Providence, Tallulah, Opelousas, and, of course, New Orleans. All told, Louisiana boasted 636 black elected officials, a figure exceeded only in Mississippi. Overall, blacks held 12.8 percent of all elective offices. In 1993 thirty-one blacks served in the state legislature, accounting for 21.5 percent of all the seats. In 1990 William Jefferson, former student leader at Southern University, became Louisiana's first black congressman, taking the New Orleans seat vacated by Lindy Boggs. Louisiana now has two black congressmen.[6]

Black political gains reflected more than raw voting strength measured by the sheer number of black voters; they also testified to the importance of the federal government in ensuring that black votes were translated into something approaching fair representation. With each decennial census, blacks brought suit in federal court to redistrict electoral boundaries in order to increase the number of majority-black districts. At the same time, the Supreme

Court's decision in *Allen* v. *State Board of Elections* (1969) enabled blacks to challenge official efforts to rig the electoral game against black candidates. In affirming that Congress intended the Voting Rights Act to prevent discrimination in the electoral process, as well as in the act of voting itself, the Court unleashed a flood of private suits against unfair electoral practices. Moreover, as Frank Parker notes, the *Allen* decision "greatly increased the voting rights enforcement role of the Justice Department," which now had clear authority to scrutinize proposed changes to the electoral laws of states and localities. The lawyers of the Civil Rights Division, writes Steven Lawson, soon became adept at spotting and challenging "sophisticated practices designed to diminish the influence of the black electorate." Despite its courting of southern white voters, the Nixon administration did not make a vigorous effort to reverse the momentum of black advances; at the national level, too, the civil rights movement had apparently evoked broad consensus rather than spirited backlash.[7]

Just as its contemporaneous *Alexander* decision proved the turning point in making school integration a social reality, the Supreme Court's ruling in *Allen* ensured that black representation went far beyond tokenism. Its most obvious consequence was that blacks successfully opposed a large number of "at-large" electoral plans at the city and parish level under which, except in rare instances where blacks were a majority, whites would continue to monopolize elective offices. Throughout the state, judges imposed single-district plans (although sometimes retaining a couple of at-large seats) on police juries, school boards, and city councils. One such decision led to a black majority on the New Orleans city council, which, until 1975, had been all white.[8]

The results of *Allen* were especially striking in north Louisiana, where whites had been most resistant to black voting and were fighting a vigorous rearguard action to keep black representation to a minimum. After being reversed by the court of appeals in a pivotal case involving East Carroll Parish, Judge Ben Dawkins sedulously struck down schemes that discriminated against black voters. Disallowing an at-large system for the Caddo Parish police jury, he insisted that "this substantial proportion of black citizenry should not have its vote diluted . . . and that it was entitled to black representation as nearly as possible to that proportion." In his most important voting rights decision, Dawkins ended a white monopoly of political power in Shreveport that had endured for a century. Declaring that Shreveport's at-large elections deprived blacks of political representation, Dawkins accused the city's white officials of systematically discriminating against blacks in every sphere of municipal life. They had virtually excluded blacks from the better-paying city jobs; their efforts to provide low-rent public housing had been minimal; their neglect of black neighborhoods was shamefully visible in ill-lit, badly drained, potholed streets. At-large elections, Dawkins argued, perpetuated "official unresponsiveness to the physical and economic needs and desires of Shreveport's black populace." Under a new city charter establishing single-member districts, three blacks won election to the city council in 1978.[9]

In a political world dominated by bloc voting, of course, whites could still place a ceiling on black representation no matter how equitable the electoral system. But if whites still routinely opposed black office seekers, the black vote could often make or break white candidates. "Maybe we could not get a person elected we wanted elected," explained Jesse Stone, "but we could defeat anybody we wanted to defeat. And that's what we did. We decided, for example, that no one who holds public office in Shreveport at this time . . . is ever going to go further along than where he is right now." The ability to mobilize black voters in this way made Shreveport representative Alphonse Jackson one of the most powerful politicians in the state. According to one study, the Jackson organization "has helped elect congressmen, sheriffs, district attorneys and mayors." It might have added governors and U.S. senators. But the showpiece of black political power was New Orleans, where a combination of bloc voting by blacks and crossover voting by whites enabled Ernest N. Morial to win the mayor's office in 1977 despite the fact that whites composed a clear majority of the electorate. Four years later Morial won reelection, again receiving near solid black support and substantial, albeit reduced, white minority support.[10]

Given the political clout wielded by black voters, it seems strange that a racial extremist like David Duke could become a serious candidate for statewide office. Biracial coalitions, however, have been difficult to construct and have always been vulnerable to the vicissitudes of white opinion. Despite appearances, race never disappeared as a political issue; it could be played down, but it could not be ignored or erased. The reappearance of overt racism also reflected, in addition to lingering rank prejudice, the failure of conventional politics to bring blacks and whites together in any real sense. Racial bloc voting does not simply reflect racial prejudice or racial chauvinism; it mirrors the inequalities and divisions that continue to inform the relationship between blacks and whites.

The persisting economic gap between the races is perhaps the most obvious source of inequality. Scholars have argued endlessly about the extent of black economic progress since the Civil Rights Act of 1964. Optimists point to the rapid growth of the black middle class, a loosely defined category that now embraces between a quarter and a third of the black population. Pessimists view black economic gains as illusory, pointing to the much larger group who suffer from unemployment and poverty and noting that the overall income gap between the races has not closed. As Steven Lawson argues, despite the gains chalked up by the middle class, "the majority of blacks had made little progress in catching up with whites." In 1992 the median income of black families stood at 58 percent of the white level, a wider gap than in 1968. According to a 1991 survey, the median white household has *ten times* the net assets of the median black household. In New Orleans, one of the poorest cities in the nation, 37 percent of black families were below the poverty level compared with 9 percent of white families. Only Mississippi has a greater percentage of poor people than Louisiana.[11]

The most ominous and controversial aspect of black poverty has been the growth of a so-called black underclass of people who have little or no hope of ever escaping from poverty. The "underclass" concept, popularized in the 1980s, revived the old association of black poverty with social pathology. It stresses that the poor are held back not only by unemployment and lack of skills, but also by crime, drug addiction, family instability, and other behavioral problems. The "underclass" is impossible to precisely define or quantify, and the term should be treated circumspectly. Still, the increasing social, physical, and economic isolation of the very poor is all too visible in urban America, and Louisiana's cities are no exception. In New Orleans, for example, the exodus of upwardly mobile blacks to formerly white neighborhoods and new suburbs has weakened both the social cohesion and the physical fabric of many older black areas. The desegregation of Canal Street and the opening of suburban shopping malls has led to the virtual extinction of black business districts.

The gap between the black middle class and the so-called underclass might, logically, militate against racial bloc voting by blacks and whites. Indeed, sociologist William Julius Wilson has argued that it is economic class, far more than race, that governs the position of blacks in contemporary America. Educated blacks, he contends, have little difficulty in finding well-paid jobs, and the major corporations are going out of their way to recruit them. Hence the unemployed, underemployed "underclass" is not so much the victim of white racism as of economic change. With the decline of traditional "smokestack" industries and the consequent shrinkage of blue-collar employment, the unskilled and uneducated are marginalized, languishing in low-wage service industries or dropping out of the labor market altogether to live on the criminal fringes of society in the decaying central cities.

If class, therefore, were to become the main determinant of political behavior, then political alliances would increasingly cut across the racial divide. After all, as the black population becomes increasingly stratified according to economic class, the basis for political unity becomes increasingly tenuous; once the novelty of electing a black candidate wears off, there is a natural tendency for the black vote to lose its cohesion. In New Orleans, for example, blacks failed to unite around a black candidate to succeed Ernest Morial as mayor: in a race contested by two blacks, the man favored by most whites, Sidney Barthelemy, won the election with only a quarter of the black vote. According to Arnold Hirsch, the Barthelemy coalition "blended the most conservative segments of each [race]."[12]

Class, rather than color, might also explain the ambivalent white perceptions of black people. Whites might fear and abhor the "underclass," but also respond positively to "respectable" middle-class blacks. This was certainly the belief of the strategists who constructed Douglas Wilder's campaign for the lieutenant governorship of Virginia. Explained one of them: "People were convinced that prejudice was based solely on the element of color. Our feeling was that that kind of prejudice was on the wane and that the real prejudice that had to be overcome was one based more on class." Whites *would*, they calculated, vote for a smooth, educated, affluent black lawyer. Wilder won his campaign for the lieutenant governorship and went on to become the first black governor of a southern state. In both races he could not have won without substantial white support.[13]

It is a fallacy, however, to argue that nonracial factors alone account for the reality that blacks still lag behind whites. Class and race do not constitute political opposites: they intersect in complex ways and in some respects reinforce each other. Even in an ideal world where racism did not exist, the overlapping of race and class would still tend to divide whites and blacks. And in practice, when the mental world of white people is already well stocked with negative images of black people, the high rate of black poverty and the association of blacks with crime make it difficult for many whites to view African-Americans as individuals rather than as members of a racial group. Color-blind judgments are rendered still more difficult by the fact that residential segregation, now more marked than ever, physically separates blacks and whites into two social worlds.

White perceptions of crime illustrate how real fears combine with racial stereotypes to reinforce divisions. The explosion of violent crime that took place during the 1970s and 1980s is an undeniable fact. Before 1966, the annual homicide figure for New Orleans never exceeded one hundred; after 1970 it never fell below that number. During the second half of the 1980s, with the spread of "crack" cocaine, the black homicide rate soared, in some cities almost doubling. During the first nine months of 1990, 229 people were murdered in New Orleans; 203 of the victims were blacks. In 1993, with 389 homicides, New Orleans became the murder capital of the United States. Louisiana had become one of two southern states, and one of seven states nationwide, where more people died by the gun than died on the roads.

Spiraling crime rates are a matter of legitimate public concern for blacks and whites alike. There is a strong tendency among whites, however, to make fear of crime their primary response to African-Americans. This association of blacks with crime helps to perpetuate racial segregation. It also fuels repressive criminal justice policies that have a disproportionate impact upon black people. Hence while the overall crime rate actually *declined* somewhat during the 1980s, America's prison population more than doubled. With over one million prisoners, the United States has the highest rate of incarceration in the world, and blacks make up almost 47 percent of those behind bars. America's renewed enthusiasm for capital punishment shows a similar effect: blacks make up 39 percent of all death-row inmates. Since the resumption of executions in 1976, the twelve leading death penalty states include all but one of the ex-Confederate states. Louisiana has executed more prisoners than any other state except Florida and Texas; in proportion to its population, it is America's leading executioner.[14]

In the white suburbs on the peripheries of predominantly black cities, fear of crime is almost an obsession, and politicians have not been slow to exploit it. Jefferson Parish, which borders New Orleans to the south and west, is typical of such areas. Almost as populous as the city itself, Jefferson is a bastion of the "white flight" mentality. In 1986 its sheriff, Harry Lee, ordered his deputies to stop and question any blacks who were seen driving through white neighborhoods in "rinky-dink cars." Two months later the commission council erected barriers across Willow and Hickory streets at the Jefferson Parish line, preventing vehicular access to and from New Orleans. The resulting furor caused both actions to be rescinded, but their authors suffered no political harm at all in a parish that is 90 percent white. In 1989 David Duke won a seat in the legislature representing Metairie, an area of Jefferson Parish in which blacks compose less than 1 percent of the population.[15]

The black vote has not, therefore, fragmented along class lines as much as one might expect. The growing black middle class has not lost its race consciousness; it remains aware of its economic vulnerability and recognizes that its advancement has resulted from racial unity as much as from individual initiative. "Although increased competition for public office sometimes proved divisive," notes Lawson, "blacks generally remained united in their unfinished goal of achieving racial equality." As long as they suffered from discrimination and prejudice, "race persisted as a crucial category for determining political choices." And middle-class blacks had ample reason to believe that whatever their economic status, they would still need to unite with other blacks to oppose racism. True, public expressions of crude racial prejudice had become unacceptable, even in the South. Granted, the only whites who openly advocated segregation were regarded as cranks. But blacks suspect a large dose of racism, albeit vicariously expressed, in the white obsession with crime, in white opposition to busing, in "white flight" from the cities, in white attacks on "affirmative action" policies, and in the general white indifference to the problems of cities and poor people.[16]

The growth of the Republican party in the South illustrates the difficulty of isolating class and race as distinct political categories. The Louisiana Republican party has not based its appeal on overt racism, but it recognizes that its strength resides almost exclusively in the white electorate, especially in suburban enclaves like Jefferson Parish (where David Duke ran as a Republican). Thus in 1979 the party elected its first governor, Dave Treen, a former Citizens Council stalwart, by splitting the interracial coalition put together by Edwin Edwards and solidifying the white vote. Nationally, too, the Republicans have become a virtually all-white party: Ronald Reagan received only 6 percent of the black vote in 1980 and barely 10 percent in 1984. The Republican party has therefore had little to lose by being unresponsive to black demands, and much to gain by opposing them. Usually, moreover, they have been able to frame their policies in such a way that, although having a disproportionately adverse impact on blacks, they are racially neutral. As Alphonso Pinkney laments in *The Myth of Black Progress*, "As long as conservatism dominates the country, there can be no progress in the area of race relations."[17]

It would be fatuous to equate conservatism and racism, yet considerations of race pervade Republican strategy and tactics at both the state and national level. During the 1986 U.S. Senate race, for example, the Republican National Committee tried to reduce the black electorate by as many as eighty thousand voters in an effort to defeat Democratic candidate John B. Breaux. The Republican "ballot integrity" program was reminiscent of the voter purge conducted by the white Citizens Councils in the late 1950s. Like that earlier effort, a federal court judged it illegal. Two years later the Republican party sensationalized the crime issue during George Bush's election campaign by framing a television commercial around a black rapist. The infamous "Willie Horton" spots typified the way in which an ostensibly nonracial issue was given a racial slant in a manner plainly calculated to arouse white fears.[18]

By catering to the white vote and writing off the black vote, the Republican party has helped to legitimate a new form of covert or coded racism. "White racial attitudes have definitely hardened during the Reagan-Bush era," writes Lawrence Powell. "Duke is the beneficiary of twenty years of Republican bottom fishing for Wallace votes." Duke sounded many of the themes that had been popularized by the Republican party; indeed, judged solely on policies, it would be difficult to distinguish Duke from Jesse Helms, archconservative senator from North Carolina, and other right-wing southern Republicans. It could even be argued that whites voted for Duke in spite of, rather than because of, his Klan and Nazi background; hence Duke advised his supporters to "stay away from the 'N' word" on the grounds that voters were repelled by racial hatred.[19]

Yet to interpret Duke as another right-wing Republican would be to underestimate the breadth and character of his appeal. Duke's electoral support in Jefferson Parish differed from that of mainstream Louisiana Republicans: he drew most of his votes from working and middle-class whites, many of them registered Democrats, not from the affluent whites who formed the backbone of the traditional Republican vote. Duke exerted a class appeal that mobilized white voters from the bottom up, not the top down. And, unlike mainstream Republicans, he explicitly encouraged those voters to project their resentments onto the black population. Lawrence Powell argues, and common sense would indicate, that it was precisely *because* of his well-known Klan background that whites of this class responded to Duke so enthusiastically.[20]

If the Republican party helped to sow what David Duke reaped, the reemergence of overt racism at the end of the 1980s still requires a fuller explanation. Perhaps, as Powell speculates, the backdrop of sharp economic decline made whites in Louisiana especially susceptible to Duke's brand of right-wing populism. Between 1974 and 1981 Louisiana enjoyed an economic boom of unprecedented magnitude: per capita income grew from 79 percent of the national average to 90 percent; nonagricultural employment increased by almost a quarter. When oil prices plummetted in 1981, however, the bubble burst, and Louisiana entered a recession of exceptional severity. By 1982 unemployment had climbed to 13.1 percent, twice the national average, and by 1988 per capita income had declined to 75 percent of the national average. As the unemployment lines lengthened, moreover, the Reagan administration slashed federal aid to the cities. New Orleans, for example, saw its annual subventions decline from $123 million in 1980 to $65 million in 1982; by 1987 the city faced a crippling budget deficit of $30 million.

Instead of class conflict, hard times produced two highly charged, racially polarized state elections. Duke "successfully focused blue- and white-collar economic resentments on programs of racial preference and the black 'underclass,'" writes Powell. And the growth of the black middle class, instead of fostering a feeling of common interest that transcended race, merely accentuated white racial resentments. Middle-class blacks lived in different areas and had little contact with white suburbanites. Moreover, as blacks were demanding a larger slice of the pie, the pie was shrinking. In a straitened economy, with rising unemployment and a contracting public sector, the economic fortunes of the black middle class became closely linked to political patronage, state spending, affirmative action, and minority "set-asides." Race-specific programs to favor black job applicants and promote black employees became one of the most politically divisive issues of the 1980s. Whites believed — and the Republican party encouraged them to believe — that "racial quotas" directly and unfairly disadvantaged them. By the time David Duke appeared on the scene it had become almost an article of faith that black gains meant white losses.[21]

Yet economic hardship and white racial resentments were hardly peculiar to Louisiana. Perhaps one should also look to Louisiana's political culture as an explanation for the Duke phenomenon. The collapse of white supremacy and the rise of the Republican party has not led to a stable two-party system. Quite the reverse: the past quarter of a century has seen the bifactionalism of the Long era give way to an anarchic multifactionalism in which party labels mean little. An "open primary" law, under which all candidates run in the same primary, regardless of party, further discourages party cohesion. The 1979 gubernatorial election, writes Paul Grosser, exemplified Louisiana's "no-party politics run amok." After the first primary, the four losing Democratic candidates all endorsed the Republican, former Citizens Council stalwart Dave Treen, and campaigned against the Democratic front-runner. After Treen's election, his Democratic backers all received plum appointments in the governor's new administration.

Dishonest elections also continue to tarnish Louisiana politics. A 1974 congressional race produced so many fraudulent votes that a state court set aside the result and ordered a new election. In 1976 Congressman Rick Tonry resigned his seat after being indicted for election fraud; two years later he began a jail sentence. The gubernatorial primary of 1978 aroused widespread suspicion, later shown to be justified, that voting machines had been tampered with. The following year a federal grand jury indicted over twenty people in the Leesville area for conspiring to buy votes on behalf of Congressman Claude Leach.[22]

Louisiana's political culture is also, as ever, riddled with corruption. In 1973 a federal judge sentenced former state attorney general Jack P. F. Gremillion to a three-year jail sentence for perjury after he falsely denied his financial interest in a savings and loan company. In 1976 a grand jury charged Shreveport public safety commissioner George D'Artois with stealing $30,000 in city funds; he was also charged with the contract murder of a political enemy. Refusing to submit to arrest, he was physically removed from his office after a sensational armed siege. (He died before standing trial.) Allegations of corruption have swirled around Edwin Edwards throughout his gubernatorial career; he twice stood trial in federal court on charges of fraud and racketeering, but juries acquitted him on each occasion. A 1980 "sting" operation by the FBI revealed the extensive influence of Mafia boss Carlos Marcello with many leading politicians and public officials. Charles Roemer, a top Edwards aide and father of future governor Buddy Roemer, went to jail for corruption. In 1991 a jury convicted Insurance Commissioner Doug Green of taking $3 million in bribes.

Black politicians have no immunity against greed, and many have readily adapted to the "enrich yourself" mentality that pervades public life. The leaders of New Orleans political organization SOUL, writes Arnold Hirsch, proved "adept at blending race and politics for profit." They demanded money in return for financial support, misused antipoverty funds, and made dubious profits from public ventures like the Superdome. Members of the state parole board gave convicts preferential treatment in exchange for money. Perhaps the most egregious case of corruption involved former civil rights lawyer Robert F. Collins. Appointed to the federal bench by President Carter, the first black federal judge in the South, Collins went to jail for taking a $16,500 bribe.[23]

Dishonesty and unprincipled opportunism provide a poor foundation upon which to build a healthy democratic politics. It is common to hear that Louisianians love a rogue, and that corruption in public life is tolerated and even admired. In his memoirs of a long political career, William J. Dodd argued that "a big-time state politician who failed to get rich and make his friends rich has been considered stupid." There is little evidence, however, that voters approve of flagrant greed and dishonesty in the state's highest officials. Corruption has not so much been tolerated by the state's voters as foisted upon them by a corrupt political system that seems incapable of reforming itself.[24]

Chaotic factionalism, stolen elections, and endemic corruption have nurtured the kind of cynicism that makes voters warm to a candidate, in this case David Duke, who seems to offer a principled stand and a clean break with the past. The corruption of Edwin Edwards's third administration alienated white voters, causing his political base to fracture along racial lines in 1987. After the failure of Buddy Roemer to ease Louisiana's wretched financial condition, many white voters needed only a little prompting to turn their economic woes into resentment against blacks. The coalition that gave Edwards, the notorious corruptionist, a precedent-breaking fourth term had little rationale other than that of denying the governorship to David Duke. The anti-Duke sticker that adorned car bumpers in 1990 — "Vote For the Crook, It's Important" — provided a rueful but telling comment on the straitened moral climate of Louisiana politics.

David Duke and Edwin Edwards exemplify the Janus face of contemporary Louisiana. Yet Duke's astonishing popularity among whites in 1990–91 should not obscure the most salient fact about his two bids for statewide office: he lost. Blacks voted in unprecedented numbers to oppose Duke: in the

1991 governor's race, black turnout actually exceeded white. Black Louisianians stopped Duke's career in its tracks, burying his hopes of statewide office and thwarting his national political ambitions. And the black vote, truly functioning as a coherent "bloc," ensured the return to the governor's mansion of Edwin W. Edwards, for twenty years the leading exponent of biracial politics. If the meteoric rise of Duke underlined the continuing vitality of white racism, his equally swift fall demonstrated the extraordinary durability and popular appeal of Edwards. It is doubtful that historians will ever write about "the Duke era." The last quarter of a century of Louisiana politics, however, can already be called "the Edwards era."

To be sure, the rise of David Duke revealed disturbing continuities in Louisiana politics, but the 1991 gubernatorial election revealed, even more clearly, how the electoral game had changed since the heyday of segregation. In 1959, to cite the last example of a campaign based solely on the race issue, Willie Rainach had prompted all the other candidates to gang up against Chep Morrison, the racial moderate. In 1991 Duke's racist campaign persuaded all the other candidates to rally around Edwards. And while the division between north and south Louisiana could be discerned in the Duke-Edwards result, it was not nearly so clear as in previous elections where race had been the dominant issue. Duke carried a bloc of rural parishes in the northern half of the state, but he failed to carry Shreveport, the traditional bastion of Louisiana conservatism. He won Winn Parish, the seat of the Long dynasty, but failed to carry Claiborne, Rainach's home parish and the birthplace of the Citizens Councils. While Duke won two former Klan strongholds in the Florida Parishes, Washington and Livingston, he lost Plaquemines Parish, the old fiefdom of Leander Perez. Duke was soundly beaten, in fact, in every part of Louisiana.[25]

The extraordinary diversity of the coalition that mobilized against him suggests that David Duke was anything but an ordinary segregationist. Only the most profound fear of the consequences of a Duke win could have persuaded business leaders, conservative Republicans, and former Dixiecrats to resurrect Edwin Edwards from his political grave. Much of the white opposition to Duke was a vote against racial extremism and a vote against Louisiana becoming a pariah state, but it was also a vote for conservatism and for the continuation of white control wherever possible. In a racially polarized mayoral election in 1990, for example, voters in Shreveport chose Hazel Beard, a white woman and a Republican, over Dr. C. O. Simpkins, the black civil rights leader who had recently returned to the city after a twenty-five year residence in New York. But the city also returned majorities against David Duke, and an outbreak of cross-burnings led to the swift apprehension and punishment of the Klan perpetrators.

Paradoxically, Duke's statewide campaigns may well have had the beneficial effect of introducing much-needed order into Louisiana's politics and of clarifying the race issue after two decades of obfuscation. Writing in 1989, historian Glen Jeansonne argued that "given the opportunity to vote class interests, as opposed to religious or racial interests, Louisianians have consistently voted the latter two." The elections of 1990 and 1991 broke that pattern, and may well mark a turning point in the state's political development.[26]

In New Orleans, the white elite's commitment to racial egalitarianism was soon put to the test. No sooner had Duke been defeated than a controversy over Carnival erupted. An ordinance passed by the majority-black city council in December 1991 gave Carnival krewes a year to demonstrate that they did not restrict their membership on the basis of race, gender, or religion. If they failed to do so, the city would, in effect, make it impossible for them to parade. Two of the oldest and most prestigious krewes, Comus and Momus, cancelled their 1992 parades in protest, others threatened to pull out, and for a time the future of Carnival was in doubt. The council responded to white anguish by appointing a committee, in which whites outnumbered blacks, to examine the controversial ordinance and try to finesse a compromise. Carnival went ahead, and blacks and whites mingled on the sidewalks, yelling "Throw me something, mister!" with no evident racial tension. New Orleans is probably the only city in America where race can be all but forgotten amid two weeks of madcap hedonism. Yet race endures as a fact of life in contemporary Louisiana, just as it does in the United States as a whole. Race and racism are not entities that can be weighed and measured; they are complicated amalgams of social relationships and social identities. They change and mutate over time; they are refracted through class and culture. Race is part of the warp and weft of American society. Like politics itself, in a democracy the struggle for racial equality is a struggle without end.[27]

NOTES

ADA	Americans for Democratic Action Papers, State Historical Society of Wisconsin, Madison
AFSC	American Friends Service Committee Papers, Philadelphia
ARC	Amistad Research Center, Tulane University
APT	A. P. Tureaud Papers, Amistad Research Center, Tulane University
CCHR	Catholic Council on Human Relations Papers, Amistad Research Center, Tulane University
CCS	Catholic Committee of the South Papers, Amistad Research Center, Tulane University
CIC	Commission on Interracial Cooperation Papers
CORE	Congress of Racial Equality Papers
CORE(SRO)	CORE Papers, Southern Regional Office files, State Historical Society of Wisconsin, Madison
FEPC	Fair Employment Practices Committee Papers (microfilm)
HRC	New Orleans Human Relations Committee files, New Orleans Public Library
LCDC	Lawyers Constitutional Defense Committee files
LBJ	Lyndon B. Johnson Presidential Papers, Lyndon B. Johnson Library, Austin, Texas
LSUS	Louisiana State University, Shreveport

NAACP	NAACP, Voting Rights, Education, Lynching, Legal Department and Central Office Records files, Manuscripts Division, Library of Congress (microfilm)
NAACP(LA)	NAACP, Papers of the NAACP Field Director for Louisiana, Amistad Research Center, Tulane University
NAACP(LC)	NAACP, Papers, Branch files, Manuscripts Division, Library of Congress
NAACP(NO)	NAACP, New Orleans Branch Records, Earl K. Long Library, University of New Orleans
NOPL	New Orleans Public Library
NUL	National Urban League Papers, Manuscripts Division, Library of Congress
OPSB	Orleans Parish School Board files, Earl K. Long Library, University of New Orleans
SCLC	Southern Christian Leadership Conference Papers, Library and Archives, Martin Luther King, Jr., Center for Nonviolent Social Change, Atlanta
SEDFRE	Congress of Racial Equality (CORE), Scholarship, Education, and Defense Fund for Racial Equality files
SHSW	State Historical Society of Wisconsin, Madison
SRC	Southern Regional Council Papers
STFU	Southern Tenant Farmers Union Papers
TU	Howard-Tilton Library, Tulane University
UCC	United Church of Christ Papers, Amisted Research Center, Tulane University

PREFACE

1. Robert J. Norrell, *Reaping the Whirlwind: The Civil Rights Movement in Tuskegee* (New York: Alfred A. Knopf, 1985); Bayard Rustin, "From Protest to Politics: The Future of the Civil Rights Movement" (1965), in Paul Jacobs and Saul Landau, eds., *The New Radicals* (London: Penguin, 1967), p. 294. For a survey of works dealing with the Roosevelt-Truman era, see Adam Fairclough, "State of the Art: Historians and the Civil Rights Movement," *Journal of American Studies* 24 (December 1990): 387–90.

2. Robin D. G. Kelley, *Hammer and Hoe: Alabama Communists during the Great Depression* (Chapel Hill: University of North Carolina Press, 1990), pp. 227–31.

3. Richard H. King, *Civil Rights and the Idea of Freedom* (New York: Oxford University Press, 1992), p. 4; Hugh Murray Jr., "Change in the South," *Journal of Ethnic Studies* 16 (Summer 1988): 119–35.

4. Mark V. Tushnet, *The NAACP's Legal Strategy against Segregated Education, 1925–1950* (Chapel Hill: University of North Carolina Press, 1987); Genna Rae McNeil, *Groundwork: Charles Hamilton Houston and the Struggle for Civil Rights* (Philadelphia: University of Pennsylvania Press, 1983); Raymond Gavins, "The NAACP in North Carolina during the Age of Segregation," in Armstead L. Robinson and Patricia L. Sullivan, eds., *New Directions in Civil Rights Studies* (Charlottesville: University Press of Virginia, 1991), p. 106. When I completed this work, the papers of the NAACP Legal Defense Fund, and those of Thurgood Marshall, were still closed. However, I had time to review the memoir of Jack Greenberg, *Crusaders in the Courts: How a Dedicated Band of Lawyers Fought for the Civil Rights Revolution* (New York: Basic

Books, 1994), which provides illuminating insights into the complex and often tense relationship between the NAACP and the NAACP Legal Defense Fund.

5. Lecture delivered by Julian Bond at the University of Virginia, 1990.

6. Andrew Young quoted in Jack Minnis to Wiley A. Branton, "Conference Held by the United Crusade for Voters, Lake Charles, Louisiana," August 20, 1963, series 6, folder 153, Southern Regional Council Papers, Woodruff Library, Atlanta University (microfilm; collection hereinafter cited as SRC); Vicki Crawford, "Women in the Mississippi Movement," paper delivered at the annual convention of the Southern Historical Association, Atlanta, November 1992.

7. Lolis E. Elie, interviewed by Jack Bass, September 28, 1979, p. 2, Jack Bass Oral History Collection, Law Library, Tulane University (hereinafter cited as Bass Collection).

8. William J. Dodd, *Peapatch Politics. The Earl Long Era in Louisiana Politics* (Baton Rouge: Claitor's Publishing Division, 1991).

9. Robin D. G. Kelley, "'We Are Not What We Seem': Black Working-Class Opposition in the Jim Crow South," *Journal of American History* 80 (June 1993): 75–112.

10. Stephen Potter, *One-Upmanship* (London: Penguin, 1962).

11. Harvey R. H. Britton, interviewed by Adam Fairclough, November 4, 1987.

12. On the relationship between local and national history, see Steven F. Lawson, "Commentary," in Charles W. Eagles, ed., *The Civil Rights Movement in America* (Jackson: University Press of Mississippi, 1986), pp. 34–35.

CHAPTER 1 : *Creole Louisiana*

1. T. Lynn Smith and Homer L. Hitt, *The People of Louisiana* (Baton Rouge: Louisiana State University Press, 1952), pp. 2–3; Leedell Wallace Neyland, "The Negro in Louisiana since 1900: An Economic and Social Study" (Ph.D. diss., New York University, 1958), pp. 23–27. In 1890 foreign-born immigrants composed 4.5 percent of Louisiana's population, a proportion far exceeding that of other southern states.

2. Gwendolyn Midlo Hall, "The Formation of Afro-Creole Culture," in Arnold R. Hirsch and Joseph Logsdon, eds., *Creole New Orleans: Race and Americanization* (Baton Rouge: Louisiana State University Press, 1992), pp. 65–68. See also the fuller treatment in Hall, *Africans in Colonial Louisiana: The Development of Afro-Creole Culture in the Eighteenth Century* (Baton Rouge: Louisiana State University Press, 1992), pp. 159–87, 277–302.

3. Hall, *Africans in Colonial Louisiana*, pp. 187–200.

4. Paul F. Lachance, "The 1809 Immigration of Saint-Domingue Refugees to New Orleans: Reception, Integration, and Impact," *Louisiana History* 29 (Spring 1988): 110–11; H. E. Sterkx, *The Free Negro in Ante-Bellum Louisiana* (Cranbury, N.J.: Associated University Presses, 1972), pp. 91–92, 198–99; Gary B. Mills, *The Forgotten People: Cane River's Creoles of Color* (Baton Rouge: Louisiana State University Press, 1977), p. xiv; John T. Gillard, *Colored Catholics in the United States* (Baltimore: Josephite Press, 1941), pp. 14–20.

5. Smith and Hitt, *People of Louisiana*, pp. 34–35, 46–47; Gilbert C. Din, *The Canary Islanders of Louisiana* (Baton Rouge: Louisiana State University Press, 1988); Frank M. Lovrich, *The Social System of a Rural Yugoslav-American Community: Oysterville* (San Francisco: R and E Research Associates, 1971), p. 59. By 1940 immigrants made up only 1.2 percent of the state's population.

6. Paul F. Lachance, "The Foreign French," in Hirsch and Logsdon, eds., *Creole New*

Orleans, pp. 101–30; Carl A. Brasseaux, *The Founding of New Acadia: The Beginnings of Acadian Life in Louisiana, 1765–1803* (Baton Rouge: Louisiana State University Press, 1987), pp. 73, 91; Brasseaux, *Acadian to Cajun: The Transformation of a People, 1803–1877* (Jackson: University Press of Mississippi, 1992), pp. 105–9, 151; Smith and Hitt, *People of Louisiana,* pp. 48–49; Nicholas Spitzer, "Cajuns and Creoles: The French Gulf Coast," *Southern Exposure* 5 (1977): 140–55; Neyland, "Negro in Louisiana," pp. 132–35.

7. Joseph Logsdon and Caryn Cossé Bell, "The Americanization of Black New Orleans, 1850–1900," in Hirsch and Logsdon, eds., *Creole New Orleans,* pp. 243–44.

8. "An Interview with Andrew Young," *Playboy,* July 1977, p. 72; Hall, *Africans in Colonial Louisiana,* pp. 115–18; Daniel H. Usner Jr., *Indians, Settlers, and Slaves in a Foreign Exchange Economy* (Chapel Hill: University of North Carolina Press, 1992), pp. 56–59, 132; Smith and Hitt, *People of Louisiana,* pp. 45–46.

9. Sterkx, *Free Negro,* pp. 285–315 passim.

10. David C. Rankin, "The Politics of Caste: Free Colored Leadership in New Orleans during the Civil War," in Robert R. Macdonald, John R. Kemp, and Edward F. Haas, eds., *Louisiana's Black Heritage* (New Orleans: Louisiana State Museum, 1979, pp. 116–17; Virginia R. Dominguez, *White by Definition: Social Classification in Creole Louisiana* (New Brunswick: Rutgers University Press, 1986), pp. 134–37.

11. Dominguez, *White by Definition,* pp. 26–31; C. Vann Woodward, "The National Decision against Equality," in *American Counterpoint: Slavery and Racism in the North-South Dialogue* (Boston: Little, Brown, 1971), pp. 212–33.

12. Rudolph Lucien Desdunes, *Our People and Our History* (Baton Rouge: Louisiana State University Press, 1972), pp. 140–46 (originally published as *Nos hommes et notre histoire,* 1911); John W. Blassingame, *Black New Orleans, 1860–1880* (Chicago: University of Chicago Press, 1973), pp. 124–29. Leland University, New Orleans University, and Straight University had been founded during Reconstruction; they were supported by, respectively, the Baptist, Methodist Episcopal, and Congregationalist churches. The Methodist church also supported the New Orleans-based *Southwestern Christian Advocate,* the sole black-edited newspaper in the Deep South during the early twentieth century.

13. C. Vann Woodward, *Origins of the New South, 1877–1913* (Baton Rouge: Louisiana State University Press, 1951, 1966), pp. 342–43; A. P. Tureaud, "Registration Practices in Louisiana," September 1, 1944; Tureaud to George Dudley, September 1, 1944, both in box 12, folder 38, A. P. Tureaud Papers, Amistad Research Center, Tulane University (collection hereinafter cited as APT).

14. James B. Lafourche, "Democracy Complex: The Danger That Arises from Impartial Universal Suffrage," *Civic Leader,* September 1929, box 18, folder 1, APT; "Lynchings in Louisiana, 1882–1900," Association of Southern Women for the Prevention of Lynching Papers, Commission on Interracial Cooperation Papers, Trevor Arnett Library, Atlanta University (microfilm, University of Virginia; collection hereinafter cited as CIC); George E. Cunningham, "The Italian: A Hindrance to White Solidarity in Louisiana, 1890–1898," *Journal of Negro History* 50 (January 1965): 35–36.

15. Dominguez, *White by Definition,* pp. 136–46.

16. Dolores Egger Labbé, *Jim Crow Comes to Church: The Establishment of Segregated Catholic Parishes in South Louisiana* (Lafayette: University of Southwestern Louisiana, 1971), pp. 51–53, 66–83; Allison Davis, "The Negro Church and Associations in the Lower South," June 1940, pp. 22–28, Carnegie-Myrdal Papers (microfilm, University of Virginia); Stephen J. Ochs, *Desegregating the Altar: The Josephites and the*

Struggle for Black Priests, 1871–1960 (Baton Rouge: Louisiana State University Press, 1990), p. 327.

17. Ochs, *Desegregating the Altar*, pp. 3–5, 164–74, 324–41.

18. Eric Foner, *Reconstruction: America's Unfinished Revolution, 1863–1877* (New York: Harper and Row, 1988), p. 437; William Ivy Hair, *Bourbonism and Agrarian Protest: Louisiana Politics, 1877–1900* (Baton Rouge: Louisiana State University Press, 1969), pp. 181–88; Bennett H. Wall, ed., *Louisiana: A History* (Arlington Heights, Ill.: Forum Press, 1984, 1990), p. 235; William Ivy Hair, *Carnival of Fury: Robert Charles and the New Orleans Riot of 1900* (Baton Rouge: Louisiana State University Press, 1976), pp. 137–55.

19. Paul Ted McCulley, "Black Protest in Louisiana, 1898–1928" (M.A. thesis, Louisiana State University, 1970), pp. 75, 89–90, 114.

20. Ibid., p. 75; Walter White, *Rope and Faggot* (New York: Alfred A. Knopf, 1927), pp. 246–47. There was another striking correlation between lynching and demography: the leading lynching parishes all had black majorities in 1910. Yet the fact that the majority-black parishes of south Louisiana had a lower incidence of lynching was no coincidence.

21. Charles C. Alexander, *The Ku Klux Klan in the Southwest* (Lexington: University of Kentucky Press, 1966), pp. 40–53, 118–21, 177–84, 211–12. Ironically, in 1956 state authorities used the anti-Klan law to attack the NAACP.

22. Forrest E. LaViolette, "The Negro in New Orleans," in Nathan Glazer and Davis McEntire, eds., *Studies in Minority Group Housing* (Berkeley and Los Angeles: University of California Press, 1960), pp. 115–16; Daphne Spain, "Race Relations and Residential Segregation in New Orleans: Two Centuries of Paradox," *Annals of the American Academy of Political and Social Science* 441 (January 1979): 86.

23. Herbert R. Northrup, *Organized Labor and the Negro* (New York: Harper and Brothers, 1944), pp. 7, 39–46; Herbert R. Northrup, "The New Orleans Longshoremen," *Political Science Quarterly* 57 (December 1942): 526–29; David Lee Wells and Jim Stodder, "A Short History of New Orleans Dockworkers," *Radical American* 10 (1976): 50–51; Daniel Rosenberg, *New Orleans Dockworkers: Race, Labor, and Unionism, 1892–1923* (Albany, N.Y.: State University of New York Press, 1988), pp. 72–75; Eric Arnesen, *Waterfront Workers of New Orleans: Race, Class, and Politics, 1863–1923* (New York: Oxford University Press, 1991), pp. viii, 183. The Bricklayers, Masons and Plasterers Union vigorously opposed racial discrimination, maintaining mixed locals in the South of which Local No. 1 in New Orleans was the strongest.

24. Dominguez, *White by Definition*, pp. 138–48; Kim Lacy Rogers, "Humanity and Desire: Civil Rights Leaders and the Desegregation of New Orleans, 1954–1966" (Ph.D. diss., University of Minnesota), 1982, pp. 13–14; John Minor Wisdom, interviewed by Jack Bass, May 22, 1979, p. 10, Bass Collection; Fourth All-Southern Negro Youth Conference, April 18–21, handwritten notes, box 3, folder 7, Harold N. Lee Papers, Howard-Tilton Library, Tulane University (library hereinafter cited as TU); Oretha Castle Haley, interviewed by Kim Lacy Rogers, November 27, 1978, recording, Amistad Research Center, Tulane University (archive hereinafter cited as ARC). In 1943 some 10,000 blacks worked as full-time domestics or servants; another 16,000 worked part time.

25. Donald E. DeVore, "The Rise from the Nadir: Black New Orleans Between the Wars, 1920–1940" (M.A. thesis, University of New Orleans, 1983), pp. 27–33; Richard B. Sherman, *The Republican Party and Black America from McKinley to Hoover, 1896–1933* (Charlottesville: University Press of Virginia, 1973), pp. 135–37, 153–54,

237–38; Arnold R. Hirsch, "Simply a Matter of Black and White: The Transformation of Race and Politics in Twentieth-Century New Orleans," in Hirsch and Logsdon, eds., *Creole New Orleans,* p. 264; Joseph Logsdon, "Oral History of A. P. Tureaud, Sr.," transcripts of tapes 7 and 10, in possession of Joseph Logsdon, University of New Orleans (material hereinafter cited as Logsdon, "Tureaud"); Ralph J. Bunche, *The Political Status of the Negro in the Age of FDR* (Chicago: University of Chicago Press, 1973), p. 540; L. Vaughan Howard and David R. Deener, *Presidential Politics in Louisiana, 1952* (New Orleans: Tulane University Press, 1954), pp. 3–4.

26. James D. Anderson, *The Education of Blacks in the South, 1860–1935* (Chapel Hill: University of North Carolina Press, 1988), p. 153; Betty Porter, "The History of Negro Education in Louisiana," *Louisiana Historical Quarterly* 25 (July 1942): 801.

27. Anderson, *Education of Blacks in the South,* p. 182; Plaintiff's Trial Brief, *U.S. v. Board of Registration of Louisiana,* Appendix E, table 4, October 5, 1964, Burke Marshall Papers, John F. Kennedy Presidential Library, Boston.

28. Abigail Curlee to C. E. Baldridge, "Louisiana education statistics," March 27, 1931, box 7, folder 165, CIC; Smith and Hitt, *People of Louisiana,* p. 89; Anderson, *Education of Blacks in the South,* pp. 153–56; Porter, "History of Negro Education in Louisiana," p. 801; Ellis D. Howard, interviewed by Miriam Feingold, 1967, recording, Feingold Collection, State Historical Society of Wisconsin, Madison (archive hereinafter cited as SHSW); Neyland, "Negro in Louisiana," pp. 100–101.

29. Gunnar Myrdal, *An American Dilemma: The Negro Problem and Modern Democracy* (New York: Harper and Brothers, 1944), 1:446–73; 2:842–49.

30. "Negro Welfare in Louisiana: Program Adopted by a Conference of White Citizens, June 16, 1920," box 52, folder 164, CIC.

31. Meetings of New Orleans CIC, 1921–31; "Reorganization of State Inter-racial Committees," 1922; Ira F. Steel to Jesse Daniel Ames, November 13, 1931, all in CIC.

32. Davis, "Negro Church and Associations in the Lower South," pp. 23–28; Logsdon, "Tureaud," p. 27.

33. John Bernard Alberts, "Black Catholic Schools: The Josephite Parishes of New Orleans during the Jim Crow Era" (M.A. thesis, University of New Orleans, 1990), pp. 6–24.

34. Neyland, "Negro in Louisiana," p. 103; "A History of the Knights and Ladies of Peter Claver in Southwest Louisiana," n.d., copy in Lake Charles public library.

35. Barbara Ann Worthy, "The Travail and Triumph of a Southern Black Civil Rights Lawyer: The Legal Career of Alexander Pierre Tureaud, 1899–1972" Ph.D. diss., Tulane University, 1984), p. 6; Logsdon, "Tureaud," pp. 21–23; Lyla Hay Owen, *Creoles of New Orleans* (New Orleans: First Quarter Publishing Company, 1987).

36. Ted Tunnell, *Crucible of Reconstruction: War, Radicalism, and Race in Louisiana, 1862–1877* (Baton Rouge: Louisiana State University Press, 1984), pp. 69–91; Mary F. Berry, "Negro Troops in Blue and Gray: The Louisiana Native Guards, 1861–1863," *Louisiana History* 8 (Spring 1967): 167–69; Mills, *Forgotten People,* pp. 230–36.

37. Labbé, *Jim Crow Comes to Church,* p. 53; Roger A. Fischer, *The Segregation Struggle in Louisiana, 1862–77* (Urbana and London: University of Illinois Press, 1974), p. 29; Logsdon and Bell, "Americanization of Black New Orleans," p. 218. "In a careful review of the social columns and editorials of New Orleans black newspapers," write Logsdon and Bell, "we find no mention of any society formed on the basis of light or dark skin color" (p. 244).

38. Logsdon, "Tureaud," p. 39.

39. Arthe Agnes Anthony, "The Creole Community in New Orleans, 1880–1920: An Oral History" (Ph.D. diss., University of California, Irvine, 1978), pp. 47–56, 108; Dominguez, *White by Definition*, pp. 162–65; Mills, *Forgotten People*, pp. xvi–xvii; Joseph H. Jones, "The People of Frilot Cove: A Study of a Racial Hybrid Community in Rural South Central Louisiana" (M.A. thesis, Louisiana State University, 1950), pp. 179–82; Sister Frances Jeanne Woods, *Marginality and Identity: A Colored Creole Family through Ten Generations* (Baton Rouge: Louisiana State University Press, 1972), pp. 200–211; Marion Overton White, interviewed by Patricia Rickels, 1979, recording, Carleton N. James Oral History Collection, University of Southwestern Louisiana, LaFayette (archive hereinafter cited as USL); *Times-Picayune,* September 1, 7, 1962; Smith and Hitt, *People of Louisiana,* p. 46.

40. Joseph H. Fichter, *Southern Parish: The Dynamics of a City Church* (Chicago: University of Chicago Press, 1951), p. 18. Fichter estimated that in a predominantly white uptown parish, about 5 percent of the black population "could pass for Nordic whites and another 10 percent for Latin-Americans."

41. Tureaud, "Experiences and Observations of a Negro Lawyer," 1940, box 12, folder 35, APT; *Eubanks v. Louisiana,* 356 U.S. 584 (1957); Leonard L. Burns, interviewed by Kim Lacy Rogers, May 14, 1979, recording, ARC; White, Rickels interview.

42. *Times-Picayune,* March 12, 1955; John E. Rousseau, "Segregationists May Never Know Extent of Integration," *Louisiana Weekly,* September 15, 1962; Virginia Collins Young, quoted in Rogers, "Humanity and Desire," p. 65.

43. Anthony, "Negro Creole Community," pp. 47–54, 107–15, 140–41; John H. Rohrer and Munro S. Edmunson, eds., *The Eighth Generation: Cultures and Personalities of New Orleans Negroes* (New York: Harper and Brothers, 1960), p. 49; Davis, "Negro Church and Associations," pp. 14–15; Ralph J. Bunche, "The Programs, Ideologies, Tactics and Achievements of Negro Betterment and Interracial Organizations, p. 127, Carnegie-Myrdal Papers.

44. NAACP, *Annual Report, 1924,* p. 23; Dr. Ernest Cherrie to William L. Andrews, July 6, 1931, part 1, series G, container 82, Branch Files, NAACP Papers, Manuscripts Division, Library of Congress (collection hereinafter cited as NAACP[LC]).

45. Warren M. Banner and J. Harvey Kerns, "A Review of the Economic and Cultural Problems of New Orleans, Louisiana, as They Relate to Conditions in the Negro Population," unpublished ms., 1950, pp. 19–20, Giles A. Hubert Papers, ARC; LaViolette, "Negro in New Orleans," pp. 115–16; Daphne Spain, "Race Relations," p. 90; Rohrer and Edmunson, *Eighth Generation,* pp. 37–39.

46. Hirsch, "Simply a Matter of Black and White," p. 266.

47. Claude F. Jacobs, "Benevolent Societies in New Orleans during the Late Nineteenth and Early Twentieth Centuries," *Louisiana History* 29 (Winter 1988): 21–33; DeVore, "Rise from the Nadir," pp. 20–23, 38–39; A. P. Tureaud and C. C. Haydel, *The Negro in Medicine in Louisiana: Souvenir Program: Forty-First Annual Session of the National Medical Association* (New Orleans: Dillard University), pp. 15–26.

48. *Tyler v. Harmon,* 273 U.S. 668 (1927); McCulley, "Black Protest in Louisiana," pp. 95–99, 116–24, 145–53; DeVore, "Rise from the Nadir," pp. 61–72; NAACP news release, April 7, 1930; James E. Gayle to Walter White, March 6, 1936; Charles H. Houston to Gayle, March 10, 1936, all in part 1, series G, container 82, NAACP(LC); George W. Lucas to Members and Friends, November 15, 1927, box 8, folder 1, APT.

49. McCulley, "Black Protest in Louisiana," p. 96; Tureaud to Walter White, October 2, 1931; Tureaud to Robert Bagnall, October 24, November 30, 1931; Bagnall to Tureaud, December 7, 1931, all in box 8, folder 2, APT; August Meier and Elliott

Rudwick, "Attorneys in Black and White: A Case Study of Race Relations within the NAACP," in the same authors' *Along the Color Line: Explorations in the Black Experience* (Urbana: University of Illinois Press, 1976), p. 161.

50. McCulley, "Black Protest," pp. 88–93, 124–30; Claude Hudson to Robert W. Bagnall, March 27, 1923, part 1, series G, container 83, NAACP(LC). The branches outside New Orleans were Shreveport (1914), Alexandria (1919), Ama (1920), Baton Rouge (1919), Clarence (1922), Lake Providence (1927), Madison Parish (1928), and Monroe (1927).

CHAPTER 2: *Race and Power in the Long Era*

1. Anthony J. Badger, "Huey Long and the New Deal," in Stephen W. Baskerville and Ralph W. Willett, eds., *Nothing to Fear: New Perspectives on America in the Thirties* (Manchester, Eng.: Manchester University Press, 1985), pp. 74–80; Michael L. Kurtz and Morgan D. Peoples, *Earl K. Long: The Saga of Uncle Earl and Louisiana Politics* (Baton Rouge: Louisiana State University Press, 1990), pp. 5–6; William Ivy Hair, *The Kingfish and His Realm: The Life and Times of Huey P. Long* (Baton Rouge: Louisiana State University Press, 1991).

2. Glen Jeansonne, *Leander Perez: Boss of the Delta* (Baton Rouge: Louisiana State University Press, 1977), pp. 14–31, 64–76, 101–19.

3. Badger, "Huey Long," pp. 73–74; Kurtz and Peoples, *Earl K. Long*, p. 65; Carleton S. Beals, *The Story of Huey P. Long* (Philadelphia: J. B. Lippincott, 1935), pp. 361–62; T. Harry Williams, *Huey Long* (New York: Bantam, 1970), p. 567; Allan P. Sindler, *Huey Long's Louisiana: State Politics, 1920–1952* (Baltimore: Johns Hopkins University Press, 1956), p. 77.

4. Roy Wilkins, "Huey Long Says — An Interview with Louisiana's Kingfish," *Crisis,* February 1935, pp. 41–42.

5. Badger, "Huey Long and the New Deal," pp. 73–74; statistics compiled by US Department of Justice, in Plaintiff's Trial Brief, *U.S. v. Louisiana*, Appendix E; Alan Brinkley, *Voices of Protest: Huey Long, Father Coughlin and the Great Depression* (New York: Vintage, 1983), p. 32.

6. Wilkins, "Huey Long Says," p. 41; Beals, *Story of Huey P. Long*, p. 363.

7. "History of the Federation of Civic Leagues," *Louisiana Weekly,* June 30, 1943; "8th Ward Civic League Meets," [1928], box 18, folder 21, APT; Logsdon, "Tureaud," tape 9; McCulley, "Black Protest," p. 3.

8. DeVore, "Rise from the Nadir," pp. 38–42; Hugh W. Robinson to William L. Andrewes, November 27, 1931, part 1, series G, container 82, NAACP(LC); *Trudeau* v. *Barnes* 65 F. 2d. 563 (1933).

9. Sindler, *Huey Long's Louisiana*, p. 90; Badger, "Huey Long," p. 74; Bunche, *Political Status of the Negro*, pp. 34–35; Gregory quoted in Edward F. Haas, "Huey Long and the Communists," *Louisiana History* 32 (Winter 1991): 33–34.

10. Harold Rouzan, interviewed by Adam Fairclough, October 30, 1990, New Orleans; Rev. Robert Perry, interviewed by Patricia Rickels, March 14, 1979, USL; Bunche, *Political Status of the Negro*, pp. 248, 312–14.

11. A. C. Terrance to Walter White, April 29, 1935, part 1, series G, container 83, NAACP(LC); August C. Terrance, "Autobiography," recording, n.d., Terrance Papers, ARC; Frederick Douglass Lewis, interviewed by Miriam Feingold, 1967, recording,

Feingold Collection; Wilkins, "Huey Long Says," p. 41. Abolition of the poll tax was approved in a referendum by 83 percent of those voting.

12. C. H. Myers to Charles H. Houston, May 3, 1938, part 1, series G, container 81, NAACP(LC).

13. William C. Havard, *The Government of Louisiana* (Baton Rouge: Louisiana State University Press, 1958), pp. 175, 180; Williams, *Huey Long*, pp. 134–35, 792–93. The sheriff was elected by the voters of the parish. In addition to his law enforcement authority, his power derived from his position as collector of state and local taxes, his ability to dispense patronage by appointing deputies and fixing their salaries, and his power to curb or tolerate gambling and prostitution.

14. *Pittsburgh Courier*, February 19, 1933; *Nashville Banner*, February 20, 1933; *Atlanta Constitution*, September 27, October 13, 1933; Beals, *Story of Huey P. Long*, pp. 354–56.

15. *New York Herald-Tribune*, January 11, 1936; *Shreveport Sun*, February 26, 1936; Carleton James, interviewed by Patricia Rickels, c. 1979, recording, USL.

16. *Louisiana Weekly*, January 26, 1935.

17. "Mr. John Wilson's account of what happened," Horace Mann Bond Papers; James E. Gayle and D. W. Taylor to Walter White, August 11, 1934; *New Orleans Times-Picayune*, July 31, August 3, 6, 1934; all in part 7, series A, file I-C-357, NAACP, Voting Rights, Education, Lynching, Legal Department and Central Office Records files, Manuscripts Division, Library of Congress (microfilm, University of Virginia) (collection hereafter cited as NAACP). According to the Gayle-Taylor report, there was some doubt about whether the shot that killed Wood had in fact been fired by Jerome Wilson; according to one account, Wood had been shot from behind by a .45-caliber pistol.

18. P. L. Prattis to Roy Wilkins, August 3, 1934, file I-C-357, NAACP. Norman Thibodeaux, who was hanged by Moore's killers but survived after being cut down by the bridge tender, appeared at an ILD antilynching rally in New York: *New York World-Telegram*, December 26, 1933, reprinted in Ralph Ginzburg, ed., *100 Years of Lynching* (New York: Lancer Books, 1962), pp. 212–14.

19. James E. Gayle to White, November 16, 1934, January 8, 1935, file I-C-357, NAACP; *State v. Wilson*, 181 La. 62, 158 So. 621 (1953).

20. *New Orleans Item*, January 11, 1935; *New York Times*, January 12, 1935.

21. White to Long, January 12; White to Roosevelt, January 12; "Mass Meeting, January 30, 1935," flyer, all in file I-C-357, NAACP; Robert L. Zangrando, *The NAACP Crusade against Lynching, 1909–1950* (Philadelphia: Temple University Press, 1980), pp. 126–28.

22. Roy Wilkins, "Huey Long Says," pp. 41, 52.

23. *Shreveport Times; New York Times; Shreveport Journal;* unidentified clipping, all October 14, 1938. According to the *Journal*, Williams's body had two hundred wounds and bore evidence of having been tortured with a hot iron or burning stick.

24. H. Horne Huggins to Walter White, October 20; Gordon McIntire to O. C. W. Taylor, October 14, 1938, file I-C-357, NAACP.

25. C. H. Myers to White, November 11, 1938; White to Bennett Champ Clark, November 15, 1938; Kester to White, January 7, 1939, all in file I-C-357, NAACP. White asked one of his friends in Congress, Senator Bennett Champ Clark of Missouri, to contact his brother-in-law, who happened to own the *New Orleans Item*. Under the editorship of Marshall Ballard, a firm liberal, the *Item* supported the passage of the federal antilynching law; perhaps, White suggested, the paper could investigate

the rumor. It appears that nothing came of this idea. Fingerprints taken by police from the corpse matched those found on the car of the murdered man: Roman Heleniak, *Soldiers of the Law: Louisiana State Police* (Topeka, Kans.: Josten's Publications, 1980), p. 38.

26. *New York Times,* October 18, 20, 1938; Zangrando, *NAACP Crusade,* p. 152; George C. Rable, "The South and the Politics of Antilynching Legislation," *Journal of Southern History* 51 (May 1985): 216; Thigpen to White, October 29, 1938, part 7, series A, file I-C-357, NAACP.

27. Jesse Daniel Ames, *The Changing Character of Lynching* (Atlanta: Commission on Interracial Cooperation, 1942), pp. 5–7; Jacquelyn Dowd Hall, *Revolt against Chivalry: Jesse Daniel Ames and the Women's Campaign Against Lynching* (New York: Columbia University Press, 1979, 1993), pp. 194–221.

28. Kelley, *Hammer and Hoe,* pp. 184–85; Robert K. Carr, *Federal Protection of Civil Rights: Quest for a Sword* (Ithaca: Cornell University Press, 1947, 1964), pp. 24–28, 152–53; Margery Dallet, "The Case of Clinton Clark," August 17, 1940, box 3, folder 19, Harold N. Lee Papers, TU. The police brutality prosecution involved the Atlanta police department.

29. *Washington Post,* May 22, 1936; *Louisiana Weekly,* August 17, 1940.

30. James A. Burran III, "Racial Violence in the South during World War II" (Ph.D. diss., University of Tennessee, 1977), pp. 31–32; *Detroit News,* November 1, 1935.

31. Gayle to Walter White, November 11, 1935; White to Edgar Stern, November 15, 1935; White to Howard Kester, November 18, 1935; Tom Tippett to White, November 16, 1935; Kester to White, November 26, 1935; White to Gayle, January 27, 1936, all in part 7, series A, file I-C-357, NAACP.

32. *Louisiana Weekly,* July 13, 1940; unidentified correspondent to Walter White, October 9, 1940, part 8, series B, Gretna file, NAACP.

33. Jeansonne, *Leander Perez,* pp. 74–84; Jeansonne, "The Apotheosis of Huey Long," *Biography* 12 (Fall 1989): 288–89.

34. Allan A. Michie and Frank Ryhlick, *Dixie Demagogues* (New York: Vanguard Press, 1939), pp. 128–37; David Lee Wells, "The ILWU in New Orleans: CIO Radicalism in the Crescent City, 1937–1957" (M.A., University of New Orleans, 1979), pp. 7–8; Bruce Nelson, *Workers on the Waterfront: Seamen, Longshoremen, and Unionism in the 1930s* (Urbana and Chicago: University of Illinois Press, 1988), pp. 224–25; Sarah Newman Shouse, *Hillbilly Realist: Herman Clarence Nixon of Possum Trot* (University: University of Alabama Press, 1986), p. 96; A. W. Brazier to NAACP, August 18, 1938, part 1, series G, container 83, NAACP(LC); William V. Moore, "Civil Liberties in Louisiana: The Louisiana League for the Preservation of Constitutional Rights," *Louisiana History* 31 (Winter 1990): 50–69; Douglas L. Smith, *The New Deal in the Urban South* (Baton Rouge: Louisiana State University Press, 1988), pp. 197–99.

35. Thomas Martin, *Dynasty: The Longs of Louisiana* (New York: G. P. Putnam's Sons, 1960), pp. 166–72; Kurtz and Peoples, *Earl K. Long,* pp. 99–101.

36. Kurtz and Peoples, *Earl K. Long,* p. 111; Jerry Purvis Sanson, "A History of Louisiana, 1939–1945" (Ph.D. diss., Louisiana State University, 1984), pp. 78–84; *Times-Picayune,* January 15, 1940; *Louisiana Weekly,* February 10, 1940; "Long Raises Race Question," Jones campaign flyer, box 18, folder 11, APT; Bunche, *Political Status of the Negro,* p. 557; *New Orleans Item,* February 14, 1940. The fake endorsements were inserted by a black freelance journalist, James B. Lafourche, ostensibly on his own initiative; he arranged to receive a 2-cent commission on every extra newspaper sold. See Sanson, p. 84.

37. Charles S. Johnson, *The Negro Public Schools,* vol. 8 of Louisiana Educational Survey Commission, *Louisiana Educational Survey* (Baton Rouge: Louisiana State University, 1942); Anderson, *Education of Blacks,* pp. 156, 176; "Louisiana Negro Schools"; Leon Lewis, ANP press release, "Charges of Fund Diversion Hurled at Louisiana Education Department," both in box 7, folder 38, CIC; Plaintiff's Trial Brief, *U.S.* v. *Louisiana,* Appendix F.

38. Plaintiff's Trial Brief, *U.S.* v. *Louisiana,* Appendix E, tables 1, 3, 5, 6; Porter, "History of Negro Education," p. 801; Julien R. Tatum et al., "The Negro in Baton Rouge," M.A. thesis, Louisiana State University, 1939–40, p. 79.

39. T. H. Harris to Charles Houston, May 4, 14, 1937; T. H. Harris to Parish Superintendents and School Board Members, April 2, 1938, all in part 4, series A, file 1-C-200, NAACP; Plaintiff's Trial Brief, *U.S.* v. *Louisiana,* Appendix E, table 7; Beals, *Story of Huey P. Long,* p. 359; Anderson, *Education of Blacks in the South,* pp. 187–221; Neyland, "Negro in Louisiana," p. 103.

40. Sue Lyles Eakins, "The Black Struggle for Education in Louisiana, 1877–1930s" (Ph.D. diss., University of Southwestern Louisiana, 1980); Keith Weldon Medley, "Gilbert Academy's Legacy of Distinction," *New Orleans Tribune* 1 (November 1985): 20–21. Gilbert Academy's alumni included lawyers Louis Berry, Lolis Elie, and Robert Collins (later a federal judge); poet Tom Dent, the son of Dillard president Albert Dent; and Andrew Young, colleague of Martin Luther King, mayor of Atlanta, congressman, and U.N. ambassador.

41. Porter, "History of Negro Education," pp. 774–75.

42. Rosa Keller, "Autobiography," vol. 2, 1977, pp. 1–2, box 12, Rosa Keller Papers, ARC; Wilma Dykeman and James Stokely, *Seeds of Southern Change: The Life of Will Alexander* (Chicago: University of Chicago Press, 1962), pp. 171–74; Raymond B. Fosdick, *Adventures in Giving: The Story of the General Education Board* (New York: Harper and Row, 1962), pp. 205–6.

43. Edgar B. Stern to Thomas F. Holgate, July 30, 1930; January 8, 1931; Stern to Fred L. Brownlee, March 16, 1931; Stern to Edwin W. Embree, January 8, 1931, all in box 191, folder 7, Julius Rosenwald Fund Papers, microfilm, ARC.

44. James D. Anderson, *Education of Blacks in the South,* pp. 240–44.

45. Fred L. Brownlee to Stern, March 3, 1931; Embree to Stern, March 20, 1931; Stern to Holgate, January 8, 1931, all in box 191, folder 7, Rosenwald Fund Papers.

46. Will W. Alexander to Fred L. Brownlee, September 18, 1934; Brownlee to Alexander, September 25, 1934; Mrs. E. R. Eastman to Alexander, November 28, 1934, all in box 84, CIC.

47. Dr. John J. Cross, "The Advantages and Disadvantages of Various Plans for Staffing a Negro College," December 4, 1934; Edgar B. Stern to Alexander, December 21, 1934; Alexander to Cross, January 3, 1935, all in folder 84, CIC. The $2 million cost of the merger and new campus was shared by the AMA, the Methodist Episcopal Church, the Rosenwald Fund, the General Education Board, and the New Orleans Community Chest.

48. Stern to Holgate, July 30, 1930; Stern to Brownlee, March 20, 1931; Stern to A. B. Freeman, May 19, 1939, all in boxes 191–92, Rosenwald Fund Papers; Clifton H. Johnson, "White Philanthropy Builds a Black School," unpublished ms., pp. 34–35, ARC.

49. W. J. Avery to H. B. Burkee, May 9, 1932; Chas. P. Manship to Ames, December 19, 1941, both in box 7, folder 165, CIC; on written correspondence, see, for example, the many letters addressed to A. P. Tureaud from white attorneys, in APT.

The Louisiana Supreme Court even had trouble uttering the full name of an African-American, often referring only to "the colored man [Smith]" or "a colored man named [Jones]."

50. H. B. Burkee to R. B. Eleazar, March 2, 1934, box 7, folder 165, CIC.

51. Harvard Sitkoff, *A New Deal for Blacks: The Emergence of Civil Rights as a National Issue* (New York: Oxford University Press, 1978), pp. 35–38; Smith, *New Deal in the Urban South,* pp. 21, 232–33; Anderson, *Education of Blacks in the South,* pp. 232–34; C. H. Myers to Charles H. Houston, June 7, 1936; May 3, 1938, both in part 1, series G, container 81, NAACP; Katherine Radke to Tureaud, 1937, box 8, folder 2, APT.

52. Neyland, "Negro in Louisiana," p. 23; Gilbert C. Fite, *Cotton Fields No More: Southern Agriculture, 1865–1980* (Lexington: University Press of Kentucky, 1984), pp. 233, 238; Milton B. Newton Jr., "The Peasant Farm of St. Helena Parish, Louisiana: A Cultural Geography" (Ph.D. diss., Louisiana State University, 1967), p. 113; Sitkoff, *New Deal for Blacks,* pp. 53–54; E. L. Fair to NAACP, December 29, 1938, part 1, series G, container 80, NAACP(LC). There is a discrepancy in the figures: according to those cited by Fite, the number of black farmers declined by 14,178 although the total number of farms fell by only 11,438.

53. Sitkoff, *New Deal for Blacks,* pp. 73–74; James Donald Holley, "The New Deal and Farm Tenancy: Rural Resettlement in Arkansas, Louisiana, and Mississippi" (Ph.D. diss., Louisiana State University, 1969), pp. 19–20, 280–81; T. Roy Reid to R. G. Tugwell, March 16, 1936; Reid to Alexander, December 22, 1939, both in Jack T. Kirby, ed., "New Deal Agencies and Black America" (microfilm, Alderman Library, University of Virginia). Of the more than 150 resettlement projects, only four were located in Louisiana.

54. Holley, "New Deal and Farm Tenancy," pp. 280–81; Logsdon, "Tureaud," tape 12; John Henry Scott, interviewed by Joseph Logsdon, 1966, pp. 47–52, Earl K. Long Library, University of New Orleans.

55. Anthony J. Badger, *The New Deal: The Depression Years, 1933–1940* (London: Macmillan, 1989), pp. 253–55; Patricia Sullivan, "Southern Reformers, the New Deal, and the Movement's Foundations," in Armstead L. Robinson and Patricia Sullivan, eds., *New Directions in Civil Rights Studies* (Charlottesville: University Press of Virginia, 1991), p. 82.

56. *Louisiana Weekly,* August 14, 1948; J. H. Scott, Logsdon interview, p. 44; Logsdon, "Tureaud," tape 10.

CHAPTER 3 : *The Labor Movement, the Left, and the Transformation of the NAACP*

1. Alexandria file; Shreveport file; N. B. Baker to William Pickens, April 2, 1932, all in part 1, series G, boxes 79, 82, 83, NAACP(LC).

2. Branch files, part 1, series G, containers 80–83, NAACP(LC).

3. Myers biography in *The Negro in Louisiana:* (New Orleans: Sepia Socialite, 1942), p. 54, copy in Louisiana Collection, TU; Myers to Houston, May 3, 6, 1938; Houston to William H. Hastie and E. P. Lovett, August 21, 1936, part 1, series G, box 80; Myers to Roy Wilkins, June 7, 1940; Myers to Lucille Black, August 3, 1945, part 2, series C, box 70, NAACP(LC); McNeill, *Groundwork,* pp. 157–70; *Steele v. Louisville & Nashville Railroad,* 323 U.S. 192 (1944).

4. J. H. Scott to NAACP, March 9, 1934; E. L. Fair to NAACP, December 29,

1938; Myers to White, June 20, 1930, all in part 1, series C, box 80, NAACP(LC).

5. Bunche, "The Programs, Ideologies, Tactics, and Achievements of Negro Better-ment and Interracial Organizations," pp. 142–55.

6. Lewis to Walter White, November 11, 1939, part 1, series G, box 83, NAACP(LC).

7. Nida H. Vital, "Dr. Rivers Fredericks and the History of Black Medicine in Louisiana" (M.A. thesis, University of New Orleans, 1978); Terrance, "Autobiogra-phy."

8. Lyle Saxon, Edward Dreyer, and Robert Tallant, eds., *Gumbo Ya-Ya* (New York: Bonanza Books, 1945), p. 5; "Mardi Gras Marred Again," editorial, *Louisiana Weekly,* February 21, 1948; Logsdon, "Tureaud," p. 43; Tureaud and Haydel, *Negro in Medicine in Louisiana.*

9. Wells, "ILWU in New Orleans," pp. 5–11; Wells and Stodder, "New Orleans Dockworkers," p. 58; Nelson, *Workers on the Waterfront,* p. 225.

10. Robert Korstad and Nelson Lichtenstein, "Opportunities Lost and Found: Labor, Radicals, and the Early Civil Rights Movement," *Journal of American History* 75 (December 1988): 787; Nelson, *Workers on the Waterfront,* p. 259; Jane Cassels Record, "The Rise and Fall of a Maritime Union," *Industrial and Labor Relations Review* 10 (October 1956): 92; Joshua B. Freeman, "The Transport Workers Union in New York City, 1933–1948" (Ph.D. diss., Rutgers University, 1983), pp. 662–65; Freeman, *In Transit: The Transport Workers Union in New York City, 1933–1966* (New York: Oxford University Press, 1989), pp. 259–60; John Beecher to Lawrence W. Cramer, "Supplement to New Orleans Report," March 16, 1942, Office Files of John Beecher, Headquarters Files, reel 78, Records of the Fair Employment Practices Com-mittee, microfilm (hereafter cited as FEPC); SAC, New Orleans, to Director, "The Communist Party of the U.S.A., New Orleans, Louisiana, District," April 14, 1941; "Communist Party, U.S.A., District 24," February 15, 1944, FBI files 100-3-47-3, 100-3-47-722. (All cited FBI files were obtained by the author under the Freedom of Information Act.)

11. "Louisiana Farmer's Union," September 27, 1941, FBI file 100-45768-1; Clyde Johnson, interviewed by H. L. Mitchell, April 4, 1976, pp. 48, 64–65, reel 13, The Green Rising, supplement to Southern Tenant Farmers Union Papers (microfilm; collection hereinafter cited as STFU).

12. Gordon McIntire and Clyde Johnson, "Statement on the St. Landry Farm Case," n.d.; Dale Rosen, "The Alabama Sharecroppers Union" (B.A. essay, Radcliffe College, 1969), p. 116, reproduced in reel 13, Green Rising, STFU.

13. Lowell K. Dyson, *Red Harvest: The Communist Party and American Farmers* (Lin-coln: University of Nebraska Press, 1982), p. 97; *Southern Farm Leader,* July, August 1936, reel 58, STFU.

14. Gordon McIntire to Bill Bachman, February 24, 1937, reel 13, Green Rising, STFU; George A. Dreyfous and Mack Swearingen, "Report to the Executive Com-mittee of the LLPCR," October 17, 1937, box 2, folder 7, Lee Papers; Edith Rosepha Ambrose, "Sarah Towles Reed and the Origins of Teacher Unions in New Orleans" (M.A. thesis, University of New Orleans, 1991).

15. Affidavit of Irene Scott, July 1937; "Statement of Terror against Farmers Union Leaders," July 2, 1937, both in part 1, series G, box 883, NAACP(LC); Elma Godchaux to the LLPCR, October 17, 1937, box 1, folder 7, Lee Papers.

16. Dreyfous and Swearingen, "Report."

17. Margery Dallet, "Case of Clinton Clark," August 17, 1940; Affidavit of Clinton Clark, August 21, 1940; Statement by Wayman Kimble to Margery Dallet, August 1940, all in box 3, folders 19, 20, Lee Papers; *Louisiana Weekly,* August 17, 24, 1940;

SAC, New Orleans, to Director, "Louisiana Farmers Union," August 6, 1943, FBI file 100-45768-10.

18. McIntire to Members and Friends, March 10, 1942, reel 13, Green Rising, STFU; SAC, New Orleans, to Director, "Louisiana Farmers Union," August 6, 1943.

19. Kelley, *Hammer and Hoe,* pp. 227–31; Dreyfous and Swearingen, "Report."

20. Bunche, "Programs," pp. 377–78; Johnetta Richards, "The Southern Negro Youth Congress: A History" (Ph.D. diss., University of Cincinnati, 1987), pp. 95–100.

21. Keith Weldon Medley, "Ernest Wright: People's Champion," *Southern Exposure,* May-June 1984, pp. 53–54; Medley, "Remembering Ernest Wright: 'The People's Champion,'" *New Orleans Tribune* 2 (February 1986): 13–14; Giles A. Hubert, "Notes on Leadership: Ernest J. Wright," July 1959, box 2, folder 11, Hubert Papers, ARC.

22. *Louisiana Weekly,* September 7, 14, 21, 28, October 5, 12, 19, 26, 1940; *New Orleans Sentinel,* September 14, 21, 28, October 12, 1940; NAACP, *Annual Report, 1940,* p. 10, copy in Alderman Library, University of Virginia; Louisiana Legislature, Joint Legislative Committee, *Subversion in Racial Unrest* (Baton Rouge, 1957), pp. 317–25; Medley, "Remembering Ernest Wright," p. 13; Harold N. Rouzan, Fairclough interview.

23. Rogers, "Humanity and Desire," pp. 61–63; SAC, New Orleans, to Director, "Ernest John Wright," January 15, 1944, FBI file 100-56308-8; *Louisiana Weekly,* October 11, 1941; December 12, 1942.

24. Smith, *New Deal,* p. 244; untitled history of the New Orleans Urban League, box 2, folder 9, Hubert Papers; Bunche, "Programs," p. 155; Katherine Martensen, "Region, Religion, and Social Action: The Catholic Committee of the South, 1939–1956," *Catholic Historical Review* 68 (April 1982): 250–53; Howard Lee to Charles H. Behre, January 11, 1940, box 22, folder 270, James A. Dombrowski Papers, Hollis Burke Frissell Library, Tuskegee University; Paul D. Williams to John F. Cronin, December 9, 1941, box 1, folder 6, Catholic Committee of the South Papers, ARC (collection hereinafter cited as CCS).

25. Smith, *New Deal in the Urban South,* pp. 250–51; Logsdon, "Tureaud," tape 9; Maurice R. Woulfe to Thurgood Marshall, November 5, December 21, 1938; Mrs. S. P. Schexnayder to Marshall, February 13, 1939, all in part 8, series A. Hugh Pierre file, NAACP; A. W. Brazier to NAACP, August 18, 1938; James B. Lafourche to Walter White, November 18, 27, 1938; William Pickens to White, November 21, 1938, all in part 1, series G, box 83, NAACP(LC).

26. James A. Hardin to Judge Michael Provosty, April 7, 1937, box 8, folder 3; Tureaud to George M. Johnson, March 14, 1951, box 10, folder 14, both in APT; John E. Rousseau Jr., interviewed by Adam Fairclough, March 16, March 31, 1992; Logsdon, "Tureaud," tape 8.

27. *New Orleans Sentinel,* July 17, August 16, 1941; Rousseau, Fairclough interview; Logsdon, "Tureaud," tape 8; Smith, *New Deal,* pp. 251–52; Dorothy K. Newman et al., *Protest, Politics, and Prosperity: Black Americans and White Institutions, 1940–75* (New York: Pantheon, 1978), p. 105.

28. Donald Jones to Walter White, July 3, 1939; Jones to Marshall, August 7, September 6, 1939; Tureaud to Marshall, July 14, 1939; Marshall to Jones, August 31, September 14, 1939, all in part 1, series G, box 83, NAACP(LC); White to Branch, November 6, 1939; Tureaud to White, November 8, 1939, both in box 8, folder 5, APT.

29. Election dodger, November 9, 1939; James Lewis to White, November 11; Brazier to White, November 28, 1939, all in part 1, series G, box 83, NAACP(LC).

30. Jones to White, November 15, 1939, part 1, series G, box 83, NAACP(LC).

31. *Louisiana Weekly*, January 27, 1940; Bunche, "Programs," p. 128. Tureaud later explained that he had a foot in both camps (Logsdon, "Tureaud," tape 8).

32. John Hope Franklin, *From Slavery to Freedom* (New York: Vintage, 1947, 1969), p. 520.

33. Frederic E. Morrow to White, April 22, 1940; White to Hubert Delaney, April 22, 1940; Morrow to Marshall, May 10, 1940, both in part 2, series C, box 70, NAACP(LC); *Louisiana Weekly*, April 20, 27, May 11, 1940; Logsdon, "Tureaud," tape 8; Rousseau, Fairclough interview.

34. Joan Redding, "The Dillard Project: The Black Unit of the Louisiana Writers' Project," *Louisiana History* 32 (Winter 1991): 54–62.

35. *New Orleans Sentinel*, June 15, July 27, August 3, 1940; *Louisiana Weekly*, June 22, July 20, 1940.

36. Rousseau, Fairclough interview; Logsdon, "Tureaud," tape 8.

37. *Louisiana Weekly*, September 21, November 16, 1940.

38. Worthy, "Travail and Triumph," p. 37; Daniel Byrd to J. K. Haynes, June 7, 1975, box 3, folder 13, Daniel E. Byrd Papers, ARC; Jones to Marshall, September 30, 1940; February 20, 1941, both in part 3, series B, box 177, NAACP.

39. Tushnet, *NAACP's Legal Strategy*, pp. 34–44; McNeil, *Groundwork*, pp. 115–16.

40. Johnson, *Negro Public Schools*, pp. 94–104.

41. Ernest J. Middleton, "The Louisiana Education Association, 1901–1970" *Journal of Negro Education* (Fall 1978): 364–67; Kurtz and Peoples, *Earl K. Long*, pp. 8–9, 83; *Alexandria Daily Town-Talk*, March 8, 1933.

42. Ernest J. Middleton, *History of the Louisiana Education Association* (Washington, D.C.: National Education Association, 1984), p. 57.

43. Jones to Marshall, November 16, 1940, part 4, series A, box 177, NAACP(LC); Rousseau, Fairclough interview.

44. Mrs. S. P. Schexnayder to NAACP, July 1, 1938, part 8, series A, reel 12, Hugh Pierre file, NAACP; *Pierre v. State*, 189 La. 764 (1938).

45. Marshall to Maurice R. Woulfe, January 26, 1939; NAACP legal staff, Memo on Pierre case, n.d., part 8, series A, reel 12, Hugh Pierre file, NAACP.

46. *Norris v. Alabama*, 294 U.S. 587 (1935); *Pierre v. Louisiana*, 306 U.S. 354 (1939).

47. *U.S. v. Classic*, 313 U.S. 299 (1941); Carr, *Federal Protection of Civil Rights*, pp. 85–93; Charles V. Hamilton, *The Bench and the Ballot: Southern Federal Judges and Black Voters* (New York: Oxford University Press, 1973), pp. 26–27; Darlene Clark Hine, *Black Victory: The Rise and Fall of the White Primary in Texas* (Millwood, N.Y.: KTO Press, 1979), pp. 202–6.

48. *Louisiana Weekly*, January 31, 1942.

49. Greenberg, *Crusaders in the Courts*, p. 246; Worthy, "Travail and Triumph of a Southern Black Civil Rights Lawyer," pp. 18–21; Logsdon, "Tureaud," p. 137; Constance Baker Motley, interviewed by Jack Bass, June 21, 1979, pp.61–63, Bass Collection.

50. Logsdon, "Tureaud," tapes 6 and 7.

51. Tushnet, *NAACP's Legal Strategy*, p. 98; Tureaud to Marshall, October 17, 1942, part 3, series B, box 177, NAACP; Ernest N. Morial, interviewed by Kim Lacy Rogers, October 30, 1987, recording, ARC; Tureaud to George M. Johnson, March 14, 1951, box 10, folder 14, APT.

52. Daniel E. Byrd, interviewed by David Legendre, October 27, 1978, pp. 2–5, ARC; Byrd, interviewed by Patricia Rickels, March 14, 1979, recording, Carleton James Collection, USL; Perry, Rickels interview.

53. Arthur J. Chapital, biographical data, box 201, NAACP, New Orleans Branch Records, Earl K. Long Library, University of New Orleans (collection hereinafter cited as NAACP(NO)); Raphael Cassimere and Joseph Logsdon, interviewed by Adam Fairclough, October 8, 1987; Britton, Fairclough interview, pp. 1–2.

54. Tureaud to Marshall, July 21, 1939, part 1, series G, box 83, NAACP(LC).

55. Neyland, "Negro in Louisiana," pp. 167–68; Logsdon and Bell, "Americanization of Black New Orleans," p. 234; *The Negro in Louisiana; Eureka Grand Lodge: 100 Years of Legitimate and Progressive Freemasonry* (1963), copy in O. C. W. Taylor Papers, ARC; Joseph A. Walkes, Jr., *JNo. G. Lewis, Jr.—End of an Era: The History of the Prince Hall Grand Lodge of Louisiana, 1842–1979* (privately published, 1986), pp. 124–85, 230–31, copy in State Library of Louisiana, Baton Rouge; Willard B. Gatewood, *Aristocrats of Color: The Black Elite, 1880–1920* (Bloomington: Indiana University Press, 1990), pp. 8, 85, 213–14; NAACP, *Southwestern Region Newsletter,* July 1, 1951, box 15, folder 29, APT; Greenberg, *Crusaders in the Courts,* pp. 179–80, 246, 350, 529n. 41.

56. *Souvenir Program, Sesquicentennial Celebration of the Grand Consistory of Louisiana, Ancient Association of Scottish Rite Freemasonry, June 19–23, 1963,* box 210, NAACP(NO); Logsdon and Bell, "Americanization of Black New Orleans," pp. 234–35, 248.

57. Doris M. White, "The Louisiana Civil Rights Movement's Pre-Brown Period, 1936–1954" (M.A. thesis, University of Southwestern Louisiana, 1976), p. 20; Middleton, *History of the Louisiana Education Association,* pp. 70–90; Daniel E. Byrd to Thurgood Marshall, April 14, 1947, box 9, folder 2, APT; Logsdon, "Tureaud," tape 11.

58. Thurgood Marshall, Memo to the Office, June 27, 1944, part 1, series G, box 70, NAACP(NO).

59. *A History of the Knights and Ladies of Peter Claver in Southwest Louisiana,* n.d., copy in Lake Charles public library.

60. Tureaud and Haydel, *The Negro in Medicine in Louisiana,* n.p.; Neyland, "Negro in Louisiana," pp. 48–61; Vital, "Dr. Rivers Fredericks," pp. 58–59. As Vital points out, the closure of Flint Medical College in New Orleans in 1911 ended all medical training for blacks in Louisiana and had disastrous consequences for the black profession. Forced to train out of state—most of them at Meharry College in Nashville—the number of black doctors in Louisiana fell from 127 in 1910 to 107 in 1930. By 1950 the number had declined to 94.

61. Neyland, "Negro in Louisiana," pp. 62–63; biography of O. C. W. Taylor, in Taylor Papers, ARC; Scott, Logsdon interview, pp. 40–41.

62. *NAACP Annual Report, 1947,* copy in Alderman Library, University of Virginia; Lucille Black to Daniel E. Byrd, April 19, 1946, part 2, series C, box 70, NAACP(LC).

CHAPTER 4: *Tremors of War*

1. Burran, "Racial Violence in the South," pp. 61–64; *New York Times,* January 12, 1943; *PM,* January 21, 1943; *Louisiana Weekly,* January 17, 24, 31, October 10, 1942; James B. Lafourche to Walter White, January 22, 1943, part 2, series A, box 504, NAACP(LC); Harvard Sitkoff, "Racial Militancy and Interracial Violence in the Second World War," *Journal of American History* (December 1971): 668–69.

2. Giles A. Hubert, "Notes on Leadership: Ernest J. Wright," Hubert Papers; Neil A. Wynn, *The Afro-American and the Second World War* (London: Paul Elek, 1976),

pp. 72, 100. See also Pete Daniel, "Going among Strangers: Southern Reactions to World War II," *Journal of American History* (December 1990): 886–911.

3. Charles S. Johnson, *To Stem This Tide: A Survey of Racial Tension Areas in the United States* (Boston: Pilgrim Press, 1943), pp. 90–101; Lee Finkle, *Forum for Protest: The Black Press during World War II* (Cranbury, N.J.: Associated University Presses, 1975), pp. 104–7, 205–9.

4. Richard Polenberg, *War and Society: The United States, 1941–1945* (Philadelphia: J. B. Lippincott, 1972), pp. 100–105; Wynn, *Afro-American and the Second World War,* pp. 21–30.

5. "Committee of Citizens Resolution," May 8, 1941, box 5, folder 12, George S. Longe Papers, ARC; *Louisiana Weekly,* May 10, 1941; *The Negro in Louisiana,* p. 18; *New Orleans Sentinel,* May 10, 17, 1941. O. C. W. Taylor to Leon G. Tujague, October 12, 1944, box 1, folder 1, Longe Papers; Finkle, *Forum for Protest,* p. 104.

6. John Morton Blum, *V Was for Victory: Politics and American Culture during World War II* (New York: Harcourt Brace Jovanovich, 1976), p. 199; *Louisiana Weekly,* January 24, 1942; Finkle, *Forum for Protest,* pp. 110–28, 212 (quotation); Patrick S. Washburn, *A Question of Sedition: The Federal Government's Investigation of the Black Press during World War II* (New York: Oxford University Press, 1986), pp. 111–12, 131, 191–92. Finkle also suggests that historians have exaggerated the influence of Du Bois's "Close Ranks" editorial. Blacks by no means ceased their egalitarian agitation during World War One, he reminds us, and Du Bois's editorials, although influential, did not appear until the war was nearly over. A cynical reading of Du Bois's motivations is offered in Mark Ellis, "'Closing Ranks' and 'Seeking Honors': W. E. B. Du Bois in World War II," *Journal of American History* 79 (June 1992): 96–124.

7. Tureaud to Frank T. Reeves, October 22, 1941, box 8, folder 10, APT.

8. Wynn, *Afro-American and the Second World War,* pp. 27–29; *Louisiana Weekly,* June 5, 1943; November 11, 1942.

9. Burran, "Racial Violence in the South," pp. 76–79; Carr, *Federal Protection of Civil Rights,* p. 129; Walter White, *A Man Called White: The Autobiography of Walter White* (London: Victor Gollancz, 1949), p. 222; Zangrando, *NAACP Crusade against Lynching,* p. 169; *Louisiana Weekly,* September 5, October 10, 31, November 11, December 5, 1942; January 16, March 20, May 8, 15, 22, July 3, August 7, 1943; May 20, 1944; *Adams v. U.S.,* 319 U.S. 312 (1943); Mark V. Tushnet, *Making Civil Rights Law: Thurgood Marshall and the Supreme Court, 1936–1961* (New York: Oxford University Press, 1994, pp. 64–66. Minutes of NAACP Statewide Meeting, January 17, 1943, box 12, folder 9, APT; Logsdon, "Tureaud," tape 12. A state conference in North Carolina was organized later in 1943. State conferences already existed in Virginia (1935), Texas (1936), and South Carolina (1940).

10. Burran, "Racial Violence in the South," pp. 211–16; McGary and Washington file, box 8, folder 25; Leroy McGary to Tureaud, March 11, 1945, both in box 8, folder 27, APT; New Orleans Press Club, news release, January 23, 1942, box 5, folder 1, Lee Papers.

11. Tureaud to C. A. Williams, October 13, 1942, box 8, folder 11, APT; Harold N. Lee to Harlan [?], November 11, 1943; Lee to Ernest J. Wright, August 14, 1943, box 5, folders 5–6, Lee Papers.

12. Georgia M. Johnson to Tureaud, August 1, 1943; Tureaud to Johnson, August 3, 1943, box 8, folder 17, APT.

13. Myrdal, *An American Dilemma,* 2:535–36; *Louisiana Weekly,* October 3, 1942.

14. Finkle, *Forum for Protest,* p. 104; Johnson, *To Stem This Tide,* p. 65; *Louisiana*

Weekly, September 5, 1942; "Excerpts from Speech Made by E. A. Stephens, Ruston, August 6, 1942"; Mrs. H. M. Barrett to Ellender, August 29, 1942; John H. Overton, "Radio Address," August 28, 1942, all in box 1819, Allen J. Ellender Papers, Nicholls State University, Thibodaux, Louisiana.

15. "History of the New Orleans Urban League," pp. 15–16, Hubert Papers; Donald Jones, Monthly Report, April 1943, part 2, series A, box 587, NAACP(LC); SAC, New Orleans, to Director, "Ernest John Wright," July 26, 1943, FBI file 100-56308-6; Hubert, "Notes on Leadership: Ernest J. Wright," p. 6.

16. *Louisiana Weekly,* July 10, November 11, 1943; May 6, 1944 (Dent quotation).

17. Johnson, *To Stem This Tide,* p. 65; *Louisiana Weekly,* September 5, 1942; Statement of F. Edward Hebert, n.d., box 15, folder 3, APT; Charles S. Johnson, *Into the Mainstream: A Survey of Best Practices in Race Relations in the South* (Chapel Hill: University of North Carolina Press, 1947), pp. 22–23; New Orleans, Institute of Race Relations, "The Good Neighbor at Home," pp. 1–4, box 82, folder 14, Race Relations Department, United Church Board for Homeland Ministries, United Church of Christ Papers, ARC (collection hereinafter cited as UCC); Albert W. Dent, interviewed by Glenda Stephens, November 11, 1978, recording, Kim Lacy Rogers–Glenda Stephens Oral History Collection, ARC.

18. Wynn, *Afro-American and the Second World War,* pp. 71–72.

19. Howard W. Odum, *Race and Rumors of Race* (Chapel Hill: University of North Carolina Press, 1943), pp. 113–28; Johnson, *To Stem This Tide,* p. 31.

20. Tureaud to Leslie Perry, February 3, 1945, box 8, folder 27, APT; *Louisiana Weekly,* January 16, October 2, 1943; May 27, 1944; Tureaud to Harold N. Lee, November 11, December 29, 1943, box 5, folders 16 and 17, Lee Papers; Tureaud to Perry, July 31, 1944, box 34, folder 6, APT; Kelley, "'We Are Not What We Seem,'" pp. 102–9.

21. Johnson, *Into the Mainstream,* pp. vii–viii; "A Basis for Inter-Racial Cooperation and Development in the South: A Statement by Southern Negroes," October 20, 1942, in Johnson, *To Stem This Tide,* p. 132; A. Philip Randolph, "March on Washington Movement Presents Program for the Negro," in Rayford W. Logan, ed., *What the Negro Wants* (Chapel Hill: University of North Carolina Press, 1944), p. 151; August Meier and Elliott Rudwick, "The Origins of Nonviolent Direct Action in Afro-American Protest: A Note on Historical Discontinuities," in *Along the Color Line,* pp. 34–49.

22. Banner and Kerns, "Review," pp. 138–39, 155–56.

23. *Louisiana Weekly,* August 14, 1943; "Resolution of the Federation of Civic Leagues in Opposition to the Protests of the Residents of Gentilly against the Use of Seabrook by Colored Residents for Bathing Purposes" [1929], box 18, folder 21, APT; Peirce F. Lewis, *New Orleans: The Making of an Urban Landscape* (Cambridge, Mass.: Ballinger, 1976), pp. 64–66.

24. Keith Weldon Medley, "1954: A Year in the Life of Lincoln Beach," *New Orleans Tribune,* September 1985, p. 20; Harold N. Lee to Fontaine Martin Jr. [1941], box 4, folder 5, Lee Papers; Robert E. Fullilove to Harold N. Lee, August 16, 1943; Lee to Base Commander, August 20, 1943; Col. J. H. Houghton to Lee, August 30, 1943, all in box 5, folder 15, Lee Papers; Daniel E. Byrd to Robert S. Maestri, August 26, 1943, box 8, folder 17, APT.

25. Sanson, "History of Louisiana," pp. 422–34.

26. Merl E. Reed, "The FEPC, the Black Worker, and the Southern Shipyards," *South Atlantic Quarterly* 74 (Autumn 1975): 446–53; John Beecher to Lawrence W.

Cramer, "Field Report on New Orleans, Louisiana," March 7, 1942, Office Files of John Beecher, Headquarters Files, reel 78, FEPC.

27. *Louisiana Weekly,* September 20, October 11, 1941; Mary Lee Muller, "The Orleans Parish School Board and Negro Education, 1940–1960" (M.A. thesis, Louisiana State University in New Orleans, 1975), p. 10; Sanson, "History of Louisiana," p. 374.

28. Beecher, "Field Report on New Orleans;" Beecher to Cramer, "Supplement to New Orleans Report," March 16, 1942, Headquarters Files, reel 78, FEPC.

29. Beecher, "Field Report;" John A. Davis to Malcolm Ross, February 29, 1944, Headquarters Files, reel 75; Joy P. Davis to John A. Davis, "New Orleans, Louisiana: Delta Shipbuilding Company," March 31, 1944, Tension File, Headquarters Files, reel 75; Don Ellinger, "Weekly Report," December 12, 1944, Field Records, reel 96, all in FEPC; *Louisiana Weekly,* February 19, 1944.

30. Raymond J. Martinez, *Racial Aspects of the Labor Supply in New Orleans* (New Orleans: Chamber of Commerce, June 12, 1943), copy in Louisiana Collection, TU; Virgil Williams to Carlos E. Castaneda, "Training and Utilization of Negro Workers in the New Orleans Area," December 18, 1943, Weekly Reports, Region 10, reel 52, FEPC; Reed, "The FEPC, the Black Workers, and the Southern Shipyards," pp. 451–55; Sanson, "History of Louisiana," p. 511.

31. Johnson, *To Stem This Tide,* pp. 24–25; Holley, "New Deal and Farm Tenancy," pp. 315–16; *Louisiana Weekly,* October 10, 1942; Anthony P. Dunbar, *Against the Grain: Southern Radicals and Prophets, 1929–1959* (Charlottesville: University Press of Virginia, 1981), pp. 200–201; Thomas Becnel, *Labor, Church, and the Sugar Establishment, Louisiana, 1887–1976* (Baton Rouge: Louisiana State University Press, 1980), pp. 84–86.

32. "Unknown Subjects; Eviction of Negro Civil Rights Leaders, New Iberia, Louisiana, May 17, 1944," June 20, 1944, FBI file 44-999-6; September 7, 1944, FBI file 44-999-10 (all reports of the same title hereinafter cited as FBI Report); J. Leo Hardy, "A Straightforward Account of the New Iberia, Louisiana, Outrage," July 3, 1944, part 2, series C, box 71, NAACP(LC); Carlos E. Castaneda to Will Maslow, January 8, 1944, Weekly Reports, Region 10, reel 52, FEPC.

33. Howard Scoggins, Ima A. Pierson, and J. Leo Hardy to NAACP, April 22, 1943; Record of Election of Officers, June 27, 1943; Hardy to NAACP, December 10, 1943, part 2, series C, box 70, NAACP(LC). Hardy's previous NAACP activity is documented in Alexandria branch records, part 1, series G, box 79; and Monroe branch records, box 80, both in NAACP(LC); Johnson, *Negro Public Schools,* pp. 163–65. Biographies of H. C. Scoggins and E. L. Dorsey in *The Negro in Louisiana,* pp. 18, 69. For Lilly see Redding, "The Dillard Project," p. 52.

34. FBI Report, June 20, 1944; Hardy, "Account."

35. Hardy to NAACP, December 10, 1943; *Louisiana Weekly,* March 18, June 3, 1944; FBI Report, September 7, 1944.

36. Castaneda to Maslow, January 8, 1944; Leonard M. Brin to Maslow, March 11, 1944, Weekly Reports, Region 10, reel 52, FEPC; L. Virgil Williams to Lloyd G. Porter, April 14, 1944; Hardy to Brin, April 22, May 11, 1944, in FBI Reports, June 20, 1944; September 21, 1944, FBI file 44-999-13.

37. Hardy's account of his expulsion is taken from Hardy to Leonard M. Brin, May [18?], 1944; affidavit of Octave Lilly Jr., May 19, 1944, both in box 34, folder 5, APT; Hardy, affidavit, June 14, 1944, in FBI report, June 20, 1944, pp. 29–32; "Why Negroes Are Angry," *New Republic,* September 25, 1944, p. 360.

38. Affidavit of Howard C. Scoggins, May 31, 1944, in box 34, folder 5, APT.

39. Affidavits of Luins H. Williams, May 20, 1944; Ima A. Pierson, May 20, 1944; Herman Joseph Faulk, May 27, 1944, all in box 34, folder 5, APT; *Sepia Socialite,* May 27, 1944; testimony of Negro barber, in FBI report, June 20, 1944, p. 27; *Louisiana Weekly,* May 27, June 3, 1944.

40. Affidavits of Lilly and Scoggins; A. P. Tureaud to Rachel B. Noel, June 15, 1944, box 34, folder 6, APT; *Louisiana Weekly,* June 10, 1944.

41. Tureaud to Thurgood Marshall, May 19, 1944; February 1, 1945, box 34, folder 6, APT; *Louisiana Weekly,* June 3, 1944; "Anon, New Iberia, Louisiana," n.d., Tension File, Headquarters Files, reel 75, FEPC; Donald Jones to Walter White, June 21, 1944, part 2, series C, box 70, NAACP(LC).

42. Tureaud to Marshall, October 11, 1944; February 1, 1945; Tureaud to Victor Rotnem, May 19, 20, 27, 1944; Tureaud to Tom C. Clark, June 7, 1944; all in box 34, folders 5, 6, 21, APT; *Louisiana Weekly,* June 3, 1944; Tom C. Clark to J. Edgar Hoover, May 25, 1944, FBI file 44-999-1; Hoover to Clark, May 29, 1944, FBI file 44-1006-1; Hoover to SAC, New Orleans, May 30, 1944, FBI file 44-999-2.

43. FBI Report, June 20, 1944, p. 4.

44. Ibid., pp. 4–5.

45. Ibid., pp. 27–31.

46. Marshall to Rotnem, July 5, 1944; Francis Biddle to Walter White, July 10, 1944; Leslie Perry to Tureaud, July 27, 1944; Tureaud to Perry, July 31, 1944, all in box 34, folder 6, APT.

47. Clark to Hoover, June 24, 1944, FBI file 44-1001-3; September 21, 1944, file 44-999-13, 14; December 8, 1944, file 44-999-31; J. C. Strickland, Memorandum for Mr. Ladd, September 20, 1944, file 44-999-9; Hoover to Tom C. Clark, September 25, 1944, file 44-999-11; Hoover to SAC, Jackson, September 26, 1944, file 44-999-12; SAC, Washington, "Foreign Inspired Agitation among the American Negroes in the Washington Field Division," October 10, 1944, file 100-135-168, pp. 8–9; Hoover to SAC, New Orleans, December 13, 1944, file 44-999-32; FBI Report, February 10, 1945, file 44-999-35; Hoover to Clark, February 16, 1945, file 44-999-35.

48. Carr, *Federal Protection of Civil Rights,* pp. 41–45, 106–14, 134–41, 152–71; Dominic J. Capeci Jr., "The Lynching of Cleo Wright: Federal Protection of Constitutional Rights during World War II," *Journal of American History* 72 (March 1986): 869–84.

49. Carr, *Federal Protection of Civil Rights,* pp. 152–53; Hoover to Attorney General, September 24, 1946, reprinted in U.S. Commission on Civil Rights, *1961 Report,* vol. 5: *Justice* (Washington, D.C.: 1961), pp. 213–15.

50. FBI Report, December 8, 1944, file 44-999-27, p. 9; FBI Report, December 28, 1944, file 44-999-33, pp. 1–2.

51. FBI Reports, September 7, 1944, file 44-999-10, pp. 1–3, 16, 27; September 21, 1944, file 44-999-13, pp. 1, 11; J. C. Strickland to Mr. Ladd, October 4, 1944, file 44-999-18; Tureaud to Marshall, October 24, 1944, box 34, folder 21, APT.

52. FBI Reports, June 20, 1944, p. 29; September 7, 1944, pp. 15–17, 32.

53. FBI Reports, June 20, 1944, p. 26; September 7, 1944, p. 13–14, 18.

54. FBI Report, June 20, 1944, pp. 25–28; Leo Hardy to Leonard M. Brin, May 8, 1944, in FBI Report, September 27, 1944, pp. 7–8; FBI Report, September 7, 1944, pp. 12–13; Sanson, "History of Louisiana," p. 206.

55. FBI Report, September 7, 1944, pp. 18, 27–28, 30–31; FBI Report, September 21, 1944, pp. 13–14; Elizabeth Wilson and Ward B. Melody, "4 Negroes Clubbed,

Driven from Louisiana Town," *PM,* June 17, 1944, p. 1. Scoggins, it seems, also received an invitation to resume his practice, but he preferred to stay in New Orleans. "I can't return," he told the leftist newspaper *PM.* "I don't trust the New Iberia kind of white democracy." Roy Palmer, the welding school instructor, was another fugitive whom Ozenne had not intended to expel. When Palmer phoned Lloyd Porter from Baton Rouge, the schools superintendent told him to return to New Iberia.

56. *Louisiana Weekly,* June 17, 1944; FBI Report, September 7, 1944, pp. 16–17; FBI Report, December 8, 1944, pp. 3–4.

57. FBI Report, September 7, 1944, pp. 2, 13–18, 26; September 21, 1944, pp. 14–15; June 20, 1944, pp. 28–29; December 8, 1944, pp. 4–5, 11. Ozenne remained sheriff of Iberia Parish until his death in 1951.

58. FBI Reports, September 7, 1944, pp. 4, 10–11, 19–20, 29; September 21, 1944, pp. 10–11, 15.

59. FBI Reports, September 7, 1944, pp. 22, 25–28; September 21, 1944, pp. 13–14; December 28, 1944, pp. 1–2.

60. Rev. F. M. Boley to Walter White, June 30, 1944; Marshall, "Memo to the Office," June 27, 1944, part 2, series C, box 70, NAACP(LC); Tureaud to Marshall, October 11, 1944, box 34, folder 21, APT.

61. Finkle, *Forum for Protest,* pp. 124–27, 168.

62. Sitkoff, "Racial Militancy and Interracial Violence," p. 679.

63. George B. Tindall, *The Emergence of the New South, 1913–1945* (Baton Rouge: Louisiana State University Press, 1967), p. 565.

64. Tushnet, *NAACP's Legal Strategy,* p. 37; Raphael Cassimere Jr., "Equalizing Teachers' Pay in Louisiana," *Integrated Education* 15 (July–August 1977): 7.

65. DeVore, "Rise from the Nadir," pp. 119–22; Marshall to Tureaud, July 7, 1942, box 49, folder 22, APT; Tureaud to Marshall, July 29, 1942; Marshall to Tureaud, July 30, 1942, part 3, series B, box 177, NAACP; *Louisiana Weekly,* September 5, 1942.

66. *Louisiana Weekly,* June 16, 1943; *Times-Picayune,* July 1, 1943; John E. Coxe to Presidents of Parish School Boards, June 19, 1943, part 3, series B, box 177, NAACP; Leon M. Wallace to Tureaud, June 30, 1943, box 8, folder 16; Iberville Parish School Board, copy of resolution, June 22, 1943, box 35, folder 12, APT.

67. Byrd to Marshall, February 29, 1944; W. W. Harleaux to Byrd, February 6, 1947, part 3, series B, box 177, NAACP.

68. J. K. Haynes to Tureaud, April 21, 1943; Tureaud to Marshall, December 20, 1943; Tureaud to Haynes, April 21, 1943; Tureaud to National War Labor Board, June 29, 1943, box 31, folder 13; John Byrne Chamberlin to Tureaud, July 1, 1943, box 19, folder 15; all in APT; *Louisiana Weekly,* October 16, 1943; White, "The Louisiana Civil Rights Movement's Pre-Brown Period," pp. 35–40.

69. Tureaud to Marshall, December 27, 1944, January 23, 1945, March 7, 1945; Marshall, memo, "Conference Re Louisiana Teachers Salary Cases," January 23, 1945, part 33, series B, box 177, NAACP; Tureaud to Haynes, January 9, 1945, box 34, folder 23; Special Committee on Educational Planning, minutes, January 23, 1945, box 35, folder 6, APT.

70. *Pittsburgh Courier,* March 10, 1945, box 35, folder 15; Tureaud to P. L. Prattis, March 16, 1945; Marshall to Tureaud, March 12, 1945; Tureaud to W. W. Harleaux, March 21, 1945, box 34, folder 34, APT; Marshall, "Memo to the Office," April 28, 1945, part 3, series B, box 177, NAACP; *Morris v. Williams,* 149 F. 2d 703 (8th Cir. 1945); *Reynolds v. Board of Public Instruction,* 148 F. 2d 754 (5th Cir. 1945). "The decision was a disaster," writes Mark V. Tushnet of the Miami case. "Unless school boards

made grotesque errors like those in Little Rock, they could use rating systems that had significant subjective elements to reproduce with only modest changes to the prior discriminatory salary patterns" (*NAACP's Legal Strategy*, p. 97).

71. *Louisiana Weekly,* August 11, 1945; "Present Status of Twenty-Four Plaintiffs," March 28, 1946, box 35, folder 7; "Procedure Used for Rating Teachers in Iberville Parish, 1945–1946," box 35, folder 10; "Temporary Ranking of White and Negro Teachers, 1944–45," box 35, folder 12; Tureaud to Marshall, November 17, 1945, box 34, folder 26; Tureaud to Marshall, August 30, 1946; W. W. Harleaux to Daniel E. Byrd, October 15, 1946, box 34, folder 28, all in APT.

72. Taylor to Tureaud, June 20, 1945, box 34, folder 25, APT.

73. *Louisiana Weekly,* May 20, 1944; Tureaud, notes of meeting to plan organization of statewide voters league, August 17, 1944, box 8, folder 22, APT; Byrd, "Speech to NAACP National Convention," June 27, 1946, box 8, folder 1, Byrd Papers.

74. *Louisiana Weekly,* September 23, 1944; Tureaud to Houston Dutton, August 14, 1944, box 8, folder 12, APT; Spencer Bradley to Marshall, February 26, 1945, part 2, series B, box 212, NAACP.

75. Tureaud, "Complaints against Practices in the Office of Registrar of Voters in Various Louisiana Parishes," September 1, 1944, box 12, folder 38, APT; R. L. Williams to Marshall, August 14, 1944, part 2, series B, box 212, NAACP.

76. Sanson, "History of Louisiana," p. 511; Tureaud to Marshall, August 29, 1944, box 8, folder 22, APT.

77. Blum, *V Was for Victory,* p. 212; Tureaud to Houston Dutton, September 30, 1944; Tom C. Clark to Tureaud, October 5, 1944; Marshall to Francis Biddle, October 3, 1944, all in box 8, folder 23, APT; *Lane* v. *Wilson,* 307 U.S. 268 (1939).

78. *Louisiana Weekly,* August 25, September 15, 1945; Tureaud, "Complaints against Practices in the Office of Registrar of Voters"; Edward T. Hall, Affidavit, n.d.; Tureaud to Marshall, October 16, 1945, both in box 56, folder 7, APT.

79. *Louisiana Weekly,* April 13, 1946; Marshall, "Memo to the Office," April 8, 1946, part 3, series B, NAACP.

80. *Hall* v. *Nagel* and *Mitchell* v. *Wright,* 154 F. 2d 924 (1946); Byrd, "Speech to NAACP National Convention," June 27, 1946, box 8, additions, Byrd.

81. Byrd "Speech"; Zelma C. Wyche, interviewed by Miriam Feingold, [1967], recording, Feingold Collection, SHSW; William Bailey Jr., interviewed by Adam Fairclough, September 29, 1987, recording.

CHAPTER 5 : *Brutality and Ballots, 1946–1956*

1. Judge Wayne G. Borah, "Final Judgment," November 7, 1947, box 35, folder 15, APT; J. E. Fleury to Tureaud, April 9, 1948; Tureaud to Thurgood Marshall, July 30, 1948, part 3, series B, folder 177, NAACP; *Louisiana Weekly,* November 15, 1947.

2. Daniel Byrd, report on East Carroll Parish schools, May 9, 1946, box 8, folder 37, APT; "Comparison of White and Negro Schools in St. Charles Parish, Louisiana," February 8, 1946, part 3, series B, NAACP.

3. Tureaud to school superintendents of Concordia, East Carroll, Madison, Morehouse, and Tensas parishes, December 29, 1952; D. W. Gibson to Tureaud, February 16, 1953; Tureaud to Gibson, February 19, 1953, box 29, APT.

4. Henry S. Weisman to P. F. O'Brien, report on Negro schools of Shreveport, October 6, 1950, Joseph B. Gremillion Papers, microfilm, Louisiana State University at Shreveport (archive hereinafter cited as LSUS).

5. Lionel J. Bourgeois, *Proposed Program for the Improvement of the Public Schools of New Orleans* (New Orleans: Orleans Parish School Board, 1948), pp. 33, 43; Muller, "Orleans Parish School Board, p. 28; *Louisiana Weekly,* June 5, 1948.

6. Haynes to Tureaud, November 9, 1945; March 30, 1946; January 22, 1948; Tureaud to Officers and Members, LEA, November 21, 1949, all in box 19, folders 15–16, APT; Tureaud to Marshall, March 27, 1948, part 3, series B, NAACP; Sindler, *Huey Long's Louisiana,* p. 210.

7. Bourgeois, *Proposed Program,* pp. 46–60; Muller, "Orleans Parish School Board," pp. 14–31; Bourgeois to Tureaud, September 30, 1947; Bourgeois to Byrd, April 23, 1948, box 43, folder 1, APT; *Louisiana Weekly,* June 5, 1948.

8. Harry S. Ashmore, *The Negro and the Schools* (Chapel Hill: University of North Carolina Press, 1954), pp. 144–45, 154; *US* v. *Louisiana,* Plaintiff's Trial Brief, Appendix E, tables 4–6.

9. Tureaud to A. Maceo Hubbard, December 27, 1944, box 8, folder 25, APT.

10. A good analysis of these incidents is provided by Burran, "Racial Violence in the South," pp. 229ff. For the Monroe, Georgia, lynching, see also W. Fitzhugh Brundage, *Lynching in the New South: Georgia and Virginia, 1880–1930* (Urbana and Chicago: University of Illinois Press, 1993), pp. 252–54.

11. Statements of Charles Harris Jr. and Mary Harris, June 7, 1946, part 8, series B, Harris file, NAACP.

12. *Louisiana Weekly,* June 1, 1946; affidavit of Johnnie A. Jones, July 9, 1946; *Southwestern Region Newsletter,* January 1950, box 15, folders 21, 27, both in APT.

13. August Meier and Elliott Rudwick, *CORE: A Study in the Civil Rights Movement* (New York: Oxford University Press, 1973), pp. 34–38; Meier and Rudwick, "The Origins of Nonviolent Direct Action," in *Along the Color Line,* p. 370; William R. Ming, "Railroad Passenger Segregation Re-Examined" [1948], box 12, folder 38, APT.

14. Oakley Johnson to William Patterson, June 6, 1950; Johnson to Aubrey Grossman, September 10, 1950, both in Oakley Johnson Papers (microfilm), Schomburg Library, New York City.

15. Banner and Kerns, "Review," pp. 174–75; *Louisiana Weekly,* August 23, 1947; Georgia Mitchell to James Dombrowski, June 13, July 15, 1946, both in box 1, folder 71, James A. Dombrowski Papers; *Southern Patriot,* December 1946.

16. "Registration and Voting in Louisiana, September 1946," folder 67, NAACP(NO); "Additional Information on the Discriminatory Practices in Louisiana," part 4, series 2, folder B-212, NAACP.

17. Daniel Byrd, Report, May 10, 1946, box 8, folder 37, APT; U.S. Commission on Civil Rights, *Hearings* (Washington, D.C., 1961), 1:17, 22–23.

18. "Registration and Voting in Louisiana"; *Louisiana Weekly,* August 17, 1946; "Plaintiff's Trial Brief," *U.S.* v. *Louisiana,* Appendix A, table C.

19. William C. Berman, *The Politics of Civil Rights in the Truman Administration* (Columbus: Ohio State University Press, 1970), pp. 31, 179, and passim.

20. Burran, "Racial Violence in the South, pp. 12–13, 290. See also Wynn, *Afro-American and the Second World War,* pp. 122–27.

21. Daniel E. Byrd, untitled report, 1946, folder 96, NAACP(NO); NAACP, *Annual Report,* 1947, 1948, 1949, 1950; Leonard P. Avery, "Annual Report of State Conference, 1952–53," box 12, folder 13; Clarence A. Laws, "Annual Report, 1955," box 12, folder 27; New Orleans Branch, "Annual Report, 1942–43," box 12, folder 25; Minutes of Southwestern Regional Advisory Board, March 12–14, 1948, box 12, folders 9, 13, 25, 27, all in APT.

22. Berman, *Politics of Civil Rights,* pp. 45–55.

23. Sanson, "History of Louisiana," pp. 426–27; Burran, "Racial Violence in the South," p. 272; Daniel E. Byrd, "Report of Investigation of Lynching of John C. Jones," part 7, series A, folder 2-A-398, NAACP (folder hereinafter cited as NAACP Minden file).

24. *New York Herald-Tribune*, August 16, 1946; Byrd, "Report of Investigation of Lynching of John C. Jones," August 17; Byrd to Madison Jones, August 18, 1946; both in NAACP Minden file; *Louisiana Weekly*, August 24, 1946; Daniel Byrd, Legendre interview, pp. 5–6, ARC.

25. Walter White, "Memo for the files," August 21, 22, 1946; Byrd, "Confidential Report," n.d., both in NAACP Minden file.

26. Walter White, "Memo on long distance call with Theron Caudle, Department of Justice," August 19, 1946; NAACP, press release, August 28, 1946; Dr. Robert S. Wilkinson, "Examination of Albert Harris, Jr.," August 28, 1946; all in NAACP Minden file; *Louisiana Weekly*, September 7, 1946.

27. Sworn statements of Albert Harris Jr. and Albert Harris Sr., August 29, 1946, NAACP Minden file; Daniel Byrd, Legendre interview, p. 5; *Shreveport Times*, February 26, 28, 1947.

28. Edward Swan, "Report of Louisiana Trip," October 16, 1946, NAACP Minden file; *New York Times*, October 19, 1946; *Louisiana Weekly*, October 26, 1946.

29. For the history of earlier federal prosecutions see Carr, *Federal Protection of Civil Rights*, pp. 106–14, 152–73; Capeci, "Lynching of Cleo Wright, pp. 859–97; John T. Eliff, "Aspects of Federal Civil Rights Enforcement: The Justice Department and the FBI, 1939–1964," in Donald Fleming and Bernard Bailyn, eds., *Perspectives in American History*, vol. 5 (Cambridge, Mass.: Charles Warren Center for Studies in American History, 1971), pp. 607–19.

30. Eliff, "Aspects of Federal Civil Rights Enforcement," pp. 621–25; Thurgood Marshall to Tom C. Clark, December 27, 1946, NAACP Minden file.

31. Clark to Marshall, January 13, 1947; Hoover to White, January 13, 1947; White to Marshall, January 26, 1947; Hoover to White, January 28, 1947; Marshall to White, January 23, 1947, all in NAACP Minden file.

32. Walter White to Tom Clark, October 24, 1946; NAACP press release, December 6, 1946, both in NAACP Minden file.

33. President's Committee on Civil Rights, *To Secure These Rights* (Washington, D.C.: 1947), p. 124. The account of the trial is based on *Louisiana Weekly*, March 1, 1946; *PM*, February 25, 1946; *Shreveport Times*, February 26, 27, 28, March 1, 2, 1946; *Shreveport Journal*, February 25, March 1, 1946; Martha Wilson to Roy Wilkins, February 26, 1946, NAACP Minden file.

34. Arthur Selwyn Miller and Jeffrey H. Bowman, "'Slow Dance on the Killing Ground': The *Willie Francis* Case Revisited," *DePaul Law Review* 32, no. 1 (1983): 1–47; Willie Francis file, part 8, series B, NAACP; *Louisiana Weekly*, May 17, 1947.

35. Gerald Horne, *Communist Front? The Civil Rights Congress, 1946–1956* (Cranbury, N.J.: Associated Universities Presses, 1988), pp. 19, 30; Oakley Johnson, "The New Orleans Story," *Centennial Review* 12 (Spring 1968): 207–8. A white and a black served as the LCCR's cochairmen: A. A. "Red" O'Brien, local head of the Food, Tobacco and Agricultural Workers Union, and Louis Brown, president of the Jefferson Parish branch of the NAACP. Also backing the LCRC were Theodore R. Means, a white organizer with the Fur and Leather Workers Union; Ernest Scott, black president of the Transport Workers Union, Local 206; and Andrew Nelson, black head of the ILWU in New Orleans. Like Johnson, they were also Communists.

36. Horne, *Communist Front?* p. 199; "Petition for the Defense of Milton Wilson,"

box 19, folder 224, Dombrowski Papers; *Pittsburgh Courier*, July 28, 1951; Oakley Johnson, notes on the Wilson case, Oakley Johnson Papers; *State* v. *Wilson*, 214 La. 318, 37 So. 2d 804 (1948); 217 La. 470, 46 So. 2d 738 (1950).

37. Horne, *Communist Front?* p. 199; "The Case of Paul Washington," Oakley Johnson Papers. The trial judge excluded three oral confessions but admitted two others.

38. Johnson to Patterson, May 4, 30, 1950; Patterson to Johnson, June 2, 1950, Oakley Johnson Papers.

39. *Daily Worker*, June 28, 1951; William O. Douglas, Stay Order, June 29, 1951; Johnson to Alice Gordon, n.d.; both in Oakley Johnson Papers; Horne, *Communist Front?* pp. 199–200; *Pittsburgh Courier*, July 19, 1952. Johnson chided Long for using the word "nigger."

40. Edward R. Dudley to Daniel Byrd, March 25, 1948; statement of Martha Morris, May 10, 1946; statement of Laura Brooks, May 10, 1946; unidentified correspondent to Walter White, October 9, 1940; *Louisiana Weekly*, March 13, 27, April 3, 1948; Dillard Oakes, "Grief in a Louisiana Shack," clipping, part 8, series B, Roy Brooks file, NAACP; Oakley Johnson, "The Facts of the Brooks Case," January 13, 1949, box 15, folder 27, APT; William Patterson to Leon Weiner, May 11, 1949; Johnson to Patterson, May 17, 1949, Oakley Johnson Papers; *Louisiana Weekly*, July 2, 1949.

41. Joseph H. Fichter, *One-Man Research: Reminiscences of a Catholic Sociologist* (New York: John Wiley, 1973), pp. 134–35; Morrison to A. A. O'Brien, January 4, 1950, Oakley Johnson Papers; Marion Wynn Perry to Alex Campbell, July 20, 1949, part 8, series B, police brutality cases, NAACP; statement of Martha Randolph Jones, November 7, 1949, box 9, folder 30, APT; Daniel Byrd and Robert Perry, Rickels interview; *Louisiana Weekly*, October 1, December 24, 1949.

42. Daniel Byrd to T. Vincent Quinn, n.d., part 4, series 2, file B-212, NAACP; interview with Rev. Victor Ragas, September 1964, box 6, folder 1, Southern Regional Office, CORE Papers, SHSW; C. G. Montgomery to Len Goldsmith, October 4, 1948, Oakley Johnson Papers.

43. "Plaintiff's Trial Brief," *U.S.* v. *Louisiana*, Appendix A, table B. In 1948, for example, both Washington and St. Landry parishes reported a single black voter. Yet when blacks registered there in, respectively, 1950 and 1952, they were reported as "firsts."

44. Louisiana State Conference of Branches, minutes, April 24, 1948, box 12, folder 12; "Report of Activities of the Progressive Voters League during the Second Primary, February 24, 1948," box 18, folder 24; E. N. Frances to Tureaud, January 20, 1948; Tureaud to Department of Justice, December 10, 1947; January 23, February 27, 1948, box 9, folders 5–6, all in APT; *Louisiana Weekly*, August 7, 1948.

45. Stuart O. Landry, ed., *Louisiana Almanac and Fact Book, 1953–54* (New Orleans: Pelican Publishing Company, 1954), p. 561; Spitzer, "Cajuns and Creoles," p. 145; handwritten note, n.d., box 15, folder 4, APT; Jones, "People of Frilot Cove," pp. 38–39; S. E. Briscoe to Tureaud, July 28, 1949, box 9, folder 2; Tureaud to Department of Justice, May 26, 1950, box 10, folder 5, both in APT.

46. Donatto to Tureaud, February 23, 1949; Tureaud to Donatto, March 25, 1949; Tureaud to Gustave Auzenne, May 5, 1950, box 56, folders 15–16, APT.

47. Tureaud to Thurgood Marshall, August 4, 1949; Donatto to Tureaud, September 2, 1949; Tureaud to Donatto, September 5, 1949; Tureaud to Gustave Auzenne, May 5, 1950, all in box 56, folders 15–16, APT.

48. E. A. Johnson to Thurgood Marshall, January 24, 1950, box 10, folder 2, APT; U. Simpson Tate, "Report on Visit to Alexandria, March 1, 1950"; Tate, "Report on Interview with Edward Honeycutt, April 13, 1950," both in Oakley Johnson Papers;

Times-Picayune, March 7, 8, 1949; *New York Times*, March 7, 1949; Transcript of Appeal, May 24, 1949, *State* v. *Honeycutt*, Louisiana Supreme Court, New Orleans; *State* v. *Honeycutt*, 216 La. 610, 44 So. 2d (1950).

49. Tate, "Report on Visit to Alexandria"; "Report on Interview with Edward Honeycutt."

50. Tureaud to E. A. Johnson, January 25, 1950, box 10, folder 2, APT.

51. *State* v. *Perkins*, 211 La. 993; *Louisiana Weekly*, May 18, 1948; *Sentinel-Informer*, May 15, 1948.

52. J. K. Haynes, Vanue LaCour, and Murphy Bell, interviewed by Patricia Rickels, c. 1979, recordings, University of Southwestern Louisiana, Lafayette. The delegation that saw Earl Long included E. A. Johnson, J. K. Haynes, and John G. Lewis.

53. Transcript of Appeal, July 18, 1950; Plaintiff's Original Brief, October 3, 1950; Original Brief on Behalf of State of Louisiana, October 5, 1950, Louisiana Supreme Court, New Orleans.

54. *State* v. *Honeycutt*, 218 La. 362 (1950); notes on Honeycutt case, n.d., Oakley Johnson Papers; *Times-Picayune*, June 9, 1951.

55. *Louisiana Weekly*, June 3, 1950; Marion O. White, Rickels interview.

56. *Louisiana Weekly*, June 24, 1950; Labbe, *Jim Crow Comes to Church*, pp. 59–60.

57. *Louisiana Weekly*, June 10, 1950; *Baton Rouge Morning Advocate*, June 7, 1950; "[Deleted]–Subjects; Alvin Hamilton Jones et al.–Victims," FBI file 44-3207-10, July 7, 1950, p. 27.

58. Auzenne to Tureaud, June 8, 1950, box 56, folder 16, APT; McInerney to J. Edgar Hoover, June 9, 1950, FBI Alvin Jones file, 33-3207-4.

59. FBI reports, June 16, 1950, file 44-3207-6, p. 26 (quotation); July 7, 1950, file 44-3207-10; September 18, 1950, file 44-3207-12.

60. *Louisiana Weekly*, November 3, 1951; William R. Valentine to Nelson C. Jackson, "Field Visit to the New Orleans Urban League, April 6–May 1, 1948," part 1, series 1, box III, National Urban League Papers, Manuscripts Division, Library of Congress (collection hereinafter cited as NUL); McInerney to Hoover, January 29, 1952, FBI file 44-3207-26; A. C. Terrance, "Autobiography."

61. *Louisiana Weekly*, March 31, 1950; October 27, 1951; November 25, 1951; Thurgood Marshall to McInerney, November 23, 1951, FBI file 44-3207-24; White, "The Louisiana Civil Rights Movement's Pre-Brown Period," p. 69. Numerous special deputies were selected by the sheriff to keep order at nightclubs and bars; they were paid by the club owner.

62. J. K. Haynes, Vanue LaCour, and Murphy Bell, Rickels interviews; *Louisiana Weekly*, October 11, 1952; Mary Alice Fontenot and Vincent Riehl, *The Cat and St. Landry: A Biography of Sheriff D. J. "Cat" Doucet of St. Landry Parish, Louisiana* (Baton Rouge: Claitor's Publishing Division, 1972), pp. 87, 100; Southern Regional Council, "Negro Voter Registration in the South," June 7, 1957, SRC; Plaintiff's Trial Brief, *U.S.* v. *Louisiana*, Appendix A, table B. It is difficult to be precise about the level of black registration and its proportion to total registration because the voting-age population can only be estimated. Using the figures from the 1960 census, black registration in 1956 stood at 87 percent.

63. Haynes, LaCour, and Bell, Rickels interviews; Fontenot and Riehl, *The Cat and St. Landry*, pp. 149–50; John H. Fenton and Kenneth N. Vines, "Negro Registration in Louisiana," *American Political Science Review* 51 (September 1957): 711–12. These observations also apply to such sheriffs as Gilbert Ozenne of Iberia Parish and Frank Clancy of Jefferson Parish.

64. "Report of Activities of the Progressive Voters League during the Second Pri-

mary, February 24, 1948," box 18, folder 24; W. B. McMillan to Tureaud, February 20, 1950, box 10, folder 3; NAACP, Louisiana State Conference, minutes, April 24, 1948, box 18, folder 2, all in APT; *Louisiana Weekly*, February 16, 1952.

65. Frederick D. Wright, "The History of Black Political Participation to 1965," in Lawrence W. Morland, Robert P. Steed, and Tod A. Baker, eds., *Blacks in Southern Politics* (New York: Praeger, 1987), p. 22; Fenton and Vines, "Negro Registration in Louisiana," pp. 704–13; U.S. Commission on Civil Rights, *1961 Report, vol. 1: Voting* (Washington, D.C.: 1961), pp. 266–69. The political history of the sugar parishes might also have been a factor in producing high black registration. As Perry H. Howard has pointed out, in the late nineteenth century many planters, desiring a high tariff on imported sugar, had been staunch Republicans, and "here the tradition of Negro voting had been nurtured longest." See Howard, *Political Tendencies in Louisiana*, p. 153.

66. Robert Garson, *The Democratic Party and the Politics of Sectionalism* (Baton Rouge: Louisiana State University Press, 1974), pp. 185–86; Daniel Byrd to J. K. Haynes, April 13, 1950, box 10, folder 5, APT; Thurgood Marshall, "The Rise and Collapse of the 'White Democratic Primary,'" *Journal of Negro Education* 26 (Summer 1957): 249–54.

67. *Louisiana Weekly*, June 10, 1950; Joe Dean to NAACP, July 27, 1946, series 2, B-212, NAACP; "Registration and Voting in Louisiana, September 1946," folder 67, NAACP(NO); Joe Dean to Louis Berry, March 20, 1950, box 10, folder 4, APT; *Bogalusa Daily News*, July 28, 1950; *Dean v. Thomas*, 93 F. Supp. 129 (1950); William Bailey, Fairclough interview.

68. *Byrd v. Brice*, 104 F. Supp. 442 (1952).

69. Plaintiff's Trial Brief, *US v. Louisiana*, Appendix A, table E.

70. William Bailey, Fairclough interview; *Louisiana Weekly*, May 18, 1948.

CHAPTER 6: *Race and Red-Baiting*

1. "Registration and Voting in Louisiana," September 1946, folder 67, NAACP(NO); Tureaud to W. B. McMillan, November 12, 1947, box 34, folder 29; *Southwestern Region Newsletter*, January 21, 1949, box 15, folder 25; Donald Jones to Roy Wilkins, January 14, 1949, box 9, folder 18, all in APT.

2. *Louisiana Weekly*, April 18, May 6, 1953; April 17, 1954; May 26, 1956; "History Made in Opelousas," n.d., box 12, folder 38, APT.

3. Ernest N. Morial, Rogers interview; Harvey R. H. Britton, Fairclough interview.

4. Daniel C. Thompson, *The Negro Leadership Class* (Englewood Cliffs, N.J.: Spectrum, 1963), pp. 112–14.

5. The phrase "tangible nucleus" was coined by Abraham Lincoln to describe the core of Union loyalists that formed the basis of the southern state governments he set up under his plan of Reconstruction.

6. Acting Executive Committee of Louisiana, SCHW, 1946, box 35, folder 524; "Alexandria Meeting," news release, June 13, 1946, box 1, folder 72; "Baton Rouge Meeting," news release, October 26, 1946, box 19, folder 224, all in Dombrowski Papers.

7. Sam Carothers(?) to Guy B. Johnson, draft, n.d., box 22, folder 270, Dombrowski Papers; Irwin Klibaner, *Conscience of a Troubled South: The Southern Conference Education Fund, 1944–1966* (Brooklyn, N.Y.: Carlson Publishing, 1989), pp. 31–33; Leo M. Favrot to Guy B. Johnson, September 12, 1946, series 1, folder 1991, SRC.

8. Georgia Mitchell to Dombrowski, February 7, June 13, 1946, box 1, folder 71, Dombrowski Papers; Dave McGuire to Morrison, n.d., DeLesseps S. Morrison Papers, TU.

9. John F. Cronin to Joseph F. Rummel, May 1, 1942; Paul D. Winter to Cronin, box 1, CCS; Wells, "ILWU in New Orleans," pp. 28–35; Martensen, "Region, Religion, and Social Action," pp. 256, 262; David Caute, *The Great Fear: The Anti-Communist Purge under Truman and Eisenhower* (New York: Simon and Schuster, 1978), p. 571.

10. Dunbar, *Against the Grain*, pp. 226–67; William B. Monroe Jr. to Sam Carothers, May 3, 1947, box 22, folder 270; Eugenie P. Schwarz to Edmonia Grant, August 23, 1947, both in Dombrowski Papers; William M. Kolb to ADA, August 8, 1947, series 3, reel 63, ADA Papers, SHSW; Thomas A. Krueger, *And Promises to Keep: The Southern Conference for Human Welfare, 1938–1948* (Nashville: Vanderbilt University Press, 1967), pp. 167–83; Harvey Klehr, *The Heyday of American Communism: The Depression Decade* (New York: Basic Books, 1984), pp. 275–76; Shouse, *Hillbilly Realist*, pp. 112–15.

11. Mrs. Paul A. Blanchard to Eugenie P. Schwarz, July 30, 1947, box 19, folder 224, Dombrowski Papers; Ruth Preston to Martha G. Robinson, January 28, 1947; Robinson to Preston, September 2, 1947; Jane Well Stubb to Blanchard, April 2, 1948, box 2, folders 97, 103, 110, League of Women Voters Papers, TU.

12. Krueger, *And Promises to Keep*, pp. 182–87; Sam Carothers(?) to Emily Blanchard, October 11, 1947, box 19, folder 224, Dombrowski Papers; Wallace for President Committee of Louisiana, Program for Paul Robeson, June 16, 1948, reel 3, Oakley Johnson Papers; *Louisiana Weekly*, September 4, 1948; Sindler, *Huey Long's Louisiana*, p. 222. Raymond Tillman and Louis Berry were among the few well-known blacks to support Wallace.

13. *Louisiana Weekly*, February 12, 1949; *Times-Picayune*, February 9, 10, June 9, 1949; Louisiana Civil Rights Congress, "Case Letter No. 1," April 17, 1949, box 15, folder 22, APT.

14. Membership lists, October 22, December 10, 1947, February 17, 1948; William L. Kolb to James Loeb, September 14, 1947, December 15, 1948; Violet M. Gunther to George Lambert, March 8, 1954, all in series 3, reel 64, ADA Papers.

15. Wells, "ILWU in New Orleans," p. 50; *New Orleans Item*, September 9, 23, 26, 29, 30, October 1, 1947; *New Orleans States*, May 6, 7, 24, June 27, 1948; *Times-Picayune*, August 4, 27, 29, 1948. The school board eventually voted three to one to "clear" Reed of promoting "un-Americanism."

16. *Louisiana Weekly*, May 29, 1948. The Mundt-Nixon Bill proposed the compulsory registration of all Communist party members with the attorney general and the denial of passports to Communists.

17. *Times-Picayune*, July 2, 1948; July 26, 30, 1949; Freeman, *In Transit*, p. 321; Arthur Selwyn Miller, *A "Capacity for Outrage": The Judicial Odyssey of J. Skelly Wright* (Westport, Conn.: Greenwood Press, 1984), pp. 129–30.

18. Wells, "ILWU in New Orleans," pp. 63–65; Freeman, *In Transit*, p. vi; Daniel Guerin, *Negroes on the March: A Frenchman's Report on the American Negro Struggle* (New York: George L. Weissman, 1956), pp. 165–74.

19. Johnson, "New Orleans Story," pp. 212–19; Johnson to Patterson, July 4, 1951; August 3, 1951; Isaac Heller to Johnson, August 1, 1951; Albert Dent to Johnson, May 1, 1951, Oakley Johnson Papers.

20. Byrd to Donald Jones, April 25, 1949, box 9, folder 22, APT; *Louisiana Weekly*,

May 5, 1949; Tureaud to Marshall, September 28, 1954, box 10, folder 24, APT; Johnson to Patterson, November 20, 1949, Oakley Johnson Papers.

21. Horne, *Communist Front?* p. 140; Roy Wilkins, with Tom Matthews, *Standing Fast: The Autobiography of Roy Wilkins* (New York: Penguin Books, 1984), p. 210; "Report of Administration on Communist Efforts Against the Association," June 22, 1950; Resolution by Forty-First Annual Convention, June 23, 1950, both in NAACP; Tureaud to Benjamin J. Stanley, June 30, 1949, box 9, folder 25; Walter White to Branches, August 29, 1950, box 10, folder 8; White to Branches, January 15, 1951, box 10, folder 12, APT.

22. "Memorandum to Mr. Current from Mr. Marshall," May 4, 1951; Marshall to Alfred Baker Lewis, May 18, 1951; June 5, 1951, part 2, series C, box 328, NAACP.

23. "Summary of Information: Clarence Alvert Laws," April 19, 1951, attached to Brigadier General C. J. Hauck Jr. to F. Edward Hebert, September 23, 1955; Department of Army to Laws, February 21, 1957, part 3, series C, folder 262, NAACP(LC); Martensen, "Region, Religion, and Social Action," pp. 65–66; Philip S. Ogilvie to Board of Governors, "Quarterly Report," April 1–June 30, 1951, CCS; Laws to Tureaud, December 9, 1960, folder 70, NAACP(NO). Laws told Congressman F. Edward Hebert that he joined the SCHW at the suggestion of Father Vincent O'Connell "in order to better observe its operation"; Hebert to Perez, October 10, 1955, Leander H. Perez Papers, Louisiana Collection, New Orleans Public Library (library hereinafter cited as NOPL).

24. Alfred Baker Lewis to Marshall, May 17, 21, 1951, part 2, series C, box 328; Louisiana State Conference, minutes, October 29–30, 1954, box 12, folder 15, APT; Tureaud quoted in Saul Gottlieb, "The Negro and the Church," *Dissent*, Spring 1956, p. 119; Frank T. Adams, *James A. Dombrowski: An American Heretic, 1897–1983* (Knoxville: University of Tennessee Press, 1992), p. 238. In New Orleans, where SCEF maintained its headquarters, the NAACP kept a polite but cold distance. "Most of us here look upon the organization with suspicion of its being associated with leftist groups," explained Tureaud (Tureaud to Ruby Hurley, April 10, 1952, box 10, folder 20, APT).

25. White to Leslie Perry, September 30, 1947; Tureaud to Ruby Hurley, April 10, 1952; Hurley to Maurice V. Shean, April 14, 1952; Wilkins to Carl R. Johnson, May 4, 1954, all in part 2, series A, box 396, NAACP(LC); Klibaner, *Conscience of a Troubled South*, pp. 178–79. The Urban League, both locally and nationally, also refused to cooperate with or defend SCEF; see Lester Granger to J. Westbrook McPherson, April 3, 1954, part 1, series 1, box 111, NUL.

26. *Times-Picayune*, March 18, 1954; Klibaner, *Conscience of a Troubled South*, pp. 73–84, 95–99; Rabbi Julian Feibelman, interviewed by Kim Lacy Rogers, November 7, 1978, Rogers-Stephens Collection; Dunbar, *Against the Grain*, pp. 227 (quotation), 234–40; Adams, *James A. Dombrowski*, pp. 222–38.

27. August Meier, "Toward a Synthesis of Civil Rights History," in Robinson and Sullivan, eds., *New Directions in Civil Rights History*, p. 216.

28. Mary L. Dudziak, "Desegregation as a Cold War Imperative," *Stanford Law Review* 41 (November 1988): 61–120.

29. Fred H. Wiegmann, "Agriculture in the Louisiana Economy," in Thomas R. Beard, ed., *The Louisiana Economy* (Baton Rouge: Louisiana State University Press, 1969), pp. 60–74; Fite, *Cotton Fields No More*, pp. 233–38; James R. Bobo and Sandra A. Etheridge, eds., *Statistical Abstract of Louisiana, 1967* (New Orleans: Louisiana State University in New Orleans, 1967), pp. 9, 151, 289, 291; Paul Grosser,

"Political Parties," in James Bolner, ed., *Louisiana Politics: Festival in a Labyrinth* (Baton Rouge: Louisiana State University Press, 1982), pp. 271–73; Jay R. Mandle, *The Roots of Black Poverty: The Southern Plantation Economy after the Civil War* (Durham: Duke University Press, 1978), p. 95.

30. Stern quoted in New Orleans Committee on Race Relations, "The Good Neighbor at Home," Institute of Race Relations, November 5–7, 1945, transcript, p. 92, box 82, folder 14, UCC.

31. Paul B. Williamson to Ellender, May 10, 1947; Ellender to J. O. Grimes, March 16, 1946, Ellender Papers.

32. *New Orleans States,* September 24, 1947; "History of the New Orleans Urban League," ms., Hubert Papers.

33. Stephen L. McDonald, "Postwar Economic Growth and Fluctuations in Louisiana," in Beard, ed., *The Louisiana Economy,* pp. 85–92; Bobo and Etheridge, eds., *Statistical Abstract of Louisiana, 1967,* pp. 262, 322; Lester Rubin, *The Negro in the Shipbuilding Industry* (Philadelphia: Wharton School of Finance and Commerce, University of Pennsylvania, 1970), p. 58; Herbert R. Northrup, *The Negro in the Paper Industry* (Philadelphia: Wharton School of Finance and Commerce, University of Pennsylvania, 1969), pp. 32–34, 45–51, 96–97; Carl B. King and Howard W. Risher Jr., *The Negro in the Petroleum Industry* (Philadelphia: Wharton School of Finance and Commerce, University of Pennsylvania, 1970), pp. 30–35.

34. Bobo and Etheridge, eds., *Statistical Abstract of Louisiana, 1967,* p. 320; King and Risher, *Negro in the Petroleum Industry,* pp. 35–36; Rubin, *Negro in the Shipbuilding Industry,* pp. 58, 63–65, 140.

35. Banner and Kerns, "Review," pp. 34–39; Thompson, *Negro Leadership Class,* p. 124; Landry, ed., *Louisiana Almanac and Fact Book,* p. 432; Bobo and Etheridge, eds., *Statistical Abstract of Louisiana, 1967,* p. 84.

36. Gene Sutherland, "H. J. Voorhies, vice-president and general manager, Esso," May 2, 1955, South Central Regional Office Files, American Friends Service Committee Papers, Philadelphia (collection hereinafter cited as AFSC).

37. Sutherland to Thelma Babbit, "Richard E. Walker, assistant director, department of commerce," March 5, 1955; "James L. Mehaffy, international representative, Communication Workers of America," March 12, 1955; "Opie Shelton, executive director, Chamber of Commerce," March 2, 1955; Merit Employment Program, Advisory Committee, summary minutes, October 19, December 10, 1955, all in AFSC.

38. Thompson, *Negro Leadership Class,* p. 124; Emmett Harold Buell, "The Politics of Frustration: An Analysis of Negro Political Leadership in East Baton Rouge Parish, 1953–1966" (M.A. thesis, Louisiana State University, 1967), p. 50; James R. Bobo and Sandra A. Etheridge, eds., *Statistical Abstract of Louisiana, 1969* (New Orleans: Louisiana State University in New Orleans, 1969), p. 169.

39. Bobo and Etheridge, eds., *Statistical Abstract of Louisiana, 1969,* pp. 10–11; Samuel Lubell, *The Future of American Politics* (New York: Harper and Brothers, 1951), pp. 118–20.

40. Sindler, *Huey Long's Louisiana,* pp. 220–25; Jeansonne, *Leander Perez,* p. 183.

41. Edward F. Haas, *DeLesseps S. Morrison and the Image of Reform: New Orleans Politics, 1946–1961* (Baton Rouge: Louisiana State University Press, 1974), pp. 137–38; "New Orleans: Race-Baiting Comes a Cropper," *New South,* January–February 1950, pp. 1–3; Carl T. Rowan, *South of Freedom* (New York: Alfred A. Knopf, 1952), p. 194.

42. Haas, *Morrison,* pp. 51–52, 69–76; W. Ray Scheuring to Morrison, March 23, 1949; Scott Wilson to Morrison, May 29, 1949, both in Morrison Papers, TU; Mayor's

Advisory Committee, minutes, June 9, July 28, 1949, Scott W. Wilson Papers, TU; Medley, "1954: A Year in the Life of Lincoln Beach," pp. 20–21. Administrative aide Ray Scheuring suggested siting a Negro golf course in Algiers, on the west bank of the Mississippi, thereby forcing "the jiggs," as he called them, to cross the river.

43. Haas, pp. 76–78; Mayor's Advisory Committee, minutes, June 15, 1949, Scott Wilson Papers; Morrison to M. Tricou, May 30, 1950, Morrison Papers, NOPL; Willie Burton, *On the Black Side of Shreveport: A History* (Shreveport: Willie Burton, 1983), pp. 85–86.

44. Numa Rousseve, interviewed by John W. Martin, July 1959, box 2, folder 13, Hubert Papers.

45. *Sweatt v. Painter,* 339 U.S. 629 (1950); Tushnet, *NAACP's Legal Strategy,* pp. 115–16, 135–36.

46. Tureaud to U. S. Tate, July 31, 1950; Haynes to Tureaud, August 23, 1950; Marshall to E. A. Johnson, September 7, 1950, box 73, folders 1–2, APT.

47. Warren Rogers, "The Man in the Fish Fry Parlor," *Look,* October 17, 1967, p. 115; Warren Rogers to Tureaud, September 6, 1950; Marshall to Tureaud, September 12, 1950, box 73, folder 2, APT; J. Skelly Wright to Charles and Rosa Keller, n.d., Rosa Keller Papers.

48. Tureaud to Marshall, November 8, 1950; January 4, 1951; Marshall to Tureaud, November 15, 1950; January 10, 1951, all in box 73, folders 2–3, APT.

49. Rogers, "The Man in the Fish Fry Parlor"; Ashmore, *Negro and the Schools,* pp. 41–42; *Louisiana Weekly,* February 27, 1954.

50. Stephen L. Wasby, Anthony A. D'Amato, and Rosemary Metrailer, *Desegregation from Brown to Alexander* (Carbondale: Southern Illinois University Press, 1977), pp. 56, 164; Logsdon, "Tureaud," tape 13; *Louisiana Weekly,* June 17, 1950.

51. Donald Jones to Roy Wilkins, January 14, 1949, box 9, folder 18; Tureaud to E. A. Johnson, July 15, 1950, box 10, folder 8, APT; Byrd to Marshall, September 12, 1951, box 1, folder 1, Byrd Papers.

52. Byrd, "Activity Report," various, 1951–54, box 4, Byrd Papers; Tureaud to Thurgood Marshall and Robert Carter, September 4, 1952, box 53, folder 1, APT.

53. *Louisiana Weekly,* November 29, December 20, 1947; September 15, 1951; *Byrd v. City of New Orleans,* February 2, 1948, box 5, folder 18; Byrd to Marshall, March 5, 1953, box 1, folder 1; Byrd, "Activity Report," March 1953, box 4, folder 1, Byrd Papers; Meier and Rudwick, "Origins of Nonviolent Direct Action," pp. 360–61.

54. Aldon D. Morris, *The Origins of the Civil Rights Movement: Black Communities Organizing for Change* (New York: Free Press, 1984), p. 17; Martin M. Grossack, "Psychological Effects of Segregation on Buses," *Journal of Negro Education* 22 (Winter 1956): 71–74; *Louisiana Weekly,* March 18, 1950.

55. Mrs. A. J. Scott to Tureaud, November 23, 1946, box 8, folder 41, APT; *Louisiana Weekly,* March 13, 1948; NAACP Legal Department, Monthly Reports, February–March, 1953, pp. 6–7; June 1–15, 1953, pp. 6–7, box 4, folder 5, Byrd Papers.

56. Morris, *Origins of the Civil Rights Movement,* pp. 17–25; Meier and Rudwick, "Origins of Nonviolent Direct Action," pp. 365–66; *New York Times,* June 16, 21, 1953; *Baton Rouge Morning Advocate,* June 16–22, 1953; *Louisiana Weekly,* June 25, 1949, July 4, 1953; *Pittsburgh Courier,* July 4, 1953; Buell, "Politics of Frustration," pp. 116–27; Plaintiff's Petition, *Jemison v. City of Baton Rouge,* box 31, folder 4, APT.

57. Notes on mass meeting, Claver Building, May 3, 1954; "To Parents and Civic Groups," May 3, 1954, folder 68, NAACP(NO); Rogers, "Humanity and Desire," pp. 96–99.

1. Ben Dawkins Jr., notes for speech, May 12, 1950, J. B. Gremillion Papers, LSUS; "The National Municipal League and *Look* Salute the All-American Cities," *Look,* February 9, 1954, p. 57; Ben C. Dawkins Jr., interviewed by Norman Provizer, March 1, 1978, pp. 4–5, LSUS; Norman W. Provizer, "The Judicial Evolution of Ben Dawkins, Jr.," in Norman W. Provizer and William D. Pederson, eds., *Grassroots Constitutionalism: Shreveport, The South, and the Supreme Court* (Lanham, Md.: University Press of America, 1988), pp. 78–80.

2. Rosa Keller, "Autobiography," vol. 2; F. LaViolette, interview with Mrs. Charles Keller, July 13, 1959, box 2, folder 12, Hubert Papers; Arthur E. Carpenter, "Social Origins of Anticommunism: The Information Council of the Americas," *Louisiana History* 30 (Spring 1989): 125–26.

3. Joe Gray Taylor, *McNeese State University, 1939–1987: A Chronicle* (Lake Charles: McNeese State University, 1990), pp. 82–84; M. Eloi Girad to Dear Friend, April 25, 1955, folder 92, Robert F. Kennon Papers, Hill Library, Louisiana State University; William Rainach to Leander Perez, November 30, 1954, Perez Papers; Associated Negro Press, December 1, 1954; Daniel Byrd, Activity Report, August 23, 1955, box 4, folder 2, Byrd Papers.

4. Rogers, "Humanity and Desire," pp. 85–90; Rosa Keller, interviewed by Vincent J. Browne, January 11, 1968, p. 20, Ralph J. Bunche Oral History Project, Moorland-Spingarn Library, Howard University, copy in ARC.

5. Byrd, Activity Reports, March, April 1953, box 4, folder 1; Byrd to Marshall, April 9, 1953, box 1, folder 3, Byrd Papers.

6. E. A. Johnson, "Report on Atlanta Meeting," in Executive Board and Regional Board, minutes, May 30, 1954, box 12, folder 15, APT; *Nashville Tennesseean,* May 23, 1954; "Suggested Program for Southern Branches, 1954–1955," box 4, folder 7, Byrd Papers.

7. Joseph T. Taylor, "Desegregation in Louisiana: One Year Later," *Journal of Negro Education* 24 (Summer 1955): 264–67.

8. Joseph B. Gremillion, "Re Supreme Court Decision," handwritten notes, n.d., Gremillion Papers.

9. Rainach to W. M. Caskey, December 5, 1955, box 1, folder 10, William M. Rainach Papers, LSUS; Ellender to Samuel Arceneaux, February (?), 1955, box 1442, Ellender Papers. Whenever a civil rights bill came up for debate, Ellender wrote to the police chief of every large city in the country for an up-to-date racial breakdown of the latest crime figures.

10. Ellender, speech outlines, 1938, 1948, boxes 1280 and 1442, Ellender Papers.

11. Perez, "Racial Integration by Court Decree," December 29, 1954, box 1, Perez Papers; Rainach to Sue Hefley, May 4, 1955, box 2, Rainach Papers.

12. Paul G. Borron to Kennon, May 31, 1954, box 4, folder 91, Kennon Papers; Robert F. Farmer to Louis Twomey, December 11, 1955, box 19, folder 17, Louis Twomey Papers, Loyola University of the South; Rogers, "Humanity and Desire," p. 150; Mrs. Harry L. Crane to Rainach, April 28, 1955, box 1, Rainach Papers.

13. Herman P. Folse to Twomey, December 8, 1955, box 19, folder 17; M. Basilico to Twomey, March 9, 1960, box 21, folder 4, Twomey Papers.

14. Deposition of Dr. Clarence Scheps, June 1955, box 44, folder 17, APT; Morrison to Henry O. Meisel, January 29, 1961, folder S61-12, Morrison Papers, NOPL.

15. Earleen May McCarrick, "Louisiana's Official Resistance to Desegregation" (Ph.D. diss., Vanderbilt University, 1964), pp. 27–40; Rainach to Rex H. Smelser, November 24, 1954, Rainach Papers.

16. Louisiana, Legislative Council, *The Government of Louisiana* (Baton Rouge, 1959), p. 12; William Rainach, interviewed by Hubert Humphreys, 1977, p. 24, LSUS. For Kennon's arm's-length approach to the ultrasegregationists, see also George T. Madison to John Sheldon Toomer, June 23, 1954; Kennon to W. L. Lawrence, December 7, 1955; Kennon to Rainach, December 27, 1955, all in Kennon Papers; Rainach to Paul G. Borron, September 24, 1955, Rainach Papers.

17. LCHR Workshop, January 11, 1955, series 1, folder 971, SRC.

18. M. C. D. D'Argonne to Guy B. Johnson, January 2, 1946; Leo M. Favrot to Johnson, September 12, 1946; Johnson, "Interracial Cooperation in Louisiana," n.d., all in series 1, folder 1991, SRC. Another interracial committee in New Orleans was formed at the initiative of M. C. D. D'Argonne, a Belgian-born sociology professor at Xavier University, but it had only six members.

19. *Louisiana Weekly,* October 10, 1949; Fichter, *One-Man Research,* p. 77; Ochs, *Desegregating the Altar,* pp. 404–5; Morton Inger, *Politics and Reality in an American City: The New Orleans School Integration Crisis of 1960* (New York: Center for Urban Education, 1969), p. 22; Joseph F. Rummel, "Blessed Are the Peacemakers," March 15, 1953, box 19, folder 15, Twomey Papers.

20. William McFerrin Stowe Jr., "William Rainach and the Defense of Segregation in Louisiana, 1954–1959" (Ph.D. diss., Texas Christian University, 1989), p. 31; Rummel to Kennon, July 1, 1954, Kennon Papers.

21. *Louisiana Weekly,* June 5, 1954; John Robert Payne, "A Jesuit Search for Social Justice: The Public Career of Louis J. Twomey, S.J., 1947–1969" (Ph.D. diss., University of Texas at Austin, 1976), pp. 204–5; *Louisiana Weekly,* September 3, 1955; James Graham Cook, *The Segregationists* (New York: Appleton-Century-Crofts, 1962), pp. 231–32; Landry, ed., *Louisiana Almanac and Fact Book,* p. 463; *Times-Picayune,* August 31, 1960. In 1952 there were 167 schools in the archdiocese with a total enrollment of 91,472. Eighty-six of them, with an enrollment of 39,359, were in New Orleans, and they included 19 black schools with 7,659 pupils. By 1959 there were 194 Catholic schools in the archdiocese with an enrollment of 86,000, including 90 in New Orleans with an enrollment of 47,000. These figures included 20 black schools in the city with an enrollment of 8,900 pupils and another 21 black schools outside the city with an enrollment of 3,800.

22. Fichter, *One-Man Research,* pp. 29–67; Fichter, *Southern Parish,* 1:16, 265–70.

23. Fichter, *One-Man Research,* pp. 78–79.

24. Ibid., pp. 76–77; Payne, "Jesuit Search for Social Justice," pp. 198–99; Twomey to Vincent A. McCormick, January 18, 1951, box 19, folder 10, Twomey Papers. In 1951 two black nuns were awarded tuition scholarships to the university extension program; Joseph H. Fichter, "The First Black Students at Loyola University: A Strategy to Obtain Teacher Certification," *Journal of Negro Education* 56 (Fall 1987): 548.

25. Fichter, *One-Man Research,* pp. 79, 91; Payne, "Jesuit Search for Social Justice," p. 64; Twomey to J. B. Janssens, December 4, 1958, box 20, folder 11, Twomey Papers; John P. Nelson, interviewed by Glenda Stephens, May 3, 1979, recording, Rogers-Stephens Collection.

26. Mary Dolan and Anne Foley, "Report on Friendship House," October 1953–October 1954, Gremillion Papers.

27. Joseph B. Gremillion, *Journal of a Southern Pastor* (Chicago: Fides, 1957), pp. 44,

146–47; Gremillion, "Southern Hospitality Wears Out," September 1955, Gremillion Papers; *Shreveport Sun,* July 30, 1955.

28. Editorial, *North-Central Louisiana Register,* July 8, 1955, copy in Harry A. Johnson, Jr. to Robert F. Kennon, July 26, 1955, Kennon Papers.

29. Martensen, "Region, Religion, and Social Action," pp. 66–72; Ochs, *Desegregating the Altar,* pp. 349–50.

30. Becnel, *Labor, Church, and the Sugar Establishment,* pp. 119–145, 186–88.

31. Gremillion, *Journal of a Southern Pastor,* pp. 284–85; John Beecher, "Magnolia Ghetto," *Ramparts,* December 1964, pp. 48–49; Twomey to Mr. and Mrs. Stephen Ryan, January 14, 1955, box 19, folder 15, Twomey Papers.

32. Muller, "Orleans Parish School Board," pp. 43–44; *New Orleans States,* September 14, 1955; Foust Richards, "Churches, Unions Lead Integration Fight," *New Leader,* November 14, 1955, p. 13; Daniel Byrd, Report, August 23, 1955, box 4, folder 3, Byrd Papers; Ochs, *Desegregating the Altar,* p. 427; Fichter, *One-Man Research,* p. 81.

33. Ochs, *Desegregating the Altar,* pp. 433–38; Warren Olney to George S. Blue, December 8, 1955, serial number unrecorded, FBI file 44-9732; *Times-Picayune,* December 8, 1955; Jules B. Jeanmard to Parishioners of Our Lady of Lourdes Church, Erath, November 26, 1955, box 19, folder 17, Twomey Papers; Fichter, *One-Man Research,* pp. 107–8; Cook, *Segregationists,* pp. 232–33.

34. Alfred J. Kronlage to Twomey, December 7, 1955, folder 17; Mrs. Edward Kultgen to Twomey, June 6, 1955, folder 15; Twomey to John J. O'Connor, December 16, 1955, folder 17, all in box 19, Twomey Papers.

35. Kurtz and Peoples, *Earl K. Long,* p. 195; Shreveport resident to Morrison, September 9, 1948, Morrison Papers, TU; Morrison campaign statement, 1960, David McGuire Papers, TU. In 1948 a Shreveport resident told Morrison that Don Ewing, publisher of the *Shreveport Times* and a temporary Earl Long ally, was shouting about Morrison's Negro support in order to divert attention from the fact that black votes had helped to elect Russell Long to the U.S. Senate.

36. Van Buren Harris, "Speech before Mass Meeting of the Joint State Conventions of the NAACP and the Progressive Voters League," October 28, 1949, box 19, folder 8, APT.

37. Donald Jones to Roy Wilkins, January 14, 1949; Tureaud to Leslie S. Perry, January 8, 1949, box 9, folder 15; *Southwest Region Newsletter,* 1949, box 15, folder 25, APT. "Both Long and Johnson are frankly fearful of the 'wool hat boys' among their electorates," Donald Jones reported after meeting the freshmen senators from Louisiana and Texas. "However . . . they agreed that on issues where they could not give us their support, they would at least not actively organize or lead opposition to us." A. P. Tureaud argued that the NAACP would do well to remain silent on Senator Long's "oratorical outbursts" in view of "the help we expect to get from his uncle, Gov. Earl Long, on the matter of registration." Weeks after being charmed by Russell Long, however, Jones received a "resentful and evil-tempered" letter from the senator that "hedged on everything promised." And by 1952 Tureaud had broken with Earl Long, convinced that he was deliberately restricting black registration in New Orleans. (Southwestern Region Newsletter [1949], p. 3, box 15, folder 25; Tureaud comment in OPPVL radio script, January 6, 1952, box 19, folder 8, both in APT.)

38. *Louisiana Weekly,* March 6, 1948; Kurtz and Peoples, *Earl K. Long,* pp. 147–52; Garson, *Democratic Party,* pp. 298–300. Garson advances a more cynical explanation of Long's opposition to the Dixiecrats, arguing that one of his motives in calling a special session of the legislature to restore Truman's name to the ballot was his desire to use the session to scrap the state's civil service laws.

39. Kurtz and Peoples, *Earl K. Long,* pp. 82–83, 130–31, 147–51; Sindler, *Huey Long's Louisiana,* pp. 258–60; *LEA Journal,* April 1949.

40. *Louisiana Weekly,* September 4, 1948; April 9, 1949; Program, OPPVL's Silver Anniversary Celebration, July 7–8, 1974, box 18, folder 24, APT; Sindler, *Huey Long's Louisiana,* p. 259; Haas, *Morrison,* pp. 80–81, 25–52. The board of the OPPVL included Clarence Laws and Alvin H. Jones of the Urban League; Dave Dennis and Avery Alexander of ILA Local 1419; Rev. A. L. Davis, pastor of the largest Negro Baptist church in the city; C. C. Dejoie Jr., owner-editor of the *Louisiana Weekly;* Jackson V. Acox, leader of the Second Ward Voters League; and A. P. Tureaud.

41. Medley, "Remembering Ernest Wright," p. 14; *Louisiana Weekly,* February 21, May 1, 1949; September 29, 1951; April 11, August 1, 1953.

42. Medley, "Ernest Wright," p. 55; "Ernest J. Wright," August 20, 1948, FBI file 100-56308-25; Sindler, *Huey Long's Louisiana,* p. 259; *Louisiana Weekly,* January 14, 1950; Haas, *Morrison,* pp. 124–38.

43. *Louisiana Weekly,* July 15, 22, 1950; Sindler, *Huey Long's Louisiana,* pp. 229–30; Haas, *Morrison,* pp. 142–47; Kurtz and Peoples, *Earl K. Long,* pp. 155–56. Haas is skeptical that a Morrison-Long deal took place; Kurtz and Peoples affirm that it did.

44. *Louisiana Weekly,* June 6, 1954; March 12, December 17, 1955; January 11, 18, 1958; Haas, *Morrison,* p. 251. Although Tureaud returned to the OPPVL fold, longshoremen's leader Dave Dennis formed his own political grouping, the Crescent City Independent Voters League (CCIVL). When Dennis was ousted from the leadership of Local 1419 amid charges that he had misappropriated union funds, Clarence "Chink" Henry took over both the union and the CCIVL. Henry became a key Morrison supporter. Dennis, after being tried and acquitted of theft, became a Baptist minister and organized the New Orleans Voters League (NOVL). Another group, the United Voters League (UVL), appeared on the scene in 1955; led by Ellis Hull, it was based in the city's Second Ward. Still another faction, the New Orleans Voters Association (NOVA), made a bow in 1958, led by Earl J. Amadee, a lawyer, and Avery C. Alexander, a minister and former ILA official.

45. Daniel E. Byrd to Thurgood Marshall, Gloster Current, and U.S. Tate, "NAACP in Louisiana" [October 1951], box 12, folder 11, APT; Sindler, *Huey Long's Louisiana,* p. 261; *Louisiana Weekly,* November 4, 18, 1950; October 31, November 24, December 22, 1951; January 23, 30, 1954; December 17, 1955; January 14, 28, 1956; March 8, August 30, 1958. Amadee ran for the Orleans Parish school board (1950), councilman-at-large (1954 and 1958), and attorney general (1955).

46. Sindler, *Huey Long's Louisiana,* p. 261.

47. Sindler, *Huey Long's Louisiana,* p. 259; Thompson, *Negro Leadership Class,* pp. 113–14; Haas, p. 232; Kurtz and Peoples, *Earl K. Long,* p. 205.

48. *Newsweek,* June 15, 1959, p. 3. On the looseness of political factions, see Sindler, *Huey Long's Louisiana,* pp. 276–85; Kurtz and Peoples, *Earl K. Long,* pp. 11–12.

49. Numan V. Bartley and Hugh D. Graham, *Southern Elections: County and Precinct Data, 1950–1972* (Baton Rouge: Louisiana State University Press, 1978), pp. 127–28; "Registered Voters in Louisiana, October 4, 1952," in Landry, ed., *Louisiana Almanac and Fact Book,* pp. 466–67; "Voter Registration in Southern States," June 7, 1957, SRC.

50. The charge of a Long-inspired "slowdown" was made by Jackson Acox, A. P. Tureaud, and Joseph O. Brien in an OPPVL radio broadcast endorsing gubernatorial candidate Hale Boggs, aired on January 6, 1952, script in box 19, folder 8, APT.

51. *Louisiana Weekly,* December 29, 1951; Alex L. Andrus to Morrison, December 16, 1958, campaign files, Morrison Papers, TU.

52. James M. Nabrit Jr., "The Future of the Negro Voter in the South," *Journal of Negro Education* 26 (Summer 1957): 420; Louisiana Council on Human Relations, Workshop, minutes, January 11, 1955, series 1, folder 971, SRC; A. P. Tureaud to Thurgood Marshall, April 10, 1958, box 34, folder 8, APT; Dr. James H. Henderson, interviewed by Adam Fairclough, September 28, 1987, New Iberia; Ernesto Galarza, "The Louisiana Sugar Cane Industry," August 1954, reel 38, STFU.

53. Rainach to Jay Murphy, October 7, 1954; Rainach to Paul G. Borron, November 26, 1955, Rainach Papers.

54. Wasby, D'Amato, and Metrailer, *Desegregation from Brown to Alexander,* pp. 120–30; Thurgood Marshall and Robert L. Carter, "The Meaning and Significance of the Supreme Court Decree," *Journal of Negro Education* 24 (Summer 1955): 403; William Greer McCall, "School Desegregation in Louisiana: An Analysis of the Constitutional Issues" (Ph.D. diss., University of Tennessee, 1973), pp. 37–38.

55. Muller, "Orleans Parish School Board," pp. 41–42; Eugene G. Sutherland, "Glen Nordyke, director of Boy Scouts," May 13, 1955; Sutherland, "Progress Report," December 22, 1955, AFSC; Committee on Stores, minutes, July 28, September 7, November 8, 1954; Negro Women's Study Group, minutes, April 4, 1955; "An Open Letter to Shreveport Stores," newsletter [June 1955], all in Gremillion Papers.

56. *New York Times,* September 4, 1954; "JLC's appearance before East Baton Rouge School Board," September 23, 1954, Rainach Papers; Directive to Branches, June 4, 1955, box 4, folder 7, Byrd Papers; Constance Baker Motley, Bass interview.

57. *NAACP Annual Report,* 1948, 1949; Clarence A. Laws, "Annual Report for 1955"; Leonard P. Avery, "Annual Report, 1952–53," box 12, folders 27 and 13, APT; New Orleans Branch, "President's Annual Report, 1950–51"; Branch meeting, minutes, October 12, 1953; Executive Committee, minutes, March 8, 1954, folders, 210 and 181, NAACP(NO); Lucille Black, "NAACP Membership in Louisiana, 1948–1958"; Lucille to Gloster B. Current, June 21, 1949; Clay A. Williams to Black, December 7, 1948, both in part 2, series C, containers 69–70, NAACP(LC); Logsdon, "Tureaud," tape 12. In 1949, when it increased the individual subscription to two dollars, the association's national membership fell from half a million to 248,000.

58. W. H. Samuel to New York Office, July 8, 1949, box 9, folder 26, APT.

59. Donald Jones to Thurgood Marshall, January 30, 1950; U. S. Tate to Marshall, January 31, 1950, both in part 8, series B, NAACP; Tureaud to Jones, box 9, folder 29, APT; Jesse N. Stone Jr., interviewed by Adam Fairclough, April 3, 1991, pp. 5–6.

60. Tureaud to Johnson, January 18, 23, 25, 1950; Johnson to W. B. McMillan, January 30, 1950; Johnson to Tureaud, January 19, 1950; Johnson to Marshall, January 24, 1950, all in box 10, folders 1–2, APT; Tate to Marshall, January 31, 1950, part 8, series B, NAACP.

61. Johnson to Tureaud, September 14, 1950, box 10, folder 9; Meeting of the NAACP and LEA, minutes, August 20, 1950; LSC Executive Board, minutes, December 9, 1951, box 20, folder 3, all in APT; Southwest Region *Newsletter,* July 1, 1951, box 15, folder 29, APT. The Prince Hall Masons had recently pledged $20,000 a year to the NAACP Legal Defense Fund.

62. Director to William F. Tompkins, November 2, 1955, FBI file 105-38567-14; Edwin Gaskell to Thelma Babbit, "Advisory Committee Chairman's Report, Baton Rouge Employment on Merit Program," December 9, 1955; Eugene G. Sutherland, "Progress Report," December 22, 1955, both in AFSC.

63. Muller, "Orleans Parish School Board," pp. 44–47; Orleans Parish school board, minutes, December 6, 22, 1955, folder 189, NAACP(NO); Julian B. Feibelman, *The Making of a Rabbi* (New York: Vantage Press, 1980), pp. 448–49.

64. Neil R. McMillen, *The Citizens Council* (Urbana: University of Illinois Press, 1971), pp. 62–65; *Times-Picayune*, April 10, 20, 1955; *New Orleans Item*, March 1, 1956; SAC, New Orleans, to Director, July 6, 1955, FBI file 105-38567; SAC to Director, November 17, 1955, file 105-38567-16; Rainach to Paul G. Borron Sr., November 26, 1955, Rainach Papers; Jeansonne, *Leander Perez*, p. 236.

65. Stowe, "William Rainach," pp. 49–51; *Richmond Times-Dispatch*, May 7, 1955; *Times-Picayune*, May 7, 22, 24, 26, 1955; Rainach to Sybil Huckaby, June 15, 1955, Rainach Papers.

66. Rainach to Morrison, September 2; G. E. Barham to Rainach, September 6, 1955; Rainach to Paul G. Borron, September 24, 1955, all in Rainach Papers; *Times-Picayune*, December 11, 1955; Hunter O'Dell, "The Political Scene in Louisiana," *Political Affairs*, August 1956, pp. 13–23; John H. Fenton, "The Negro Voter in Louisiana," *Journal of Negro Education* 26 (Summer 1957): 325–26; Howard, *Political Tendencies in Louisiana*, pp. 288–90; Dave McGuire to Alex George, March 30, 1956, McGuire Papers; *Louisiana Weekly*, January 28, 1956.

67. W. Scott Wilkinson to Rainach, June 13, 1955; Rainach to Wade O. Martin, April 18, 1955; Paul G. Borron to Rainach, November 21, 1955; Rainach to Borron, November 26, 1955, all in Rainach Papers.

68. Wilkinson to Rainach, June 13, 1955; Rainach to Members, JLC, June 11, 1955, Rainach Papers; Rainach to Kennon, June 11, 1955; Kennon to Rainach, June 13, 1955, both in Kennon Papers; Perez to Rainach, June 28, 1955; Rainach to Fred S. LeBlanc, July 10, 1955; Perez to Duncan Kemp, August 16, 1955, all in Rainach Papers; *Louisiana Weekly*, September 10, 1955. The plaintiffs in the NAACP suit were Dr. William R. Adams and C. C. Dejoie Jr.

69. Byrd to Marshall, "Intimidation of Plaintiffs in Louisiana," August 23, 1955, box 10, folder 26, APT.

70. William Rainach, notes of meetings, "$100,000 Segregation Suit, etc.," November 3, 1955; "Action against the NAACP by State of Louisiana for violation of Louisiana laws," November 29, 1955, Rainach Papers; Stowe, "William Rainach," pp. 53–54.

71. Stowe, "William Rainach," pp. 80–81; Association of Citizens Councils of Louisiana, Articles of Incorporation, January 27, 1956, in New Orleans report, April 30, 1956, FBI file 105-44536.

CHAPTER 8: *Counterattack*

1. Combre to Gloster B. Current, April 29, 1956, part 3, series C, box 55, NAACP(LC).

2. Clarence A. Laws to Branch Presidents, March 22, 1956; Arthur J. Chapital to Allen K. Chalmers, March 28, April 4, 1956; Audrey C. Robertson to Chapital, February 5, 1956, all in folder 68, NAACP(NO); Logsdon, "Tureaud," tape 12.

3. A. P. Tureaud and Robert L. Carter, "Defendants' Answer"; "On Rule for Preliminary Injunction," March 29, 1956, transcript of hearings; J. Coleman Lindsey, "Writ of Injunction," March 29, 1956; April 24, 1956; J. Skelly Wright, "On Application for Injunction," April 4, 1956, all in boxes 67 and 68, APT; *Louisiana Weekly*, March 10, April 7, 28, 1956. Some organizations had, in fact, filed membership lists in recent years. In 1942, for example, the Louisiana League for the Preservation of Constitutional Rights had done so (Fontaine Martin Jr. to Secretary of State, January 3, 1942, box 5, folder 1, Lee Papers). On April 4 Judge Skelly Wright declined to dissolve

Lindsey's injuction even though the state court had acted beyond its jurisdiction. His reasoning was extraordinary. "That court has already failed to recognize the removal of this matter to this court. There is no reason to believe it would be more apt to recognize the dissolution of its injunction by this court." In other words, as Lindsey had already ignored him once, he would only do so again.

4. Stowe, "William Rainach," pp. 109–10; *Birmingham News,* May 23, 1956; *Atlanta Journal,* May 27, 1956; Havard, *The Government of Louisiana,* p. 30.

5. Kenneth N. Vines, "A Louisiana Parish: Wholesale Purge," in Margaret Price, ed., *The Negro and the Ballot in the South* (Atlanta: Southern Regional Council, 1959), pp. 38–40; Rainach to Walter M. Hester, December 5, 1955, Rainach Papers.

6. *Monroe News-Star,* March 5, 1956; Vines, pp. 40–41; "Supplemental Statement by Assistant Attorney General Warren Olney III," October 10, 1956, in House, Subcommittee on Constitutional Rights of the Committee of the Judiciary, *Hearings: Civil Rights-1957,* 85th Cong., 1st sess., pp. 237–39; Commission on Civil Rights, *Hearings Held in New Orleans, Louisiana 1960–61,* 1:80–85; *Louisiana Weekly,* May 19, 1956.

7. Haynes to John G. Lewis, May 2, 1956, box 2, folder 10; Byrd, Activity Report, April 1956, box 4, folder 3, both in Byrd Papers.

8. *Times-Picayune,* January 11, 1956; Joseph F. Rummel, "The Morality of Racial Segregation," February 11, 1956, part 3, series A, box 102, NAACP(LC); Fichter, *One-Man Research,* pp. 84–85.

9. Clarence A. Laws to Archbishop Rummel, February 23, 1956, box 20, folder 2, Twomey Papers.

10. Cook, *Segregationists,* pp. 235–39; Rummel to Emile Wagner, March 19, 28, 1956; Jackson G. Ricau to Rummel, April 12, 1956; Rummel to Ricau, April 14, 23, 1956, all in Twomey Papers; *New Orleans States,* March 21, 1956; Jackson Ricau, "The Tragic Truth about the Catholic Race-Mixing Program in New Orleans," July 25, 1962, in reel 27, Right-Wing Collection of the University of Iowa Libraries (microfilm).

11. *Times-Picayune,* May 25, 1956; Convention of Delegates Organizing the Citizens Councils of America, minutes, April 7, 1956, box 5, Rainach Papers; Twomey to Rev. David Cantwell, May 29, 1956, box 20, folder 5, Twomey Papers.

12. Feibelman, *Making of a Rabbi,* pp. 451–52; *Times-Picayune,* March 22, 1956.

13. Fichter, *One-Man Research,* pp. 84–96; Juliette Joray to Perez, February 24, 1956, Perez Papers; *Times-Picayune,* June 11, 1956; *New Orleans States,* June 14, 15, 1956.

14. Senate Subcommittee to Investigate the Administration of the Internal Security Act of the Committee of the Judiciary, *Scope of Soviet Activity in the United States,* 84th Cong., 2d sess, parts 11, 12, 13; *Times-Picayune,* March 20, 28, 29, 31; April 4, 5, 6, 7, 9, 12, 1956; February 5, 6, 7, 8, 9, 23; March 26; April 4, 1957; Haas, *Morrison,* p. 213. For evidence of Banister's mental instability, see Haas, p. 216. One of the witnesses lost her job as assistant librarian at Isidore Newman school, two others were fired from WDSU, the "liberal" television station owned by the Stern family, five faced charges of criminal anarchy and subversion, and one received a three-month jail sentence for contempt of Congress. Isidore Newman is a prestigious and expensive private school in uptown New Orleans.

15. Fichter, *One-Man Research,* p. 91.

16. Ibid., pp. 101–2; Fichter to David F. Freeman, June 29, 1956; Fichter to Rummel, July 26, 1956; Gladys Williams to Fichter, June (?), 1956; Fichter to Williams, June 30, 1956, all in box 46, folder 7, Joseph H. Fichter Papers, Loyola University.

17. Cook, *Segregationists,* pp. 241–42; "Parents! Protect Your Children," Citizens Council advertisement, in *Times-Picayune,* September 7, 1956; Rummel, "Integration in the Catholic Schools," July 31, 1956; Twomey to Most Rev. Peter Comisius Van

Lierde, December 21, 1957, April 23, 1958, box 20, folders 5, 9, and 10, Twomey Papers.

18. McMillen, *Citizens' Council,* p. 67.

19. Nelson C. Jackson to Lester B. Granger, "Field Visit to New Orleans, April 25–May 2, 1956," box 3, series 1; Jackson to Granger, "The Current Southern Scene," May 13, 1957, box 4, series 1; Helen Mervis to Granger, April 30, 1957, box 22, series 2; "Confidential Report on the National Urban League Leadership Conference on Southern Problems," December 9–10, 1957, series 1, box 4, all in part 1, NUL; New Orleans Urban League, condensed minutes, May 29, June 2, 1956, Hubert Papers.

20. McCarrick, "Louisiana's Official Resistance," pp. 47–57; Charles A. Reynard, "Legislation Affecting Segregation," *Louisiana Law Review* 17 (1956–57): 101–22.

21. Belden opinion poll, in Benjamin Muse, "Confidential Memorandum: Lester Kabacoff – Judge J. Skelly Wright, Nov. 2–6, 1959," November 16, 1959, series 1, folder 1835, SRC.

22. McCarrick, "Louisiana's Official Resistance," p. 46; *Louisiana Weekly,* June 9, 1956; O'Dell, "The Political Scene in Louisiana," p. 20. The "right-to-work," issue might also have played a part in their defeat; part of the Morrison ticket, and hence saddled with Morrison's endorsement of "right-to-work," Bruns and Engert had been opposed by organized labor, which backed Earl Long's ticket.

23. Vines, "A Louisiana Parish: Wholesale Purge," p. 39; *Louisiana Weekly,* May 26, 1956; "Statement of Billye L. Adams," October 10, 1962, in Plaintiff's Trial Brief, *U.S.* v. *Louisiana;* "Statement of Albin P. Lassiter," April 27, 1961, Civil Rights Commission, *Hearings in New Orleans,* 2:745–46.

24. Stowe, "William Rainach" pp. 58–59; *Times-Picayune,* June 2, 1956; Logsdon, "Tureaud," tape 15; Kurtz and Peoples, *Earl K. Long,* pp. 184–86. The bill Long vetoed required couples to produce birth certificates in order to obtain a marriage license.

25. Commission on Civil Rights, *With Liberty and Justice for All* (Washington, D.C.: GPO, 1959), pp. 76–77; *1961 Report, vol. 1: Voting,* p. 61 (quotation); Plaintiff's Trial Brief, *U.S.* v. *Louisiana,* pp. 17–21, and Appendix A, table D; *Minden Herald,* July 5, 1956.

26. Stowe, "William Rainach," pp. 48, 116–17; *Richmond Times-Dispatch,* November 15, 1956; Reynard, "Legislation Affecting Segregation," p. 114; *Nashville Banner,* December 16, 1956.

27. Clarence A. Laws to Wilkins, May 25, 1956, box 3-A-277, NAACP(LC); Rogers, "Humanity and Desire," p. 136; Thompson, *Negro Leadership Class,* p. 104; Albert Dent, Stephens interview.

28. Doretha A. Combre to Gloster Current, April 29, 1956; Current to Roy Wilkins, July 24, 1956, box 1-C-55; Arthur J. Chapital to Roy Wilkins, August 3, 1956, part 3, series A, box 277; Wilkins to Current, June 18, 1956, box 3-C-262, all in NAACP(LC); New Orleans Improvement League, minutes, June 18, 21, 28, July 5, 1956, folder 68, NAACP(NO); *Louisiana Weekly,* July 7, 1956.

29. *Times-Picayune,* November 27, December 13, 1956; *Louisiana Weekly,* December 1, 1956; Wilkins to Branch Officers, November 30, 1956; Executive Board meeting, minutes, December 12, 1956, folders 68 and 181, NAACP(NO).

30. *Times-Picayune,* December 20, 1956; *Louisiana Weekly,* December 22, 1956; Wilkins to A. J. Chapital, December 14, 1956; Jack P. F. Gremillion to Chapital, December 18, 1956, folders 68 and 125, NAACP(NO).

31. John G. Lewis to Wilkins, December 18, 1956; Carter to Tureaud and Laws, December 26, 1956, both in box 67, folder 17, APT. Lewis suggested filing the names

of only those members who agreed to renew their membership in 1957, but Carter insisted that only a list of *all* current members would satisfy the law; anybody unwilling to have his name on the list would have to resign.

32. New Orleans branch membership list, December 31, 1956, folder 125; Clarence Laws to Branch Members, January 3, 1957, folder 68, both in NAACP(NO); Robert Carter to Chapital, January 4, 1957, box 10, folder 29; C. W. Anderson to Combre, December 19, 1956, box 68, folder 10, APT.

33. "Affidavit of Gloster B. Current," November 12, 1959; "Affidavit of Clarence A. Laws," November 12, 1959; "Affidavit of Arthur J. Chapital, Sr.," November 13, 1959, all in box 68, folder 12, APT; Lucille Black, "Membership in Louisiana, 1948–1958," box 3-C-55, NAACP(LC).

34. Laws to Current, July 25, 1957, box 3-C-262; Tureaud to Combre, September 13, 1957; Combre to Laws, September 11, 1957; Combre to Wilkins, September 15, 1957, box 3-A-277, NAACP(LC); Chapital to Wilkins, September 4, 1957; Combre to Tureaud, September 11, 1957; Wilkins to Branch Officers, September 24, 1957, folders 69 and 129, NAACP(NO).

35. Jack P. F. Gremillion to Rainach, November 14, 1956; October 15, 1958; Flournoy to Rainach, January 9, 1958; Flournoy to Alexander Lee, January 9, 1958; Rainach to Morgan Murphy, January 28, 1958, all in Rainach Papers; "Affidavit of Frank Davis," November 10, 1959, in box 68, folder 12, APT.

36. Clarence Laws to Gloster Current, March 21, 1958, box 3-C-262, NAACP(LC); H. W. Belton to Doretha Combre, March 17, 1958, box 68, folder 10; "Affidavit of R. L. Williams," November 10, 1959; "Affidavit of Joseph N. Blankenship," November 10, 1959, box 68, folder 12, APT; Burton, *Black Side of Shreveport,* p. 104.

37. Adam Fairclough, *To Redeem the Soul of America: The Southern Christian Leadership Conference and Martin Luther King, Jr.* (Athens: University of Georgia Press, 1987), pp. 32–34, 42–43.

38. Rogers, "Humanity and Desire," pp. 61–63.

39. *Times-Picayune,* March 18, 1956; *Louisiana Weekly,* March 24, 1956.

40. Dave McGuire to Col. Alex George, March 30, 1956, McGuire Papers; Gottlieb, "The Negro and the Church," p. 118; *Times-Picayune,* December 1, 1956.

41. *Times-Picayune,* January 10, 21, 1957; *New Orleans States,* May 15, 1958; *Louisiana Weekly,* May 31, 1958; Tureaud to Robert Carter, January 18, 1957; J. Skelly Wright, Minute Entry, May 15, 1957; Judgment, May 24, 1957; Minute Entry, May 30, 1958, all in box 49, folders 1–7, APT; *Morrison v. Davis,* 252 F. 2d 102 (1958); "Leadership Study: Dr. Ernest Cherrie" [1959], box 2, folder 11, Hubert Papers.

42. *Charleston News and Courier,* June 1, 1958; *Montgomery Advertiser,* June 1, 1958; *Louisiana Weekly,* July 19, 1958; Sidney L. Ferry to Rainach, June 1, 1958, box 6, Rainach Papers; *St. Petersburg Times,* June 27, 1958.

43. *Shreveport Journal,* June 15, 1957; Burton, *Black Side of Shreveport,* p. 95.

44. James Gardner, interviewed by Hubert Humphreys, June 14 and October 11, 1977, LSUS; *Shreveport Journal,* June 17, 1957; Complaint, *Simpkins v. Gardner,* December 14, 1957, in box 27, folder 30, APT.

45. United Christian Movement, news release [July 1958], box 27, folder 28, APT; *Shreveport Sun,* July 17, 1958; Burton, *Black Side of Shreveport,* p. 96.

46. *Shreveport Journal,* July 21, 1958; *Shreveport Times,* July 25, 1958; Statement of Princella Bender, July 25, 1958, box 28, folder 4, APT.

47. Provizer, "The Judicial Evolution of Ben Dawkins, Jr.," p. 82.

48. Transcript of Proceedings, August 29, 1958, *Simpkins v. Gardner,* box 28, folder 1, APT.

49. Simpkins to Tureaud, October 9, 27, 1958, July 5, 1959; "Shreveport Trolley Reports," November 8, 1958; Jesse N. Stone to Tureaud, February 19, July 13, 1959, box 27, folders 28–29; Statement of Dorothy Simpkins, n.d., box 28, folder 4, all in APT; Burton, *Black Side of Shreveport*, pp. 96–97.

50. "Resolution of Lake Charles Citizens Committee," August 11, 1958; Leo McDaniel to Tureaud, March 6, 1959; "Transcript of Proceedings," September 18, 1959, and "Judgment," n.d., *Brown v. Gray*, all in box 28, folders 5–8 and 12, APT.

51. *Judges of the United States* (Washington, D.C.: Government Printing Office, 1983); "political navel": Tom Sancton, quoted in A. J. Liebling, *The Earl of Louisiana: Profile of an Eccentric* (London: W. H. Allen, 1962), p. 84.

52. William Rainach to Gervaise and Rex [H. Smelser], November 24, 1955, box 2, Rainach Papers; "Southern Gentlemen" [March 1956], FBI File 105-38567-18; "Minutes of Joint Legislative Committee, Jackson, Mississippi, May 2–3, 1960," box 15, Rainach Papers.

53. *Times-Picayune*, December 29, 1956, January 4, 5, 1957; "Motion for Summary Judgment," March 14, 1960, *Jemison v. Christian*, box 31, folder 6, APT; *Jemison v. Christian*, 303 F. 2d 52 (1962); Catherine A. Barnes, *Journey from Jim Crow: The Desegregation of Southern Transit* (New York: Columbia University Press, 1983), pp. 189–91.

54. Buell, "Politics of Frustration," p. viii.

55. Tureaud to Alex Pitcher, September 20, 1957, box 29, folder 22, APT; *State v. Jemison*, December 12, 1960, 240 La. 787, 125 So. 2d 363.

56. Frank T. Read and Lucy S. McGough, *Let Them Be Judged: The Judicial Integration of the Deep South* (Metuchen, N.J.: Scarecrow Press, 1978), pp. 31, 55–57; biographical entries in *Judges of the United States*.

57. Read and McGough, *Let Them Be Judged*, 38–57; Robert F. Burk, *The Eisenhower Admonistration and Black Civil Rights* (Knoxville: University of Tennessee Press, 1984), pp. 199–200. For Wisdom's role in Republican politics, see L. Vaughan Howard and David R. Deneer, *Presidential Politics in Louisiana, 1952* (New Orleans: Tulane University Press, 1954), pp. 3–14, 41–46.

58. Read and McGough, *Let Them Be Judged*, pp. 118–23; *Bush v. Orleans Parish School Board*, 138 F. Supp. 337.

59. Read and McGough, *Let Them Be Judged*, pp. 197–201; *Times-Picayune*, February 8, April 17, 1957; *Nashville Tennesseean*, February 14, 1958; Kurtz and Peoples, *Earl K. Long*, p. 202; *Louisiana Weekly*, October 25, December 12, 1958; *Ludley v. Board of Supervisors of LSU*, 150 F. Supp. 900 (1957), 252 F. 2d 372 (1957); *New Orleans City Park Improvement Association v. Detiege*, 252 F. 2d 122 (1958), 358 U.S. 54 (1958); *Dorsey v. State Athletic Commission*, 168 F. Supp. 149 (1958).

60. J. W. Anderson, *Eisenhower, Brownell, and the Congress: The Tangled Origins of the Civil Rights Bill of 1956–1957* (University: University of Alabama Press, 1964), pp. 4–5, 34–43; Burk, *Eisenhower Administration and Black Civil Rights*, pp. 208–14.

61. Burk, *Eisenhower Administration and Black Civil Rights*, pp. 218–19; Warren Olney III, "Supplemental Statement," October 10, 1956, in House Subcommittee on Constitutional Rights, *Hearings, Civil Rights-1957*, pp. 237–40.

62. [Deleted] to A. H. Belmont, December 7, 1956; Director to Attorney General, December 11, 1956; Belmont to L. V. Boardmen, December 14, 1956, all in "Citizens Councils of Louisiana," FBI file 105-44536; *Times-Picayune*, December 6, 1956.

63. Director to SAC, New Orleans, September 25, 1956, FBI file 105-44536-18; SAC, New Orleans, to Director, December 12, 1956, file 105-44536-19; Director to SAC, New Orleans, March 7, 1957, "Southern Gentlemen," file 105-38567. The FBI

opened files on the Southern Gentlemen in July 1955; on the Citizens Council of Greater New Orleans in September 1955; and on the Association of Citizens Councils of Louisiana in February 1956.

64. *Times-Picayune,* January 24, February 7, 1957; Stowe, "William Rainach," pp. 112–15; *Reddix v. Lucky,* February 11, 1957, 148 F. Supp. 108; *Sharp v. Lucky,* January 30, 1957, 148 F. Supp. 8.

65. Warren Olney III to Hon. Emmanuel Celler, February 21, 1957, House Subcommittee on Constitutional Rights, in *Hearings, Civil Rights-1957,* pp. 240–43.

66. Samuel Lubell, "The Future of the Negro Voter in the United States," *Journal of Negro Education* 26 (Summer 1957): 416.

67. Ibid., p. 408; Howard, *Political Tendencies in Louisiana,* pp. 331–33; *Louisiana Weekly,* August 29, 1956; Anderson, *Eisenhower, Brownell, and the Congress,* pp. 137–39; Kurtz and Peoples, *Earl K. Long,* p. 199.

68. Wilkins to Branch Presidents, August 1, 1958, box 28, folder 67, NAACP(NO).

69. Joint Legislative Committee, *Subversion in Racial Unrest,* part 1, pp. 7–13; part 2, p. 206, copy in Louisiana Collection, TU; SAC, New Orleans to Director, January 31, 1956, "Leander Perez," FBI file 44–9732. On Kornfeder and Johnson, see Caute, *The Great Fear,* pp. 126–29.

70. George S. Mitchell to Albert D'Orlando, November 24, 1954; D'Orlando to Mitchell, January 4, 1955; Mitchell to D'Orlando, March 8, 1955, folder 341, series 4, SRC; House Committee on Un-American Activities, *Investigation of Communist Activities in the New Orleans Area,* Hearings, February 15, 1957 (Washington, D.C.: GPO, 1957); *Times-Picayune,* March 26, April 4, 1957; March 21, 22, 25, 1958; Badeaux to Rainach, March 25, 1957; March 8, 1958, box 3, Rainach Papers; Thompson, *Negro Leadership Class,* p. 74; Albert D'Orlando, interviewed by Kim Lacy Rogers, recording, May 16, 1979, Rogers-Stephens Collection, ARC.

71. *Times-Picayune,* March 17, 1957; *Shreveport Journal,* January 7, 1957; *Progress and Portents: NAACP Annual Report for 1958* (New York: NAACP, 1959), p. 71; Wilkins to George Shannon, March 28, 1957, part 3, series A, box 277; Clarence A. Laws to A. B. Cox, n.d.; Henry Lee Moon to Ellis A. Bryant, n.d., both in part 3, series C, box 55, NAACP(LC).

72. L.R.S. 14: 385-14: 388 (Act 1958, no. 260), in *Louisiana Revised Statutes, 1950, 1962,* Cumulative Supplement, vol. 1, pp. 341–42; Robert L. Carter to Arthur J. Chapital, September 23, 1958; Alma Valley and Chapital to Rev. A. W. Ricks, April 15, 1959, box 28, folders 69–70, NAACP(NO); "Plaintiff's Motion for Temporary Restraining Order and Preliminary Injunction," *Louisiana v. NAACP,* in box 68, folder 1, APT; Burton, *Black Side of Shreveport,* pp. 104–5; *Louisiana Weekly,* October 17, 31, 1959.

73. *Louisiana ex rel Gremillion v. NAACP,* 181 F. Supp. 37 (1960), 81 S. Ct. 1333 (1960).

74. Stowe, "William Rainach," pp. 130–34; deposition of Mary C. Flournoy, October 8, 1962, in Plaintiff's Trial Brief, *U.S. v. Louisiana,* Appendix B; Flournoy to Rainach, January 19, 1959, box 6, Rainach Papers. Between 1956 and 1960 black registration in Winn Parish declined from 1,430 to 1,096; figures in Margaret Price, *The Negro and the Ballot in the South* (Atlanta: Southern Regional Council, 1959), p. 71; 1961 Commission on Civil Rights, *1961 Report,* vol. 1: *Voting,* pp. 268–69.

75. Plaintiff's Trial Brief, *U.S. v. Louisiana,* pp. 37–39, and "Statement of Charles S. Kilbourne," in Appendix B.

76. M. M. Coleman and J. A. Philips to Roy Wilkins, April 1, 1958, box 270, series A, part C, NAACP(LC); *Louisiana Weekly,* March 29, 1958.

77. Stowe, "William Rainach," pp. 135–39; "Minutes of First and Second Congressional Districts Conference on Uniform Enforcement of Louisiana Voter Qualification Laws," February 12, 1959, reprinted in Exhibit J, Commission on Civil Rights, *Hearings Held in New Orleans*, 2:484–90. Seven meetings took place between December 17, 1958, and February 12, 1959, all of them following the same format.

78. Commission on Civil Rights, *Hearings Held in New Orleans*, 1:327–32; C. A. Barnett, "Reasons for Judgment," April 6, 1959, *Thomas* v. *McElveen*, in ibid., 2:458–62; Rainach to Saxon Farmer, November 8, 1958, and handwritten annotation of March 2, 1959, box 6, Rainach Papers; Stowe, "William Rainach," p. 142; Clarence Laws, "Report," March 29, 1959, part 3, series C, box 62, NAACP; Bailey, Fairclough interview.

79. Kurtz and Peoples, *Earl K. Long*, p. 206; Stowe, "William Rainach," p. 129.

80. McCarrick, "Louisiana's Official Resistance," pp. 93–102; Harris Wofford, *Of Kennedys and King: Making Sense of the Sixties* (New York: Farrar, Straus and Giroux, 1980), p. 162; Commission on Civil Rights, *With Liberty and Justice for All*, pp. 76–79; Kurtz and Peoples, *Earl K. Long*, pp. 207–10; Liebling, *The Earl of Louisiana*, pp. 28–32.

81. Rainach to Rosamund Berryman, June 11, 1959, box 3, Rainach Papers.

82. *Louisiana Weekly*, July 18, 1959; Rainach to Bob Angers, July 9, 1959; Rainach to Jules Ashlock, July 11, 1959, box 3, Rainach Papers; Stowe, "William Rainach," p. 146.

83. William Bailey Jr., Fairclough interview; Wade O. Martin to Bailey, June 3, 1959; U. Simpson Tate to Tureaud, April 28, 1959; Tureaud to Tate, April 30, May 14, June 16, 1959; Tureaud to John G. Lewis, May 28, 1949; W. Wilson White to M. Hepburn Many, [June 1959], all in box 62, folder 11, APT.

84. Commission on Civil Rights, *With Liberty and Justice for All*, pp. 77–79; Donald S. Strong, *Negroes, Ballots, and Judges: National Voting Rights Legislation in the Federal Courts* (University: University of Alabama Press, 1968), pp. 4–5.

85. *U.S.* v. *McElveen*, 180 F. Supp. 10 (1960).

86. "Minutes of Meeting of State-Wide Organization," December 6, 1959; Kenneth J. Walker to Morrison, January 19, 1960; Vance Thompson to Morrison, November 5, 1959, all in 1959–60 campaign records, Morrison Papers, TU; McGuire to Morrison, November 13, 1959, McGuire Papers. Thompson insisted that Camille Gravel, a former Long ally now backing Morrison, should not venture north of Alexandria.

87. Noe-Long campaign leaflet, McGuire Papers; Glen S. Jeansonne, *Race, Religion and Politics: The Louisiana Gubernatorial Elections of 1959–60*, University of Southwestern Louisiana History Series, no. 10 (Lafayette: University of Southwestern Louisiana, 1977), pp. 28–29, 65; McGuire to Morrison, [Analysis of First Primary], December 7, 1959, McGuire Papers; Bartley and Graham, *Southern Elections*, pp. 129–30.

88. McGuire to Morrison, December 1, 1959; McGuire to Ted Maloy, [Analysis of Second Primary], January 25, 1960; Morrison, statement on result of first primary; Morrison advertisement for second primary, all in McGuire Papers; Kurtz and Peoples, *Earl K. Long*, pp. 204–5; Jeansonne, *Race, Religion and Politics*, pp. 105–12. For other analyses of this election, with particular reference to race, see Howard, *Political Tendencies in Louisiana*, pp. 339–55; William C. Havard, Rudolf Heberle and Perry H. Howard, *The Louisiana Elections of 1960* (Baton Rouge: Louisiana State University Press, 1963), pp. 42–52.

89. Keller to Morrison, December 19, 1959; Morrison to Keller, December 21, 1959, 1959–60 campaign files, Morrison Papers, TU; Albert Dent, summary of interview by John Youngblut, January 11, 1960, College Program, Reports, South Central Office, AFSC.

90. Black registration stood at 150,000; Rainach polled 143,000 votes.

91. Donald H. Wollett, "Race Relations," *Louisiana Law Review* 21 (1960–61): 86–87.

CHAPTER 9: *The New Orleans Schools Crisis*

1. Donald E. DeVore and Joseph Logsdon, *Crescent City Schools: Public Education in New Orleans, 1841–1991* (Lafayette: Center for Louisiana Studies, University of Southwestern Louisiana, 1991), pp. 236–37. In April 1960 the board asked parents if they preferred to "see the schools closed rather than integrated" or "kept open even though a small amount of integration is necessary." This postcard poll resulted in a slim majority in favor of open schools. With astonishing arrogance, however, the board discounted the 11,407 black parents who voted for open schools, heeding only the white parents, 82 percent of whom had voted for closure rather than integration. "I will abide by the wishes of the white people," explained board president Lloyd J. Rittiner, "because they are the people who support the school system and elect us."

2. Inger, *Politics and Reality*, pp. 19, 101; Mary Lee Muller, "New Orleans Public School Desegregation," *Louisiana History* 17 (Winter 1976): 75–79; *New Orleans States-Item*, August 26, 1960.

3. Robert L. Crain, ed., *The Politics of School Desegregation* (Garden City, N.Y.: Doubleday, 1969), p. 267.

4. *Times-Picayune*, August 17, 1960.

5. Paul Rilling to Mrs. Moise Cahn, August 4, 1959, January 12, 1960; Cahn to Rilling, March 21, 1960, folder 340, series 4, SRC; Save Our Schools, minutes, February 24, March 23, May 9, 1960, SOS Papers, ARC.

6. Inger, *Politics and Reality*, p. 25; C. A. Rogers to Paul Rilling, folder 341, series 4, SRC.

7. Paul Rilling to Harold Fleming, "New Orleans, No. 2," August 16, 1960; "Report of New Orleans School Project," August 30, 1960, folder 326, series 4, SRC; Crain, ed., *Politics of School Desegregation*, pp. 268–80; Inger, *Politics and Reality*, p. 28; Warren Breed, "The Emergence of Pluralistic Public Opinion in a Community Crisis," in Alvin W. Gouldner and S. M. Miller, eds., *Applied Sociology: Opportunities and Problems* (New York: Free Press, 1965), pp. 134–36.

8. Rittiner quoted in *New Orleans States-Item*, August 9, 1960; Orleans Parish school board, summary of minutes, August 14, 1960, Orleans Parish School Board files, Earl K. Long Library, University of New Orleans (collection hereinafter cited as OPSB); Paul Rilling to Harold Fleming, "New Orleans, No. 3," August 23, 1960, folder 326, series 4, SRC; Read and McGough, *Let Them Be Judged*, p. 134; *Times-Picayune*, August 18, 1960.

9. *Baton Rouge Morning Advocate*, August 26, 1960; *New Orleans States*, August 26, 27, 1960; *Times-Picayune*, August 28, 1960; Read and McGough, *Let Them Be Judged*, pp. 134–35.

10. *Times-Picayune*, August 31, 1960; *States-Item*, August 31, 1960; Jack Bass, *Unlikely Heroes* (Tuscaloosa: University of Alabama Press, 1981, 1990), pp. 132–34.

11. Robert N. Kelso, "Pupil Placement Law and How it May Be Applied," *States-Item*, September 3, 1960; "Administrative Plan Assignment of Grade One Pupils," OPSB; Byrd to Marshall, n.d., box 43, folder 26, APT; Furey quoted in Rogers, "Humanity and Desire," p. 197.

12. *States-Item*, September 13, 30, 1960; *Times-Picayune*, September 13, 1960; Rilling

to Mary Sand et al., September 13, 1960; Rilling to Harold Fleming, October 10, 1960, folder 326, series 4, SRC; Save Our Schools, minutes, September 8, 19, 1960, SOS Papers; SAC, New Orleans, to Director, September 6, 1960, "Integration of Public Schools in Orleans Parish; Racial Matters," FBI file 157-4-33-28.

13. Crain, ed., *Politics of School Desegregation,* pp. 260–61; Louisiana State Advisory Committee to the U.S. Commission on Civil Rights, *The New Orleans Schools Crisis* (Washington, D.C.: Government Printing Office, 1961), pp. 35–36; Benjamin Muse, "New Orleans Times-Picayune, November 3, 1959," November 17, 1959, series 1, folder 1835; Paul Rilling to Harold Fleming, August 8, 1960, folder 326, series 4, SRC.

14. Crain, ed., *Politics of School Desegregation,* pp. 276–77; Read and McGough, *Let Them Be Judged,* pp. 140–41; Betty Wisdom to Paul Rilling, [October 1960], folder 326, series 4, SRC.

15. Benjamin Muse, "New Orleans Chamber of Commerce," November 5–6, 1960, folder 1835, series 1, SRC.

16. *States-Item,* June 17, September 1, 1960; *Times-Picayune,* August 21, 1960; Benjamin Muse, "New Orleans, Baton Rouge, Lafayette, La., October 9–14, 1960," October 16, 1960, folder 1835, series 4, SRC; *Times-Picayune,* November 13, 1960.

17. Inger, *Politics and Reality,* pp. 42–43; *Times-Picayune,* November 1, 2, 4, 1960; *States-Item,* October 31, 1961; Betty Wisdom to Paul Rilling, October 24, 1960, folder 326, series 4, SRC. Sutherland faced three other candidates, and his supporters worried that a fragmented vote might prevent him from winning on the first ballot, for a new law required runoff elections if no school board candidate polled a majority of the votes. As things turned out, the divided opposition worked to Sutherland's advantage.

18. *Baton Rouge Morning Advocate,* November 3, 1960; *States-Item,* November 9; Crain, ed., *Politics of School Desegregation,* p. 288. The legislation passed by this and the four succeeding special sessions is conveniently summarized in Louisiana Advisory Committee, *New Orleans Schools Crisis,* Appendix 2. Appendix 1 of the same report includes a concise summary of the litigation.

19. Read and McGough, *Let Them Be Judged,* p. 139.

20. *States-Item,* August 12, 1960; *Times-Picayune,* November 11, 1960; *Baton Rouge Morning Advocate,* November 12, 1960; Rogers to Davis; Rogers to Morrison, both in Department of Justice press release, November 12, 1960.

21. *Times-Picayune,* November 13, 1960; *States-Item,* November 14, 1960; *Baton Rouge Morning Advocate,* November 14, 1960.

22. J. Skelly Wright, interviewed by Glenda Stephens, December 9, 1978, recording, Rogers-Stephens Collection, ARC; SAC, New Orleans, to Director, November 13, 1960, FBI file 157-4-33-77; Letter Head Memorandum, November 17, 1960, FBI file 157-4-33-150; *Times-Picayune,* November 15, 1960.

23. *Times-Picayune,* November 16, 17, 1960; *States-Item,* November 16, 1960.

24. *States-Item,* November 16, 18, 1960; *Baton Rouge Morning Advocate,* November 17, 1960; *Shreveport Journal,* November 18, 1960; *Times-Picayune,* November 24, 1960.

25. W. J. Weatherby, "The Conscience of New Orleans," *Manchester Guardian,* [November ? 1960], clipping in Louisiana Collection, TU.

26. Skelly Wright, Stephens interview.

27. Logsdon, "Tureaud," tape 15.

28. *States-Item,* November 16, 18, 23, December 20, 21, 1960; January 20, 23, 1961; *Times-Picayune,* November 23, December 3, 9, 19, 1960; January 24, 1961; *Shreveport*

Times, February 26, 1961; Burke Marshall to Attorney General, February 13, 1961; Department of Justice, press release, February 16, 1961, both in reel 1, part 2, Marshall Papers; Morrison to Robert F. Kennedy, February 27, 1961, folder S61-13, Morrison Papers, NOPL; Inger, *Politics and Reality,* pp. 54–55.

29. Byrd to Thurgood Marshall, December 3, 1960, box 43, folder 26, APT; Read and McGough, *Let Them Be Judged,* pp. 135, 153; "Integration in New Orleans: An Interview with James F. Redmond," *Cambridge 38,* April 1991, p. 25, in box 38, OPSB.

30. *Times-Picayune,* November 17, 1960.

31. Bill Monroe to Burke Marshall, copy of lecture to Tulane Association, April 17, 1962, reel 1, part 2, Marshall Papers; Steinbeck quoted in Inger, *Politics and Reality,* pp. 57–58; *States-Item,* November 29, 1960.

32. DeVore and Logsdon, *Cresent City Schools,* p. 250; Betty Wisdom to Paul Rilling, August 1, 1961, series 4, folder 326, SRC; Robert Coles, *Children of Crisis: A Study of Courage and Fear* (Boston: Little, Brown, 1967), pp. 74–86.

33. *Times-Picayune,* December 3, 9, 1960; *States-Item,* December 9, 1960; *Washington Post,* December 11, 1960; Paul Rilling to Harold C. Fleming, "New Orleans," December 4, 1960, series 4, folder 326, SRC; "Save Our Schools, Inc., Report by Mary Sand at Conference on Education held by U.S. Commission on Civil Rights," February 1961, SOS Papers; Harold R. Tyler to J. Edgar Hoover, December 1, 1960, FBI file 154-4-33-148.

34. *Washington Post,* December 8, 9, 1960; *States-Item,* December 9, 1960; *New York Herald-Tribune,* December 11, 1960; Harold D. Tyler to Hoover, December 1, 1960, FBI file 157-4-33-148; Betty Wisdom to Paul Rilling, n.d., December 22, 1960, series 4, folder 326, SRC; Alan Wieder, "One Who Stayed: Margaret Conner and the New Orleans School Crisis," *Louisiana History,* Spring 1985, p. 198.

35. SAC [Wade Bromwell], New Orleans, to Hoover, November 30, December 10, 1960; Al Rosen to Mr. Parsons, December 2, 7, 1960; Harold D. Tyler to Hoover, December 6, 1960; Hoover to Tyler, December 8, 1960; Bromwell to Hoover, December 10, 1960; [name deleted] to Rosen, December 13, 1960; Hoover to Bromwell, November 28, December 15, 1960, all in "Integration of Public Schools in Orleans Parish," FBI file 154-4-33.

36. *States-Item,* December 7, 1960; *Shreveport Times,* January 31, 1961; *Jackson Daily News,* February 1, 1961; Ira Mothner, "Exodus from New Orleans," *Look,* March 14, 1961, pp. 53–58; Read and McGough, *Let Them Be Judged,* pp. 146–47; Wisdom to Paul Rilling, December 22, 1960, series 3, folder 326, SRC. By March 1961 white attendance at Frantz had edged up to fourteen. In that month Morrison, apparently at the urging of Robert Kennedy, ordered the police to disperse the demonstrators around the school.

37. Read and McGough, *Let Them Be Judged,* p. 138; Inger, *Politics and Reality,* pp. 34–39; Muller, "New Orleans Public School Desegregation," pp. 87–88; *Times-Picayune,* June 18, 1993.

38. Telephone callers quoted in Rickey Dixon to Thomas Heier, November 14, 1960, folder SPR60-3, Morrison Papers, NOPL.

39. "Integration in New Orleans: An Interview with James F. Redmond," *Cambridge 38,* April 1961, p. 26, OPSB.

40. Haas, *Morrison,* pp. 257–62; *Times-Picayune,* September 1, 1960; Morrison to Mildred Bradford, September 16, 1960, folder SPR60-1; Tom Farrar to Morrison, November 14, 1960, folder SPR60-3, Morrison Papers, NOPL.

41. Morrison to Arthur J. Chapital and Ernest N. Morial, April 18, 1960, McGuire Papers; Morrison to James W. Sweeney, February 16, 1961, folder S61-12; Morrison

to George Healy et al., December 2, 1960, folder SPR60-3, Morrison Papers, NOPL; Haas, *Morrison*, p. 274. Morrison added that the Gabrielles and the Thompsons might have "attracted harassment" because "they were so prominent in the news."

42. Marion R. Henriquez to Morrison, November 29, 1960; Kurt M. Esser to Morrison, December 5, 1960, folder SPR60-2; Dave McGuire to Tommy Heier, November 14, 1960, folder SPR60-3, Morrison Papers, NOPL.

43. Nelson to Dennis Clark, November 29, 1960; "Two Southerners Speak Their Minds," transcript of discussion, [1961], box 1, folder 1, John P. Nelson Papers, ARC; Twomey to John M. Daley, December 10, 1959; Twomey to Clement McNaspy, November 23, 1960; Twomey to Charles O'Neill, December 14, 1960; Twomey to John Waldo, April 3, 1961, box 21, folders 3, 4, 8, Twomey Papers. Rummel had apparently given tentative approval for integration to begin on November 21, a week after public school integration. Emile Wagner and Leander Perez exposed the plan at the November 15 Citizens Council rally. See *Times-Picayune*, November 16, 1960; Nicholas Gorman, "Scandal of New Orleans," *Commonweal*, April 28, 1961, pp. 127–28.

44. Crain, ed., *Politics of School Desegregation*, pp. 280, 304–22; Inger, *Politics and Reality*, pp. 70–88; Betty Wisdom to Paul Rilling, October 26, 1960, series 4, folder 326, SRC.

45. Twomey to J. J. McCarthy, October 6, 1961, box 21, folder 10, Twomey Papers.

46. Inger, *Politics and Reality*, pp. 67–68, text of statement at 105. For the background of the Committee for Public Schools and the "Declaration of Principles," see Louis G. Riecke to Ivor A. Trapolin, May 2, 1960, box 1, OPSB; Gabriel M. Gelb, press release, "Citizens for Public Schools," n.d.; Betty Wisdom to Paul Rilling, August 11, 1960, series 4, folders 341 and 326, SRC; Ed Guthman to Robert Kennedy, August 14, 1960, Marshall Papers. The men behind the statement were Raburn Monroe, lawyer and uncle of WDSU news editor Bill Monroe; Charles Keller, contractor and husband of Rosa Keller; Clifford Favrot, real estate owner and prominent Jimmie Davis supporter; John Tims, publisher of the *Times-Picayune*; Richard Freeman, head of the local Coca-Cola business and brother of Rosa Keller; Darwin Fenner, chairman of the Merrill Lynch stockbroker group; A. L. Schlesinger, a lawyer; Charles Smither, an insurance salesman; and Lester Kabacoff, lawyer to Mrs. Edith Stern and the Stern Family Fund. Favrot and Fenner were considered the two most influential businessmen in New Orleans.

47. Inger, *Politics and Reality*, pp. 67–69; New Orleans Police Department, "Public Schools, No. 3," n.d.; St. John Barrett to Burke Marshall, August 11, 17, 1961, both in Marshall Papers; SAC to Hoover, August 8, 23, 24, 25, 1960, all in "Integration of Public Schools in Orleans Parish," FBI files 154-4-33-463, 474, 476, 479. The school board's agreement to admit eight additional black applicants rather than five helped persuade the NAACP to accept a postponement of the hearings.

48. SAC to Director, September 5, 6, 8, 11, 20, 29, 1961, "Integration of Public Schools in Orleans Parish," FBI files 154-4-33-481, 486, 487-89, 499, 502, 544, 553.

49. Rosen to Belmont, September 1, 1961, FBI file 154-4-33-513. Wright and Many dropped their request when the first few days of the new school year passed off peacefully.

50. *Catholic Action*, April 2, 1961.

51. Letters to Cabirac from James J. Walsh, June 22; Philip M. Hannan, August 14; Charles M. Williams, May 9, August 11; Vincent H. Harris, May 22, June 8, October 17; George E. Lynch, May 24, July 28; Patrick S. Molloy, May 13; William M. Drumm, June 27; J. L. Manning, June 14; Joseph L. Benardin, September 21, all 1961, box 1, Catholic Council on Human Relations Papers, ARC (collection hereinafter

cited as CCHR). On the council's change of strategy: Cabirac to Henican, October 18, 1961, box 3; Cabirac to William Hughes, May 14, 1962, box 1, CCHR.

52. "Report of the Southern Field Service of the National Catholic Conference on Interracial Justice," n.d., box 2; Cabirac to Henican, November 1, 1961, box 3; "Meeting of Sub-Committee of the Research Committee," minutes, November 25, 1961, box 2, CCHR.

53. Cabirac to Henican, November 29, 1961, box 3, CCHR.

54. Cabirac to Henican, October 1, 11, 1961; November 29, 1961; December 1, 1961; box 3; Cabirac to Bezou, March 9, 1962, box 1, CCHR. The council initially proposed that some transfers might take place in January 1961: by quietly transferring a few black children, it reasoned, the church could present the ultrasegregationists with a fait accompli when Rummel subsequently announced the plan for general desegregation. In this way, the council believed, the danger of legislative retaliation in the fall would be minimized.

55. Henican to Rummel, January 2, 1962, box 1; Cabirac to Henican, February 7, 1962, box 3; Cabirac to Matthew Ahmann, February 12, 1962, box 1, CCHR.

56. Cabirac to Rummel, January 23, 1962; George E. Lynch to Cabirac, February 15, 1962; Ahmann to Rummel, February 7, 1962, box 1; Cabirac to Henican, March 28, April 4, June 5, 1962, box 3; "Report of the Southern Field Service of the National Catholic Conference for Interracial Justice," n.d., box 2, CCHR.

57. Rummel to Mrs. B. J. Gaillot, March 31, 1962, box 3, CCHR; *Times-Picayune,* April 17, 1961. Ricau headed the Citizens Councils of South Louisiana, which broke away from the Perez-dominated Citizens Councils of Greater New Orleans because of the latter's anti-Semitism.

58. Alfred P. Giarrusso, "Desegregation of the Orleans Parish School System" (D.Ed. diss., University of Arkansas, 1969), pp. 115–18; Cabirac to Henican, April 26, 1962, box 3, CCHR; *Southern School News,* September 1962.

59. Benjamin Muse, "Parochial School Desegregation," April 27, 1962, series 4, folder 1835, SRC; Jeansonne, *Leander Perez,* pp. 267–70; Betty Wisdom to Paul Rilling, September 7, 1962, series 4, folder 326, SRC; *Times-Picayune,* August 31, September 1, 5, 7, 1962; August 28, 1963. For a brief but evocative description of the ethnic, racial, and religious peculiarities of Plaquemines Parish, see Etienne Barrois, "King of the River People," *Commonweal,* July 6, 1962, pp. 365–66.

60. *Morgan City Review,* September 5, 1962; *St. Mary and Franklin Banner,* September 6, 1962; Cabirac to Henican, October 19, December 7, 20, 1962, box 3, CCHR.

61. *St. Joseph Magazine,* April 1963, in scrapbook, CCHR.

62. James W. Sweeney to Msgr. Lucien J. Caillouet, April 9, 1962, box 21, folder 12, Twomey Papers; Cabirac to Henican, June 14, July 5, October 4, 1962, box 3; Henican to Cody, December 13, 1962, box 1, CCHR.

63. Rogers, "Humanity and Desire," pp. 248–49; *PAR Analysis,* October 1963, in scrapbook, CCHR; McCall, "School Desegregation in Louisiana," p. 137.

64. Morrison to Henry O. Meisel, January 29, 1961, folder S61-12, Morrison Papers, NOPL; Twomey to Donald Zewe, January 11, 1960, box 21, folder 3, Twomey Papers; Miller, *A "Capacity for Outrage,"* p. 79.

65. Rogers, "Humanity and Desire," pp. 287–94; Cheryl V. Cunningham, "The Desegregation of Tulane University" (M.A. thesis, University of New Orleans, 1982); John P. Nelson, Bass interview, pp. 16–23; Betty Wisdom to Paul Rilling, July 21, 1961, April [?] 1962, folder 32, series 4, SRC; Albert Dent, Stephens interview.

66. McCall, "School Desegregation in Louisiana," pp. 137, 164–97, 208 (quotation); Betty Wisdom to Paul Rilling, [April 1962], series 4, folder 326, SRC.

67. Adolph L. Reed, "Crisis on the Negro Campus," *Nation,* February 10, 1962, p. 113; Skelly Wright, remarks in "Amistad Symposium on Southern Civil Rights Litigation Records for the 1960s," Dillard University, December 8–9, 1978, pp. 8–9.

CHAPTER 10: *Nonviolent Direct Action, 1960–1962*

1. Robert Penn Warren, *Who Speaks for the Negro?* (New York: Random House, 1965), pp. 14–15; Melinda Bartley, "Southern University Activism, 1960–63, Revisited" (M.A. thesis, Southern University, 1973), pp. 33–34; Iris Johnson Perkins, "Felton Grandison Clark: Louisiana Educator" (Ed.D. diss., Louisiana State University, 1976), p. 71; Eugene Sutherland to Thelma Babbit, "Felton Clark," February 16, 1955; Wade Mackie to Barbara Moffett, "Felton Clark," December 16, 1969, AFSC.
2. Editorial, *Louisiana Weekly,* March 26, 1960.
3. Chronology of Southern University demonstrations, March 7–April 1, 1960, Felton G. Clark Papers, Southern University, Baton Rouge ("sit-in chronology"); *Morning-Advocate,* March 16, 1960; *Louisiana Weekly,* March 12, 1960; Lewis W. Jones, "Dillard University," September 1961, box 15, UCC. Heeding a warning from President Dent that absence from class would lead to dismissal, the Dillard students held their demonstrations between classes and their parades off campus.
4. Sit-in chronology; Major Johns to Gordon Carey, March 15, 1960; Carey to Johns, March 21, 1960, series 5, reel 20, file 42, Congress of Racial Equality Papers, microfilm (collection hereinafter cited as CORE); Felton Clark to Mrs. Davis and Mrs. Wallace and Other Members of the Southern University Family of Chicago, April 29, 1960, Clark Papers.
5. Sit-in chronology; "Recommendations from University Disciplinary Committee," n.d.; Citizens Committee for Cooperative Action, resolution, March 31, 1960, both in Clark Papers; Major Johns and Ronnie Moore, *It Happened in Baton Rouge* (New York: Congress of Racial Equality, April 1962), series 6, reel 49, file 16, CORE; Felton Clark, "Statement by the President," April 2, 1960, box 67, folder 16, APT; *Baton Rouge Morning Advocate,* March 29, 30, 31, April 2, 3, 1960; Wade Mackie, "Final Report of Sit-In Effects," May 9, 1960, AFSC.
6. McCain to James R. Robinson, April 3, 1960, series 5, reel 36, file 258, CORE; Mackie, "Report on Sit-Ins," April 11, 1960, AFSC.
7. Perkins, "Felton Grandison Clark," p. 72; Clark to Davis and Wallace, April 29, 1960, Clark Papers.
8. McCain, Report, March 29–April 9, 1960, CORE; Brice F. Taylor to Clark, n.d., Clark Papers.
9. WDSU editorial, April 6, 1960, box 28, folder 70, NAACP(NO); *Baton Rouge Morning Advocate,* March 31, 1960; Wollett, "Race Relations," pp. 93–101; McGuire to Morrison, March 17, 1960, McGuire Papers.
10. Rogers, "Humanity and Desire," pp. 177–82; Rogers, "'You Came Away with Some Courage:' Three Lives in the Civil Rights Movement," *Mid-America* 71 (October 1989): 180–81; Oretha Castle Haley, Rogers interview; Rudy Lombard, interviewed by Rogers, May 9, 1979, recordings, Rogers-Stephens Collection; *Louisiana Weekly,* March 26, June 4, 1960; McCain to James R. Robinson, April 16, 1960; McCain, Report, "New Orleans, March 11–May 1, 1960," series 5, reel 36, file 258; Marvin Robinson to James Robinson, July 29, 1960, series 5, reel 37, file 265, CORE.
11. Clarence Laws to Doretha A. Combre, "1960 Membership," March 11,

1961; Edward Stewart to Arthur Chapital, November 14, 1960, folders 128, 70, NAACP(NO).

12. Committee on Branch Participation in Sit-Ins, Report, n.d., folder 52; Chapital to Tureaud, October 19, 1960; Tureaud to Chapital, February 1, 1960, folder 70, all in NAACP(NO); Tureaud quoted in Thompson, *Negro Leadership Class,* p. 39; Lewis W. Jones, "Dillard University," UCC.

13. Meier and Rudwick, *CORE,* pp. 112–13; Hugh T. Murray Jr., "The Struggle for Civil Rights in New Orleans in 1960: Reflections and Recollections," *Journal of Ethnic Studies* 6 (Spring 1978): 37–41.

14. McGuire to Morrison, with annotation by Morrison, September 7, 1960, McGuire Papers; John T. Toler to New Orleans Branch NAACP, October 3, 1960; Chapital to Roy Wilkins, November 9, 1962, folders 70, 73, NAACP(NO).

15. McCain, Report, September 8–25, 1960, series 5, reel 36, file 258; McCain to Marvin Rich, September 28, 1960; Rudy Lombard to Rich, n.d., reel 20, file 44, all in CORE; *Louisiana Weekly,* September 17, 24, 1960; Morrison, press release, September 12, 1960, folder S61-8, Morrison (NOPL).

16. Carey to Lombard, October 12, 1960, series 5, reel 20, file 44, CORE.

17. McCain, Report, September 26–October 13, 1960, series 5, reel 36, file 258, CORE; *Louisiana Weekly,* November 11, December 17, 1960.

18. Thomas Gaither, Field Report, November 11–28, 1960, series 4, file 44, CORE; Hugh T. Murray Jr., "Autobiography," unpublished ms., TU, pp. 33, 74–75.

19. Raphael Cassimere Jr., interviewed by Kim Lacy Rogers, May 2, 1979, recording, ARC; Lester Granger, "Report on Visit to New Orleans," December 15, 1960, series 1, box 112, NUL.

20. J. Harvey Kerns, "Report of Community Activities," n.d., part 1, series 1, box 112; Kerns to Granger, February 7, 1961, part 2, series 1, box 73, NUL; Liebling, *The Earl of Louisiana,* p. 246; *LEA Journal,* September–October 1960, p. 2; Canon John Collins to Roy Wilkins, September 17, 1960; Shad Polier to Wilkins, November 27, 1960; Clarence Mitchell to Wilkins, December 15, 1960, box 3-A-277, NAACP(LC); Newman et al., *Protest, Politics, and Prosperity,* p. 262.

21. Thompson, *Negro Leadership Class,* pp. 170–71; organizational documents of the CCGNO, box 8, folder 2, Hubert Papers; *Louisiana Weekly,* December 24, 1960, February 11, 25, 1961.

22. "New Orleans: Summary of Activities, 1961," series 5, folder 44, CORE; *Louisiana Weekly,* March 11, 18, 1961; "Proposals for the Execution of Boycott against NOPSI," n.d.; Avery C. Alexander, Consumers League of Greater New Orleans to Members, August 7, 1961, both in box 28, folder 72, NAACP(NO).

23. Meier and Rudwick, *CORE,* p. 144; Rogers, "Humanity and Desire," pp. 267–70.

24. Connie Bradford, "Report of New Orleans Action," April 16, 1961, series 5, folder 44, CORE; Rogers, "'You Came Away With Some Courage,'" p. 188.

25. *Garner* v. *Louisiana,* 368 U.S. 157 (1961). A. P. Tureaud represented the plaintiffs.

26. *State* v. *Smith,* 146 So. 2d 152 (1962); *Lombard* v. *Louisiana,* 373 U.S. 267 (1963); Nils R. Douglas, "Talk to Annual Law Institute, Southern University, April 30–May 2, 1964," box 1, folder 8, Nils R. Douglas Papers, ARC. In 1941, after the police shot a black prisoner in suspicious circumstances, Cocke privately encouraged the NAACP to ask for the body to be exhumed for forensic examination (John E. Rousseau, Fairclough interview).

27. Haas, *Morrison,* pp. 285–88. Morrison campaigned for an amendment that would have lifted the two-term restriction that he himself had inserted into the

city charter. In April 1961, however, the overwhelmingly white electorate narrowly defeated it.

28. Charles McCord, "The Anatomy of a Registration Drive: A Success Story from New Orleans," *Interracial Review,* May 1962, pp. 1–11; *Louisiana Weekly,* December 16, 1961, January 13, 1962; Plaintiff's Trial Brief, *U.S. v. Louisiana.*

29. Inger, *Politics and Reality,* pp. 66–70, 89; Council for a Better Louisiana, *Report of Organization* (New Orleans, 1962), copy in vertical file, Louisiana Collection, TU.

30. Chapital to Wilkins, November 9, 1962, box 28, folder 73, NAACP(NO); *Louisiana Weekly,* January 13, 1962; Betty Wisdom to Paul Rilling, December 13, 1961, series 4, folder 326, SRC.

31. Wilkins to Chapital, January 5, 15, 1962; Chapital to Wilkins, January 8, 1962, folder 72, NAACP(NO).

32. Minutes of special meeting of Executive Committee, February 26, 1962; Raphael Cassimere and Dorothy Mouton to Wilkins, November 7, 1962; Chapital to Wilkins, November 9, 1962; Current to Chapital, December 11, 1962, folder 73, NAACP(NO); Current to Wilkins, May 21, 1962; Clarence Laws to Current, May 22, 1962; June 19, 1962, folder 3-C-55, NAACP(LC). For Wilkins's disdain for nonviolent direct action, see James Peck to Wilkins, January 26, 1958, reel 9; Stanley D. Levison to Wilkins, [September-October 1958], reel 9, both in Bayard Rustin Papers (microfilm).

33. Rogers, "Humanity and Desire," pp. 310–31; R. G. Graves to Mayor Morrison, April 27, 1961, folder S61-12, Morrison Papers (NOPL); statements of Joyce Taylor, Ruthie Wells, and George Raymond Jr., January 7, 1962, folder 72, NAACP(NO); Marvin Robinson to Fredericka Teer, May 22, 1962, series 5, folder 265; Lolis Elie to Richard Haley, June 6, 1962, series 5, folder 44, both in CORE; Elie to Haley, July 18, 1962, part 3, series A, CORE, Scholarship, Educational and Defense Fund (microfilm; sub-collection hereinafter cited as SEDFRE).

34. John Minor Wisdom, interviewed by Jack Bass, May 22, 1979, pp. 12–13, Bass Collection.

35. Bill Monroe, lecture to Tulane Association, enclosed in Monroe to Burke Marshall, April 17, 1962, reel 1, Marshall Papers; Numan V. Bartley, *The Rise of Massive Resistance* (Baton Rouge: Louisiana State University Press, 1969) pp. 313–14; Inger, *Politics and Reality,* p. 85.

36. J. J. McCarthy to Louis Twomey, October 3, 1961, box 21, folder 10, Twomey Papers.

37. McMillen, *Citizens Councils,* pp. 71–72.

38. John R. Martzell, interviewed by Adam Fairclough, October 1, 1987, p. 24.

39. James Gardner, Humphreys interview, pp. 20–23.

40. Martzell, Fairclough interview, p. 24; *Times-Picayune,* May 29, 1990; Harvey R. H. Britton, Fairclough interview.

41. J. R. Yungblut, interviews with Rev. Jolly Harper and Dean Vogel, November 11, 1959, College Program Reports, South Central Regional Office, AFSC; J. J. McCarthy to Louis Twomey, November 24, 1961, box 21, folder 10, Twomey Papers.

42. J. J. McCarthy to Louis Twomey, October 3, November 11, 1961; Ethel Daniell to Twomey, October 28, December 1, 1961; Burke Marshall to Twomey, November 28, 1961, all in box 21, folder 10, Twomey Papers; *Shreveport Times,* July 24, 1961; Mrs J. R. Daniell, "Boycott of J. R. Daniell, Shreveport, Louisiana," n.d., in reel 1, Marshall Papers.

43. Tureaud to Jesse N. Stone, July 22, 1959, box 27, folder 29; Tureaud to Constance Baker Motley, November 11, 1959, box 53, folder 1; Alton L. Curtis to Tureaud, January 26, 1962, box 64, folder 6, all in APT; L. C. Bates to Robert L. Carter, Febru-

ary 16, 1962, box 3-C-55, NAACP(LC). Tureaud delayed pressing the bus integration suit in 1959–60 so as not to embarrass Chep Morrison in his campaign for governor. In January 1962 Dawkins dismissed the suit for lack of prosecution. The Shreveport trade school was enjoined to admit blacks in 1960, but it defied the ruling and continued to exclude them.

44. Ella J. Baker to John L. Tilley, box 32, folder 8, Southern Christian Leadership Conference Papers, Library and Archives, Martin Luther King, Jr., Center for Non-violent Social Change, Atlanta (collection hereinafter cited as SCLC); "Chronology of Some Events at Shreveport," Committee of Inquiry into the Administration of Justice in the Freedom Struggle, May 25–27, 1962, series 5, folder 3, CORE.

45. Meier and Rudwick, *CORE,* p. 166; David Dennis to Cyril Simon, November 10, 1961; Dennis to Carey, November 11, 1961, both in series 5, folder 245, CORE; Burke Marshall to Robert F. Kennedy, May 23, 1962, reel 1, Marshall Papers; *U.S.* v. *City of Shreveport,* 210 F. Supp. 708 (1962); "Minutes of the SCLC Field Secretaries Meeting, December 19–21, 1962," box 138, folder 11, SCLC. In *Taylor* v. *Louisiana,* 370 U.S. 154 (1962), the Supreme Court set aside the convictions of six people who had been arrested for breach of the peace while attempting to integrate the Trailways bus station.

46. Stone, Fairclough interview; "Chronology of Some Events."

47. Martin Luther King Jr. [Wyatt Walker], "New Harassment: The Lunacy Test," June 23, 1962, box 27, folder 10; Andrew Young to Jack Minnis, February 26, 1963, box 138, folder 2, both in SCLC; Joseph Russell to CORE, June 9, 1962; March 4, 1963, series 5, folder 352, CORE.

48. Meier and Rudwick, *CORE,* pp. 166–67; Dave Dennis to Marvin Rich, November 25, 26, 1961; Weldon Rougeau to Gordon Carey, December 4, 1961, series 5, folder 42; Dennis to Carey, November 25, 1961, folder 245, CORE; W. M. Pass to Mr. Kraft, November 30, 1961, Clark Papers.

49. The best summary of these events is in *Cox* v. *Louisiana,* 379 U.S. 537 (1965). See also testimony of Ronnie Moore, Weldon Rougeau, and B. Elton Cox to Committee of Inquiry, series 5, folder 2, CORE.

50. Johns and Moore, *It Happened in Baton Rouge,* n.p., series 6, folder 16; State Board of Education, directive, December 16, 1961, series 5, folder 42; Adolph L. Reed to Felton G. Clark, January 24, 1962, series 5, folder 349, all in CORE; W. M. Pass to Kraft, January 15, 1962, Clark Papers; D'Army Bailey to Julian Bond, August 4, 1962, folder A-4-40, SNCC Papers, Martin Luther King, Jr. Center for Nonviolent Social Change, Atlanta; Reed, "Crisis on the Negro Campus," pp. 111–13; Woodward quoted in Warren, *Who Speaks for the Negro?* pp. 15–16; American Association of University Professors, "Academic Freedom and Tenure: Late Notice Cases, 1961 and 1962," pp. 5–6, series 1, folder 1, CORE.

51. *State* v. *Cox,* 245 La. 303, 158 So. 2d 172.

52. "The Speech of Rev. B. Elton Cox," *Louisiana* v. *Cox,* reel 17, Lawyers Constitutional Defense Committee Files (microfilm, collection hereinafter cited as LCDC); *State* v. *Cox,* 243 La. 917, 148 So. 2d 608 (1962); James Farmer to Friends of CORE, February 6, 1963, series 5, folder 42, CORE.

53. Collins, Douglas, and Elie to Rich, January 25, 1963, *Louisiana* v. *Cox,* reel 17, LCDC; Benjamin E. Smith to James Farmer, *Clemmons* v. *CORE,* reel 27, LCDC; Johnnie Jones to Elie, March 1, 1962, series 5, folder 4; Dave Dennis to James Farmer, May 1, 1963, folder 124, CORE; Meier and Rudwick, *CORE,* pp. 168–69; Leon Friedman, ed., *Southern Justice* (New York: Pantheon, 1965), pp. 116–17; *Garrison* v. *Louisiana,* 379 U.S. 64 (1964); *Cox* v. *Louisiana,* 348 F. 2d 750; 379 U.S. 537, 559 (1965).

54. *Clemmons* v. *CORE*, 201 F. Supp. 737 (1962); *CORE* v. *Clemmons*, 323 F. 2d 54 (1963); Rachlin to Roosevelt, April 16, 1962; series 5, folder 2; Rachlin to Patricia Ann Tate, September 27, 1962, series 5, folder 42, CORE. Cox was by no means the only victim of the legal crackdown in Baton Rouge. Others included Ronnie Moore, convicted for disturbing the peace and criminal anarchy, later rearrested along with Patricia Ann Tate on the charge of defaming the grand jury that indicted Cox; SNCC field secretary Dion Diamond, arrested on the Southern campus for vagrancy and then charged with criminal anarchy; SNCC chairman Charles McDew, arrested for criminal anarchy while trying to visit Diamond in jail; and SNCC field secretary Robert Zellner, who was accompanying McDew.

55. "Articles of Incorporation, Association of Citizens Councils of Louisiana," January 27, 1956, *Louisiana* v. *Cox*, reel 17, LCDC; Victor Navasky, *Kennedy Justice* (New York: Atheneum, 1977), p. 246.

56. Winfield Pate to Kennedy, January 18, 1962, folder HU2/ST13, John F. Kennedy Papers, in Steven F. Lawson, ed., "Civil Rights During the Kennedy Admnistration," part 1," microfilm; Marshall to St. John Barrett, February 7, 1962, reel 1, Marshall Papers; Wofford, *Of Kennedys and Kings*, pp. 164–65.

57. Meier and Rudwick, *CORE*, p. 169; Fairclough, *To Redeem the Soul of America*, p. 108. In Alabama, a state court enjoined CORE from operating anywhere in the state.

58. Meier and Rudwick, *CORE*, pp. 173–74.

59. Mackie to Jean Fairfax, "Current Developments in School Desegregation in Baton Rouge," March 18, 1962, AFSC; McCain to Teer, May 10, 1962, series 5, folder 258, CORE; Ronnie Moore to McCain, July 30, September 4, 1962, series F, folder 134, addendum, CORE.

60. Rogers, "Humanity and Desire," pp. 278–83; Murray, "Autobiography," pp. 106–7; Carlene T. Smith to McCain, February 22, 1962; McCain to New Orleans CORE, March 13, 1962, both in series 5, folder 351, CORE; Oretha Castle Haley, Rogers interview; Meier and Rudwick, *CORE*, p. 265.

CHAPTER 11: *The Movement, 1963–1964*

1. David J. Garrow, "Commentary," Charles W. Eagles, ed., *The Civil Rights Movement in America* (Jackson: University Press of Mississippi, 1986), p. 59.

2. Stan Weschler and Debbie Bernstein, "Assorted Papers Prepared for Use in Informal Discussion Workshops for Volunteers and Supporters of CORE's Southern Summer Project, 1965," box 9, folder 12, CORE Papers, Southern Regional Office Files, SHSW (collection hereinafter cited as CORE(SRO)); Dan Rosenberg, "Community Development Field Fellowship Report," October 14, 1965, SEDFRE; Mary Aiken Rothschild, *A Case of Black and White: Northern Volunteers and the Southern Freedom Summers, 1964–1965* (Westport, Conn.: Greenwood Press, 1982), pp. 137–39; Spiver Gordon, Field Report, October 2, 1964, box 3, folder 2, Monroe Project Files, CORE Papers, SHSW.

3. Rothschild, p. 54; Miriam Feingold, notebook entry, June 21, 1964, Miriam (Mimi) Feingold Papers, reel 2, microfilm collection 845, SHSW.

4. Frederick Brooks to Oretha Castle, "Jackson Parish," n.d., box 3, folder 2, Monroe Project Files, CORE Papers.

5. Feingold to Family, July 17, 23, 31, October 15, 1963, reel 1, Feingold Papers. On police and other harassment, see for example, "Intimidations and Harassment Against

Negroes and CORE Workers, Summer 1963 to Summer 1964," July 17, 1964, series 5, folder 41, CORE.

6. Harleaux to Branton, October 16, 1962, series F, folder 134, addendum, CORE; Kenny Johnson, unidentified interviewer, [1988], recording, ARC.

7. Newton, "Peasant Farm of St. Helena Parish," pp. 15–22, 59–64; Commission on Civil Rights, *Voting, 1961 Report,* vol. 1: pp. 266–67.

8. Testimony of Quitman Crouch, in Commission on Civil Rights, *Hearings Held in New Orleans,* 2: 327–33; Plaintiff's Trial Brief, *U.S. v. Louisiana,* pp. 36–37, and testimony of Charles S. Kilbourne in appendix B, reel 1, Marshall Papers.

9. "Number of Farms and Farm Operators, 1959," box 9, folder 10, CORE(SRO); Moore to McCain, November 11, December 10, 1962; January 13, 1963, series F, folder 133, addendum, CORE. In 1959 there were 48 black farm owners in West Feliciana Parish, 12 part-owners, and 275 tenants or sharecroppers.

10. Ed Vickery to Jim McCain, October 31, 1963, addendum, CORE; Meier and Rudwick, *CORE,* p. 262; "Contacts: Clinton," August 4, 1963; "Field Report: Direct Action, Economic Boycotts, and Related Activity, September 1963," both in box 4, folder 1, CORE(SRO); Feingold to Family, July 31, August 5, 19, 1963; Hazel P. Matthews to Feingold, October 6, 1963, all in reel 1, Feingold Papers; Miriam Feingold, "Chronicling the 'Movement,'" *Reviews in American History* 11 (March 1974): 159.

11. Ronnie Moore, "Triumph Over Harassments," n.d., part 3, series A, SEDFRE; Rev. Joseph Carter, interviewed by Miriam Feingold, n.d., recording, Feingold Collection; Warren, *Who Speaks for the Negro?* pp. 3–10.

12. Moore to Wiley Branton, January 10, 1964, series 5, folder 124, CORE; Civil Rights Commission, *Hearings Held in New Orleans, 1960–1961,* pp. 33–37; John Henry Scott, Logsdon interview, pp. 67–69; Louis Berry to Scott, September 21, 1954; April 10, 1956, both in John Henry Scott Papers, University of New Orleans.

13. East Carroll: *U.S. v. Manning,* 205 F. Supp. 172 (1962); Madison: *U.S. v. Ward,* 222 F. Supp. 617 (1962); West Feliciana: *U.S. v. Palmer* (1963); Beinville: *U.S. v. Association of Citizens Councils,* 196 F. Supp. 908 (1961); Red River: *U.S. v. Crawford,* 229 F. Supp. 898 (1964); Jackson: *U.S. v. Wilder,* 222 F. Supp. 749 (1963); Washington: *U.S. v. McElveen,* 180 F. Supp. 10 (1960).

14. Civil Rights Commission, *Hearings Held in New Orleans,* pp. 793–800; *Louisiana Weekly,* September 1, 1962; John Henry Scott, Logsdon interview, pp. 86–94; *Lake Providence Banner-Democrat,* February 5, 1965.

15. Act no. 613 (1960); Act no. 61 (1962); Act no. 63 (1962), *Louisiana Revised Statutes;* Plaintiff's Trial Brief, *U.S. v. Louisiana,* pp. 53–54, 106–7, reel 1, Marshall Papers; Louisiana Citizenship Test; John M. Brooks to Wiley Branton, January 11, 1963, both in series 6, folder 109, SRC.

16. Feingold to Family, July 31, October 15, 1963, reel 1, Feingold Papers; Kenneth Johnson interview.

17. William H. Kyles to Wiley Branton, "Lake Charles," November 11, 1964; Mrs. Joseph Sarpy to Branton, "Shreveport," January 17, February 6, 1964; Yvonne A. Minor to Branton, "New Orleans," April 16, August 31, September 4, 1964, series 6, folders 110, 375, SRC.

18. Minor to Branton, April 16, October 27, 1964.

19. Louisiana Board of Registration, voter registration reports, September 30, 1962; March 31, 1964; October 31, 1964, Attorney General of Louisiana Papers, State Archives, Baton Rouge.

20. *U.S. v. Louisiana,* 225 F. Supp. 353 (1963); 85 S. Ct. 817 (1965).

21. Kenneth O'Reilly, *"Racial Matters": The FBI's Secret File on Black America, 1960–1972* (New York: Free Press, 1989), pp. 51–61.

22. Marshall to Kennedy, September 6, 1961, reel 1, Marshall Papers.

23. *U.S. v. Wilder,* 222 F. Supp. 749 (1963); *U.S. v. Crawford,* 229 F. Supp. 898 (1964); *U.S. v. Lucky,* 239 F. Supp. 233 (1965); *U.S. v. Association of Citizens Councils of Louisiana,* 196 F. Supp. 908 (1961).

24. *Atlanta Daily World,* July 29, 1962; David J. Garrow, *Protest at Selma: Martin Luther King, Jr., and the Voting Rights Act of 1965* (New Haven: Yale University Press, 1978), p. 29.

25. Moore to Barbara Whitaker, May 21, 1964, box 10, folder 1, CORE(SRO).

26. Plaintiff's Trial Brief, *U.S. v. Louisiana; U.S. v. Louisiana,* 225 F. Supp. 353 (1963) at 386.

27. Moore to McCain, [April 1963], series 5, folder 125, CORE; Vickery to Farmer, October 31, 1963, series F, folder 216, CORE (Addendum).

28. Mike Lesser to Val Coleman, January 15, 1964, series 5, folder 43, CORE; minutes of staff meeting, March 29, 1964, box 9, folder 12, CORE(SRO); Spiver Gordon, VEP field report, October 2, 1964, box 3, folder 2, Monroe Project Files, CORE Papers.

29. Peter Teachout, "West Monroe: The Legal Situation," June 19–25, 1964, series 5, folder 43, CORE; Peter Teachout, "Louisiana Underlaw," in Friedman, ed., *Southern Justice,* pp. 67–71.

30. Meier and Rudwick, *CORE,* p. 267; Daniel Mitchell, "Field Report, Jonesboro," July 15, 1964, series 5, folder 42, CORE; "Special Report on Jonesboro," July 1964, box 1, folder 10, Jackson Parish Files, CORE Papers, SHSW.

31. "CORE-VEP Field Report: North Louisiana, February 1 to March 14, 1964," box 4, folder 1, CORE(SRO).

32. Mimi Feingold, Field Report, St. Helena, East Feliciana, and West Feliciana parishes, June 28–July 5, 1964; Loria Davis, Field Report, Tangipahoa Parish, July 15–30, 1964; Spiver Gordon, Field Report, Iberville Parish, July 10, 1964; Feingold, Freedom Registration Report, July 27–August 5, 1964; Marvin Rich to Ronnie Moore, April 20, 1964; Moore, Field Report, September 1964–January 1965, all in series 5, folder 124, CORE; Summary field report, September 1963, box 4, folder 1, CORE(SRO); Meier and Rudwick, *CORE,* p. 268.

33. Field Summary Reports, Iberville Parish, December 15, 1963, box 4, folder 1, CORE(SRO); Jack Minnis to Wiley A. Branton, "Report on Visit to Baton Rouge," August 23, 1963, p. 7; "Visit to Plaquemine," August 30, 1963, pp. 2–3; "Conference Held by the United Crusade for Voters in Lake Charles," August 20, 1963, p. 2; Jack Brady, "Report from Louisiana," November 1, 1963, all in series 6, folder 153, SRC. Jack Brady (1902–85) was a midwesterner who became a schoolteacher in Lake Charles; he owned and edited the *Lake Charles Beacon* from 1954(?) to 1960. In its early years the paper reflected Brady's opposition to cigarettes, pollution, the medical profession, and chemical additives and preservatives in foodstuffs. After Minnis joined the staff in 1958, the paper adopted a harder political edge. It attacked the political machine of Sheriff "Hamm" Reid and in 1960 supported the student sit-ins. By the time of its demise it was reprinting articles from liberal-left magazines like the *Nation,* but it had lost nearly all of its advertising. Biographical information on Brady in Mary Margaret Morgan to Kathie Bordelon, January 5, 1989, with *Beacon* file, McNeese State University.

34. *U.S. v. Louisiana,* 225 F. Supp. 353 (1963), at 360; Steven F. Lawson, *Black Ballots:*

Voting Rights in the South, 1944–1969 (New York: Columbia University Press, 1976), p. 285; Feingold, "Chronicling the 'Movement,'" p. 155; Kenneth Johnson interview; Spiver Gordon, unidentified interviewer, January 14, 1984, recording, ARC.

35. Stan Weschler and Debbie Bernstein, discussion paper; King, *Civil Rights and the Idea of Freedom*, p. 57.

36. Plaintiff's Trial Brief, *U.S.* v. *Louisiana*, Appendix A, table C; Final VEP Report [draft, 1964], series 6, folder 36, SRC.

37. Garrow, *Protest at Selma*, pp. 29–30.

38. O'Reilly, *"Racial Matters,"* pp. 69–77; Wofford, *Of Kennedys and Kings,* pp. 160–64; Lawson, *Black Ballots,* p. 289; Commission on Civil Rights, *1961 Report,* vol. 1: *Voting,* pp. 56–57.

39. Plaintiff's Trial Brief, *U.S.* v. *Louisiana*, Appendix B.

40. David J. Garrow, "The Voting Rights Act in Historical Perspective," *Georgia Historical Quarterly* 74 (Fall 1990): 386–90; Lawson, *Black Ballots,* pp. 307–9; Nicholas Katzenbach to Lyndon B. Johnson, January 29, 1965, box 1, legislative background to Voting Rights Act, Lyndon B. Johnson Presidential Papers, Lyndon B. Johnson Library, Austin, Texas (collection hereinafter referred to as LBJ).

41. Meier and Rudwick, *CORE,* p. 223; Steven F. Lawson, "Commentary" in Eagles, ed., *Civil Rights Movement in America,* pp. 34–35; Garrow, "Commentary," in ibid., p. 59.

42. Feingold, "Chronicling the 'Movement,'" p. 152.

43. McMillen, *Citizens Council,* pp. 71–72; Jeansonne, *Leander Perez,* p. 240; Rainach, Humphreys interview, p. 25.

44. John Kenneth Price, "The Impact of Black Voter Participation on the Politics of Louisiana and Virginia" (Ph.D. diss., University of Texas at Austin, 1978), pp. 137–38; John F. Kennedy and James H. Davis, telephone conversation, June 3, 1963, transcript, belt 21A, Presidential recordings, John F. Kennedy Presidential Library, Boston.

45. Irwin Klibaner, "The Southern Conference Education Fund: A History" (Ph.D. diss., University of Wisconsin, 1971), pp. 368–90; Pamela Jean Turner, "Civil Rights and Anti-Communism in New Orleans, 1946–1965" (M.A. thesis, University of New Orleans, 1981) pp. 67–74; Jack Peebles, "Subversion and the Southern Conference Education Fund" (M.A. thesis, University of New Orleans, 1970), pp. 52–53. The police, guns drawn, also raided Smith's law office.

46. Turner, "Civil Rights and Anti-Communism," p. 67; Louisiana Legislature, House Concurrent Resolution no. 54, 1960; Joint Legislative Committee on Un-American Activities, *The Case of Dr. Waldo F. McNeir* (Baton Rouge, May 8, 1961); Louisiana State Department of Education, *Americanism versus Communism: A Unit of Work in American History* (Baton Rouge, 1960); State Sovereignty Commission, *Why Segregation?* (Baton Rouge, n.d.); Carol E. Jensen, *The Network of Control: State Supreme Courts and State Security Statutes, 1920–1970* (Westport, Conn.: Greenwood Press, 1982), pp. 83, 160.

47. SAC, New Orleans, to Hoover, January 31, 1956, FBI Perez file, 44-9732; Twomey to Rev. R. C. Hartnet, April 27, 1956, box 20, folder 4; *Boston Globe,* August 31, 1964, box 2, folder 3, both in Twomey Papers.

48. John P. Nelson to Burke Marshall, October 9, 1963, box 21, folder 15, Twomey Papers; *Dombrowski* v. *Pfister,* 227 F. Supp. 556 (1964).

49. *Dombrowski* v. *Pfister,* 380 U.S. 479 (1965); Jensen, *Network of Control,* pp. 55–57, 158–60; Arthur Kinoy, *Rights on Trial: The Odyssey of a People's Lawyer* (Cambridge: Harvard University Press, 1983), pp. 158, 193–94; William Kunstler, *Deep In My Heart*

(New York: William Morrow, 1966), pp. 22–23, 199–200; Lolis E. Elie, Bass interview, pp. 2–3; Greenberg, *Crusaders in the Courts,* pp. 351–52. The 1964 Civil Rights Act explicitly affirmed this right to appeal remand orders.

50. Robert F. Collins, Nils R. Douglas, and Lolis E. Elie, "Clinton, Louisiana," in Friedman, ed., *Southern Justice,* pp. 120–21; Judge John R. Rarick, Order, October 24, 1963; "Memorandum of Fact," January 26, 1965, *CORE* v. *Clinton,* both in reel 16, LCDC; Robert F. Collins, interviewed by Jack Bass, May 23, 1979, pp. 16–19, Bass Collection; Lolis E. Elie, Bass interview, pp. 20–21.

51. Meier and Rudwick, *CORE,* p. 262; Collins, Douglas, and Elie, "Clinton," p. 125; *The Watchman,* November 1, 1963; Laura Spears and James Bell, interviewed by Miriam Feingold, 1967, recording, Feingold Collection; Feingold, notebook entry, December 4, 1963, reel 2, Feingold Papers.

52. Jeansonne, *Leander Perez,* pp. 271–78; "Plaintiff's Post-Trial Brief," April 8, 1968, *Sobol* v. *Perez,* reel 65, LCDC; *States-Item,* January 23, 1968; *Washington Post,* January 29, 1968; Mary Hamilton to James McCain, "Activities in Plaquemines Parish, New Orleans, and Jackson," January 12, 1964, CORE (Addendum).

53. Chapital to James Ivy, September 21, 1961, folder 72, NAACP(NO); Hamilton to McCain, "Plaquemines Parish," March 1, 1964, box 6, folder 1, CORE(SRO); Jeansonne, *Leander Perez,* pp. 279–81.

54. Meier and Rudwick, *CORE,* pp. 221–23; James Farmer, *Lay Bare the Heart: An Autobiography of the Civil Rights Movement* (New York: Arbor House, 1985), pp. 244–54; Murphy W. Bell, "Key Points on Cross Examination," Murphy W. Bell Papers (microfilm), SHSW; Citizens Committee to Mayor Charles P. Schebelen, August 16, 1963, reel 27, LCDC; *Griffon* v. *CORE, Race Relations Law Reporter* 8, 1963, 863; "The Story of Plaquemine"; statements of Gertrude Jones and Larry Dayries, all in series 5, folder 45, CORE; notes on August 19 demonstration, reel 16, LCDC; Feingold to Danny, September 5, 1963, reel 1, Feingold Papers; Spiver Gordon interview.

55. The girls to Feingold, n.d., reel 1, Feingold Papers.

56. Feingold, notebook entries, September 25, 27, 1963, reel 1, Feingold Papers; "Intimidations and Harassment," series 5, folder 41; Farmer, *Louisiana Story,* pamphlet, n.p., series 6, folder 10, CORE; Kenny Johnson interview; Spiver Gordon, "Field Report: Iberville Parish," n.d., box 5, folder 3, CORE(SRO); Meier and Rudwick, *CORE,* p. 223.

57. Daniel Harrell, "Report from Louisiana," [August 1963]; Major Johns, field reports, May 10, June 14, 1963, box 140, folders 13, 15, SCLC.

58. Henry W. Wallingford to Paul Anthony, July 6, 1963, series 4, folder 341, SRC; Gardner, Humphreys interview, pp. 30–33.

59. Gloster Current to Roy Wilkins, September 23, 1963, box 3-A-277, NAACP; *Shreveport Times,* September 23, 24, 1963; Lavert H. Taylor, report from Iberia, Louisiana, October 30, 1963, series 6, folder 335, SRC; *Chicago Defender,* October 28, 1963; Ike Reynolds, report from Shreveport, n.d., series 5, folder 263, CORE; Burton, *The Black Side of Shreveport,* p. 101.

60. William Douthard, field report, Shreveport [November 1963]; James McCain to Douthard, November 20, 1963; Ike Reynolds to McCain, January 26, 1964; Reynolds to Marcia McKenna, March 11, 1964, series 5, folders 246, 263, CORE; Claudia Edwards and Frank Battiste, field report, Caddo Parish, November 12–December 11, 1964, box 4, folder 5, CORE(SRO); Burton, *The Black Side of Shreveport,* p. 107.

61. Loria Davis, Miriam Feingold, and Howard Messing, Field Report: Tangipahoa Parish, [spring 1964], box 7, folder 2, CORE(SRO); Jack Brady, Report from Louisiana, November 1, 1963, series 6, folder 335, SRC.

62. Crain, ed., *Politics of School Desegregation*, p. 248; Wade Mackie and Yvonne Coleman, "Negro Leadership: Baton Rouge," February 20, 1963; Wade Mackie to Garnet Guild, "Comprehensive Report, Community Relations Program, Baton Rouge," November 4, 1963, South Central Regional Office files, AFSC.

63. Gloster Current to Roy Wilkins, January 17, April 25, 1963; Clarence Laws to Current, "Meeting in New Orleans on Baton Rouge Situation," May 31, 1963, all in box 3-C-53, NAACP; Jack Minnis, "Field Trip, May 28–June 1, 1963;" Minnis to Wiley Branton, "Report on Visit to Baton Rouge," August 23, 1963, both in series 6, folder 153, SRC.

64. Mackie, "Comprehensive Report"; *Davis* v. *East Baton Rouge Parish School Board*, 219 F. Supp. 876.

65. Frank M. Dunbaugh to Burke Marshall, November 21, 1963, reel 1, Marshall Papers.

66. *Barthe* v. *City of New Orleans*, 219 F. Supp. 789 (1963); *Bynum* v. *Schiro* (1963); Johnnie A. Jones to Norman Amaker, October 5, 1962, box 64, folder 11, APT.

67. Raphael Cassimere, employment survey, July 18, 1963; Ernest N. Morial to Lolis E. Elie, July 22, 1963; Milton L. Upton to A. M. Trudeau, August 20, 1963; Trudeau to Upton, August 22, 1963; Roy Wilkins to Horace C. Bynum, August 22, 1963, all in Ernest N. Morial Papers, ARC; Morial to Elie, September 4, 1963, folder 74; Executive Committee minutes, April 2, September 3, 1963, folder 182, NAACP(NO); Leonard L. Burns, interviewed by Kim Lacy Rogers, May 14, 1979, recording, ARC; Raphael Cassimere, Rogers interview.

68. Rogers, "Humanity and Desire," p. 328; Burns, Rogers interview; Ellis Henican to Cody, July 24, 1963, box 2, CCHR.

69. Jack Minnis to Wiley Branton, "New Orleans," August 23, 1963, series 4, folder 153, SRC; Rogers, "Humanity and Desire," p. 318. Minnis's articles on Lake Charles appeared in the *Lake Charles Beacon* between February 2 and May 29, 1959.

70. Rogers, "Humanity and Desire," pp. 329–32; notes of meeting with mayor, August 29, 1963; memo for meeting with mayor, n.d., both in Morial Papers; Winter Trapolin to Victor Schiro, September 6, 1963; Stephen Lemann to Darwin Fenner, September 19, October 3, 1963; Fenner to Lemann, September 25, October 15, 1963, reel 1, Marshall Papers; CORE press release, February 27, 1964, CORE (Addendum)

71. Howard, *Political Tendencies in Louisiana*, pp. 360–89; Henry Cabirac to Ellis Henican, November 27, 1962, box 3, CCHR; Fred Dent, "Continuation of Report on Rapides Parish," June 21, 1963; Morrison to Personal Friends, July 9, 1963, both in box 15, Scott Wilson Papers; Red River Parish speech, n.d.; campaign speech, n.d.; "Morrison Works to Destroy Segregation"; "All Smiles," all in 1963–64 campaign files, Morrison Papers, TU; Glen S. Jeansonne, "Longism: Mainstream Politics or Aberration? Louisiana before and after Huey Long," *Mid-America* 71 (April–July 1989): 90.

72. Frank Gibney, "New Orleans Speech," October 9, 1964; Bill Moyers to Jack Valenti, October 9, 1964, both in box 24, Bill Moyers Papers, LBJ; Merle Miller, *Lyndon: An Oral Biography* (New York: Ballantine Books, 1980), p. 485; Roman Heleniak, "Lyndon Johnson in New Orleans," *Louisiana History* 21 (Summer 1980): 263–75. According to Heleniak, the tape of the speech clearly shows that Johnson said "Negro," not "nigger" or "nigra." Heleniak suggests that Johnson had already written Louisiana off.

73. *Baton Rouge State-Times*, July 3, 7, 14, 15, 23, 1964; May 5, 1965; *Times-Picayune*, July 16, 18, 1964.

74. *Baton Rouge State-Times*, June 17, 1965; Urban League of New Orleans, "Facing

the Facts of the Racial Relations Dilemma in 1964"; Beecher, "Magnolia Ghetto," p. 46.

75. SAC, New Orleans, to Hoover, November 11, 1963; April 18, 30, May 5, 1964, "Original Knights of the Ku Klux Klan," FBI file 105-71801; *Atlanta Constitution,* July 19, 1964.

76. John Henry Scott to Roy Wilkins, June 30, 1963, box C-24-270, NAACP(LC); Scott, Logsdon interview, pp. 98–99; Meier and Rudwick, *CORE,* p. 267; typed note on Jonesboro, n.d., series 5, folder 43, CORE; "Deacons for Defense," August 17, 1965, FBI file 157-2466.

77. Wynn Craig Wade, *The Fiery Cross: The Ku Klux Klan in America* (New York: Simon and Schuster, 1987), pp. 333–34.

78. Weschler and Bernstein, discussion paper (see note 2); Wade Mackie, "CORE Workers Non-Violent Workshop," April 8, 1964, AFSC.

79. "Staff meeting," November 24, 1963, notebook entry, reel 1, Feingold Papers.

80. Louisiana summer task force, staff meeting, minutes, July 15, 1964, series 5, folder 467, CORE.

81. Daniel Mitchell, "Jonesboro, Louisiana," box 4, folder 4, Monroe Project Files, CORE Papers; "Deacons for Defense and Justice," January 6, March 25, 1965, FBI file 157-2466; Elmo Jacobs, interviewed by Miriam Feingold, recording, Feingold Collection.

82. *New York Times,* January 21, 1965; Meldon Acheson to parents, July 30, 1965, Meldon Acheson Papers, Ferriday Freedom Movement Files, CORE Papers, SHSW; Fred Powledge, *Free at Last? The Civil Rights Movement and the People Who Made It* (Boston: Little, Brown, 1991), p. 573.

83. Father August Thompson to Mimi Feingold, December 21, 1964, reel 1, Feingold Papers; *Louisiana Weekly,* January 2, 1965; Don Whitehead, *Attack on Terror: The FBI against the Ku Klux Klan in Mississippi* (New York: Funk and Wagnalls, 1970), pp. 25–230.

CHAPTER 12: *North to Bogalusa*

1. *Bogalusa Golden Jubilee: Official Program* (1964), n.d.; C. W. Goodyear, *Bogalusa Story* (Buffalo, N.Y.: privately printed, 1950), p. 81, both in Louisiana Collection, TU.

2. Vera Rony, "Bogalusa: The Economics of Tragedy," in Jeremy Larner and Irving Howe, eds., *Poverty: Views from the Left* (New York: William Morrow, 1968), pp. 281–82; James Francis Fouche, "The Bogalusa Quasi-Riot of 1919: A Microcosm of National and Regional Hysteria" (M.A. thesis, Louisiana State University at New Orleans, 1972), pp. 26–27; Judge Frederick Heebe, quoted in Transcript of Hearings, *Hicks v. Weaver,* June 10, 1968, reel 35, LCDC.

3. Goodyear, *Bogalusa Story,* pp. 7–11, 76–87, 134; Fouche, "Bogalusa Quasi-Riot," pp. 42–44. The mob also killed at least three other union men.

4. Judy Nussbaum to Ronnie Moore, November 27, 1964, box 9, CORE(SRO).

5. Robert Hicks, interviewed by Miriam Feingold, 1967, recording, Feingold Collection.

6. A. Z. Young, interviewed by Miriam Feingold, 1967, recording, Feingold Collection.

7. Wisdom, Christenberry, and Ainsworth, Judgment, *U.S. v. Original Knights of the Ku Klux Klan,* December 1, 1965.

8. SAC, New Orleans, to Director, "Original Knights of the Ku Klux Klan," April 30; May 31, 1964, FBI files 105-71801-254, 260; Paul Good, "Klantown, USA," *Nation*, February 1, 1964, p. 112; Tureaud to Cutrer; Tureaud to Justice Department, June 3, 1964, box 11, folder 16, APT.

9. Northrup, *Negro in the Paper Industry*, pp. 96–97; A. Z. Young, Feingold interview; Rony, "Bogalusa," pp. 282–83.

10. Rony, "Bogalusa," p. 283.

11. Ibid., pp. 284–85; *U.S. v. Local 189, United Papermakers and Paperworkers, AFL-CIO; and Crown-Zellerbach Corporation*, 301 F. Supp. 906 (1969), in Northrup, *Negro in the Paper Industry*, p. 203; "Memorandum of Position on Employment at Crown-Zellerbach's Bogalusa Plant," June 1965; Jeremish S. Gutman, "Memorandum of notes of meeting held at the home of Robert Hicks, June 17, 1966," both in reel 30, LCDC.

12. Mimi Feingold, Loria Davis, and Howard Messing, Scouting Report, Washington Parish, n.d., box 7, folder 5, CORE(SRO); Mimi Feingold, notes on Bogalusa, n.d., reel 2, Feingold Papers.

13. Rony, "Bogalusa," p. 285; Moore to Cutrer, July 18, 1964, box 7, folder 5, CORE(SRO); Gayle Jenkins, interviewed by Miriam Feingold, 1967, recording, Feingold Collection.

14. *Bogalusa Daily News*, August 10, 11, 13, 16, 17, 1964.

15. *New York Times*, January 9, 1965; Klan circular, n.d., enclosed with James H. Morrison to Cartha D. DeLoach, August 25, 1964; FBI Laboratory to New Orleans, October 13, 1964; SAC, New Orleans, to Director, September 30, 1964; December 11, 1964, all in "Original Knights of the Ku Klux Klan," FBI files 105-71801-281, 295, 320; *New York Times*, April 20, 1965.

16. Charles L. Weltner, "The Terror of Bogalusa: A Case in Point," reprinted from the *Congressional Record*, n.d., in reel 5, LCDC; LeRoy Collins to Hubert H. Humphrey, April 7, 1965, box 3, Lee C. White Papers, LBJ.

17. Collins to Humphrey, April 7, 1965; Good, "Klantown, USA," pp. 110–13; Klan leaflet, n.d., enclosed with John Doar to Director, September 6, 1965, "Public Accommodations (Interference), Civil Rights Act of 1964," FBI file 173-2015-21; *Baton Rouge State-Times*, January 6, 1965; *New York Times*, January 9, 1965; *States-Item*, September 9, 1965.

18. John A. Griffin to LeRoy Collins, "Bogalusa, La.," January 29, 1965, box 3, Lee White Papers; "CORE in Bogalusa," February 28, 1965, reel 9, LCDC; "Fact Sheet on Bogalusa, La.," February 17, 1965; "Bogalusa Chronology, January 25–February 29, 1965," both in series 5, folder 43, CORE; "Who Bought Jesse Cutrer?" Klan leaflet, in Doar to Director, September 9, 1965; *States-Item*, September 9, 1965; Rony, "Bogalusa," pp. 286–87; Feingold interviews with Gayle Jenkins, Robert Hicks, and A. Z. Young; Good, "Klantown, USA," p. 110; Meier and Rudwick, *CORE*, pp. 347–48.

19. "Fact sheet on Bogalusa," CORE; "Bogalusa Chronology"; *Birmingham News*, April 4, 1965; *Wall Street Journal*, April 1, 1965; *Times-Picayune*, March 20, 1965; *New York Times*, July 22, December 30, 1965.

20. *Times-Picayune*, March 20, 1965; *Baton Rouge State-Times*, March 25, 1965; *Wall Street Journal*, April 1, 1965; Collins to Humphrey, April 7, 1965.

21. SAC, New Orleans, "Deacons for Defense and Justice," February 24, 26, March 4, 1965, FBI files 157-2466-4, 7, 8; "Fact Sheet on Bogalusa," CORE; *Los Angeles Times*, June 13, 1965; *Newsweek*, August 2, 1965, p. 28.

22. *Los Angeles Times*, June 14, 1965; Director to SAC, New Orleans, "Deacons for Defense and Justice," February 26, 1965, FBI file 157-2466-6. Newspapers reporting

the claims of 50 chapters and 5,000 to 15,000 members included *Los Angeles Times,* June 13; *Wall Street Journal,* July 12; *Newsweek,* August 2, 1965.

23. Fred S. Baumgardner to William C. Sullivan, July 15, 1965; SAC, New Orleans to Director, July 15; August 17, 1965, FBI files 157-2466-23, 26, 41.

24. SAC, New Orleans, to Director, August 17, 1965, FBI file 157-2466-41; "Bogalusa Chronology"; *Wall Street Journal,* July 12, 1965; *Los Angeles Times,* July 13, 1965; *Birmingham News,* April 4, 1965; Young, Feingold interview; Martzell, Fairclough interview.

25. CORE staff meeting, minutes, April 12, 1965, box 9, folder 12, CORE(SRO); Shana Alexander, "Visit Bogalusa and You Will Look for Me," *Life,* July 2, 1965, p. 28; Lolis Elie, interviewed by Adam Fairclough, January 29, 1992.

26. Charles Currier to Marvin Rich, "Preliminary Report on Crown-Zellerbach Corporation," February 17, 1965; James Farmer to P. T. Sinclair, February 19, 1965, both in box 20, folder 42, CORE; Shirley Mesher, Committee for Concern, minutes, February 18, 1965; reel 9, LCDC.

27. *Bogalusa Golden Jubilee: Official Program.*

28. *Business Week,* August 7, 1965, pp. 102–6; *Wall Street Journal,* April 1, 1965; Bill Yates to Shirley Mesher, February 25, 1965, reel 30, LCDC; Steven M. Gelber, *Black Men and Businessmen: The Growing Awareness of a Social Responsibility* (Port Washington, N.Y.: Kennikat Press, 1974), p. 78.

29. Steve Miller to Committee for Concern, March 4, 1965, box 7, folder 5, CORE(SRO); "Bogalusa Chronology"; Klan boycott rules, enclosed with John Doar to J. Edgar Hoover, September 6, 1965, FBI file 173-2015-21; "Additions to Bogalusa Intimidations List, February 28–March 30, 1965," reel 9, LCDC.

30. "Summary of Incidents in Bogalusa, April 7–9;" notes on Bogalusa situation, April 7–9, both in reel 9, LCDC; *Baton Rouge State-Times, Times-Picayune,* April 9, 1965; *New York Times,* April 8, 9, 1965.

31. *Times-Picayune,* April 14, 15, 1965; *Baton Rouge State-Times,* April 12, 15, 16, 21, 22, 1965; *Louisiana Weekly,* May 1, 1965; LeRoy Collins to Hubert H. Humphrey, April 7, 1965, box 3, Lee White Papers; *New York Times,* April 25, 1965; "Memorandum re meeting with Mayor's Office," April 14, 1965, reel 9, LCDC; "Strategy for Mayor's Meeting #2," April 20, 1965; notes of Type 1 meeting #2, both in box 1, folder 2, Bogalusa Voters League (BVL) files, CORE Papers, SHSW.

32. Martzell, Fairclough interview; *Times-Picayune,* April 23, 24, 1965.

33. Joel Rubinstein to Ed Hollander, April 28, 1965, box 7, folder 5, CORE(SRO); *State-Times,* April 27, 30, 1965; John R. Martzell to Lolis E. Elie, April 29, 1965, reel 9, LCDC; Elie, Fairclough interview; Martzell, Fairclough interview.

34. John P. Nelson, Stephens interview; Elie, Fairclough interview.

35. Martzell, Fairclough interview; "Agreement reached between the Mayor and Commission Council of the City of Bogalusa and the Bogalusa Voters League," May 16, 1965, reel 9, LCDC; *Time,* June 7, 1965; Elie, Fairclough interview; *Louisiana Weekly,* July 31, 1965.

36. Elie, Fairclough interview; "Who Bought Jesse Cutrer?" Klan leaflet, in Doar to Hoover, September 6, 1965.

37. Statement of Sam Barnes, May 19, 1965; statement of Terry Friedman, n.d., reels 8 and 35, LCDC; Transcript of Hearings, June 28, July 1–2, *Hicks* v. *Knight,* passim, E.D. La., New Orleans Div., Civil Action 15727, case records, Federal Records Center, Fort Worth, Texas.

38. *Birmingham News,* May 30, 1965; *State-Times,* June 1, 2, 1965; *Time,* June 11, 1965; *Louisiana Weekly,* June 12, 1965; Transcript, *Hicks* v. *Knight,* pp. 50, 268–72.

39. *Time,* August 6, 1965; H. L. Mitchell, *Mean Things Happening in the Land: The Life and Times of H. L. Mitchell, Co-Founder of the Southern Tenant Farmers Union* (Montclair, N.J.: Allanheld, Osmun, 1979), pp. 283–84; Alvin J. Bronstein, interviewed by Jack Bass, January 16, 1979, pp. 35–36, Bass Collection; *Times-Picayune,* June 29, 1965; Transcript, *Hicks* v. *Knight,* pp. 34 and 370; Christenberry, Preliminary Injunction, July 10, 1965, *Hicks* v. *Knight,* reel 35, LCDC.

40. Statements of Henry Austin, Milton Johnson, Samuel F. Fleming, Donald L. Keith, Joseph Jefferson, Gardner Compton, and Leneva Tiedman, all in *Austin and Johnson* v. *Louisiana,* reel 5, LCDC.

41. *New York Times,* July 11, 19, 1965.

42. *New York Times,* July 13, 14, 15, 1965; Roy Reed, "Bogalusa Negroes on March," *New York Times,* July 18, 1965; *Louisiana Weekly,* July 31, 1965; *Time,* July 23, 1965; A. Z. Young, Feingold interview; John J. McKeithen, interviewed by Adam Fairclough, October 7, 1987; Martzell, Fairclough interview.

43. Marvin Watson to Lyndon B. Johnson, July 14, 1965; Cutrer to Johnson, July 14, 1965, box 26, Ex. HU2/ST13, LBJ.

44. Agent's report, July 20, 1965, FBI file NO 173-201; Heleniak, *Soldiers of the Law,* pp. 96–97.

45. Ibid, p. 94; Martzell, Fairclough interview.

46. *New York Times,* July 17, 18, 1965; Statement of George Tuttle, July 16, 1965, reel 8, LCDC; Agent's report, "Original Knights of the Ku Klux Klan," July 16–17, 1965, FBI file 105-71801-403.

47. Hubert Humphrey to Lyndon B. Johnson, July 16, 1965; Jack Rosenthal to Bill Moyers, July 19, 1965, both in box 1, Voting Rights Act of 1965, LBJ.

48. *New York Times,* July 27, 28, 1965; Judgment of Civil Contempt, July 30, 1965, *Hicks* v. *Knight,* in *Race Relations Law Reporter* 10 (Winter 1965).

49. Doar to Hoover, August 18, 1965; SAC, New York, to Hoover, September 1, 1965; Doar to Hoover, September 6, 1965, all in "Original Knights of the Ku Klux Klan, et al., Subjects; [deleted], et al., Victim-RM," FBI files 173-2015-1, 6, 21.

50. *Times-Picayune,* September 8, 10, 12, 1965; *States-Item,* September 7, 8, 9, 1965; *New York Times,* September 8, 9, 12, 1965; Mitchell, *Mean Things Happening in the Land,* p. 227.

51. Judgment, December 1, 1965, *U.S.* v. *Original Knights of the Ku Klux Klan,* Civil Action No. 15793, E.D. La., New Orleans Division; Docket entries of case, U.S. District Court House, New Orleans; Martzell, Fairclough interview.

52. *Louisiana Weekly,* July 31, 1965; *New York Times,* July 5, 11, September 11, 1965; Louisiana Legislature, Joint Committee on Un-American Activities, *Activities of the Ku Klux Klan and Certain Other Organizations in Louisiana* (Baton Rouge, July 26, 1965), pp. 87–89. In 1966 Rarick defeated veteran Congressman Jimmie H. Morrison, a racial moderate.

53. Inspector [deleted] to W. C. Sullivan, "Injunction Proceedings against the Ku Klux Klan and Other Racial-Type Organizations," September 13, 1965, FBI file 173-2015-26; Martzell, Fairclough interview; Wade, *The Fiery Cross,* pp. 361–62; "Log of events in investigation of the Donald Ray Sims shooting," police report, March 12, 1965, in *Hicks* v. *Knight* court records (see n. 37 above); Petition for Removal, July 21, 1966, *Griffin* v. *Louisiana,* reel 26, LCDC; Jenkins, Feingold interview.

54. Alvin J. Bronstein to Richard B. Sobol, June 7, 1966, *Hicks* v. *Cutrer,* reel 34; Judge Jim W. Richardson, Order, October 19, 1965; handwritten notes; chronology of demonstrations, all in *Bogalusa School Board* v. *Bogalusa Voter League,* reel 9, LCDC; police reports, October 13 and 20, 1965; statement of Henry Austin, October 21, 1965;

Transcript of Hearings, December 28–30, 1965, pp. 1898–99, all in court records, *Hicks* v. *Knight;* Bronstein, Bass interview, pp. 21–23; Hattie Mae Hill, interviewed by Miriam Feingold, 1967, recording, Feingold Collection; *Times-Picayune,* October 19, 20, 22, 1965; SAC, New Orleans, to Hoover, "Integration of Public Schools in Bogalusa," October 20, 1965, FBI file 173-2015-33.

55. Transcript of Hearings, pp. 349–50; *New York Times,* December 29, 30, 1965.

56. Christenberry, Minute Entry, November 1, 1966; Opinion Order, March 22, 1967; Minute Entry; February 24, 1969, court records, *Hicks* v. *Knight; New South,* Winter 1967, pp. 74–75; Bronstein, Bass interview, pp. 23–24. The Justice Department also filed charges against deputy sheriff Sidney J. Lyons and city policeman John Hill, but neither stood trial.

57. Lolis Elie, Fairclough interview; Transcript of Proceedings, June 10, 1968, pp. 205–44, *Hicks* v. *Weaver,* reel 35, LCDC; Harris David to Sargent Shriver, July 8, 1966; handwritten notes on Bogalusa poverty program, both in reel 9, LCDC; *States-Item,* July 12, 1966.

58. David to Jeremiah Gutman, October 19, 1965, reel 9, LCDC; police report, April 26, 1966, in court records, *Hicks* v. *Knight;* Statement of Robert Hicks, September 12, 1966, *Jenkins* v. *Bogalusa School Board,* reel 39; *Monroe News-Star,* September 13, 1966; Judge Heebe, Order, July 19, 1967, *Hicks* v. *Cutrer,* U.S. District Court, E.D. La, N.O. Div., C.A. 66225, reel 34; Judge Cassibry, Temporary Restraining Order, May 17, 1968; Judge Heebe, Preliminary Injunction, May 31, 1969, *Hicks* v. *Weaver,* U.S. District Court, E.D. La., N.O. Div. C.A. 68987, reel 35, all in LCDC.

59. "Minutes of Meeting between Representatives of Crown-Zellerbach and Representatives of the Bogalusa Voters League," July 15, 1965, reel 30, LCDC.

60. Jeremiah Gutman to Don Slaiman, July 20, 1965; Gutman to Robert Collins, August 3, 1965, reel 30, LCDC.

61. *U.S.* v. *Local 189, United Papermakers and Paperworkers, Crown-Zellerbach Corp., et al.,* 282 F. Supp. 39; 301 F. Supp. 906; U.S.C.A., 5th Cir., July 28, 1969, reprinted in Northrup, *Negro in the Paper Industry,* pp. 189–227; Judge Heebe, Opinion, November 7, 1970, *Hicks* v. *Crown-Zellerbach,* reel 36, LCDC; Lolis Elie, Fairclough interview.

62. *State-Times,* July 23, 1965.

63. John McKeithen, Fairclough interview; Council for a Better Louisiana, *Report of Organization,* 1962, vertical file, NOPL; CABL, *1965 Report,* Louisiana Collection, TU.

64. Frank J. Price, *Troy H. Middleton: A Biography* (Baton Rouge: Louisiana State University Press, 1974), pp. 375–76; Albert W. Dent, Stephens interview.

CHAPTER 13: *Making Rights Real*

1. Ronnie Moore to Marvin Rich, "The State of CORE," August 8, 1966, SEDFRE; Meier and Rudwick, *CORE,* p. 411.

2. Raymond J. Lockett, "A History of Black Leadership and Participation in Local Politics in St. Mary Parish, 1950–1970" (M.A. thesis, Southern University, 1971), pp. 41, 57; John Zippert, "Chronology of Events in the Formation and Development of the Grand Marie Vegetable Producers Cooperative," July 20, 1966, SEDFRE.

3. Judith R. Berzon, *Neither Black nor White: The Mulatto Character in American Fiction* (New York: New York University Press, 1978). For expressions of the cliché by black writers, see, for example, Frank Smalls, "The Octoroon"; Pauli Murray, "Mu-

latto's Dilemma"; Octave Lilly Jr., "Song of the Mulatto," all in *Opportunity,* March, June, November, 1938. *Opportunity* was published by the National Urban League.

4. Hirsch, "Simply a Matter of Black and White, pp. 292–316; Dominguez, *White by Definition,* pp. 172–74; Britton, Fairclough interview, p. 13.

5. For a brief history of the LCDC, see Bass, *Unlikely Heroes,* p. 293.

6. Report, "Proposed March of Bogalusa Voters League in Bogalusa, Louisiana, to Franklinton, Louisiana," August 11, 1966, FBI file 157-5844; Feingold to Russell, August 12, 1967, reel 1, Feingold Papers. In 1968 the FBI concluded that the Deacons for Defense were now "of little or no significance" and discontinued its surveillance; see R. W. Smith to William C. Sullivan, March 26, 1968; SAC, New Orleans, to Hoover, December 13, 1968, FBI file 157-2466.

7. Martzell, Fairclough interview, pp. 20–21.

8. Carson, "Civil Rights Reform and the Black Freedom Struggle," in Eagles, ed., *Civil Rights Movement in America,* pp. 26–27.

9. Rustin, "From Protest to Politics," pp. 25–31.

10. *Times-Picayune,* November 7, 1965; A. L. Davis to Marvin Rich, November 3, 1965, SEDFRE; *Louisiana Weekly,* August 21, 28, September 4, October 2, 1965; *Blacks United for Lasting Leadership* v. *City of Shreveport,* 71 F.R.D. 623 (1976); Commission on Civil Rights, *The Voting Rights Act: The First Months* (Washington, D.C.: GPO, 1965), p. 38; *U.S.* v. *Louisiana,* 265 F. Supp. 603 (1966); John Doar to James H. Morrison, August 13, 1966, box 74, folder 15, James H. Morrison Papers, University of Southeastern Louisiana, Hammond; Jack P. F. Gremillion to Louis Lyons, August 3, 1966, box 986, Louisiana Attorney General's Papers, Louisiana State Archives, Baton Rouge.

11. *U.S.* v. *Louisiana;* Price, "Impact of Black Voter Participation," p. 93.

12. James T. McCain to Marvin Rich, "Louisiana and South Carolina Reports," December 18, 1967, SEDFRE; "Leander H. Perez, Sr.," FBI file 44-37688; Garrow, *Protest at Selma,* pp. 19, 200; Voter Education Project, "Voter Registration in the South: Autumn, 1970," December 1970, SRC; James R. Bobo and Jesse M. Charlton Jr., eds., *Statistical Abstract of Louisiana* (New Orleans: Division of Business and Economic Research, University of New Orleans, 1974). p. 246.

13. Pat Watters and Reese Cleghorn, *Climbing Jacob's Ladder: The Arrival of Negroes in Southern Politics* (New York: Harcourt, Brace and World, 1967), pp. 33–34; Mark Doherty, "Hale Boggs and Civil Rights: A Case Study of a Southern Moderate" (B.A. honors thesis, Tulane University, 1983), pp. 66–67.

14. Jack Bass and Walter DeVries, *The Transformation of Southern Politics: Social Change and Political Consequences Since 1945* (New York: Meridian, 1977), pp. 167–70.

15. Jules Witcover, "Who's Afraid of Those Negro Voters?" *New Republic,* October 30, 1965, p. 10; "'Black Power' v. Americanism," Rarick campaign flyer; Speech of James H. Morrison, July 25, 1966, reprinted from *Congressional Quarterly,* both in James H. Morrison Papers; *New South,* Fall 1966, pp. 101–3.

16. Stone, Fairclough interview, p. 5; Watters and Cleghorn, *Climbing Jacob's Ladder,* pp. 35–36; Wall, *Louisiana,* p. 349.

17. Stone, Fairclough interview, pp. 4–7; Ronnie Moore to Acie Belton, August 23, 1966, SEDFRE.

18. Stone, Fairclough interview, p. 6; Hirsch, "Simply a Matter of Black and White," p. 291; Nils R. Douglas to Marvin Rich, December 27, 1966, SEDFRE.

19. Hirsch, "Simply a Matter of Black and White," p. 289; Addison C. Carey, "Black Political Participation in New Orleans" (Ph.D. diss., Tulane University, 1971), pp. 55–56; Wilfred Aubert, "Narrative Report," July 26, 1967, folder 289, NAACP(NO).

20. Lockett, "History of Black Leadership," pp. 33–54. In 1979 a federal grand jury

indicted over thirty people in Leesville for conspiracy to buy votes in the election that put Claude "Buddy" Leach into Congress. They included the town's mayor and top officials, as well as a former president of the NAACP branch. Most pleaded guilty or were convicted.

21. *Lake Providence Banner-Democrat,* May 22, 1970; Harvey Britton to Nathaniel Jones, May 25, 1970, box 8, folder 6, Papers of the NAACP Field Director for Louisiana, ARC, collection hereinafter cited as NAACP(LA).

22. James T. McCain to Marvin Rich, "Louisiana and South Carolina Report," December 18, 1967, SEDFRE.

23. Hirsch, "A Simple Matter of Black and White," p. 298.

24. "Field Report on Project Head Start," July 1965, SEDFRE; David Dyer Massey, "The Federation of Southern Cooperatives," *Southern Exposure,* Fall 1974, pp. 39–47; Harris David to Sargent Shriver, July 8, 1966; notes on Bogalusa poverty program, June 8, August 19, 1966, reel 9, LCDC.

25. Mike Lesser, "Let's Have a Peoples' Conference," May 1965, box 9, folder 12, CORE(SRO); Lawrence Stewart to Harvey Britton, August 7, 1965, box 1, folder 1, NAACP(LA); Lockett, "History of Black Leadership," p. 12.

26. William H. Samuel to Ronnie Moore, October 11, 1967; "Roster of Negro Candidates," 1967, both in SEDFRE.

27. Stanislaus Anthony Halpin Jr., "The Anti-Gerrymander: The Impact of Section 5 of the Voting Rights Act upon Louisiana Parish Redistricting" (Ph.D. diss., George Washington University, 1978), p. 174; Commission on Civil Rights, *The Voting Rights Act: Ten Years After* (Washington, D.C.: GPO 1975), pp. 205–6.

28. Marvin Rich, "Civil Rights Progress out of the Spotlight," *Reporter,* March 7, 1968; Charles L. Sanders, "Black Lawman in KKK Territory," *Ebony,* January 1970, p. 57.

29. Catherine Cortez to Oretha Castle, Field Report, November 8–10, 1964, box 3, folder 2, Monroe Project files, CORE Papers.

30. *Louisiana Weekly,* November 13, 1965; Zelma Wyche, Moses Williams, Harrison H. Brown Jr., Rev. F. W. Wilson, Rev. T. I. Israel, interviewed by Miriam Feingold, [1966], recording, Feingold Collection; L. H. Whittemore, *Together: A Reporter's Journey into the New Black Politics* (New York: William Morrow, 1971), pp. 206–7; "Madison Parish School Boycott Injunction," January 14, 1966, *Madison Parish School Board* v. *Madison Parish Voters League* file, reel 98, LCDC; New Orleans to Director, September 1, 1966, teletype, FBI file 157-6-33-4410; Martzell, Fairclough interview, p. 20.

31. Armin Rosecranz to Harris David, April 17, 1966, Madison Parish file, reel 48, LCDC; Sanders, "Black Lawman," p. 64.

32. Files on *Brown* v. *Post, U.S.A.* v. *Post, Wyche* v. *Post,* reel 74, LCDC; Research Project, University of Chicago Law Review, *Voting Rights: A Case Study of Madison Parish, Louisiana* (Chicago: American Bar Foundation, 1971), pp. 764–74; Read and McGough, *Let Them Be Judged,* pp. 314–15.

33. Donald A. Juneau, Memo, December 20, 1965, in Zelma Wyche: Aggravated Assault file; Note of Evidence, September 28, 1966, and other materials in *Louisiana* v. *Wyche* file, all in reel 73, LCDC.

34. Whittemore, *Together,* pp. 206–8; Bruce Baines, unidentified interviewer, [1984?], recording, ARC.

35. University of Chicago Law Review, *Voting Rights,* pp. 767-76; *A SEDFRE Report: Tallulah, Louisiana,* n.d., SEDFRE.

36. Elaine Dundy, *Ferriday, Louisiana* (New York: Donald I. Fine, 1991); Martzell,

Fairclough interview, p. 19; *Louisiana Weekly,* December 4, 1965; CORE news release, December 19, 1965, box 1, folder 2, Ferriday Freedom Movement files, CORE Papers, SHSW (collection hereinafter cited as CORE(FFM); SAC, New Orleans, to Director, "Ferriday Freedom Movement," August 4, 1965, FBI file 517-5133; Keesing's Research Reports, no. 4, *Race Relations in the USA* (New York: Charles Scribner's Sons, 1970), p. 214.

37. John Hamilton to Richard Haley, [May 1966], box 1, folder 5, CORE(FFM); Meldon Acheson to parents, July 10, 1965; "The Firey Cross Extinguisher," Meldon Acheson Papers, CORE(FFM); Louisiana State Conference of Branches, minutes, February 27, 1966, folder 134, NAACP(NO).

38. Meldon Acheson to parents, July 10, 14, 30, August 10, 1965; Acheson to Garry Greenberg, July 27, August 17, 1965, all in Acheson Papers; David Whatley, Field Report, n.d.; John Hamilton to Richard Haley, May 18, 1966, both in box 1, folder 5, CORE(FFM); Robert Lewis to Mary Jamieson, June 28, 1966, box 1, folder 7; NAACP news releases, August 8, 31, 1966, box 34, folder 24, all in NAACP(LA).

39. John Hamilton to Richard Haley, Field Report, April 2–7, 1966, box 1, folder 5, CORE(FFM); David L. Whatley to Mary Jamieson, June 21, 1966; Harvey Britton to Gloster Current, January 15, 1967, box 1, folders 7, 13; Britton to Rhennie Whittle, October 24, 1969, box 7, folder 4, all in NAACP(LA); Britton, Fairclough interview, p. 1.

40. Calvin Kytle to Wiley Branton, July 22, 1965, box 3, Lee White Papers; Price, *Troy H. Middleton,* p. 378; Harvey Britton to Mayor L. W. Davis, March 23, 1967; Britton, Monthly Report, April 13, 1967, box 2, folders 3, 4, NAACP(LA); Martzell, Fairclough interview, p. 19; *Wallace* v. *House,* 337 F. Supp. 1192 (1974).

41. Roy Wilkins quoted in Fairclough, *To Redeem the Soul of America,* p. 320; Current to Branch Department Staff, May 31, 1966, box 1, folder 5, NAACP(LA).

42. Logsdon, "Tureaud," tape 20; Mary Jamieson to Current, June 20, 1966; Jamieson to Richard L. Dockery, n.d., box 1, folders 7, 10, NAACP(LA).

43. Marion Overton White, Rickels interview; Current to Jamieson, June 16, 22, September 26, October 13, 1966, in box 1, folders 9–11, NAACP(LA).

44. Britton's biographical details in Britton to Donald Avery, March 7, 1967, box 2, folder 2, NAACP(LA); Britton, Fairclough interview, pp. 13–14.

45. Britton, Monthly Report, October 17, 1967, Annual Report, November 29, 1967, box 3, folders 3, 4; Monthly Report, April 15, 1968, box 4, folder 1, all in NAACP(LA). On the reluctance of teachers to join the NAACP, see Anthony G. Pierre (Lafeyette) to Jamieson, April 27, 1966, box 1, folder 3; Linton J. Carmouche (Marksville) to Britton, October 22, 1968, box 5, folder 2; Robert Clark and Dessie Lee Patterson (De Soto Parish) to Britton, April 5, 1969, box 6, folder 2, all in NAACP(LA).

46. Brendan Sexton and Bill Brown, Parish Scouting Report, Opelousas, St. Landry Parish, November 22, 1963, box 7, folder 1, CORE(SRO); White, Rickels interview; "A Brief History of the St. Landry NAACP," [1967], box 38, folder 7, NAACP(LA); Fontenot and Riehl, *The Cat and St. Landry,* pp. 145–46.

47. James H. Henderson, Fairclough interview; Louisiana State Conference of Branches, minutes, February 27, 1966, folder 134, NAACP(NO); Emmitt J. Douglas, "Newsletter," April 21, 1967; Britton to Current, April 26, 1967, both in box 2, folder 5; Britton to Charles E. Bryant, August 1, 1968; Current to Britton, August 8, 1968, both in box 4, folder 8, all in NAACP(LA); *Baton Rouge Morning-Advocate,* August 13, 1969.

48. Henderson, Fairclough interview; Britton, Monthly Report, February 14, 1968, box 3, folder 7, NAACP(LA).

49. Stanley J. Lewis to B. J. Mason, June 27, 1968; Mason to Lewis, July 27, 1968, box 4, folder 7; Britton to Current, June 25, 1969, box 6, folder 7; Shreveport NAACP, news releases, May 2, July 30, 1968, box 38, folder 9; Britton, Monthly Report, November 19, 1968; Britton to Current, December 16, 1968, box 5, folders 3, 4; B. J. Mason to Alfred Mitchell, March 4, 1969, box 5, folder 8; Britton, Monthly Report, May 15, 1969, box 6, folder 9, all in NAACP(LA); *Shreveport Sun*, June 13, 1968; Notes on picketing of Sliman's liquor store, December 12–29, 1968; Petition for Writ of Habeas Corpus and Bail, May 1969, *Cooper* v. *Goslin* file, reel 16, LCDC; Britton, Fairclough interview, p. 7; Burton, *The Black Side of Shreveport*, pp. 109–12.

50. Britton, Fairclough interview, p. 5; Meier and Rudwick, *CORE*, p. 349; Stone, Fairclough interview, tape 2, p. 2.

51. Britton, Fairclough interview, pp. 1, 11.

52. Harvey Britton, "Chronicle of Events Leading to the Establishment of an NAACP Military Complaints Center in Leesville, Louisiana, May 17, 1969," May 22, 1969; Britton to Gloster Current, "NAACP Mass Rally, Leesville, June 1, 1969," June 3, 1969, box 6, folders 5, 6, NAACP(LA); Britton, Fairclough interview, p. 4; John J. McKeithen, Fairclough interview.

53. Stone, Fairclough interview, pp. 2, 7.

54. George Frazier IV, "100 Yards and 60 Minutes of Black Power," *Esquire*, October 1967, pp. 95–99; list of demands, April 7, 1967; R. W. E. Jones and William M. Zanders, Agreement, April 10, 1967, all in Grambling College file, reel 75, LCDC.

55. "The Grambling Protest Movement," n.d.; The Informers, "Awaken Black Brothers and Sisters," leaflet, n.d.; notes of Interdepartmental Council meeting, October 26, 1967; *Monroe Morning World*, November 1, 1967; *Wall Street Journal*, November 3, 1967, all in reel 75, LCDC.

56. Martzell, Fairclough interview, pp. 22–23; *Shreveport Times*, November 1, 1967.

57. Price, *Troy H. Middleton*, pp. 377–78; Martzell, Fairclough interview, p. 21; *Homer* v. *Alexander* file, reel 1, LCDC. Creation of the Alexandria BRC is mentioned in Louis Berry, Annual Report of the State Attorney, January 8, 1968, box 3, folder 6, NAACP(LA). The New Orleans BRC was appointed in August 1967; eight white members were nominated by labor, religious, and civil organizations; an equal number of black members by colleges, civil rights organizations, labor, and the ministerial alliance. In early 1968 another six members of each race were chosen in public elections, with voters casting ballots by race (New Orleans Human Relations Council Files, NOPL; collection hereinafter cited as HRC).

58. Stone, Fairclough interview, tape 1, pp. 7–8.

59. Martzell, Fairclough interview, pp. 18–19. Interestingly, while the commission's white director, Martzell, recalled that the commission met frequently and that the meetings were useful, according to Stone, the black associate director, the commission met infrequently and the meetings did not achieve all that much.

60. Ibid., p. 16; *Times-Picayune*, August 15, 1967; Brown quoted in Keesing's Research Reports, *Race Relations in the USA*, p. 252.

61. Martzell, Fairclough interview, pp. 12, 16–17; *Times-Picayune*, August 15–21, 1967.

62. Louisiana Commission on Human Relations, minutes, August 28, 1967; meeting of subcommittee with Civil Service Commission, minutes, November 7, 1967, both in box 21, folder 24, APT.

63. Nils R. Douglas, "An Impartial Look at the Biracial Commission and the Present Status of the Negro Under Governor McKeithen," n.d.; Speech to Lyceum Committee, Tulane University Center, December 9, 1966, both in Douglas Papers; Camille Gravel, interviewed by Jim Brown, "Louisiana Politics" series, NOETC Higher Education Channel, broadcast February 17, 1992; Louis, Bowles, and Grace, "Study of Racial Attitudes in Louisiana, Fall of 1966: Principal Findings," p. 11, box 5, Gene Geisert Papers, OPSB; Henderson, Fairclough interview.

64. Martzell and Stone, "Position Paper on the Louisiana Commission on Human Relations, Rights, and Responsibilities," February 9, 1967, box 21, folder 27, APT; Price, *Troy H. Middleton*, p. 380.

65. John Hampton Carson, "A Quantitative and Qualitative Analysis of Racial Employment Discrimination in Louisiana, 1950–1971" (Ph.D., diss., Louisiana State University, 1973), pp. 99–127; *Baton Rouge Morning Advocate*, August 13, 1969; *Blacks United for Lasting Leadership* v. *Shreveport*, 71 F.R.D. 623 (1976).

66. *Louisiana Weekly*, January 2, 1965.

67. Britton, Monthly Report, October 17, 1967, box 3, folder 3, NAACP(LA); Britton, Fairclough interview, pp. 2–3.

68. Stone, Fairclough interview, p. 6; Scott, Logsdon interview, p. 113; *Lake Providence Banner-Democrat*, February 5, 1965; *Louisiana Weekly*, February 6, 1965; Lockett, "History of Black Political Leadership," pp. 13–14; Martzell, Fairclough interview, p. 20.

69. Joseph H. Fichter, with the collaboration of Brian Jordan, *Police Handling of Arrestees: A Research Study of Police Arrestees in New Orleans* (New Orleans: Loyola University of the South, 1964), pp. 3–7, 32, 46–58, copy in box 5, folder 9, Longe Papers; Fichter, *One-Man Research*, pp. 121–54.

70. Statement of Rose Mary Harris, April 18, 1967; Britton to Current, April 19, 1967, box 2, folder 5; Britton, Monthly Report, June 14, 1967, box 2, folder 7; Britton to Robert L. Carter, December 11, 1967, box 3, folder 5; Joan Franklin to Britton, March 22, 1968, box 3, folder 10, all in NAACP(LA); Henderson, Fairclough interview.

71. Britton, Annual Report, November 29, 1967, box 3, folder 4; Britton to John E. Rousseau, June 13, 1967, box 2, folder 7; Velesta Jenkins, "River Road: A Rural Black Community in Southeastern Louisiana" (Ph.D. diss., Louisiana State University, 1969), pp. 101–2; Britton to Rowland C. Halstead, October 20, 1971; Hurley to Britton, November 2, 1971, box 12, folders 3, 4, all in NAACP(LA).

72. *Scott* v. *Walker*, 358 F. 2d 561 (1966); *State* v. *Goree*, 139 So. 2d 531 (1962); *Labat* v. *Bennett*, 365 F. 2d 698 (1966); Read and McGough, *Let Them Be Judged*, pp. 336–44; Carroll J. Dugas, "The Dismantling of De Jure Segregation in Louisiana, 1954–1974" (Ph.D. diss., Louisiana State University, 1989). After 1963, however, the death penalty fell into disuse in Louisiana. This development reflected a national trend: in 1967, in a decision that had national application, the U.S. Supreme Court ruled that the death penalty, as then carried out, was unconstitutional.

73. Alvin J. Bronstein interviews with Ben Smith and John P. Nelson, January 5, 1968; Plaintiff's Pre-Trial Brief, April 8, 1968, all in *Sobol* v. *Perez* file, reel 65, LCDC. Midlo was an officer of SCEF and the National Lawyers Guild who had been practicing in New Orleans since the 1930s.

74. Bass, *Unlikely Heroes*, pp. 286–92; Post-Trial Memorandum of Defendant-Intervenor Louisiana State Bar Association," *Sobol* v. *Perez* file, reel 65, LCDC.

75. *Times-Picayune*, February 7, 1968; Bass, *Unlikely Heroes*, p. 291.

76. *Sobol v. Perez,* 289 F. Supp. 392 (1968); *Duncan v. Louisiana,* 391 U.S. 145 (1968); *Duncan v. Perez,* 321 F. Supp. 181 (1970).

77. Britton to John E. Rousseau, June 13, 1967, box 2, folder 7; Sargent Pitcher Jr. to Chief of Police Eddie Bauer, September 19, 1969, box 34, folder 8, both in NAACP(LA).

78. W. Scott Miller to Rev. Herman Farr, December 29, 1970, box 10, folder 2; Tony Pierre to U.S. Attorney General, October 19, 1971, box 12, folder 3, both in NAACP(LA); James Duffy to Richard Kennion, May 17, 1976, general correspondence files, HRC.

79. *Baton Rouge Morning Advocate,* July 26, 27, 31, August 1, 2, 3, 7, 8, 12, 13, 14, 1969; memo on Baton Rouge situation, n.d., Morial Papers; D'Orsay Bryant, "Open Letter," August 8, 1969; Pitcher to Bauer, September 16, 1969, box 34, folders 7, 8, NAACP(LA).

80. Patricia B. Miller to Paul Anthony, March 20, 1968, series 1, file 1140, SRC.

81. Robert Weisbrot, *Freedom Bound: A History of America's Civil Rights Movement* (New York: W. W. Norton, 1990), pp. 236–37.

82. Joseph I. Giarusso to Moon Landrieu, "Intelligence Information on Black Panther Party," July 17, 30, August 5, 20, 1970, HRC.

83. *Times-Picayune,* September 15, 16, 17, 18, 19, 26, 1970; *States-Item,* September 15, 16, 17, 18, October 10, 1970; *Louisiana Weekly,* September 19, 1970; SAC, New Orleans, to Director, "Black Panther Party," September 8, 1970, FBI file 105-165706-33-151. The FBI intercepted all the telephone calls between the Black Panther headquarters in New Orleans and the national headquarters in Oakland.

84. *Times-Picayune,* November 20, 26, 30, 1970; *NOLA Express,* December 1, 1970; E. J. Keyes, reports from Desire Project, November 20, 24, 25, 1970, HRC; New Orleans to Director, "Black Panther Party," November 19; November 27, 1970, FBI file 105-165706-174, 182.

85. Margery Stitch to Moon Landrieu, n.d.; Concerned Black Citizens, press release, n.d.; F. Winter Trapolin to Clarence Giarusso, December 1, 1970, all in HRC; Harvey Britton, "Open Letter to Moon Landrieu," September 22, 1970, box 9, folder 4, NAACP(LA); *States-Item,* September 16, 1970.

86. Regional Planning Committee for Jefferson, Orleans, and St. Bernard Parishes, *Community Leaders Attitude Survey Report* (New Orleans, May 1970), p. 145, copy in Earl K. Long Library, University of New Orleans.

87. Roy Wilkins, "Steady As She Goes," reprinted in A. C. Littleton and M. W. Burger, eds., *Black Viewpoints* (New York: Mentor, 1971), pp. 295–96; *Times-Picayune,* September 16, 1970.

88. William Chafe, *Civilities and Civil Rights: Greensboro, North Carolina, and the Black Struggle for Freedom* (New York: Oxford University Press, 1981), pp. 197–99.

89. Gene Bourg, "Black Politics," *States-Item,* February 12, 13, March 2, 1973; Beverly H. Wright, "New Orleans: A City that Care Forgot," in Robert D. Bullard, ed., *In Search of the New South: The Black Urban Experience in the 1970s and 1980s* (Tuscaloosa: University of Alabama Press, 1987), p. 69; Hirsch, "Simply a Matter of Black and White," pp. 296–301.

90. Rogers, "Humanity and Desire," pp. 350–51; Ellis P. Henican to John P. Sissons, January 27, 1965; Sisson to Henican, March 5, 1965, box 3, CCHR; Summary of Deliberations of Interim Committee for Creating Biracial Committee, [1967]; Joseph I. Giarusso to Mayor Schiro, February 27, 1970, public accommodations file, all in HRC.

1. Hugh T. Murray Jr., "Black Eruption: Southern Style," pp. 13–14, Murray Collection, Rare Books and Manuscripts Division, TU.

2. Martzell, Fairclough interview, pp. 23–24; *Times-Picayune,* April 3, 1969.

3. Murray, "Black Eruption," pp. 16–24; Harvey Britton, Monthly Report, March 13–April 14, 1969, box 6, folder 3, NAACP(LA); *Times-Picayune,* April 7, 10, 1969.

4. Murray, "Black Eruption," pp. 25–160; *Times-Picayune,* May 10, 13, 15, 21, 1969.

5. Murray, "Black Eruption," pp. 79–84, 136; *Times-Picayune,* May 20, 1969; McKeithen, Fairclough interview.

6. Murray, "Black Eruption," pp. 4, 82.

7. *AAUP Bulletin,* 54, no. 1 (1968): 22–34.

8. Raphael Cassimere Jr., "Crisis of Public Higher Education in Louisiana," *Integrated Education* 13 (September 1975), p. 10; Murray, "Black Eruption," pp. 5–6.

9. George S. Haggar, "Letter to a Soul Brother," n.d., in *Haggar v. Bashfull* file, reel 27, LCDC; Murray, "Autobiography," pp. 230–31.

10. List of demands in *TABU SUNO,* [March 31, 1969], copy in *Haggar v. Bashfull* file, reel 27, LCDC; Murray, "Black Eruption," p. 111.

11. Robert Carter to Board Member, October 16, 1968; Roy Wilkins to National Board of Directors, October 31, 1968, both in box 5, folder 2, NAACP(LA); Wilkins, *Standing Fast,* pp. 330–32.

12. Alfred Baker Lewis to Britton, February 21, 1969; Britton to Gloster Current, February 25, 1969; to B. J. Mason, March 3, 1969, box 5, folders 7 and 8, NAACP(LA).

13. Britton, Monthly Report, March 13, 1969, box 5, folder 8; Richard L. Dockery to Paul Stewart, June 5, 1970, box 8, folder 7; Britton to Allison Chapital, Lucius Newell, and Claude Gasper, May 20, 1972, box 13, folder 8, all in NAACP(LA). In both Shreveport and Lake Charles, he suspected that older individuals encouraged Youth Council insurgency in order to further their own personal ambitions within the branch.

14. *Times-Picayune,* July 1, 1984.

15. Judge Frank Ellis forbade the Orleans Parish school board from applying the Pupil Placement Act until the dual school system had been completely dissolved. This 1962 decision effectively nullified the act.

16. Gary Orfield, *The Reconstruction of Southern Education: The Schools and the 1964 Civil Rights Act* (London: John Wiley, 1969), pp. 72–74, 110; McCall, "School Desegregation in Louisiana," pp. 198–201.

17. Tureaud to West, May 15, 1964, box 53, folder 2, APT; Navasky, *Kennedy Justice,* pp. 246–47; McCall, "School Desegregation in Louisiana," pp. 257–82; Ellis D. Howard to Daniel E. Byrd, August 13, 1964; Byrd T. Norman Amaker, August 17, 1964, both in box 2, folder 16, Byrd Papers.

18. McCall, "School Desegregation in Louisiana," p. 263; *Davis v. East Baton Rouge Parish School Board,* 214 F. Supp. 624 (1963).

19. McCall, "School Desegregation in Louisiana," p. 233; Donald W. Williamson and C. L. Perry to Jesse N. Stone Jr., April 27, 1965, box 1, folder 11, E. L. McGuire Papers, LSUS; Harold Howe II to Russell B. Long, April 22, 1966, Long file, White House Confidential File, LBJ; Henry H. Wilson to Joseph Califano, April 5, 1966, box 4, Ex HU2, LBJ; Southern Regional Council, *Lawlessness and Disorder: Fourteen Years of Failure* (Atlanta: Southern Regional Council, 1967), p. 55.

20. Orfield, *Reconstruction of Southern Education,* pp. 99–100; Lee C. White to Lyndon B. Johnson, August 6, 7, 1964, box HU2/ST13, LBJ; Burke Marshall to

J. Edgar Hoover, August 7, 1964; A. Rosen to A. H. Belmont, August 7, 1964; SAC, New Orleans, to Director, August 17, 1964, all in "Integration of St. Helena Parish, Louisiana, Public Schools-Racial Matter," FBI files 173-3230-47, 48, 76.

21. Dani Ostrow, "Compliance with Court Integration Order in Union Parish," [1967], in *Cleveland* v. *Union Parish School Board* file, reel 15; Ostrow, reports on East Feliciana Parish, June 22, 1968; West Feliciana Parish, June 23, 1968; Winn Parish, June 24, 1968, in *George* v. *Davis* file, reel 19; Ostrow,"Compliance with Court Integration Order in Bogalusa," September 28, 1967, in *Jenkins* v. *City of Bogalusa* file, reel 39, all in LCDC; James H. Henderson to A. P. Tureaud, September 8, 1966, box 33, folder 15, APT. For Heebe and Bogalusa (and Washington Parish), see Dugas, "Dismantling of De Jure Segregation," pp. 231–32, 238–39; for Christenberry and Plaquemines Parish, see Jeansonne, *Leander Perez*, pp. 284–308.

22. *United States* v. *Jefferson County Board of Education,* 372 F. 2d 836 (1966); Southern Regional Council, *Lawlessness and Disorder*, pp. 29–54; Bass, *Unlikely Heroes*, pp. 297–307.

23. Wisdom, Bass interviews, May 22, 1979, p. 44; September 28, 1979, p. 15.

24. *Green* v. *County School Board of New Kent County,* 391 U.S. 430 (1968); Read and McGough, *Let Them Be Judged*, pp. 474, 615; Bass, *Unlikely Heroes*, pp. 307–8.

25. Dugas, "Dismantling of De Jure Segregation" pp. 238–39; Read and McGough, *Let Them Be Judged*, pp. 476–77; Haley M. Carter and A. Clayton James to Louisiana School Superintendents, February 12, 1968, E. L. McGuire Papers.

26. Judges Dawkins, Hunter, and Putnam, Order, November 13, 1968, in *Andrews* v. *City of Monroe* file, reel 4, LCDC; Brief for the Appellants, *Trahan* v. *Lafayette Parish School Board,* box 5, folder 18, Byrd Papers; Brief for the United States, *Hall* v. *St. Helena Parish School Board and Companion Cases,* box 53, folder 15, APT; McCall, "School Desegregation in Louisiana," pp. 314–26.

27. "Background and Introduction of Desegregation Recommendations for Caddo Parish Independent School District," [1969], box 3, folder 92; D. L. Kennedy to Caddo Parish School Board, June 16, 1969, box 9, folder 150; HEW, "A Desegregation Plan for Caddo Parish School District," [1969]; Caddo Parish School Board, minutes, July 21, 1969, box 9, folder 155, all in E. L. McGuire Papers; *Lake Charles American Press,* July 4, 1969 (this and other citations of the *American Press* refer to "Schools in Crisis," a scrapbook of clippings in the Lake Charles public library); Brief for the Appellants, in the U.S. Court of Appeals for the Fifth Circuit, No. 28061, in *Jenkins* v. *City of Bogalusa* file, reel 39, LCDC.

28. Charlton H. Lyons to E. L. McGuire, June 23, 1969, box 9, folder 151, E. L. McGuire Papers; Leon H. Panetta and Peter Gall, *Bring Us Together: The Nixon Team and Civil Rights* (Philadelphia: J. B. Lippincott, 1971), pp. 233, 325. In the 88th Congress, Waggoner had supported the Democratic administration in only one vote out of four, a record of siding with the Republicans matched only by Otto Passman, representing the Monroe area. Louisiana had eight congressmen at that time; their voting records are analyzed in Louisiana briefing book, box 121, Moyers Papers, LBJ. It should be noted, however, that all of Louisiana's congressmen, with the exception of Hale Boggs, lobbied the Nixon administration to slow down desegregation (McCall, "School Desegregation in Louisiana," p. 346).

29. "Statement by Ben C. Dawkins, Jr.," July 3, 1969, in *Andrews* v. *City of Monroe* file, reel 5, LCDC; *Lake Charles American Press,* July 21, 1969.

30. *Times-Picayune,* June 25, 1969; *Lake Charles American-Press,* July 16, 1969; McCall, "School Desegregation in Louisiana," pp. 347–48; Harvey Britton, Summer Report, June 14–September 15, 1969, pp. 4–6, box 7, folder 2, NAACP(LA).

31. *States-Item,* September 3, 8, 9, 1969; *Times-Picayune,* September 9, 11; October 13, 15; November 11, 1969; McGough and Read, *Let Them Be Judged,* pp. 483–509.

32. *Times-Picayune,* February 17, 19, 24, 1970; Harvey Britton, Annual Report, November 18, 1970, box 9, folder 8, NAACP(LA). The "freedom-of-choice" act was declared unconstitutional by a federal district court in October 1970.

33. Price, *Troy H. Middleton,* pp. 382–83; Stone, Fairclough interview; Jewel L. Prestage and Carolyn Sue Williams, "Blacks in Louisiana Politics," in Bolnar, ed., *Louisiana Politics,* pp. 307–8. McKeithen's hard-line stand spelled the end of the state biracial commission, which ceased functioning in 1970.

34. *Times-Picayune,* October 31, 1969; *States-Item,* August 1, 1969; E. Gordon West, Speech to Louisiana School Board Association, March 13–15, 1969, box 2, material of unknown provenance, OPSB; Alexandria *Daily Town Talk,* April 28, 1970.

35. Read and McGough, *Let Them Be Judged,* p. 616.

36. Allen H. Plummer to Ben C. Dawkins, March 10, 1970; Dawkins to Plummer, March 12, 1970, box 8, folder 1; analysis of school registration in selected parishes, December 2, 1970, box 9, folder 9, all in NAACP(LA).

37. James R. Bobo and Sandra A. Etheridge, eds., *Statistical Abstract of Louisiana, 1969* (New Orleans: Division of Business and Economic Research, University of New Orleans, 1969), p. 105; Bobo and Etheridge, eds., *Statistical Abstract of Louisiana, 1974,* p. 116; Vincent Maruggi and Susanne D. Harti, eds., *Statistical Abstract of Louisiana, 1981* (New Orleans: Division of Business and Economic Research, University of New Orleans, 1981), p. 80; *Poindexter* v. *Louisiana Financial Assistance Commission,* 275 F.Supp. 833 (1967); Judges Wisdom, Heebe and Gordon, *Brumfield* v. *Dodd,* December 2, 1975, box 6, folder 1, Byrd Papers; *Green* v. *Kennedy* file, reel 26, LCDC. Evidence of substantial segregation in the Catholic schools is contained in *Auzenne* v. *School Board of the Diocese of Lafayette,* reel 6, LCDC.

38. "NEA Task Force Report on School Desegregation in Louisiana, February 15–22, 1970," pp. 4–7, box 8, older 6, NAACP(LA); Johnny S. Butler, "Black Educators in Louisiana: A Question of Survival," *Journal of Negro Education* 43 (Winter 1974): 13–23. In 1966–67 black children composed 39 percent of the public school registration in Louisiana, and blacks made up 36 percent of the teachers. In 1975–76 the proportion of black children had increased to 40 percent but the proportion of black teachers had fallen to 34 percent.

39. Alvin R. Childress to St. Bernard Parish School Board, March 25, 1969, box 2, material of unknown provenance, OPSB; *States-Item,* August 28, 1969; "NEA Report Task Force Report," pp. 12–13.

40. Imy Viquire to NAACP Legal Defense Fund, December 18, 1969, box 7, folder 6; Harvey Britton, Monthly Report, February 17, 1970, box 7, folder 10; Robert Lee Lewis to Harvey Britton, January 16, box 10, folder 2; Concerned Parents of Rayne to Britton, February 17, 1971, box 10, folder 5, all in NAACP(LA); Concerned Citizens for Equal Education to Caddo Parish School Board, August 1972, box 5, folder 5, Byrd Papers.

41. Johnnie Mae Walton to Britton, October 21, 1970, box 9, folder 6; Rayne parents to Emmitt J. Douglas, December 28, 1970, box 10, folder 1, both in NAACP(LA); Commission on Civil Rights, Louisiana Advisory Committee, *School Desegregation in Bogalusa,* p. 44.

42. *Times-Picayune,* September 10, 1968; Phil Trice to Samuel I. Rosenberg, November 6, 1972, OPSB; anonymous teacher to Carl Dolce, July 4, 1965, box 2, folder 17, Byrd Papers.

43. Britton, Summer Report, September 14, 1970, box 25, folder 5, NAACP(LA).

44. Harvey Britton, "Chronological Summary of Events of Student Demonstrations at Alcee Fortier High School," January 17–28, 1969, box 5, folder 6; "Report of the Special Committee by the Orleans Parish School System and Superintendant Carl Dolce on the Fortier High School Crisis," March 17, 1969, box 6, folder 1, both in NAACP(LA); Veronica B. Hill to Orleans Parish School Board, n.d., box 2, material of unknown provenance, OPSB.

45. *New Orleans States-Item,* August 27, 1969; Christopher H. Foreman, Annual Report, New Iberia NAACP, December 30, 1969; Wilfred L. Lambert, Report of the Committee on Political Action, New Iberia NAACP, January 5, 1970, both in box 39, folder 24; "NAACP Newsletter," Plaquemine Branch, February 15, 1970, box 38, folder 8, all in NAACP(LA); *Baton Rouge Morning Advocate,* February 4, 18, 20; March 10, 26; April 2, 1970; *Baton Rouge State-Times,* February 18, 19, 1970; SAC, New Orleans, to Director, "Iberville Parish, Louisiana, Schools," March 13, 1970, FBI file 173-7262-2; SAC, New Orleans, to Director, "James Williams vs. Iberville Parish School Board," FBI file 173-2110-86; Harvey Britton, Annual Report, November 18, 1970, box 9, folder 8, NAACP(LA).

46. *Bogalusa Daily News,* October 18[?], 23, 1969; September 14, 15, 1970; *Washington Post,* November 23, 1969; notes on Bogalusa demonstrations, October 17, 1969; Judge Heebe, Temporary Restraining Order, October 18, 22, 28, 1969; Minute Entry and Order, May 2, 1970; Temporary Restraining Order, September 21, 30; October 9, 16, 1970; Welton Seal, Petition for Temporary Restraining Order, September 19, 1970; Memo in Support of Motion for Preliminary Injunction, n.d., 1970, all in *Jenkins* v. *City of Bogalusa* file, reel 40, LCDC.

47. Daniel Byrd, Special Report, Vermilion Parish, January 14, 1972, box 4, folder 9; Byrd to Margaret Ford, November 11, December 16, 1972, box 3, folder 8; Byrd, Activity Report, December 1972, box 4, folder 3; Byrd to J. K. Haynes, January 21, 1975, box 3, folder 12, all in Byrd Papers.

48. *Times-Picayune,* July 11, 1984.

49. Summary of Citizens Committee Plan, 1973; "Problems Associated with Integrating Black Girls into the School Activities Program," n.d.; advice to athletics coaches, n.d., all in box 2, Charles T. Beaird Papers, LSUS.

50. Byrd to Norman Chachkin, Special Report, March 31, 1973; Special Report, Lafourche Parish, April 7, 1973; Special Report, Vermilion Parish, January 14, 1972, box 4, folder 9, Byrd Papers.

51. Carl J. Dolce to Orleans Parish School Board, August 20, 1968, box 2, material of unknown provenance, OPSB; *Times-Picayune,* July 19, 1971; May 29, 31, 1972; July 11, 1984.

52. Activity Report, December 1972, box 4, folder 3, Byrd Papers; Motley, Bass interview, pp. 72–74.

53. Statement of John W. Davis, Special Director, Department of Teacher Information and Security, June 20, 1955, box 5, folder 1; Davis, Review and Report, February 8, 1963, box 2, folder 21; J. K. Haynes to Byrd, box 2, folder 4; Haynes to Byrd, March 7, 1968; Jack Greenberg to Leon Panetta, July 25, 1969; Davis to Norman Chachkin, December 21, 1970; Byrd to Chachkin, January 9, 1971; Byrd to Haynes, February 5, 1971; Byrd to Greenberg, November 29, 1972, box 3, folders 2–8, all in Byrd Papers.

54. Britton to Johnnie Mae Walton, November 2, 1970, box 9, folder 7; Britton, Fairclough interview, p. 9; White, Rickels interview; Basile Miller to Byrd, [1967], box 4, folder 2, Byrd Papers.

55. Herman Schwarz, Hearing Memo, July 11, 1969; Judge Heebe, Memorandum

Opinion and Order, July 22, 1969, both in *Jenkins* v. *City of Bogalusa* file, reel 39, LCDC.

56. Byrd to Chachkin, "Re: Jones v. Caddo Parish School Board," [1973], box 3, folder 9, Byrd Papers.

57. Memo in Support of Motion for Appointment and Designation of the United States as Amicus Curiae, February 16, 1970; Affidavit of Charles K. Howard, February 16, 1970, both in *Adams* v. *City of Monroe* file, reel 4, LCDC; Charles T. Beaird, handwritten notes concerning desegregation of Caddo Parish schools, May 3, 22, 1973; Summary of Citizens Committee Plan, both in Beaird Papers; Beaird, Humphreys interview, p. 19–21.

58. *Times-Picayune*, May 29, 1972; Summary of Citizens Committee Plan, box 2, Beaird Papers; *Davis* v. *East Baton Rouge School Board*, 398 F. Supp. 1013 (1975); Jeansonne, *Leander Perez*, p. 308; Commission on Civil Rights, Louisiana Advisory Committee, *School Desegregation in Bogalusa*.

59. W. E. Solomon to John W. Davis, March 23, 1967; Davis to Byrd, April 27, 1976; Irvamae Applegate to J. K. Haynes and N. B. Hackett, May 25, 1967; George Fischer to Haynes, February 12, 1969; June 25, 1969, all in box 3, folders 1–3, Byrd Papers.

60. Middleton, *History of the Louisiana Education Association*, pp. 115–53; Cassimere and Logsdon, Fairclough interview; Haynes to Byrd, April 26, 1974, box 3, folder 10, Byrd Papers.

61. Cassimere "Crisis of Public Higher Education, p. 11; Panetta and Gall, *Bring Us Together*, p. 330; Howell T. Humphrey to Harvey Britton, November 25, 1971, box 12, folder 5; Special Committee on Desegregation of Higher Education, minutes, December 19, 1971, box 41, folder 17; Raphael Cassimere Jr., Report of the Chairman, April 23, 1972; Britton, Monthly Report, May 22–June 21, 1972, box 14, folder 2, all in NAACP(LA); Report of the NAACP Special Committee on Desegregation of Public-Supported Higher Education in Louisiana, November 12, 1972, box 4, folder 8, Byrd Papers.

62. *Baton Rouge Morning Advocate*, November 17, 18, 19, 20, 21, 1972; Nicholas C. Chriss, "A Moderate's First Test," *Nation*, December 18, 1972, 622–23; Cornish Rogers, "Ironies and Deaths at Southern," *Christian Century* 84 (December 18, 1972): 1263–64; Pat Watters, "Toward Justice in Louisiana," *Christian Century* 90 (January 31, 1973): 115; William J. Guste Jr., *Report of the Attorney General's Special Commission of Enquiry of the Southern University Tragedy of November 16, 1972* (Baton Rouge, 1973), copy in Law Library, University of Virginia.

63. Wright, "New Orleans: A City That Care Forgot," p. 64. The Supreme Court's decision in a Mississippi case, *U.S.* v. *Fordice*, 120 L. Ed 2d 575 (1992), has revived pressure for the two systems to merge.

64. Ibid., pp. 65–67; Roger Biles, "A Bittersweet Victory: Public School Desegregation in Memphis," *Journal of Negro Education* 55 (Fall 1986): 470–83; Robert A. Pratt, "A Promise Unfulfilled: School Desegregation in Richmond, Virginia, 1956–1986," *Virginia Magazine of History and Biography* 99 (October 1991): 415–48; Ronald P. Formisano, *Boston against Busing: Race, Class and Ethnicity in the 1960s and 1970s* (Chapel Hill: University of North Carolina Press, 1991), pp. 210–11, 222–23; *Times-Picayune*, July 11, 1984. It is not my intention to address the debate on the extent to which busing caused or exacerbated the decline in white enrollment. A consensus seems to be emerging that busing was indeed counterproductive. Yet in Louisiana's big cities, where busing was not extensively employed, whites left the public schools in comparable numbers.

65. *Times-Picayune*, August 21, 1988; November 23, 1991; January 12, 1992.

66. *Zippert* v. *Sylvester,* RRLR, 12 (1967), 1445; *Times-Picayune,* January 11, 1988; John P. Nelson, Stephens interview; David R. Fine, text of speech, September 19, 1985, box 4, folder 10, records of New Orleans Community Relations Council, ARC. By 1986 the number of interracial marriages had risen to five hundred, or 1.4 percent.

CHAPTER 15: *Struggle without End*

1. Elizabeth A. Rickey, "The Nazi and the Republicans: An Insider View of the Response of the Louisiana Republican Party to David Duke," in Douglas D. Rose, ed., *The Emergence of David Duke and the Politics of Race* (Chapel Hill: University of North Carolina Press, 1992), pp. 64–74. Duke took 58 percent of the white vote in 1990 and 55 percent in 1991.

2. Bass and DeVries, *Transformation of Southern Politics,* pp. 167–68; Price, "Impact of Black Voter Participation," pp. 115–18; Alexander P. Lamis. *The Two-Party South* (New York: Oxford University Press, 1990), pp. 110–11; Prestage and Williams, "Blacks in Louisiana Politics," pp. 307–8. Edwards rewarded his black allies with important appointments. Jackson, elected to the state legislature in 1971—the first black representative from north Louisiana—became Edwards's floor manager. Stone became president of Southern University. A. Z. Young, former leader of the Bogalusa Voters League, received a top administrative position in the Department of Health and Human Resources.

3. Bass and DeVries, *Transformation of Southern Politics,* pp. 177, 180. The victor in the runoff, W. Henson Moore, was a conservative Republican with the reputation of a racial moderate.

4. Ibid., p. 176; Price, "Impact of Black Voter Participation," p. 177; *Times-Picayune,* June 9, July 6, 1972; Anne L. Simon, "Inequality under the Law: The Louisiana Story," *Southern Studies* 16 (1977): 293–96; Mark T. Carleton, "The Louisiana Constitution of 1974," in Bolner, ed., *Louisiana Politics,* p. 27. The New Orleans public accommodations ordinance was passed in December 1969 and came into effect the following month.

5. Pat Bryant, "A Long Time Coming," *Southern Exposure* 10 (May-June 1982): 83–89; *New York Times,* February 25, 1980; May 11, 1981; *Times-Picayune,* February 24, March 20, August 3, December 11, 12, 1987.

6. *Bogalusa Daily News,* December 5, 1979; Dundy, *Ferriday,* pp. 194–96; Joint Center for Political Studies, *Black Elected Officials: A National Roster* (Washington, D.C.: Joint Center for Political Studies, 1993). Reapportionment created another black-majority district stretching along the Mississippi and Red River.

7. Frank R. Parker, *Black Votes Count: Political Empowerment in Mississippi after 1965* (Chapel Hill: University of North Carolina Press, 1990), pp. 97–100; Steven F. Lawson, *In Pursuit of Power: Southern Blacks and Electoral Politics, 1965–1982* (New York: Columbia University Press, 1985), pp. 135–40, 189–90.

8. Halpin, "The Anti-Gerrymander," pp. 206–8.

9. *Blacks United for Lasting Leadership* v. *City of Shreveport,* 71 F.R.D. 623 (1976); Burton, *The Black Side of Shreveport,* pp. 122–23.

10. Stone, Fairclough interview; Louisiana Governmental Studies, *The Grass Roots Guide, Vol 2: Lobbying the Louisiana Legislature, 1988–1992* (Lafayette: Louisiana Governmental Studies, 1988), pp. 140–41, copy in Louisiana Collection, TU; Alvin J. Schexnider, "Political Mobilization in the South: The Election of a Black Mayor in New Orleans," in Michael B. Preston, Lenneal J. Henderson Jr., and Paul Puryear,

eds., *The New Black Politics: The Search for Political Power* (New York: Longman, 1982), pp. 227–31; Hirsch, "Simply a Matter of Black and White," p. 314. According to Stone, an exception was made for Pike Hall, who became a justice of the state supreme court.

11. Steven F. Lawson, *Running for Freedom: Civil Rights and Black Politics in America since 1941* (Philadelphia: Temple University Press, 1991), p. 262; Wright, "New Orleans: A City That Care Forgot," pp. 60–61; *Washington Post,* January 11, 1991; *New York Times,* April 10, 1994.

12. William Julius Wilson, *The Declining Significance of Race: Blacks and Changing American Institutions* (Chicago: University of Chicago Press, 1978), pp. 93–103; Hirsch, "Simply a Matter of Black and White," pp. 317–18.

13. *New York Times,* January 12, 1986; Lamis, *Two-Party South,* pp. 288–89, 316–18. Wilder picked up 44 percent of the white vote in 1986 and 41 percent in 1989.

14. Maruggi and Harti, eds., *Statistical Abstract of Louisiana, 1981,* p. 133; *Washington Post,* October 14, 1990; January 5, 1991; *Times-Picayune,* November 17, 1993; *Guardian* (London), June 1, 1994; Coramae Richey Mann, *Unequal Justice: A Question of Color* (Bloomington and Indianapolis: Indiana University Press, 1993), pp. 46, 202–3, 222–23.

15. *Times-Picayune,* January 11, February 22, 24, 1987; Lawrence N. Powell, "Slouching toward Baton Rouge: The 1989 Legislative Election of David Duke," in Douglas D. Rose, ed., *The Emergence of David Duke and the Politics of Race,* pp. 16–17.

16. Lawson, *Running for Freedom,* p. 244.

17. Alphonso Pinkney, *The Myth of Black Progress* (Cambridge: Cambridge University Press, 1984), p. 179.

18. *Times-Picayune,* October 25, 1986; Lamis, *The Two-Party South,* pp. 277–78.

19. Powell, "Slouching toward Baton Rouge," pp. 16–17; Douglas D. Rose with Gary Esolen, "DuKKKe for Governor: 'Vote for the Crook. It's Important,'" in Douglas D. Rose, ed., *The Emergence of David Duke and the Politics of Race,* p. 211.

20. Powell, "Slouching toward Baton Rouge," pp. 22–25.

21. Ibid., pp. 28–29; James R. Adams, "The Sunbelt," in John B. Boles, ed., *Dixie Dateline: A Journalistic Portrait of the Contemporary South* (Houston: Rice University Studies, 1983), pp. 148–49; Wright, "New Orleans: A City That Care Forgot," p. 61; Powell, "Slouching toward Baton Rouge," pp. 28–29; Monte Piliawsky, "The Limits of Power: New Orleans," *Southern Exposure* 12 (February 1984): 72.

22. Paul Grosser, "Political Parties," in James Bolner, ed., *Louisiana Politics,* pp. 258–77; Wall, *Louisiana,* p. 365; Lamis, *The Two-Party South,* pp. 114–16, 355; *New York Times,* July 6, 18, 21, 1979; January 5, 1980. The "open primary" rule, moreover, provides that the top two candidates in the first primary, regardless of party affiliation, should face each other in the runoff election. The rule has made a nonsense of the two-party system.

23. *New York Times,* May 20, September 26, 1971; *New York Times,* January 5, 1973; Lamis, *The Two-Party South,* p. 280; Hirsch, "Simply a Matter of Black and White," pp. 300–2; *Washington Post,* June 30, 1991; John H. Davis, *Mafia Kingfish: Carlos Marcello and the Assassination of John F. Kennedy* (New York: Signet, 1989), pp. 486–92, 549; *Southern Exposure,* Summer 1991, p. 2. If they do not take bribes or steal public monies, politicians still commonly exploit public office to favor friends, relatives, and business associates. In 1992, for example, it emerged that state legislators, who each have the right to award a Tulane scholarship to a deserving student, have routinely chosen their own family members. Mayor Sidney Barthelemy awarded one to his son.

24. Dodd, *Peapatch Politics,* pp. 5–6.

25. *Times-Picayune,* November 17, 18, 1991; Iris Kelso, "Black Solidarity Wins it

for Edwards and Louisiana," *Times-Picayune,* November 18, 1991; Rose and Esolen, "DuKKKe for Governor," pp. 227–31. Black turnout reached nearly 80 percent, 3 or 4 percentage points above white turnout.

26. *Times-Picayune,* May 29, November 8, 1990; February 1, 1992.

27. *Times-Picayune,* January 12, 19, 20, 21, 22, 1992.

BIBLIOGRAPHY

PAPERS AND ARCHIVAL COLLECTIONS

Americans for Democratic Action Papers, State Historical Society of Wisconsin, Madison (microfilm at University of Ulster, Jordanstown).
American Friends Service Committee Papers, Philadelphia.
Attorney General of Louisiana Papers, Louisiana State Archives, Baton Rouge.
Jack Bass Oral History Collection, Law Library, Tulane University, New Orleans.
Charles T. Beaird Papers, Louisiana State University, Shreveport.
Murphy W. Bell Papers, State Historical Society of Wisconsin, Madison (microfilm).
Horace Mann Bond Papers, University of Massachusetts, Amherst (microfilm at Perkins Library, Duke University).
Daniel E. Byrd Papers, Amistad Research Center, Tulane University, New Orleans.
Catholic Committee of the South Papers, Amistad Research Center, Tulane University, New Orleans.
Catholic Council on Human Relations Papers, Amistad Research Center, Tulane University, New Orleans.
Commission on Interracial Cooperation Papers (microfilm at Alderman Library, University of Virginia, Charlottesville).
Congress of Racial Equality (CORE) Papers (microfilm at Amistad Research Center, Tulane University, New Orleans).
Congress of Racial Equality (CORE) Papers, Scholarship, Education and Defense

Fund for Racial Equality files (microfilm at Alderman Library, University of Virginia, Charlottesville).

Congress of Racial Equality (CORE) Papers, Southern Regional Office files, State Historical Society of Wisconsin, Madison.

Congress of Racial Equality (CORE) Papers, Monroe Project files, State Historical Society of Wisconsin, Madison.

Congress of Racial Equality (CORE) Papers, Ferriday Freedom Movement files, State Historical Society of Wisconsin, Madison.

Congress of Racial Equality (CORE) Papers, Homer files, State Historical Society of Wisconsin, Madison.

Congress of Racial Equality (CORE) Papers, Jackson Parish files, State Historical Society of Wisconsin, Madison.

Congress of Racial Equality (CORE) Papers, Bogalusa Voters League files, State Historical Society of Wisconsin, Madison.

Congress of Racial Equality (CORE) Papers, Meldon Acheson Papers, State Historical Society of Wisconsin, Madison.

James A. Dombrowski Papers, Hollis Burke Frissell Library, Tuskegee University.

Nils R. Douglas Papers, Amistad Research Center, Tulane University, New Orleans.

Allen J. Ellender Papers, Nicholls State University, Thibodaux, Louisiana.

Fair Employment Practices Committee Papers (microfilm at Alderman Library, University of Virginia, Charlottesville).

Miriam Feingold Papers, State Historical Society of Wisconsin, Madison.

Joseph H. Fichter Papers, Loyola University of the South, New Orleans.

Joseph B. Gremillion Papers, Louisiana State University, Shreveport.

Joseph A. Hardin Papers, Amistad Research Center, Tulane University, New Orleans.

Giles A. Hubert Papers, Amistad Research Center, Tulane University, New Orleans.

Carleton N. James Oral History Collection, University of Southwestern Louisiana, Lafayette.

Lyndon B. Johnson Presidential Papers, Lyndon B. Johnson Library, Austin, Texas.

Oakley C. Johnson Papers, Schomberg Library, New York, New York.

Rosa Keller Papers, Amistad Research Center, Tulane University, New Orleans.

Robert F. Kennon Papers, Hill Memorial Library, Louisiana State University, Baton Rouge.

Kirby, Jack T., ed. *New Deal Agencies and Black America,* microfilm at Alderman Library, University of Virginia.

Lawson, Steven F., ed. *Civil Rights during the Kennedy Administration* (microfilm at Alderman Library, University of Virginia, Charlottesville).

Lawyers Constitutional Defense Committee files (microfilm at Amistad Research Center, Tulane University, New Orleans).

League of Women Voters Papers, Howard-Tilton Library, Tulane University, New Orleans.

Harold N. Lee Papers, Howard-Tilton Library, Tulane University, New Orleans.

George S. Longe Papers, Amistad Research Center, Tulane University, New Orleans.

Dave McGuire Papers, Howard-Tilton Library, Tulane University, New Orleans.

E. L. McGuire Papers, Louisiana State University, Shreveport.

Harry C. McPherson Papers, Lyndon B. Johnson Library, Austin, Texas.

Burke Marshall Papers, John F. Kennedy Presidential Library, Boston.

Ernest N. Morial Papers, Amistad Research Center, Tulane University, New Orleans.

DeLesseps S. Morrison Papers, Louisiana Collection, New Orleans Public Library.

DeLesseps S. Morrison Papers, Howard-Tilton Library, Tulane University, New Orleans.

James H. Morrison Papers, University of Southeastern Louisiana, Hammond.

Bill Moyers Papers, Lyndon B. Johnson Library, Austin, Texas.

National Association for the Advancement of Colored People (NAACP) Papers, Branch files, Library of Congress Manuscript Division.

National Association for the Advancement of Colored People (NAACP), Papers of the NAACP Field Director for Louisiana, Amistad Research Center, Tulane University, New Orleans.

National Association for the Advancement of Colored People (NAACP), New Orleans Branch Records, Earl K. Long Library, University of New Orleans.

National Association for the Advancement of Colored People (NAACP), Voting Rights, Education, Lynching, Legal Department and Central Office Records files, Library of Congress Manuscript Division (microfilm at Alderman Library, University of Virginia, Charlottesville).

National Urban League Papers, Library of Congress.

John P. Nelson Papers, Amistad Research Center, Tulane University, New Orleans.

New Orleans Community Relations Council Papers, Amistad Research Center, Tulane University, New Orleans.

New Orleans Human Relations Council, Louisiana Collection, New Orleans Public Library.

Orleans Parish School Board files, Earl K. Long Library, University of New Orleans.

Leander H. Perez Papers, Louisiana Collection, New Orleans Public Library.

William M. Rainach Papers, Louisiana State University, Shreveport.

Right-Wing Collection of the University of Iowa Libraries (microfilm at University of Ulster, Jordanstown).

Kim Lacy Rogers–Glenda Stephens Oral History Collection, Amistad Research Center, Tulane University, New Orleans.

Rosenwald Fund Papers (microfilm at Amistad Research Center, Tulane University, New Orleans).

Bayard Rustin Papers (microfilm at Alderman Library, University of Virginia, Charlottesville).

Save Our Schools Papers, Amistad Research Center, Tulane University, New Orleans.

John Henry Scott Papers, Earl K. Long Library, University of New Orleans.

Southern Christian Leadership Conference Papers, Library and Archives, Martin Luther King, Jr., Center for Nonviolent Social Change, Atlanta.

Southern Regional Council Papers (microfilm at Alderman Library, University of Virginia, Charlottesville).

Southern Tenant Farmers Union Papers (microfilm at Alderman Library, University of Virginia, Charlottesville).

Southern University Archives, Southern University, Baton Rouge.

Alexander Pierre Tureaud Papers, Amistad Research Center, Tulane University, New Orleans.

Louis Twomey Papers, Loyola University of the South, New Orleans.

United Church of Christ Papers, Amistad Research Center, Tulane University, New Orleans.

Marvin Watson Papers, Lyndon B. Johnson Library, Austin, Texas.

Lee C. White Papers, Lyndon B. Johnson Library, Austin, Texas.

Scott W. Wilson Papers, Howard-Tilton Library, Tulane University, New Orleans.
John Zippert Papers, Amistad Research Center, Tulane University, New Orleans.

FEDERAL BUREAU OF INVESTIGATION FILES

44-0-8149	Leander H. Perez Sr.
44-0-10686	Leander H. Perez Sr.
44-999	Unknown Subjects; Eviction of Negro Civic Leaders, New Iberia, Louisiana
44-3207	Racial Incident, Opelousas, Louisiana (Alvin Jones, Victim)
44-9732	Leander H. Perez Sr.
44-10956	White Citizens Council, Colfax, Louisiana
44-11324	Citizens Council of Louisiana
44-30670	Leander H. Perez Sr.
44-38137	Richard Sobol v. Leander H. Perez Sr.
56-1211	Leander H. Perez Sr.
61-10149	Civil Rights Congress
61-3176	Communist Infiltration of the National Association for the Advancement of Colored People, New Orleans
62-5-7437	Name Check, Leander H. Perez Sr.
72-1285	Integration of Public Schools in Orleans Parish
72-1286	Integration of Public Schools in Orleans Parish
100-232896	People's Defense League
100-3-47	Communist Party of the USA, New Orleans District
100-326-33	Communist Party of Louisiana
100-33049-33	Communist Infiltration of CIO Industrial Union Councils, New Orleans
100-38567	Southern Gentlemen
100-45768	Louisiana Farmers' Union
100-56308	Ernest John Wright
105-40774	Citizens Council of Greater New Orleans
105-44536	Citizens Council of Louisiana
105-45268	Shreveport Citizens Council
105-47564	Citizens Council of Ouachita Parish
105-47575	Natchitoches Parish Citizens Council
105-48034	Choudrant Citizens Council
105-48558	Arcadia Citizens Council
105-49733	Sarepta Citizens Council
105-49758	Citizens Council of Athens
105-49764	Bossier Citizens Council
105-49770	Citizens Council of Homer
105-49798	Citizens Council of Shongaloo
105-49832	Citizens Council of Haynesville, Louisiana
105-49845	Citizens Council of Dubberly
105-49846	Citizens Council of Summerfield
105-49936	Citizens Council of West Carroll Parish
105-50153	Springhill Citizens Council
105-50206	Benton Citizens Council
105-50210	Plain Dealing Citizens Council

105-51477	Cotton Valley Citizens Council
105-50956	Caldwell Parish Citizens Council
105-52227	Farmerville Citizens Council
105-52533	Minden Citizens Council
105-71801	Original Knights of the Ku Klux Klan
105-165706	Black Panther Party, New Orleans Division
157-4-33	Integration of Public Schools, Orleans Parish
157-2466	Deacons of Defense and Justice
157-4517	Anti-Communist Christian Association
157-5844	Proposed March of Bogalusa Voters League
157-7984	Rabble Rouser Index, Leander H. Perez Sr.
173-987	Racial Situation, Bogalusa, Louisiana
173-134	Jackson Parish Public Library, Jonesboro
173-1342	Jackson Parish Courthouse, Jonesboro, La.
173-1720	Desegregation of Schools, Washington Parish
173-1784	Jackson Parish School Board, School Desegregation
173-1887	Desegregation of Public Schools, Claiborne Parish
173-2015	Original Knights of the Ku Klux Klan
173-2110	Desegregation of Public Schools, Iberville Parish
173-2607	Webster Parish, La.
173-3230	Desegregation of St. Helena Parish Public Schools
173-5897	Desegregation of Public Schools, East Carroll Parish
173-7262	Racial Incidents, Iberville Parish
173-8032	Transfer of Public School Property to Private Schools, Lake Providence

Cross References J. Leo Hardy
Cross References Madison Parish Voters League

SELECTED BOOKS

Adams, Frank T. *James A. Dombrowski: An American Heretic, 1897–1983*. Knoxville: University of Tennessee Press, 1992.

Alexander, Charles C. *The Ku Klux Klan in the Southwest*. Lexington: University of Kentucky Press, 1966.

Ames, Jesse Daniel. *The Changing Character of Lynching*. Atlanta: Commission on Interracial Cooperation, 1942.

Amistad Symposium on Southern Civil Rights Litigation Records for the 1960s. New Orleans, Amistad Research Center, 1978.

Anderson, James D. *The Education of Blacks in the South, 1860–1935*. Chapel Hill: University of North Carolina Press, 1988.

Anderson, J. W. *Eisenhower, Brownell, and the Congress: The Tangled Origins of the Civil Rights Bill of 1956–57*. University: University of Alabama Press, 1964.

Arnesen, Eric. *Waterfront Workers of New Orleans: Race, Class, and Politics, 1863–1923*. New York: Oxford University Press, 1991.

Ashmore, Harry S. *The Negro and the Schools*. Chapel Hill: University of North Carolina Press, 1954.

Badger, Anthony J. *The New Deal: The Depression Years, 1933–1940*. London: Macmillan, 1989.

Barnes, Catherine A. *Journey from Jim Crow: The Desegregation of Southern Transit.* New York: Columbia University Press, 1983.

Bartley, Numan V. *The Rise of Massive Resistance.* Baton Rouge: Louisiana State University Press, 1969.

Bartley, Numan V., and Hugh D. Graham. *Southern Elections: County and Precinct Data, 1950–1972.* Baton Rouge: Louisiana State University Press, 1978.

Baskerville, Stephen W., and Ralph Willet, eds. *Nothing Else to Fear: New Perspectives on America in the Thirties.* Manchester: Manchester University Press, 1985.

Bass, Jack. *Unlikely Heroes.* Tuscaloosa: University of Alabama Press, 1981, 1990.

Bass, Jack, and Walter DeVries. *The Transformation of Southern Politics: Social Change and Political Consequences since 1945.* New York: Meridian, 1977.

Beals, Carleton S. *The Story of Huey P. Long.* Philadelphia: J. B. Lippincott, 1935.

Beard, Thomas R., ed. *The Louisiana Economy.* Baton Rouge: Louisiana State University Press, 1969.

Becnel, Thomas. *Labor, Church, and the Sugar Establishment: Louisiana, 1887–1976.* Baton Rouge: Louisiana State University Press, 1980.

Berman, William C. *The Politics of Civil Rights in the Truman Administration.* Columbus: Ohio State University Press, 1970.

Berzon, Judith R. *Neither White nor Black: The Mulatto Character in American Fiction.* New York: New York University Press, 1978.

Blassingame, John W. *Black New Orleans, 1860–1880.* Chicago: University of Chicago Press, 1973.

Blum, John Morton. *V Was for Victory: Politics and American Culture during World War II.* New York: Harcourt Brace Jovanovich, 1976.

Bobo, James R., and Jesse M. Charlton Jr., eds. *Statistical Abstract of Louisiana.* New Orleans: Division of Business and Economic Research, University of New Orleans, 1974.

Bobo, James R., and Sandra A. Etheridge, eds. *Statistical Abstract of Louisiana.* New Orleans: Division of Business and Economic Research, University of New Orleans, 1967.

———, eds. *Statistical Abstract of Louisiana.* New Orleans: Division of Business and Economic Research, University of New Orleans, 1969.

Boles, John B., ed. *Dixie Dateline: A Journalistic Portrait of the Contemporary South.* Houston: Rice University Studies, 1983.

Bolner, James, ed. *Louisiana Politics: Festival in a Labyrinth.* Baton Rouge: Louisiana State University Press, 1982.

Bourgeois, Lionel J. *Proposed Program for the Improvement of Public Schools in New Orleans.* New Orleans: Orleans Parish Public School Board, 1948.

Brasseaux, Carl A. *The Founding of New Acadia: The Beginnings of Acadian Life in Louisiana, 1765–1803.* Baton Rouge: Louisiana State University Press, 1987.

———. *Acadian to Cajun: The Transformation of a People, 1803–1877.* Jackson: University Press of Mississippi, 1992.

Brinkley, Alan. *Voices of Protest: Huey Long, Father Coughlin, and the Great Depression.* New York: Vintage, 1983.

Brundage, W. Fitzhugh. *Lynching in the New South: Georgia and Virginia, 1880–1930.* Urbana and Chicago: University of Illinois Press, 1993.

Bunche, Ralph J. *The Political Status of the Negro in the Age of FDR.* Edited by Dewey W. Grantham. Chicago: University of Chicago Press, 1973.

Burk, Robert F. *The Eisenhower Administration and Black Civil Rights.* Knoxville: University of Tennessee Press, 1984.

Burton, Willie. *On the Black Side of Shreveport: A History.* Shreveport: Willie Burton, 1983.

Calcasieu Parish Public Schools. Nashville: George Peabody College, 1969.

Carr, Robert K. *Federal Protection of Civil Rights: Quest for a Sword.* Ithaca: Cornell University Press, 1947, 1964.

Caute, David. *The Great Fear: The Anti-Communist Purge under Truman and Eisenhower.* New York: Simon and Schuster, 1978.

Chafe, William H. *Civilities and Civil Rights: Greensboro, North Carolina, and the Black Struggle for Freedom.* New York: Oxford University Press, 1980.

Citizens' Planning Committee for Public Education in New Orleans. *The New Orleans Study and Program of Public Education.* New Orleans: privately published, 1939.

Coles, Robert. *Children of Crisis: A Study of Courage and Fear.* Boston: Little, Brown, 1967.

Cook, James Graham. *The Segregationists.* New York: Appleton-Century-Crofts, 1962.

Crain, Robert L., ed. *The Politics of School Desegregation.* Garden City, N.Y.: Doubleday, 1969.

Dalfiume, Richard M. *Desegregation of the U.S. Armed Forces: Fighting on Two Fronts, 1939–1953.* Columbia: University of Missouri Press, 1969.

Davis, John H. *Mafia Kingfish: Carlos Marcello and the Assassination of John F. Kennedy.* New York: Signet, 1989.

Desdunes, Rudolph Lucien. *Our People and Our History.* Baton Rouge: Louisiana State University Press, 1973. Originally published as *Nos hommes et notre histoire* (1911).

DeVore, Donald E., and Joseph Logsdon. *Crescent City Schools: Public Education in New Orleans, 1841–1991.* Lafayette: Center for Louisiana Studies, University of Southwestern Louisiana, 1991.

Din, Gilbert C. *The Canary Islanders of Louisiana.* Baton Rouge: Louisiana State University Press, 1988.

Dodd, William J. *Peapatch Politics: The Earl Long Era in Louisiana Politics.* Baton Rouge: Claitor's Publishing Division, 1991.

Dominguez, Virginia R. *White by Definition: Social Classification in Creole Louisiana.* New Brunswick, N.J.: Rutgers University Press, 1986.

Dunbar, Anthony P. *Against the Grain: Southern Radicals and Prophets, 1929–1959.* Charlottesville: University Press of Virginia, 1981.

Dundy, Elaine. *Ferriday, Louisiana.* New York: Donald I. Fine, 1991.

Duram, James C. *A Moderate among Extremists: Dwight D. Eisenhower and the School Desegregation Crisis.* Chicago: Nelson-Hall, 1981.

Dykeman, Wilma, and James Stokely. *Seeds of Southern Change: The Life of Will Alexander.* Chicago: University of Chicago Press, 1962.

Dyson, Lowell K. *Red Harvest: The Communist Party and the American Farmers.* Lincoln: University of Nebraska Press, 1982.

Eagles, Charles W. *Jonathan Daniels and Race Relations: The Evolution of a Southern Liberal.* Knoxville: University of Tennessee Press, 1982.

———, ed. *The Civil Rights Movement in America.* Jackson: University Press of Mississippi, 1986.

Fairclough, Adam. *To Redeem the Soul of America: The Southern Christian Leadership Conference and Martin Luther King, Jr.* Athens: University of Georgia Press, 1987.

Farmer, James. *Lay Bare the Heart: An Autobiography of the Civil Rights Movement.* New York: Arbor House, 1985.

Feibelman, Julian B. *The Making of a Rabbi.* New York: Vantage Press, 1980.

Fichter, Joseph J. *Southern Parish: The Dynamics of a City Church.* Chicago: University of Chicago Press, 1951.

———. *Police Handling of Arrestees: A Research Study of Police Arrestees in New Orleans.* New Orleans: Loyola University of the South, 1964.

———. *One-Man Research: Reminiscences of a Catholic Sociologist.* New York: John Wiley, 1973.

Finkle, Lee. *Forum for Protest: The Black Press during World War II.* Cranbury, N.J.: Associated University Presses, 1975.

Fischer, Roger A. *The Segregation Struggle in Louisiana, 1862–77.* Urbana: University of Illinois Press, 1974.

Fite, Gilbert C. *Cotton Fields No More: Southern Agriculture, 1865–1980.* Lexington: University Press of Kentucky, 1984.

Foner, Eric. *Reconstruction: America's Unfinished Revolution, 1863–1877.* New York: Harper and Row, 1988.

Fontenot, Mary Alice, and Vincent Riehl. *The Cat and St. Landry: A Biography of Sheriff D. J. "Cat" Doucet of St. Landry Parish, Louisiana.* Baton Rouge: Claitor's Publishing Division, 1972.

Formisano, Ronald P. *Boston against Busing: Race, Class and Ethnicity in the 1960s and 1970s.* Chapel Hill: University of North Carolina Press, 1991.

Fosdick, Raymond B. *Adventures in Giving: The Story of the General Education Board.* New York: Harper and Row, 1962.

Freeman, Joshua B. *In Transit: The Transport Workers Union in New York City, 1933–1966.* New York: Oxford University Press, 1989.

Friedman, Leon, ed. *Southern Justice.* New York: Pantheon Books, 1965.

Garrow, David J. *Protest at Selma: Martin Luther King, Jr., and the Voting Rights Act of 1965.* New Haven: Yale University Press, 1978.

Garson, Robert. *The Democratic Party and the Politics of Sectionalism.* Baton Rouge: Louisiana State University Press, 1974.

Gatewood, Willard B. *Aristocrats of Color: The Black Elite, 1880–1920.* Bloomington: Indiana University Press, 1990.

Gelber, Steven M. *Black Men and Businessmen: The Growing Awareness of a Social Responsibility.* Port Washington, N.Y.: Kennikat Press, 1974.

Gillard, John T. *Colored Catholics in the United States.* Baltimore: Josephite Press, 1941.

Goodyear, C. W. *Bogalusa Story.* Buffalo, New York: privately published, 1950.

Greenberg, Jack. *Crusaders in the Courts: How a Dedicated Band of Lawyers Fought for the Civil Rights Revolution.* New York: Basic Books, 1994.

Gremillion, Joseph B. *Journal of a Southern Pastor.* Chicago: Fides, 1957.

Guerin, Daniel. *Negroes on the March: A Frenchman's Report on the American Negro Struggle.* New York: George L. Weissman, 1956.

Haas, Edward F. *DeLesseps S. Morrison and the Image of Reform: New Orleans Politics, 1946–1961.* Baton Rouge: Louisiana State University Press, 1974.

Hacker, Andrew. *Two Nations: Black and White, Separate, Hostile, Unequal.* New York: Ballantine Books, 1992.

Hair, William Ivy. *Bourbonism and Agrarian Protest: Louisiana Politics, 1877–1900.* Baton Rouge: Louisiana State University Press, 1969.

————. *Carnival of Fury: Robert Charles and the New Orleans Race Riot of 1900.* Baton Rouge: Louisiana State University Press, 1976.

————. *The Kingfish and His Realm: The Life and Times of Huey P. Long.* Baton Rouge: Louisiana State University Press, 1991.

Hall, Gwendolyn Midlo. *Africans in Colonial Louisiana: The Development of Afro-Creole Culture in the Eighteenth Century.* Baton Rouge: Louisiana State University Press, 1992.

Hall, Jacquelyn Dowd. *Revolt against Chivalry: Jesse Daniel Ames and the Women's Campaign against Lynching.* New York: Columbia University Press, 1979, 1993.

Hamilton, Charles V. *The Bench and the Ballot: Southern Federal Judges and Black Voters.* New York: Oxford University Press, 1973.

Havard, William C. *The Government of Louisiana.* Baton Rouge: Louisiana State University Press, 1958.

Havard, William C., Rudolf Heberle and Perry H. Howard. *The Louisiana Elections of 1960.* Baton Rouge: Louisiana State University Press, 1963.

Heleniak, Roman. *Soldiers of the Law: Louisiana State Police.* Topeka, Kans.: Josten's Publications, 1980.

Hine, Darlene Clark. *Black Victory: The Rise and Fall of the White Primary in Texas.* Millwood, N.Y.: KTO Press, 1979.

Hirsch, Arnold R., and Joseph Logsdon, eds. *Creole New Orleans: Race and Americanization.* Baton Rouge: Louisiana State University Press, 1992.

Honey, Michael K. *Southern Labor and Black Civil Rights: Organizing Memphis Workers.* Urbana and Chicago: University of Illinois Press, 1993.

Horne, Gerald. *Communist Front? The Civil Rights Congress, 1946–1956.* Cranbury, N.J.: Associated University Presses, 1988.

Howard, L. Vaughan, and David R. Deener. *Presidential Politics in Louisiana, 1952.* New Orleans: Tulane University Press, 1954.

Howard, Perry H. *Political Tendencies in Louisiana.* Baton Rouge: Louisiana State University Press, 1971.

Inger, Morton. *Politics and Reality in an American City: The New Orleans School Integration Crisis of 1960.* New York: Center for Urban Education, 1969.

Jeansonne, Glen S. *Leander Perez: Boss of the Delta.* Baton Rouge: Louisiana State University Press, 1977.

————. *Race, Religion and Politics: The Louisiana Gubernatorial Elections of 1959–60.* University of Southwestern Louisiana History Series, no. 10. Lafayette: University of Southwestern Louisiana, 1977.

Jensen, Carol E. *The Network of Control: State Supreme Courts and State Security Statutes, 1920–1970.* Westport, Conn.: Greenwood Press, 1982.

Johns, Major, and Ronnie Moore. *It Happened in Baton Rouge.* New York: Congress of Racial Equality, 1962.

Johnson, Charles S. *The Negro Public Schools.* vol. 8 of Louisiana Educational Survey Commission, *Louisiana Educational Survey.* Baton Rouge: Louisiana State University, 1942.

————. *To Stem This Tide: A Survey of Racial Tension Areas in the United States.* Boston and Chicago: Pilgrim Press, 1943.

————. *Into the Mainstream: A Survey of Best Practices in Race Relations in the South.* Chapel Hill: University of North Carolina Press, 1947.

Joint Center for Political Studies. *Black Elected Officials: A National Roster.* Washington, D.C.: Joint Center for Political Studies, 1993.

Judges of the United States. Washington, D.C.: Government Printing Office, 1983.

Keesing's Research Reports. no. 4. *Race Relations in the USA*. New York: Charles
    Scribner's Sons, 1970.
Kelley, Robin D. G. *Hammer and Hoe: Alabama Communists during the Great
    Depression*. Chapel Hill: University of North Carolina Press, 1990.
King, Carl B., and Howard W. Risher Jr. *The Negro in the Petroleum Industry*.
    Philadelphia: University of Pennsylvania, Wharton School of Finance and
    Commerce, 1969.
King, Richard H. *Civil Rights and the Idea of Freedom*. New York: Oxford University
    Press, 1992.
Kinoy, Arthur. *Rights on Trial: The Odyssey of a People's Lawyer*. Cambridge: Harvard
    University Press, 1983.
Klehr, Harvey. *The Heyday of American Communism: The Depression Decade*. New
    York: Basic Books, 1984.
Klibaner, Irwin. *Conscience of a Troubled South: The Southern Conference Education
    Fund, 1944–1966*. Brooklyn, N.Y.: Carlson Publishing, 1989.
Kluger, Richard. *Simple Justice: The History of Brown v. Board of Education and Black
    America's Struggle for Equality*. New York: Alfred A. Knopf, 1976.
Krueger, Thomas A. *And Promises to Keep: The Southern Conference for Human
    Welfare, 1938–1948*. Nashville: Vanderbilt University Press, 1967.
Kunstler, William. *Deep in My Heart*. New York: William Morrow, 1966.
Kurtz, Michael L. and Morgan D. Peoples. *Earl K. Long: The Saga of Uncle Earl and
    Louisiana Politics*. Baton Rouge: Louisiana State University Press, 1990.
Labbé, Dolores E. *Jim Crow Comes to Church: The Establishment of Segregated Catholic
    Parishes in South Louisiana*. Lafayette: University of Southwestern Louisiana, 1971.
Lamis, Alexander P. *The Two-Party South*. New York: Oxford University Press, 1990.
Landry, Stuart O., ed. *Louisiana Almanac and Fact Book, 1953–54*. New Orleans:
    Pelican Publishing Company, 1954.
Lawson, Steven F. *Black Ballots: Voting Rights in the South, 1944–1969*. New York:
    Columbia University Press, 1976.
————. *In Pursuit of Power: Southern Blacks and Electoral Politics, 1965–1982*. New
    York: Columbia University Press, 1985.
————. *Running for Freedom: Civil Rights and Black Politics in America since 1941*.
    Philadelphia: Temple University Press, 1990.
Lewis, Pierce F. *New Orleans: The Making of an Urban Landscape*. Cambridge, Mass.:
    Ballinger, 1976.
Liebling, A. J. *The Earl of Louisiana: Profile of an Eccentric*. London: W. H.
    Allen, 1962.
Lipsitz, George. *A Life in the Struggle: Ivory Perry and the Culture of Opposition*.
    Philadelphia: Temple University Press, 1988.
Logan, Rayford W., ed. *The Attitude of the Southern White Press toward Negro Suffrage,
    1932–1940*. Washington, D.C.: Foundation Publishers, 1940.
————, ed. *What the Negro Wants*. Chapel Hill: University of North Carolina
    Press, 1944.
Louisiana Civil Liberties Union. *Analysis of Part 1 of the Joint Legislative Committee to
    Investigate Louisiana State University*. Baton Rouge, 1959.
Louisiana Governmental Studies. *The Grass Roots Guide, Vol. 2: Lobbying the Louisiana
    Legislature, 1988–92*. Lafayette: University of Southwestern Louisiana, 1988.
Lovrich, Frank M. *The Social System of a Rural Yugoslav-American Community:
    Oysterville*. San Francisco: R and E Research Associates, 1971.

Lubell, Samuel. *The Future of American Politics*. New York: Harper and
Brothers, 1951.

Macdonald, Robert R., John R. Kemp, and Edward F. Haas, eds. *Louisiana's Black
Heritage*. New Orleans: Louisiana State Museum, 1979.

Mandle, Jay R. *The Roots of Black Poverty: The Southern Plantation Economy after the
Civil War*. Durham: Duke University Press, 1978.

Mann, Coramae Richey. *Unequal Justice: A Question of Color*. Bloomington and
Indianapolis: Indiana University Press, 1993.

Martin, Thomas. *Dynasty: The Longs of Louisiana*. New York: G. P. Putnam's
Sons, 1960.

Martinez, Raymond. *Racial Aspects of the Labor Supply in New Orleans*. New Orleans:
Chamber of Commerce, 1943.

Maruggi, Vincent, and Susanne D. Harti, eds. *Statistical Abstract of Louisiana*. New
Orleans: Division of Business and Economic Research, University of New
Orleans, 1981.

Mays, Benjamin E., and Joseph W. Nicholson. *The Negro's Church*. 1933. Reprint.
New York: Russell and Russell, 1969.

McAdam, Doug. *Political Process and the Development of Black Insurgency, 1930–1970*.
Chicago: University of Chicago Press, 1982.

McDougall, Curtis D. *Gideon's Army*. 3 vols. New York: Marzani and Munsell, 1965.

McGovern, James R. *Anatomy of a Lynching: The Killing of Claude Neal*. Baton
Rouge: Louisiana State University Press, 1982.

McMillen, Neil R. *The Citizens Council*. Urbana: University of Illinois Press, 1971.

McNeil, Genna Rae. *Groundwork: Charles Hamilton Houston and the Struggle for Civil
Rights*. Philadelphia: University of Pennsylvania Press, 1983.

Meier, August, and Elliott Rudwick. *CORE: A Study in the Civil Rights Movement,
1942–1968*. New York: Oxford University Press, 1973.

———. *Along the Color Line: Explorations in the Black Experience*. Urbana: University
of Illinois Press, 1976.

Michie, Allan, and Frank Ryhlick. *Dixie Demagogues*. New York: Vanguard
Press, 1939.

Middleton, Ernest J. *History of the Louisiana Education Association*. Washington, D.C.:
National Education Association, 1984.

Miller, Arthur Selwyn. *A "Capacity for Outrage:" The Judicial Odyssey of J. Skelly
Wright*. Westport, Conn.: Greenwood Press, 1984.

Miller, Merle. *Lyndon: An Oral Biography*. New York: Ballantine Books, 1980.

Mills, Gary B. *The Forgotten People: Cane River's Creoles of Color*. Baton Rouge:
Louisiana State University Press, 1977.

Mitchell, H. L. *Mean Things Happening in the Land: The Life and Times of H. L.
Mitchell, Co-Founder of the Southern Tenant Farmers Union*. Montclair, N.J.:
Allanheld, Osmun, 1979.

Morris, Aldon D. *The Origins of the Civil Rights Movement: Black Communities
Organizing for Change*. New York: Free Press, 1984.

Murray, Hugh T. Jr. *Civil Rights History-Writing and Anti-Communism: A Critique*.
New York: American Institute for Marxist Studies, 1975.

Myrdal, Gunnar. *An American Dilemma: The Negro Problem and Modern Democracy*.
2 vols. New York: Harper and Brothers, 1944.

Nalty, Bernard C. *Strength for the Fight: A History of Black Americans in the Military*.
New York: Free Press, 1986.

Navasky, Victor S. *Kennedy Justice*. New York: Atheneum, 1977.

The Negro in Louisiana. New Orleans: Sepia Socialite, June 1942.

Nelson, Bruce. *Workers on the Waterfront: Seamen, Longshoremen, and Unionism in the 1930s*. Urbana and Chicago: University of Illinois Press, 1988.

Newman, Dorothy K., Nancy J. Amidei, Barbara L. Carter, Dawn Day, William J. Kruvent, and Jack S. Russell. *Protest, Politics, and Prosperity: Black Americans and White Institutions, 1940–75*. New York: Pantheon, 1978.

New Orleans Population Handbook, 1950. New Orleans: Urban Life Research Institute, Tulane University, 1953.

Norrell, Robert J. *Reaping the Whirlwind: The Civil Rights Movement in Tuskegee*. New York: Alfred A. Knopf, 1985.

Northrup, Herbert R. *Organized Labor and the Negro*. New York: Harper and Brothers, 1944.

———. *The Negro in the Paper Industry*. Philadelphia: Wharton School of Finance and Commerce, University of Pennsylvania, 1969.

Ochs, Stephen J. *Desegregating the Altar: The Josephites and the Struggle for Black Priests, 1871–1960*. Baton Rouge: Louisiana State University Press, 1990.

Odum, Howard W. *Race and Rumors of Race*. Chapel Hill: University of North Carolina Press, 1943.

O'Reilly, Kenneth. *"Racial Matters": The FBI's Secret File on Black America, 1960–1972*. New York: Free Press, 1989.

Orfield, Gary. *The Reconstruction of Southern Education: The Schools and the 1964 Civil Rights Act*. London: John Wiley, 1969.

Owen, Lyla Hay. *Creoles of New Orleans*. New Orleans: First Quarter Publishing Company, 1987.

Panetta, Leon E., and Peter Gall. *Bring Us Together: The Nixon Team and Civil Rights*. Philadelphia: J. B. Lippincott, 1971.

Parker, Frank R. *Black Votes Count: Political Empowerment in Mississippi after 1965*. Chapel Hill: University of North Carolina Press, 1990.

Perkins, A. E. *Who's Who In Colored Louisiana*. Baton Rouge: Douglas Loan Co., 1930.

Pinkney, Alphonso. *The Myth of Black Progress*. Cambridge: Cambridge University Press, 1984.

Polenberg, Richard. *War and Society: The United States, 1941–1945*. Philadelphia: J. B. Lippincott, 1972.

Powledge, Fred. *Free at Last? The Civil Rights Movement and the People Who Made It*. Boston: Little, Brown, 1991.

Preston, Michael B., Lenneal J. Henderson and Paul Puryear, eds. *The New Black Politics: The Search for Political Power*. New York: Longman, 1982.

Price, Frank J. *Troy H. Middleton: A Biography*. Baton Rouge: Louisiana State University Press, 1974.

Price, Margaret. *The Negro and the Ballot in the South*. Atlanta: Southern Regional Council, 1959.

Provizer, Norman, and William D. Pederson, eds. *Grassroots Constitutionalism: Shreveport, the South, and the Supreme Court*. Lanham, Md.: University Press of America, 1988.

Public Affairs Research Council. *Citizens Guide to the 1960 Legislature*. Baton Rouge, 1960.

Read, Frank T., and Lucy S. McGough. *Let Them Be Judged: The Judicial Integration of the Deep South*. Metuchen, N.J.: Scarecrow Press, 1978.

Reed, Merl E. *Seedtime for the Modern Civil Rights Movement: The President's*

Committee on Fair Employment Practice, 1941–1946. Baton Rouge: Louisiana State University Press, 1991.

Regional Planning Commission for Jefferson, Orleans and St. Bernard Parishes. *Community Leaders Attitude Survey Report.* New Orleans, 1970.

Report of the Committee of Investigation of Certain Phases of Negro Education in Louisiana. 1930. Copy in TU.

Robinson, Armstead L., and Patricia Sullivan, eds. *New Directions in Civil Rights History.* Charlottesville: University Press of Virginia, 1991.

Rogers, Kim Lacy. *Righteous Lives: Narratives of the New Orleans Civil Rights Movement.* New York: New York University Press, 1993.

Rohrer, John H., and Munro S. Edmonson, eds. *The Eighth Generation: Cultures and Personalities of New Orleans Negroes.* New York: Harper and Brothers, 1960.

Rose, Douglas D., ed. *The Emergence of David Duke and the Politics of Race.* Chapel Hill: University of North Carolina Press, 1992.

Rosenberg, Daniel. *New Orleans Dockworkers: Race, Labor, and Unionism, 1892–1923.* Albany: State University of New York Press, 1988.

Rothschild, Mary Aiken. *A Case of Black and White: Northern Volunteers and the Southern Freedom Summers, 1964–1965.* Westport, Conn.: Greenwood Press, 1982.

Rousseve, Charles Barthelemy. *The Negro in Louisiana: Aspects of His History and His Literature.* 1937. Reprint. New Orleans: Johnson Reprint Corporation, 1970.

Rowan, Carl T. *South of Freedom.* New York: Alfred A. Knopf, 1952.

Rubin, Lester. *The Negro in the Shipbuilding Industry.* Philadelphia: Wharton School of Finance and Commerce, University of Pennsylvania, 1970.

Saxon, Lyle, Edward Dreyer, and Robert Tallant, eds. *Gumbo Ya-Ya.* New York: Bantam Books, 1945.

Shapiro, Herbert. *White Violence and Black Response: From Reconstruction to Montgomery.* Amherst: University of Massachusetts Press, 1988.

Sherman, Richard B. *The Republican Party and Black America from McKinley to Hoover, 1896–1933.* Charlottesville: University Press of Virginia, 1973.

Sherrill, Robert. *Gothic Politics in the Deep South.* New York: Grossman Publishers, 1968.

Shouse, Sarah Newman. *Hillbilly Realist: Herman Clarence Nixon of Possum Trot.* University: University of Alabama Press, 1986.

Sims, Patsy. *The Klan.* New York: Dorset Press, 1978.

———. *Cleveland Benjamin's Dead: A Struggle for Dignity in Louisiana's Cane Country.* New York: E. P. Dutton, 1981.

Sindler, Allan P. *Huey Long's Louisiana: State Politics, 1920–1952.* Baltimore: Johns Hopkins University Press, 1956.

Sitkoff, Harvard. *A New Deal for Blacks: The Emergence of Civil Rights as a National Issue.* New York: Oxford University Press, 1978.

Smead, Howard. *Blood Justice: The Lynching of Charles Mack Parker.* New York: Oxford University Press, 1986.

Smith, Douglas L. *The New Deal in the Urban South.* Baton Rouge: Louisiana State University Press, 1988.

Smith, T. Lynn, and Homer L. Hitt. *The People of Louisiana.* Baton Rouge: Louisiana State University Press, 1952.

Southern Regional Council. *Lawlessness and Disorder: Fourteen Years of Failure.* Atlanta: Southern Regional Council, 1967.

Stanley, Harold W. *Voter Mobilization and the Politics of Race: The South and Universal Suffrage, 1952–1984.* Westport, Conn.: Greenwood Press, 1987.

Sterkx, H. E. *The Free Negro in Ante-Bellum Louisiana*. Cranbury, N.J.: Associated University Presses, 1972.

Strong, Donald S. *Negroes, Ballots and Judges: National Voting Rights Legislation in the Federal Courts*. University: University of Alabama Press, 1968.

Taylor, Joe Gray. *Louisiana: A Bicentennial History*. New York: W. W. Norton, 1976.

———. *McNeese State University, 1939–1987: A Chronicle*. Lake Charles: McNeese State University, 1990.

Thompson, Daniel C. *The Negro Leadership Class*. Englewood-Cliffs, N.J.: Spectrum, 1963.

Tindall, George B. *The Emergence of the New South, 1913–1945*. Baton Rouge: Louisiana State University Press, 1967.

Tunnell, Ted. *Crucible of Reconstruction: War, Radicalism, and Race in Louisiana, 1862–1877*. Baton Rouge: Louisiana State University Press, 1984.

Tushnet, Mark V. *The NAACP's Legal Strategy against Segregated Education, 1925–1950*. Chapel Hill: University of North Carolina Press, 1987.

———. *Making Civil Rights Law: Thurgood Marshall and the Supreme Court, 1936–1961*. New York: Oxford University Press, 1994.

University of Chicago Law Review. Research Project. *Voting Rights: A Case Study of Madison Parish*. Chicago: American Bar Foundation, 1971.

Vincent, Charles. *Black Legislators in Louisiana during Reconstruction*. Baton Rouge: Louisiana State University Press, 1976.

Wade, Wynn Craig. *The Fiery Cross: The Ku Klux Klan in America*. New York: Simon and Schuster, 1987.

Walkes, Joseph A. *JNo. G. Lewis, Jr. — End of an Era: The History of the Prince Hall Grand Lodge of Louisiana, 1842–1979*. Privately published, 1986.

Wall, Bennett H., ed. *Louisiana: A History*. Arlington Heights, Ill.: Forum Press, 1984, 1990.

Warren, Robert Penn. *Who Speaks for the Negro?* New York: Random House, 1965.

Wasby, Stephen L., Anthony A. D'Amato, and Rosemary Metrailer. *Desegregation from Brown to Alexander*. Carbondale: Southern Illinois University Press, 1977.

Washburn, Patrick S. *A Question of Sedition: The Federal Government's Investigation of the Black Press during World War II*. New York: Oxford University Press, 1986.

Watters, Pat, and Reese Cleghorn. *Climbing Jacob's Ladder: The Arrival of Negroes in Southern Politics*. New York: Harcourt, Brace and World, 1967.

Weisbrot, Robert. *Freedom Bound: A History of America's Civil Rights Movement*. New York: W. W. Norton, 1990.

White, Walter. *Rope and Faggot*. New York: Alfred A. Knopf, 1927.

———. *A Man Called White: The Autobiography of Walter White*. London: Victor Gollancz, 1949.

Whitehead, Don. *Attack on Terror: The FBI against the Ku Klux Klan in Mississippi*. New York: Funk and Wagnalls, 1970.

Whittemore, L. H. *Together: A Reporter's Journey into the New Black Politics*. New York: William Morrow, 1971.

Wilkins, Roy, with Tom Matthews. *Standing Fast: The Autobiography of Roy Wilkins*. New York: Penguin Books, 1984.

Williams, T. Harry. *Huey Long*. New York: Bantam, 1970.

Williamson, Joel. *New People: Miscegenation and Mulattoes in the United States*. New York: Free Press, 1980.

Wilson, William Julius. *The Declining Significance of Race: Blacks and Changing American Institutions*. Chicago: University of Chicago Press, 1978.

———. *The Truly Disadvantaged: The Inner City, the Underclass, and Public Policy*. Chicago: University of Chicago Press, 1987, 1990.

Wofford, Harris. *Of Kennedys and Kings: Making Sense of the Sixties*. New York: Farrar, Straus and Giroux, 1980.

Woods, Sister Frances Jeanne. *Marginality and Identity: A Colored Creole Family through Ten Generations*. Baton Rouge: Louisiana State University Press, 1972.

Woodward, C. Vann. *Origins of the New South, 1977–1913*. Baton Rouge: Louisiana State University Press, 1951, 1966.

Wynn, Neil A. *The Afro-American and the Second World War*. London: Paul Elek, 1976.

Zangrando, Robert L. *The NAACP Crusade against Lynching, 1909–1950*. Philadelphia: Temple University Press, 1980.

ARTICLES

Adams, James R. "The Sunbelt." In John B. Boles, ed., *Dixie Dateline: A Journalistic Portrait of the Contemporary South*, 141–57. Houston: Rice University Studies, 1983.

Ahmann, Matthew. "Catholics and Race." *Commonweal* 73 (December 2, 1960): 247–50.

Alexander, Shana. "Visit Bogalusa and You Will Look for Me." *Life*, July 2, 1965, 28.

Badger, Anthony J. "Huey Long and the New Deal." In Stephen W. Baskerville and Ralph Willet, eds., *Nothing Else to Fear: New Perspectives on America in the Thirties*, 65–103. Manchester: Manchester University Press, 1985.

Bailes, Lloyd H. "Negroes in Major Occupations and Industry." *Journal of Negro Education* 22 (Summer 1953): 297–321.

Baker, Riley E. "Negro Voter Registration in Louisiana, 1879–1964." *Southern Studies* 4 (Winter 1965): 332–50.

Barrois, Etienne. "King of the River People." *Commonweal*, July 6, 1962, 365–66.

Beecher, John. "A Little Night Music." *Nation*, October 28, 1964, 272–75.

———. "Magnolia Ghetto." *Ramparts*, December 1964, 45–50.

Beezer, Bruce. "Black Teachers' Salaries and the Federal Courts before *Brown* v. *Board of Education:* One Beginning for Equality." *Journal of Negro History* 55 (Spring 1986): 200–213.

Berry, Mary Frances. "Negro Troops in Blue and Gray: The Louisiana Native Guards, 1861–1863." *Louisiana History* 8 (Spring 1967): 165–90.

Biles, Roger. "A Bittersweet Victory: Public School Desegregation in Memphis." *Journal of Negro Education* 55 (Fall 1986): 470–83.

Boulard, Gary. "Louisiana Governor Joins HBCU Leaders in Forging Desegregation Plan." *Black Issues in Higher Education* 9 (October 8, 1992): 11.

Breed, Warren. "The Emergence of Pluralistic Public Opinion in a Community Crisis." In Alvin W. Gouldner and S. M. Miller, eds., *Applied Sociology: Opportunities and Problems*, 127–46. New York: Free Press, 1965.

Bryant, Pat. "A Long Time Coming." *Southern Exposure* 10 (May–June 1982): 83–89.

Butler, Johnny S. "Black Educators in Louisiana: A Question of Survival." *Journal of Negro Education* 43 (Winter 1974): 9–24.

Capeci, Dominic J., Jr. "The Lynching of Cleo Wright: Federal Protection of Constitutional Rights during World War II." *Journal of American History* 72 (March 1986): 859–97.

Carleton, Mark T. "The Louisiana Constitution of 1974." In James Bolner, ed.,
  Louisiana Politics: Festival in a Labyrinth, 15–41. Baton Rouge: Louisiana State
  University Press, 1982.
Carpenter, Arthur E. "Social Origins of Anticommunism: The Information Council
  of the Americas." *Louisiana History* 30 (Spring 1989): 117–43.
Cassimere, Raphael, Jr. "Crisis of Public Higher Education in Louisiana." *Integrated
  Education* 13 (September 1975): 8–13.
————. "Equalizing Teachers' Pay in Louisiana." *Integrated Education* 15
  (July–August 1977): 3–8.
————. "*Plessy* Revisited: Louisiana's Separate and Unequal University System."
  Equity and Excellence 24 (Fall 1988): 12–21.
Cater, Douglass. "The Lessons of William Frantz and McDonogh 19." *Reporter*,
  February 16, 1961, 36–38.
Chandler, David. "McKeithen." *New Orleans*, January 1967, 20.
————. "The 'Little Man' Is Bigger Than Ever." *Life*, April 10, 1970, 30–36.
Chriss, Nicholas C. "A Moderate's First Test." *Nation*, December 18, 1972, 622–23.
Clift, Eleanor. "Black Land Loss: 6 Million Acres and Fading Fast." *Southern
  Exposure* 2 (Fall 1974): 108–21.
Collins, Robert F., Nils R. Douglas, and Lolis E. Elie. "Clinton, Louisiana." In
  Leon Friedman, ed., *Southern Justice*, 112–26. New York: Pantheon Books, 1965.
Cunningham, George E. "The Italian: A Hindrance to White Solidarity in Louisiana,
  1890–1898." *Journal of Negro History* 50 (January 1965): 22–36.
Dalcher, Louisa. "A Time of Worry in the 'City Care Forgot.'" *Reporter*, March 8,
  1956, 17–20.
Day, Dorothy. "Southern Pilgrimage." *Commonweal*, March 31, 1961, 10–12.
Dudziak, Mary L. "Desegregation as a Cold War Imperative." *Stanford Law Review*
  41 (November 1988): 61–120.
Eliff, John T. "Aspects of Federal Civil Rights Enforcement: The Justice Department
  and the FBI, 1939–1964." In Donald Fleming and Bernard Bailyn, eds., *Perspectives
  in American History*, vol. 5, 605–73. Cambridge: Charles Warren Center for Studies
  in American History, 1971.
Ellis, Mark. "'Closing Ranks' and 'Seeking Honors': W. E. B. Du Bois in World
  War I." *Journal of American History* 79 (June 1992): 96–124.
Everard, Wayne M. "Bourbon City: New Orleans, 1878–1900." *Louisiana Studies* 11
  (1972): 240–51.
Fairclough, Adam. "State of the Art: Historians and the Civil Rights Movement."
  Journal of American Studies 24 (December 1990): 387–98.
Feingold, Miriam. "Chronicling the 'Movement.'" *Reviews in American History* 11
  (March 1974): 152–60.
Fenton, John H. "The Negro Voter in Louisiana." *Journal of Negro Education* 26
  (Summer 1957): 319–28.
Fenton, John H., and Kenneth N. Vines. "Negro Registration in Louisiana."
  American Political Science Review 51 (September 1957): 704–13.
Fichter, Joseph H. "The First Black Students at Loyola University: A Strategy to
  Obtain Teacher Certification." *Journal of Negro Education* 56 (Fall 1987): 535–49.
Frazier, George. "100 Yards and 60 Minutes of Black Power." *Esquire*, October 1967,
  95–99.
Gandy, Samuel L. "Desegregation of Higher Education in Louisiana." *Journal of
  Negro Education* 58 (Summer 1958): 269–74.

Garrow, David J. "The Voting Rights Act in Historical Perspective." *Georgia Historical Quarterly* 74 (Fall 1990): 377–98.

Gavins, Raymond. "The NAACP in North Carolina during the Age of Segregation." In Armstead L. Robinson and Patricia L. Sullivan, eds., *New Directions in Civil Rights Studies*, 105–25. Charlottesville: University Press of Virginia, 1991.

Good, Paul. "Klantown, USA." *Nation*, February 1, 1965, 110–13.

Gorman, Nicholas. "Scandal of New Orleans." *Commonweal* 74 (April 28, 1961): 127–28.

Gottlieb, Saul. "The Negro and the Church." *Dissent*, Spring 1956: 118–20.

Grossack, Martin M. "Psychological Effects of Segregation on Buses." *Journal of Negro Education* 22 (Winter 1956): 71–74.

Guillory, Ferrel. "Baton Rouge Desegregates." *America* 122 (June 20, 1970): 650–52.

———. "Emerging Black Politics." *America* 127 (September 9, 1972): 147–49.

Haas, Edward F. "Huey Long and the Communists." Louisiana History 32 (Winter 1991): 29–46.

Hall, Bob, and Louisa Seibel. "The South in Congress." *Southern Exposure* 12 (February 1984): 15–19.

Hall, Gwendolyn Midlo. "The Formation of Afro-Creole Culture." In Arnold R. Hirsch and Joseph Logsdon, eds., *Creole New Orleans: Race and Americanization*, 58–87. Baton Rouge: Louisiana State University Press, 1992.

Hawkins, B. Denise. "Southern University Board Abstains from Voting on Louisiana Desegregation Plan." *Black Issues in Higher Education* 9 (December 31, 1992): 16–17.

Heleniak, Roman. "Lyndon Johnson in New Orleans." *Louisiana History* 21 (Summer 1980): 263–75.

Hine, Darlene Clark. "The Pursuit of Professional Equality: Meharry Medical School, 1921–1938, a Case Study." In Vincent P. Franklin and James D. Anderson, eds., *New Perspectives in Black Educational History*, 173–92. Boston: G. K. Hall, 1978.

Hirsch, Arnold R. "Simply a Matter of Black and White: The Transformation of Race and Politics in Twentieth-Century New Orleans." In Arnold R. Hirsch and Joseph Logsdon, eds., *Creole New Orleans: Race and Americanization*, 262–319. Baton Rouge: Louisiana State University Press, 1992.

Inverarity, James M. "Populism and Lynching in Louisiana, 1889–1896." *American Sociological Review* 41 (April 1976): 262–80.

Jacobs, Claude F. "Benevolent Societies in New Orleans during the Late Nineteenth and Early Twentieth Centuries." *Louisiana History* 29 (Winter 1988): 21–33.

Jeansonne, Glen S. "Racism and Longism in Louisiana: The 1959–60 Gubernatorial Elections." *Louisiana History* 11 (Summer 1970): 259–70.

———. "Longism: Mainstream Politics or Aberration? Louisiana before and after Huey Long." *Mid-America* 71 (April–July 1989): 89–100.

———. "The Apotheosis of Huey Long." *Biography* 12 (Fall 1989): 283–301.

———. "Huey Long and Racism." *Louisiana History* 33 (Summer 1992): 265–82.

Johnson, Oakley. "The New Orleans Story." *Centennial Review* 12 (Spring 1968): 194–219.

Jones, Lewis W. "The Negro Farmer." *Journal of Negro Education* 22 (Summer 1953): 322–32.

Jupiter, Clare. "Lost Lives? A Profile of Death Row." *Southern Exposure* 6 (Winter 1978): 76–78.

Kane, Harnett T. "Dilemma of the Crooner-Governor." *New York Times Magazine,* January 1, 1961, 8.

Kelley, Robin D. G. "'We Are Not What We Seem:' Rethinking Black Working-Class Opposition in the Jim Crow South." *Journal of American History* 80 (June 1993): 75–112.

Korstad, Robert, and Nelson Lichtenstein. "Opportunities Lost and Found: Labor, Radicals, and the Early Civil Rights Movement." *Journal of American History* 75 (December 1988): 786–811.

Kunkel, Paul A. "Modifications in Louisiana Negro Legal Status under Louisiana Constitutions, 1812–1957." *Journal of Negro History* 44 (January 1959): 1–25.

Kurtz, Michael L. "DeLesseps S. Morrison: Political Reformer." *Louisiana History* 17 (1976): 19–39.

LaChance, Paul F. "The 1809 Immigration of Saint-Domingue Refugees to New Orleans: Reception, Integration and Impact." *Louisiana History* 29 (Spring 1988): 109–41.

———. "The Foreign French." In Arnold R. Hirsch and Joseph Logsdon, eds., *Creole New Orleans: Race and Americanization,* 101–30. Baton Rouge: Louisiana State University Press, 1992.

LaViolette, Forrest E. "The Negro in New Orleans." In Nathan Glazer and Davis McEntire, eds., *Studies in Minority Group Housing,* 110–34. Berkeley and Los Angeles: University of California Press, 1960.

Lawrence, James. "Scandal of New Orleans." *Commonweal,* February 3, 1961, 475–76.

Logsdon, Joseph. "Americans and Creoles in New Orleans: The Origins of Black Citizenship in the United States." *Amerikastudien* 34 (1989): 187–202.

Logsdon, Joseph, and Caryn Cossé Bell. "The Americanization of Black New Orleans, 1850–1900." In Arnold R. Hirsch and Joseph Logsdon, eds., *Creole New Orleans: Race and Americanization,* 201–61. Baton Rouge: Louisiana State University Press, 1992.

Lubell, Samuel. "The Future of the Negro Voter in the United States." *Journal of Negro Education* 26 (Summer 1957): 408–17.

Marshall, Thurgood. "The Rise and Collapse of the 'White Democratic Primary.'" *Journal of Negro Education* 26 (Summer 1957): 249–54.

Marshall, Thurgood, and Robert L. Carter. "The Meaning and Significance of the Supreme Court Decree." *Journal of Negro Education* 24 (Summer 1955): 397–404.

Martensen, Katherine. "Region, Religion, and Social Action: The Catholic Committee of the South, 1939–1956." *Catholic Historical Review* 68 (April 1982): 249–67.

Massey, David Dyer. "The Federation of Southern Cooperatives." *Southern Exposure* 2 (Fall 1974): 38–47.

McCord, Charles. "The Anatomy of a Registration Drive: A Success Story from New Orleans." *Interracial Review,* May 1962, 1–11.

McTeague, Geraldine. "Patterns of Residence: Housing Distribution by Color in Two Louisiana Towns, 1860–1880." *Louisiana Studies* 15 (Winter 1976): 345–88.

Medley, Keith Weldon. "Ernest Wright: People's Champion." *Southern Exposure* (May/June 1984): 52–55.

———. "A Year in the Life of Lincoln Beach." *New Orleans Tribune* 1 (September 1985): 20–21.

———. "Gilbert Academy's Legacy of Distinction." *New Orleans Tribune* 1 (November 1985): 20–21.

―――. "Remembering Ernest Wright: 'The People's Champion.'" *New Orleans Tribune* 2 (February 1986): 13–14.

―――. "Black New Orleans: A Twenty Year Retrospective." *New Orleans Tribune* 2 (April 1986): 18–21.

Middleton, Ernest J. "The Louisiana Education Association, 1901–1970." *Journal of Negro Education* (Fall 1978): 363–78.

Miller, Arthur Selwyn, and Jeffrey H. Bowman. "'Slow Dance on the Killing Ground': The *Willie Francis* Case Revisited." *DePaul Law Review* 32 (1983): 1–73.

Moore, William V. "Civil Liberties in Louisiana: The Louisiana League for the Preservation of Constitutional Rights." *Louisiana History* 31 (Winter 1990): 59–81.

Mothner, Ira. "Exodus from New Orleans." *Look,* March 14, 1961, 53–58.

Muller, Mary Lee. "New Orleans Public School Desegregation." *Louisiana History* 17 (Winter 1976): 69–88.

Murrah, Bill. "Llano Cooperative Colony, Louisiana." *Southern Exposure* 13 (Winter 1974): 87–104.

Murray, Hugh T., Jr. "The Struggle for Civil Rights in New Orleans in 1960: Reflections and Recollections." *Journal of Ethnic Studies* 6 (Spring 1978): 25–41.

Nabrit, James M., Jr. "The Future of the Negro Voter in the South." *Journal of Negro Education* 26 (Summer 1957): 418–23.

Northrup, Herbert R. "The New Orleans Longshoremen." *Political Science Quarterly* 57 (December 1942): 526–44.

O'Dell, Hunter. "The Political Scene in Louisiana." *Political Affairs,* August 1956, 13–23.

O'Gara, James. "An Outsider's View." *Commonweal* 76 (June 1, 1962): 248.

Osborne, John. "The Nixon Watch." *New Republic* 163 (August 22, 1970): 7–9.

Piliawsky, Monte. "The Limits of Power: New Orleans." *Southern Exposure* 12 (February 1984): 70–76.

Planer, Ed. "Louisiana: The Expensive Way to Fight Integration." *Reporter,* October 11, 1962, 37.

Pope, Whitney, and Charles Ragin. "Mechanical Solidarity, Repressive Justice, and Lynchings in Louisiana." *American Sociological Review* 42 (April 1977): 363–69.

Porter, Betty. "The History of Negro Education in Louisiana." *Louisiana Historical Quarterly* 25 (July 1942): 728–821.

Powell, Lawrence N. "Slouching toward Baton Rouge: The 1989 Legislative Election of David Duke." In Douglas D. Rose, ed., *The Emergence of David Duke and the Politics of Race.* Chapel Hill: University of North Carolina Press, 1992.

Pratt, Robert A. "A Promise Unfulfilled: School Desegregation in Richmond, Virginia, 1956–1986." *Virginia Magazine of History and Biography* 99 (October 1991): 415–48.

Prestage, Jewel L., and Carolyn Sue Williams. "Blacks in Louisiana Politics." In James Bolner, ed., *Louisiana Politics: Festival in a Labyrinth,* 285–317. Baton Rouge: Louisiana State University Press, 1982.

Rable, George C. "The South and the Politics of Antilynching Legislation." *Journal of Southern History* 51 (May 1985).

Rankin, David C. "The Origins of Black Leadership in New Orleans during Reconstruction." *Journal of Southern History* 40 (August 1974): 417–40.

―――. "The Politics of Caste: Free Colored Leadership in New Orleans during the Civil War." In Robert R. Macdonald, John R. Kemp, and Edward F. Haas, eds., *Louisiana's Black Heritage,* 107–46. New Orleans: Louisiana State Museum, 1979.

Record, Jane Cassels. "The Rise and Fall of a Maritime Union." *Industrial and Labor Relations Review* 10 (October 1956): 81–92.

Redding, Joan. "The Dillard Project: The Black Unit of the Louisiana Writers' Project." *Louisiana History* 32 (Winter 1991): 47–62.

Reed, Adolph L. "Crisis on the Negro Campus." *Nation,* February 10, 1962, 111–13.

Reed, Germaine A. "Race Legislation in Louisiana, 1864–1920." *Louisiana History* 6 (Fall 1965): 379–92.

Reed, Merl E. "The FEPC, the Black Worker, and the Southern Shipyards." *South Atlantic Quarterly* 74 (Autumn 1975): 446–87.

Reynard, Charles A. "Legislation Affecting Segregation." *Louisiana Law Review* 17 (1956–57): 101–22.

Rickey, Elizabeth. "The Nazi and the Republicans: An Insider View of the Response of the Louisiana Republican Party to David Duke." In Douglas D. Rose, ed., *The Emergence of David Duke and the Politics of Race,* 64–74. Chapel Hill: University of North Carolina Press, 1992.

Rogers, Cornish. "Ironies and Deaths at Southern." *Christian Century* 84 (December 18, 1972): 1263–64.

Rogers, Kim Lacy. " 'You Came Away with Some Courage': Three Lives in the Civil Rights Movement." *Mid-America* 71 (October 1989): 175–94.

Roney, Vera. "Bogalusa: The Economics of Tragedy." In Jeremy Larner and Irving Howe, eds., *Poverty: Views From the Left,* 280–92. New York: William Morrow, 1968.

Rose, Douglas D., with Gary Esolen. "DuKKKe for Governor." In Douglas D. Rose, ed., *The Emergence of David Duke and the Politics of Race.* Chapel Hill: University of North Carolina Press, 1992.

Rushton, Bill. "New Orleans Elects a Black Mayor." *Southern Exposure* 5 (1978): 3–4.

Rustin, Bayard. "From Protest to Politics: The Future of the Civil Rights Movement." *Commentary* 39 (February 1965): 25–31.

Sanders, Charles L. "Black Lawman in KKK Territory." *Ebony,* January 1970, 57–66.

Schexnider, Alvin J. "Political Mobilization in the South: The Election of a Black Mayor in New Orleans." In Michael B. Preston, Lenneal J. Henderson Jr., and Paul Puryear, eds., *The New Black Politics: The Search for Political Power,* 224–34. New York: Longman, 1982.

Schott, Matthew J. "Class Conflict in Louisiana Voting Since 1877." *Louisiana History* 12 (Spring 1971): 149–65.

———. "Progressives Against Democracy: Electoral Reform in Louisiana, 1894–1921." *Louisiana History* 20 (1979): 247–60.

Shea, William L., and Merill R. Pritchett. "The Wehrmacht in Louisiana." *Louisiana History* 23 (Winter 1982): 5–19.

Sherman, George. "The Nightmare Comes to New Orleans." *Reporter,* December 8, 1960, 24–27.

Simon, Anne L. "Inequality under the Law: The Louisiana Story." *Southern Studies* 16 (1977): 293–96.

Sitkoff, Harvard. "Racial Militancy and Interracial Violence in the Second World War." *Journal of American History* 58 (December 1971): 661–81.

Slovenko, Ralph. "The Jury System in Louisiana." *Louisiana Law Review* 17 (1956–57): 665–729.

Spain, Daphne. "Race Relations and Residential Segregation in New Orleans: Two Centuries of Paradox." *Annals of the American Academy of Political and Social Science* 441 (January 1979): 82–96.

Spitzer, Nicholas. "Cajuns and Creoles: The French Gulf Coast." *Southern Exposure* 5 (1977): 140–55.

Taylor, Joseph T. "Desegregation in Louisiana: One Year Later." *Journal of Negro Education* 24 (Summer 1955): 258–74.

———. "Desegregation in Louisiana: 1956." *Journal of Negro Education* 25 (Summer 1956): 262–71.

Tregle, Joseph G. "Another Look at Shugg's Louisiana." *Louisiana History* 17 (1976): 245–81.

Vincent, Charles. "Black Louisianians during the Civil War and Reconstruction: Aspects of Their Struggles and Achievements." In Robert R. Macdonald, John R. Kemp, and Edward F. Haas, eds., *Louisiana's Black Heritage*, 85–106. New Orleans: Louisiana State Museum, 1979.

Vines, Kenneth N. "A Louisiana Parish: Wholesale Purge." In Margaret Price, ed., *The Negro and the Ballot in the South*. Atlanta: Southern Regional Council, 1959.

Vodicka, John. "Prison Plantation: The Story of Angola." *Southern Exposure* 6 (Winter 1978): 32–38.

Watters, Pat. "Toward Justice in Louisiana." *Christian Century* 90 (January 31, 1973): 115.

Weisberger, Andrew D. "A Reappraisal of the Constitutionality of Miscegenation Statutes." *Journal of Negro Education* 26 (Fall 1957): 435–46.

Wells, David Lee, and Jim Stodder. "A Short History of New Orleans Dockworkers." *Radical America* 10 (1976): 43–69.

Wieder, Alan. "One Who Stayed: Margaret Conner and the New Orleans Schools Crisis." *Louisiana History* (Spring 1985): 194–201.

Wilkins, Roy. "The Future of the Negro Voter in the United States." *Journal of Negro Education* 26 (Summer 1957): 424–31.

Wisdom, Betty. "Letter from a New Orleans Mother." *Nation,* November 4, 1961, 353.

Wollett, Donald H. "Race Relations." *Louisiana Law Review* 21 (1960–61): 85–105.

Wool, Robert. "Clams, Complacency, Corruption." *Look,* December 8, 1959, 42–46.

Wright, Beverly H. "New Orleans: A City That Care Forgot." In Robert D. Bullard, ed., *In Search of the New South: The Black Urban Experience in the 1970s and 1980s,* 45–74. Tuscaloosa: University of Alabama Press, 1987.

Wright, Frederick D. "The History of Black Political Participation to 1965." In Lawrence W. Morland, Robert P. Steed, and Tod A. Baker, eds., *Blacks in Southern Politics,* 9–30. New York: Praeger, 1987.

U.S. GOVERNMENT DOCUMENTS

President's Committee on Civil Rights. *The Report of the President's Committee on Civil Rights: To Secure These Rights.* Washington: Government Printing Office, 1947.

U.S. Commission on Civil Rights. *With Liberty and Justice for All: An Abridgement of the Report of the United States Commission on Civil Rights.* Washington: Government Printing Office, 1959.

———. *Hearings Held in New Orleans, Louisiana, 1960–1961.* Washington: Government Printing Office, 1961.

———. *1961 Commission on Civil Rights Report: vol 1: Voting.* Washington: Government Printing Office, 1961.

———. *1961 Commission on Civil Rights Report: vol 5: Justice*. Washington: Government Printing Office, 1961.

———. *The Voting Rights Act: The First Months*. Washington: Government Printing Office, 1965.

———. *Southern School Desegregation, 1966–67*. Washington: Government Printing Office, 1967.

———. *Political Participation*. Washington: Government Printing Office, 1968.

———. *The Voting Rights Act: Ten Years After*. Washington: Government Printing Office, 1975.

———. *The Black/White Colleges: Dismantling the Dual System of Higher Education*. Washington: Government Printing Office, 1981.

———. *The Voting Rights Act: Unfulfilled Goals*. Washington: Government Printing Office, 1981.

———. *Statement of the U.S. Civil Rights Commission on School Desegregation*. Washington: Government Printing Office, 1982.

———. Louisiana Advisory Committee. *The New Orleans Schools Crisis*. Washington: Government Printing Office, 1961.

———. Louisiana Advisory Committee. *School Desegregation in Bogalusa*. Washington: Government Printing Office, 1977.

U.S. Congress. House of Representatives. Subcommittee on Constitutional Rights of the Committee of the Judiciary. *Hearings, Civil Rights — 1957*. 85th Congress, 1st session, 1957.

———. House of Representatives. Committee on Un-American Activities. *Investigation of Communist Activities in the New Orleans Area*. 85th Congress, 1st Session, 1957.

———. Senate. Subcommittee to Investigate the Administration of the Internal Security Act of the Committee of the Judiciary. *Scope of Soviet Activity in the United States*. 84th Congress, 2d session, 1956.

LOUISIANA, STATE DOCUMENTS

Guste, William J. Jr. *Report of the Attorney General's Special Commission of Enquiry of the Southern University Tragedy of November 16, 1972*. Baton Rouge, 1973.

Louisiana. *Constitution of the State of Louisiana*. 1921, 1942.

Louisiana. Joint Legislative Committee. *Subversion in Racial Unrest*. Baton Rouge, 1957.

Louisiana. Joint Legislative Committee on Un-American Activities. *The Case of Dr. Waldo F. McNeir*. Baton Rouge, May 8, 1961.

———. *Activities of the "Ku Klux Klan" and Certain Other Organizations in Louisiana*. Baton Rouge, July 26, 1965.

———. *Aspects of the Poverty Program in Louisiana*. Baton Rouge, April 14, 1967.

———. *Students for a Democratic Society and the New Left*. Baton Rouge, February 11, 1969.

Louisiana. Legislative Council. *Interim Committees of the Louisiana Legislature, October 1958*. Baton Rouge, 1958.

———. *The Government of Louisiana*. Baton Rouge, April 1959.

Louisiana Revised Statutes, 1950, 1962. Cumulative supplement, vol. 1.

Louisiana. State Department of Education. *Americanism versus Communism: A Unit of Work in American History*. Baton Rouge, 1960.

Louisiana. State Sovereignty Commission. *Why Segregation?* n.d.

Alberts, John Bernard. "Black Catholic Schools: The Josephite Parishes of New Orleans during the Jim Crow Era." M.A. thesis, University of New Orleans, 1990.

Ambrose, Edith Rosepha. "Sarah Towles Reed and the Origins of Teacher Unions in New Orleans." M.A. thesis, University of New Orleans, 1991.

Anthony, Arthe Agnes. "The Negro Creole Community in New Orleans, 1880–1920: On Oral History." Ph.D. dissertation, University of California, Irvine, 1978.

Bartley, Melinda. "Southern University Activism, 1960–63, Revisited." M.A. thesis, Southern University, 1973.

Buell, Emmett Harold. "The Politics of Frustration: An Analysis of Negro Political Leadership in East Baton Rouge Parish, 1953–1966." M.A. thesis, Louisiana State University, 1967.

Burran, James A., III. "Racial Violence in the South during World War II." Ph.D. dissertation, University of Tennessee, 1977.

Butler, Loretta Myrtle. "A History of Catholic Elementary Education for Negroes in the Diocese of Lafayette, Louisiana." Ph.D. dissertation, Catholic University of America, 1963.

Carey, Addison C. "Black Political Participation in New Orleans." Ph.D. dissertation, Tulane University, 1971.

Carson, John Hampton. "A Quantitative and Qualitative Analysis of Racial Employment Discrimination in Louisiana, 1950–1971." Ph.D. dissertation, Louisiana State University, 1973.

Cunningham, Cheryl V. "The Desegregation of Tulane University." M.A. thesis, University of New Orleans, 1982.

DeVore, Donald E. "The Rise from the Nadir: Black New Orleans between the Wars, 1920–1940." M.A. thesis, University of New Orleans, 1983.

———. "Race Relations and Community Development: The Education of Blacks in New Orleans, 1862–1960." Ph.D. dissertation, Louisiana State University, 1989.

Doherty, Mark J. "Hale Boggs and Civil Rights: A Case Study of a Southern Moderate." B.A. honors thesis, Tulane University, 1983.

Dugas, Carroll J. "The Dismantling of De Jure Segregation in Louisiana, 1954–1974." Ph.D. dissertation, Louisiana State University, 1989.

Eakins, Sue Lyles. "The Black Struggle for Education in Louisiana, 1877–1930s." Ph.D. dissertation, University of Southwestern Louisiana, 1980.

Field, Betty M. "The Politics of the New Deal in Louisiana." Ph.D. dissertation, Tulane University, 1973.

Fouche, James Francis. "The Bogalusa Quasi-Riot of 1919: A Microcosm of National and Regional Hysteria." M.A. thesis, Louisiana State University at New Orleans, 1972.

Freeman, Joshua B. "The Transport Workers Union in New York City, 1933–1948." Ph.D. dissertation, Rutgers University, 1983.

Giarusso, Alfred P. "Desegregation of the Orleans Parish School System." D.Ed. dissertation, University of Arkansas, 1969.

Gillette, Michael L. "The NAACP in Texas, 1937–1957." Ph.D. dissertation, University of Texas at Austin, 1984.

Halpin, Stanislaus Anthony, Jr. "The Anti-Gerrymander: The Impact of Section 5 of the Voting Rights Act of 1965 upon Louisiana Parish Redistricting." Ph.D. dissertation, George Washington University, 1978.

Halstead, Michael N. "Ideology and Identity: Black Youth in New Orleans." Ph.D. dissertation, Tulane University, 1972.

Holley, James Donald. "The New Deal and Farm Tenancy: Rural Resettlement in Arkansas, Louisiana, and Mississippi." Ph.D. dissertation, Louisiana State University, 1969.

Jenkins, Velesta. "River Road: A Rural Black Community in Southeastern Louisiana." Ph.D. dissertation, University of California, Berkeley, 1976.

Jones, Joseph H. "The People of Frilot Cove: A Study of a Racial Hybrid Community in Rural South Central Louisiana." M.A. thesis, Louisiana State University, 1950.

Kurtz, Michael L. "The 'Demagogue' and the 'Liberal': A Study of the Political Rivalry of Earl Long and DeLesseps Morrison." Ph.D. dissertation, Tulane University, 1971.

Lockett, Raymond J. "A History of Black Leadership and Participation in Local Politics in St. Mary Parish, 1950–1970." M.A. thesis, Southern University, 1971.

Martensen, Katherine. "Region, Religion, and Social Action: The Catholic Committee of the South, 1939–1956." M.A. thesis, University of New Orleans, 1978.

McCall, William Greer. "School Desegregation in Louisiana: An Analysis of the Constitutional Issues." Ph.D. dissertation, University of Tennessee, 1973.

McCarrick, Earleen May. "Louisiana's Official Resistance to Desegregation." Ph.D. dissertation, Vanderbilt University, 1964.

McCulley, Paul Ted. "Black Protest in Louisiana, 1898–1928." M.A. thesis, Louisiana State University, 1970.

Muller, Mary Lee. "The Orleans Parish School Board and Negro Education, 1940–1960." M.A. thesis, Louisiana State University at New Orleans, 1975.

Newton, Milton B., Jr. "The Peasant Farm of St. Helena Parish, Louisiana: A Cultural Geography." Ph.D. dissertation, Louisiana State University, 1967.

Neyland, Leedell Wallace. "The Negro in Louisiana since 1900: An Economic and Social Study." Ph.D. dissertation, New York University, 1958.

Payne, John Robert. "A Jesuit Search for Social Justice: The Public Career of Louis J. Twomey, S.J., 1947–1969." Ph.D. dissertation, University of Texas at Austin, 1976.

Peebles, Jack. "Subversion and the Southern Conference Education Fund." M.A. thesis, University of New Orleans, 1970.

Perkins, Iris J. "Felton Grandison Clark: Louisiana Educator." Ed.D. dissertation, Louisiana State University, 1976.

Price, John Kenneth. "The Impact of Black Voter Participation on the Politics of Louisiana and Virginia." Ph.D. dissertation, University of Texas at Austin, 1978.

Rehder, John B. "Sugar Plantation Settlements of Southern Louisiana: A Cultural Geography." Ph.D. dissertation, Louisiana State University, 1971.

Richards, Johnetta. "The Southern Negro Youth Congress: A History." Ph.D. dissertation, University of Cincinnati, 1987.

Rogers, Kim Lacy. "Humanity and Desire: Civil Rights Leaders and the Desegregation of New Orleans, 1954–1966." Ph.D. dissertation, University of Minnesota, 1982.

Sanson, Jerry Purvis. "A History of Louisiana, 1939–1945." Ph.D. dissertation, Louisiana State University, 1984.

Schindler, Inez Agnes. "The History of Education in Lake Charles from 1907–1937." M.A. thesis, Louisiana State University, 1940.

Scott, Wilbur J. "An Ecological Analysis of the Organizational Factor in the

Expansion of Political Action: The Case of New Orleans." Ph.D. dissertation, Louisiana State University, 1976.

Stowe, William McFerrin, Jr. "William Rainach and the Defense of Segregation in Louisiana, 1954–1959." Ph.D. dissertation, Texas Christian University, 1989.

Turner, Pamela Jean. "Civil Rights and Anti-Communism in New Orleans, 1946–1965." M.A. thesis, University of New Orleans, 1981.

Vital, Nida H. "Dr. Rivers Fredericks and the History of Black Medicine in New Orleans." M.A. thesis, University of New Orleans, 1978.

Wells, David Lee. "The ILWU in New Orleans: CIO Radicalism in the Crescent City, 1937–1957." M.A. thesis, University of New Orleans, 1979.

White, Doris M. "The Louisiana Civil Rights Movement's Pre-Brown Period, 1936–1954." M.A. thesis, University of Southwestern Louisiana, 1976.

Williams, Ernest R. "The Florida Parish Ellises and Louisiana Politics." Ph.D. dissertation, University of Southern Mississippi, 1969.

Worthy, Barbara Ann. "The Travail and Triumph of a Southern Black Civil Rights Lawyer: The Legal Career of Alexander Pierre Tureaud, 1899–1972." Ph.D. dissertation, Tulane University, 1984.

INTERVIEWS

ARC   Amistad Research Center, Tulane University, New Orleans
LSUS Louisiana State University, Shreveport
SHSW State Historical Society of Wisconsin, Madison
USL   University of Southwestern Louisiana, Lafayette
TU   Law Library, Tulane University.

Bailey, William. Adam Fairclough, September 29, 1987.
Baines, Bruce. Unidentified interviewer, 1984, recording. ARC.
Beaird, Charles T. Hubert Humphreys, September 12, 1978. LSUS.
Bell, James. Miriam Feingold, 1967, recording. SHSW.
Bell, Murphy W. Patricia Rickels, 1979, recording. USL.
Britton, Harvey R. H. Adam Fairclough, November 4, 1987.
Bronstein, Alvin. Jack Bass, January 16, 1979. TU.
Brown, Harrison H. Miriam Feingold, 1967, recording. SHSW.
Brown, John R. Jack Bass, January 16, 1979. TU.
Brownell, Herbert. Jack Bass, October 17, 1979. TU.
Burns, Leonard L. Kim Lacy Rogers, May 14, 1979, recording. ARC.
Burris, Royan. Miriam Feingold, 1967, recording. SHSW.
Byrd, Daniel E. David Legendre, October 27, 1978. ARC.
Byrd, Daniel E. Patricia Rickels, March 14, 1979, recording. USL.
Carter, Rev. Joseph. Miriam Feingold, 1967, recording. SHSW.
Carter, Robert L. Jack Bass, June 20, 1979. TU.
Cassimere, Raphael, Jr. Kim Lacy Rogers, November 9, 1978; May 2, 1979, recordings. ARC.
Cassimere, Raphael, Jr. Adam Fairclough, October 8, 1987.
Chapital, Arthur J. Daniel Thompson(?), February 28, 1987. ARC.
Cherrie, Ernest. Daniel Thompson(?), 1959/60. ARC.
Clancy, Father Thomas H. Adam Fairclough, November 1, 1987.

Collins, Robert L. Jack Bass, May 23, 1979. TU.
Dawkins, Ben C. Norman Provizer, March 1 and March 28, 1978; June 12, 1979. LSUS.
Dent, Albert W. Glenda Stephens, November 11, 1978, recording. ARC.
Dent, Tom. Adam Fairclough, 1991.
D'Orlando, Albert. Kim Lacy Rogers, May 16, 1979, recording, ARC.
Elie, Lolis. Kim Lacy Rogers, April 25 and May 22, 1979, recordings. ARC.
Elie, Lolis. Jack Bass, September 28, 1979. TU.
Elie, Lolis. Adam Fairclough, January 29, 1992.
Ellender, Allen J. T. H. Baker, July 30, 1969. Johnson Presidential Library.
Feibelman, Rabbi Julian B. Kim Lacy Rogers, November 7, 1978, recording. ARC.
Gardner, James. Hubert Humphreys, July 14; October 11, 1977. LSUS.
Gordon, Spiver. Unidentified interviewer, January 14, 1984, recording. ARC.
Gravel, Camille. Jim Brown, "Louisiana Politics," broadcast on Tulane University television channel, February 17, 1992.
Greenberg, Jack. Jack Bass, June 21, 1979. TU.
Haley, Oretha Castle. Kim Lacy Rogers, November 27, 1979, recording. ARC.
Haynes, J. K. Patricia Rickels, 1979, recording. USL.
Henderson, James H. Adam Fairclough, September 28, 1987.
Henry, Clarence. Daniel Thompson, 1959/60. ARC.
Hicks, Robert. Miriam Feingold, 1967, recording. SHSW.
Hill, Hattie Mae. Miriam Feingold, 1967, recording. SHSW.
Howard, Ellis D. Miriam Feingold, 1967, recording. SHSW.
Israel, Rev. T. I. Miriam Feingold, 1967, recording. SHSW.
Jacobs, Elmo. Miriam Feingold, 1967, recording. SHSW.
James, Carleton. Patricia Rickels, 1979, recording. USL.
Jemison, Rev. T. J. Judy Barton, April 12, 1972. King Library, Atlanta.
Jenkins, Gayle. Miriam Feingold, 1967, recording. SHSW.
Johnson, Annie. Miriam Feingold, 1967, recording. SHSW.
Johnson, Kenny. Unidentified interviewer, 1988, recording. ARC.
Jones, Johnnie. Judy Barton, April 12, 1972. King Library, Atlanta.
Jones, Johnnie. Patricia Rickels, 1979. USL.
Keller, Rosa. Forrest LaViolette, June 23, 30, 1959. ARC.
Keller, Rosa. Vincent J. Browne, January 11, 1968. Moorland-Spingarn Library, Howard University.
Kerns, J. Harvey. Daniel Thompson, 1959. ARC.
LaCour, Vanue. Patricia Rickels, 1979. USL.
Lewis, Frederick Douglass. Miriam Feingold, 1967, recording. SHSW.
Logsdon, Joseph. Adam Fairclough, October 8, 1987.
Lombard, Rudy. Kim Lacy Rogers, May 9, 1979, recording. ARC.
Martzell, John. Adam Fairclough, October 1, 1987.
McKeithen, John J. Adam Fairclough, October 7, 1987, recording.
Mervis, Helen. Kim Lacy Rogers, November 18, 1978, recording. ARC.
Morial, Ernest N. Kim Lacy Rogers, October 30, 1987, recording. ARC.
Motley, Constance Baker. Jack Bass, June 21, 1979. TU.
Nelson, John P. Kim Lacy Rogers, April 23, May 3, 1979, recordings. ARC.
Nelson, John P. Glenda Stephens, June 27, 1979, recording. ARC.
Nelson, John P. Jack Bass, November 16, 1979. TU.
Oliver, James. Patricia Rickels and Barry Ancelet, n.d. USL.

Perry, Robert. Patricia Rickels, March 14, 1979. USL.

Rainach, William N. Hubert Humphreys, June 28, August 19, October 7, 1977. LSUS.

Rickels, Milton. Sharme Darden, November 16, 20, 1987. USL.

Riehl, Joseph A. Michael Foret, March 16, 1981. USL.

Rousseau, John E., Jr. Adam Fairclough, March 16, 31, 1992.

Rousseve, Numa. John W. Martin, 1959. ARC.

Rouzan, Harold N. Adam Fairclough, October 30, 1990, recording.

Scott, Rev. J. H. Joseph Logsdon, 1966. University of New Orleans.

Spears, Laura. Miriam Feingold, 1967, recording. SHSW.

Stone, Jesse N. Adam Fairclough, April 3, 1992.

Strickler, George. Jack Bass, November 15, 1979. TU.

Terrance, Dr. A. C. Unidentified interviewer, n.d., recording. ARC.

Tureaud, A. P. Joseph Logsdon, numerous dates, 1968–71.

White, Marion O. Patricia Rickels, 1979, recording. USL.

Williams, Moses. Miriam Feingold, 1967, recording. SHSW.

Wilson, Rev. F. W. Miriam Feingold, 1967, recording. SHSW.

Wisdom, Bonnie. Jack Bass, September 27, 1979. TU.

Wisdom, John Minor. Jack Bass, May 22, September 28, 1979. TU.

Wright, Ernest J. Giles Hubert, July 1959. ARC.

Wright, J. Skelly. Glenda Stephens, December 9, 1978, recording. ARC.

Wyche, Zelma. Miriam Feingold, 1967, recording. SHSW.

Young, A. Z. Miriam Feingold, 1967, recording. SHSW.

Young, A. Z. Patricia Rickels, March 20, 1979, recording. USL.

INDEX

Aaron, Julia, 280, 289
Acadiana, 4, 8, 303, 383
Acheson, Meldon, 400–401
Acox, Jackson V., 211, 512 (n. 40)
Adams, Billy, 199
Adams, Cliff, 396
Adams, Kenneth, 53
Adams, Richard, 78
Adams, Vertrees, 366, 371, 375
Affirmative action, 439, 473–74
AFL. *See* American Federation of Labor
Afro-American Association, 430
Agricultural Adjustment Act, 43
Agricultural Stabilization Conservation
  Program, 347
Ahmann, Matthew, 258
Aid to Dependent Children, 233, 277
Ainsworth, Robert, 372
Alabama, xiv
Alabama Dry Dock Co., 86
Alabama Sharecroppers Union, 51
Albany, Ga., 292, 294
Alexander, Avery C., 272, 275, 391, 411,
  513 (n. 44)
Alexander, Will, 39–41, 43, 337–38
Alexander v. *Holmes County Board of
  Elections* (1969), 443
Alexandria, xviii, 87, 136; NAACP in,
  46, 78–79; 1942 riot in, 74–75; voter
  registration in, 102–3, 132; picketing
  of courthouse, 156
Allen Parish, 79
Allen v. *State Board of Education* (1969),
  466–67
Allport, Gordon, 173
Amadee, Earl, 183, 327, 513 (n. 44)
Amalgamated Meat Cutters, 347
American Association of University
  Professors, 291, 432
American Civil Liberties Union, 34
American Dilemma, 49, 79–80
American Federation of Labor, 34, 42,
  47, 137

American Federation of Teachers, 100
American Friends Service Committee,
  150–51, 191–92, 332–35
American Independence Party, 442
American Missionary Association,
  39–40
Americans for Democratic Action, 139,
  141
Ames, Jesse Daniel, 13
Anderson, C. W., 209
Anderson, Dupuy, 334
Anderson, Fletcher, 374
Anderson, Herbert, 79
Anderson, James D., 36, 39
Anderson, Marian, 59–60
Angers, Robert, Jr., 229, 260
Angola state penitentiary, 304
Anticommunism, 137–47, 163, 223–25,
  323–25, 417
Anti-Communist Christian Association,
  356, 372. *See also* Ku Klux Klan
Anti-Semitism, 237, 244, 254, 324, 526
  (n. 57)
Ascension Parish, 103, 303
Association of Catholic Laymen, 201
Association of Citizens Councils of
  Louisiana, 195, 199
Association of Southern Women for the
  Prevention of Lynching, 13, 31
Atlanta, Ga., 236, 261, 461
At-large elections, 394, 466–68
Atlas, Joseph, 307
Audubon Park, 83, 152
Austin, Henry, 368–69, 374
Autocrat Club, 18, 58
Auzenne, Gustave, 130
Avery, Leonard P., 189
Avoyelles Parish, 4, 124
Aycock, C. C. "Taddy," 444

Babylon, Edwin, 141
Badeaux, Hubert, 202–3, 223–24

Cherrie, Ernest, 18

Chicago Defender, 73

Chiles (FBI agent), 221

Christenberry, Herbert W., 93, 107, 133, 142, 146, 216, 219, 238, 246, 335, 337; and Bogalusa, 367–69, 371–72, 374–75; and Plaquemines Parish schools, 438

Christian, Jack, 217

Christian, Marcus, 60

Christmas, Charles, 355, 372–73

CIO Political Action Committee, 102

Citizens Committee (New Orleans), 335–36, 427

Citizens Committee on Race Relations (New Orleans), 81–82

Citizens Committee for Equal Education, 101–2

Citizens Committee for Quality Education, 442

Citizens Council of Webster Parish, 197

Citizens Councils, 8, 191–96, 280; purges black voters, 197–99, 206–7, 220–22, 226–31, 303, 309; Catholic Church, 199–204; attacks Urban League, 204–5; power of, 205–6; opposes New Orleans school integration, 236, 244, 247–53; decline of, 261, 321, 323; in Shreveport, 285–87. *See also* Rainach, William M.

Citizens Councils of Greater New Orleans, 192, 195, 526 (n. 57)

Citizens Councils of South Louisiana, 526 (n. 57)

Citizens for Public Schools (New Orleans), 254

Citizens Forum on Integration (New Orleans), 192

Citizens Improvement Council (Lake Charles), 208

City Park (New Orleans), 83, 106, 111, 152, 171, 219

Civil Rights Act (1957), 223, 230

Civil Rights Act (1960), 312

Civil Rights Act (1964), 318–19, 322, 343; effects of, 339–40; implementation of, 345–46, 351–52, 363, 371–72, 374, 378–80, 384; and school integration, 436

Civil Rights Act (1968), 423

Civil Rights Bill (1956–57), 219–20

Civil Rights Commission. *See* U.S. Commission on Civil Rights

Civil Rights Congress, xvi, 120–21, 125, 129, 136, 142–43, 158, 190–91, 502 (n. 35)

Civil Rights Division. *See* Department of Justice

Civil rights movement: interpretations of, ix–xvi; character of post-1945, 124; and Black Power, 381–87. *See also* Congress of Racial Equality; National Association for the Advancement of Colored People; Nonviolent direct action

Claiborne Parish, 25, 184, 476

Clancy, Frank, 32, 121, 185

Clark, Clinton, 31, 53

Clark, Ed, 295

Clark, Felton G., 154, 266–71, 289–91, 432

Clark, Jim, 364

Clark, Joseph S., 266

Clark, Tom, 91–92, 116–17, 207

Clarke, Thompson, 184

Classroom Teachers Federation of New Orleans, 52, 137, 141

Clement, Winnie P., 197–98, 207

Clemmons, Bryan, 290

Clinton, East Feliciana Parish, 301–2, 304–5, 326–27

Close, Carl B., 136

Coalition of Patriotic Societies, 34

Cobb, Alvin A., 151–52

Cocke, Bernard, 123, 141, 280, 528 (n. 26)

Cody, John P., 258–61, 336

Cohen, Walter L., 10–11, 19, 66

Cold War, xi, 112, 137, 140, 145–46, 242

Cole, Reuben, 52

Coles, Robert, 248

Coleman, M. M., 226

Colfax massacre, 8

Collins, Corrie, 304

Collins, LeRoy, 352, 357

Collins, Robert F., 279, 292, 326, 364; on Perez, 327; convicted of bribery, 475

Columbia, Tenn., 109

Combre, Doretha A., 190, 196, 209–10, 283

Comité des Citoyens, 6, 15, 70

Commission on Human Relations, Rights, and Responsibilities. *See* Biracial Commission (Louisiana)

Commission on Interracial Cooperation, xiv, 11–13, 41, 138

Committee for a Better Louisiana, 282, 379

Committee for Industrial Organization, 34, 50–51, 54–55

Committee for Public Education (New Orleans), 237–38, 240, 254

Communist Control Law, 325–26

Communist Party, xi, xvi, 51–52, 56, 111, 120, 220, 223; leaders prosecuted, 137; and labor unions, 139, 142; and Southern Conference for Human Welfare, 139–40; and Progressive Party, 140; and HUAC, 202; and Civil Rights Congress, 502 (n. 35)

Community action programs, 393–94

Community Chest (New Orleans), 205

Community Relations Council (New Orleans), 336, 416

Community Relations Service, 352, 354, 363, 378, 402, 436

Compton, Gardner, 368

Concordia Parish, 53

Congress of Industrial Organizations, 138, 142, 150

Congress of Racial Equality, xvi, 83, 110; in Baton Rouge, 267–70, 289–94; in New Orleans, 272–76, 278–80, 282–84, 295–96; role of lawyers in, 279–80; in Shreveport, 288–89, 332; "Committee of Inquiry," 292; and Voter Education Project, 294–95, 302–10, 313–17; interracial tensions in, 295–96, 299; role of field staff, 297–98, 320–21; field secretaries in, 298–99; sexual tensions in, 299–300; role of whites in, 299–302; in Madison Parish, 300, 314, 395–98; police harassment, 302; in Plaquemine, 302, 309, 315, 328–30; in Felicianas, 303–6, 314; in Monroe and West Monroe, 313–14; in Jonesboro,

314, 341, 432–43; voter registration work assessed, 316–17; relationship to local movements, 320–21; role of nonviolent direct action, 321; in Plaquemines Parish, 327–28; and philosophy of nonviolence, 341–42, 381–82; and guns, 342–43, 382; in Bogalusa, 350–51, 353–70 passim; and Black Power, 381–82; decline of, 381–82; and War on Poverty, 393–94; in Ferriday, 399–402

Connor, Bull, 330–31

Consumers League of Greater New Orleans, 272, 275–76, 278, 282

Coon, John E., 136, 206

Cooper, Larry N., 407–8, 434

Cooper v. *Aaron* (1958), 255–56

Coordinating Council of Greater New Orleans, 277–78, 283, 309

Copelin, Sherman, 475

Corpus Christi Parish, 7, 14

Corruption, 33–35, 474–75, 554 (n. 23). *See also* Perez, Leander

Cortez, Cathy, 395

Coss, John J., 40

Costello, Father (Catholic priest), 201

Costigan-Wagner antilynching bill, 29–30

Council of Federated Organizations, 315

Council of Social Agencies (New Orleans), 81

COUP, 393

Coushatta, Red River Parish, 210

Cox, B. Elton, 290–92

Cox, Harold, 311, 319

"Crack" cocaine, 470

Crandell, William, 172

Craven, Gary, 300, 395

Crawford, Vicki, xvi

Creole: definition of, 2, 6, 10

Creoles of color, xi, xix, 2–3, 5–6, 10, 125; and Roman Catholic Church, 13–14; and color distinctions, 14–18, 383, 484 (n. 37); militancy of, 15, 383; Creole-American division, 58–59; and Black Power, 383–84; "tragic mulatto," 383, 541 (n. 3)

Crescent City Independent Voters League, 513 (n. 44)

Crime, 470–71

Johns, Major, 267–69
Johnson, Charles S., 62, 88
Johnson, Clyde, 51
Johnson, E. A. (physician), 70, 72, 127, 154, 167, 189, 180, 189, 405; dispute with Tureaud, 190–91
Johnson, Frank M., 310, 377
Johnson, Georgia M., 78–79
Johnson, James Weldon, 66
Johnson, Kenny, 302, 329–30
Johnson, Lyndon B., 136, 352, 512 (n. 37); administration of, 319, 378; New Orleans speech, 339, 536 (n. 72); and Bogalusa, 370, 373; and Ku Klux Klan, 377; and War on Poverty, 416
Johnson, Manning, 223
Johnson, Milton, 368
Johnson, Oakley, 111, 120–21, 143
Johnston, J. Bennett, 464
Joint Legislative Committee on Un-American Activities, 323, 373
Joint Legislative Committee to Maintain Segregation, 170, 187–88, 194, 199, 205–6, 223–24, 226–29
Jones, Alvin H., 129–30, 137, 512 (n. 40)
Jones, Donald, 10, 57–58, 61, 63, 65, 80, 91, 135, 155, 190
Jones, Herman, 226
Jones, John C., 113–18
Jones, Johnnie A., 110, 159, 188, 267, 292
Jones, Joseph H., 125
Jones, Ralph Waldo Emerson, 410–11
Jones, Sam, 35, 198
Jonesboro, xvii; black voting in, 124; CORE in, 314, 341–43; Deacons for Defense in, 341–42, 357–58
Josephites, 7, 177, 278
Jugger, Ocie, 120–21
Juries: exclusion of blacks from, 56, 63–64, 79, 127–29, 419
Justice, Department of, xviii, 132, 185; New Iberia investigation, 84–85, 91–93; and voting rights, 103–4, 220–22, 229–30, 306–7, 310–13, 317–19; and Minden lynching, 115–17; and St. Landry Parish, 125, 130; and New Orleans school integration, 237–38, 243, 246, 249–50, 255, 258; and Bogalusa crisis, 349, 363, 370–78; and

Voting Rights Act, 388; and Madison Parish, 396–98; and Sobol case, 421; and school integration, 436, 451; and integration of higher education, 460

Kabacoff, Lester, 237, 240
Kansas City Call, 72
Karenga, Ron, 386
Kelleher, Harry, 336
Keller, Charles, 152, 525 (n. 46)
Keller, Rosa, 165–66, 232, 236, 240, 262–63
Kelley, Robin D. G., xi, xv, 82
Kelso, Robert, 240
Kennedy, Donald L., 440
Kennedy, John F., 322–33; administration of, 246, 258–59, 280, 293–94, 306, 378; judicial appointments of, 311; and civil rights commission, 318; assassination of, 338, 342
Kennedy, Robert F., 247, 318, 524 (n. 36)
Kennon, Robert, 168, 170–71, 185–86, 193–95, 338, 510 (n. 9)
Kerns, J. Harvey, 277, 416
Kester, Howard, 30, 32–33, 113
Kilbourne, Charles S., 226
Kilbourne, Richard, 326
King, Martin Luther, Jr., ix–xiii, 161–62, 212, 281–82, 289, 292, 294, 319; opposed by Joseph H. Jackson, 333; Letter from Birmingham City Jail, 335; attitude of CORE workers toward, 342; and Selma campaign, 362, 377; and Vietnam, 417; assassination of, 423, 427
King, Richard H., xi, 316
Kinoy, Arthur, 325
Kirkpatrick, F. D., 357
Kitchen, A. P., 91–92
Knight, Claxton, 355, 357, 360, 366, 371, 374
Knights of Peter Claver, 14, 69, 72, 102, 123
Kolb, William, 139, 141
Korean War, 144
Kornfeder, Joseph Zack, 223
Ku Klux Klan, xviii, 8–9, 109, 197, 390; in Shreveport, 287–89, 476; revival

of, 323, 340–43; murders Frank
Morris, 343; in Bogalusa, 345, 348–57,
359, 362–63, 365–66, 369, 370–71;
and murder of O'Neal Moore, 367,
373; prosecuted by Department of
Justice, 371–74, 377; bombing
campaign, 373; and Johnson
administration, 377; in Madison
Parish, 397; in Ferriday, 399–401; in
Florida Parishes, 412–13; in St.
Helena Parish, 436; and David Duke,
462–63; supports John Rarick, 465
Kwaanza, 386

Labat, George, 19
Labor unions, xiv–xvi, 9–10, 34,
LaCour, Vanue, 128, 130
Lafargue, J. B., 62–63
Lafargue, Malcolm, 115–18, 182
Lafayette, xviii, 33, 112, 124, 156, 165,
322; black voting in, 309; biracial
committee formed, 379
Lafourche, James B., 6, 56, 488 (n. 36)
Lafourche Parish, 185
Lake Charles, xviii, 33, 112, 322;
described, 215–16; black voting in,
309; school integration in, 441, 442
Lake Charles Beacon, 315, 337, 533 (n. 33)
Lakefront controversy, 83–84, 152
Lake Providence, East Carroll Parish,
43; riot in, 382, 392; police brutality
in, 417
Landrieu, Maurice "Moon," 174, 257,
392–93; and Black Panthers, 424–26;
appoints blacks, 425
Landry, Norbert "Baba," 422
Lane v. *Wilson*, 104
Lassiter, Albin P., 206
Lautenschlaeger, Lester J., 152
Laws, Clarence, 58–59, 182, 200, 208–
10, 298, 334, 512 (n. 40); allegations
of communism, 144, 224, 507 (n. 23);
arrested in Shreveport, 331
Lawson, Steven F., 146, 316, 320,
467–68
Lawyers Constitutional Defense
Committee, xviii, 298, 367, 384, 396,
398, 421–42
Leach, Claude, 474

League for the Preservation of
Constitutional Rights, 53, 79
League of Women Voters, 140
LeBeau, Pierre, 129
Lebeau, St. Landry Parish, 129
LeBlanc, Dudley, 22
LeBlanc, Fred, 159, 194, 197, 291–93
Leche, Richard W., 35
Ledoux, Ariel, 126
Lee, Eula Mae, 107
Lee, Harold Newton, 79, 137, 141
Lee, Harry (sheriff), 471
Leipziger, Emil, 81, 141
Leland University, 482 (n. 12)
Lesser, Mike, 300, 305, 313–14, 342
Lewis, Alfred Baker, 144
Lewis, Frederick Douglass, 25,
Lewis, Gerald, 178
Lewis, James, Jr., 70
Lewis, James, Sr., 70
Lewis, Jerry Lee, 399
Lewis, John G., Jr., 10, 70, 190, 209, 269
Lewis, John G., Sr., 70
Lewis, Leon, 80
Lewis, Robert Lee, 399, 401, 448
Lewis, Scott, 70
Liebling, A. J., 277
Lilly, Octave, Jr., 60, 88, 91, 94
Lincoln Beach, 152
Lincoln Parish, 100
Lindsey, J. Coleman, 194, 197, 208, 515
(n. 3)
Little Rock, Ark., 223, 235
Liuzzo, Viola, 377
Livingston Parish: carried by Duke, 476
Loe, Newt, 314
Logsdon, Joseph, 70–71
Lomax, Louis, 369–70
Lombard, Rudy, 272, 275–76, 305, 328,
382
Lombard v. *Louisiana* (1963), 280
Long, Earl, 35, 108, 120, 128, 151, 251,
306, 364; and black voting, 132, 179–
86, 198, 228–29, 512 (n. 37); supports
Truman, 180, 512 (n. 38); and 1955
election, 193, 196; and Rainach, 206,
228–29; on A. L. Davis, 212; vetoes
segregation bill, 213; 1959–60
governor's race, 231–32; on sit-ins,
271; and Washington Parish, 348

Long, Huey, 21, 125; racism of, 22–23; and blacks, 22–23, 25, 35–36, 44–45; Share Our Wealth movement, 22–23, 34; and lynching, 25, 29

Long, Russell B., 135, 155, 182, 259, 512 (n. 37)

Longe, George S., 63, 71

Longshoremen, 9–10, 50–51

Louisiana: distinctiveness of, xvii–xviii, 1–5; farm population, 147–48; economic change, 147–51; manufacturing, 148–49; oil industry, 149; 1973 state constitution, 465; crime in, 470–71; economic decline of, 473–74; corruption in, 474–75

Louisiana Association for the Progress of Negro Citizens, 55

Louisiana Bar Association, 188, 420

Louisiana Colored Teachers Association. See Louisiana Education Association

Louisiana Committee on Human Rights, 170–71, 224

Louisiana Education Association, 62–63, 71, 99–101, 190, 552 (n. 60); and War on Poverty, 393–94; fights dismissals of black teachers, 454–55; merges with LTA, 457–58

Louisiana Farmers Union, xvi, 30–31, 51–53, 303

Louisiana Human Relations Council, 423

Louisiana Industrial Life Insurance Co., 48, 61

Louisiana League for the Preservation of Constitutional Rights, 53

Louisiana Medical Association, 204

Louisiana Progressive Voters League, 102, 129, 132

Louisiana State Conference of NAACP Branches, 67–73, 78, 112, 127, 189–91, 196, 283; Legal Redress Committee, 190; in Ferriday, 399; and Emmitt Douglas, 405–6; and Leesville arrests, 419; and integration of higher education, 458–60

Louisiana state legislature, 169–70, 205, 225, 228–29, 232; and voter registration, 233, 307–8; and New Orleans schools integration, 235–36, 239, 242–47, 257; and sit-ins, 271–72;

and "freedom of choice," 443–44; repeals segregation laws, 465

Louisiana State University, 265, 431–32; integration of, 106, 154–55, 205, 219, 339; and anticommunism, 323–24; current status of integration, 458–61

Louisiana State University in New Orleans, 206, 219, 461

Louisiana Supreme Court, 28, 64, 111, 127–29, 280, 291

Louisiana Teachers Association, 100, 457–58

Louisiana Weekly, 19, 54–55, 61, 74, 87, 96, 100, 129, 144, 295; and Dejoie family, 15; passes into white ownership, 42; opposes NAACP, 59; and "Double V" campaign, 77; on police brutality, 80; on Thurgood Marshall, 104; on Supreme Court, 155; in 1950s, 188; on sit-ins, 267; on Felton Clark, 270; on Zulus, 278

Loyola University, 172; integration of, 171, 173–74, 511 (n. 24); WWL radio, 174, 203

Lubell, Samuel, 151

Lucas, George W., 19

Lucky, Mae, 198–99, 208, 221, 311

Lynch, Connie, 369

Lynching, 8–9, 25–33, 76, 347, 483 (n. 20); decline of, 31–33, 118–19; "legal lynchings," 119–21

—victims: Nelson Cash (1933), 26; Henry Freeman (1935), 32–33; Dave Hart (1935), 32–33; John C. Jones (1946), 113–18; Freddy Moore (1933), 26, 28, 32; Claude Neal (1934), 30; Mack Parker (1959), 344; John White (1933), 26; W. C. Williams (1938), 29–31, 487 (n. 25); Jerome Wilson (1935), 26–29, 347, 487 (n. 17)

Lyons, Charlton H., 441

Mackie, Wade, 266, 269, 294, 332, 334–35

Macon County, Ala., 230

Maddry, Sam, Jr., 114–17

Maddry, Mrs. Sam, Jr., 114–17

Maddry, Sam, Sr., 115–17

Madison Parish, 43, 105, 199; black

voting in, 184, 307–8, 388, 394–98;
CORE in, 314, 395–98; direct action
in, 395–96; Justice Department and,
396; private schools in, 445
Madison Parish Voters League. *See*
Madison Parish
Maestri, Robert S., 34, 81
Magee, Johnny, 372
Major, Lou, 351, 353–54
Malcolm X, 383
Maloney, Harry, 177
Mandle, Jay, 148
Manship, Douglas, 332–33
Many, M. Hepburn, 146, 229–30,
237–38, 243, 246, 249
Marcello, Carlos, 474
March on Washington, 328
Mardi Gras. *See* Carnival
Mardi Gras Indians, 4–5
Marshall, Burke, 255, 258, 287, 293
Marshall, Thurgood, x, xii, 50, 108, 125,
166, 177, 239, 454–55; and salary
equalization suits, 58, 62–63, 99–102,
499 (n. 70); as Mason, 70; and LEA,
71–99; and New Iberia incident, 91–
92, 98; and Minden lynching, 116–17;
and Hoover, 116–17; and
anticommunism, 143–44; integration
of LSU, 154–55; and *Brown* decision,
167, 187–88; defends Tureaud, 190;
increasing influence of, 191; on sit-ins,
270; and word "black," 433–34
Martensen, Katherine Anne, 176
Martin, Teddy, 303
Martin, Wade O., 225
Martzell, John R., 286: in Bogalusa,
363–65, 369, 375, 429; in Tallulah,
386, 396; on Ferriday, 399; and
biracial commission, 409–15; in
Grambling, 411; on Avery Alexander,
411; and Bogalusa to Baton Rouge
march, 412–13
Mason, B. J., 406–8
Mason, Ira, 422
Mater Dolorosa Church (New Orleans),
172–73
Matthews, Hazel, 304
McCain, James T., 267–70, 272–75,
294–95, 313, 342, 388, 392
McCall, Harold, 240

McCall, William G., 263
McCarthy, Joseph, 137
McCarthyism, xi, 144, 146–47, 187, 223,
267
McComb, Miss., 352
McDaniel, Leo F., 215
McDew, Charles, 531 (n. 54)
McDonogh, John, 162
McDonogh Day, 162–63, 188
McDonogh No. 19 school, 244, 246–50,
255
McElveen, Ernest Ray, 367
McGary, Leroy, 78
McGill, Ralph, 285
McGough, Lucy, 243
McGuire, David, 138, 152, 193, 212, 231–
32, 252, 262; and sit-ins, 272,
274–75
McIlhenny Co., 406
McInerney, James M., 130
McIntire, Gordon, 30, 51–53
McKeithen, John J., 338–39, 343; and
Bogalusa crisis, 345, 359, 364–66,
369–70, 375; creates biracial
commission, 378–80; and voter
registration, 388; and black vote, 389–
90, 402; opposes school integration,
389–90, 442–44; and biracial
commission, 408–15; and Leesville
affair, 409; and Grambling strike,
410–11; and Bogalusa to Baton
Rouge march, 412–14; reelected,
414–15; and Baton Rouge crisis, 423;
and Southern University, 430–31;
Troy Middleton on, 444; runs for
Senate, 464
McKelpin, Joseph, 63
McKnight, Albert, 393
McLemore, James, 193
McManus, Eugene, 202, 257
McMillen, Neil R., 285
McNamara, Robert, 327
McNeese State College, 165–66
McNeil, Genna Rae, xv
McNeir, Waldo F., 323–24
Meadows, J. L., 166–67, 194
Means, Theodore R., 502 (n. 35)
Meharry College, 494 (n. 60)
Meier, August, 146, 278, 293, 330
Melton, John W., 137–38

Natchez, Miss.: boycott in, 401
Natchitoches, 31, 53, 72, 132
National Agricultural Workers Union, 177
National Alliance of Postal Employees, 57, 61
National Association for the Advancement of Colored People: importance of, xii–xvi; and lynching, 28–33, 113–19; weaknesses of, 48–49, 188–91, 273, 297–98, 404; expansion of, 50, 69–73, 112–13; equalization strategy, 107–9, 153; and nonviolent direct action, 110–11, 273, 282–83; anticommunism of, 143–47, 507 (n. 24); prosecuted by State of Louisiana, 195–97, 207–11, 223–26, 515 (n. 3); Youth Councils, 272, 275, 279–80, 283, 296, 336, 384, 401, 407–8, 417, 434, 548 (n. 13); and Black Power, 383, 402–3, 434; and biracial commission, 385, 408–9; and War on Poverty, 393–94; sectarianism of, 402–3; Harvey Britton on, 404; and black teachers, 404, 455–56; decline in membership, 514 (n. 57)
—branches: Alexandria, 46, 189, 404; Baton Rouge, 30, 47–48, 73, 189, 216–18, 333–34, 404, 423; Ferriday, 399–402; Friendship, 211; Jefferson Parish, 143; Jennings, 47, 209; Lake Charles, 47, 73, 190, 209, 216, 434; Lake Providence, East Carroll Parish, 43, 47–48, 72, 111–12, 157; Leesville, 189; Monroe, 25, 42, 47–48, 73, 189, 313, 404, 434; Natchitoches, 189; New Iberia, 72, 88–98, 406, 418–19; New Orleans, 17–19, 24, 28–30, 31–32, 46, 48–49, 56–63, 65–73, 143–45, 156, 189, 209, 273, 279–80, 282–83, 296, 404, 417–17; New Roads, 405–6; Plaquemine, 47; Plaquemines Parish, 327; Red River Parish, 210; St. Helena Parish, 194; St. Landry Parish, 129–30, 405; Shreveport, 8, 20, 46, 73, 114, 189, 209, 211, 289, 330–32, 404, 406–8, 434. See also Britton, Harvey R. H.; Byrd, Daniel E.; Chapital, Arthur J.; Louisiana State

Conference of NAACP Branches; Marshall, Thurgood; Tureaud, Alexander Pierre
National Association for the Advancement of Colored People, Legal Defense and Educational Fund, xiii, 62, 298, 480–81 (n. 4); and LEA, 71, 99; seeks integration, 153–56; legal strategy of, 191; hostile to National Lawyers Guild, 326; Department of Teacher Information and Security, 454; and black teachers, 454–55
National Association for the Advancement of White People, 463–64
National Baptist Convention, 159, 217, 333
National Catholic Conference for Interracial Justice, 258
National Citizens Committee for Community Relations, 352
National Conference of State Teachers Associations, 454
National Education Association, 447, 457–58
National Labor Relations Board, 142
National Lawyers Guild, 324–26
National Maritime Union, 51, 142
National States Rights Party, 367, 369
National Union of Marine Cooks and Stewards, 51, 142
National Urban League, 56, 58, 80–81, 86, 130, 144, 148, 218, 237, 277, 416; attacked by Citizens Council, 204–5; and communism, 224
National War Labor Board, 101
Nelson, Andrew, 142, 502 (n. 35)
Nelson, John P., 174, 236, 253, 256, 262–63, 364–65, 420
Nelson, William Stuart, 40
Netterville, Leon G., 430, 432, 460
New Deal, x–xi, 43–44, 85, 103, 136–37, 147
New Iberia, 84–98 passim, 186, 406, 418–19, 498 (n. 55)
New Llano, Vernon Parish, 137
New Orleans, xv, 8, 9–10; in World War II, 76–86; black voting in, 103, 112, 123, 183–86, 308–9, 312, 318;

Stanley, Eugene, 31, 53
State Board of Registration, 184, 198, 227
State legislature. *See* Louisiana state legislature
State Sovereignty Commission, 323, 465
State v. Perkins (1947), 127–28
Steimel, Edward, 379
Steinbeck, John, 248
Stern, Edgar B., 32, 38–40, 138–39, 143, 148, 152
Stern Family Fund, 236–37, 294
Stevens, E. A., 80
Stitch, Arlene, 140
Stone, Jesse N., 190, 288, 331, 437; and George D'Artois, 390–31, 417; and biracial commission, 408–12; political influence of, 464, 468, 553 (n. 2)
Stoner, J. B., 369
Stouffer, Samuel, 173
Straight University, 38, 482 (n. 12)
Strong, Donald, 230
Student Nonviolent Coordinating Committee, xiv, 381
Sugarcane workers, 8, 176–77, 185–86
Sullivan, Patricia, 44
Sullivan, William Henry, 346–47
Superdome, 475
Sutherland, Gene, 150, 191
Swaggart, Jimmy, 399
Swan, Edward, 115
Swann v. Charlotte-Mecklenburg (1970), 456
Swearingen, Mack, 34, 53
Sweatt, Herman, 153
Sweatt v. Painter (1950), 153–55

Taconic Foundation, 294
Taft-Hartley Act, 142
Tallahassee, Fla., 214
Talley, Bascom D., 352–54, 421
Tallulah, Madison Parish, 6, 386, 396. *See also* Madison Parish
Tangipahoa Parish, 103, 303; black voting in, 111, 132, 181, 308, 315
Tate, Patricia Ann, 289, 530 (n. 54)
Tate, U. Simpson, 127
Taylor, B. B., Jr., 333

Taylor, Rev. C. C., 61
Taylor, Dorothy Mae, 465
Taylor, Gardner C., 56, 101–2, 159
Taylor, Lavert, 289
Taylor, O. C. W., 73, 76
Taylor v. Louisiana (1962), 529 (n. 45)
Teachout, Peter, 314
Teasley, Harvey, 213, 287
Tensas Parish, 306
Terrance, A. C., 25, 49, 72
Terrebonne, Linus P., 101–2, 107
Terrell, L. C., 366
Texas Southern University, 153–54
Thibodeaux, Lafourche Parish, 8, 146
Thierry, Louis, 125
Thigpen, Bryan, 29–31
Thomas, Curtis, 133, 227–30, 348
Thomas, Ernest, 357–58
Thomas, Norman, 61, 292
Thompson, August, 401–2
Thompson, Daniel C., 136
Thompson, John H., 250, 252
Thompson, Vance, 231
Thornton, Joseph A., 105
Thurmond, Strom, 151, 180, 441
Tillman, Raymond R., 54, 120, 139, 142, 506 (n. 12)
Tims, John F., 240, 525 (n. 46)
Tindall, George B., 99
Tippett, Tom, 32
Todd-Johnson shipyard, 148
Tonry, Rick, 474
Total Community Action, 393
Tracy, Bishop, 258
Trailways (bus company), 157
Transport Workers Union, 51, 53, 139, 142
Transylvania Project, 43
Treen, Dave, 464, 472, 474
Triche, Risley, 465
Trudeau, A. M., 19, 24
Trudeau, A. M., Jr., 208, 327
Trudeau v. Barnes, 104–5
Truman, Harry S., 112–13, 132–33, 137, 146; 1948 election, 140, 151, 180
Tucker, Robert, 268
Tulane University, 139–41, 169, 237, 262–63
Tunnell, Ted, 15

Tureaud, Alexander Pierre, xii, 10, 13, 14–16, 19, 56–57, 61, 77–79, 81, 88, 91, 137, 157, 206, 208, 212, 217, 271, 283, 349, 383; and voting, 24–25, 102–4; on Huey Long, 44–45; on lower-class culture, 49; and Creole legacy, 60; and salary equalization suits, 63, 73, 99–102, 108; profile of, 63–69; and Thurgood Marshall, 66; and Communists, 67, 139, 143–45, 507 (n. 24); and Catholic Church, 68–69, 173; and LEA, 71, 99; on wartime tensions, 77, 82–83; on police brutality, 79; and FBI, 94, 98; on black schools, 107; on Home Guard, 109; and Minden lynching, 114; on St. Landry Parish, 125, 130; and politics, 135, 182, 512 (n. 37), 513 (n. 44); integration of LSU, 154–55; on integration strategy, 156; and St. Helena Parish suit, 166, 436; on *Brown II,* 187; dispute over cases, 189–91; and attack on NAACP, 197, 209–10; Shreveport bus suit, 214, 287, 528 (n, 43); and New Orleans schools crisis, 235, 245–46; and sit-ins, 273, 279; supports Schiro, 391; death of, 455
Tureaud, Alexander Pierre, Jr., 155
Tushnet, Mark V., xv, 66
Tuskegee, Ala., xii
Twomey, Louis J., 146, 174, 177–79, 201, 204, 253–54, 262, 324
Tyler, Gary, 452
Tyson, Bertrand, 302

"Underclass," black, 469
United Christian Movement, 213–15, 228, 287–89
United Clubs, 208, 278
United Defense League, 159–62
United Fruit Co., 138
United Office and Professional Workers (CIO), 55
United Papermakers and Paperworkers, 348, 350
United Pulp and Sulphite Workers, 348, 355
U.S. Commission on Civil Rights, 228–30, 307, 317–18

U.S. Supreme Court, 63–65, 78, 119–20, 153–54, 161, 187, 212, 421, 440–41; and sit-ins, 280, 292; *Alexander* decision, 443; *Swann* decision, 456; legalizes interracial marriage, 462
U.S. v. *Board of Registration of Louisiana,* 312, 318
U.S. v. *Classic* (1941), 65
U.S. v. *Jefferson* (1966), 439–40
U.S. v. *Louisiana* (1963), 310, 312, 316, 388
United Steelworkers (AFL), 151
United Voters League, 513 (n. 44)
University of New Orleans, 206, 219, 461
University of Texas Law School, 153–54
Ussery, Wilfred, 360

Verret, J. Emile, 95
Vickery, Ed, 304, 313
Vietnam, 381, 417
Vilitz, Lawrence, 87, 89
Vines, Kenneth N., 132
Volter, Franzella, 88, 91, 406
Voodoo, 4, 49, 260
Vote-buying, 392, 474, 542 (n. 20)
Voter Education Project, 294–95, 302–17, 384
Voter registration, 6, 106; in 1930s, 23–25; "understanding clause," 24, 207, 227; 1940 right-to-vote campaign, 54–55; in 1944, 102–4; in 1946, 105, 111–12; in 1947–48, 123–24; in 1950, 129–30; in 1951–56, 130–34; and Earl Long, 132; and Catholic Church, 132; and federal government, 132–34; Citizens Council purge of black voters, 197–99, 206–7, 220–22, 226–31, 303, 309; in New Orleans, 277–78, 281, 308–9, 311, 387–88; in 1962–64, 303–19 passim; "good character" clause, 307, 388; application form, 307–8, 312; "citizenship test," 308, 311; U.S. v. *Louisiana* (1963), 310, 312, 316, 388; U.S. v. *Board of Registration,* 312, 318. *See also* Department of Justice; Federal Bureau of Investigation; Federal Judiciary; Voter Education Project; Voting, black;

Voting Rights Act; *names of individual parishes*

Voting, black: in Shreveport, 103, 111, 228, 309; in New Orleans, 103, 112, 123, 183–86, 308–9, 312, 318; in Baton Rouge, 103, 185, 315; in Tangipahoa Parish, 111, 132, 181, 308, 315; in St. Bernard Parish, 123; in Jefferson Parish, 123, 185; in Plaquemines Parish, 123, 318, 388; in Avoyelles Parish, 124; in Jonesboro, 124; in Iberia Parish, 124, 185–86; in St. Landry Parish, 129–31, 185, 228–29, 309, 405; in Pointe Coupee Parish, 132; Earl Long and, 132, 179–86, 198, 228–29, 512 (n. 37); and Roman Catholic Church, 132, 278, 392; in Bossier Parish, 133–34; in Washington Parish, 133–34, 227–31, 303, 347, 376, 388; in St. Helena Parish, 134, 227, 303, 314–15; and Chep Morrison, 179–86; in East Carroll Parish, 184, 306–7, 312, 390, 392, 467; in Madison Parish, 184, 307–8, 388, 394–98; sheriffs and, 185; purges of black voters, 197–99, 206–7, 220–22, 226–31, 303, 309; in East Feliciana Parish, 226, 303, 308, 313; in Iberville Parish, 302, 309–10, 315, 394; in Ascension Parish, 303; in West Feliciana Parish, 303–6, 310, 466; in Tensas Parish, 306; and Leander Perez, 307–8, 388; in Lafayette, 309; in Lake Charles, 309; in Monroe, 310–11; in St. Mary Parish, 383, 393; in Morehouse Parish, 388; in West Carroll Parish, 388; and McKeithen, 389–90, 402; in Ferriday, 402

Voting Rights Act, xvii, 186, 222, 311–12, 317, 319, 377; effects of, 384, 387–92, 394–98, 428, 466–67; New Orleans, 387–88, 467; Plaquemines Parish, 388; Shreveport, 467–68

Waggoner, Joe D., 441–42, 549 (n. 28)
Wagner, Emile, 177, 192, 200–204, 235, 237, 239, 247
Wagner, Robert, 340
Walker, E. L. (judge), 30
Walker, Edwin A., 373

Walker, Gus, 90, 92, 94
Walker, Kenneth, 231
Walker, Wyatt T., 289
Wallace, George C., 441–42, 472
Walzer, Bruce, 323–24
Ward, Katherine, 395
Waring, J. Waties, 133
War Manpower Commission, 87
War on Poverty, 384, 393–94
Wascom, Haynes "Twister," 368, 375
Washburn, Fannie, 159
Washington, Booker T., 39
Washington, D.C., 461
Washington, Paul, 120–22
Washington Parish: black voting in, 133–34, 227–31, 303, 347, 376, 388; carried by Duke, 476
Wattigny, Gerald, 185
WDSU television, 240, 247, 271
Weatherby, W. J., 245
Webb, Jesse L., Jr., 217
Webster Parish, 197, 207
Wells, Dave Lee, 51
West, E. Gordon, 291–94, 311, 318, 324, 326, 328, 333–34, 336, 374, 436–37, 440, 444, 451
West Carroll Parish, 388
West Feliciana Parish, xvi, 52–53; black voting in, 303–6, 310, 466
West Monroe, 313–14
Whatley, David, 400–401, 403
White, Marion O., 17, 129, 403, 455
White, Walter, 28–29, 32–33, 48, 58, 78, 91, 98; and Minden lynching, 114; and Hoover, 116–17; and anticommunism, 143, 145; death of, 210
White Castle, Iberville Parish, 16
White Knights of the Ku Klux Klan, 341
Wilder, Douglas, 470, 554 (n. 13)
Wilkins, J. Edwin, 58–61
Wilkins, Roy, 22, 23, 28–29, 209–10, 341, 434; on Faubus victory, 223; and communism, 225; criticizes Chapital, 282–83; denounces Black Power, 402
Wilkinson, W. Scott, 193
William J. Frantz school, 244, 246–50
Williams, Adell, 398
Williams, Luins H., 88, 90, 94, 96
Williams, Moses, 307
Williams, R. L., 211, 225